The Pearson Series in Finance

Bekaert/Hodrick
International Financial Management

Berk/DeMarzo
Corporate Finance*

Berk/DeMarzo
Corporate Finance: The Core*

Berk/DeMarzo/Harford
Fundamentals of Corporate Finance*

Brooks
Financial Management: Core Concepts*

Copeland/Weston/Shastri
Financial Theory and Corporate Policy

Dorfman/Cather
Introduction to Risk Management and Insurance

Eiteman/Stonehill/Moffett
Multinational Business Finance

Fabozzi
Bond Markets: Analysis and Strategies

Fabozzi/Modigliani
Capital Markets: Institutions and Instruments

Fabozzi/Modigliani/Jones
Foundations of Financial Markets and Institutions

Finkler
Financial Management for Public, Health, and Not-for-Profit Organizations

Frasca
Personal Finance

Gitman/Zutter
Principles of Managerial Finance*

Gitman/Zutter
Principles of Managerial Finance—Brief Edition*

Goldsmith
Consumer Economics: Issues and Behaviors

Haugen
The Inefficient Stock Market: What Pays Off and Why

Haugen
The New Finance: Overreaction, Complexity, and Uniqueness

Holden
Excel Modeling in Corporate Finance

Holden
Excel Modeling in Investments

Hughes/MacDonald
International Banking: Text and Cases

Hull
Fundamentals of Futures and Options Markets

Hull
Options, Futures, and Other Derivatives

Hull
Risk Management and Financial Institutions

Keown
Personal Finance: Turning Money into Wealth*

Keown/Martin/Petty
Foundations of Finance: The Logic and Practice of Financial Management*

Kim/Nofsinger
Corporate Governance

Madura
Personal Finance*

Marthinsen
Risk Takers: Uses and Abuses of Financial Derivatives

McDonald
Derivatives Markets

McDonald
Fundamentals of Derivatives Markets

Mishkin/Eakins
Financial Markets and Institutions

Moffett/Stonehill/Eiteman
Fundamentals of Multinational Finance

Nofsinger
Psychology of Investing

Ormiston/Fraser
Understanding Financial Statements

Pennacchi
Theory of Asset Pricing

Rejda
Principles of Risk Management and Insurance

Seiler
Performing Financial Studies:
A Methodological Cookbook

Smart/Gitman/Joehnk
Fundamentals of Investing*

Solnik/McLeavey
Global Investments

Stretcher/Michael
Cases in Financial Management

Titman/Keown/Martin
Financial Management: Principles and
Applications*

Titman/Martin
Valuation: The Art and Science of Corporate
Investment Decisions

Weston/Mitchel/Mulherin
Takeovers, Restructuring, and Corporate
Governance

*denotes MyFinanceLab titles   Log onto www.myfinancelab.com to learn more.

Principles of Finance

Baruch College
Zicklin School of Business

Taken from:
Fundamentals of Investing, Twelfth Edition
by Scott Smart, Lawrence Gitman, Michael Joehnk

Financial Management: Principles and Applications, Twelfth Edition
by Sheridan Titman, Arthur J. Keown, John D. Martin

Cover Art: Courtesy of Getty/Photodisc.

Taken from:

Fundamentals of Investing, Twelfth Edition
by Scott Smart, Lawrence Gitman, Michael Joehnk
Copyright © 2014, 2011, 2008 by Pearson Education, Inc.
Published by Pearson
Upper Saddle River, New Jersey 07458

Financial Management: Principles and Applications, Twelfth Edition
by Sheridan Titman, Arthur J. Keown, John D. Martin
Copyright © 2014, 2011, 2008 by Pearson Education, Inc.
Published by Pearson
Upper Saddle River, New Jersey 07458

This special edition published in cooperation with Pearson Learning Solutions.

All trademarks, service marks, registered trademarks, and registered service marks are the property of their respective owners and are used herein for identification purposes only.

Pearson Learning Solutions, 501 Boylston Street, Suite 900, Boston, MA 02116
A Pearson Education Company
www.pearsoned.com

Printed in the United States of America

9 10 V092 18 17 16 15

000200010271918516

RD

ISBN 10: 1-269-94697-8
ISBN 13: 978-1-269-94697-1

Brief Contents

Contents

MARKETS IN CRISIS
Rating Agencies Miss a Big One 59

MARKETS IN CRISIS
Implicit Guarantee Becomes Explicit 60

Chapter 3
Securities Markets and Transactions 88

MARKETS IN CRISIS
No Time to Go Public 93

MARKETS IN CRISIS
SEC Bans Short Selling 115

Chapter 4
Firms and the Financial Market 125

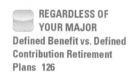

Chapter 5
Time Value of Money—The Basics 147

Chapter 9
Stock Valuation 292

Chapter 10
Return and Risk 331

**MARKETS IN
CRISIS**
Recession Pushes Prices
Down 335

Opening Vignette 331

The Concept of Return 332

Components of Return 332 / Why Return Is Important 333 / Level
of Return 334 / Historical Returns 335 / Time Value of Money
and Returns 336

Measuring Return 338

Real, Risk-Free, and Required Returns 339 / Holding Period
Return 341 / Yield: The Internal Rate of Return 343 / Finding
Growth Rates 346

Risk: The Other Side of the Coin 348

Sources of Risk 348 / Risk of a Single Asset 351 / Assessing
Risk 354 / Steps in the Decision Process: Combining Return
and Risk 356

**Summary 357 / Discussion Questions 359 / Problems 359 /
Case Problem 10.1 363 / Case Problem 10.2 364 / Excel with
Spreadsheets 365 / Chapter-Opening Problem 366**

Chapter 11
Modern Portfolio Concepts 368

**MARKETS IN
CRISIS**
Bulging Betas 383

Opening Vignette 368

Principles of Portfolio Planning 369

Portfolio Objectives 369 / Portfolio Return and Standard
Deviation 369 / Correlation and Diversification 372 / International
Diversification 377

The Capital Asset Pricing Model 379

Components of Risk 379 / Beta: A Measure of Undiversifiable
Risk 380 / The CAPM: Using Beta to Estimate Return 383

Traditional Versus Modern Portfolio Management 386

The Traditional Approach 386 / Modern Portfolio
Theory 387 / Reconciling the Traditional Approach and MPT 393

**Summary 394 / Discussion Questions 396 / Problems 397 /
Case Problem 11.1 403 / Case Problem 11.2 404 / Excel with
Spreadsheets 406 / Chapter-Opening Problem 407**

CFA Exam Questions 409

Chapter 12
More on Risk and Return—Capital Market Theory 412

P PRINCIPLE 2: There Is a Risk–Return Tradeoff 412

P PRINCIPLE 4: Market Prices Reflect Information 412

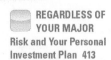

Chapter 13
Options: Puts and Calls 446

Preface

"Great firms aren't great investments unless the price is right." Those words of wisdom come from none other than Warren Buffett, who is, without question, one of the greatest investors ever. The words of Mr. Buffett sum up very nicely the essence of this book—namely, to help students learn to make informed investment decisions, not only when buying stocks but also when investing in bonds, mutual funds, or any other type of investment.

The fact is, investing may sound simple, but it's not. Investors in today's turbulent financial markets confront many challenges when deciding how to invest their money. After the 2008 meltdown in financial markets, investors have become more wary of risk than they have been in many years. This book is designed to help students understand the risks inherent in investing and to give them the tools they need to answer the fundamental questions that help shape a sound investment strategy. For example, students want to know, what are the best investments for me? Should I buy individual securities, mutual funds, or exchange-traded funds? What's the market outlook in the next few years? What about risk? Do I need professional help with my investments, and can I afford it? Clearly, investors need answers to questions like these to make informed decisions.

The language, concepts, and strategies of investing are foreign to many. In order to become informed investors, students must first become conversant with the many aspects of investing. Building on that foundation, they can learn how to make informed decisions in the highly dynamic investment environment. This thirteenth edition of *Fundamentals of Investing* provides the information and guidance needed by individual investors to make such informed decisions and to achieve their investment goals.

This book meets the needs of professors and students in the first investments course offered at colleges and universities, junior and community colleges, professional certification programs, and continuing education courses. Focusing on both individual securities and portfolios, *Fundamentals of Investing* explains how to develop, implement, and monitor investment goals after considering the risk and return of both markets and investment vehicles. A conversational tone and liberal use of examples guide students through the material and demonstrate important points.

New for the Thirteenth Edition

Our many adopters are interested in how we have changed the content from the twelfth to the thirteenth edition. We hope that this information will also interest potential adopters because it indicates our mandate to stay current in the field of investments and to continue to craft a book that will truly meet the needs of students and professors.

The most dramatic change in the thirteenth edition is the positioning of Scott Smart as the book's lead author. Scott received his Ph.D. from Stanford University in 1991, and he has been a member of the finance faculty at Indiana University since then. He is currently Associate Chair of the MBA Program at Indiana University's Kelley School of Business. His scholarly articles have appeared in the *Journal of Financial Economics*, the *Journal of Finance*, *Financial Management*, the *Financial Review*, the

Journal of Accounting and Economics, and other scholarly journals. He has been recognized as an outstanding teacher by *Business Week*, and he has won more than a dozen teaching awards. Readers will see Scott's imprint on every page.

Some of the major changes made in the thirteenth edition are the following:

- Updated all real-world data through 2012, including text, tables, and figures.

- Adopted a new, tablet-like design and included many new digital features that students can use on their own to enhance their learning.

- Added a new feature called An Adviser's Perspective. Available on MyFinanceLab, this feature consists of short video clips of professional investment advisers, including some of national prominence (such as Jim Grant of Grant's Interest Rate Observer), talking about the investments topics covered in each chapter.

- Added new QR codes in the margins of each chapter. Students can scan these codes with their smart phones to gain access to videos and other web content that enhance the topical coverage of each chapter.

- Added a new feature called Investor Mistakes. These boxes appear in the margins of most chapters and highlight investment lessons gleaned from the behavioral finance literature.

- Updated numerous Investor Facts boxes from the eleventh edition and incorporated entirely new ones in most chapters.

- Updated the Markets in Crisis feature, highlighting various aspects of the recent financial crisis and recession.

- Step-by-step video tutorials featuring author Scott Smart can be found in MyFinanceLab as a learning aid for select end-of-chapter questions.

- Expanded the use of real-world data in examples.

- Expanded and updated coverage of behavioral finance, particularly but not exclusively in Chapter 7.

- Revised or replaced every chapter opener, and in many chapters, included an end-of-chapter problem that ties back to the chapter opener.

Hallmarks of *Fundamentals of Investing*

Using information gathered from academicians and practicing investment professionals, plus feedback from adopters, the thirteenth edition reflects the realities of today's investment environment. At the same time, the following characteristics provide a structured framework for successful teaching and learning.

Clear Focus on the Individual Investor

Today, about half of all U.S. households own stock either directly or indirectly through mutual funds or participation in 401(k)s. That percentage has been growing for many years and is likely to continue. The focus of *Fundamentals of Investing* has always been on the individual investor. This focus gives students the information they need to develop, implement, and monitor a successful investment program. It also provides students with a solid foundation of basic concepts, tools, and techniques. Subsequent courses can build on that foundation by presenting the advanced concepts, tools, and techniques used by institutional investors and money managers.

Comprehensive Yet Flexible Organization

The text provides a firm foundation for learning by first describing the overall investment environment, including the various investment markets, information, and transactions. Next, it presents conceptual tools needed by investors—the concepts of return and risk and the basic approaches to portfolio management. It then examines the most popular types of investments—common stocks, bonds, and mutual funds. Following this series of chapters on investment vehicles is a chapter on how to construct and administer one's own portfolio. The final section of the book focuses on derivative securities—options and futures—which require more expertise. Although the first two parts of the textbook are best covered at the start of the course, instructors can cover particular investment types in just about any sequence. The comprehensive yet flexible nature of the book enables instructors to customize it to their own course structure and teaching objectives.

We have organized each chapter according to a decision-making perspective, and we have been careful always to point out the pros and cons of the various investments and strategies we present. With this information, individual investors can select the investment actions that are most consistent with their objectives. In addition, we have presented the various investments and strategies in such a way that students learn the decision-making implications and consequences of each investment action they contemplate.

Timely Topics

Various issues and developments constantly reshape financial markets and investment vehicles. Virtually all topics in this book take into account changes in the investment environment. For example, in every chapter we've continued and updated a feature that was new to the eleventh edition called Markets in Crisis. This feature highlights various aspects of the recent and historic financial crisis, the government's response to that crisis, and the deep recession that followed the crisis. Fundamentally, investing is about the tradeoff between risk and return, and the Markets in Crisis feature serves as a reminder to students that they should not focus exclusively on an investment's returns.

In addition, the thirteenth edition provides students access to short video clips from professional investment advisers. In these clips, which are carefully integrated into the content of each chapter, students will hear professionals sharing the lessons that they have learned through years of experience working as advisers to individual investors.

Globalization

One issue that is reshaping the world of investing is the growing globalization of securities markets. As a result, *Fundamentals of Investing* continues to stress the global aspects of investing. We initially look at the growing importance of international markets, investing in foreign securities (directly or indirectly), international investment performance, and the risks of international investing. In later chapters, we describe popular international investment opportunities and strategies as part of the coverage of each specific type of investment vehicle. This integration of international topics helps students understand the importance of maintaining a global focus when planning, building, and managing an investment portfolio. Global topics are highlighted by a globe icon in the margin.

Comprehensive, Integrated Learning System

Another feature of the thirteenth edition is its comprehensive and integrated learning system, which makes clear to students what they need to learn in the chapter and helps them focus their study efforts as they progress through the chapter. For more detailed discussion of the learning system, see the feature walkthrough later in the preface (beginning on page xvii).

CFA Questions

We are pleased to include CFA questions in the thirteenth edition, both in the written text and in MyFinanceLab. CFA exam questions appear in the text at the end of three of the book's 13 chapters. These questions offer students an opportunity to test their investment knowledge against that required for the CFA Level-I exam.

Also added to this edition are three Sample CFA Exams in MyFinanceLab. Each of these exams is patterned after the CFA Level-I exam and comes with detailed guideline answers. The exams deal only with topics that are actually covered in the thirteenth edition of *Fundamentals of Investing* and are meant to replicate as closely as possible the types of questions that appear on the standard Level-I Exam. The Sample CFA Exams on MyFinanceLab come in three lengths: 30 questions, 40 questions, and 50 questions. Each exam is unique and consists of a different set of questions, so you can take any one or all of the exams without running into any duplicate questions. For the most part, these questions are adapted from the 2009 CFA Candidate Study Notes. Answers are included for immediate reinforcement.

MyFinanceLab

MyFinanceLab is a fully integrated online homework and tutorial system. MyFinanceLab offers flexible instructor tools like the easy-to-use homework manager for test, quiz, and homework assignments, automatic grading, and a powerful online Gradebook. Students can take preloaded Sample Tests for each chapter and their results generate an individualized Study Plan that helps focus and maximize their study time. Students will find ample opportunities to solve problems (some with help from author Scott Smart on video) and to explore investments-related content on the Internet through features like Smart's Tour of the Web. Please visit www.myfinancelab.com for more information or to register.

The Smart, Gitman, & Joehnk

PROVEN TEACHING/LEARNING/MOTIVATIONAL SYSTEM

Users of *Fundamentals of Investing* have praised the effectiveness of the Smart/Gitman/Joehnk teaching and learning system, which has been hailed as one of its hallmarks. In the twelfth edition we have retained and polished the system, which is driven by a set of carefully developed learning goals. Users have also praised the rich motivational framework that underpins each chapter. Key elements of the pedagogical and motivational features are illustrated and described below.

THE LEARNING GOAL SYSTEM

The Learning Goal system begins each chapter with **six Learning Goals**, labeled with numbered icons. These goals anchor the most important concepts and techniques to be learned. The Learning Goal icons are then tied to key points in the chapter's structure, including

- First-level headings
- Summary
- Discussion Questions
- Problems
- Cases

This tightly knit structure provides a clear road map for students—they know what they need to learn, where they can find it, and whether they've mastered it by the end of the chapter.

An **opening story** sets the stage for the content that follows by focusing on an investment situation involving a real company or real event, which is in turn linked to the chapter topics. Students see the relevance of the vignette to the world of investments.

In many cases, an end-of-chapter problem draws students back to the chapter opener and asks them to use the data in the opener to make a calculation or draw a conclusion to demonstrate what they learned in the chapter.

What Is a P/E Ratio?

In the margins of each chapter students will find new **QR codes**. By scanning these codes with their smart phones, students will be taken to websites with useful information to enhance their understanding of the topics covered in the textbook. For example, many of these QR codes link students with free online video tutorials covering a range of topics.

INVESTOR MISTAKES

What's in a Name?—Confusion over ticker symbols can cause investors to make embarrassing and costly mistakes. One study discovered that investors who intended to buy shares in a company called MCI Communications (which was widely known simply by the initials MCI but traded under the ticker symbol MCIC) mistakenly purchased shares in Massmutual Corporate Investors. The reason for this error was that Massmutual's ticker symbol is MCI.

Also new to this edition, **Investor Mistakes** boxes appear in the margins of most chapters and highlight investment lessons gleaned from the behavioral finance literature.

Each chapter contains a handful of **Investor Facts**—brief sidebar items that give an interesting statistic or cite an unusual investment experience. These facts add a bit of seasoning to the concepts under review and capture a real-world flavor. The Investor Facts sidebars include material focused on topics such as art as an investment, the downgrade of the U.S. government's credit rating, the use of financial statements to detect accounting fraud, and recent issues of unusual securities such as bonds with 100-year maturities.

An Adviser's Perspective consists of short video clips of professional investment advisers discussing the investments topics covered in each chapter. Students can access the video clips on MyFinanceLab.

INVESTOR FACTS

Detecting Fraud—Researchers have discovered that information published in financial statements can be helpful in predicting which firms are most likely to commit accounting fraud. Firms that are most likely to commit fraud include those with the following characteristics:

- Declining receivables turnover
- Falling gross profit margins
- Rapidly growing sales (because fast-growing firms may face great temptation to commit fraud in order to raise more capital)
- Rising debt ratios
- Net income that exceeds cash flow from operations

Ethics boxes—short, boxed discussions of real-life scenarios in the investments world that focus on ethics—appear in nine selected chapters and on the book's website. Many ethics boxes contain a Critical Thinking Question for class discussion, with guideline answers given in the Instructor's Manual.

ETHICS IN INVESTING

Cooking the Books: What Were They Thinking?

Recent scandals involving fraudulent accounting practices have resulted in public outrage, not only in the United States but around the world as well. In February 2012 the San Francisco–based maker of products such as Kettle Chips and Pop Secret Popcorn, Diamond Foods, fired its CEO and CFO after discovering $80 million in payments to walnut growers that had been accounted for improperly. Diamond's stock fell nearly 40% in a single day on news of the accounting fraud. In January 2009 Ramalinga Rau, Chairman of the Indian tech company Satyam Computer Services, confessed that the firm's books had been falsified and overstated the firm's revenues and assets while understating its expenses. Satyam's stock lost more than 90% of its value between 2008 and 2009 as the scandal unfolded.

These were hardly the first cases of accounting fraud leading to financial ruin. It appears that creative and unethical accounting practices kept real costs and

debts off the books at Enron, WorldCom, Xerox, Qwest Communications, Conseco, and dozens of other public companies. When the reality finally caught up with the fantasy, thousands of investors and employees lost their life savings.

Unscrupulous executives used a number of accounting tricks to deceive the public including capitalizing operating expenses on the balance sheet, recognizing fictitious or premature revenues, creating off-balance-sheet liabilities, using off-balance-sheet derivative transactions to understate risk, and writing off goodwill as extraordinary loss rather than amortizing it over time to manipulate future earnings growth.

Critical Thinking Question One of the steps to strengthen corporate reporting is to separate internal and external audits of a company by not permitting an auditor to provide both internal and external audits to the same client. Will this regulation be able to eliminate conflict of interest? Discuss.

WITHIN THE CHAPTER

Each chapter features a short **Markets in Crisis** item that discusses some element of the recent financial crisis and the recession that followed. These items help students see the breadth of the financial crisis and the depth of its impact around the world.

MARKETS IN CRISIS

SEC Bans Short Selling

In September 2008, as the financial crisis grew deeper, the Securities and Exchange Commission announced a temporary ban on short sales of almost 800 financial stocks from September 19 to October 9. Research shows that the prices of stocks affected by the ban rose significantly, but those price increases were largely reversed when the ban was lifted. The vulnerability of stock markets to excessive short selling in times of crisis has led the SEC to implement rules aimed at preventing significant downward price pressure but allowing for unfettered price discovery. The alternative uptick rule (Rule 201) approved in 2010 imposes restrictions on short selling only when a stock has triggered a circuit breaker by experiencing a price decline of at least 10% in one day. At that point, short selling would be permitted if the price of the security were above the current national best bid.

Key Equations are screened in green throughout the text to help readers identify the most important mathematical relationships.

Equation 6.1

$$EPS = \frac{\text{Net profit after taxes} - \text{Preferred dividends}}{\text{Number of shares of common stock outstanding}}$$

Smart's Tour of the Web is a short video discussion (included as part of MyFinanceLab) of several websites that have useful information related to content in each chapter.

Smart's Tour of the Web

To watch author Scott Smart discuss key websites for this chapter, visit www.myfinancelab.com

Calculator Keystrokes At appropriate spots in the text the student will find sections on the use of financial calculators, with marginal calculator graphics that show the inputs and functions to be used.

Input	Function
−1000	PV
2	N
8	I
	CPT
	FV

Solution
1,166.40

CONCEPTS IN REVIEW

Answers available at
www.pearsonhighered.com/smart

7.1 Identify the three major parts of security analysis and explain why security analysis is important to the stock selection process.

7.2 What is intrinsic value? How does it fit into the security analysis process?

7.3 How would you describe a satisfactory investment? How does security analysis help in identifying investment candidates?

7.4 Would there be any need for security analysis if we operated in an efficient market environment? Explain.

Concepts in Review questions appear at the end of each section of the chapter. These review questions allow students to test their understanding of each section before moving on to the next section of the chapter. Answers for these questions are available at the book's website and by review of the preceding text.

The **end-of-chapter summary** makes *Fundamentals of Investing* an efficient study tool by integrating chapter contents with online learning resources available in **MyFinanceLab**. A thorough summary of the key concepts—What You Should Know—is directly linked with the text and online resources—Where to Practice. **Learning Goal** icons precede each summary item, which begins with a boldfaced restatement of the learning goal.

Discussion Questions, keyed to Learning Goals, guide students to integrate, investigate, and analyze the key concepts presented in the chapter. Many questions require that students apply the tools and techniques of the chapter to investment information they have obtained and then make a recommendation with regard to a specific investment strategy or vehicle. These project-type questions are far broader than the Concepts in Review questions within the chapter. Answers to odd-numbered questions are available to students on the book's website.

Expanded and Revised Problem Sets offer additional review and homework opportunities and are keyed to Learning Goals. Answers to odd-numbered Problems are available to students on the book's website, while all answers/solutions are available for instructors in the Instructor's Manual.

MyFinanceLab

Here is what you should know after reading this chapter. MyFinanceLab will help you identify what you know and where to go when you need to practice.

What You Should Know	Key Terms	Where to Practice
LG1 Review the concept of return, its components, the forces that affect the level of return, and historical returns. Return is the reward for investing. The total return provided by an investment includes income and capital gains (or losses). Return is commonly calculated on a historical basis and then used to project expected returns. The level of return depends on internal characteristics and external forces, which include the general level of price changes. Significant differences exist among the average annual rates of return realized over time on various types of security investments.	deflation, p. 121 expected return, p. 120 income, p. 118 inflation, p. 121 return, p. 118 total return, p. 119	MyFinanceLab Study Plan 4.1 Excel Table 4.3
LG2 Discuss the role of time value of money in measuring return and defining a satisfactory investment. Because investors have opportunities to earn interest on their funds, money has a time value. Time value concepts should be considered when making investment decisions. Financial calculators and electronic spreadsheets can be used to streamline time value calculations. A satisfactory investment is one for which the present value of its benefits equals or exceeds the present value of its costs.	satisfactory investment, p. 123	MyFinanceLab Study Plan 4.2 Excel Table 4.5

Discussion Questions

LG1 Q4.1 Choose a publicly traded company that has been listed on a major exchange or in the over-the-counter market for at least 5 years. Use any data source of your choice to find the annual cash dividend, if any, paid by the company in each of the past 5 calendar years. Also find the closing price of the stock at the end of each of the precedings 6 years.
   a. Calculate the return for each of the five 1-year periods.
   b. Create a graph that shows the return that the investment earned on the *y*-axis and the year in which the return was earn on the *x*-axis.
   c. On the basis of the graph in part **b**, estimate the return for the coming year, and explain your answer.

LG2 Q4.2 Two investments offer a series of cash payments over the next 4 years, as shown in the following table:

Investment	Year 1	Year 2	Year 3	Year 4
1	$100	$200	$300	$400
2	$250	$250	$250	$250

   a. What is the total amount of money paid by each investment over the 4 years?
   b. From a time value of money perspective, which of these investments is more attractive?
   c. Can you think of a reason why investors might prefer Investment 1?

LG4 Q4.3 Access appropriate estimates of the expected inflation rate over the next year, and the current yield on 1-year, risk-free securities (the yield on these securities is referred to as the *nominal* rate of interest). Use the data to estimate the current risk-free *real* rate of interest.

LG3 LG6 Q4.4 Choose 3 NYSE-listed stocks and maintain a record of their dividend payments, if any, and closing prices each week over the next 6 weeks.
   a. At the end of the 6-week period, calculate the 1-week HPRs for each stock for each of

Problems

All problems are available on www.myfinancelab.com

LG1 P4.1 How much would an investor earn on a stock purchased 1 year ago for $45 if it paid an annual cash dividend of $2.25 and had just been sold for $52.50? Would the investor have experienced a capital gain? Explain.

LG1 P4.2 An investor buys a bond for $10,000. The bond pays $300 interest every 6 months. After 18 months, the investor sells the bond for $9,500. Describe the types of income and/or loss the investor had.

LG1 P4.3 Assuming you purchased a share of stock for $50 one year ago, sold it today for $60, and during the year received 3 dividend payments totaling $2.70, calculate the following.
   a. Income
   b. Capital gain (or loss)
   c. Total return
      (1) In dollars
      (2) As a percentage of the initial investment

AT CHAPTER END

Case Problem 6.1   Sara Decides to Take the Plunge

 1 **6**

Sara Thomas is a child psychologist who has built up a thriving practice in her hometown of Boise, Idaho. Over the past several years she has been able to accumulate a substantial sum of money. She has worked long and hard to be successful, but she never imagined anything like this. Even so, success has not spoiled Sara. Still single, she keeps to her old circle of friends. One of her closest friends is Terry Jenkins, who happens to be a stockbroker and who acts as Sara's financial adviser.

Not long ago Sara attended a seminar on investing in the stock market, and since then she's been doing some reading about the market. She has concluded that keeping all of her money in low-yielding savings accounts doesn't make sense. As a result, Sara has decided to move part of her money to stocks. One evening, Sara told Terry about her decision and explained that she

Two Case Problems, keyed to the Learning Goals, encourage students to use higher-level critical thinking skills: to apply techniques presented in the chapter, to evaluate alternatives, and to recommend how an investor might solve a specific problem. Again, Learning Goals show the student the chapter topics on which the case problems focus.

Excel with Spreadsheets problems, appearing at the end of all chapters, challenge students to solve financial problems and make decisions through the creation of spreadsheets. In Chapter 1 students are directed to the website www.myfinancelab.com, where they can complete a spreadsheet tutorial, if needed. In addition, this tutorial and selected tables within the text carrying a spreadsheet icon are available in spreadsheet form on the text's website.

Excel with Spreadsheets

You have just learned about the mechanics of margin trading and want to take advantage of the potential benefits of financial leverage. You have decided to open a margin account with your broker and to secure a margin loan. The specifics of the account are as follows:

- Initial margin requirement is 70%.
- Maintenance margin is 30%.
- You are informed that if the value of your account falls below the maintenance margin, your account will be subject to a margin call.

You have been following the price movements of a stock over the past year and believe that it is currently undervalued and that the price will rise in the near future. You feel that the opening of a margin account is a good investment strategy. You have decided to purchase 3 round lots (i.e., 100 shares per round lot) of the stock at its current price of $25 per share.

Create a spreadsheet similar to the spreadsheet for Table 2.3, which can be viewed at www.myfinancelab.com, to model and analyze the following market transactions.

CFA Questions from the 2010 Level One Curriculum and the *CFA Candidate Study Notes, Level 1, Volume 4* are now at the end of each part of the book, starting at Part Two. These questions are also assignable in MyFinanceLab.

CFA Exam Questions

Being certified as a Chartered Financial Analyst (CFA) is globally recognized as the highest professional designation you can receive in the field of professional money management. The CFA charter is awarded to those candidates who successfully pass a series of 3 levels of exams, with each exam lasting 6 hours and covering a full range of investment topics. The CFA program is administered by the CFA Institute in Charlottesville, VA. (For more information about the CFA program, go to www.cfainstitute.org.)

Starting with this Part (2) of the text, and at the end of each part hereafter, you will find a small sample of questions similar to those that you might encounter on the Level 1 exam.

The Investment Environment and Conceptual Tools

Following is a sample of questions similar to ones that you might find on the CFA exam, Level 1. These questions deal with many of the topics covered in Parts 1 and 2 of this text, including the time value of money, measures of risk and return, securities markets, and portfolio management. (When answering the questions, give yourself 1½ minutes for each question; the objective is to correctly answer 8 of the 11 questions in 16½ minutes.)

1. Liquidity is best described as:
   a.   wanting a portfolio to grow over time in real terms to meet future needs.
   b.   converting an asset into cash without much of a price concession.
   c.   wanting to minimize the risk of loss and maintain purchasing power.

2. A portfolio consists of 75% invested in Security A with an expected return of 35% and 25% invested in Security B with an expected return of 7%. Compute the expected return on the portfolio.

3. Stocks A and B have standard deviations of 8% and 15%, respectively. The correlation between the two stocks' returns has historically been 0.35. What is the standard deviation of a portfolio consisting of 60% invested in Stock A and 40% invested in Stock B?

4. Which of the following portfolios would be off the efficient frontier?

Portfolio	Expected Return (%)	Risk (%)
A	13	17
B	12	18
C	18	30

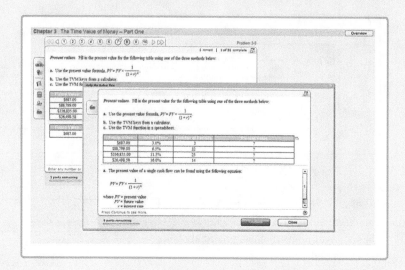

MyFinanceLab is a fully integrated homework and tutorial system which solves one of the biggest teaching problems in finance courses—students learn better with lots of practice, but grading complex multipart problems is time-consuming for the instructor. In MyFinanceLab, students can work the end-of-chapter problems with algorithmically generated values for unlimited practice and instructors can create assignments that are automatically graded and recorded in an online Gradebook.

MyFinanceLab also contains brief videos of author Scott Smart walking students through step-by-step solutions of select end-of-chapter problems.

MyFinanceLab: hands-on practice, hands-off grading.

Supplemental Materials

We recognize the key role of a complete and creative package of materials to supplement a basic textbook. We believe that the following materials, offered with the twelfth edition, will enrich the investments course for both students and instructors.

Fundamentals of Investing Companion Website

The book's Companion Website offers students and professors an up-to-date source of supplemental materials. This resource is located at www.pearsonhighered.com/smart. Visitors will find calculator keystrokes tutorials; answers to Concepts in Review questions; answers to odd-numbered Discussion Questions and Problems; a comprehensive list of the QR codes that appear in the text; and other readings and material that are beyond the normal scope of the first-level investments course.

Also at the book's website are three complete online chapters that appeared in earlier editions of this book: "Investing in Preferred Stocks," "Tax-Advantaged Investments," and "Real Estate and Other Tangible Investments." These highly informative chapters have been updated and moved to the website in response to user, reviewer, and our own preference that the text focus solely on securities investing. In addition to its improved focus, moving these chapters to the website allows us to both tighten and improve a number of text discussions and to shorten the text's overall length. We feel this change improves the text's effectiveness in terms of both content and length.

Instructor's Manual

Revised by Robert J. Hartwig of Worcester State College, the *Instructor's Manual* contains chapter outlines; lists of key concepts discussed in each chapter; detailed chapter overviews; answers/suggested answers to all Concepts in Review and Discussion Questions, Problems, and Critical Thinking Questions to Ethics in Investing boxes; solutions to the Case Problems; and ideas for outside projects.

Test Item File

Revised for the twelfth edition, also by Robert J. Hartwig of Worcester State College, the *Test Item File* includes a substantial number of questions. Each chapter features true-false and multiple-choice questions, as well as several problems and short-essay questions. The *Test Item File* is also available in Test Generator Software (TestGen with QuizMaster). Fully networkable, this software is available for Windows and Macintosh. TestGen's graphical interface enables instructors to easily view, edit, and add questions; export questions to create tests; and print tests in a variety of fonts and forms. Search and sort features let the instructor quickly locate questions and arrange them in a preferred order. QuizMaster, working with your school's computer network, automatically grades the exams, stores results on disk, and allows the instructor to view or print a variety of reports.

PowerPoint Lecture Slides

To facilitate classroom presentations, PowerPoint slides of all text images and classroom lecture notes are available for Windows and Macintosh. The slides were revised by textbook author Scott Smart.

CourseSmart for Instructors

CourseSmart goes beyond traditional expectations by providing instant, online access to the textbooks and course materials you need at a lower cost to students. And, even as students save money, you can save time and hassle with a digital textbook that allows you to search the most relevant content at the very moment you need it. Whether it's evaluating textbooks or creating lecture notes to help students with difficult concepts, CourseSmart can make life a little easier. See how when you visit www.coursesmart .com/instructors.

CourseSmart for Students

CourseSmart goes beyond traditional expectations by providing instant, online access to the textbooks and course materials students need at a lower cost. They can also search, highlight, and take notes anywhere at any time. See all the benefits to students at www.coursesmart.com/students.

Acknowledgments

Many people gave their generous assistance during the initial development and revisions of *Fundamentals of Investing*. The expertise, classroom experience, and general advice of both colleagues and practitioners have been invaluable. Reactions and suggestions from students throughout the country—comments we especially enjoy receiving—sustained our belief in the need for a fresh, informative, and teachable investments text.

A few individuals provided significant subject matter expertise in the initial development of the book. They are Terry S. Maness of Baylor University, Arthur L. Schwartz, Jr., of the University of South Florida at St. Petersburg, and Gary W. Eldred. Their contributions are greatly appreciated. In addition, Pearson obtained the advice of a large group of experienced reviewers. We appreciate their many suggestions and criticisms, which have had a strong influence on various aspects of this volume. Our special thanks go to the following people, who reviewed all or part of the manuscript for the previous eighth editions of the book.

Kevin Ahlgrim
M. Fall Ainina
Joan Anderssen
Felix O. Ayadi
Gary Baker
Harisha Batra
Richard B. Bellinfante
Cecil C. Bigelow
Robert J. Boldin
Paul Bolster
A. David Brummett
Gary P. Cain
Gary Carman
Daniel J. Cartell
P. R. Chandy
Steven P. Clark
David M. Cordell
Timothy Cowling
Robert M. Crowe
Richard F. DeMong
Clifford A. Diebold
Steven Dolvin
James Dunn
Betty Marie Dyatt
Steven J. Elbert
Robert Eldridge
Imad Elhaj
Thomas Eyssell
Frank J. Fabozzi
Robert A. Ford
Albert J. Fredman
John Gerlach

Tom Geurts
Chaim Ginsberg
Joel Gold
Terry Grieb
Frank Griggs
Brian Grinder
Harry P. Guenther
Tom Guerts
Robert Hartwig
Mahboubul Hassan
Gay Hatfield
Robert D. Hollinger
Sue Beck Howard
Ping Hsiao
Roland Hudson, Jr.
Raad Jassim
Donald W. Johnson
Samuel Kyle Jones
Rajiv Kalra
Ravindra R. Kamath
Bill Kane
Daniel J. Kaufmann, Jr.
Burhan Kawosa
Nancy Kegelman
Phillip T. Kolbe
Sheri Kole
Christopher M. Korth
Marie A. Kratochvil
Thomas M. Krueger
Wendy Ku
George Kutner
Blake LeBaron

Robert T. LeClair
Chun I. Lee
William Lepley
Steven Lifland
Ralph Lim
James Lock
Larry A. Lynch
Weston A. McCormac
David J. McLaughlin
Anne Macy
James Mallett
Keith Manko
Timothy Manuel
Kathy Milligan
Warren E. Moeller
Homer Mohr
Majed R. Muhtaseb
Joseph Newhouse
Michael Nugent
Joseph F. Ollivier
Michael Palermo
John Palffy
John Park
Thomas Patrick
Michael Polakoff
Barbara Poole
Ronald S. Pretekin
Stephen W. Pruitt
Mark Pyles
S. P. Umamaheswar Rao
Rathin Rathinasamy
William A. Richard

Linda R. Richardson
William A. Rini
Roy A. Roberson
Tammy Rogers
Edward Rozalewicz
William J. Ruckstuhl
David Russo
Arthur L. Schwartz, Jr.
William Scroggins
Daniel Singer
Keith V. Smith
Pat R. Stout
Nancy E. Strickler
Glenn T. Sweeney
Amir Tavakkol
Phillip D. Taylor
Wenyuh Tsay
Robert C. Tueting
Howard E. Van Auken
P. V. Viswanath
Doug Waggle
John R. Weigel
Sally Wells
Peter M. Wichert
John C. Woods
Michael D. Woodworth
Robert J. Wright
Richard H. Yanow
Ali E. Zadeh
Edward Zajicek

The following people provided extremely useful reviews and input to the thirteenth edition:

Anand K. Bhattacharya, Arizona State University
Denis O. Boudreaux, University of Louisiana-Lafayette
William Compton, University of North Carolina-Wilmington
Scott Ehrhorn, Liberty University
Arthur S. Guarino, Rutgers University
John Guess, Delgado Community College
Dan Hess, Seattle Pacific University
Barry Marchman, Georgia Tech
Hsinrong Wei, Bronx Community College

Because of the wide variety of topics covered in the book, we called upon many experts for advice. We thank them and their firms for allowing us to draw on their insights and awareness of recent developments to ensure that the text is as current as possible. In particular, we want to mention Bill Bachrach, Bachrach & Associates, San Diego, CA; John Markese, President, American Association of Individual Investors, Chicago, IL; Frank Hatheway, CFA, Chief Economist, Nasdaq, New York, NY; George Ebenhack, Oppenheimer & Co., Los Angeles, CA; Mark D. Erwin, ChFC, Commonwealth Financial Network, San Diego, CA; David M. Love, C. P. Eaton and Associates, La Jolla, CA; Michael R. Murphy, Sceptre Investment Counsel, Toronto, Ontario, Canada; Mark S. Nussbaum, CFP®, Wells Fargo Advisors, Inc., La Jolla, CA; Richard Russell, Dow Theory Letters, La Jolla, CA; and Michael J. Steelman, Merrill Lynch, Bonsall, CA.

To create the new video feature, An Adviser's Perspective, we relied on the generosity of many investment professionals from around the country. We are especially thankful to David Hays of CFCI and Ed Slott of Ed Slott and Company for helping us to do a great deal of the videotaping for this feature at the 2012 Ed Slott conference in Phoenix, Arizona. We are thankful to all of the investment professionals who participated in this project on video:

Catherine Censuello, Founder, CMC Wealth Management
Joseph A. Clark, Managing Partner, Financial Enhancement Group
Ron Courser, CFO, Ron Courser and Associates
Bob Grace, President, Grace Tax Advisory Group
James Grant, Founder, Grant's Interest Rate Observer
Bill Harris, Founder, WH Cornerstone Investments
James Johnson, President, All Mark Insurance Services
Mary Kusske, President, Kusske Financial Management
Rick Loek, CEO, Calrima Financial and Insurance Agency
Ryan McKeown, Senior VP, Wealth Enhancement Group
Thomas O'Connell, President, International Financial Advisory Group
Phil Putney, Owner, AFS Wealth Management
Tom Riquier, Owner, The Retirement Center
Rob Russell, CEO, Russell and Company
Carol Schmidlin, President, Franklin Planning
Ed Slott, CEO, Ed Slott and Company
Bryan Sweet, Owner, Sweet Financial Services
Steve Wright, Managing Member, The Wright Legacy Group

Special thanks to Robert Hartwig of Worcester State College for revising and updating the *Test Item File* and *Instructor's Manual*.

The staff at Pearson, particularly Donna Battista, contributed their creativity, enthusiasm, and commitment to this textbook. Pearson Project Managers Emily Biberger and Jill Kolongowski managed and pulled together the various strands of the project. Other dedicated Pearson staff, including production supervisor Alison Eusden, media producer Melissa Honig, content lead for MyFinanceLab Miguel Leonarte, media project manager Lisa Rinaldi, marketing manager Jami Minard, and permissions supervisor Jill Dougan, warrant special thanks for shepherding the project through the development, production, marketing, permissions, and website construction stages. Without their care and concern, this text would not have evolved into the teachable and interesting text and package we believe it to be.

Finally, our wives, Susan, Robin, and Charlene, played important roles by providing support and understanding during the book's development, revision, and production. We are forever grateful to them, and we hope that this edition will justify the sacrifices required during the many hours we were away from them working on this book.

SCOTT B. SMART
LAWRENCE J. GITMAN
MICHAEL D. JOEHNK

1

Common Stocks

LEARNING GOALS

After studying this chapter, you should be able to:

LG1 Explain the investment appeal of common stocks and why individuals like to invest in them.

LG2 Describe stock returns from a historical perspective and understand how current returns measure up to historical standards of performance.

LG3 Discuss the basic features of common stocks, including issue characteristics, stock quotations, and transaction costs.

LG4 Understand the different kinds of common stock values.

LG5 Discuss common stock dividends, types of dividends, and dividend reinvestment plans.

LG6 Describe various types of common stocks, including foreign stocks, and note how stocks can be used as investment vehicles.

In recent years, stock markets in the United States and around the world have been extremely volatile. From October 2007 to March 2009, U.S. stocks lost more than half their value, and in many markets around the world, the results were even worse. Those declining stock values mirrored the state of the world economy, as country after country slipped into a deep recession. U.S. firms responded by cutting dividends. Standard and Poor's reported that a record number of firms cut their dividend payment in the first quarter of 2009, and a record low number announced plans to increase their dividends.

Fortunately, from its March 2009 low, the U.S. stock market nearly doubled over the next 2 years, hitting a post-recession peak in April 2011. The run-up in stock prices coincided with an increase in dividend payouts. Of the 500 firms included in the S&P 500 stock index, 154 increased their dividend payment in 2010 or 2011, compared to just 3 firms who cut payments over the same period. Even so, the good news for stocks didn't last very long. In the spring of 2011, concern about a looming economic crisis in Europe sent U.S. stocks lower again. The S&P 500 Index fell by more than 17% from April to August in 2011. The market largely recovered its losses over the next year.

Throughout this volatile period, some companies managed to increase their dividends each year. Standard and Poor's tracks the performance of a portfolio of firms that it calls "dividend aristocrats" because these firms have managed to increase their dividends for at least 25 consecutive years. Including household names such as Johnson & Johnson, Exxon Mobil, and AFLAC, the dividend aristocrat index displays ups and downs that mirror those of the overall market, but at least investors in these firms have enjoyed consistently rising dividends.

(Sources: IROC Press Release, August 10, 2009, CNWTelbec, www.cnw.ca/fr/releases/archive/August2009/10/c3719; Stephen Bernard, S&P: Record Number of Firms Cut Dividends in 1st Quarter," *Pittsburgh Post Gazette*, April 7, 2009; "S&P 500 Dividend Payers Rose to Dozen Year High," May 1, 2012, http://seekingalpha.com/article/545451-s-p-500-dividend-payers-rise-to-dozen-year-high; http://www.standardandpoors.com/indices/sp-500-dividend-aristocrats/en/us/?indexId=spusa-500dusdff--p-us----&ffFix=yes)

What Stocks Have to Offer

 Common stock enables you to participate in the profits of a firm. Every shareholder is a part owner of the firm and, as such, has a claim on the wealth created by the company. This claim is not without limitations, however, because common stockholders are really the **residual owners** of the company. That is, their claim is subordinate to the claims of other investors, such as lenders, so for stockholders to get rich, the firm must first meet all its other financial obligations. Accordingly, as residual owners, holders of common stock have no guarantee that they will receive any return on their investment.

The Appeal of Common Stocks

Even in spite of the steep decline in the U.S. stock market in 2008 and 2009, common stocks remain a popular investment choice among both individual and institutional investors. For most investors, the allure of common stocks is the prospect that they will increase in value over time and generate significant capital gains. Many stocks do pay dividends, thereby providing investors with a periodic income stream. For most stocks, however, the dividends paid in any particular year pale in comparison to the capital gains (and capital losses) that are the natural consequence of stock price fluctuations.

Putting Stock Price Behavior in Perspective

Given the nature of common stocks, when the market is strong, you can generally expect to benefit from price appreciation. A good example is the performance that took place in 2009 and 2010, when the market, as measured by the Dow Jones Industrial Average (DJIA), went up by more than 19% and 11%, respectively. Unfortunately, when markets falter, so do investor returns. Just look at what happened in 2008, when the market (again, as measured by the DJIA) fell by almost 34%. Excluding dividends, that means a $100,000 investment declined in value to a little more than $66,000. That hurts!

Make no mistake about it: The market does have its bad days, and sometimes those bad days seem to go on for months. Even though it may not always appear to be so, bad days are the exception rather than the rule. That was certainly the case over the 56-year period from 1956 through 2011, when the Dow went down (for the year) just 17 times—about 30% of the time. The other 70% of the time, the market was up—anywhere from 2% on the year to nearly 40%. True, there is some risk and price

MARKETS IN CRISIS

The Lumbering Bear

Bear markets occur when stock prices are falling. But not all falling markets end up as bears. A drop of 5% or more in one of the major market indexes, like the Dow Jones Industrial Average, is called a routine decline. Such declines are considered routine because they typically occur several times a year. A correction is a drop of 10% or more in an index, whereas the term *bear market* is reserved for severe market declines of 20% or more. Bear markets occur every 3 to 4 years on average, although that pattern does not make it easy to predict bear markets. For example, the 1990s were totally bear-free. The most recent bear market began in October 2007 when the S&P 500 peaked a little shy of 1,600. The next 20 months witnessed one of the worst bear markets in U.S. history, with the S&P 500 falling almost 57% by March 2009.

TABLE 1.1   HISTORICAL RETURNS ON THE STANDARD AND POOR'S 500, 1950–2010

	Rate of Return from Dividends (%)	Rate of Return from Capital Gains (%)	Total Return (%)
1950s	5.4	13.2	19.3
1960s	3.3	4.4	7.8
1970s	4.3	1.6	5.8
1980s	4.6	12.6	17.3
1990s	2.7	15.3	18.1
2000s	1.8	−2.7	−1.0
1950–2010	3.6	7.2	11.0

Note: The total return is higher than the sum of the dividend return and the capital gain return because we assume dividends are reinvested when received.

(Source: www.simplestockinvesting.com/SP500-historical-real-total-returns.htm)

volatility (even in good markets), but that's the price you pay for all the upside potential. For example, from 1982 through early 2000, in one of the longest bull markets in history, the DJIA grew (over 18 years) at an average annual rate of nearly 17%. Yet, even in this market, there were some off days, and even a few off years. But, clearly, they were the exception rather than the rule.

From Stock Prices to Stock Returns

Our discussion so far has centered on stock prices. However, more important than stock prices are *stock returns*, which take into account both price behavior and dividend income. Table 1.1 uses the Standard and Poor's 500 Index (S&P 500) to illustrate how the U.S. stock market has performed since 1950. Like the DJIA, the S&P 500 is a barometer of the overall stock market. As its name implies, the S&P 500 tracks 500 companies (most of which are large firms), so most experts consider it a better indicator of the market's overall performance than the DJIA, which tracks just 30 firms. In addition to total returns, the table breaks market performance down into the two basic sources of return: dividends and capital gains. These figures, of course, reflect the general behavior of the market as a whole, not necessarily that of individual stocks. Think of them as the return behavior on a well-balanced portfolio of common stocks.

The table shows several interesting patterns. First, the returns from capital gains range from an average of 15.3% during the booming 1990s to −2.7% in the 2000s. Returns from dividends vary too, but not nearly as much, ranging from 5.4% in the 1950s to 1.8% in the 2000s. Breaking down the returns into dividends and capital gains reveals, not surprisingly, that the big returns (or losses) come from capital gains.

Second, stocks generally earn positive total returns over long time periods. From 1950 to 2010, the average total return on the S&P 500 was 11.0% per year. At that rate, you could double their money every 6 or 7 years. To look at the figures another way, if you had invested $10,000 in the S&P 500 in 1950, your investment would have grown to $5.2 million over the next 60 years. You can get rich by investing in the stock market, as long as you are patient!

Third, investing in stocks is clearly not without risk. After 5 decades in which the average annual return on stocks was positive, the beginning of the 21st century witnessed a prolonged period with negative average returns. From 2000 through 2009, the U.S. stock market's average annual return was −1.0% per year! In other words, if you had invested $10,000 in stocks in 1950, your portfolio would have grown to $5.7 million over the next 50 years, but in the 10 years after that, your portfolio would have fallen to just under $5.2 million. That's still a lot of money, suggesting that stocks may be a very good investment in the long run, but that was little consolation to investors who saw their wealth fall dramatically in the early years of the 21st century.

Now keep in mind that the numbers here represent market performance; individual stocks can and often do perform quite differently. But at least the averages give us a benchmark against which we can assess current stock returns and our own expectations. For example, if a return of about 11% can be considered a good long-term estimate for stocks, then sustained returns of 16% to 18% should definitely be viewed as extraordinary. (These higher returns are possible, of course, but to get them, you very likely will have to take on more risk.) Likewise, long-run stock returns of only 4% to 6% should probably be viewed as substandard. If that's the best you think you can do, then you may want to consider sticking with bonds, where you'll earn almost as much, but with less risk.

A Real Estate Bubble Goes Bust and So Does the Market

An old investment tip is, "Buy land because they aren't making any more of it." For many years, it appeared that this advice applied to housing in the United States, as home prices enjoyed a long, upward march. According to the Standard and Poor's Case-Shiller Home Price Index, a measure of the average value of a single-family home in the United States, the average home price peaked in May 2006. Over the next 3 years, home prices fell sharply, falling 32% by the summer of 2009. As prices fell, some homeowners realized that they owed more on their mortgages than their homes were worth, and mortgage defaults began to rise. Unfortunately, some of the biggest investors in home mortgages were U.S. commercial and investment banks. As homeowners fell behind on their mortgage payments, the stock prices of financial institutions began to drop, raising serious concerns about the health of the entire U.S. financial system. Those fears seemed to have been realized when a top-tier investment bank, Lehman Brothers, filed for bankruptcy in September 2008. That event sparked a free fall in the stock market.

The House Price Puzzle

Figure 1.1 (on page 5) shows that U.S. stocks rose along with housing prices for many years, but when weakness in the housing sector spilled over into banking, stock prices plummeted, and the world economy fell into a deep recession that continued through the spring of 2009. The stock market signaled that a recovery might be on the horizon, rising for 6 consecutive months starting in March 2009. Indeed, the recession officially ended in June 2009, but by historical standards the economic recovery was somewhat anemic. By September 2012, the stock market had still not recovered all of its losses, unemployment remained near 8%, and house prices showed no real sign of improvement.

The Pros and Cons of Stock Ownership

Investors own stocks for all sorts of reasons: the potential for capital gains, their current income, or perhaps the high degree of market liquidity. But as with any investment, there are pros and cons to these securities.

The Advantages of Stock Ownership One reason stocks are so appealing is the possibility for substantial returns that they offer. As we just saw, stocks generally provide relatively high returns over the long haul. Indeed, common stock

FIGURE 1.1   **A Snapshot of U.S. Stock and Housing Indexes (mid-2003 through mid-2012)**

From mid-2003 through 2005 U.S. stocks rose along with housing prices, but when crumbling U.S. housing prices began to spill over into banking, stock prices plummeted, wiping out all the gains accumulated over the prior 6 years. Three years after the stock market hit bottom, it had still not reached its precrisis peak, nor had house prices rebounded from their crisis lows to any significant degree.
(Source: Data from Yahoo! Finance and Standard & Poor's.)

returns compare very favorably to other investments such as long-term corporate bonds and U.S. Treasury securities. For example, over the last century, high-grade corporate bonds earned annual returns that were about half as large as the returns on common stocks. Although long-term bonds outperform stocks in some years, the opposite is true more often than not. Stocks typically outperform bonds, and usually by a wide margin. Stocks also provide protection from inflation because over time their returns exceed the inflation rate. In other words, by purchasing stocks, you gradually increase your purchasing power.

Stocks offer other benefits as well: They are easy to buy and sell, and the costs associated with trading stocks are modest. Moreover, information about stock prices and the stock market is widely disseminated in the news and financial media. A final advantage is that the unit cost of a share of common stock is typically fairly low. Unlike bonds, which normally carry minimum denominations of at least $1,000, and some mutual funds that have fairly hefty minimum investments, common stocks don't have such minimums. Instead, most stocks today are priced at less than $50 or $60 a share—and you can buy any number of shares that you want.

The Disadvantages of Stock Ownership There are also some disadvantages to common stock ownership. Risk is perhaps the most significant. Stocks are subject to various types of risk, including business and financial risk, purchasing power risk, market risk, and event risk. All of these can adversely affect a stock's earnings and dividends, its price appreciation, and, of course, the rate of return that you earn. Even the best of stocks possess elements of risk that are difficult to eliminate because company earnings are subject to many factors, including government control and regulation, foreign competition, and the state of the economy. Because such factors affect sales and profits, they also affect stock prices and (to a lesser degree) dividend payments.

All of this leads to another disadvantage: stock returns are highly volatile and very hard to predict, so it is difficult to consistently select top performers. The stock selection process is complex because so many elements affect how a company will perform. In addition, the price of a company's stock today reflects investors' expectations about how the company will perform. In other words, identifying a stock that will earn high returns requires that you not only identify a company that will exhibit strong future financial performance (in terms of sales and earnings) but also that you can spot that opportunity before other investors do and bid up the stock price.

A final disadvantage is that stocks generally distribute less current income than some other investments. Several types of investments—bonds, for instance—pay more current income and do so with much greater certainty. Figure 1.2 compares the dividend yield on common stocks with the coupon yield on high-grade corporate bonds. It

---

FIGURE 1.2   **The Current Income of Stocks and Bonds**

The current income (dividends) paid to stockholders falls far short of interest income paid to bondholders. The dividend yield is the average dividend yield for stocks in the S&P 500 Index, and the bond yield is for high-quality corporate bonds.
(Source: Data from Federal Reserve Board of Governors and www.multpl.com/s-p-500-dividend-yield/table.)

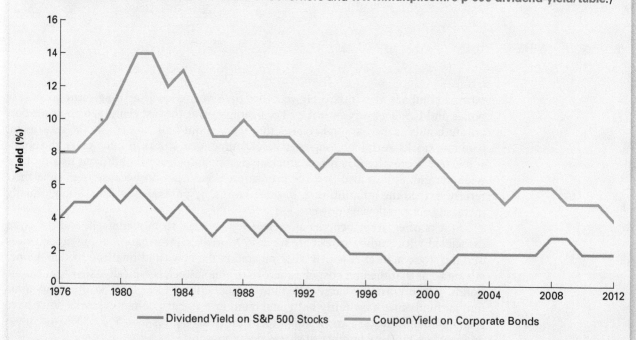

shows the degree of sacrifice common stock investors make in terms of current income. Clearly, even though the yield gap has narrowed a great deal in the past few years, common stocks still have a long way to go before they catch up with the current income levels available from bonds and most other types of fixed-income securities.

CONCEPTS IN REVIEW
Answers available at
www.pearsonhighered.com/
smart

1.1 What is a common stock? What is meant by the statement that holders of common stock are the residual owners of the firm?

1.2 What are 2 or 3 of the major investment attributes of common stocks?

1.3 Briefly describe the behavior of the U.S. stock market over the last half of the 20th century and the early part of the 21st century.

1.4 How important are dividends as a source of return to common stock? What about capital gains? Which is more important to total return? Which causes wider swings in total return?

1.5 What are some of the advantages and disadvantages of owning common stock? What are the major types of risks to which stockholders are exposed?

Basic Characteristics of Common Stock

LG3 LG4 Each share of common stock represents an equity (or ownership) position in a company. It's this equity position that explains why common stocks are often referred to as *equity securities* or **equity capital**. Every share entitles the holder to an equal ownership position and participation in the corporation's earnings and dividends, an equal vote (usually), and an equal voice in management. Together the common stockholders own the company. The more shares an investor owns, the bigger his or her ownership position. Common stock has no maturity date—it remains outstanding indefinitely.

Common Stock as a Corporate Security

All corporations "issue" common stock of one type or another. But the shares of many, if not most, corporations are never traded because the firms either are too small or are family controlled. The stocks of interest to us in this book are **publicly traded issues**— the shares that are readily available to the general public and that are bought and sold in the open market. The firms issuing such shares range from giants like Apple Inc. and Exxon Mobil Corporation to much smaller regional and local firms. The market for publicly traded stocks is enormous. According to the World Federation of Stock Exchanges, the value of all U.S. stocks in early 2012 was more than $16 trillion.

Issuing New Shares Companies can issue shares of common stock in several ways. The most widely used procedure is the **public offering**. When using this procedure, the corporation offers the investing public a certain number of shares of its stock at a certain price. Figure 1.3 (on page 8) shows an announcement for such an offering. Note in this case that Angie's List is offering 8,793,408 shares of stock at a price of $13 per share. Of the 8,793,408 shares being offered, 6,250,000 are newly issued shares sold by the company to investors. At $13 per share, the offering will raise more than $81.2 million. The remaining 2,543,408 shares are being sold by existing shareholders to new investors. The cash raised from selling these shares goes to the firm's existing shareholders and not to the company.

FIGURE 1.3   **An Announcement of a New Stock Issue**

This announcement indicates that the company—Angie's List—is issuing 8,793,408 million shares of stock at a price of $13 per share. For this leading provider of reviews of professional service providers, the new issue will mean $81.3 million in fresh capital.
(Source: *Angie's List*, Initial Public Offer prospectus, http://www.thinkequity.com/banking/prospectus-pdf/Angies-List-Prospectus-11-22-11.pdf.)

PROSPECTUS

8,793,408 Shares

Angie's list.

Common Stock

This is Angie's List, Inc.'s initial public offering. We are selling 6,250,000 shares of our common stock and the selling stockholders, including members of our senior management, are selling 2,543,408 shares of our common stock. We will not receive any proceeds from the sale of shares to be offered by the selling stockholders.

Prior to this offering, there has been no public market for the shares. The shares of our common stock have been approved for listing on the NASDAQ Global Market under the symbol "ANGI."

Investing in our common stock involves risks that are described in the "Risk Factors" section beginning on page 10 of this prospectus.

	Per Share	Total
Public offering price	$13.00	$114,314,304
Underwriting discount[1]	$.91	$8,002,001
Proceeds, before expenses, to us	$12.09	$75,562,500
Proceeds, before expenses, to the selling stockholders	$12.09	$30,749,803

(1) We refer you to "Underwriting" beginning on page 124 for additional information regarding total underwriter compensation.

The underwriters may also exercise their option to purchase up to an additional 1,319,011 shares from us at the public offering price, less the underwriting discount, for 30 days after the date of this prospectus to cover overallotments, if any.

Neither the Securities and Exchange Commission nor any state securities commission has approved or disapproved of these securities or determined if this prospectus is truthful or complete. Any representation to the contrary is a criminal offense.

The shares will be ready for delivery on or about November 22, 2011.

BofA Merrill Lynch

Allen & Company LLC	**Stifel Nicolaus Weisel**		**RBC Capital Markets**
Janney Montgomery Scott	**Oppenheimer & Co.**	**ThinkEquity LLC**	**CODE Advisors**

The date of this prospectus is November 16, 2011.

Companies also can issue new shares of stock using what is known as a **rights offering**. In a rights offering, existing stockholders are given the first opportunity to buy the new issue. In essence, a stock right gives a shareholder the right (but not the obligation) to purchase new shares of the company's stock in proportion to his or her current ownership position.

For instance, if a stockholder currently owns 1% of a firm's stock and the firm issues 10,000 additional shares, the rights offering will give that stockholder the opportunity to purchase 1% (100 shares) of the new issue. If the investor does not want to use the rights, he or she can sell them to someone who does. The net result of a rights offering is the same as that of a public offering: The firm ends up with more equity in its capital structure, and the number of shares outstanding increases.

Stock Spin-Offs Perhaps one of the most creative ways of bringing a new issue to the market is through a **stock spin-off**. Basically, a spin-off occurs when a company gets rid of one of its subsidiaries or divisions. For example, Sears did this when it spun off its Orchard Supply Hardware subsidiary in December 2011. The company doesn't just sell the subsidiary to some other firm. Rather, it creates a new stand-alone company and then distributes stock in that company to its existing stockholders. Thus, every Sears shareholder received 1 share in the newly created, and now publicly traded, Orchard Supply for every 22 shares of Sears stock that they held.

Smart's Tour of the Web
To watch author Scott Smart discuss key websites for this chapter, visit www.myfinancelab.com

There have been hundreds of stock spin-offs in the last 10 to 15 years. Some of the more notable recent ones are the spin-off of Madison Square Garden by Cablevision Systems and the TripAdvisor spin-off by Expedia. Normally, companies execute stock spin-offs if they believe the subsidiary is no longer a good fit or if they feel they've become too diversified and want to focus on their core products. The good news is that such spin-offs often work very well for investors, too.

Stock Splits Companies can also increase the number of shares outstanding by executing a **stock split**. In declaring a split, a firm merely announces that it will increase the number of shares outstanding by exchanging a specified number of new shares for each outstanding share of stock. For example, in a 2-for-1 stock split, 2 new shares of stock are exchanged for each old share. In a 3-for-2 split, 3 new shares are exchanged for every 2 old shares outstanding. Thus, a stockholder who owned 200 shares of stock before a 2-for-1 split becomes the owner of 400 shares; the same investor would hold 300 shares if there had been a 3-for-2 split.

A company uses a stock split when it wants to enhance its stock's trading appeal by lowering its market price. Normally, the price of the stock falls roughly in proportion to the terms of the split (unless the stock split is accompanied by a big increase in the level of dividends). For example, using the ratio of the number of old shares to new, we can expect a $100 stock to trade at or close to $50 a share after a 2-for-1 split. Specifically, we divide the original price per share by the ratio of new shares to old. That same $100 stock would trade at about $67 after a 3-for-2 split—that is, $100 \div 3/2 = $100 \div 1.5 = 67. (Later in this chapter we will discuss a variation of the stock split, known as a stock dividend.)

Example

On June 26, 2012, Dollar Tree Inc. split its shares 2-for-1. On the day before the split, Dollar Tree shares sold for $110.98. Theoretically, after a 2-for-1 split the stock price should fall by half to $55.49. In fact, once the split went into effect, the price of 1 Dollar Tree share fell to $55.59.

Treasury Stock Instead of increasing the number of outstanding shares, corporations sometimes find it desirable to reduce the number of shares by buying back their own stock. Generally speaking, firms repurchase their own stock when they view it as undervalued in the marketplace. When that happens, the company's own stock becomes an attractive investment candidate.

Firms usually purchase their stock in the open market, like any other individual or institution. When acquired, these shares become known as **treasury stock**. Technically, treasury stocks are simply shares of stock that have been issued and subsequently repurchased by the issuing firm. Treasury stocks are kept by the corporation and can be used at a later date for several purposes. For example, they could be used to pay for mergers and acquisitions, to meet employee stock option plans, or as a means of paying stock dividends. Or the shares can simply be held in treasury for an indefinite time.

The short-term impact of these share repurchases—or *buybacks*, as they're sometimes called—is generally positive, meaning that stock prices generally go up when firms announce their intentions to conduct share repurchases. The long-term impact is less settled, with some research indicating that share repurchases are followed by periods of above-average stock returns and other research contesting that conclusion.

Classified Common Stock For the most part, all the stockholders in a corporation enjoy the same benefits of ownership. Occasionally, however, a company will issue different classes of common stock, each of which entitles holders to different privileges and benefits. These issues are known as **classified common stock**. Hundreds of publicly traded firms, including well-known tech companies such as Google and Facebook, have created such stock classes. Although issued by the same company, each class of common stock may have unique characteristics.

Firms that issue multiple classes of stock usually do so to grant different voting rights to different groups of investors. For instance, when Facebook conducted its 2012 IPO, it issued Class A and Class B shares. The Class A shares, available for purchase by the public, were entitled to 1 vote per share. Class B shares, held by Facebook CEO and founder Mark Zuckerberg (and other Facebook insiders) were entitled to 10 votes per share. This ensured that Zuckerberg would have voting control of the company even if Facebook issued many more Class A shares over time in subsequent stock offerings. On rare occasions firms may use classified stock to grant different dividend rights to different investors.

Regardless of the specifics, whenever there is more than one class of common stock outstanding, you should take the time to determine the privileges, benefits, and limitations of each class.

Buying and Selling Stocks

To be an informed stock trader, you need a basic awareness of how stock prices are quoted. You also need to understand the transaction costs associated with buying and selling stock. Certainly, keeping track of current prices is an essential element in buy-and-sell decisions. Prices help you monitor the market performance of your security holdings. Similarly, transaction costs are important because of the impact they have on investment returns. Indeed, the costs of executing stock transactions can sometimes consume most (or all) of the profits from an investment. You should not take these costs lightly.

Reading the Quotes Investors in the stock market have come to rely on a highly efficient information system that quickly disseminates market prices to the public. The stock quotes that appear daily in the financial press and online are a vital part of that

FIGURE 1.4 A Stock Quote for Abercrombie & Fitch

This figure shows a stock quote for Abercrombie & Fitch on August 23, 2012.
(Source: Yahoo! Finance, http://finance.yahoo.com/q?s=ANF&ql=0.)

Abercrombie & Fitch Co. (ANF) - NYSE

35.55 ↓0.83 (2.27%) 4:00PM EDT | After Hours: **35.55** ↓0.01 (0.03%) 4:11PM EDT - Nasdaq Real Time Price

Prev Close:	36.38	Day's Range:	35.48 - 36.42
Open:	36.35	52wk Range:	28.64 - 77.49
Bid:	35.40 x 100	Volume:	2,332,560
Ask:	35.72 x 100	Avg Vol (3m):	3,472,700
1y Target Est:	38.23	Market Cap:	2.94B
Beta:	2.19	P/E (ttm):	34.35
Next Earnings Date:	N/A	EPS (ttm):	1.03
		Div & Yield:	0.70 (2.20%)

information system. To see how to read and interpret stock price quotations, consider the quotes that appear at Yahoo! Finance. These quotes give not only the most recent price of each stock but also a great deal of additional information.

Figure 1.4 illustrates a basic quote for Abercrombie & Fitch Co. stock, which trades under the ticker symbol ANF. The quote was taken after trading hours on Thursday, August 23, 2012. On that day, the price of Abercrombie common stock closed at $35.55 per share, down $0.83 (or about 2.3%) from the previous day's close of $36.38. Notice that the stock opened on Thursday at $36.35, reaching an intraday high of $36.42 and an intraday low of $35.48. Figure 1.4 also reveals that during the preceding 52 weeks Abercrombie stock traded as high as $77.49 and as low as $28.64. Trading volume for the stock on August 23 was 2.3 million shares, considerably less than the average daily volume over the previous 3 months of just under 3.5 million shares.

A few other items from Figure 1.4 are noteworthy. Abercrombie's stock has a beta of 2.19, meaning that it is more than twice as risky (i.e., has more than twice as much systematic risk) as the average stock in the market (as the very wide trading range over the past year would also indicate). Abercrombie's total *market capitalization* (or market cap) is $2.94 billion. Remember, a company's market cap is simply its share price times the number of shares outstanding. In its most recent reporting period, the company earned $1.03 per share, and given the closing price of $35.55, the price-to-earnings ratio of Abercrombie stock was just over 34.)

Transaction Costs Investors can buy and sell common stock in round or odd lots. A *round lot* is 100 shares of stock or multiples thereof. An *odd lot* is a transaction involving fewer than 100 shares. For example, the sale of 400 shares of stock would be a round-lot transaction; the sale of 75 shares would be an odd-lot transaction. Trading 250 shares of stock would involve a combination of two round lots and an odd lot.

An investor incurs certain transaction costs when buying or selling stock. In addition to some modest transfer fees and taxes paid by the seller, the major cost is the brokerage fee paid—by both buyer and seller—at the time of the transaction. As a rule, brokerage fees can amount to just a fraction of 1% to as much as 2% or more, depending on whether you use the services of a discount broker or full-service broker. But they can go even higher, particularly for very small trades. Historically, transactions involving odd lots required a specialist called an *odd-lot dealer* and triggered an extra cost called an *odd-lot differential*. Today, electronic trading systems make it easier to process odd-lot transactions, so these trades do not increase trading costs as much as they once did. Not surprisingly, odd-lot trades have become more common in recent years. For example, roughly one-third of all trades of Google shares involve odd lots.

Another type of transaction cost is the *bid-ask spread*, the difference between the bid and ask prices for a stock. In Figure 1.4, you can see that the last quoted ask price for Abercrombie stock was $35.72 and the bid price was $35.40, so the spread between these two prices was $0.32 (or a little less than 1% of the value of the stock). Remember that the ask price represents what you would pay to buy the stock and the bid price is what you receive if you sell the stock, so the difference between them is a kind of transaction cost that you incur when you make a roundtrip (i.e., a purchase and then later a sale) trade. Of course, these prices change throughout the trading day as does the spread between them, but the current bid-ask spread gives you at least a rough idea of the transaction cost that you pay to the market maker or dealer who makes a living buying and selling shares every day.

Common Stock Values

The worth of a share of common stock can be described in a number of ways. Terms such as *par value*, *book value*, *market value*, and *investment value* are all found in the financial media. Each designates some accounting, investment, or monetary attribute of a stock.

Par Value A stock's **par value** is an arbitrary amount assigned to the stock when it is first issued. It has nothing to do with the stock's market price, but instead represents a minimum value below which the corporate charter does not allow a company to sell shares. Because par value establishes a kind of floor for the value of a stock, companies set par values very low. For example, in Facebook's 2012 IPO, the par value of its shares was set at $0.000006. Except for accounting purposes, par value is of little consequence. Par value is a throwback to the early days of corporate law, when it was used as a basis for assessing the extent of a stockholder's legal liability. Because the term has little or no significance for investors, many stocks today are issued without a par value.

Book Value Another accounting measure, **book value** is the stockholders' equity in the firm as reported on the balance sheet (and sometimes expressed on a per share basis). Remember that on the balance sheet, stockholders' equity is just the difference between the value of the firm's assets and its liabilities (less any preferred stock). The book value represents the amount of capital that shareholders contributed to the firm when it initially sold shares as well as any profits that have been reinvested in the company over time.

Example

Social Networks Incorporated (SNI) lists assets worth $100 million on its balance sheet along with $60 million in liabilities. There is no preferred stock, but the company has 10 million common shares outstanding. The book value of SNI's stockholders' equity is $40 million, or $4 per common share. Of the $40 million in stockholders' equity, $30 was raised in the company's initial public offering of common stock and the other $10 million represents profits that the company earned and reinvested in the business since its IPO.

A stock's book value is inherently a backward-looking estimate of its value because it focuses on things that happened in the past (like the original sale of stock and profits earned and reinvested in earlier periods). In contrast, a stock's market value is forward-looking and reflects investors' expectations about how the company will perform in the future.

Market Value A stock's **market value** is simply its prevailing market price. It reflects what investors as a group are willing to pay to acquire the company today, and it is essentially independent of the book value. In fact, stocks usually trade at market prices that exceed their book values, sometimes to a very great degree.

As you have already learned, by multiplying the market price of the stock by the number of shares outstanding, you can calculate a firm's market capitalization, which represents the total market value of claims held by shareholders. A firm's market capitalization is somewhat analogous to the stockholders' equity figure on the balance sheet, except that the market capitalization represents what the firm's equity is actually worth in today's market, whereas the stockholders' equity balance is a backward-looking assessment of shareholders' claims.

Example

Investors believe that prospects for Social Networking Incorporated are very bright and that the company will rapidly increase its revenues and earnings for the next several years. As a result, investors have bid up the market price of SNI's stock to $20, which is 5 times greater than the company's book value per share. With 10 million common shares outstanding, SNI's market capitalization is $200 million compared to the book value of stockholders' equity of just $40 million.

When a stock's market value drops below its book value, it is usually because the firm is dealing with some kind of financial distress and does not have good prospects for growth. Some investors like to seek out stocks that are trading below book value in the hope that the stocks will recover and earn very high returns in the process. While such a strategy may offer the prospect of high returns, it also entails significant risks.

Investment Value **Investment value** is probably the most important measure for a stockholder. It indicates the worth investors place on the stock—in effect, what they think the stock should be trading for. Determining a security's investment value is a complex process based on expectations of the return and risk characteristics of a stock. Any stock has two potential sources of return: dividend payments and the capital gains that arise from appreciation in market price. In establishing investment value, investors try to determine how much money they will make from these two sources. They then use those estimates as the basis for formulating the return potential of the stock. At the same time, they try to assess the amount of risk to which they will be exposed by holding the stock. Such return and risk information helps them place an investment value on the stock. This value represents the maximum price an investor should be willing to pay for the issue. Investment value is the major topic in Chapter 9.

1.6 What is a stock split? How does a stock split affect the market value of a share of stock? Do you think it would make any difference (in price behavior) if the company also changed the dividend rate on the stock? Explain.

1.7 What is a stock spin-off? In very general terms, explain how a stock spin-off works. Are these spin-offs of any value to investors? Explain.

1.8 Define and differentiate between the following pairs of terms.

  a. Treasury stock versus classified stock
  b. Round lot versus odd lot
  c. Par value versus market value
  d. Book value versus investment value

1.9 What is an odd-lot differential? How can you avoid odd-lot differentials? Which of the following transactions would involve an odd-lot differential?

  a. Buy 90 shares of stock
  b. Sell 200 shares of stock
  c. Sell 125 shares of stock

Common Stock Dividends

LG5 In 2011, U.S. corporations paid out billions in dividends. Counting only the companies included in the S&P 500 stock index, dividends that year totaled more than $240 billion. Yet, in spite of these numbers, dividends still don't get much attention. Many investors, particularly younger ones, often put very little value on dividends. To a large extent, that's because capital gains provide a much bigger source of return than dividends—at least over the long haul.

But attitudes toward dividends are beginning to change. The protracted bear market of 2007 through 2009 revealed just how uncertain capital gains can be and, indeed, that all those potential profits can turn into substantial capital losses. Dividend payments do not fluctuate as much as stock prices do. Plus, dividends provide a nice cushion when the market stumbles (or falls flat on its face). Moreover, recent changes in the (federal) tax laws put dividends on the same plane as capital gains. Both now are taxed at the same (maximum 15%) tax rate, although it seems likely that this provision of the tax code will change. If the Bush tax cuts expire as scheduled in 2012, then the tax rate on long-term capital gains will be lower than the tax rate on dividends.

The Dividend Decision

By paying out dividends, typically on a quarterly basis, companies share some of their profits with stockholders. Actually, a firm's board of directors decides how much to pay in dividends. The directors evaluate the firm's operating results and financial condition to determine whether dividends should be paid and, if so, in what amount. They also consider whether the firm should distribute some of its cash to investors by paying a dividend or by repurchasing some of the firm's outstanding stock. If the directors decide to pay dividends, they also establish several important payment dates. In this section we'll look at the corporate and market factors that go into the dividend decision. Then we'll briefly examine some of the key payment dates.

Corporate versus Market Factors When the board of directors assembles to consider the question of paying dividends, it weighs a variety of factors. First, the board looks at the firm's earnings. Even though a company does not have to show a profit to pay dividends, profits are still considered a vital link in the dividend decision.

With common stocks, the annual earnings of a firm are usually measured and reported in terms of **earnings per share (EPS)**. Basically, EPS translates aggregate corporate profits into profit per share. It provides a convenient measure of the amount of earnings available to stockholders. Earnings per share is found by using the following formula:

Equation 1.1

$$EPS = \frac{\substack{\text{Net profit} \\ \text{after taxes}} - \text{Preferred dividends}}{\substack{\text{Number of shares of} \\ \text{common stock outstanding}}}$$

For example, if a firm reports a net profit of $1.25 million, pays $250,000 in dividends to preferred stockholders, and has 500,000 shares of common stock outstanding, it has an EPS of $2 (($1,250,000 − $250,000)/500,000). Note in Equation 1.1 that preferred dividends are subtracted from profits because they must be paid before any funds can be made available to common stockholders.

While assessing profits, the board also looks at the firm's growth prospects. It's very likely that the firm will need some of its earnings for investment purposes and to help finance future growth. In addition, the board will take a close look at the firm's cash position, making sure that paying dividends will not lead to a cash shortfall. Furthermore, the firm may be subject to a loan agreement that legally limits the amount of dividends it can pay.

After looking at internal matters, the board will consider certain market effects and responses. Most investors feel that if a company is going to retain earnings rather than pay them out in dividends, it should reinvest those funds to achieve faster growth and higher profits. The market's message is clear: If the firm is investing the money wisely and at a high rate of return, fine; otherwise, pay a larger portion of earnings out in the form of dividends.

Moreover, to the extent that different types of investors tend to be attracted to different types of firms, the board must make every effort to meet the dividend expectations of its shareholders. For example, income-oriented investors are attracted to firms that generally pay high dividends. Failure to meet those expectations might prompt some investors to sell their shares, putting downward pressure on the stock price. In addition, some institutional investors (e.g., certain mutual funds and pension funds) are restricted to investing only in companies that pay a dividend. This is a factor in some companies' decisions to initiate a dividend payment.

Some Important Dates Let's assume the directors decide to declare a dividend. Once that's done, they must indicate the date of payment and other important dates associated with the dividend. Three dates are particularly important to the stockholders: date of record, payment date, and ex-dividend date. The **date of record** is the date on which the investor must be a registered shareholder of the firm to be entitled to a dividend. All investors who are official stockholders as of the close of business on that date will receive the dividends that have just been declared. These stockholders are often referred to as *holders of record*. The **payment date**, also set by the board of directors, generally follows the date of record by a week or two. It is the actual date on which the company will mail dividend checks to holders of record (and is also known as the *payable date*).

Because of the time needed to make bookkeeping entries after a stock is traded, the stock will sell without the dividend (ex-dividend) for 3 business days up to and including the date of record. The **ex-dividend date** will dictate whether you were an official shareholder and therefore eligible to receive the declared dividend. If you sell a stock on or after the ex-dividend date, you receive the dividend. The reason is that the buyer of the stock (the new shareholder) will not have held the stock on the date of record. Instead, you (the seller) will still be the holder of record. Just the opposite will occur if you sell the stock before the ex-dividend date. In this case, the new shareholder (the buyer of the stock) will receive the dividend because he or she will be the holder of record.

To see how this works, consider the following sequence of events. On June 3, the board of directors of Cash Cow, Inc., declares a quarterly dividend of 50 cents per share to holders of record on June 18. Checks will be mailed out on the payment date, June 30. The calendar below shows these dividend dates. In this case, if you bought 200 shares of the stock on June 15, you would receive a check in the mail sometime after June 30 in the amount of $100. On the other hand, if you purchased the stock on June 16, the seller of the stock would receive the check because he or she, not you, would be recognized as the holder of record.

June

S	M	T	W	T	F	S	
	1	2	3	4	5	6	— Declaration date
7	8	9	10	11	12	13	
14	15	16	17	18	19	20	— Date of record
21	22	23	24	25	26	27	— Ex-dividend date
28	29	30					— Payment date

Types of Dividends

Normally, companies pay dividends in the form of cash. Sometimes they pay dividends by issuing additional shares of stock. The first type of distribution is known as a **cash dividend**; the second is a **stock dividend**. Occasionally, companies pay dividends in other forms, such as a stock spin-off (discussed earlier in this chapter) or perhaps even samples of the company's products. But these other forms of dividend payments are relatively rare compared to cash dividends.

Cash Dividends More firms pay cash dividends than any other type of dividend. A nice by-product of cash dividends is that they tend to increase over time, as companies' earnings grow. In fact, for companies that pay cash dividends, the average annual increase in dividends is around 3% to 5%. This trend represents good news for investors, because a steadily increasing stream of dividends tends to shore up stock returns in soft markets.

A convenient way of assessing the amount of dividends received is to measure the stock's **dividend yield**. Basically, this is a measure of dividends on a relative (percentage) basis rather than on an absolute (dollar) basis. A stock's dividend yield measures its current income as a percentage of its price. The dividend yield is computed as follows:

Equation 1.2

$$\text{Dividend yield} = \frac{\text{Annual dividends received per share}}{\text{Current market price of the stock}}$$

Thus, a company that annually pays $2 per share in dividends to its stockholders, and whose stock is trading at $40, has a dividend yield of 5%.

Example

> In May 2012, Radio Shack paid its quarterly dividend of $0.125 per share, which translates into an annual dividend of $0.50. At that time, Radio Shack's share price was about $4, so its dividend yield was 12.5% ($0.50 ÷ $4.00), which is an unusually high level for common stock.

Firms generally do not pay out all of their earnings as dividends. Instead, they distribute some of their earnings as dividends and retain some to reinvest in the business. The **dividend payout ratio** measures the percentage of earnings that a firm pays in dividends. It is computed as follows:

Equation 1.3

$$\text{Dividend payout ratio} = \frac{\text{Dividends per share}}{\text{Earnings per share}}$$

A company would have a payout ratio of 50% if it had earnings of $4 a share and paid annual dividends of $2 a share. Although stockholders like to receive dividends, they normally do not like to see payout ratios over 60%. Payout ratios that high are difficult to maintain and may lead the company into trouble.

Example

> In the 12 months ending in June 2012, The Coca-Cola Company paid dividends of $1.96 per share to investors. Over the same period, the company's earnings per share were $3.76, so Coca-Cola's dividend payout ratio was approximately 52%. In other words, Coca-Cola used about half of its earnings to pay dividends and it reinvested the other half.

The appeal of cash dividends took a giant leap forward in 2003, when the federal tax code changed to reduce the tax on dividends. Prior to this time, cash dividends were taxed as ordinary income, meaning they could be taxed at rates as high as 35%. For that reason, many investors viewed cash dividends as a relatively unattractive source of income, especially because capital gains (when realized) were taxed at much lower preferential rates. After 2003, both dividends and capital gains were taxed at the same low, preferential rate (of 15% or less). That, of course, makes dividend-paying stocks far more attractive, even to investors in higher tax brackets. Firms responded to the tax change in two ways. First, firms that already paid dividends increased them. Total dividends paid by U.S. companies increased by 30% from 2003 to 2005. Second, many firms that had never paid dividends began paying them. In the year leading up to the tax cut, about 4 firms per quarter announced plans to initiate dividend payments. In the following year, the number of firms initiating dividends surged to 29 companies per quarter, an increase of roughly 700%! However, the tax break on dividends enacted in 2003 was set to expire in 2012, and it remains to be seen whether Congress and a newly elected president will extend the low dividend tax rates or allow them to go back to their pre-2003 levels.

Stock Dividends Occasionally, a firm may declare a stock dividend. A stock dividend simply means that the firm pays its dividend by distributing additional shares of stock.

For instance, if the board declares a 10% stock dividend, then you will receive 1 new share of stock for each 10 shares that you currently own.

Stock dividends are similar to stock splits in the sense that when you receive a stock dividend, you receive no cash. As the number of shares outstanding increases due to the dividend, the share price falls, leaving the total value of your holdings in the company basically unchanged. As with a stock split, a stock dividend represents primarily a cosmetic change because the market responds to such dividends by adjusting share prices downward according to the terms of the stock dividend. Thus, in the example above, a 10% stock dividend normally leads to a decline of around 10% in the stock's share price. If you owned 200 shares of stock that were trading at $100 per share, the total market value of your investment would be $20,000. After a 10% stock dividend, you would own 220 shares of stock (i.e., 200 shares $\times$ 1.10), but each share would be worth about $90.91. You would own more shares, but they would be trading at lower prices, so the total market value of your investment would remain about the same (i.e., 220 $\times$ $90.91 = $20,000.20). There is, however, one bright spot in all this: Unlike cash dividends, stock dividends are not taxed until you actually sell the stocks.

Dividend Reinvestment Plans

Do you want to have your cake and eat it too? When it comes to dividends, there is a way to do just that. You can participate in a **dividend reinvestment plan** (**DRIP**). In these corporate-sponsored programs, shareholders can have their cash dividends automatically reinvested into additional shares of the company's common stock. (Similar reinvestment programs are offered by mutual funds, and by some brokerage houses such as Bank of America and Fidelity.) The basic investment philosophy is that *if the company is good enough to invest in, it's good enough to reinvest in*. As Table 1.2 demonstrates, such an approach can have a tremendous impact on your investment position over time.

TABLE 1.2   CASH OR REINVESTED DIVIDENDS?

Situation: You buy 100 shares of stock at $25 a share (total investment, $2,500); the stock currently pays $1 a share in annual dividends. The price of the stock increases at 8% per year; dividends grow at 5% per year.

Investment Period (yr.)	Number of Shares Held	Market Value of Stock Holdings ($)	Total Cash Dividends Received ($)
Take Dividends in Cash			
5	100	3,672	552
10	100	5,397	1,258
15	100	7,930	2,158
20	100	11,652	3,307
Full Participation in Dividend Reinvestment Plan (100% of cash dividends reinvested)			
5	115.59	4,245	0
10	135.66	7,322	0
15	155.92	12,364	0
20	176.00	20,508	0

Today more than 1,000 companies (including most major corporations) offer dividend reinvestment plans. These plans provide investors with a convenient and inexpensive way to accumulate capital. Stocks in most DRIPs are acquired free of brokerage commissions, and most plans allow partial participation. That is, participants may specify a portion of their shares for dividend reinvestment and receive cash dividends on the rest. Some plans even sell stocks to their DRIP investors at below-market prices—often at discounts of 3% to 5%. In addition, most plans will credit fractional shares to the investor's account, and many will even allow investors to buy additional shares of the company's stock. For example, once enrolled in the General Mills plan, investors can purchase up to $3,000 worth of the company's stock each quarter, free of commissions.

Shareholders can join dividend reinvestment plans by simply sending a completed authorization form to the company. (Generally, it takes about 30 to 45 days for all the paperwork to be processed.) Once you're enrolled, the number of shares you hold will begin to grow with each dividend. There is a catch, however: Even though these dividends take the form of additional shares of stock, you must still pay taxes on them as though they were cash dividends. Don't confuse these dividends with stock dividends—reinvested dividends are treated as taxable income in the year they're received, just as though they had been received in cash. But as long as the preferential tax rate on dividends remains in effect, paying taxes on stock dividends, will be much less of a burden than it used to be.

CONCEPTS IN REVIEW

Answers available at
www.pearsonhighered.com/
smart

1.10 Briefly explain how the dividend decision is made. What corporate and market factors are important in deciding whether, and in what amount, to pay dividends?

1.11 Why is the ex-dividend date important to stockholders? If a stock is sold on the ex-dividend date, who receives the dividend—the buyer or the seller? Explain.

1.12 What is the difference between a cash dividend and a stock dividend? Which would be more valuable to you? How does a stock dividend compare to a stock split? Is a 200% stock dividend the same as a 2-for-1 stock split? Explain.

1.13 What are dividend reinvestment plans, and what benefits do they offer to investors? Are there any disadvantages?

Types and Uses of Common Stock

LG6 Common stocks appeal to investors because they offer the potential for everything from current income and stability of capital to attractive capital gains. The market contains a wide range of stocks, from the most conservative to the highly speculative. Generally, the kinds of stocks that investors seek depend on their investment objectives and investment programs. We will examine several of the more popular types of common stocks here, as well as the various ways such securities can be used in different types of investment programs.

Types of Stocks

Not all stocks are alike, and the risk and return profile of each stock depends on the characteristics of the company that issued it. Some of the characteristics include whether the company pays a dividend, the company's size, how rapidly the company is growing, and how susceptible its earnings are to changes in the business cycle. Over time, investors have developed a classification scheme that helps them place a particular stock into one of several categories. Investors use these categories to help design their portfolios to achieve a good balance of risk and return. Some of the categories that you hear about most often are blue chip stocks, income stocks, growth stocks, tech stocks, cyclical stocks, defensive stocks, large-cap stocks, mid-cap stocks, and small-cap stocks.

Blue-Chip Stocks Blue chips are the cream of the common stock crop. They are stocks issued by companies that have a long track record of earning profits and paying dividends. **Blue-chip stocks** are issued by large, well-established firms that have impeccable financial credentials. These companies are often the leaders in their industries.

Not all blue chips are alike, however. Some provide consistently high dividend yields; others are more growth-oriented. Good examples of blue-chip growth stocks are Nike, Procter & Gamble, Home Depot, Walgreen's, Lowe's Companies, and United Parcel Service. Figure 1.5 (on page 21) shows some basic operating and market information about P&G's stock, as obtained from the introductory part of a typical Zacks Investment Research report. Examples of high-yielding blue chips include such companies as AT&T, Chevron, Merck, Johnson & Johnson, McDonald's, and Pfizer.

While blue-chip stocks are not immune from bear markets, they are less risky than most stocks. They tend to appeal to investors who are looking for quality, dividend-paying investments with some growth potential. Blue chips appeal to investors who want to earn higher returns than bonds typically offer without taking a great deal of risk.

AN ADVISER'S PERSPECTIVE

Bill Harris
Founder,
WH Cornerstone Investments

"Blue chips are companies that pay a dividend and increase it over time."

MyFinanceLab

Income Stocks Some stocks are appealing simply because of the dividends they pay. This is the case with **income stocks**. These issues have a long history of regularly paying higher-than-average dividends. Income stocks are ideal for those who seek a relatively safe and high level of current income from their investment capital. But there's more: Holders of income stocks (unlike bonds and preferred stocks) can expect the dividends they receive to increase regularly over time. Thus, a company that paid, say, $1.00 a share in dividends in 1997 would be paying just over $1.80 a share in 2012, if dividends had been growing at around 4% per year. Dividends that grow over time provide investors with some protection from the effects of inflation.

The major disadvantage of income stocks is that some of them may be paying high dividends because of limited growth potential. Indeed, it's not unusual for income securities to exhibit relatively low earnings growth. This does not mean that such firms are unprofitable or lack future prospects. Quite the contrary: Most firms whose shares qualify as income stocks are highly profitable organizations with excellent prospects. A number of income stocks are among the giants of U.S. industry, and many are also classified as quality blue chips. Many public utilities, such as American Electric Power, Duke Energy, Oneok, Scana, DTE Energy, and Southern Company, are in this group. Also in this group are selected industrial and financial issues like Conagra Foods, General Mills, and Altria Group. By their very nature, income stocks are not exposed to a great deal of business and market risk. They are, however, subject to a fair amount of interest rate risk.

Growth Stocks Shares issued by companies that are experiencing rapid growth in revenues and earnings are known as **growth stocks**. A good growth stock might exhibit a sustained earnings growth of 15% to 18% when most common stocks are growing at 6% to 8% per year. Generally speaking, established growth companies combine steady

FIGURE 1.5 A Blue-Chip Stock

ZACKS
INVESTMENT RESEARCH

July 10, 2012

Procter & Gamble (PG-NYSE)

Current Recommendation	**UNDERPERFORM**
Prior Recommendation	Neutral
Date of Last Change	07/10/2012
Current Price (07/09/12)	$61.55
Target Price	**$56.00**

SUMMARY

Procter & Gamble recently lowered its sales and earnings outlook for the final quarter of fiscal 2012 marking the second successive cut in the company's guidance in the last two months. Management blamed the latest guidance cut on lower-than-expected top-line growth due to a slowing global economy, sluggish market share growth in the developed countries and China, and foreign exchange headwinds. P&G is witnessing sluggish growth in the developed nations, principally in North America and Western Europe, due to weak economic conditions and market share declines. Moreover, rising commodity costs are constantly hurting the company's margins. Moreover, the company has also failed to make a break-through in the recent past which is hurting growth. Other short term headwinds include business disruptions in Venezuela, import restrictions in Argentina and negative impact of foreign exchange. We have thus downgraded our rating on P&G from Neutral to Underperform as most of these issues are expected to persist and pressure earnings in the near term.

SUMMARY DATA

52-Week High	$67.90
52-Week Low	$58.51
One-Year Return (%)	-1.55
Beta	0.44
Average Daily Volume (sh)	13,965,574
Shares Outstanding (mil)	2,740
Market Capitalization ($mil)	$168,647
Short Interest Ratio (days)	2.32
Institutional Ownership (%)	52
Insider Ownership (%)	0
Annual Cash Dividend	$2.25
Dividend Yield (%)	3.65
5-Yr. Historical Growth Rates	
Sales (%)	0.9
Earnings Per Share (%)	4.7
Dividend (%)	10.2
P/E using TTM EPS	15.7
P/E using 2012 Estimate	16.2
P/E using 2013 Estimate	15.8
Zacks Rank *: Short Term 1 – 3 months outlook	4 - Sell

* Definition / Disclosure on last page

Risk Level *	Low
Type of Stock	Large-Blend
Industry	Soap&Clng Preps
Zacks Industry Rank *	177 out of 267

ZACKS CONSENSUS ESTIMATES

Revenue Estimates
(In millions of $)

	Q1 (Sep)	Q2 (Dec)	Q3 (Mar)	Q4 (Jun)	Year (Jun)
2010	19,807 A	21,027 A	19,178 A	18,926 A	78,938 A
2011	20,122 A	21,347 A	19,893 A	20,860 A	82,559 A
2012	21,917 A	22,135 A	20,194 A	20,310 E	83,918 E
2013	21,217 E	21,664 E	20,565 E	20,651 E	84,469 E

Earnings Per Share Estimates
(EPS is operating earnings before non-recurring items, but including employee stock options expenses)

	Q1 (Sep)	Q2 (Dec)	Q3 (Mar)	Q4 (Jun)	Year (Jun)
2010	$0.97 A	$1.10 A	$0.89 A	$0.71 A	$3.67 A
2011	$1.02 A	$1.13 A	$0.94 A	$0.84 A	$3.93 A
2012	$1.03 A	$1.10 A	$0.94 A	$0.77 E	$3.80 E
2013	$1.04 E	$1.08 E	$0.95 E	$0.84 E	$3.90 E

Q210,Q310 EPS and rev has been restated. Future quarter results will be restated as and when the company reports.

Projected EPS Growth - Next 5 Years %   8

earnings growth with high returns on equity. They also have high operating margins and plenty of cash flow to service their debt. Amazon.com, Apple, Google, eBay, Berkshire Hathaway, and Starbucks are all prime examples of growth stocks. As this list suggests, some growth stocks also rate as blue chips and provide quality growth, whereas others represent higher levels of speculation.

Growth stocks normally pay little or no dividends. Their payout ratios seldom exceed 10% to 15% of earnings. Instead, these companies reinvest most of their profits to help finance additional growth. Thus, investors in growth stocks earn their returns through price appreciation rather than dividends—and that can have both a good side and a bad side. When the economy is strong and the stock market is generally rising, these stocks are particularly hot. When the markets turn down, so do these stocks, often in a big way. Growth shares generally appeal to investors who are looking for attractive capital gains rather than dividends and who are willing to bear more risk.

Tech Stocks Over the past 20 years or so, tech stocks have become such a dominant force in the market (both positive and negative) that they deserve to be put in a class all their own. **Tech stocks** basically represent the technology sector of the market. They include companies that produce computers, semiconductors, data storage devices, and software. They also include companies that provide Internet services, networking equipment, and wireless communications. Some of these stocks are listed on the NYSE and Amex, although the vast majority are traded on the Nasdaq. Tech stocks, in fact, dominate the Nasdaq market and, thus, the Nasdaq Composite Index.

These stocks would probably fall into either the growth stock category or the speculative stock class, although some of them are legitimate blue chips. Tech stocks may offer the potential for very high returns, but they also involve considerable risk and are probably most suitable for the more risk-tolerant investor. Included in the tech-stock category you'll find some big names, like Apple, Cisco Systems, Google, and Intel. You'll also find many not-so-big names, like NVIDIA, Marvell Technology, LinkedIn, SanDisk, Advantest, L-3 Communications, and Electronic Arts (see Figure 1.6 on page 23).

Speculative Stocks Shares that lack sustained records of success but still offer the potential for substantial price appreciation are known as **speculative stocks**. Perhaps investors' hopes are spurred by a new management team that has taken over a troubled company or by the introduction of a promising new product. Other times, it's the hint that some new information, discovery, or production technique will favorably affect the growth prospects of the firm. Speculative stocks are a special breed of securities, and they enjoy a wide following, particularly when the market is bullish.

Generally speaking, the earnings of speculative stocks are uncertain and highly unstable. These stocks are subject to wide swings in price, and they usually pay little or nothing in dividends. On the plus side, speculative stocks such as Sirius XM Radio, Dreamworks Animation, Liberty Media, and Under Armour offer attractive growth prospects and the chance to "hit it big" in the market. To be successful, however, an investor has to identify the big-money winners before the rest of the market does. Speculative stocks are highly risky; they require not only a strong stomach but also a considerable amount of investor know-how. They are used to seek capital gains, and investors will often aggressively trade in and out of these securities as the situation demands.

Cyclical Stocks **Cyclical stocks** are issued by companies whose earnings are closely linked to the overall economy. They tend to move up and down with the business cycle.

FIGURE 1.6 A Tech Stock
(Source: Copyright ©2012 Zacks Investment Research. All rights reserved. www.zacks.com, July 10, 2012.)

June 13, 2012

Electronic Arts Inc.

(EA-NASDAQ)

Current Recommendation	NEUTRAL
Prior Recommendation	Underperform
Date of Last Change	03/17/2010
Current Price (06/12/12)	$12.79
Target Price	**$13.00**

SUMMARY

EA reported a mixed fourth quarter with earnings comfortably beating the Zacks Consensus Estimate but revenue missing by miles. The guidance was also disappointing. We believe that EA's shift in focus to the digital format, its diversified portfolio and strong product pipeline will drive top-line growth going forward. However, a sluggish video game market keeps us on the sidelines. Moreover, EA faces stiff competition in both digital and packaged goods, which are expected to hurt profitability going forward. We don't foresee any turnaround in the near term and the long-term outlook is murky. Thus, we have a Neutral rating and set a price target of $13.00.

SUMMARY DATA

52-Week High	$25.20
52-Week Low	$12.79
One-Year Return (%)	-44.86
Beta	1.24
Average Daily Volume (sh)	5,036,886
Shares Outstanding (mil)	318
Market Capitalization ($mil)	$4,065
Short Interest Ratio (days)	2.15
Institutional Ownership (%)	90
Insider Ownership (%)	6
Annual Cash Dividend	$0.00
Dividend Yield (%)	0.00
5-Yr. Historical Growth Rates	
Sales (%)	2.5
Earnings Per Share (%)	-18.0
Dividend (%)	N/A
P/E using TTM EPS	36.5
P/E using 2013 Estimate	18.5
P/E using 2014 Estimate	14.4
Zacks Rank *: Short Term 1 – 3 months outlook	4 - Sell

* Definition / Disclosure on last page

Risk Level *	Average,
Type of Stock	Large-Value
Industry	Toys/Game/Hobby
Zacks Industry Rank *	71 out of 267

ZACKS CONSENSUS ESTIMATES

Revenue Estimates
(In millions of $)

	Q1	Q2	Q3	Q4	Year
	(Jun)	(Sep)	(Dec)	(Mar)	(Mar)
2011	539 A	884 A	1,410 A	995 A	3,828 A
2012	524 A	1034 A	1,651 A	977 A	4,186 A
2013	957 E	837 E	1,263 E	1,029 E	4,086 E
2014					4,539 E

Earnings Per Share Estimates
(EPS is operating earnings before non-recurring items, but including employee stock options expenses)

	Q1	Q2	Q3	Q4	Year
	(Jun)	(Sep)	(Dec)	(Mar)	(Mar)
2011	-$0.44 A	-$0.02 A	$0.46 A	$0.20 A	$0.20 A
2012	-$0.57 A	-$0.06 A	$0.87 A	$0.11 A	$0.35 A
2013	-$0.51 E	$0.06 E	$0.92 E	$0.22 E	$0.69 E
2014					$0.89 E

Projected EPS Growth - Next 5 Years %   18

Companies that serve markets tied to capital equipment spending by business or to consumer spending for big-ticket, durable items like houses and cars typically head the list of cyclical stocks. Examples include Alcoa, Caterpillar, Genuine Parts, Lennar, Brunswick, and Timken.

Cyclical stocks generally do well when the economy is moving ahead, but they tend to do especially well when the country is in the early stages of economic recovery. Likewise, they perform poorly when the economy begins to weaken. Cyclical stocks are probably most suitable for investors who are willing to trade in and out of these stocks as the economic outlook dictates and who can tolerate the accompanying exposure to risk.

Defensive Stocks Sometimes it is possible to find stocks whose prices remain stable or even increase when general economic activity is tapering off. These securities are known as **defensive stocks**. They tend to be less susceptible to downswings in the business cycle than the average stock.

Defensive stocks include the shares of many public utilities, as well as industrial and consumer goods companies that produce or market such staples as beverages, foods, and drugs. An excellent example of a defensive stock is Walmart. This recession-resistant company is the world's leading retailer. Other examples are Checkpoint Systems, a manufacturer of antitheft clothing security clips, WD-40, the maker of that famous all-purpose lubricant, and Extendicare, a leading provider of long-term care and assisted-living facilities. Defensive shares are commonly used by more aggressive investors, who tend to "park" their funds temporarily in defensive stocks while the economy remains soft or until the investment atmosphere improves.

Mid-Cap Stocks A stock's size is based on its market value—or, more commonly, its market capitalization. This value is calculated as the market price of the stock times the number of shares outstanding. Generally speaking, the U.S. stock market can be broken into three segments, as measured by a stock's market cap:

Small-cap	less than $2 billion
Mid-cap	$2 billion up to $10 billion
Large-cap	more than $10 billion

The large-cap stocks are the corporate giants such as Walmart, Exxon Mobil, and Apple. Although large-cap stocks are few in number, these companies account for more than 75% of the market value of all U.S. equities. But as the saying goes, bigger isn't necessarily better. Nowhere is that statement more accurate than in the stock market. On average, small-cap stocks tend to earn higher returns than do large-caps.

Mid-cap stocks offer investors some attractive return opportunities. They provide much of the sizzle of small-stock returns, without as much price volatility. (We'll look at small-cap stocks soon.) At the same time, because mid-caps are fairly good-sized companies and many of them have been around for a long time, they offer some of the safety of the big, established stocks. Among the ranks of the mid-caps are such well-known companies as Dick's Sporting Goods, Hasbro, Safeway, and Williams-Sonoma. Although these securities offer a nice alternative to large stocks without the uncertainties of small-caps, they probably are most appropriate for investors who are willing to tolerate a bit more risk and price volatility than large-caps have.

One type of mid-cap stock of particular interest is the so-called baby blue chip. Also known as "baby blues," these companies have all the characteristics of a regular blue chip except size. Like their larger counterparts, baby blues have rock-solid balance sheets, modest levels of debt, and several years of steady profit growth. Baby blues normally pay a modest level of dividends, but like most mid-caps, they tend to emphasize growth. Thus, they're considered ideal for investors seeking quality long-term growth. Some well-known baby blues are Logitech, American Eagle Outfitters, and Garmin Ltd.

Small-Cap Stocks Some investors consider small companies to be in a class by themselves in terms of attractive return opportunities. In many cases, this has turned out to be true. Known as **small-cap stocks**, these companies generally have annual revenues of less than $250 million. But because of their size, spurts of growth can have dramatic effects on their earnings and stock prices. Callaway Golf, Wendy's, and Shoe Carnival are some of the better-known small-cap stocks.

Although some small-caps are solid companies with equally solid financials, that's not the case with most of them. Indeed, because many of these companies are so small, they don't have a lot of stock outstanding, and their shares are not widely traded. In addition, small-company stocks have a tendency to be "here today and gone tomorrow." Although some of these stocks may hold the potential for high returns, investors should also be aware of the very high-risk exposure that comes with many of them.

A special category of small-cap stocks is the initial public offering (IPO). Most IPOs are small, relatively new companies that are going public for the first time. (Prior to their public offering, these stocks were privately held and not publicly traded.) Like other small-company stocks, IPOs are attractive because of the substantial capital gains that investors can earn. Of course, there's a catch: To stand a chance of buying some of the better, more attractive IPOs, you need to be either an active trader or a preferred client of the broker. Otherwise, the only IPOs you're likely to hear of will be the ones these investors don't want. Without a doubt, IPOs are high-risk investments, with the odds stacked against the investor. Because there's no market record to rely on, only investors who know what to look for in a company and who can tolerate substantial risk should buy these stocks.

AN ADVISER'S PERSPECTIVE

Thomas O'Connell
President,
International Financial Advisory Group

"Unless you're a high net worth client, you're not getting in at the IPO price."

MyFinanceLab

Investing in Foreign Stocks

One of the most dramatic changes to occur in U.S. financial markets in the past 20 years was the trend toward globalization. Indeed, globalization became the buzzword of the 1990s, and nowhere was that more evident than in the world's equity markets. Consider, for example, that in 1970 the U.S. stock market accounted for fully two-thirds of the world market. In essence, the U.S. stock market was twice as big as all the rest of the world's stock markets combined. That's no longer true: By 2012, the U.S. share of the world equity market had dropped to approximately 33%.

Today the world equity markets are dominated by just 6 markets, which together account for about 80% of the global total. The United States, by far, has the biggest equity market, which in 2012 had a total value of close to $16 trillion. Vying for second place are Japan, China, and the United Kingdom, all of which have stock markets valued in excess of $3 trillion. Other equity markets worth more than $1 trillion can be found in Switzerland, Germany, Spain, Hong Kong, and Canada.

Comparative Returns The United States still dominates the world equity markets in terms of sheer size, as well as in the number of listed companies (more than 10,000 of them). But that leaves unanswered an important question: How has the U.S. equity market performed in comparison to the rest of the world's major stock markets? In 2011, which was generally a poor year for stock returns, the U.S. market eked out a

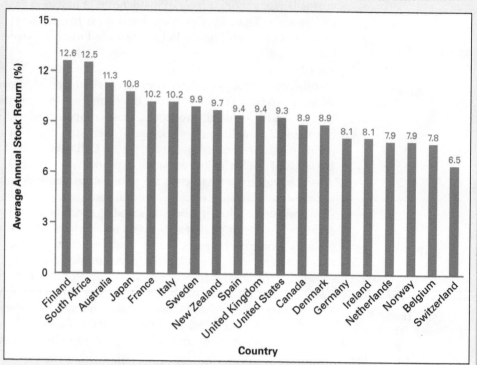

FIGURE 1.7

Average Annual Stock Returns Around the World (1900 to 2011)

(Source: Elroy Dimson, Paul Marsh, and Mike Staunton, Credit Suisse Global Investment Returns Sourcebook 2012, https://www.credit-suisse.com/investment_banking/doc/cs_global_investment_returns_yearbook.pdf.)

2% gain (as measured by the S&P 500 Index). That doesn't sound like much, but it was one of the best performing markets that year. Around the world, most stock markets experienced double-digit losses, including the major stock markets in Spain, Australia, Canada, Japan, South Africa, China, Germany, and many other countries. One year is probably not the best way to judge the performance of a country's stock market, so Figure 1.7 plots the average annual return on stocks from 1900 to 2011 for 19 countries. Over that period the U.S. stock market earned an average annual return of 9.3%, performance that ranked roughly in the middle of the countries listed in Figure 1.7. In other words, over a long period of time, stock returns in the United States have been unremarkable relative to stock returns in other markets. If we looked on a year-by-year basis, we would see that 2011 was an exception in that U.S. stocks rarely earn the highest returns in any given year. Translated, that means there definitely are attractive returns awaiting those investors who are willing to venture beyond our borders.

Going Global: Direct Investments Basically, there are two ways to invest in foreign stocks: through direct investments or through ADRs.

Without a doubt, the most adventuresome way is to buy shares directly in foreign markets. Investing directly is *not* for the uninitiated, however. You have to know what you're doing and be prepared to tolerate a good deal of market risk. Although most major U.S. brokerage houses are set up to accommodate investors interested in buying foreign securities, there are still many logistical problems to face. To begin with, you have to cope with currency fluctuations that can have a dramatic impact on your returns. But that's just the start. You also have to deal with different regulatory and accounting standards. The fact is that most foreign markets, even the bigger ones, are not as closely regulated as U.S. exchanges. Investors in foreign markets, therefore, may have to put up with insider trading and other practices that can create disadvantages for foreign investors. Finally, there are the obvious language barriers, tax issues, and general "red tape" that all too often plague international transactions. The returns from direct foreign investments can be substantial, but so can the obstacles.

Going Global with ADRs Fortunately, there is an easier way to invest in foreign stocks, and that is to buy American Depositary Receipts (ADRs). ADRs are dollar-denominated instruments (or certificates) that represent ownership of a certain number of shares in a specific foreign company (the number of shares can range from a fraction of a share to 20 shares or more). ADRs are great for investors who want to own foreign stocks but don't want the hassles that often come with them. Actually, ADRs trade in the market as American depositary shares (or ADSs). Although the terms *ADR* and *ADS* are often used interchangeably, technically there is a difference between the two: An ADR is the legal document that describes the security, whereas an ADS is the vehicle through which you invest in the security. Thus, ADSs represent shares in a given ADR and are the securities that are traded in the market.

How Do ADRs Work?

American depositary receipts are bought and sold on U.S. markets just like stocks in U.S. companies. Their prices are quoted in U.S. dollars. Furthermore, dividends are paid in U.S. dollars. Although there are about 400 foreign companies whose shares are directly listed on U.S. exchanges, most foreign companies are registered in this country as ADRs. Indeed, shares of some 2,100 companies, from more than 50 countries, are traded as ADSs on the NYSE, Amex, Nasdaq, and OTC markets.

To see how ADRs are structured, take a look at BP, the British oil and gas firm, whose ADRs trade on the NYSE. Each BP ADR represents ownership of 6 shares of BP stock. These shares are held in a custodial account by a U.S. bank (or its foreign correspondent), which receives dividends, pays any foreign withholding taxes, and then converts the net proceeds to U.S. dollars, which it passes on to investors. Other foreign stocks that can be purchased as ADRs include Sony (Japan), Ericsson Telephone (Sweden), Nokia (Finland), Royal Dutch Shell (Netherlands), Nestle (Switzerland), Elan Corporation (Ireland), Suntech Power (China), BASF (Germany), Hutchison Wampoa, Ltd. (Hong Kong), Teva Pharmaceuticals (Israel), Norsk Hydro (Norway), Diageo (U.K.), and Grupo Televisa (Mexico). You can even buy ADRs on Russian companies, such as Vimpel-Communications, a Moscow-based cellular phone company whose shares trade (as ADRs) on the NYSE.

Putting Global Returns in Perspective Whether you buy foreign stocks directly or through ADRs, the whole process of global investing is a bit more complicated and more risky than domestic investing. When investing globally, you have to pick both the right stock and the right market. Basically, foreign stocks are valued much the same way as U.S. stocks. Indeed, the same variables that drive U.S. share prices (earnings, dividends, and so on) also drive stock values in foreign markets. On top of this, each market reacts to its own set of economic forces (inflation, interest rates, level of economic activity), which set the tone of the market. At any given time, some markets are performing better than others. The challenge facing global investors is to be in the right market at the right time.

As with U.S. stocks, foreign shares produce the same two basic sources of returns: dividends and capital gains (or losses). But with global investing, there is a third variable—currency exchange rates—that affects returns to U.S. investors. In particular, as the U.S. dollar weakens or strengthens relative to a foreign currency, the returns to U.S. investors from foreign stocks increase or decrease accordingly. In a global context, total return to U.S. investors in foreign securities is defined as follows:

Equation 1.4

$$\begin{matrix} \text{Total returns} \\ (\text{in U.S. dollars}) \end{matrix} = \begin{matrix} \text{Current income} \\ (\text{dividends}) \end{matrix} + \begin{matrix} \text{Capital gains} \\ (\text{or losses}) \end{matrix} \pm \begin{matrix} \text{Changes in currency} \\ \text{exchange rates} \end{matrix}$$

Because current income and capital gains are in the "local currency" (the currency in which the foreign stock is denominated, such as the euro or the Japanese yen), we can shorten the total return formula to:

Equation 1.5

$$\begin{matrix} \text{Total return} \\ (\text{in U.S. dollars}) \end{matrix} = \begin{matrix} \text{Returns from current} \\ \text{income and capital gains} \\ (\text{in local currency}) \end{matrix} \pm \begin{matrix} \text{Returns from} \\ \text{changes in currency} \\ \text{exchange rates} \end{matrix}$$

Thus, the two basic components of total return are those generated by the stocks themselves (dividends plus change in share prices) and those derived from movements in currency exchange rates.

Measuring Global Returns Employing the same two basic components noted in Equation 1.5, we can compute total return in U.S. dollars by using the following holding period return (HPR) formula, as modified for changes in currency exchange rates.

Equation 1.6

$$\begin{matrix} \text{Total return} \\ (\text{in U.S. dollars}) \end{matrix} = \left[\frac{\begin{matrix}\text{Ending value of} \\ \text{stock in foreign} \\ \text{currency}\end{matrix} + \begin{matrix}\text{Amount of dividends} \\ \text{received in} \\ \text{foreign currency}\end{matrix}}{\begin{matrix}\text{Beginning value of stock} \\ \text{in foreign currency}\end{matrix}} \times \frac{\begin{matrix}\text{Exchange rate} \\ \text{at } end \text{ of} \\ \text{holding period}\end{matrix}}{\begin{matrix}\text{Exchange rate} \\ \text{at } beginning \text{ of} \\ \text{holding period}\end{matrix}} \right] - 1.00$$

In Equation 1.6, the "exchange rate" represents the value of the foreign currency in U.S. dollars—that is, how much one unit of the foreign currency is worth in U.S. money.

This modified HPR formula is best used over investment periods of 1 year or less. Essentially, the first component of Equation 1.6 provides returns on the stock in local currency, and the second element accounts for the impact of changes in currency exchange rates.

To see how this formula works, consider a U.S. investor who buys several hundred shares of Siemans AG, the German electrical engineering and electronics company that trades on the Frankfurt Stock Exchange. Since Germany is part of the European Community (EC), its currency is the euro. Let's assume that the investor paid a price per share of 90.48 euros for the stock, at a time when the exchange rate between the U.S. dollar and the euro (U.S.$/€) was $0.945, meaning 1 euro was worth almost 95 (U.S.) cents. The stock paid annual dividends of 5 euros per share. Twelve months later, the stock was trading at 94.00 euros, when the U.S.$/€ exchange rate was $1.083. Clearly, the stock went up in price and so did the euro, so the investor must have done all right. To find out just what kind of return this investment generated (in U.S. dollars), we'll have to use Equation 1.6.

$$\begin{aligned} \text{Total return} \atop \text{(in U.S. dollars)} &= \left[\frac{\text{€94.00} + \text{€5.00}}{\text{€90.48}} \times \frac{\$1.083}{\$0.945} \right] - 1.00 \\ &= [1.0942 \times 1.1460] - 1.00 \\ &= [1.2540] - 1.00 \\ &= 25.4\% \end{aligned}$$

With a return of 25.4%, the investor obviously did quite well. However, most of this return was due to currency movements, not to the behavior of the stock. Look at just the first part of the equation, which shows the return (in local currency) earned on the stock from dividends and capital gains: $1.0942 - 1.00 = 9.42$. Thus, the stock itself produced a return of less than 9.50%. All the rest of the return—about 16% (i.e., $25.40 - 9.42$)—came from the change in currency values. In this case, the value of the U.S. dollar went down relative to the euro and thus added to the return.

Currency Exchange Rates As we've just seen, exchange rates can have a dramatic impact on investor returns. They can convert mediocre returns or even losses into very attractive returns—and vice versa. Only one thing determines whether the so-called currency effect is going to be positive or negative: the behavior of the U.S. dollar relative to the currency in which the security is denominated. In essence, a stronger dollar has a negative impact on total returns to U.S. investors, and a weaker dollar has a positive impact. Thus, other things being equal, the best time to be in foreign securities is when the dollar is falling.

Of course, the greater the amount of fluctuation in the currency exchange rate, the greater the impact on total returns. The challenge facing global investors is to find not only the best-performing foreign stock(s) but also the best-performing foreign currencies. You want the value of both the foreign stock and the foreign currency to go up over your investment horizon. And note that this rule applies both to direct investment in foreign stocks and to the purchase of ADRs. (Even though ADRs are denominated in dollars, their quoted prices vary with ongoing changes in currency exchange rates.)

Alternative Investment Strategies

Basically, common stocks can be used as (1) a "storehouse" of value, (2) a way to accumulate capital, and (3) a source of income. Storage of value is important to all investors, as nobody likes to lose money. However, some investors are more concerned about losses than are others. They rank safety of principal as their most important stock selection criterion. These investors are more quality-conscious and tend to gravitate toward blue chips and other nonspeculative shares.

Accumulation of capital, in contrast, is generally an important goal to those with long-term investment horizons. These investors use the capital gains and/or dividends that stocks provide to build up their wealth. Some use growth stocks for this purpose, while others do it with income shares, and still others use a little of both.

Finally, some investors use stocks as a source of income. To them, a dependable flow of dividends is essential. High-yielding, good-quality income shares are usually their preferred investment vehicle.

Individual investors can use various investment strategies to reach their investment goals. These include buy-and-hold, current income, quality long-term growth, aggressive stock management, and speculation and short-term trading. The first 3 strategies appeal to investors who consider storage of value important. Depending on the temperament of the investor and the time he or she has to devote to an investment program, any of these strategies might be used to accumulate capital. In contrast, the current-income strategy is the logical choice for those using stocks as a source of income.

We discuss these strategies in more detail below. You should understand these strategies so that you can choose which one suits your needs.

Buy-and-Hold Buy-and-hold is the most basic of all investment strategies and certainly one of the most conservative. The objective is to place money in a secure investment (safety of principal is vital) and watch it grow over time. In this strategy, investors select high-quality stocks that offer attractive current income and/or capital gains and hold them for extended periods—perhaps as long as 10 to 15 years. This strategy is often used to finance retirement funds, to meet the educational needs of children, or simply to accumulate capital over the long haul. Generally, investors pick a portfolio of good stocks and invest in them on a regular basis for long periods of time—until either the investment climate or corporate conditions change dramatically.

Buy-and-hold investors regularly add fresh capital to their portfolios (many treat them like savings plans). Most also plow the income from annual dividends back into the portfolio and reinvest in additional shares (often through dividend reinvestment plans). Long popular with so-called value-oriented investors, this approach is used by quality-conscious individuals who are looking for competitive returns over the long haul.

Current Income Some investors use common stocks to seek high current income. Common stocks are desirable for this purpose, not so much for their high dividend yields but because their dividends tend to increase over time. In this strategy, safety of principal and stability of income are vital; capital gains are of secondary importance. Quality income shares are the obvious choice for this strategy. Some investors adopt it simply as a way of earning high (and relatively safe) returns on their investment capital. More often, however, the current-income strategy is used by those who are trying to supplement their income. Indeed, many of these investors plan to use the added income for consumption purposes, such as a retired couple supplementing their retirement benefits.

Quality Long-Term Growth This strategy is less conservative than either of the first two in that it seeks capital gains as the primary source of return. A fair amount of trading takes place with this approach. Most of the trading is confined to quality growth stocks (including some of the better tech stocks, as well as baby blues and other mid-caps). These stocks offer attractive growth prospects and the chance for considerable price appreciation. Although a number of growth stocks also pay dividends, this strategy emphasizes capital gains as the principal way to earn big returns.

This approach involves greater risk because of its heavy reliance on capital gains. Therefore, a good deal of diversification is often used. Long-term accumulation of capital is the most common reason for using this approach, but compared to the buy-and-hold tactic, the investor aggressively seeks a bigger payoff by doing considerably more trading and assuming more market risk.

A variation of this investment strategy combines quality long-term growth with high income. This is the total-return approach to investing. Although solidly anchored in long-term growth, this approach also considers dividend income as a source of return. Investors who use the total-return approach seek attractive long-term returns from both dividend income and capital gains by holding both income stocks and growth stocks in their portfolios. Or they may hold stocks that provide both dividends and capital gains. In the latter case, the investor doesn't necessarily look for high-yielding stocks but for stocks that offer the potential for high rates of growth in their dividend streams.

Total-return investors are very concerned about quality. Indeed, about the only thing that separates them from current-income and quality long-term growth investors is that total-return investors care more about the amount of return than about the source of return. For this reason, total-return investors seek the most attractive returns wherever they can find them, be it from a growing stream of dividends or from appreciation in the price of a stock.

Aggressive Stock Management Aggressive stock management also seeks attractive rates of return through a fully managed portfolio. An investor using this strategy aggressively trades in and out of stocks to achieve eye-catching returns, primarily from capital gains. Blue chips, growth stocks, big-name tech stocks, mid-caps, and cyclical issues are the primary investments. More aggressive investors might even consider small-cap stocks, including some of the more speculative tech stocks, foreign shares, and ADRs.

This approach is similar to the quality long-term growth strategy. However, it involves considerably more trading, and the investment horizon is generally much shorter. For example, rather than waiting 2 or 3 years for a stock to move, an aggressive stock trader would go after the same investment payoff in 6 to 12 months. Timing security transactions and turning investment capital over fairly rapidly are both key elements of this strategy. These investors try to stay fully invested in stocks when the market is bullish. When the market weakens, they put a big chunk of their money into defensive stocks or even into cash and other short-term debt instruments.

This aggressive strategy has substantial risks and trading costs. It also places real demands on the individual's time and investment skills. But the rewards can be substantial.

Speculation and Short-Term Trading Speculation and short-term trading characterize the least conservative of all investment strategies. The sole objective of this strategy is capital gains. The shorter the time in which the objective can be achieved, the better. Although investors who use this strategy confine most of their attention to speculative or small-cap stocks and tech stocks, they are not averse to using foreign shares (especially those in so-called emerging markets) or other forms of common stock if they offer attractive short-term opportunities. Many speculators feel that information about the industry or company is less important than market psychology or the general tone of the market. It is a process of constantly switching from one position to another as new opportunities unfold.

Because the strategy involves so much risk, many transactions yield little or no profit, or even substantial losses. The hope is, of course, that when one does hit, it will be in a big way, and returns will be more than sufficient to offset losses. This strategy obviously requires considerable knowledge and time. Perhaps most important, it also requires the psychological and financial fortitude to withstand the shock of financial losses.

CONCEPTS IN REVIEW
Answers available at www.pearsonhighered.com/smart

1.14 Define and briefly discuss the investment merits of each of the following.
a. Blue chips
b. Income stocks
c. Mid-cap stocks
d. American depositary receipts
e. IPOs
f. Tech stocks

1.15 Why do most income stocks offer only limited capital gains potential? Does this mean the outlook for continued profitability is also limited? Explain.

1.16 With all the securities available in this country, why would a U.S. investor want to buy foreign stocks? Briefly describe the two ways in which a U.S. investor can buy stocks in a foreign company. As a U.S. investor, which approach would you prefer? Explain.

1.17 Which investment approach (or approaches) do you feel would be most appropriate for a quality-conscious investor? What kind of investment approach do you think you'd be most comfortable with? Explain.

MyFinanceLab

Here is what you should know after reading this chapter. MyFinanceLab will help you identify what you know and where to go when you need to practice.

What You Should Know	Key Terms	Where to Practice
LG1 Explain the investment appeal of common stocks and why individuals like to invest in them. Common stocks have long been a popular investment vehicle, largely because of the attractive return opportunities they provide. From current income to capital gains, there are common stocks available to fit any investment need.	residual owners, *p. 2*	MyFinanceLab Study Plan 1.1
LG2 Describe stock returns from a historical perspective and understand how current returns measure up to historical standards of performance. Stock returns consist of both dividends and capital gains, although price appreciation is the key component. Over the long run, stocks have provided investors with annual returns of around 10% to 12%. The decade of the 1990s was especially rewarding, as stocks generated returns of anywhere from around 20% (on the Dow) to nearly 30% in the tech-heavy Nasdaq market. That situation changed in early 2000, when one of the biggest bull markets in history came to an abrupt end. From 2000 through late 2002, the DJIA fell some 38%, the S&P 500 fell nearly 50%, and the Nasdaq fell an eye-popping 77%.		MyFinanceLab Study Plan 1.2
LG3 Discuss the basic features of common stocks, including issue characteristics, stock quotations, and transaction costs. Common stocks are a form of equity capital, with each share representing partial ownership of a company. Publicly traded stock can be issued via a public offering or through a rights offering to existing stockholders. Companies can also increase the number of shares outstanding through a stock split. To reduce the number of shares in circulation, companies can buy back shares, which are then held as treasury stock. Occasionally, a company issues different classes of common stock, known as classified common stock.	classified common stock, *p. 10* equity capital, *p. 7* public offering, *p. 7* publicly traded issues, *p. 7* rights offering, *p. 9* stock spin-off, *p. 9* stock split, *p. 9* treasury stock, *p. 10*	MyFinanceLab Study Plan 1.3 Video Learning Aid for Problem P1.1

What You Should Know	Key Terms	Where to Practice
LG4 **Understand the different kinds of common stock values.** There are several ways to calculate the value of a share of stock. Book value represents accounting value. Market value is a security's prevailing market price. Investment value is the amount that investors think the stock should be worth.	book value, *p. 12* investment value, *p. 13* market value, *p. 13* par value, *p. 12*	MyFinanceLab Study Plan 1.4
LG5 **Discuss common stock dividends, types of dividends, and dividend reinvestment plans.** Companies often share their profits by paying out cash dividends to stockholders. Companies pay dividends only after carefully considering a variety of corporate and market factors. Sometimes companies declare stock dividends rather than, or in addition to, cash dividends. Many firms that pay cash dividends have dividend reinvestment plans, through which shareholders can automatically reinvest cash dividends in the company's stock.	cash dividend, *p. 16* date of record, *p. 15* dividend yield, *p. 16* dividend payout ratio, *p. 17* dividend reinvestment plan (DRIP), *p. 18* earnings per share (EPS), *p. 15* ex-dividend date, *p. 16* payment date, *p. 15* stock dividend, *p. 16*	MyFinanceLab Study Plan 1.5
LG6 **Describe various types of common stocks, including foreign stocks, and note how stocks can be used as investment vehicles.** Depending on their needs and preferences, investors can choose blue chips, income stocks, growth stocks, tech stocks, speculative issues, cyclicals, defensive shares, mid-cap stocks, small-cap stocks, and initial public offerings. Also, U.S. investors can buy common stock of foreign companies either directly on foreign exchanges or on U.S. markets as American depositary shares (ADSs). Generally, common stocks can be used as a storehouse of value, as a way to accumulate capital, or as a source of income. Investors can follow different investment strategies (buy-and-hold, current income, quality long-term growth, aggressive stock management, and speculation and short-term trading) to achieve these objectives.	blue-chip stocks, *p. 20* cyclical stocks, *p. 22* defensive stocks, *p. 24* growth stocks, *p 20* income stocks, *p. 20* mid-cap stocks, *p. 24* small-cap stocks, *p. 25* speculative stocks, *p. 22* tech stocks, *p. 22*	MyFinanceLab Study Plan 1.6 Video Learning Aid for Problem P1.14

Log into MyFinanceLab, take a chapter test, and get a personalized Study Plan
that tells you which concepts you understand and which ones you need to
review. From there, MyFinanceLab will give you further practice, tutorials,
animations, videos, and guided solutions.
Log into **www.myfinancelab.com**

Discussion Questions

LG1 Q1.1 Look at the record of stock returns in Table 1.1 (page 3), particularly the return performance during the 1970s, 1980s, 1990s, and 2000 through 2010.

    a. How would you compare the returns during the 1970s with those produced in the 1980s? How would you characterize market returns in the 1990s? Is there anything that stands out about this market? How does it compare with the market that existed from early 2000 through 2010?

    b. Considering the average annual returns that have been generated over holding periods of 5 years or more, what rate of return do you feel is typical for the stock market in general? Is it unreasonable to expect this kind of return, on average, in the future? Explain.

LG2 Q1.2 Given the information in Figure 1.4 (page 11), answer the following questions for Abercrombie & Fitch Co.

    a. On what day did the trading activity occur?

    b. At what price did the stock sell when the market closed at 4:00 P.M. on Thursday, August 23, 2012?

    c. What is the firm's price-to-earnings ratio? What does that indicate?

    d. What is the first price at which the stock traded on the date quoted?

    e. What was the dividend paid per share for the previous year?

    f. What are the highest and lowest prices at which the stock traded during the latest 52-week period?

    g. How many shares of stock were traded on the day quoted?

    h. How much, if any, of a change in price took place between the day quoted and the immediately preceding day? At what price did the stock close on the immediately preceding day?

LG4 Q1.3 Listed below are 3 pairs of stocks. Look at each pair and select the security you would like to own, given that you want to select the one that's worth more money. Then, after you make all 3 of your selections, use the *Wall Street Journal* or some other source to find the latest market value of the securities in each pair.

    a. 50 shares of Berkshire Hathaway (stock symbol BRKA) or 150 shares of Coca-Cola (stock symbol KO). (Both are listed on the NYSE.)

    b. 100 shares of WD-40 (symbol WDFC—a Nasdaq National Market issue) or 100 shares of Nike (symbol NKE—a NYSE stock).

    c. 150 shares of Walmart (symbol WMT) or 50 shares of Sprint Nextel Corp. (symbol S). (Both are listed on the NYSE.)

How many times did you pick the one that was worth more money? Did the price of any of these stocks surprise you? If so, which one(s)? Does the price of a stock represent its value? Explain.

LG6 Q1.4 Assume that a wealthy woman comes to you looking for some investment advice. She is in her early forties and has $250,000 to put into stocks. She wants to build up as much capital as she can over a 15-year period and is willing to tolerate a "fair amount" of risk.

    a. What types of stocks do you think would be most suitable for this investor? Come up with at least 3 types of stocks, and briefly explain the rationale for each.

    b. Would your recommendations change if you were dealing with a smaller amount of money—say, $50,000? What if the investor were more risk-averse? Explain.

LG6 Q1.5 Identify and briefly describe the 3 sources of return to U.S. investors in foreign stocks. How important are currency exchange rates? With regard to currency exchange rates, when is the best time to be in foreign securities?

    a. Listed below are exchange rates (for the beginning and end of a hypothetical 1-year investment horizon) for the British pound (B£), the Australian dollar (A$), and the Mexican peso (Mp).

	Currency Exchange Rates	
Currency	Beginning of Investment Horizon	End of 1-Year Investment Horizon
British pound (B£)	1.55 U.S.$ per B£	1.75 U.S.$ per B£
Australian dollar (A$)	1.35 A$ per U.S.$	1.25 A$ per U.S.$
Mexican peso (Mp)	0.10 U.S.$ per Mp	0.08 U.S.$ per Mp

From the perspective of a U.S. investor holding a foreign (British, Australian, or Mexican) stock, which of the above changes in currency exchange rates would have a positive effect on returns (in U.S. dollars)? Which would have a negative effect?

b. ADRs are denominated in U.S. dollars. Are their returns affected by currency exchange rates? Explain.

LG6 Q1.6 Briefly define each of the following types of investment programs and note the kinds of stock (blue chips, speculative stocks, etc.) that would best fit with each.
   a. A buy-and-hold strategy
   b. A current-income portfolio
   c. Long-term total return
   d. Aggressive stock management

Problems

All problems are available on www.myfinancelab.com

LG3 P1.1 An investor owns some stock in Harry's Pottery Inc. The stock recently underwent a 5-for-4 stock split. If the stock was trading at $50 per share just before the split, how much is each share most likely selling for after the split? If the investor owned 200 shares of the stock before the split, how many shares would she own afterward?

LG3 P1.2 An investor deposits $20,000 into a new brokerage account. The investor buys 1,000 shares of Tipco stock for $19 per share. Two weeks later, the investor sells the Tipco stock for $20 per share. When the investor receives his brokerage account statement, he sees that there is a balance of $20,900 in his account:

Item	Number of Shares	Price per Share ($)	Total Transaction ($)	Account Balance ($)
1. Deposit			20,000	20,000
2. Tipco purchase	1,000	19	(19,000)	20,000
3. Tipco sale	1,000	20	20,000	21,000
4.				
5. Balance				20,900

What belongs in item 4 on this statement?

LG4 P1.3 Ron's Rodents Co. has total assets of $5 million, total short- and long-term debt of $2.8 million, and $400,000 worth of 8% preferred stock outstanding. What is the firm's total book value? What would its book value per share be if the firm had 50,000 shares of common stock outstanding?

LG4 P1.4 Lockhart's Bookstores is trading at $35 per share. There are 280 million shares outstanding. What is the market capitalization of this company?

LG5 **P1.5** The MedTech Company recently reported net profits after taxes of $15.8 million. It has 2.5 million shares of common stock outstanding and pays preferred dividends of $1 million per year.

    a. Compute the firm's earnings per share (EPS).

    b. Assuming that the stock currently trades at $60 per share, determine what the firm's dividend yield would be if it paid $2 per share to common stockholders.

    c. What would the firm's dividend payout ratio be if it paid $2 per share in dividends?

LG5 **P1.6** On January 1, 2010, an investor bought 200 shares of Gottahavit, Inc., for $50 per share. On January 3, 2011, the investor sold the stock for $55 per share. The stock paid a quarterly dividend of $0.25 per share. How much (in $) did the investor earn on this investment, and, assuming the investor is in the 33% tax bracket, how much will she pay in income taxes on this transaction?

LG4 LG5 **P1.7** Consider the following information about Truly Good Coffee, Inc.

Total assets	$240 million
Total debt	$115 million
Preferred stock	$ 25 million
Common stockholders' equity	$100 million
Net profits after taxes	$22.5 million
Number of preferred stock outstanding	1 million shares
Number of common stock outstanding	10 million shares
Preferred dividends paid	$2 per share
Common dividends paid	$0.75 per share
Market price of the preferred stock	$30.75 per share
Market price of the common stock	$25.00 per share

Use the information above to find the following.

    a. The company's book value

    b. Its book value per share

    c. The stock's earnings per share (EPS)

    d. The dividend payout ratio

    e. The dividend yield on the common stock

    f. The dividend yield on the preferred stock

LG5 **P1.8** East Coast Utilities is currently trading at $28 per share. The company pays a quarterly dividend of $0.28 per share. What is the dividend yield?

LG5 **P1.9** West Coast Utilities had a net profit of $900 million. It has 900 million shares outstanding and paid annual dividends of $0.90 per share. What is the dividend payout ratio?

LG5 **P1.10** Wilfred Nadeau owns 200 shares of Consolidated Glue. The company's board of directors recently declared a cash dividend of 50 cents a share payable April 18 (a Wednesday) to shareholders of record on March 22 (a Thursday).

    a. How much in dividends, if any, will Wilfred receive if he sells his stock on March 20?

    b. Assume Wilfred decides to hold on to the stock rather than sell it. If he belongs to the company's dividend reinvestment plan, how many new shares of stock will he receive if the stock is currently trading at $40 and the plan offers a 5% discount on the share price of the stock? (Assume that all of Wilfred's dividends are diverted to the plan.) Will Wilfred have to pay any taxes on these dividends, given that he is taking them in stock rather than cash?

LG5 **P1.11** Southern Cities Trucking Company has the following 5-year record of earnings per share.

Year	EPS ($)
2009	1.40
2010	2.10
2011	1.00
2012	3.25
2013	0.80

Which of the following procedures would produce higher dividends to stockholders over this 5-year period?
a. Paying out dividends at a fixed ratio of 40% of EPS
b. Paying out dividends at a fixed rate of $1 per share

LG4 LG5 **P1.12** Using the resources at your campus or public library or on the Internet, select any 3 common stocks you like and determine the latest book value per share, earnings per share, dividend payout ratio, and dividend yield for each. (Show all your calculations.)

LG4 LG5 **P1.13** In January 2009 an investor purchased 800 shares of Engulf & Devour, a rapidly growing high-tech conglomerate. From 2009 through 2013, the stock turned in the following dividend and share price performance.

Year	Share Price Beginning of Year ($)	Dividends Paid during Year ($)	Share Price End of Year ($)
2009	42.50*	0.82	54.00
2010	54.00	1.28	74.25
2011	74.25	1.64	81.00
2012	81.00	1.91	91.25
2013	91.25	2.30	128.75

*Investor purchased stock in 2009 at this price.

On the basis of this information, find the annual holding period returns for 2009 through 2013. (*Hint*: See Chapter 10 for the HPR formula.)

LG4 **P1.14** George Robbins considers himself an aggressive investor. He's thinking about investing in some foreign securities and is looking at stocks in (1) Bayer AG, the big German chemical and health-care firm, and (2) Swisscom AG, the Swiss telecommunications company.

Bayer AG, which trades on the Frankfurt Exchange, is currently priced at 53.25 euros per share. It pays annual dividends of 1.50 euros per share. Robbins expects the stock to climb to 60.00 euros per share over the next 12 months. The current exchange rate is 0.9025€/U.S.$, but that's expected to rise to 1.015€/U.S.$. The other company, Swisscom, trades on the Zurich Exchange and is currently priced at 71.5 Swiss francs (Sf) per share. The stock pays annual dividends of 1.5 Sf per share. Its share price is expected to go up to 76.0 Sf within a year. At current exchange rates, one Sf is worth $0.75 U.S., but that's expected to go to $0.85 by the end of the 1-year holding period.

a. Ignoring the currency effect, which of the 2 stocks promises the higher total return (in its local currency)? Based on this information, which looks like the better investment?
b. Which of the 2 stocks has the better total return in U.S. dollars? Did currency exchange rates affect their returns in any way? Do you still want to stick with the same stock you selected in part a? Explain.

LG6 **P1.15** Bruce buys $25,000 of UH-OH Corporation stock. Unfortunately, a major newspaper reveals the very next day that the company is being investigated for accounting fraud, and the stock price falls by 50%. What is the percentage increase now required for Bruce to get back to $25,000 of value?

Visit **www.myfinancelab.com** for web exercises, spreadsheets, and other online resources.

Case Problem 1.1   Sara Decides to Take the Plunge

LG1 LG6 Sara Thomas is a child psychologist who has built up a thriving practice in her hometown of Boise, Idaho. Over the past several years she has been able to accumulate a substantial sum of money. She has worked long and hard to be successful, but she never imagined anything like this. Even so, success has not spoiled Sara. Still single, she keeps to her old circle of friends. One of her closest friends is Terry Jenkins, who happens to be a stockbroker and who acts as Sara's financial adviser.

Not long ago Sara attended a seminar on investing in the stock market, and since then she's been doing some reading about the market. She has concluded that keeping all of her money in low-yielding savings accounts doesn't make sense. As a result, Sara has decided to move part of her money to stocks. One evening, Sara told Terry about her decision and explained that she had found several stocks that she thought looked "sort of interesting." She described them as follows:

- *North Atlantic Swim Suit Company.* This highly speculative stock pays no dividends. Although the earnings of NASS have been a bit erratic, Sara feels that its growth prospects have never been brighter—"what with more people than ever going to the beaches the way they are these days," she says.

- *Town and Country Computer.* This is a long-established computer firm that pays a modest dividend yield (of about 1.50%). It is considered a quality growth stock. From one of the stock reports she read, Sara understands that T&C offers excellent long-term growth and capital gains potential.

- *Southeastern Public Utility Company.* This income stock pays a dividend yield of around 5%. Although it's a solid company, it has limited growth prospects because of its location.

- *International Gold Mines, Inc.* This stock has performed quite well in the past, especially when inflation has become a problem. Sara feels that if it can do so well in inflationary times, it will do even better in a strong economy. Unfortunately, the stock has experienced wide price swings in the past. It pays almost no dividends.

Questions

a. What do you think of the idea of Sara keeping "substantial sums" of money in savings accounts? Would common stocks make better investments for her than savings accounts? Explain.

b. What is your opinion of the 4 stocks Sara has described? Do you think they are suitable for her investment needs? Explain.

c. What kind of common stock investment program would you recommend for Sara? What investment objectives do you think she should set for herself, and how can common stocks help her achieve her goals?

Case Problem 1.2   Wally Wonders Whether There's a Place for Dividends

LG5 LG6   Wally Wilson is a commercial artist who makes a good living by doing freelance work—mostly layouts and illustrations—for local ad agencies and major institutional clients (such as large department stores). Wally has been investing in the stock market for some time, buying mostly high-quality growth stocks as a way to achieve long-term growth and capital appreciation. He feels that with the limited time he has to devote to his security holdings, high-quality issues are his best bet. He has become a bit perplexed lately with the market, disturbed that some of his growth stocks aren't doing even as well as many good-grade income shares. He therefore decides to have a chat with his broker, Al Fried.

During their conversation, it becomes clear that both Al and Wally are thinking along the same lines. Al points out that dividend yields on income shares are indeed way up and that, because of the state of the economy, the outlook for growth stocks is not particularly bright. He suggests that Wally seriously consider putting some of his money into income shares to capture the high dividend yields that are available. After all, as Al says, "the bottom line is not so much where the payoff comes from as how much it amounts to!" They then talk about a high-yield public utility stock, Hydro-Electric Light and Power. Al digs up some forecast information about Hydro-Electric and presents it to Wally for his consideration:

Year	Expected EPS ($)	Expected Dividend Payout Ratio (%)
2013	3.25	40
2014	3.40	40
2015	3.90	45
2016	4.40	45
2017	5.00	45

The stock currently trades at $60 per share. Al thinks that within 5 years it should be trading at $75 to $80 a share. Wally realizes that to buy the Hydro-Electric stock, he will have to sell his holdings of CapCo Industries—a highly regarded growth stock that Wally is disenchanted with because of recent substandard performance.

Questions

a. How would you describe Wally's present investment program? How do you think it fits him and his investment objectives?

b. Consider the Hydro-Electric stock.

   1. Determine the amount of annual dividends Hydro-Electric can be expected to pay over the years 2013 to 2017.
   2. Compute the total dollar return that Wally will make from Hydro-Electric if he invests $6,000 in the stock and all the dividend and price expectations are realized.
   3. If Wally participates in the company's dividend reinvestment plan, how many shares of stock will he have by the end of 2017? What will they be worth if the stock trades at $80 on December 31, 2017? Assume that the stock can be purchased through the dividend reinvestment plan at a net price of $50 a share in 2013, $55 in 2014, $60 in 2015, $65 in 2016, and $70 in 2017. Use fractional shares, to 2 decimals, in your computations. Also, assume that, as in part **b**, Wally starts with 100 shares of stock and all dividend expectations are realized.

c. Would Wally be going to a different investment strategy if he decided to buy shares in Hydro-Electric? If the switch is made, how would you describe his new investment program? What do you think of this new approach? Is it likely to lead to more trading on Wally's behalf? If so, can you reconcile that with the limited amount of time he has to devote to his portfolio?

Excel with Spreadsheets

Build a spreadsheet containing the following quoted information. Based on the information given, what is the firm's current market cap? What was the firm's net income?

City National Corp. (CYN)   NYSE

Comprehensive Quote: 11/16/09 04:00 PM EST

Last	Change	% Change	Volume
37.95	0.66	1.77%	**658,323**

Open	High	Low	Prior Day's Volume
37.57	**38.40**	**37.57**	**394,981**

52-Week High	52-Week Low	Prior Day's Close
48.99	**22.59**	**37.29**
(12/31/2008)	(03/05/2009)	

Snapshot quotes reflect real-time trades reported through Nasdaq only: comprehensive quotes reflect trading in all markets and are delayed at least 15 minutes. Volume updates from 4:00 a.m. - 8:00 p.m. ET. (More Info)

Other Prices

U.S. Germany Xetra

Historical Quotes

Closing prices since 1/2/1970.

date: [   ] [Go]

52-Week High	52-Week Low	Prior Day's Close
48.99	**22.59**	**37.29**
(12/31/2008)	(03/05/2009)	

Snapshot quotes reflect real-time trades reported through Nasdaq only: comprehensive quotes reflect trading in all markets and are delayed at least 15 minutes. Volume updates from 4:00 a.m. - 8:00 p.m. ET. (More Info)

Other Prices

U.S. Germany Xetra

Historical Quotes

Closing prices since 1/2/1970.

date: [   ] [Go]

Stock Data

Market Cap(Mil)	**1920.56**
P/E Ratio	**151.96**
Dividend Yield	**1.07%**
Latest Dividend	**$0.1**
Pay Date of Latest Dividend	**11/18/09**

Chapter-Opening Problem

Note: In April 2012 Exxon Mobil announced plans to cut its quarterly dividend by 21% to $0.57 per share.

a. If Exxon Mobil has 4.7 billion shares outstanding, how much cash will it pay in dividends in 1 year?

b. In the 2 days surrounding Exxon's announcement, its stock fell from $85.72 to $85.48 per share. What is the decline in Exxon's total market value over this period?

c. Does the answer to part b seem appropriate given the answer to part a? Why or why not?

2

Fixed-Income Securities

LEARNING GOALS

After studying this chapter, you should be able to:

LG1 Explain the basic investment attributes of bonds and their use as investments.

LG2 Describe the essential features of a bond, note the role that bond ratings play in the market, and distinguish among different types of call, refunding, and sinking-fund provisions.

LG3 Explain how bonds are priced in the market and why some bonds are more volatile than others.

LG4 Identify the different types of bonds and the kinds of investment objectives these securities can fulfill.

LG5 Discuss the global nature of the bond market and the difference between dollar-denominated and non-dollar-denominated foreign bonds.

LG6 Describe the basic features and characteristics of convertible securities and measure the value of a convertible security.

In a sign of the severity of the global recession, Standard & Poor's Ratings Services stripped General Electric of its coveted AAA bond rating in March 2009. That marked the first time in more than 50 years that GE's bonds fell below the highest possible investment-grade rating. Later the same day, another ratings company, Fitch, issued a downgrade on the debt of Warren Buffett's firm, Berkshire Hathaway, from AAA to AA. Those actions left just 5 U.S. corporations with AAA-rated debt (Automatic Data Processing, ExxonMobil, Johnson & Johnson, Microsoft, and Pfizer), and by 2012 Pfizer would also be downgraded.

Corporations were not the only ones receiving downgrades, on August 5, 2011, Standard & Poor's lowered its long-term sovereign credit rating on the United States of America from AAA to AA+. Standard & Poor's indicated that the U.S. downgrade was prompted by a negative view of the rising public debt burden and a perception of greater policymaking uncertainty.

The global recession led to downgrades for countless companies and several countries, and 3 years after the recession's end, downgrades were still a problem. On Friday, January 13, 2012, the sovereign credit of 9 European countries was downgraded. In addition to France's loss of its highly valued AAA credit rating, the ratings of Austria, Malta, Slovakia, and Slovenia were knocked down a notch and, even worse, the ratings of Cyprus, Italy, Portugal, and Spain were knocked down by 2 notches. For Cyprus and Portugal, the downgrades meant that their treasury bonds were now "junk" bonds.

Before you invest in debt securities, whether issued by corporations or countries, you'll want to consider credit quality, interest rates, maturity, and other relevant factors. Chapters 2 and 8 will provide the background you need to make wise choices in the bond market.

(Sources: "And Then There Were Six," Seeking Alpha, March 12, 2009, seekingalpha.com/article/125625-aaa-rated-companies-and-then-there-were-six; "GE, Berkshire Lose AAA Ratings; Ranks of Top Firms Thinning," *The China Post*, March 14, 2009, www.chinapost.com.tw/business/americas/2009/03/14/200120/GE-Berkshire.htm; Standard & Poor's, Global Credit Portal Ratings Direct, August 5, 2011, **S&P | RatingsDirect**® on the **Global Credit Portal** | Americas, www.standardandpoors.com/ratingsdirect; "S&P Downgrades the Credit of Nine European Countries, Including France," January 13, 2012, www.npr.org/blogs/thetwo-way/2012/01/13/145178453/s-p-downgrades-france-deals-a-blow-to-eurozone.)

Why Invest in Bonds?

LG1 In contrast to stocks, bonds are liabilities—publicly traded IOUs where the bondholders are actually lending money to the issuer. Technically, **bonds** are negotiable, publicly traded, long-term debt securities. They are issued in various denominations, by a variety of borrowing organizations, including the U.S. Treasury, agencies of the U.S. government, state and local governments, and corporations. Bonds are often referred to as *fixed-income securities* because the debt payments of the issuers are usually fixed. That is, in most cases the issuing organization agrees to pay a fixed amount of interest periodically and to repay a fixed amount of principal at maturity.

Like stocks, bonds can provide two kinds of income: (1) current income and (2) capital gains. The current income comes from the periodic interest payments paid over the bond's life. The capital gains component is a little different. Because the companies issuing bonds promise to repay a fixed amount when the bonds mature, bond prices do not typically rise in step with a firm's profits as stocks do. However, bond prices do rise and fall as market interest rates change. A basic relationship that you must keep in mind is that interest rates and bond prices move in opposite directions. When interest rates rise, bond prices fall, and when rates drop, bond prices move up. We'll have more to say about this relation later in the chapter, but here's the intuition behind it. Imagine that you buy a brand-new bond, issued by a company like GE, paying 6% interest. Suppose that a month later market rates have risen, and new bonds pay investors 7% interest. If you want to sell your GE bond, you're likely to experience a capital loss because investors will not want to buy a bond paying 6% interest when the going rate in the market is 7%. With fewer buyers interested in them, GE bonds will decline in value. Happily, the opposite outcome can occur if market rates fall. When the going rate on bonds is 5%, your GE bond paying 6% would command a premium in the market. Taken together, the current income and capital gains earned from bonds can lead to attractive returns.

A wide variety of bonds are available in the market, from relatively safe issues sought by conservative investors (e.g., General Electric bonds) to highly speculative securities appropriate for investors who can tolerate a great deal of risk (e.g., Sirius XM bonds). In addition, the risks and returns offered by all types of bonds depend in part upon the volatility of interest rates. Because interest rate movements cause bond prices to change, higher interest rate volatility makes bond returns less predictable.

Other bonds have special features designed to appeal to certain types of investors. Investors in high tax brackets who want to shelter income from taxes find tax-exempt bonds appealing. Municipal bonds, for example, pay interest that is not subject to federal income taxation, and interest on Treasury bonds is exempt from state income tax. Despite the term *fixed income*, some bonds make interest payments that vary through time according to a formula. In a sense, the term *fixed income* is still appropriate for these bonds because the formula that determines their interest payments is contractually fixed. For example, governments in the United States and many other countries issue inflation-indexed bonds with interest payments that rise with inflation. As the inflation rate changes, the payments on these bonds will change, but investors know in advance exactly how the interest payments will adjust as inflation occurs. Those bonds appeal to investors who want some protection from the risk of rising inflation.

Putting Bond Market Performance in Perspective

Interest rates drive the bond market. In fact, the behavior of interest rates is the most important influence on bond returns. Interest rates determine not only the current income investors will receive but also the capital gains (or losses) they will incur. It's not surprising, therefore, that bond-market participants follow interest rates closely. When commentators in the news media describe how the market has performed on a particular day, they usually speak in terms of what happened to bond yields that day rather than what happened to bond prices.

Figure 2.1 provides a look at interest rates on bonds issued by U.S. corporations and the U.S. government from 1963 through 2011. It shows that rates rose steadily through the 1960s and 1970s, peaking in the early 1980s at more than 3 times their 1963 levels. Rates then began a long downward slide, and by the end of 2011 rates were lower than they had ever been (a trend which continued into October 2012 as this book was going to press). Keep in mind that rising interest rates lead to falling bond prices, so during the 1970s investors who held bonds that had been issued in the 1960s endured capital losses. By the same token, investors who purchased bonds when interest rates were very high in the early 1980s earned large capital gains as market interest rates subsequently declined.

FIGURE 2.1   **The Behavior of Interest Rates over Time, 1962 through 2011**

Interest rates rose dramatically from 1963 to the early 1980s before starting a long-term decline that continued through 2012. Rates on corporate bonds tend to mirror rates on government bonds, although corporate rates are higher due to the risk of default by the issuing corporation. Note that the gap, or "spread," between U.S. corporate bonds and U.S. Treasury bond yields was particularly wide in 2008 during the financial crisis. (Source: Aswath Damodaran, The Data Page, http://pages.stern.nyu.edu/~adamodar/.)

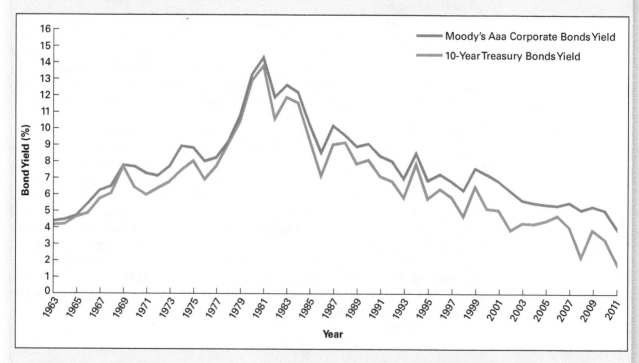

Figure 2.1 shows that rates on corporate and government bonds tend to move together, but corporate bond rates are higher. Higher rates on corporate bonds provide compensation for the risk that corporations might default on their debts. The difference between the rate on corporate bonds and the rate on government bonds is called the *yield spread* or the *credit spread*. When business conditions are weak and the risk of defaults on corporate bonds increases, the yield spread widens as it did in 2008.

Historical Returns As with stocks, total returns in the bond market are made up of both current income from the bond's interest payments and capital gains (or losses) from changes in the bond's value. Table 2.1 lists year-end bond yields and annual total returns for U.S. government bonds from 1962 through 2011. Note how different the year-end yields can be from the total returns. The differences are attributable to the inverse relation between changes in the market interest rate and bond values. When market interest rates rise, bond values fall. During a period of rising rates, total returns on bonds include capital losses that can sometimes exceed the bonds' current income,

TABLE 2.1	HISTORICAL ANNUAL YIELDS AND TOTAL RETURNS FOR TREASURY BONDS				
Year	Year-End T-Bond Yield (%)	T-Bond Annual Total Return (%)	Year	Year-End T-Bond Yield (%)	T-Bond Annual Total Return (%)
1962	3.9	5.7	1987	9.0	−5.0
1963	4.1	1.7	1988	9.1	8.2
1964	4.2	3.7	1989	7.8	17.7
1965	4.6	0.7	1990	8.1	6.2
1966	4.8	2.9	1991	7.1	15.0
1967	5.7	−1.6	1992	6.8	9.4
1968	6.0	3.3	1993	5.8	14.2
1969	7.7	−5.0	1994	7.8	−8.0
1970	6.4	16.8	1995	5.7	23.5
1971	5.9	9.8	1996	6.3	1.4
1972	6.4	2.8	1997	5.8	9.9
1973	6.7	3.7	1998	4.7	14.9
1974	7.4	2.0	1999	6.4	−8.3
1975	8.0	3.6	2000	5.1	16.7
1976	6.9	16.0	2001	5.1	5.6
1977	7.7	1.3	2002	3.8	15.1
1978	9.0	−0.8	2003	4.3	0.4
1979	10.4	0.7	2004	4.2	4.5
1980	12.8	−3.0	2005	4.4	2.9
1981	13.7	8.2	2006	4.7	2.0
1982	10.5	32.8	2007	4.0	10.2
1983	11.8	3.2	2008	2.2	20.1
1984	11.5	13.7	2009	3.8	−11.1
1985	9.3	25.7	2010	3.3	8.5
1986	7.1	24.3	2011	1.9	16.0

Source: Aswath Damodaran, The Data Page, http://pages.stern.nyu.edu/~adamodar/.

resulting in a negative total return. Total returns on U.S. Treasury bonds were negative in 8 out of 50 years, and as you can see in Table 2.1, the years with negative total returns on bonds were years in which bond yields rose. In contrast, bond returns were extraordinarily high in years when interest rates were falling such as 1982, 1984 to 1986, and more recently in 2008.

We can use the return data from Table 2.1 to look at average bond returns over different investment horizons, as shown below:

Holding Period	Average Annual Returns (%)
5 years: 2007–2011	8.7
10 years: 2002–2011	6.9
20 years: 1992–2011	7.4
30 years: 1982–2011	9.7

These figures show that the last 30 years were generally good to bond investors. This was mostly due to the fact that the U.S. economy was in a sustained period of declining interest rates, which in turn produced hefty capital gains and above-average returns. In fact, in 14 of the last 30 years, bonds earned double-digit total returns. Whether market interest rates will (or even can) continue on that path is, of course, the big question. Given the current record low yields, most market observers expect below-average returns on bonds over the next several years.

Bonds versus Stocks Compared to stocks, bonds are generally less risky and provide higher current income. Bonds, like stocks, are issued by a wide range of companies as well as various governmental bodies, so investors can construct well-diversified portfolios with bonds, just as they do with stocks. On the other hand, the potential for very high returns on bonds is much more limited compared to stocks, even though the last 2 decades have been exceptional for bonds.

Figure 2.2 (on page 47) illustrates some of the performance differences between stocks and bonds by showing how a $10,000 investment in either stocks or bonds would have grown from 1992 to 2011. Although the investment in bonds slightly outpaced stocks in the early 1990s, investors in stocks were far better off in the late 1990s as the equity market boomed. The investment in stocks peaked in August 2000 and then fell sharply. The stock value fell even more after the terrorist attacks on September 11, 2001, and eventually hit bottom in September 2002. By 2002, the bond investment was back in front, but only for a brief time. The stock investment peaked again in October 2007 only to have the U.S. housing bubble burst and the financial crisis begin. With the stock market in free fall in 2008, the stock investment hit bottom again in February 2009. Once the financial crisis began to ease, the stock investment began a rocky rebound and by the end of 2011 was within a few thousand dollars of the investment value in bonds.

Figure 2.2 illustrates that stock returns are much more volatile than bond returns are. If stocks are riskier, then investors should, on average, earn higher returns on stocks than on bonds, and stocks have outperformed bonds over long horizons. Still, Figure 2.2 shows that bonds can outperform stocks even over periods as long as a decade, or two. In fact, we see in Figure 2.2 that the average annual return on the bond investment, in spite of being less risky, was 6.3% versus 5.8% for stocks. The biggest differences in

FIGURE 2.2   Comparative Performance of Stocks and Bonds, 1992 through 2011

This graph shows what happened to $10,000 invested in bonds and $10,000 invested in stocks over the 20-year period from January 1992 through December 2011. Clearly, while stocks held a commanding lead through the late 1990s, the ensuing bear market more than erased that advantage. That pattern repeated itself as stocks outperformed bonds from 2003 to late 2007, only to fall sharply through the end of 2008. From early 2009 through the end of 2011, stocks took a bumpy path toward rebounding.

Note: Performance figures and graphs are based on fully compounded rates of return and include reinvested current income (dividends and interest) as well as capital gains (or losses); taxes have been ignored in all calculations.

returns between stocks and bonds usually come during bear markets when stock returns are negative. In part, this reflects a phenomenon called "flight to quality" in which investors pull their funds out of the stock market to invest in less risky securities such as bonds. For example, while Figure 2.2 shows that investors in stocks lost roughly 40% of their money in 2008, Table 2.1 (on page 45) shows that government bond investors made 20% that year.

Many investors argue that even if bonds earn lower returns than stocks on average, that's a low price to pay for the level of stability that bonds bring to a portfolio. The fact is, bond returns are far more stable than stock returns, plus they possess excellent portfolio diversification properties. As a general rule, adding bonds to a portfolio will, up to a point, reduce the portfolio's risk without dramatically reducing its return. Investors don't buy bonds for their high returns, except when they think interest rates are heading down. Rather, investors buy them for their current income and for the stability they bring to a portfolio.

Exposure to Risk

Like all other investments, bonds are subject to a variety of risks. Generally speaking, bonds are exposed to 5 major types of risk: interest rate risk, purchasing power risk, business/financial risk, liquidity risk, and call risk.

- *Interest Rate Risk.* Interest rate risk is the most important risk that fixed-income investors face because it's the major cause of price volatility in the bond market. For bonds, interest rate risk translates into market risk, meaning that the behavior of interest rates affects nearly all bonds and cuts across all sectors of the market, even the U.S. Treasury market. When market interest rates rise, bond prices fall, and vice versa. As interest rates become more volatile, so do bond prices.

- *Purchasing Power Risk.* Inflation erodes the purchasing power of money, and that creates purchasing power risk. Naturally investors are aware of this, so market interest rates on bonds compensate investors for the rate of inflation that they expect over a bond's life. When inflation is low and predictable, bonds do pretty well because their returns exceed the inflation rate by an amount sufficient to provide investors with a positive return, even after accounting for inflation's effect on purchasing power. When inflation takes off unexpectedly, as it did in the late 1970s, bond yields start to lag behind inflation rates, and the interest payments made by bonds fail to keep up. The end result is that the purchasing power of the money that bond investors receive falls faster than they anticipated. That's what the term *purchasing power risk* means. Of course, risk cuts both ways, so when the inflation rate falls unexpectedly, bonds do exceptionally well.

- *Business/Financial Risk.* This is basically the risk that the issuer will default on interest or principal payments. Also known as *credit risk* or *default risk*, business/financial risk has to do with the quality and financial health of the issuer. The stronger the financial position of the issuer, the less business/financial risk there is to worry about. Default risk is negligible for some securities. Historically, investors have viewed U.S. Treasury securities as being free of default risk, although the growing debt of the United States has raised some concern about the potential for a default. For other types of bonds, such as corporate and municipal bonds, default risk is a much more important consideration.

- *Liquidity Risk.* Liquidity risk is the risk that a bond will be difficult to sell at a reasonable price if the investor wants to sell it. In certain sectors of the market, this can be a big problem. Even though the bond market is enormous, many bonds do not trade actively once they are issued. U.S. Treasury bonds are the exception to the rule, but most corporate and municipal bonds are relatively illiquid.

- *Call Risk.* Call risk, or *prepayment risk*, is the risk that a bond will be "called" (retired) long before its scheduled maturity date. Issuers often prepay their bonds when interest rates fall. (We'll examine call features later in this chapter.) When issuers call their bonds, the bondholders get their cash back and have to find another place for their funds—and there's the problem. Because bonds are nearly always called for prepayment after interest rates have fallen, comparable investments just aren't available. Thus, investors have to replace high-yielding bonds with much lower-yielding bonds.

The returns on bonds are, of course, related to risk—other things being equal, the more risk embedded in a bond, the greater the expected return. The risks of investing in bonds depend upon the characteristics of the bond and the entity that issued it. For example, as we'll see later in the chapter, there's more interest rate risk with a long-term bond than with a short-term bond. In addition, for particular bonds, the characteristics that affect risk may have offsetting effects, and that makes risk comparisons of bonds difficult. That is, one issue could have more interest rate and call risk but less credit and liquidity risk than another issue. We'll examine the various features that affect a bond's risk exposure as we work our way through this chapter.

CONCEPTS IN REVIEW

Answers available at www.pearsonhighered.com/smart

2.1 What appeal do bonds hold for investors? Give several reasons why bonds make attractive investment outlets.

2.2 How would you describe the behavior of market interest rates and bond returns over the last 30 years? Do swings in market interest rates have any bearing on bond returns? Explain.

2.3 Identify and briefly describe the 5 types of risk to which bonds are exposed. What is the most important source of risk for bonds in general? Explain.

Essential Features of a Bond

LG2 LG3 A bond is a negotiable, long-term debt instrument that carries certain obligations (the payment of interest and the repayment of principal) on the part of the issuer. If you purchase a bond, you are only lending money to the issuer, so you are not entitled to any of the rights and privileges associated with common stock, such as the right to vote at shareholders' meetings. But as a bondholder you do have a number of well-defined rights and obligations that together define the essential features of a bond. We'll now take a look at some of these features. As you will see, when it comes to bonds, it's especially important to know what you're getting into, for many seemingly insignificant features can have dramatic effects on price behavior and investment return.

Bond Interest and Principal

Bonds make periodic interest and principal payments. Most bonds pay interest every 6 months, although some make monthly interest payments, and some pay interest annually. A bond's **coupon** defines the annual interest income that the issuer will pay to the bondholder. For instance, if a bond with a principal (or par value) of $1,000 pays $80 in interest each year, we say that $80 is the coupon and 8% ($80 ÷ $1,000) is the coupon rate. If the bond makes semiannual payments, there would be a $40 interest payment every 6 months. Likewise, if the bond made monthly payments, the $80 coupon would be paid as 12 equal monthly interest payments totaling $80. The bond's **current yield** measures the interest component of a bond's return relative to the bond's market price. The current yield equals the annual coupon divided by the bond's market price.

Example

Suppose that an 8% bond with a $1,000 par value is currently priced in the market at $875. You can calculate the bond's current yield as follows:

$$\frac{\$1,000 \times 0.08}{\$875} = 0.0914$$

Notice that the 9.14% current yield is greater than the bond's coupon rate. That's because the bond's market price is below its par value.

The *principal* of a bond, also known as an issue's *par value*, specifies the amount of capital that the bond issuer must repay at maturity. A bond's principal is also often referred to as its *face value* or *maturity value*. Note that a bond's market price need not, and usually does not, equal its par value. As we have discussed, bond prices fluctuate as interest rates move, yet a bond's par value remains fixed over its life.

Maturity Date

Unlike common stock, all debt securities have limited lives and will mature on some future date, the issue's **maturity date**. Whereas bond issuers may make interest payments annually or semiannually over the life of the issue, they repay principal only at maturity. The maturity date on a bond is fixed. It not only defines the life of a new issue but also denotes the amount of time remaining for older, outstanding bonds. Such a life span is known as an issue's *term to maturity*. For example, a new issue may come out as a 25-year bond; 5 years later, it will have 20 years remaining to maturity.

We can distinguish 2 types of bond offerings based on the issuer's plans to mature the debt: term and serial bond issues. A **term bond** issue has a single, fairly lengthy maturity date for all of the bonds being issued and is the most common type of bond issue. A **serial bond** issue, in contrast, has a series of bonds with different maturity dates, perhaps as many as 15 or 20, within a single bond offering. For example, an offering of 20-year term bonds issued in 2010 all have a single maturity date of 2030. That same issue conducted for serial bonds might have 20 annual maturity dates, extending from 2010 through 2030. At each of these annual maturity dates, a certain portion of the issue (i.e., a certain number of bonds) would mature.

Debt instruments with different maturities go by different names. A debt security that's originally issued with a maturity of 2 to 10 years is known as a **note**, whereas a bond technically has an initial term to maturity of more than 10 years. In practice, notes are often issued with maturities of 5 to 7 years, whereas bonds normally carry maturities of 20 to 30 years, or more.

Principles of Bond Price Behavior

Practice Pricing Bonds

The price of a bond is a function of its coupon, its maturity, and the level of market interest rates. Figure 2.3 (on page 51) captures the relationship of bond prices to market interest rates. Basically, the graph reinforces the *inverse relationship* that exists between bond prices and market rates: Lower rates lead to higher bond prices.

Figure 2.3 also shows the difference between premium and discount bonds. A **premium bond** is one that sells for more than its par value. A premium results when market interest rates drop below the bond's coupon rate. A **discount bond**, in contrast, sells for less than par value. The discount is the result of market interest rates being greater than

FIGURE 2.3 The Price Behavior of a Bond

A bond will sell at its par value so long as the prevailing market interest rate remains the same as the bond's coupon—in this case, 10%. However, even when the market rate does not equal the coupon rate, as a bond approaches its maturity, the price of the issue moves toward its par value.

Smart's Tour of the Web

To watch author Scott Smart discuss key websites for this chapter, visit www.myfinancelab.com

the issue's coupon rate. Thus, the 10% bond in Figure 2.3 trades at a premium when the market requires 8%, but at a discount when the market rate is 12%.

When a bond is first issued, it usually sells at a price that equals or is very close to par value because bond issuers generally set the coupon rate equal or close to the market's required interest rate at the time of the issue. Likewise, when the bond matures—some 15, 20, or 30 years later—it will once again be priced at its par value. What happens to the price of the bond in between is of considerable interest to most bond investors. In this regard, the extent to which bond prices move depends not only on the direction of change in market interest rates but also on the magnitude of such change. The greater the moves in interest rates, the greater the swings in bond prices.

However, bond price volatility also varies according to an issue's coupon and maturity. That is, bonds with lower coupons and/or longer maturities have more price volatility and are more responsive to changes in market interest rates. (Note in Figure 2.3 that for a given change in interest rates—for example, from 10% to 8%—

the largest change in price occurs when the bond has the greatest number of years to maturity.) Therefore, if you expect a decline in interest rates, you should buy bonds with lower coupons and longer maturities to maximize capital gains. When interest rates move up, you should do just the opposite: Purchase bonds with high coupons and short maturities. This choice will minimize price variation and act to preserve as much capital as possible.

Actually, the maturity of an issue has a greater impact on price volatility than the coupon does. For example, suppose there are 2 different bonds that both pay an 8% coupon rate, but one bond matures in 5 years while the other matures in 25 years. Look what happens to the price of these bonds when market interest rates move up or down:

	Percentage Change in the Price of an 8% Coupon Bond When Market Interest Rates Are 5% to 10%					
Interest Rate (%)	5	6	7	9	10	11
Bond Maturity (yr)						
5	13.0	8.4	4.1	−3.9	−7.6	−11.1
25	42.3	25.6	11.7	−9.8	−18.2	−25.3

The prices of both bonds rise when interest rates fall, but the effect is much larger for the 25-year bond. Similarly, both bonds fall in value when rates rise, but the 25-year bond falls a lot more than the 5-year bond does. Such behavior is universal with all fixed-income securities and is very important. It means that if investors want to reduce their exposure to capital losses or, more to the point, to lower the price volatility in their bond holdings, then they should buy bonds with shorter maturities.

Quoting Bond Prices

Unlike stocks, the vast majority of bonds—especially corporate and municipal bonds—rarely change hands in the secondary markets. As a result, with the exception of U.S. Treasury and some agency issues, bonds are not widely quoted in the financial press, not even in the *Wall Street Journal*. Prices of all types of bonds are usually expressed as a percent of par, meaning that a quote of, say, 85 translates into a price of 85% of the bond's par value or $850 for a bond with a $1,000 par value (most corporate and municipal bonds have $1,000 par values). Also, the price of any bond depends on its coupon and maturity, so those two features are always a part of any listed price.

In the corporate and municipal markets, bonds are expressed in decimals, using 3 places to the right of the decimal point. Thus, a quote of 87.562, as a percent of a $1,000 par bond, converts to a price of $875.62. Similarly, a quote of 121.683 translates into a price of $1,216.83. In contrast, U.S. Treasury and agency bond quotes are stated in thirty-seconds of a point (where 1 point equals $10). For example, you might see the price of a T-bond listed at 94:16. Translated, that means the bond is priced at 94 16/32, or 94.5% of par—in other words, at $945.00. With government bonds, the figures to the right of the colon (:) show the number of thirty-seconds embedded in the price. Consider another bond that's trading at 141:08. This bond is being priced at 141 8/32, or 141.25 percent of par. Thus, the price of this bond in dollars is $1,412.50.

Call Features—Let the Buyer Beware!

Consider the following situation: You've just made an investment in a high-yielding, 25-year bond. Now you can sit back and let the cash flow in, right? Well, perhaps.

Certainly, that will happen for the first several years. But if market interest rates drop, it's also likely that you'll receive a notice from the issuer that the bond is being called—that the issue is being retired before its maturity date. There's really nothing you can do but turn in the bond and invest your money elsewhere. Every bond is issued with a **call feature**, which stipulates whether and under what conditions a bond can be called in for retirement prior to maturity.

Basically, there are 3 types of call features:

1. A bond can be *freely callable*, which means the issuer can prematurely retire the bond at any time.

2. A bond can be *noncallable*, which means the issuer is prohibited from retiring the bond prior to maturity.

3. The issue could carry a *deferred call*, which means the issue cannot be called until after a certain length of time has passed from the date of issue. In essence, the issue is noncallable during the deferment period and then becomes freely callable thereafter.

Call features allow bond issuers to take advantage of declines in market interest rates. Companies usually call outstanding bonds paying high rates and then reissue new bonds at lower rates. In other words, call features work for the benefit of the issuers. When a bond is called, the net result is that the investor is left with a much lower rate of return than would be the case if the bond could not be called.

Investors who find their bonds called away from them do receive a small amount of extra compensation called the **call premium**. If the issue is called, the issuer will pay the call premium to investors, along with the issue's par value. The sum of the par value plus the call premium represents the issue's **call price**. This is the amount the issuer must pay to retire the bond prematurely. As a general rule, call premiums usually equal about 8 to 12 months' interest at the earliest date of call and then become progressively smaller as the issue nears maturity. Using this rule, the initial call price of a 9% bond could be as high as $1,090, where $90 represents the call premium.

In addition to call features, some bonds may carry **refunding provisions**. These are much like call features except that they prohibit just one thing: the premature retirement of an issue from the proceeds of a lower-coupon bond. For example, a bond could come out as freely callable but nonrefundable for 5 years. In this case, the bond would probably be sold by brokers as a *deferred refunding issue*, with little or nothing said about its call feature. The distinction is important, however: It means that a nonrefunding or deferred refunding issue can still be called and prematurely retired for any reason other than refunding. Thus, an investor could face a call on a high-yielding nonrefundable issue so long as the issuer has "clean cash" to retire the bond prematurely.

Sinking Funds

Another provision that's important to investors is the **sinking fund**, which stipulates how the issuer will pay off the bond over time. This provision applies only to term bonds, of course, because serial issues already have a predetermined repayment schedule. Not all (term) bonds have sinking-fund requirements, but for those that do, the sinking fund specifies the annual repayment schedule that will be used to pay off the issue. It indicates how much principal will be retired each year.

Sinking-fund requirements generally begin 1 to 5 years after the date of issue and continue annually thereafter until all or most of the issue is paid off. Any amount not repaid (which might equal 10% to 25% of the issue) would then be retired with a single "balloon" payment at maturity. Unlike a call or refunding provision, the issuer generally does not have to pay a call premium with sinking-fund calls. Instead, the bonds are normally called at par for sinking-fund purposes.

There's another difference between sinking-fund provisions and call or refunding features. That is, whereas a call or refunding provision gives the issuer the right to retire a bond prematurely, a sinking-fund provision obligates the issuer to pay off the bond systematically over time. The issuer has no choice. It must make sinking-fund payments in a prompt and timely fashion or run the risk of being in default.

Secured or Unsecured Debt

A single issuer may have a number of different bonds outstanding at any given point in time. In addition to coupon and maturity, one bond can be differentiated from another by the type of collateral behind the issue. Issues can be either junior or senior. **Senior bonds** are secured obligations, which are backed by a legal claim on some specific property of the issuer. Such issues include the following:

- **Mortgage bonds,** which are secured by real estate

- **Collateral trust bonds,** which are backed by financial assets owned by the issuer but held in trust by a third party

- **Equipment trust certificates,** which are secured by specific pieces of equipment (e.g., boxcars and airplanes) and are popular with railroads and airlines

- **First and refunding bonds,** which are basically a combination of first mortgage and junior lien bonds (i.e., the bonds are secured in part by a first mortgage on some of the issuer's property and in part by second or third mortgages on other properties).

Note that first and refunding bonds are less secure than, and should not be confused with, straight first-mortgage bonds.

Junior bonds, on the other hand, are backed only by the promise of the issuer to pay interest and principal on a timely basis. There are several classes of unsecured bonds, the most popular of which is a **debenture**. For example, a major company like Hewlett-Packard could issue $500 million worth of 20-year debenture bonds. Being a debenture, the bond would be totally unsecured, meaning there is no collateral backing up the obligation, other than the good name of the issuer. In the final analysis, it's the quality of the issuer that matters. For that reason, highly regarded firms have no trouble selling billion-dollar debenture bond issues and at highly competitive rates.

Subordinated debentures can also be found in the market. These issues have a claim on income secondary to other debenture bonds. **Income bonds,** the most junior of all bonds, are unsecured debts requiring that interest be paid only after a certain amount of income is earned. With these bonds, there is no legally binding requirement to meet interest payments on a timely or regular basis so long as a specified amount of income has not been earned. These issues are similar in many respects to revenue bonds found in the municipal market.

Bond Ratings

To many investors, an issue's *agency rating* is just as important in defining the characteristics of a bond as are its coupon, maturity, and call features. These ratings indicate the amount of credit risk embedded in a bond and are widely used by fixed-income investors. **Bond ratings** are like grades: A letter grade that designates investment quality is assigned to an issue on the basis of extensive financial analysis. Ratings are an important part of the municipal and corporate bond markets, where issues are regularly evaluated and rated by one or more of the rating agencies. Even some agency issues, like the Tennessee Valley Authority (TVA), are rated, although they always receive ratings that confirm the obvious—that the issues are prime grade. The two largest and best-known rating agencies are Moody's and Standard & Poor's; another lesser known but still important bond-rating agency is Fitch Investors Service.

How Ratings Work Every time a large new issue comes to the market, it is analyzed by a staff of professional credit analysts who estimate the likelihood that the issuer will default on its obligations to pay principal and interest. The rating agency studies the financial records of the issuing organization and assesses its prospects. As you might expect, the firm's financial strength and stability are very important in determining the appropriate bond rating. Although there is far more to setting a rating than cranking out a few financial ratios, a strong relationship does exist between the operating results and financial condition of the firm and the rating its bonds receive. Generally, higher ratings are associated with more profitable companies that rely less on debt as a form of financing, are more liquid, have stronger cash flows, and have no trouble servicing their debt in a prompt and timely fashion.

Table 2.2 lists the various ratings assigned to bonds by 2 major services. In addition to the standard rating categories noted in the table, Moody's uses numerical modifiers

TABLE 2.2   BOND RATINGS

Moody's	S&P	Definition
Aaa	AAA	High-grade investment bonds. The highest rating assigned, denoting extremely strong capacity to pay principal and interest. Often called "gilt-edge" securities.
Aa	AA	High-grade investment bonds. High quality but rated lower primarily because the margins of protection are not quite as strong as AAA bonds.
A	A	Medium-grade investment bonds. Many favorable investment attributes, but elements may be present that suggest susceptibility to adverse economic changes.
Baa	BBB	Medium-grade investment bonds. Adequate capacity to pay principal and interest but possibly lacking certain protective elements against adverse economic conditions.
Ba	BB	Speculative issues. Only moderate protection of principal and interest in varied economic times. (This is one of the ratings carried by junk bonds.)
B	B	Speculative issues. Generally lacking desirable characteristics of investment bonds. Assurance of principal and interest may be small; this is another junk-bond rating.
Caa	CCC	Default. Poor-quality issues that may be in default or in danger of default.
Ca	CC	Default. Highly speculative issues, often in default or possessing other market shortcomings.
C		Default. These issues may be regarded as extremely poor in investment quality.
	C	Default. Rating given to income bonds on which no interest is paid.
	D	Default. Issues actually in default, with principal or interest in arrears.

(Source: Moody's Investors Service and Standard & Poor's Ratings Services.)

(1, 2, or 3) on bonds rated Aa to Caa, while S&P uses plus (+) and minus (−) signs on the same rating classes to show relative standing within a major rating category. For example, A+ (or A1) means a strong, high A rating, whereas A− (or A3) indicates that the issue is on the low end of the A rating scale.

Note that the top 4 ratings (Aaa through Baa, or AAA through BBB) designate investment-grade bonds. Such ratings are highly coveted by issuers because they indicate financially strong, well-run companies. Companies and governmental bodies that want to raise money by issuing bonds save money if they have an investment-grade rating because investors will accept lower coupon rates on these bonds compared to those with lower ratings. Bonds with below-investment-grade ratings are called high-yield bonds or junk bonds. The issuers of these bonds generally lack the financial strength that backs investment-grade issues. Most of the time, when Moody's and S&P assign ratings to a particular bond issue, their ratings agree. Sometimes, however, an issue carries different ratings. For example, an issue might be rated Aa by Moody's but A or A+ by S&P. These **split ratings** are viewed simply as "shading" the quality of an issue one way or another.

Also, just because a bond receives a certain rating at the time of issue doesn't mean it will keep that rating for the rest of its life. Ratings change as the financial condition of the issuer changes. In fact, all rated issues are reviewed regularly to ensure that the assigned rating is still valid. Many issues do carry a single rating to maturity, but it is not uncommon for ratings to be revised up or down. As you might expect, the market responds to rating revisions by adjusting bond yields accordingly. For example, an upward revision (e.g., from A to AA) causes the market yield on the bond to drop, as a reflection of the bond's improved quality. By the same token, if a company's financial condition deteriorates, ratings on its bonds may be downgraded. In fact, there is a special name given to junk bonds that once had investment-grade ratings—fallen angels. Although it may appear that the firm is receiving the rating, it is actually the issue that receives it. As a result, a firm's different issues can have different ratings. The senior securities, for example, might carry one rating and the junior issues another, lower rating.

What Ratings Mean Investors pay close attention to agency ratings because ratings can affect not only market behavior but comparative market yields as well. Specifically, the higher the rating, the lower the yield, other things being equal. For example, whereas an A-rated bond might offer a 7.5% yield, a comparable AAA issue would probably yield something like 7%. Furthermore, investment-grade securities are far more interest-sensitive and tend to exhibit more uniform price behavior than junk bonds and other lower-rated issues.

Perhaps most important, bond ratings serve to relieve individual investors of the drudgery of evaluating the investment quality of an issue on their own. Large institutional investors often have their own staff of credit analysts who independently assess the creditworthiness of various corporate and municipal issuers. Individual investors, in contrast, have little if anything to gain from conducting their own credit analysis. After all, credit analysis is time-consuming and costly, and it demands a good deal more expertise than the average individual investor possesses. Two words of caution are in order, however. First, bear in mind that bond ratings are intended to measure only an issue's default risk, which has no bearing whatsoever on an issue's exposure to interest rate risk. Thus, if interest rates increase, even the highest-quality issues go down in price, subjecting investors to capital loss and market risk. Second, ratings agencies do make mistakes, and during the recent financial crisis, their mistakes made headlines.

Yield Spreads Approach Records

One interesting indicator of the state of the economy is the yield spread between low-risk government bonds and high-risk corporate bonds, sometimes called junk bonds. During the 1990–1991 recession, this yield spread set a record of 10.5%. That means that if investors require a 5% interest rate on government bonds, then they will demand a 15.5% rate on the most risky corporate bonds. In 2008, the junk bond credit spread widened again, reaching a new high of 14.68%, eclipsing the 1990s record. Interestingly, both of these episodes corresponded with a major crisis in the investment banking industry. In 1990 it was the failure of Drexel Burnham Lambert and the fall of junk-bond king Michael Milken that led to wide spreads on junk bonds. In 2008, the yield spreads reflected investors' concerns following the 2007 failure of Lehman Brothers and bailouts of several other large financial institutions. In part due to the growing crisis in Europe, junk bond credit spreads began climbing again in 2011. Although the spread topped 7% in October of 2011, it subsided during the remainder of the year and into 2012.

(Source: New York University Salomon Center and FRED Economic Data, St. Louis Fed.)

CONCEPTS IN REVIEW

Answers available at www.pearsonhighered.com/smart

2.4 Can issue characteristics (such as coupon and call features) affect the yield and price behavior of bonds? Explain.

2.5 What is the difference between a call feature and a sinking-fund provision? Briefly describe the 3 types of call features. Can a bond be freely callable but nonrefundable?

2.6 What is the difference between a premium bond and a discount bond? What 3 attributes are most important in determining an issue's price volatility?

2.7 Bonds are said to be quoted "as a percent of par." What does that mean? What is 1 point worth in the bond market?

2.8 What are bond ratings, and how can they affect investor returns? What are split ratings?

2.9 From the perspective of an individual investor, what good are bond ratings? Do bond ratings indicate the amount of market risk embedded in a bond? Explain.

The Market for Debt Securities

LG4 LG5 Thus far, our discussion has dealt with basic bond features. We now shift our attention to a review of the market in which these securities are traded. To begin with, the bond market is chiefly over-the-counter in nature, as listed bonds represent only a small portion of total outstanding obligations. In addition, this market is far more stable than the stock market. Indeed, although interest rates—and therefore bond prices—do move up and down over time, when bond price activity is measured on a daily basis, it is remarkably stable. Two other things that stand out about the bond market are its size and its growth rate. From a $250 billion market in 1950, it has grown to the point where, in March of 2012, the amount of bonds outstanding in the United States totaled $36.9 trillion! That makes the U.S. bond market more than twice the size of the U.S. stock market.

Here's what the U.S. bond market looked like in March 2012:

	Amount Outstanding ($ in trillions)
U.S. Treasury bonds	10.1
Agency bonds	2.3
Municipal bonds	3.7
Corporate bonds	8.1
Other	12.7
Total	36.9

(Source: *Securities Industry and Financial Markets Association,* "U.S. Bond Market Outstanding—Quarterly Data to Q1 2012," June 2012.)

AN ADVISER'S PERSPECTIVE

Bill Harris
Founder, WH Cornerstone Investments

"For us there are really three categories: treasuries, municipals, and corporate bonds."

MyFinanceLab

More about Treasury Bills

Major Market Segments

There are bonds available in today's market to meet almost any investment objective and to suit just about any type of investor. As a matter of convenience, the domestic bond market is normally separated into 4 major segments, according to type of issuer: Treasury, agency, municipal, and corporate. As we shall see, each sector has developed its own features, as well as its own trading characteristics.

Treasury Bonds "Treasuries" (or "governments," as they are sometimes called) are a dominant force in the fixed-income market. If not the most popular type of bond, they certainly are the best known. In addition to T-bills (a popular short-term debt security), the U.S. Treasury issues notes and bonds. It also issues *inflation-indexed securities.*

All Treasury obligations are of the highest quality because they are all backed by the "full faith and credit" of the U.S. government. This backing, along with their liquidity, makes them very popular with individual and institutional investors both in the United States and abroad. Indeed, U.S. Treasury securities are traded in all the major markets of the world, from New York to London to Sydney and Tokyo.

Treasury notes are issued with maturities of 2, 3, 5, 7, and 10 years, whereas **Treasury bonds** carry 30-year maturities. All Treasury notes and bonds pay interest semiannually. Interest income from these securities is subject to normal federal income tax but is exempt from state and local taxes. The Treasury today issues only noncallable securities; the last time it issued callable debt was in 1984. It issues its securities at regularly scheduled auctions, the results of which are widely reported by the financial media (see Figure 2.4). The Treasury establishes the initial yields and coupons on the securities it issues through this auction process.

FIGURE 2.4 Auction Results for a 30-Year Treasury Bond

Treasury auctions are closely followed by the financial media. The number of bids submitted generally far exceeds the size of the issue, so the spread between the highest and lowest bids is quite small—sometimes as small as 2 basis points, or 2/100 of 1%. (Source: Department of the Treasury—Bureau of Public Debt—Washington, DC 20239, February 9, 2012.)

U.S. Treasury Auction Results February 15, 2012	
Type of security	30-Year Bond
Coupon rate	3.125%
Auction price[1]	97.80394
Yield	3.24%
Total bids submitted ($ billion)	$41.45
Competitive bids accepted ($ billion)	$15.96
Noncompetitive bids accepted ($ billion)	$0.36

[1] Auction price of 97.80394 corresponds to $97,803.94 per $100,000 of par value.

Investors participating in an auction have a choice of 2 bidding options—competitive and noncompetitive. Investors who place competitive bids specify the yield that they are willing to accept (and hence, the price that they are willing to pay). Investors submitting competitive bids may be allocated securities in any given auction depending on how their bids compare to bids submitted by others. In a noncompetitive bid, investors agree to accept securities at the yield established in the auction. To conduct an auction, the Treasury first accepts all noncompetitive bids and then accepts competitive bids in ascending order in terms of their yield (i.e., descending order in terms of price) until the quantity of accepted bids reaches the full offering amount. All bidders receive the same yield as the highest accepted bid.

MARKETS IN CRISIS

Rating Agencies Miss a Big One

Mortgage-backed securities, essentially debt instruments with returns that depended upon payments on an underlying pool of residential real estate mortgages, played a central role in the financial crisis that began in 2007 and the Great Recession that followed. Moody's and Standard & Poor's provided ratings on these instruments, just as they did with corporate bonds. Rating these securities was much more complex than rating corporate bonds for a variety of reasons, among them the fact that rating agencies knew relatively little about the creditworthiness of the individual homeowners whose mortgages were in the pool. The rating agencies gave many mortgage-backed securities investment-grade ratings, and those ratings prompted investors of all kinds, including large financial institutions, to pour money into those assets. As real estate prices began to decline, the values of "toxic" mortgage-backed securities plummeted. That led to the failure of Lehman Brothers and bailouts of other large financial institutions.

Inflation-Protected Securities The newest form of Treasury security (first issued in 1997) is the **Treasury Inflation-Protected Securities**, also known as **TIPS**. They are issued with 5-, 10-, and 30-year maturities, and they pay interest semiannually. They offer investors the opportunity to stay ahead of inflation by periodically adjusting their returns for any inflation that has occurred. The adjustment occurs through the bond's principal or par value. That is, the par value rises over time at a pace that matches the inflation rate. Coupon payments rise, too, because the coupon rate is paid on the inflation-adjusted principal.

Example

> Suppose you purchased a 30-year TIPS with a par value of $1,000 and a 2% coupon rate. You expect to receive $20 in interest per year ($1,000 × 0.020), paid in two $10 semiannual installments. However, 1 year after you purchased the bond, inflation has caused the prices of goods and services to increase by 3%. The par value of your bond will increase by 3% to $1,030, and your interest payments will rise to $20.60 per year ($1,030 × 0.020). Notice that your interest payments have increased by 3%, thus compensating you for the inflation that occurred while you held the bond.

Because this type of bond offers payments that automatically adjust with inflation, investors do not have to guess what the inflation rate will be over the bond's life. In other words, TIPS eliminate purchasing power risk. Because they are less risky than ordinary bonds, TIPS generally offer lower coupon rates than ordinary Treasury bonds do.

Agency Bonds   **Agency bonds** are debt securities issued by various agencies and organizations of the U.S. government, such as the Federal Home Loan Bank, the Federal Farm Credit Systems, the Small Business Administration, the Student Loan Marketing Association, and the Federal National Mortgage Association. Although these securities are the closest things to Treasuries, they are not obligations of the U.S. Treasury and technically should not be considered the same as Treasury bonds. Even so, they are very high-quality securities that have almost no risk of default. In spite of the similar default risk, however, these securities usually provide yields that are slightly above the market rates for Treasuries. Thus, they offer a way to increase returns with little or no real difference in risk.

MARKETS IN CRISIS

Implicit Guarantee Becomes Explicit

Debt securities issued by agencies such as the Federal National Mortgage Association (Fannie Mae) and the Federal Home Loan Mortgage Corporation (Freddie Mac) have generally had an implicit guarantee from the federal government, meaning that investors believed that the government would not allow a default on any of these instruments even if they were not "officially" backed by the full faith and credit of the U.S. government as Treasury bills, notes, and bonds are. In 2007, as residential mortgage defaults began to rise, Fannie Mae and Freddie Mac came under severe financial distress. On September 7, 2008, the federal government effectively took over these institutions, injecting $100 billion of new capital into each to stabilize them and to reassure investors that these giants of the mortgage industry, who held or guaranteed about $5.5 trillion in residential mortgage debt, would not disappear. Although the capital infusion helped initially, investor confidence in the two government-sponsored enterprises was rocked again on August 8, 2011, when their credit ratings were downgraded. Standard & Poor's said that the downgrade reflected their "direct reliance on the U.S. government," which had seen its own credit rating downgraded three days earlier.

TABLE 2.3 CHARACTERISTICS OF SOME POPULAR AGENCY ISSUES

Type of Issue	Minimum Denomination ($)	Initial Maturity	Tax Status* Federal	State	Local
Federal Farm Credit System	1,000	13 months to 15 years	T	E	E
Federal Home Loan Bank	10,000	1 to 20 years	T	E	E
Federal Land Banks	1,000	1 to 10 years	T	E	E
Farmers Home Administration	25,000	1 to 25 years	T	T	T
Federal Housing Administration	50,000	1 to 40 years	T	T	T
Federal Home Loan Mortgage Corp.** ("Freddie Mac")	25,000	18 to 30 years	T	T	T
Federal National Mortgage Association** ("Fannie Mae")	25,000	1 to 30 years	T	T	T
Government National Mortgage Association** (GNMA—"Ginnie Mae")	25,000	12 to 40 years	T	T	T
Student Loan Marketing Association ("Sallie Mae")	10,000	3 to 10 years	T	E	E
Tennessee Valley Authority (TVA)	1,000	5 to 50 years	T	E	E
U.S. Postal Service	10,000	25 years	T	E	E
Federal Financing Corp.	1,000	1 to 20 years	T	E	E

*T = taxable; E = tax-exempt.
**Mortgage-backed securities.

There are basically 2 types of agency issues: government-sponsored and federal agencies. Six government-sponsored organizations and more than 2 dozen federal agencies offer agency bonds. To overcome some of the problems in the marketing of many relatively small federal agency securities, Congress established the Federal Financing Bank to consolidate the financing activities of all federal agencies. (As a rule, the generic term *agency* is used to denote both government-sponsored and federal agency obligations.)

Table 2.3 presents selected characteristics of some of the more popular agency bonds. As the list of issuers shows, most of the government agencies support either agriculture or housing. Although agency issues are not direct liabilities of the U.S. government, a few of them do carry government guarantees and therefore represent the full faith and credit of the U.S. Treasury. Even those issues that do not carry such guarantees are viewed as moral obligations of the U.S. government, implying it's highly unlikely that Congress would allow one of them to default. Agency issues are normally noncallable or carry lengthy call deferment features. One final point: Since 1986 all new agency (and Treasury) securities have been issued in book entry form. This means that no certificate of ownership is issued to the buyer of the bonds. Rather, the buyer receives a confirmation of the transaction, and his or her name is entered in a computerized logbook, where it remains as long as that investor owns the security.

Municipal Bonds Municipal bonds are the issues of states, counties, cities, and other political subdivisions (such as school districts and water and sewer districts). This is a $2.7 trillion market today, and it's the only segment of the bond market where the individual investor plays a major role: About 40% of municipal bonds are directly held by individuals. These bonds are often issued as *serial obligations*, which means the issue is broken into a series of smaller bonds, each with its own maturity date and coupon.

Municipal bonds ("munis") are brought to the market as either general obligation or revenue bonds. **General obligation bonds** are backed by the full faith, credit, and taxing power of the issuer. **Revenue bonds,** in contrast, are serviced by the income generated from specific income-producing projects (e.g., toll roads). The vast majority of munis today come out as revenue bonds, accounting for about 70% to 75% of the new-issue volume. Municipal bonds are customarily issued in $5,000 denominations.

The distinction between a general obligation bond and a revenue bond is important because the issuer of a revenue bond is obligated to pay principal and interest only if a sufficient level of revenue is generated. If the funds aren't there, the issuer does not have to make payment on the bond. General obligation bonds, however, are required to be serviced in a timely fashion irrespective of the level of tax income generated by the municipality. Obviously, revenue bonds involve more risk than general obligations, and because of that, they provide higher yields.

A somewhat unusual aspect of municipal bonds is the widespread use of **municipal bond guarantees.** With these guarantees, a party other than the issuer assures the bondholder that principal and interest payments will be made in a timely manner. The third party, in essence, provides an additional source of collateral in the form of insurance, placed on the bond at the date of issue, which is nonrevocable over the life of the obligation. This additional collateral improves the quality of the bond. The 2 principal insurers are the Municipal Bond Investors Assurance Corporation (MBIA) and the American Municipal Bond Assurance Corporation (AMBAC). These guarantors will normally insure any general obligation or revenue bond as long as it carries an S&P rating of BBB or better. Municipal bond insurance results in higher ratings (usually AAA) and improved liquidity for these bonds, which are generally more actively traded in the secondary markets. Insured bonds are especially common in the revenue market, where the insurance markedly boosts their attractiveness. That is, whereas an uninsured revenue bond lacks certainty of payment, a guaranteed issue is very much like a general obligation bond because the investor knows that principal and interest payments will be made on time.

Tax Advantages Without a doubt, the thing that makes municipal securities unique is the fact that, in most cases, their interest income is exempt from federal income taxes. That's why these issues are known as tax-free, or tax-exempt, bonds. Normally, the obligations are also exempt from state and local taxes in the state in which they were issued. For example, a California issue is free of California tax if the bondholder lives in California, but its interest income is subject to state tax if the investor resides in Arizona. Note that capital gains on municipal bonds are not exempt from taxes.

Individual investors are the biggest buyers of municipal bonds, and the tax-free yield that these bonds offer is a major draw. When you think about buying municipal bonds, you should compare the tax-free yield offered by the municipal and compare it to the after-tax yield that you could earn on a similar taxable bond.

Example

Suppose you are in the 25% tax bracket, so each dollar of interest that you earn triggers $0.25 in taxes, allowing you to keep $0.75. Suppose a tax-free municipal bond offers a yield of 9%. What yield would a taxable bond have to offer to give you the same 9% return after taxes that you could earn on the municipal bond? The after-tax yield on a taxable bond is just the stated yield times 1 minus the tax rate:

After-tax yield = Yield on taxable bond × (1 − tax rate)

If you desire an after-tax yield of 9% (because that's what the municipal bond offers) and your tax rate is 25%, then we can calculate the yield that you would need to earn on a taxable bond as follows:

$$0.09 = \text{Yield on taxable bond} \times (1 - 0.25)$$
$$\text{Yield on taxable bond} = 0.09 \div (1 - 0.25)$$
$$= 0.12$$

If the taxable bond offers 12% and the municipal bond offers 9%, then you are essentially indifferent between the 2 securities as long as they are similar in terms of risk (and not counting any tax benefit on your state income taxes). Notice that this value is highlighted in Table 2.4.

Table 2.4 shows how the yield that a taxable bond would have to offer to remain competitive with a municipal bond depends on the investor's *marginal tax rate*. Intuitively, the tax break that municipal bonds offer is more appealing to investors in higher tax brackets who face higher marginal tax rates. For these investors, taxable bonds are not very attractive unless their yields are much higher than the yields on municipal bonds. To put it another way, investors facing high tax rates will gladly purchase municipal bonds even if they offer yields that are somewhat lower than yields on taxable bonds. For example, Table 2.4 shows that an investor in the 10% tax bracket would be indifferent between a municipal bond offering a 6% yield and a taxable bond offering a slightly higher 6.67% yield. In contrast, an investor in the 35% tax bracket would prefer the 6% municipal bond unless the yield on the taxable bond was much higher at 9.23%. Not surprisingly, investors subject to high tax rates are the main purchasers of municipal bonds. Individuals in lower tax brackets generally do not invest as heavily in municipal bonds because for them, the higher yield on taxable bonds more than offsets the benefit of earning tax-free income. The favorable tax status given to municipal bonds allows state and local governments to borrow money at lower rates than they would otherwise be able to obtain in the market.

Taxable Equivalent Yields As you can see from the previous example and from Table 2.4, it is possible to determine the return that a fully taxable bond would have to

TABLE 2.4   TAXABLE EQUIVALENT YIELDS FOR VARIOUS TAX-EXEMPT RETURNS

Taxable Income*			Tax-Free Yield (%)					
Joint Returns ($000)	Individual Returns ($000)	Federal Tax Bracket (%)	5%	6%	7%	8%	9%	10%
0–$16.7	0–$8.35	10	5.56	6.67	7.78	8.89	10.00	11.11
16.7–$67.9	8.35–$33.95	15	5.88	7.06	8.24	9.41	10.59	11.76
67.9–$137.05	33.95–$82.25	25	6.67	8.00	9.33	10.67	12.00	13.33
137.05–$208.85	82.25–$171.55	28	6.94	8.33	9.72	11.11	12.50	13.89
208.85–$372.95	171.55–$372.95	33	7.46	8.96	10.45	11.94	13.43	14.93
372.95 and above	372.95 and above	35	7.69	9.23	10.77	12.31	13.85	15.38

*Taxable income and federal tax rates effective January 1, 2009.

provide in order to match the return provided by a tax-free bond. The taxable yield that is equivalent to a municipal bond's lower, tax-free yield is called the municipal's **taxable equivalent yield**. The taxable equivalent yield allows you to quickly compare the yield on a municipal bond with the yield offered by any number of taxable issues. The following formula shows how to calculate the taxable equivalent yield given the yield on the municipal bond and the investor's tax rate:

Equation 2.1

$$\text{Taxable equivalent yield} = \frac{\text{Yield on municipal bond}}{1 - \text{Marginal federal tax rate}}$$

For example, if a municipal offered a yield of 6.5%, then an individual in the 35% tax bracket would have to find a fully taxable bond with a yield of 10.0% (i.e., 6.5%/0.65 = 10.0%) to reap the same after-tax returns as the municipal.

Note, however, that Equation 2.1 considers federal taxes only. As a result, the computed taxable equivalent yield applies only to certain situations: (1) to states that have no state income tax; (2) to the investor who is looking at an out-of-state bond (which would be taxable by the investor's state of residence); or (3) to the investor who is comparing a municipal bond to a Treasury (or agency) bond—in which case both the Treasury and the municipal bonds are free from state income tax. Under any of these conditions, the only tax that's relevant is federal income tax, so using Equation 2.1 is appropriate.

But what if you are comparing an in-state bond to a corporate bond? In this case, the in-state bond would be free from both federal and state taxes, but the corporate bond would not. As a result, Equation 2.1 would not calculate the correct taxable equivalent yield. Instead, you should use a form of the equivalent yield formula that considers both federal and state income taxes:

Equation 2.2

$$\begin{matrix}\text{Taxable equivalent yield} \\ \text{for both federal and} \\ \text{state taxes}\end{matrix} = \frac{\text{Municipal bond yield}}{1 - [\text{Federal tax rate} + \text{State tax rate}(1 - \text{Federal tax rate})]}$$

Notice that the inclusion of state taxes means that the denominator of Equation 2.2 is slightly smaller than the denominator of Equation 2.1, which in turn means that the taxable equivalent yield will be higher with state taxes as part of the analysis. Intuitively this makes sense because if municipal bonds offer tax advantages at both the federal and state levels, then taxable yields must be even higher to remain competitive.

Example

Suppose your marginal federal tax rate is 35% and your state income tax rate is 3%. There is a municipal bond issued by your state that offers a yield of 6.305%. According to Equation 2.2, the taxable-equivalent yield is 10%:

$$\frac{0.06305}{1 - [0.35 + 0.03(1 - 0.35)]} = 0.10$$

Just to confirm that this is correct, suppose you purchased a $1,000 bond paying a 10% coupon rate. In the first year, you would receive $100 in interest income that is fully taxable at both the state and federal levels. Remember that taxes paid to state governments may be deducted from income before you pay federal taxes. How much of the $100 coupon payment will you have to pay in combined federal and state taxes?

Income	$100.00
State taxes (3%)	3.00
Taxable income (federal)	97.00
Federal taxes (35%)	33.95
Net	$ 63.05

After paying $3 in state taxes and $33.95 in federal taxes, you get to keep $63.05 of the bond's $100 coupon payment. Given that you paid $1,000 for the bond, your return is 6.305%. In other words, as you found by using Equation 2.2, a 6.305% yield on a tax-free bond is equivalent to a 10% yield on a taxable bond.

Notice that if there had been no state tax in this example, the taxable equivalent yield would have been 9.7%. That's not a huge difference, but the difference would be higher for a higher state tax rate, and some U.S. states have tax rates that go as high as 11%.

Corporate Bonds Corporations are the major nongovernmental issuers of bonds. The market for corporate bonds is customarily subdivided into 4 segments: *industrials* (the most diverse of the groups), *public utilities* (the dominant group in terms of volume of new issues), *rail and transportation bonds*, and *financial issues* (e.g., banks, finance companies). In this sector of the bond market investors can find bonds from high-quality AAA-rated issues to junk bonds in or near default, and there is also a wide assortment of bonds. These range from first-mortgage obligations to convertible bonds (which we'll examine later in this chapter), debentures, subordinated debentures, senior subordinated issues, capital notes (a type of unsecured debt issued by banks and other financial institutions), and income bonds. Interest on corporate bonds is paid semiannually, and sinking funds are fairly common. The bonds usually come in $1,000 denominations and are issued on a term basis with a single maturity date. Maturities usually range from 25 to 40 years or more. Many corporate bonds, especially the longer ones, carry call deferment provisions that prohibit prepayment for the first 5 to 10 years. Corporate issues are popular with individuals because of their relatively attractive yields.

While most corporate issues fit the general description above, one that does not is the *equipment trust certificate*, a security issued by railroads, airlines, and other transportation concerns. The proceeds from equipment trust certificates are used to purchase equipment (e.g., jumbo jets and railroad engines) that serves as the collateral for the issue. These bonds are usually issued in serial form and carry uniform annual installments throughout. They normally carry maturities that range from 1 year to a maximum of 17 years. Despite a near-perfect payment record that dates back to pre-Depression days, these issues generally offer above-average yields to investors.

Specialty Issues

In addition to the basic bonds described above, investors can choose from a number of specialty issues—bonds that possess unusual issue characteristics. These bonds have coupon or repayment provisions that are out of the ordinary. Most are issued by corporations, although they are being used increasingly by other issuers as well. Four of the most actively traded specialty issues today are zero-coupon bonds, mortgage-backed securities, asset-backed securities, and high-yield junk bonds. All of these rank as some of the more popular bonds on Wall Street.

Zero-Coupon Bonds As the name implies, **zero-coupon bonds** have no coupons. Rather, these securities are sold at a discount from their par values and then increase in value over time at a compound rate of return. Thus, at maturity, they are worth more than their initial investment, and this difference represents the bond's yield. Other things being equal, the cheaper the zero-coupon bond, the greater the return an investor can earn: For example, a bond with a 6% yield might cost $420, but one with a 10% yield might cost only $240.

Because they do not have coupons, these bonds do not pay interest semiannually. In fact, they pay nothing at all until the issue matures. As strange as it might seem, this feature is the main attraction of zero-coupon bonds. Because there are no coupon payments, there is no need to worry about reinvesting interest income twice a year. Instead, the rate of return on a zero-coupon bond is virtually guaranteed to be the yield that existed at the time of purchase as long as the investor holds the bond to maturity. For example, in mid-2012, U.S. Treasury zero-coupon bonds with 10-year maturities were available at yields of around 1.66%. For around $848, you could buy a bond that would be worth $1,000 at maturity in 10 years. That 1.66% yield is a fully compounded rate of return that's locked in for the life of the issue.

The foregoing advantages notwithstanding, zeros do have some serious disadvantages. One is that if market interest rates move up, you won't be able to participate in the higher return. (You'll have no interest income to reinvest.) In addition, zero-coupon bonds are subject to tremendous price volatility. If market rates climb, you'll experience a sizable capital loss as the prices of zero-coupons plunge. (Of course, if interest rates drop, you'll reap enormous capital gains if you hold long-term zeros. Indeed, such issues are unsurpassed in capital gains potential.) A final disadvantage is that the IRS has ruled that zero-coupon bondholders must pay tax on interest as it is accrued, even though no interest is actually received.

Zeros are issued by corporations, municipalities, and federal agencies. Actually, the Treasury does not issue zero-coupon bonds. Instead, it allows government securities dealers to sell regular coupon-bearing notes and bonds in the form of zero-coupon securities known as **Treasury strips**. Essentially, the interest payments are stripped from a Treasury bond and then sold separately as zero-coupon bonds. For example, a 10-year Treasury note has 20 semiannual interest payments, plus 1 principal payment. These 21 cash flows can be sold as 21 different zero-coupon securities, with maturities that range from 6 months to 10 years. The minimum par value needed to strip a Treasury note or bond is $100 and any par value to be stripped above $100 must be in a multiple of $100. Treasury strips with the same maturity are often bundled and sold in minimum denominations (par values) of $10,000. Because there's an active secondary market for Treasury strips, investors can get in and out of these securities with ease just about anytime they want. Strips offer the maximum in issue quality, a wide array of maturities, and an active secondary market—all of which explains why they are so popular.

Mortgage-Backed Securities Simply put, a **mortgage-backed bond** is a debt issue that is secured by a pool of residential mortgages. An issuer, such as the Government National Mortgage Association (GNMA), puts together a pool of home mortgages and then issues securities in the amount of the total mortgage pool. These securities, also known as *pass-through securities* or *participation certificates*, are usually sold in minimum denominations of $25,000. Although their maturities can go out as far as 30 years, the average life is generally much shorter (perhaps as short as 8 years) because many of the mortgages are paid off early.

As an investor in one of these securities, you hold an undivided interest in the pool of mortgages. When a homeowner makes a monthly mortgage payment, that payment is essentially passed through to you, the bondholder, to pay off the mortgage-backed bond you hold. Although these securities come with normal coupons, the interest is paid monthly rather than semiannually. Actually, the monthly payments received by bondholders are, like mortgage payments, made up of both principal and interest. Because the principal portion of the payment represents return of capital, it is considered tax-free. The interest portion, however, is subject to ordinary state and federal income taxes.

Mortgage-backed securities are issued primarily by 3 federal agencies. Although there are some state and private issuers (mainly big banks and S&Ls), agency issues dominate the market and account for 90% to 95% of the activity. The major agency issuers of mortgage-backed securities (MBSs) are:

- *Government National Mortgage Association (GNMA).* Known as Ginnie Mae, it is the oldest and largest issuer of MBSs.

- *Federal Home Loan Mortgage Corporation (FHLMC).* Known as Freddie Mac, it was the first to issue pools containing conventional mortgages.

- *Federal National Mortgage Association (FNMA).* Known as Fannie Mae, it's the leader in marketing seasoned/older mortgages.

One feature of mortgage-backed securities is that they are self-liquidating investments; that is, a portion of the monthly cash flow to the investor is repayment of principal. Thus, you are always receiving back part of the original investment capital, so that at maturity, there is no big principal payment. To counter this effect, a number of mutual funds invest in mortgage-backed securities but automatically reinvest the capital/principal portion of the cash flows. Mutual fund investors therefore receive only the interest from their investments and their capital remains fully invested.

Collateralized Mortgage Obligations Loan prepayments are another problem with mortgage-backed securities. In fact, it was in part an effort to diffuse some of the prepayment uncertainty in standard mortgage-backed securities that led to the creation of **collateralized mortgage obligations (CMOs)**. Normally, as pooled mortgages are prepaid, all bondholders receive a prorated share of the prepayments. The net effect is to sharply reduce the life of the bond. A CMO, in contrast, divides investors into classes (called *tranches*, which is French for "slice"), depending on whether they want a short-, intermediate-, or long-term investment. Although interest is paid to all bondholders, all principal payments go first to the shortest tranche until it is fully retired. Then the next class in the sequence becomes the sole recipient of principal, and so on, until the last tranche is retired.

Basically, CMOs are *derivative securities* created from traditional mortgage-backed bonds, which are placed in a trust. Participation in this trust is then sold to the investing public in the form of CMOs. The net effect of this transformation is that CMOs look and behave very much like any other bond: They offer predictable interest payments and have (relatively) predictable maturities. However, although they carry the same AAA ratings and implicit U.S. government backing as the mortgage-backed bonds that underlie them, CMOs represent a quantum leap in complexity. Some types of CMOs can be as simple and safe as Treasury bonds. Others can be far more volatile—and risky—than the standard MBSs they're made from. That's because when putting CMOs together, Wall Street performs the financial equivalent of gene splicing: Investment bankers isolate the interest and principal payments from the underlying MBSs and rechannel them to the different tranches. It's not issue quality or risk of default that's the problem here, but rather prepayment, or call, risk. All the bonds will be paid off; it's just a matter of when. Different types of CMO tranches have different levels of prepayment risk. The overall risk in a CMO cannot, of course, exceed that of the underlying mortgage-backed bonds, so in order for there to be some tranches with very little (or no) prepayment risk, others have to endure a lot more. The net effect is that while some CMO tranches are low in risk, others are loaded with it.

Investors discovered just how complex and how risky these securities could be as the financial crisis unfolded in 2007 and 2008. As homeowner defaults on residential mortgages began to rise, the values of CMOs plummeted. Trading in the secondary market dried up, so it was difficult to know what the underlying values of some CMOs really were. Investment and commercial banks that had invested heavily in these securities came under intense pressure as doubts about their solvency grew into a near panic. Everyone wanted to know which institutions held these "toxic assets" on their balance sheets and how large their losses were on these instruments. Lehman Brothers, Bear Stearns, Merrill Lynch, and many other financial institutions went bankrupt or were acquired under distress by other institutions, and the federal government poured hundreds of billions of dollars into the banking system to try to prevent total collapse.

Asset-Backed Securities The creation of mortgage-backed securities and CMOs quickly led to the development of a new market technology—the process of **securitization**, whereby various lending vehicles are transformed into marketable securities, much like a mortgage-backed security. In recent years, investment bankers sold billions of dollars' worth of pass-through securities, known as **asset-backed securities (ABS)**, which are backed by pools of auto loans, credit card bills, and home equity lines (3 of the principal types of collateral), as well as computer leases, hospital receivables, small business loans, truck rentals, and even royalty fees.

These securities, first introduced in the mid-1980s, are created when an investment bank bundles some type of debt-linked asset (such as loans or receivables), and then sells to investors—via asset-backed securities—the right to receive all or part of the future payments made on that debt. For example, GMAC, the financing arm of General Motors, is a regular issuer of collateralized auto loan securities. When it wants to get some of its car loans off its books, GMAC takes the monthly cash flow from a pool of auto loans and pledges them to a new issue of bonds, which are then sold to investors. In similar fashion, credit card receivables are regularly used as collateral for these bonds (indeed, they represent the biggest segment of the ABS market), as are home equity loans, the second-biggest type of ABS.

Investors are drawn to ABSs for a number of reasons. One is the relatively high yields they offer. Another is their short maturities, which often extend out no more than 5 years. A third is the monthly, rather than semiannual, principal/interest payments that accompany many of these securities. Also important to investors is their high credit quality. That's due to the fact that most of these deals are backed by generous credit protection. For example, the securities are often over collateralized: the pool of assets backing the bonds may be 25% to 50% larger than the bond issue itself. For whatever reason, the vast majority of ABSs receive the highest credit rating possible (AAA) from the leading rating agencies.

Junk Bonds   Junk bonds (or high-yield bonds, as they're also called) are highly speculative securities that have received low, sub-investment-grade ratings (typically Ba or B). These bonds are issued primarily by corporations and also by municipalities. Junk bonds often take the form of *subordinated debentures*, which means the debt is unsecured and has a low claim on assets. These bonds are called "junk" because of their high risk of default. The companies that issue them generally have excessive amounts of debt in their capital structures and their ability to service that debt is subject to considerable doubt.

Probably the most unusual type of junk bond is something called a **PIK bond**. PIK stands for *payment in kind* and means that rather than paying the bond's coupon in cash, the issuer can make annual interest payments in the form of additional debt. This "financial printing press" usually goes on for 5 or 6 years, after which time the issuer is supposed to start making interest payments in real money.

Why would any rational investor be drawn to junk bonds? The answer is simple: They offer very high yields. Indeed, in a typical market, relative to investment-grade bonds, you can expect to pick up anywhere from 2.5 to 5 percentage points in added yield. For example, not long ago, investors were getting 10% or 12% yields on junk bonds, compared to 7% or 8% on investment-grade corporates. Obviously, such yields are available only because of the correspondingly higher exposure to risk.

However, there's more to bond returns than yield alone: The returns you actually end up with don't always correspond to the yields you went in with. Junk bonds are subject to a good deal of risk, and their prices are unstable. Indeed, unlike investment-grade bonds, whose prices are closely linked to the behavior of market interest rates, junk bonds tend to behave more like stocks. As a result, the returns are highly unpredictable. Accordingly, only investors who are thoroughly familiar with the risks involved, and who are comfortable with such risk exposure, should use these securities.

A Global View of the Bond Market

Globalization has hit the bond market, just as it has the stock market. Foreign bonds have caught on with U.S. investors because of their high yields and attractive returns. There are risks with foreign bonds, of course, but high risk of default is not necessarily one of them. Instead, the big risk with foreign bonds has to do with the impact that currency fluctuations can have on returns in U.S. dollars.

The United States has the world's biggest debt market, accounting for about half of the global market. Following the United States is Euroland (principally Germany, Italy, and France); close behind is Japan, followed by the United Kingdom, and then Canada. Together, these issuers account for more than 90% of the world bond market. Worldwide, various forms of government bonds (e.g., Treasuries, agencies, and munis) dominate the market.

U.S.-Pay versus Foreign-Pay Bonds   There are several ways to invest in foreign bonds (excluding foreign bond mutual funds). From the perspective of a U.S. investor, we can divide foreign bonds into 2 broad categories on the basis of the currency in which the bond is denominated: *U.S.-pay* (or dollar-denominated) bonds, and *foreign-pay* (or non-dollar-denominated) bonds. All the cash flows—including purchase price, maturity value, and coupon income—from dollar-denominated foreign bonds are in U.S. dollars. The cash flows from non-dollar bonds are designated in a foreign currency, such as the euro, British pound, or Swiss franc.

Dollar-Denominated Bonds Dollar-denominated foreign bonds are of 2 types: Yankee bonds and Eurodollar bonds. **Yankee bonds** are issued by foreign governments or corporations or by so-called supernational agencies, like the World Bank and the InterAmerican Bank. These bonds are issued and traded in the United States; they're registered with the SEC, and all transactions are in U.S. dollars. Not surprisingly, Canadian issuers dominate the Yankee-bond market. Buying a Yankee bond is really no different from buying any other U.S. bond: These bonds are traded on U.S. exchanges and the OTC market, and because everything is in dollars, there's no currency exchange risk to deal with. The bonds are generally very high in quality (which is not surprising, given the quality of the issuers) and offer highly competitive yields to investors.

Eurodollar bonds, in contrast, are issued and traded outside the United States. They are denominated in U.S. dollars, but they are not registered with the SEC, which means underwriters are legally prohibited from selling new issues to the U.S. public. (Only "seasoned" Eurodollar issues can be sold in this country.) The Eurodollar market today is dominated by foreign-based investors (though that is changing) and is primarily aimed at institutional investors.

Foreign-Pay Bonds From the standpoint of U.S. investors, foreign-pay international bonds encompass all those issues denominated in a currency other than dollars. These bonds are issued and traded overseas and are not registered with the SEC. Examples are German government bonds, which are payable in euros; Japanese bonds, issued in yen; and so forth. When investors speak of foreign bonds, it's this segment of the market that most of them are thinking of.

Foreign-pay bonds are subject to changes in currency exchange rates, which can dramatically affect total returns to U.S. investors. The returns on foreign-pay bonds are a function of 3 things: (1) the level of coupon (interest) income earned on the bonds; (2) the change in market interest rates, which determine the level of capital gains (or losses); and (3) the behavior of currency exchange rates. The first 2 variables are the same as those that drive bond returns in this country. They are, of course, just as important to foreign bonds as they are to domestic bonds. Thus, if you're investing overseas, you still want to know what the yields are today and where they're headed. It's the third variable that separates the return behavior of dollar-denominated from foreign-pay bonds.

We can assess returns from foreign-pay bonds by employing the following equation:

Equation 2.3

$$\text{Total return (in U.S. dollars)} = \left[\frac{\begin{array}{c}\text{Ending value of} \quad \text{Amount of interest}\\ \text{bond in foreign} + \quad \text{received in}\\ \text{currency} \quad \text{foreign currency}\end{array}}{\begin{array}{c}\text{Beginning value of bond}\\ \text{in foreign currency}\end{array}} \times \frac{\begin{array}{c}\text{Exchange rate}\\ \text{at } \textit{end} \text{ of}\\ \text{holding period}\end{array}}{\begin{array}{c}\text{Exchange rate}\\ \text{at } \textit{beginning} \text{ of}\\ \text{holding period}\end{array}} \right] - 1.00$$

For example, assume a U.S. investor purchased a Swedish government bond, in large part because of the attractive 7.5% coupon it carried. If the bond was bought at par and market rates fell over the course of the year, the security itself would have provided a return in excess of 7.5% (because the decline in rates would provide some capital gains). However, if the Swedish krona (SEK) fell relative to the dollar, the total return (in U.S. dollars) could have actually ended up at a lot less than 7.5%, depending on what happened to the U.S.$/SEK exchange rate. To find out exactly how this investment turned out, you could use the equation above. Like foreign stocks, for-eign-pay bonds can pay off from both the behavior of the security and the behavior of the currency. That combination, in many cases, means superior returns to U.S. investors. Knowledgeable investors find these bonds attractive not only because of their competitive returns but also because of the positive diversification effects they have on bond portfolios.

CONCEPTS IN REVIEW

Answers available at www.pearsonhighered.com/smart

2.10 Briefly describe each of the following types of bonds: (a) Treasury bonds, (b) agency issues, (c) municipal securities, and (d) corporate bonds. Note some of the major advantages and disadvantages of each.

2.11 Briefly define each of the following and note how they might be used by fixed-income investors: (a) zero-coupon bonds, (b) CMOs, (c) junk bonds, and (d) Yankee bonds.

2.12 What are the special tax features of (a) Treasury securities, (b) agency issues, and (c) municipal bonds?

2.13 Describe an asset-backed security (ABS) and identify some of the different forms of collateral used with these issues. Briefly note how an ABS differs from an MBS. What is the central idea behind securitization?

2.14 What's the difference between dollar-denominated and non-dollar-denominated (foreign-pay) bonds? Briefly describe the 2 major types of U.S.-pay bonds. Can currency exchange rates affect the total return of U.S.-pay bonds? Of foreign-pay bonds? Explain.

Convertible Securities

LG6 In addition to the many types of bonds covered in the preceding material, there is still another type of fixed-income security that merits discussion at this point—namely, **convertible bonds**. Issued only by corporations, convertibles are different from most other types of corporate debt because even though these securities may start out as bonds, they usually end up as shares of common stock. That is, while these securities are originally issued as bonds (or even preferred stock), they contain a provision that gives investors the option to convert their bonds into shares of the issuing firm's stock. Convertibles are *hybrid securities* because they contain attributes of both debt and equity. But even though they possess the features and performance characteristics of both fixed-income and equity securities, convertibles should be viewed primarily as a form of equity. That's because most investors commit their capital to such obligations not for the yields they provide but rather for the potential price performance of the stock side of the issue. In fact, it is always a good idea to determine whether a corporation has convertible issues outstanding whenever you are considering a common stock investment. In some circumstances, the convertible may be a better investment than the firm's common stock. (Preferred stocks represent another type of hybrid security because they too have features and characteristics of both equity and fixed-income securities.)

Convertibles as Investment Outlets

Convertible securities are popular with investors because of their **equity kicker**—the right to convert these bonds into shares of the company's common stock. Because of this feature, the market price of a convertible has a tendency to behave very much like the price of its underlying common stock. Convertibles are used by all types of companies and are issued either as convertible bonds (by far the most common type) or as convertible *preferreds*. Convertibles enable firms to raise equity capital at fairly attractive prices. That is, when a company issues stock in the normal way (by selling more shares in the company), it does so by setting a price on the stock that's slightly below prevailing market prices. For example, it might be able to get $25 for a stock that's currently priced in the market at, say, $27 a share. In contrast, when it issues the stock indirectly through a convertible issue, the firm can set a price that's above the prevailing market—for example, it might be able to get $35 for the same stock. In this case, convertible bond investors will only choose to convert their bonds into shares if the market price of the shares subsequently increases above $35. As a result, the company can raise the same amount of money by issuing a lot less stock. Thus, companies issue convertibles not as a way of raising debt capital but as a way of raising equity. Because they are eventually converted into shares of the issuing company's common stock, convertibles are usually viewed as a form of **deferred equity**.

Convertible bonds and convertible preferreds are both linked to the equity position of the firm, so they are usually considered interchangeable for investment purposes. Except for a few peculiarities (e.g., preferreds pay dividends rather than interest and do so on a quarterly basis rather than semiannually), convertible bonds and convertible preferreds are evaluated in much the same way. Because of their similarities, the discussion that follows will be couched largely in terms of bonds, but the information and implications apply equally well to convertible preferreds.

Convertible Notes and Bonds Convertible bonds are usually issued as subordinated debentures and carry the provision that within a stipulated time period, the bond may be converted into a certain number of shares of the issuing company's common stock. (Convertibles that are issued as notes are just like convertible bonds except that the debt portion of the security carries a shorter maturity—usually of 5 to 10 years. Other than the life of the debt, there is no real difference between the 2 types of issues: They're both unsecured debt obligations, and they're usually subordinated to other forms of debt.)

Generally speaking, there is little or no cash involved at the time of conversion. You merely trade in the convertible bond (or note) for a stipulated number of shares of common stock. For example, assume that a certain convertible security recently came to the market, and it carried the provision that each $1,000 note could be converted into shares of the issuing company's stock at $62.55 a share. Thus, regardless of what happens to the market price of the stock, you can redeem each note for 15.98 shares of the company's stock ($1,000 ÷ $62.55 = 15.98 shares). So, if the company's stock is trading in the market at, say, $125 a share at the time of conversion, then you would have just converted a $1,000 debt obligation into $1,997.50 worth of stock (15.98 × $125 = $1,997.50). Not surprisingly, this conversion privilege comes at a price: the low coupon (or dividend) that convertibles usually carry. That is, when new convertible issues come to the market, their coupons are normally just a fraction of those on comparable straight (nonconvertible) bonds. Indeed, the more attractive the conversion feature, the lower the coupon.

Actually, while it's the bondholder who has the right to convert the bond at any time, more often than not, the issuing firm initiates conversion by calling the bonds—a practice known as **forced conversion**. To provide the corporation with the flexibility to retire the debt and force conversion, most convertibles come out as freely callable issues, or they carry very short call deferment periods. To force conversion, the corporation would call for the retirement of the bond and give the bondholder two options: Either convert the bond into common stock or redeem it for cash at the stipulated call price (which, in the case of convertibles, contains very little call premium). So long as the convertible is called when the market value of the stock exceeds the call price of the bond (which is almost always the case), seasoned investors would never choose the second option. Instead, they would opt to convert the bond, as the firm wants them to. Then they can hold the stocks if they want to or they can sell their new shares in the market (and end up with more cash than they would have received by taking the call price). After the conversion is complete, the bonds no longer exist; instead, there is additional common stock in their place.

Conversion Privilege The key element of any convertible is its **conversion privilege**, which stipulates the conditions and specific nature of the conversion feature. To begin with, it states exactly when the debenture can be converted. With some issues, there may be an initial waiting period of 6 months to perhaps 2 years after the date of issue, during which time the security cannot be converted. The **conversion period** then begins, and the issue can be converted at any time. The conversion period typically extends for the remaining life of the debenture, but in some instances, it may exist for only a certain number of years. This is done to give the issuing firm more control over its capital structure. If the issue has not been converted by the end of its conversion period, it reverts to a straight-debt issue with no conversion privileges.

From the investor's point of view, the most important piece of information is the conversion price or the conversion ratio. These terms are used interchangeably and specify, either directly or indirectly, the number of shares of stock into which the bond can be converted. The **conversion ratio** denotes the number of common shares into which the bond can be converted. The **conversion price** indicates the stated value per share at which the common stock will be delivered to the investor in exchange for the bond. When you stop to think about these 2 measures, it becomes clear that a given conversion ratio implies a certain conversion price, and vice versa.

Example

> Suppose that a certain $1,000 convertible bond stipulates a conversion ratio of 20, which means that the bond can be converted into 20 shares of common stock. In effect, if you give up your $1,000 bond in exchange for 20 shares, you are essentially buying 20 shares of stock for $1,000, or $50 per share. In other words, the conversation ratio of 20 is equivalent to a conversion price of $50. (One basic difference between a convertible debenture and a convertible preferred relates to conversion ratio: The conversion ratio of a debenture generally deals with large multiples of common stock, such as 15, 20, or 30 shares. In contrast, the conversion ratio of a preferred is generally very small, often less than 1 share of common and seldom more than 3 or 4 shares.)

The conversion ratio is normally adjusted for stock splits and significant stock dividends. As a result, if a firm declares, say, a 2-for-1 stock split, the conversion ratio of any of its outstanding convertible issues also doubles. And when the conversion ratio includes a fraction, such as 33.5 shares of common, the conversion privilege specifies how any fractional shares are to be handled. Usually, the investor can either put up the additional funds necessary to purchase another full share of stock at the conversion price or receive the cash equivalent of the fractional share (at the conversion price).

LYONs Leave it to Wall Street to take a basic investment product and turn it into a sophisticated investment vehicle. That's the story behind LYONs, which some refer to as "zeros on steroids." Start with a zero-coupon bond, throw in a conversion feature and a put option, and you have a **LYON** (the acronym stands for **liquid yield option note**). LYONs are zero-coupon convertible bonds that are convertible, at a fixed conversion ratio, for the life of the issue. Thus, they offer the built-in increase in value over time that accompanies any zero-coupon bond (as it moves toward its par value at maturity), plus full participation in the equity side of the issue via the equity kicker. Unlike most convertibles, there's no current income with a LYON (because it is a zero-coupon bond). On the other hand, however, it does carry an option feature that enables you to "put" the bonds back to the issuer (at specified values). That is, the put option gives you the right to redeem your bonds periodically at prespecified prices. Thus, you know you can get out of these securities, at set prices, if things move against you.

Although LYONs may appear to provide the best of all worlds, they do have some negatives. True, LYONs provide downside protection (via the put option feature) and full participation in the equity kicker. But like all zero-coupon bonds, they don't generate current income. And you have to watch out for the put option. Depending on the type of put option, the payout does not have to be in cash—it can be in stocks or bonds. One other important issue to be aware of is that because the conversion ratio on the LYON is fixed, the conversion price on the stock increases over time. This occurs because the value of the zero-coupon bond increases as it reaches maturity. Thus, the market price of the stock had better go up by more than the bond's rate of appreciation or you'll never be able to convert your LYON.

Sources of Value

Because convertibles are fixed-income securities linked to the equity position of the firm, they are normally valued in terms of both the stock and the bond dimensions of the issue. Thus, it is important to both analyze the underlying common stock and formulate interest rate expectations when considering convertibles as an investment outlet. Let's look first at the stock dimension.

Convertible securities trade much like common stock whenever the market price of the stock starts getting close to (or exceeds) the stated conversion price. When that happens, the convertible will exhibit price behavior that closely matches that of the underlying common stock. If the stock goes up in price, so does the convertible, and vice versa. In fact, the absolute price change of the convertible will exceed that of the common because of the conversion ratio, which will define the convertible's rate of change in price. For example, if a convertible carries a conversion ratio of, say, 20, then for every point the common stock goes up (or down) in price, the price of the convertible will move in the same direction by roughly that same multiple (in this case, 20). In essence, whenever a convertible trades as a stock, its market price will approximate a multiple of the share price of the common, with the size of the multiple being defined by the conversion ratio.

When the market price of the common is well below the conversion price, the convertible loses its tie to the underlying common stock and begins to trade as a bond. When that happens, the convertible becomes linked to prevailing bond yields, and investors focus their attention on market rates of interest. However, because of the equity kicker and their relatively low agency ratings, convertibles generally do not possess high interest rate sensitivity. Gaining more than a rough idea of what the prevailing yield of a convertible obligation ought to be is often difficult. For example, if the issue is rated Baa and the market rate for this quality range is 9%, then the convertible should be priced to yield something around 9%, plus or minus perhaps half a percentage point. Because of the interest and principal payments that they offer, convertible bonds essentially have a price floor, meaning that convertible values generally cannot drop as much as the underlying stock can. If a company experiences financial problems that cause its stock price to drop dramatically, the firm's convertible bonds will retain much of their value because investors are still entitled to receive interest and principal payments. That is, the price of the convertible will not fall to much less than its price floor because at that point, the issue's bond value will kick in. (More on this later.)

Measuring the Value of a Convertible

In order to evaluate the investment merits of convertible securities, you must consider both the bond and the stock dimensions of the issue. Fundamental security analysis of the equity position is, of course, especially important in light of the key role the equity kicker plays in defining the price behavior of a convertible. In contrast, market yields and agency ratings are used in evaluating the bond side of the issue. But there's more: In addition to analyzing the bond and stock dimensions of the issue, it is essential to evaluate the conversion feature itself. The 2 critical areas in this regard are conversion value and investment value. These measures have a vital bearing on a convertible's price behavior and therefore can have a dramatic effect on an issue's holding period return.

Conversion Value In essence, **conversion value** indicates what a convertible issue would trade for if it were priced to sell on the basis of its stock value. Conversion value is easy to find:

Equation 2.4
$$\text{Conversion value} = \text{Conversion ratio} \times \text{Current market price of the stock}$$

Example
Suppose that a particular convertible bond has a conversion ratio of 20. If the price of the company's stock is $60 per share, then the conversion value of the bond is $1,200 (20 × $60 = $1,200).

Sometimes analysts use an alternative measure that computes the **conversion equivalent**, also known as **conversion parity**. The conversion equivalent indicates the price at which the common stock would have to sell in order to make the convertible security worth its present market price. The conversion equivalent is calculated as follows:

Equation 2.5
$$\text{Conversion equivalent} = \frac{\text{Current market price of the convertible bond}}{\text{Conversion ratio}}$$

Example
If a convertible bond has a current market price of $1,400 and a conversion ratio of 20, the conversion equivalent of the common stock would be $70 per share ($1,400 ÷ 20 = $70). Although convertible bonds can trade above par value simply because of a decline in interest rates, as a practical matter, it would be unusual for a bond to trade as high as $1,400 based only on an interest rate drop. Accordingly, you would expect the current market price of the common stock in this example to be at or near $70 per share in order to support a convertible trading at $1,400.

Conversion Premium Convertible issues seldom trade precisely at their conversion values. Rather, they usually trade at prices that exceed the bond's underlying conversion value. The extent to which the market price of the convertible exceeds its conversion value is known as the *conversion premium*. The absolute size of an issue's conversion premium is found by taking the difference between the convertible's market price and its conversion value (per Equation 2.4). To place the premium on a relative basis, simply divide the dollar amount of the conversion premium by the issue's conversion value. That is,

Equation 2.6

$$\text{Conversion premium (in \$)} = \begin{array}{c}\text{Current market price}\\\text{of the convertible bond}\end{array} - \begin{array}{c}\text{Conversion}\\\text{value}\end{array}$$

where conversion value is found according to Equation 2.4. Then

Equation 2.7

$$\text{Conversion premium (in \%)} = \frac{\text{Conversion premium (in \$)}}{\text{Conversion value}}$$

Example

Suppose that a convertible bond trades at $1,400 and its conversion value equals $1,200. This bond has a conversion premium of $200 ($1,400 − $1,200 = $200). That $200 represents a conversion premium of 16.7% ($200/$1,200 = 0.167) relative to the bond's conversion value.

Conversion premiums are common in the market and can often amount to 30% to 40% (or more) of an issue's conversion value. Investors are willing to pay a premium because of the added current income that a convertible provides relative to the underlying common stock and because of the convertible's upside potential. An investor can recover this premium either through the added current income or by selling the issue at a premium equal to or greater than that which existed at the time of purchase. Unfortunately, the latter source of recovery is tough to come by because conversion premiums tend to fade away as the price of the convertible goes up. That means that if you purchase a convertible for its potential price appreciation, then you must accept the fact that all or a major portion of the price premium is very likely to disappear as the convertible appreciates over time and moves closer to its true conversion value. Thus, if you hope to recover any conversion premium, it will probably have to come from the added current income that the convertible provides.

Payback Period The size of the conversion premium can obviously have a major impact on investor return. When picking convertibles, one of the major questions you should ask is whether the premium is justified. One way to assess conversion premium is to compute the issue's **payback period**, a measure of the length of time it will take to recover the conversion premium from the extra interest income earned on the convertible. Because this added income is a principal reason for the conversion premium, it makes sense to use it to assess the premium. The payback period can be found as follows:

Equation 2.8

$$\text{Payback period} = \frac{\text{Conversion premium (in \$)}}{\begin{array}{c}\text{Annual interest}\\\text{income from the}\\\text{convertible bond}\end{array} - \begin{array}{c}\text{Annual dividend}\\\text{income from the}\\\text{underlying common stock}\end{array}}$$

In this equation, annual dividends are found by multiplying the stock's latest annual dividends per share by the bond's conversion ratio.

Example

In the previous example, the bond had a conversion premium of $200. Assume this bond (which carries a conversion ratio of 20) has an 8.5% coupon ($85 per year), and the underlying stock paid dividends this past year of 50 cents a share. Given this information, you can use Equation 2.8 to find the payback period.

$$\text{Payback period} = \frac{\$200}{\$85 - (20 \times \$0.50)}$$

$$= \frac{\$200}{\$85 - (\$10.00)} = 2.7 \text{ years}$$

In essence, you would recover the premium in 2.7 years (a fairly short payback period).

As a rule, everything else being equal, the shorter the payback period, the better. Also, watch out for excessively high premiums (of 50% or more). You may have real difficulty ever recovering such astronomical premiums. Indeed, to avoid such premiums, most experts recommend that you look for convertibles that have payback periods of 5 to 7 years, or less. Be careful when using this measure, however. Some convertibles will have very high payback periods simply because they carry very low coupons (of 1% to 2%, or less).

Investment Value The price floor of a convertible is defined by its bond properties and is the focus of the investment value measure. It's the point within the valuation process where we focus on current and expected market interest rates. **Investment value** is the price at which the bond would trade if it were nonconvertible and if it were priced at or near the prevailing market yields of comparable nonconvertible bonds.

We will cover the mechanics of bond pricing in more detail in Chapter 8, but suffice it to say at this point that the investment value of a convertible is found by discounting the issue's coupon stream and its par value back to the present, using a discount rate equal to the prevailing yield on comparable nonconvertible issues. In other words, using the yields on comparable nonconvertible bonds as the discount rate, find the present value of the convertible's coupon stream, add that to the present value of its par value, and you have the issue's investment value. In practice, because the convertible's coupon and maturity are known, the only additional piece of information needed is the market yield of comparably rated issues.

For example, if comparable nonconvertible bonds were trading at 9% yields, we could use that 9% return as the discount rate in finding the present value (i.e., "investment value") of a convertible. Thus, if a particular 20-year, $1,000 par value convertible bond carried a 6% annual-pay coupon, its investment value (using a 9% discount rate) can be found using a financial calculator as shown in the margin. The resulting value of the convertible would be about $726. This figure indicates how far the convertible will have to fall before it hits its price floor and begins trading as a straight-debt instrument.

Other things being equal, the greater the distance between the current market price of a convertible and its investment value, the farther the issue can fall in price and, as a result, the greater the downside risk exposure.

Input	Function
60	PMT
1000	FV
20	N
9	I
	CPT
	PV

Solution
−726.14

CONCEPTS IN REVIEW

Answers available at
www.pearsonhighered.com/
smart

2.15 What is a convertible debenture? How does a convertible bond differ from a convertible preferred?

2.16 Identify the equity kicker of a convertible security and explain how it affects the value and price behavior of convertibles.

2.17 Explain why it is necessary to examine both the bond and stock properties of a convertible debenture when determining its investment appeal.

2.18 What is the difference between conversion parity and conversion value? How would you describe the payback period on a convertible? What is the investment value of a convertible, and what does it reveal?

MyFinanceLab

Here is what you should know after reading this chapter. MyFinanceLab will help you identify what you know and where to go when you need to practice.

What You Should Know	Key Terms	Where to Practice
LG1 **Explain the basic investment attributes of bonds and their use as investment vehicles.** Bonds are publicly traded debt securities that provide investors with 2 basic sources of return: (1) current income and (2) capital gains. Current income is derived from the coupon (interest) payments received over the life of the issue. Capital gains can be earned whenever market interest rates fall. Bonds also can be used to shelter income from taxes and for the preservation and long-term accumulation of capital. The diversification properties of bonds are such that they can greatly enhance portfolio stability.	bonds, *p. 43*	MyFinanceLab Study Plan 2.1
LG2 **Describe the essential features of a bond, note the role that bond ratings play in the market, and distinguish among different types of call, refunding, and sinking-fund provisions.** All bonds carry some type of coupon, which specifies the annual rate of interest the issuer will pay. Bonds also have predetermined maturity dates: Term bonds carry a single maturity date, and serial bonds have a series of maturity dates. Municipal and corporate issues are rated for bond quality by independent rating agencies. These ratings indicate a bond's risk of default: The lower the rating, the higher the risk and the higher the expected return. Every bond is issued with some type of call feature, be it freely callable, noncallable, or deferred callable. Call features spell out whether an issue can be prematurely retired and, if so, when. Some bonds (temporarily) prohibit the issuer from paying off one bond with the proceeds from another by including a refunding provision. Others are issued with sinking-fund provisions, which specify how a bond is to be paid off over time.	bond ratings, *p. 55* call feature, *p. 53* call premium, *p. 53* call price, *p. 53* collateral trust bonds, *p. 54* coupon, *p. 49* current yield, *p. 49* debenture, *p. 54* discount bond, *p. 50* equipment trust certificates, *p. 54* first and refunding bonds, *p. 54* income bonds, *p. 54* junior bonds, *p. 54* maturity date, *p. 50* mortgage bonds, *p. 54* note, *p. 50* premium bond, *p. 50* principal, *p. 50* refunding provisions, *p. 53* senior bonds, *p. 54* serial bond, *p. 50* sinking fund, *p. 53* split ratings, *p. 56* subordinated debentures, *p. 54* term bond, *p. 50*	MyFinanceLab Study Plan 2.2 Video Learning Aid for Problem P2.8

What You Should Know	Key Terms	Where to Practice
LG3 **Explain how bonds are priced in the market and why some bonds are more volatile than others.** Bonds are priced in the market as a percentage of par and are driven by the issue's coupon and maturity, along with prevailing market yields. When interest rates go down, bond prices go up, and vice versa. The extent to which bond prices move up or down depends on the coupon and maturity of an issue. Bonds with lower coupons and/or longer maturities generate larger price swings.		MyFinanceLab Study Plan 2.3
LG4 **Identify the different types of bonds and the kinds of investment objectives these securities can fulfill.** The bond market is divided into 4 major segments: Treasuries, agencies, municipals, and corporates. Treasury bonds are issued by the U.S. Treasury and are virtually default-free. Agency bonds are issued by various subdivisions of the U.S. government and make up an increasingly important segment of the bond market. Municipal bonds are issued by state and local governments in the form of either general obligation or revenue bonds. Corporate bonds make up the major nongovernment sector of the market and are backed by the assets and profitability of the issuing companies. Generally speaking, Treasuries are attractive because of their high quality; agencies and corporates, because of the added returns they provide; and munis, because of the tax shelter they offer.	agency bonds, *p. 60* asset-backed securities (ABS), *p. 68* collateralized mortgage obligation (CMO), *p. 67* Eurodollar bonds, *p. 70* general obligation bonds, *p. 62* junk bonds, *p. 69* mortgage-backed bond, *p. 66* municipal bond guarantees, *p. 62* municipal bonds, *p. 61* PIK bond, *p. 69* revenue bonds, *p. 62* securitization, *p. 68* taxable equivalent yield, *p. 64* Treasury bonds, *p. 58* Treasury Inflation-Protected Securities (TIPS), *p. 60* Treasury notes, *p. 58* Treasury strips *p. 66* Yankee bonds, *p. 70* zero-coupon bonds, *p. 66*	MyFinanceLab Study Plan 2.4
LG5 **Discuss the global nature of the bond market and the difference between dollar-denominated and non-dollar-denominated foreign bonds.** Foreign bonds, particularly foreign-pay securities, offer highly competitive yields and returns. Foreign-pay bonds cover all issues that are denominated in some currency other than U.S. dollars. These bonds have an added source of return: currency exchange rates. In addition, there are dollar-denominated foreign bonds—Yankee bonds and Eurodollar bonds—which have no currency exchange risk because they are issued in U.S. dollars.		MyFinanceLab Study Plan 2.5

What You Should Know	Key Terms	Where to Practice
LG6 Describe the basic features and characteristics of convertible securities, and measure the value of a convertible. Convertible securities are initially issued as bonds (or preferreds), but can subsequently be converted into shares of common stock. These securities offer investors a stream of fixed income (annual coupon payments), plus an equity kicker (a conversion feature). The value of a convertible is driven by the price behavior of the underlying common stock (when the stock price is at or above its conversion price), or by market interest rates and the behavior of bonds (when the stock's price is well below its conversion price). The key values of a convertible are (1) its conversion (stock) value and (2) its investment (bond) value.	conversion equivalent (conversion parity), *p. 75* conversion period, *p. 73* conversion price, *p. 73* conversion privilege, *p. 73* conversion ratio, *p. 73* conversion value, *p. 75* convertible bonds, *p. 71* deferred equity, *p. 72* equity kicker, *p. 71* forced conversion, *p. 72* investment value, *p. 77* LYON (liquid yield option note), *p. 74* payback period, *p. 76*	MyFinanceLab Study Plan 2.6 Video Learning Aid for Problem P2.20

Log into MyFinanceLab, take a chapter test, and get a personalized Study Plan
that tells you which concepts you understand and which ones you need to
review. From there, MyFinanceLab will give you further practice, tutorials,
animations, videos, and guided solutions.
Log into **www.myfinancelab.com**

Discussion Questions

LG1   Q2.1   Using the bond returns in Table 2.1 as a basis of discussion:
   a. Compare the returns during the 1970s to those produced in the 1980s. How do you explain the differences?
   b. How did the bond market do in the 1990s? How does the performance in this decade compare to that in the 1980s? Explain.
   c. What do you think would be a reasonable rate of return to expect from bonds in the future? Explain.
   d. Assume that you're out of school and hold a promising, well-paying job. How much of your portfolio (in percentage terms) would you want to hold in bonds? Explain. What role do you see bonds playing in your portfolio, particularly as you go farther and farther into the future?

LG4 LG5   Q2.2   Identify and briefly describe each of the following types of bonds.
   a. Agency bonds
   b. Municipal bonds
   c. Zero-coupon bonds
   d. Junk bonds
   e. Foreign bonds
   f. Collateralized mortgage obligations (CMOs)

What type of investor do you think would be most attracted to each?

LG1 LG4   Q2.3   "Treasury securities are guaranteed by the U.S. government. Therefore, there is no risk in the ownership of such bonds." Briefly discuss the wisdom (or folly) of this statement.

LG4 LG5 Q2.4 Select the security in the left-hand column that best fits the investor's desire described in the right-hand column.

a. 5-year Treasury note	1. Lock in a high-coupon yield
b. A bond with a low coupon and a long maturity	2. Accumulate capital over a long period of time
c. Yankee bond	3. Generate a monthly income
d. Insured revenue bond	4. Avoid a lot of price volatility
e. Long-term Treasury strips	5. Generate tax-free income
f. Noncallable bond	6. Invest in a foreign bond
g. CMO	7. Go for the highest yield available
h. Junk bond	8. Invest in a pool of credit card receivables
i. ABS receivables	9. Go for maximum price appreciation

LG6 Q2.5 Why do companies like to issue convertible securities? What's in it for them?

LG6 Q2.6 Describe LYONs, and note how they differ from conventional convertible securities. Are there any similarities between LYONs and conventional convertibles? Explain.

LG6 Q2.7 Using the resources at your campus or public library or on the Internet, find the information requested below.

a. Select any 2 convertible debentures (notes or bonds) and determine the conversion ratio, conversion parity, conversion value, conversion premium, and payback period for each.

b. Select any two convertible preferreds and determine the conversion ratio, conversion parity, conversion value, conversion premium, and payback period for each.

c. In what way(s) are the 2 convertible bonds and the 2 convertible preferreds you selected similar? Are there any differences? Explain.

Problems

All problems are available on www.myfinancelab.com

LG2 P2.1 An 8%, 10-year bond is callable in 2 years at a call price of $1,080. The bond is currently priced in the market at $888.89. What is the issue's current yield?

LG2 P2.2 A certain bond has a current yield of 6.5% and a market price of $846.15. What is the bond's coupon rate?

LG2 P2.3 Zack buys a 10% corporate bond with a current yield of 6%. How much did he pay for the bond?

LG4 P2.4 An investor is in the 28% tax bracket and lives in a state with no income tax. He is trying to decide which of 2 bonds to purchase. One is a 7.5% corporate bond that is selling at par. The other is a municipal bond with a 5.25% coupon that is also selling at par. If all other features of these bonds are comparable, which should the investor select? Why? Would your answer change if this were an in-state municipal bond and the investor lived in a place with high state income taxes? Explain.

LG4 P2.5 An investor lives in a state with a 3% tax rate. Her federal income tax bracket is 35%. She wants to invest in 1 of 2 bonds that are similar in terms of risk (and both bonds currently sell at par value). The first bond is fully taxable and offers a yield of 10%. The second bond is exempt from both state and federal taxes and offers a yield of 7%. In which bond should she invest?

LG4 P2.6 Maria Lopez is a wealthy investor who's looking for a tax shelter. Maria is in the maximum (35%) federal tax bracket and lives in a state with a very high state income tax. (She pays the maximum of 11½% in state income tax.) Maria is currently looking at 2 municipal bonds, both of which are selling at par. One is a AA-rated in-state bond that carries a coupon of 6⅜%. The other is a AA-rated out-of-state bond that carries a 7⅛% coupon. Her broker has informed her that comparable fully taxable corporate bonds are currently available with yields of 9¾%. Alternatively, long Treasuries are now available at yields of 9%. She has $100,000 to invest, and because all the bonds are high-quality issues, she wants to select the one that will give her maximum after-tax returns.

    a. Which one of the 4 bonds should she buy?

    b. Rank the 4 bonds (from best to worst) in terms of their taxable equivalent yields.

LG4 P2.7 Wesley Jenkins is looking for a fixed-income investment. He is considering 2 bond issues:

    a. A Treasury with a yield of 5%

    b. An in-state municipal bond with a yield of 4%

Wesley is in the 33% federal tax bracket and the 8% state tax bracket. Which bond would provide Wesley with a higher tax-adjusted yield?

LG2 P2.8 Which of the following bonds offers the highest current yield?

    a. A 9½%, 20-year bond quoted at 97¾

    b. A 16%, 15-year bond quoted at 164⅝

    c. A 5¼%, 18-year bond quoted at 54

LG2 P2.9 Assume that you pay $850 for a long-term bond that carries a 7½% coupon. Over the course of the next 12 months, interest rates drop sharply. As a result, you sell the bond at a price of $962.50.

    a. Find the current yield that existed on this bond at the beginning of the year. What was it by the end of the 1-year holding period?

    b. Determine the holding period return on this investment. (See Chapter 11 for the HPR formula.)

LG3 P2.10 Colwyn buys a 10% corporate bond with a current yield of 6%. When he sells the bond 1 year later, the current yield on the bond is 7%. How much did Col make on this investment?

LG1 P2.11 In early January 2007, you purchased $30,000 worth of some high-grade corporate bonds. The bonds carried a coupon of 8⅛% and mature in 2021. You paid $94.125 when you bought the bonds. Over the 5-year period from 2007 through 2011, the bonds were priced in the market as follows:

Year	Quoted Prices		Year-End Bond Yields
	Beginning of the Year ($)	End of the Year ($)	
2007	94.125	100.625	8.82
2008	100.625	102.000	8.70
2009	102.000	104.625	8.48
2010	104.625	110.125	8.05
2011	110.125	121.250	7.33

Coupon payments were made on schedule throughout the 5-year period.

    a. Find the annual holding period returns for 2007 through 2011. (See Chapter 11 for the HPR formula.)

    b. Use the return information in Table 2.1 to evaluate the investment performance of this bond. How do you think it stacks up against the market? Explain.

LG4 P2.12 Rhett purchased a 13% zero-coupon bond with a 15-year maturity and a $20,000 par value 15 years ago. The bond matures tomorrow. How much will Rhett receive in total from this investment, assuming all payments are made on these bonds as expected?

LG4 P2.13 Nate purchased an interest-bearing security last year, planning to hold it until maturity. He received interest payments, and, to his surprise, a sizable amount of the principal was paid back in the first year. This happened again in year 2. What type of security did Nate purchase?

P2.14 Letticia Garcia, an aggressive bond investor, is currently thinking about investing in a foreign (non-dollar-denominated) government bond. In particular, she's looking at a Swiss government bond that matures in 15 years and carries a 9½% coupon. The bond has a par value of 10,000 Swiss francs (CHF) and is currently trading at 110 (i.e., at 110% of par).

Letticia plans to hold the bond for 1 year, at which time she thinks it will be trading at 117½—she's anticipating a sharp decline in Swiss interest rates, which explains why she expects bond prices to move up. The current exchange rate is 1.58 CHF/U.S.$, but she expects that to fall to 1.25 CHF/U.S.$. Use the foreign investment total return formula (Equation 2.3) to find the following information.

    a. Ignoring the currency effect, find the bond's total return (in its local currency).
    b. Now find the total return on this bond in U.S. dollars. Did currency exchange rates affect the return in any way? Do you think this bond would make a good investment? Explain.

P2.15 Red Electrica España SA (E.REE) is refinancing its bank loans by issuing Eurobonds to investors. You are considering buying $10,000 of these bonds, which will yield 6%. You are also looking at a U.S. bond with similar risk that will yield 5%. You expect that interest rates will not change over the course of the next year, after which time you will sell the bonds you purchase.

    a. How much will you make on each bond if you buy it, hold it for 1 year, and then sell it for $10,000 (or the Eurodollar equivalent)?
    b. Assume the dollar/euro exchange rate goes from 1.11 to 0.98. How much will this currency change affect the proceeds from the Eurobond? (Assume you receive annual interest at the same time you sell the Eurobond.)

P2.16 A certain convertible bond has a conversion ratio of 21 and a conversion premium of 20%. The current market price of the underlying common stock is $40. What is the bond's conversion equivalent?

P2.17 You are considering investing $800 in Higgs B. Technology Inc. You can buy common stock at $25 per share; this stock pays no dividends. You can also buy a convertible bond ($1,000 par value) that is currently trading at $790 and has a conversion ratio of 30. It pays $40 per year in interest. If you expect the price of the stock to rise to $33 per share in 1 year, which instrument should you purchase?

P2.18 A certain 6% annual pay convertible bond (maturing in 20 years) is convertible at the holder's option into 20 shares of common stock. The bond is currently trading at $800. The stock (which pays 75¢ a share in annual dividends) is currently priced in the market at $35 a share.

    a. What is the bond's conversion price?
    b. What is its conversion ratio?
    c. What is the conversion value of this issue? What is its conversion parity?
    d. What is the conversion premium, in dollars and as a percentage?
    e. What is the bond's payback period?
    f. If comparably rated nonconvertible bonds sell to yield 8%, what is the investment value of the convertible?

P2.19 An 8% convertible bond carries a par value of $1,000 and a conversion ratio of 20. Assume that an investor has $5,000 to invest and that the convertible sells at a price of $1,000 (which includes a 25% conversion premium). How much total income (coupon plus capital gains) will this investment offer if, over the course of the next 12 months, the price of the stock moves to $75 per share and the convertible trades at a price that includes a conversion premium of 10%? What is the holding period return on this investment? Finally, given the information in the problem, determine what the underlying common stock is currently selling for.

P2.20 Assume you just paid $1,200 for a convertible bond that carries a 7½% coupon and has 15 years to maturity. The bond can be converted into 24 shares of stock, which are now trading at $50 a share. Find the bond investment value of this issue, given that comparable nonconvertible bonds are currently selling to yield 9%.

LG1   **P2.21** Find the conversion value of a convertible preferred stock that carries a conversion ratio of 1.8, given that the market price of the underlying common stock is $40 a share. Would there be any conversion premium if the convertible preferred were selling at $90 a share? If so, how much (in dollar and percentage terms)? Also, explain the concept of conversion parity, and then find the conversion parity of this issue, given that the preferred trades at $90 per share.

Visit **www.myfinancelab.com** for web exercises, spreadsheets, and other online resources.

Case Problem 2.1   Max and Veronica Develop a Bond Investment Program

LG1 LG4   Max and Veronica Shuman, along with their teenage sons, Terry and Thomas, live in Portland, Oregon. Max is a sales rep for a major medical firm, and Veronica is a personnel officer at a local bank. Together they earn an annual income of around $100,000. Max has just learned that his recently departed rich uncle has named him in his will to the tune of some $250,000 after taxes. Needless to say, the family is elated. Max intends to spend $50,000 of his inheritance on a number of long-overdue family items (like some badly needed remodeling of their kitchen and family room, the down payment on a new Porsche Boxster, and braces to correct Tom's overbite). Max wants to invest the remaining $200,000 in various types of fixed-income securities.

Max and Veronica have no unusual income requirements or health problems. Their only investment objectives are that they want to achieve some capital appreciation, and they want to keep their funds fully invested for at least 20 years. They would rather not have to rely on their investments as a source of current income but want to maintain some liquidity in their portfolio just in case.

Questions

a. Describe the type of bond investment program you think the Shuman family should follow. In answering this question, give appropriate consideration to both return and risk factors.

b. List several types of bonds that you would recommend for their portfolio and briefly indicate why you would recommend each.

c. Using a recent issue of the *Wall Street Journal* or *Barron's*, construct a $200,000 bond portfolio for the Shuman family. Use real securities and select any bonds (or notes) you like, given the following ground rules:

1. The portfolio must include at least one Treasury, one agency, and one corporate bond; also, in total, the portfolio must hold at least 5 but no more than 8 bonds or notes.

2. No more than 5% of the portfolio can be in short-term U.S. Treasury bills (but note that if you hold a T-bill, that limits your selections to just 7 other notes/bonds).

3. Ignore all transaction costs (i.e., invest the full $200,000) and assume all securities have par values of $1,000 (although they can be trading in the market at something other than par).

4. Use the latest available quotes to determine how many bonds/notes/bills you can buy.

d. Prepare a schedule listing all the securities in your recommended portfolio. Use a form like the one shown below and include the information it calls for on each security in the portfolio.

e. In one brief paragraph, note the key investment attributes of your recommended portfolio and the investment objectives you hope to achieve with it.

Security Issuer-Coupon-Maturity	Latest Quoted Price	Number of Bonds Purchased	Amount Invested	Annual Coupon Income	Current Yield
Example: U.S. Treas - 8½%-'18	146%₃₂	15	$21,937.50	$1,275	5.81%
1.					
2.					
3.					
4.					
5.					
6.					
7.					
8.					
Totals	—	_____	$200,000.00	$ _____	% _____

Case Problem 2.2   The Case of the Missing Bond Ratings

LG2   It's probably safe to say that there's nothing more important in determining a bond's rating than the underlying financial condition and operating results of the company issuing the bond. Just as financial ratios can be used in the analysis of common stocks, they can also be used in the analysis of bonds—a process we refer to as credit analysis. In credit analysis, attention is directed toward the basic liquidity and profitability of the firm, the extent to which the firm employs debt, and the ability of the firm to service its debt.

A Table of Financial Ratios

(All ratios are real and pertain to real companies.)

Financial Ratio	Company 1	Company 2	Company 3	Company 4	Company 5	Company 6
1. Current ratio	1.13 ×	1.39 ×	1.78 ×	1.32 ×	1.03 ×	1.41 ×
2. Quick ratio	0.48 ×	0.84 ×	0.93 ×	0.33 ×	0.50 ×	0.75 ×
3. Net profit margin	4.6%	12.9%	14.5%	2.8%	5.9%	10.0%
4. Return on total capital	15.0%	25.9%	29.4%	11.5%	16.8%	28.4%
5. Long-term debt to total capital	63.3%	52.7%	23.9%	97.0%	88.6%	42.1%
6. Owners' equity ratio	18.6%	18.9%	44.1%	1.5%	5.1%	21.2%
7. Pretax interest coverage	2.3 ×	4.5 ×	8.9 ×	1.7 ×	2.4 ×	6.4 ×
8. Cash flow to total debt	34.7%	48.8%	71.2%	20.4%	30.2%	42.7%

Notes:
1. Current ratio = current assets / current liabilities
2. Quick ratio = (current assets − inventory) / current liabilities
3. Net profit margin = net profit / sales
4. Return on total capital = pretax income / (equity + long-term debt)
5. Long-term debt to total capital = long-term debt / (long-term debt + equity)
6. Owner's equity ratio = stockholders' equity / total assets
7. Pretax interest coverage = earnings before interest and taxes / interest expense
8. Cash flow to total debt = (net profit + depreciation) / total liabilities

The financial ratios shown above are often helpful in carrying out such analysis. The first 2 ratios measure the liquidity of the firm, the next 2 its profitability, the following 2 the debt load, and the final 2 the ability of the firm to service its debt load. (For ratio 5, the lower the ratio, the better. For all the others, the higher the ratio, and the better.) The table lists each of these ratios for 6 companies.

Questions

a. Three of these companies have bonds that carry investment-grade ratings. The other 3 companies carry junk-bond ratings. Judging by the information in the table, which 3 companies have the investment-grade bonds and which 3 have the junk bonds? Briefly explain your selections.

b. One of these 6 companies is an AAA-rated firm and one is B-rated. Identify those companies. Briefly explain your selections.

c. Of the remaining 4 companies, 1 carries an AA rating, 1 carries an A rating, and 2 have BB ratings. Which companies are they?

Excel with Spreadsheets

The cash flow component of bond investments is made up of the annual interest payments and the future redemption value or its par value. Just like other time-value-of-money considerations, the bond cash flows are discounted back in order to determine their present value.

In comparing bonds to stocks, many investors look at the respective returns. The total returns in the bond market are made up of both current income and capital gains. Bond investment analysis should include the determination of the current yield as well as a specific holding period return.

On January 13, 2013, you gather the following information on 3 corporate bonds issued by the General Pineapple Corporation (GPC). Remember that corporate bonds are quoted as a percentage of their par value. Assume the par value of each bond to be $1,000. These debentures are quoted in eighths of a point. **Create a spreadsheet** that will model and answer the following bond investment problems.

Bonds	Current Yield	Volume	Close
GPC 5.3 13	?	25	105⅞
GPC 6.65s 20	?	45	103
GPC 7.4 22	?	37	104⅝

Questions

a. Calculate the current yields for these 3 GPC corporate debentures.

b. Calculate the holding period returns under the following scenarios:
   1. Purchased the 5.3 bonds for $990 on January 13, 2012
   2. Purchased the 6.65s for $988 on January 13, 2012
   3. Purchased the 7.4 bonds for $985 on January 13, 2010

c. As of January 13, 2013, GPC common stock had a close price of $26.20. The price of GPC stock in January 2010 was $25.25. The stock paid a 2010 dividend of $0.46, a 2011 dividend of $0.46, and a 2012 dividend of $0.46.

    1. Calculate the current (January 13, 2013) dividend yield for this security.

    2. Assuming you purchased the stock in January 2010, what is the holding period return as of January 2012?

Chapter-Opening Problem

The chart shows the number of bond issues for which Standard & Poor's issued ratings upgrades or downgrades every year from 1981 to 2011.

a. What is the trend in the number of ratings changes (both upgrades and downgrades) over time? Why?

b. Which type of ratings change, upgrade or downgrade, is most common in most years? Why do you think that is so?

c. In what years does the ratio of downgrades/upgrades appear to be particularly high? Why?

3

Securities Markets and Transactions

LEARNING GOALS

After studying this chapter, you should be able to:

LG1 Identify the basic types of securities markets and describe their characteristics.

LG2 Explain the initial public offering (IPO) process.

LG3 Describe broker markets and dealer markets, and discuss how they differ from alternative trading systems.

LG4 Review the key aspects of the globalization of securities markets and discuss the importance of international markets.

LG5 Discuss trading hours and the regulation of securities markets.

LG6 Explain long purchases, margin transactions, and short sales.

"Wall Street" is an early 17th-century testament to the global beginnings of U.S. financial markets. Wall Street was originally the northern boundary of a Dutch colonial settlement founded in 1625 called New Amsterdam, which after coming under English rule in 1664 became New York City. The U.S. financial markets that we know today began to take shape in the late 18th century as stockbrokers and speculators informally gathered on Wall Street under a buttonwood tree to trade. In 1792 twenty-four stockbrokers signed the Buttonwood Agreement, agreeing to trade securities on a commission basis, thus becoming the first organized American securities exchange. In 1817 the Buttonwood organization renamed itself the New York Stock & Exchange Board and rented rooms on Wall Street to establish the first centralized exchange location of what in 1863 became known as the New York Stock Exchange (NYSE). Jumping ahead 143 years, the NYSE and Archipelago Holdings, Inc., merged in 2006 to create the NYSE Group, Inc., a publicly traded company. Archipelago Holdings comprised the Archipelago Exchange and Pacific Stock Exchange. Although the merger with Archipelago was the largest ever among securities exchanges at the time, it was to be outdone. NYSE Euronext was formed in 2007 through a merger of NYSE Group, Inc., and Euronext N.V., thus creating the first global stock exchange. Euronext brought a consortium of European exchanges to the merger, including the Paris, Brussels, Lisbon, and Amsterdam stock exchanges and the London-based electronic derivatives market Euronext.liffe, which is known now as NYSE Liffe. In 2008 NYSE Liffe U.S. was launched, offering a wide range of U.S. derivatives contracts. Further expansion occurred in 2008 when NYSE Euronext acquired the American Stock Exchange. As a result of the acquisition, more than 500 Amex-listed companies joined NYSE Euronext. Through a series of acquisitions and mergers, the Buttonwood Agreement has become the world's largest and most liquid exchange group.

From the trading under a buttonwood tree in a Dutch colonial settlement in 1792 to the NYSE's introduction of 3-D trading floors in 1999, to the launch of the NYSE Euronext's Universal Trading Platform in 2008, to the more than 8,000 listed issues on NYSE Euronext (representing one-third of the world's equities trading in 2012), Wall Street remains a truly global marketplace.

(Sources: "Who We Are," www.nyx.com, accessed April 12, 2012; "Wall Street," en.wikipedia.org/wiki/Wall_street, accessed April 12, 2012; and "NYSE Group and Euronext N.V. Agree to a Merger of Equals," NYSE press release, June 2, 2006, http://www.euronext.com/fic/000/001/891/18919.pdf, accessed April 12, 2012.)

Securities Markets

LG1 LG2 LG3 **Securities markets** are markets that allow suppliers and demanders of securities to make financial transactions. Their goal is to permit such transactions to be made quickly and at a fair price. In this section we will look at the various types of securities markets and their general characteristics.

Types of Securities Markets

In general, securities markets are broadly classified as either **money markets** or **capital markets**. The money market is the market where *short-term* debt securities (with maturities less than 1 year) are bought and sold. Investors use the money market for short-term borrowing and lending. Investors turn to the capital market to buy and sell *long-term* securities (with maturities of more than 1 year), such as stocks and bonds. In this book we will devote most of our attention to the capital market. There investors can make transactions in a wide variety of financial securities, including stocks, bonds, mutual funds, exchange-traded funds, options, and futures. Capital markets are classified as either *primary* or *secondary*, depending on whether securities are being sold initially to investors by the issuer (primary market) or resold among investors (secondary market).

Before offering its securities for public sale, the issuer must register them with and obtain approval from the **Securities and Exchange Commission (SEC)**. This federal regulatory agency must confirm both the adequacy and the accuracy of the information provided to potential investors. In addition, the SEC regulates the securities markets.

The Primary Market The market in which *new issues* of securities are sold to investors is the **primary market**. In the primary market, the issuer of the equity or debt securities receives the proceeds of sales. The most significant transaction in the primary market is the **initial public offering (IPO)**, which marks the first public sale of a company's stock and results in the company's taking on a public status. In large part due to the "Great Recession," considered by many economists to be the worst recession since the Great Depression of the 1930s, only 82 companies sold stock to the public for the first time in the primary market in the United States during 2011. That number is nearly four times the number of IPOs in 2008, the first full year of the Great Recession, but compares unfavorably with the 160 companies that "went public" in 2007. The primary markets also provide a forum for the sale of additional stock, called *seasoned equity issues*, by already public companies.

To sell its securities in the primary market, a firm has three choices. It may make (1) a **public offering**, in which the firm offers its securities for sale to public investors; (2) a **rights offering**, in which the firm offers shares to existing stockholders on a pro rata basis (each outstanding share gets an equal proportion of new shares); or (3) a **private placement**, in which the firm sells securities directly without SEC registration to select groups of private investors such as insurance companies, investment management funds, and pension funds.

Hear about
LinkedIn's IPO

Going Public: The IPO Process Most companies that go public are small, fast-growing companies that require additional capital to continue expanding. For example, Yelp, Inc., a company that provides more than 30 million user-generated reviews for almost every type of local business, raised about $107 million when it went public in March 2012 at $15 per share. Alternatively, large companies may decide to spin off a unit into a separate public corporation. The liquor company Beam, Inc. (formally Fortune

Brands) did this when it spun off its home products and hardware business, Fortune Brands Home & Security, Inc., in October 2011.

When a company decides to go public, it first must obtain the approval of its current shareholders, the investors who own its privately issued stock. Next, the company's auditors and lawyers must certify that all financial disclosure documents for the company are legitimate. The company then finds an investment bank willing to *underwrite* the offering. This bank is the lead underwriter and is responsible for promoting the company's stock and facilitating the sale of the company's IPO shares. The lead underwriter often brings in other investment banking firms to help underwrite and market the company's stock. We'll discuss the role of the investment banker in more detail in the next section.

The underwriter also assists the company in filing a registration statement with the SEC. One portion of this statement is the **prospectus**. It describes the key aspects of the securities to be issued, the issuer's management, and the issuer's financial position. Once a firm files a prospectus with the SEC, a *quiet period* begins, during which the firm faces a variety of restrictions on what it can communicate to investors. While waiting for the registration statement's SEC approval, prospective investors may receive a preliminary prospectus. This preliminary version is called a **red herring** because a notice printed in red on the front cover indicates the tentative nature of the offer. The purpose of the quiet period is to make sure that all potential investors have access to the same information about the company—that which is presented in the preliminary prospectus—but not to any unpublished data that might provide an unfair advantage. The quiet period ends when the SEC declares the firm's prospectus to be effective. The cover of the preliminary prospectus describing the 2012 stock issue of Yelp, Inc., appears in Figure 3.1 on page 91. Note the red herring printed across the top of the front page.

During the registration period and before the IPO date, the investment bankers and company executives promote the company's stock offering through a *road show*, which consists of a series of presentations to potential investors—typically institutional investors—around the country and sometimes overseas. In addition to providing investors with information about the new issue, road shows help the investment bankers gauge the demand for the offering and set an expected price range. Once all of the issue terms have been set, including the price, the SEC must approve the offering before the IPO can take place.

Table 3.1 (on page 92) shows the number of IPOs, the average first-day return (the percentage difference between the offer price in the prospectus and the closing price of the stock on its first trading day), and the gross proceeds raised in each year between 1999 and 2011. Note the exceptionally high first-day returns and large number of offerings during 1999 and 2000, part of a technology-stock-driven bull market. When the market began to fall from its 2000 peak, the IPO market cooled as well. The cycle repeated itself over the next decade, with the number of IPOs hitting another low during the depths of the financial crisis in 2008.

Investing in IPOs is risky business, particularly for individual investors who can't easily acquire shares at the offering price. Most of those shares go to institutional investors and brokerage firms' best clients. Although news stories may chronicle huge first-day gains, IPO stocks are not necessarily good long-term investments.

The Investment Banker's Role Most public offerings are made with the assistance of an investment banker. The **investment banker** is a financial intermediary (such as Goldman, Sachs & Co.) that specializes in assisting companies issuing new securities and advising firms with regard to major financial transactions. The main activity of the investment

FIGURE 3.1

Cover of a Preliminary Prospectus for a Stock Issue

Some of the key factors related to the 2012 Class A common stock issue by Yelp, Inc., are summarized on the cover of the prospectus. The disclaimer statement across the top of the page is normally printed in red, which explains its name "red herring." (Source: Yelp, Inc., "Form S-1 Registration Statement," November 17, 2011, p. 2.)

The information in this preliminary prospectus is not complete and may be changed. These securities may not be sold until the registration statement filed with the Securities and Exchange Commission is effective. This preliminary prospectus is not an offer to sell nor does it seek an offer to buy these securities in any jurisdiction where the offer or sale is not permitted.

Subject To Completion. Dated November 17, 2011

Shares

Class A Common Stock

This is an initial public offering of shares of Class A common stock of Yelp Inc.

Yelp is offering   of the shares to be sold in the offering. The selling stockholders identified in this prospectus are offering an additional   shares. Yelp will not receive any of the proceeds from the sale of the shares being sold by the selling stockholders.

Prior to this offering, there has been no public market for the Class A common stock. It is currently estimated that the initial public offering price per share will be between $ and $. Application has been made for quotation on the   under the symbol "YELP".

See "_Risk Factors_" beginning on page 14 to read about factors you should consider before buying shares of the Class A common stock.

Neither the Securities and Exchange Commission nor any other regulatory body has approved or disapproved of these securities or passed upon the accuracy or adequacy of this prospectus. Any recommendation to the contrary is a criminal offense.

	Per Share	Total
Initial public offering price	$	$
Underwriting discount	$	$
Proceeds, before expenses, to Yelp	$	$
Proceeds, before expenses, to the selling stockholders	$	$

To the extent that the underwriters sell more than   shares of Class A common stock, the underwriters have the option to purchase up to an additional   shares from Yelp at the initial public offering price less the underwriting discount.

The underwriters expect to deliver the shares against payment in New York, New York on   , 2012.

Goldman, Sachs & Co.   **Citigroup**

Jefferies

Allen & Company LLC   **Oppenheimer & Co.**

Prospectus dated   , 2012

banker is **underwriting.** This process involves purchasing the securities from the issuing firm at an agreed-on price and bearing the risk of reselling them to the public. The investment banker also provides the issuer with advice about pricing and other important aspects of the issue.

In the case of large security issues, the lead or originating investment banker brings in other bankers as partners to form an **underwriting syndicate.** The syndicate shares the financial risk associated with buying the entire issue from the issuer and reselling the new securities to the public. The lead investment banker and the syndicate members put together a **selling group,** normally made up of themselves and a large number of brokerage firms. Each member of the selling group is responsible for selling a certain portion of the issue and is paid a commission on the securities it sells. The selling process for a large security issue is depicted in Figure 3.2 on page 92.

TABLE 3.1   ANNUAL IPO DATA, 1999–2011

| Year | Number of IPOs | Aggregate | |
		Average First-Day Return (%)	Gross Proceeds ($ billion)
1999	476	71.0	64.8
2000	380	56.4	64.8
2001	79	14.2	34.2
2002	66	9.1	22.0
2003	62	12.1	9.5
2004	174	12.3	31.3
2005	160	10.2	28.3
2006	157	12.1	30.5
2007	160	13.9	35.7
2008	21	6.4	22.8
2009	41	9.8	13.0
2010	92	9.2	29.9
2011	81	13.3	27.0

(Source: Jay R. Ritter, "Initial Public Offerings: Underpricing Statistics Through 2011," bear.warrington.ufl.edu/ritter/IPOs2011Statistics70512.pdf, Table 1, accessed July 18, 2012.)

FIGURE 3.2

The Selling Process for a Large Security Issue

The lead investment banker hired by the issuing firm may form an underwriting syndicate. The underwriting syndicate buys the entire security issue from the issuing corporation at an agreed-on discount to the public offering price. The investment banks in the underwriting syndicate then bear the risk of reselling the issue to the public at a public offering price. The investment banks' profit is the difference between the price they guaranteed the issuer and the public offering price. Both the lead investment bank and the other syndicate members put together a selling group to sell the issue on a commission basis to investors.

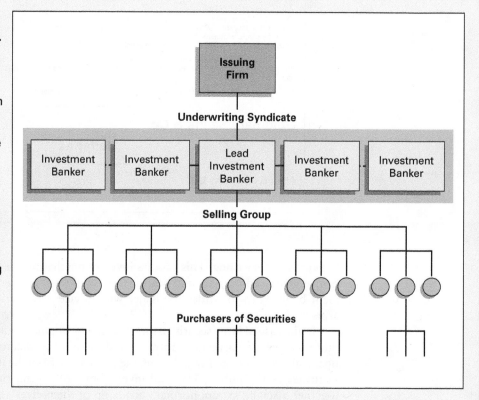

The relationships among the participants in this process can also be seen on the cover of the November 17, 2011, preliminary prospectus for the common stock offering for Yelp, Inc., in Figure 3.1 on page 91. The layout of the prospectus cover indicates the roles of the various participating firms. Placement and larger typefaces differentiate the originating underwriter or underwriting syndicate members (Goldman, Sachs & Co., Citigroup Global Markets, Inc., and Jefferies & Company, Inc.) from the selling group, whose names appear in a smaller font below. Goldman, Sachs & Co. is the lead investment bank for Yelp's IPO.

MARKETS IN CRISIS

No Time to Go Public

After three lean years, IPO markets surged from 2004 to 2007. However, due largely to the outbreak of the financial crisis, IPO volume dropped to a 29-year low in 2008. When financial markets are in crisis, issuing new securities to the public can be difficult for companies. During times of crisis investors and regulators alike take actions that make selling new securities more difficult. Investors tend to withdraw from the markets because they are more unsure than usual about the future prospects of publicly listed companies. At the same time regulators tend to impose new rules which companies need time to fully understand.

Until they do, firms may opt to avoid issuing new securities. Typically, smaller firms are the ones most affected by a financial crisis since they often lack the track record necessary to satisfy the financial market's creditors and investors. Table 3.1 supports this notion. Notice that the average IPO size, calculated by dividing the yearly aggregate gross proceeds by the yearly number of IPOs, was much higher in 2008 than in any other year. IPO volume looked to be returning in 2010 with 92 new issues, but the drop in deals during 2011 showed that the IPO market had not yet fully recovered.

Compensation for underwriting and selling services typically comes in the form of a discount on the sale price of the securities. For example, an investment bank, acting as a lead underwriter, may pay an issuing firm $24 for stock that investors will ultimately purchase for $26. Having guaranteed the issuer $24 per share, the lead underwriter may then sell the shares to the underwriting syndicate members for $24.25 per share. The additional 25 cents per share represents the lead underwriter's management fee. Next the underwriting syndicate members sell the shares to members of the selling group for $25.25 per share. That $1 difference represents the underwriters' discount, which is their profit per share. Finally, members of the selling group earn a selling concession of 75 cents per share when they sell shares to investors at $26 per share. The difference between the price per share paid to the issuer and that paid by the investor (in this case, $26 sale price − $24 purchase price = $2) is the *gross spread*, which comprises the lead underwriter's management fee, the syndicate underwriters' discounts, and the selling group's selling concession. Although the issuer places (or sells) some primary security offerings directly, the majority of new issues are sold through public offering via the process just described.

The Secondary Market The **secondary market**, or the *aftermarket*, is the market in which securities are traded *after they have been issued*. Unlike the primary market, secondary-market transactions do not involve the corporation that issued the securities. Instead, the secondary market permits an investor to sell his or her holdings to another investor. The secondary market provides an environment for continuous pricing of securities that helps to ensure that security prices reflect the securities' true values on the basis of the best available information at any point in time. The ability to make securities transactions quickly and at a fair price in the secondary market provides securities traders with *liquidity*.

One major segment of the secondary market consists of various *national securities exchanges*, which are markets, registered with the SEC, in which the buyers and sellers of *listed securities* come together to execute trades. There are fifteen national securities exchanges registered with the SEC under Section 6(a) of the Exchange Act. The **over-the-counter (OTC) market**, which involves trading in smaller, *unlisted securities*, represents the other major segment of the secondary market. The Financial Industry Regulatory Authority (FINRA) regulates securities transactions in the OTC market. FINRA is the largest independent regulator of securities firms doing business in the United States. FINRA's mission is to protect investors by making sure that the approximately 4,430 brokerage firms, 162,155 branch offices, and 629,530 registered securities representatives it oversees operate fairly and honestly.

Broker Markets and Dealer Markets

Historically, the secondary market has been divided into two segments on the basis of how securities are traded: broker markets and dealer markets. Figure 3.3 depicts the makeup of the secondary market in terms of broker or dealer markets. As you can see, the **broker market** consists of national and regional securities exchanges, whereas the **dealer market** is made up of the Nasdaq OMX and OTC trading venues.

FIGURE 3.3

Broker and Dealer Markets

On a typical trading day, the secondary market is a beehive of activity, where literally billions of shares change hands. The market consists of two distinct parts—the broker market and the dealer market. As shown, each of these markets is made up of various exchanges and trading venues.

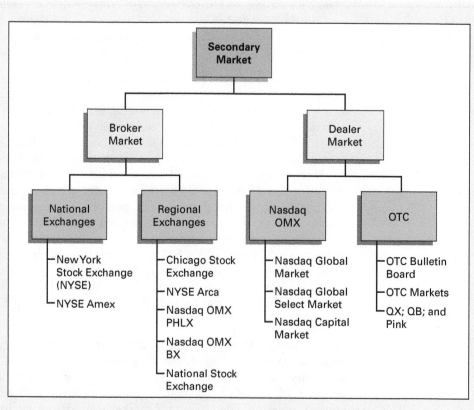

Before we look at these markets in more detail, it's important to understand that probably the biggest difference in the two markets is a technical point dealing with the way trades are executed. That is, when a trade occurs in a broker market, the two sides to the transaction, the buyer and the seller, are brought together—the seller sells his or her securities directly to the buyer. With the help of a *broker*, the securities effectively change hands on the floor of the exchange.

In contrast, when trades are made in a dealer market, buyers' orders and sellers' orders are never brought together directly. Instead, their buy/sell orders are executed by **market makers**, who are *securities dealers* that "make markets" by offering to buy or sell a certain amount of securities at stated prices. Essentially, two separate trades are made: The seller sells his or her securities (for example, in Intel Corp.) to a dealer, and the buyer buys his or her securities (in Intel Corp.) from another, or possibly even the same, dealer. Thus, there is always a dealer (*market maker*) on one side of a dealer-market transaction.

As the secondary market continues to evolve, the distinction between broker and dealer markets continues to fade. In fact, since the 21st century began there has been unprecedented consolidation of trading venues and their respective trading technologies to the point where most exchanges in existence today function as broker-dealer markets. Broker-dealer markets seamlessly facilitate both broker and dealer functions as necessary to provide liquidity for investors in the secondary market.

Broker Markets If you're like most people, when you think of the stock market, the first thing that comes to mind is the New York Stock Exchange (NYSE), which is a national securities exchange. Actually, the NYSE is the dominant broker market. Also included in this market are the NYSE Amex (formally the American Stock Exchange), another national securities exchange, and several so-called regional exchanges. Regional exchanges are national securities exchanges that reside outside New York City, such as the Chicago Stock Exchange. One thing that these exchanges have in common is that all the trading takes place on centralized trading floors. These exchanges account for about 60% of the *total dollar volume* of all shares traded in the U.S. stock market.

Known as "the Big Board," the NYSE is, in fact, the largest stock exchange in the world. In 2011 more than 2,300 firms with an aggregate market value of greater than $13 trillion listed on the NYSE.

The NYSE Amex is the second largest U.S. stock exchange in terms of the number of listed companies. NYSE Amex is home to more than 500 listed stocks and handles about 4% of the annual dollar volume of shares traded on all U.S. securities exchanges. In contrast, the NYSE handles around 90% of the common shares traded on organized exchanges, so the NYSE Amex is far smaller than the NYSE in terms of size and stature. Even so, the NYSE Amex has created a strong market niche for itself through listing and trading the very popular exchange-traded funds (ETFs), a type of index-based mutual fund.

Smart's Tour of the Web

To watch author Scott Smart discuss key websites for this chapter, visit www.myfinancelab.com

In addition to the NYSE and NYSE Amex, a handful of so-called regional exchanges are part of the broker market. The number of securities listed on each of these exchanges is typically in the range of 100 to 500 companies. As a group, they handle around 6% of the shares traded on organized exchanges. The best known of these are the Chicago Stock Exchange, NYSE Arca (formally the Pacific Stock Exchange), Nasdaq OMX PHLX (formally the Philadelphia Stock Exchange), Nasdaq OMX BX (formally the Boston Stock Exchange), and National Stock Exchange. The largest of these exchanges is the Chicago Stock Exchange, which is actually larger than the NYSE Amex in terms of the dollar volume of trading. These exchanges deal primarily in securities with local and regional appeal. Most are modeled after the NYSE, but their membership and listing requirements are considerably more lenient. To enhance their trading activity, regional exchanges often list securities that are also listed on the NYSE or NYSE Amex.

Other broker markets include foreign stock exchanges that list and trade shares of firms in their own foreign markets (we'll say more about these exchanges later in this chapter). Also, separate domestic exchanges exist for trading in options and in futures. Next we consider the basic structure, rules, and operations of each of the major exchanges in the broker markets.

The New York Stock Exchange Most organized securities exchanges are modeled after the New York Stock Exchange. Before the NYSE became a for-profit, publicly traded company in 2006, an individual or firm had to own or lease one of the 1,366 "seats" on the exchange to become a member of the exchange. The word *seat* comes from the fact that until the 1870s, members sat in chairs while trading. On December 30, 2005, in anticipation of becoming a publicly held company, the NYSE ceased having member seats. Each existing seat owner received $500,000 cash and 77,000 shares in the newly public NYSE Group, Inc., for its seat. Now part of the NYSE Euronext group of exchanges, the NYSE sells one-year trading licenses to trade directly on the exchange. As of January 1, 2012, a 1-year trading license cost $40,000 per license for the first two licenses and $25,000 per additional license held by a member organization. Investment banks and brokerage firms comprise the majority of trading license holders, and each typically holds more than one trading license.

Firms such as Merrill Lynch designate officers to hold trading licenses. Only such designated individuals can make transactions on the floor of the exchange. The two main types of floor broker are commission broker and independent broker. *Commission brokers* execute orders for their firm's customers. An *independent broker* works for herself and handles orders on a fee basis, typically for smaller brokerage firms or large firms that are too busy to handle their own orders.

Trading Activity The floor of the NYSE is an area about the size of a football field. Its operation is typical of the various exchanges (although details vary). The NYSE floor has trading posts. Certain stocks trade at each post. Bonds and less active stocks are traded in an annex. Around the perimeter are telephones and electronic equipment that transmit buy and sell orders from brokers' offices to the exchange floor and back again after members execute the orders.

All transactions on the floor of the exchange occur through an auction process. The goal is to fill all buy orders at the lowest price and to fill all sell orders at the highest price with supply and demand determining the price. The actual auction takes place at the post where the particular security trades. Members interested in purchasing a given security publicly negotiate a transaction with members interested in selling that security. The job of the **designated market maker (DMM)**—an exchange member who specializes in making transactions in one or more stocks—is to manage the auction process. The DMM buys or sells (at specified prices) to provide a continuous, fair, and orderly market in those securities assigned to her.

Listing Policies To list its shares on a stock exchange, a domestic firm must file an application and meet minimum listing requirements. Some firms have **dual listings,** or listings on more than one exchange.

To be listed on the NYSE, a U.S. firm must have at least 400 stockholders owning 100 or more shares and a minimum of 1.1 million shares of publicly held stock outstanding; aggregate pretax earnings of at least $10 million over the previous 3 years, of at least $2 million in the previous 2 years, and positive for the first of the last 2 years

See the NYSE's New iPad App

(an alternative earnings test of aggregate pretax earnings of at least $12 million over the previous 2 years, of at least $5 million in the most recent year, and of at least $2 million in the next most recent year); and a minimum market value of public shares of $100 million (a $40 million minimum market value is acceptable for IPOs and spin offs). Foreign companies are subject to similar listing requirements under the domestic listing criteria. The firm also must pay an original listing fee between $125,000 and $250,000. Once the NYSE accepts a firm's securities for listing, the company must continue to meet SEC requirements for exchange-listed securities and pay an annual listing fee between $38,000 and $500,000. Listed firms that fail to meet the requirements may be *delisted* from the exchange.

NYSE Amex The NYSE Amex has organization and procedures similar to those of the NYSE. Because its listing requirements are less stringent, many smaller and younger firms choose to list on the NYSE Amex, which has approximately 500 listed stocks.

In recent years the NYSE Amex has reinvented itself to focus on more specialized market securities. Today about two-thirds of its daily volume comes from exchange-traded funds, a security pioneered by NYSE Amex more than 16 years ago. These ETFs are baskets of securities that are designed to generally track an index of the broad stock or bond market, a stock industry sector, or an international stock, but that trade like a single stock. Trading in stock options accounts for another large segment of the NYSE Amex's business.

Regional Stock Exchanges Most regional exchanges are modeled after the NYSE, but their membership and listing requirements are considerably more lenient. Trading costs are also lower. The majority of securities listed on regional exchanges are also listed on the NYSE or the NYSE Amex. About 100 million NYSE shares pass through one of the regional exchanges on a typical trading day. This dual listing may enhance a security's trading activity. In addition, the *Intermarket Trading System (ITS)* links nine markets—five regional exchanges, the NYSE, the NYSE Amex, the Nasdaq OMX market (Nasdaq Global Select Market; Nasdaq Global Market; and Nasdaq Capital Market), and the Chicago Board Options Exchange—through an electronic communications network that allows brokers and dealers to make transactions at the best prices.

Options Exchanges *Options* allow their holders to sell or to buy another security at a specified price over a given period of time. The dominant options exchange is the Chicago Board Options Exchange (CBOE). Options are also traded on the NYSE Amex, on Nasdaq OMX BX, NYSE Arca, and Nasdaq OMX PHLX exchanges, and on the International Securities Exchange (ISE). Usually an option to sell or buy a given security is listed on all five options exchanges. Options exchanges deal only in security options. Other types of options (not discussed in this text) result from private transactions made directly between sellers and buyers.

Futures Exchanges *Futures* are contracts that guarantee the delivery of a specified commodity or financial instrument at a specific future date at an agreed-on price. The dominant exchange for trading commodity and financial futures is the Chicago Board of Trade (CBT). There are numerous other futures exchanges, some of which specialize in certain commodities and financial instruments rather than handling the broad spectrum listed on the CBT. The largest of these exchanges are the New York Mercantile Exchange; the Chicago Mercantile Exchange; the Deutsche Terminboerse; the London International Financial Futures and Options Exchange; the New York Coffee, Sugar &

Cocoa Exchange; the New York Cotton Exchange; the Kansas City Board of Trade; and the Minneapolis Grain Exchange.

Dealer Markets   One of the key features of the *dealer market* is that it has no centralized trading floors. Instead it is made up of a large number of market makers who are linked via a mass telecommunications network. Each market maker is actually a securities dealer who makes a market in one or more securities by offering to buy or sell them at stated bid/ask prices. The **bid price** and **ask price** represent, respectively, the highest price offered to purchase a given security and the lowest price offered to sell a given security. An investor pays the ask price when *buying* securities and receives the bid price when *selling* them. The dealer market is made up of both the Nasdaq OMX and the OTC markets, which account for about 40% of the shares traded in the U.S. market—with the Nasdaq OMX market accounting for the overwhelming majority of those trades. As an aside, the *primary market* is also a dealer market because all new issues—IPOs and **secondary distributions**, which involve the public sale of large blocks of previously issued securities held by large investors—are sold to the investing public by securities dealers acting on behalf of the investment banker.

Nasdaq   The largest dealer market is made up of a large list of stocks that are listed and traded on the National Association of Securities Dealers Automated Quotation System, typically referred to as Nasdaq. Founded in 1971, Nasdaq had its origins in the OTC market but is today considered a totally separate entity that's no longer a part of the OTC market. In fact, in 2006 Nasdaq was formally recognized by the SEC as a national securities exchange, giving it pretty much the same stature and prestige as the NYSE.

To be traded on Nasdaq, all stocks must have at least two market makers, although the bigger, more actively traded stocks, like Cisco Systems, have many more than that. These dealers electronically post all their bid/ask prices so that when investors place market orders, they are immediately filled at the best available price.

The Nasdaq listing standards vary depending on the Nasdaq listing market. The 1,000 or so stocks traded on the Nasdaq Global Select Market meet the world's highest listing standards. Created in 2006, the Global Select Market is reserved for the biggest and the "bluest"—highest quality—of the Nasdaq stocks. In 2012 Facebook elected to list on Nasdaq Global Select rather than on the NYSE, further cementing Nasdaq's position as the preferred listing exchange for leading technology companies.

The listing requirements are also fairly comprehensive for the roughly 1,000 stocks traded on the Nasdaq Global Market. Stocks included on these two markets are all widely quoted, actively traded, and, in general, have a national following. The trades, all executed electronically, are every bit as efficient as they are on the floor of the NYSE. Indeed, the big-name stocks traded on the Nasdaq Global Select Market, and to some extent, on the Nasdaq Global Market, receive as much national visibility and are as liquid as those traded on the NYSE. As a result, just as the NYSE has its list of big-name players (e.g., ExxonMobil, GE, Citigroup, Walmart, Pfizer, IBM, Procter & Gamble, Coca-Cola, Home Depot, and UPS), so too does Nasdaq. Its list includes companies like Microsoft, Intel, Cisco Systems, Dell, eBay, Google, Yahoo!, Apple, Starbucks, and Staples. Make no mistake: Nasdaq competes head-to-head with the NYSE for listings. In 2012, 13 companies with a combined market capitalization of $82 billion moved their listings from the NYSE to Nasdaq. Some well-known companies that moved to Nasdaq include Viacom, Kraft Foods, and Texas Instruments. The Nasdaq Capital Market is still another Nasdaq market; it makes a market in about 600 or 700 stocks that, for one reason or another, are not eligible for the Nasdaq Global Market. In total, 30 countries are represented by approximately 3,000 companies listed on Nasdaq as of 2012.

The Over-the-Counter Market The other part of the dealer market is made up of securities that trade in the over-the-counter (OTC) market. These non-Nasdaq issues include mostly small companies that either cannot or do not wish to comply with Nasdaq's listing requirements. They trade on either the OTC Bulletin Board (OTCBB) or OTC Markets Group. The OTCBB is an electronic quotation system that links the market makers who trade the shares of small companies. The OTCBB provides access to more than 3,300 securities, includes more than 230 participating market makers, and electronically transmits real-time quote, price, and volume information in traded securities. The Bulletin Board is regulated by the FINRA, which, among other things, requires all companies traded on this market to file audited financial statements and comply with federal securities law.

The OTC Markets is an unregulated segment of the market, where the companies are not even required to file with the SEC. This market is broken into three tiers. The biggest is OTC Pink, which is populated by many small and often questionable companies that provide little or no information about their operations. Securities in the OTC QB tier must provide SEC, bank, or insurance reporting and be current in their disclosures. The top tier, OTC QX, albeit the smallest, is reserved for companies that choose to provide audited financial statements and other required information. If a security has been the subject of promotional activities and adequate current information concerning the issuer is not publicly available, OTC Markets will label the security "Caveat Emptor" (buyers beware). Promotional activities, whether they are published by the issuer or a third party, may include spam e-mail or unsolicited faxes or news releases.

Alternative Trading Systems

Some individual and institutional traders now make direct transactions outside of the broker and dealer markets in the third and fourth markets. The **third market** consists of over-the-counter transactions made in securities listed on the NYSE, the NYSE Amex, or one of the other exchanges. These transactions are typically handled by market makers that are not members of a securities exchange. They charge lower commissions than the exchanges and bring together large buyers and sellers. Institutional investors, such as mutual funds, pension funds, and life insurance companies, are thus often able to realize sizable savings in brokerage commissions and to have minimal impact on the price of the transaction.

The **fourth market** consists of transactions made through a computer network, rather than on an exchange, directly between large institutional buyers and sellers of securities. Unlike third-market transactions, fourth-market transactions bypass the market maker. **Electronic communications networks (ECNs)** are at the heart of the fourth market. Archipelago (part of the NYSE Arca), Bloomberg Tradebook, Island, Instinet, and MarketXT are some of the many ECNs that handle these trades. As with the exchanges, ECNs have undergone much consolidation. For example, in 2002 Island was merged with Instinet and then in 2005 Instinet was acquired by Nasdaq.

ECNs are most effective for high-volume, actively traded securities, and they play a key role in after-hours trading, discussed later in this chapter. They automatically match buy and sell orders that customers place electronically. If there is no immediate match, the ECN, acting like a broker, posts its request under its own name on an exchange or with a market maker. The trade will be executed if another trader is willing to make the transaction at the posted price.

ECNs can save customers money because they charge only a transaction fee, either per share or based on order size. For this reason, money managers and institutions such as pension funds and mutual funds with large amounts of money to invest favor ECNs. Many also use ECNs or trade directly with each other to find the best prices for their clients.

General Market Conditions: Bull or Bear

Conditions in the securities markets are commonly classified as "bull" or "bear," depending on whether securities prices are rising or falling over time. Changing market conditions generally stem from changes in investor attitudes, changes in economic activity, and government actions aimed at stimulating or slowing down economic activity. **Bull markets** are normally associated with rising prices, investor optimism, economic recovery, and government stimulus. **Bear markets** are normally associated with falling prices, investor pessimism, economic slowdown, and government restraint. The beginning of 2003 marked the start of a generally bullish market cycle that peaked before turning sharply bearish in October 2007. Although far from having fully recovered, the bearish market appears to have bottomed out in March 2009 and has since been generally bullish. As of March 2012, 458 of the 479 stocks that have been in the S&P 500 since March 2009 have risen.

In general, investors experience higher (or positive) returns on common stock investments during a bull market. However, some securities are bullish in a bear market or bearish in a bull market. Market conditions are difficult to predict and usually can be identified only after they exist.

CONCEPTS IN REVIEW

Answers available at
www.pearsonhighered.com/smart

3.1 Differentiate between each of the following pairs of terms:

    a. *Money market* and *capital market*
    b. *Primary market* and *secondary market*
    c. *Broker market* and *dealer market*

3.2 Briefly describe the IPO process and the role of the investment banker in underwriting a public offering. Differentiate among the terms *public offering*, *rights offering*, and *private placement*.

3.3 For each of the items in the left-hand column, select the most appropriate item in the right-hand column. Explain the relationship between the items matched.

a. NYSE Amex	1. Trades unlisted securities
b. CBT	2. Is a futures exchange
c. NYSE	3. Is an options exchange
d. Boston Stock Exchange	4. Is a regional stock exchange
e. CBOE	5. Is second largest organized U.S. exchange
f. OTC	6. Has the most stringent listing requirements

3.4 Explain how the dealer market works. Be sure to mention market makers, bid and ask prices, the Nasdaq market, and the OTC market. What role does the dealer market play in initial public offerings (IPOs) and secondary distributions?

3.5 What are the third and fourth markets?

3.6 Differentiate between a bull market and a bear market.

Globalization of Securities Markets

 LG4

Today investors, issuers of securities, and securities firms look beyond the markets of their home countries to find the best returns, lowest costs, and best international business opportunities. The basic goal of most investors is to earn the highest return with the lowest risk. This outcome is achieved through **diversification**—the inclusion of a number of different securities in a portfolio to increase returns and reduce risk. An investor can greatly increase the potential for diversification by holding (1) a wider range of industries and securities, (2) securities traded in a larger number of markets, and (3) securities denominated in different currencies, and the diversification is even greater if the investor does these things for a mix of domestic and foreign securities. The smaller and less diversified an investor's home market is, the greater the potential benefit from prudent international diversification. However, even investors in the United States and other highly developed markets can benefit from global diversification.

In short, globalization of the securities markets enables investors to seek out opportunities to profit from rapidly expanding economies throughout the world. Here we consider the growing importance of international markets, international investment performance, ways to invest in foreign securities, and the risks of investing internationally.

Growing Importance of International Markets

Securities exchanges now operate in over 100 countries worldwide. Both large (Tokyo Stock Exchange) and small (South Pacific Stock Exchange), they are located not only in the major industrialized nations such as Japan, Great Britain, Canada, and Germany but also in emerging economies such as Brazil, Chile, India, South Korea, Malaysia, Mexico, Poland, Russia, and Thailand. The top four securities markets worldwide (based on dollar volume) are the NYSE, Nasdaq, London Stock Exchange, and Tokyo Stock Exchange. Other important foreign exchanges include the Shanghai Stock Exchange, Osaka Securities Exchange, Toronto Stock Exchange, Montreal Exchange, Australian Securities Exchange, Hong Kong Exchanges and Clearing Ltd., Swiss Exchange, and Taiwan Stock Exchange Corp.

The economic integration of the European Monetary Union (EMU), along with pressure from financial institutions that want an efficient process for trading shares across borders, is changing the European securities market environment. Instead of many small national exchanges, countries are banding together to create cross-border markets and to compete more effectively in the pan-European equity-trading markets. The Paris, Amsterdam, Brussels, and Lisbon exchanges, plus a derivatives exchange in London, merged to form Euronext, and the Scandinavian markets formed Norex. In mid-2006, Euronext and the NYSE Group—the NYSE parent—signed an agreement to combine their businesses in a merger of equals. Some stock exchanges—for example, Tokyo and Australian—are forming cooperative agreements. Others are discussing forming a 24-hour global market alliance, trading the stocks of selected large international companies via an electronic order-matching system. Nasdaq, with joint ventures in Japan, Hong Kong, Canada, and Australia, plans to expand into Latin America and the Middle East. The increasing number of mergers and cooperative arrangements represent steps toward a worldwide stock exchange.

Bond markets, too, have become global, and more investors than ever before regularly purchase government and corporate fixed-income securities in foreign markets. The United States dominates the international government bond market, followed by Japan, Germany, and Great Britain.

International Investment Performance

A motive for investing overseas is the lure of high returns. In fact, only once since 1980 did the United States finish first among the major stock markets of the world in the rate of increase in its stock price index. For example, in 2005, an overall good year, investors would have earned higher returns in many foreign markets. During that year the Dow Jones Global Index in U.S. dollars for South Korea increased 58%; for Mexico, 40%; for Japan, 25%; for Finland, 14%; for France, 9%; for Germany, 8%; and for Thailand, 5%. By comparison, the U.S. stock price index increased about 4%. Of course, foreign securities markets tend to be riskier than U.S. markets. A market with high returns in one year may not do so well in the next. However, even in 2008, one of the worst years on record for stock market investors, more than a dozen foreign exchanges earned returns higher than the NYSE Euronext.

Investors can compare activity on U.S. and foreign exchanges by following market indexes that track the performance of those exchanges. For instance, the Dow Jones averages and the Standard & Poor's indexes are popular measures of the U.S. markets, and indexes for more than 20 different stock markets are available. *The Wall Street Journal* publishes daily reports on most major U.S. and foreign stock indexes, and on currency exchange rates.

Ways to Invest in Foreign Securities

Investors can make foreign security transactions either indirectly or directly. One form of *indirect* investment is to purchase shares of a U.S.-based multinational corporation with substantial foreign operations. Many U.S.-based multinational firms, such as ExxonMobil, IBM, Citigroup, Dow Chemical, Coca-Cola, Colgate-Palmolive, and Hewlett-Packard, receive more than 50% of their revenues from overseas operations. By investing in the securities of such firms, an investor can achieve a degree of international diversification. Purchasing shares in a mutual fund or exchange-traded fund that invests primarily in foreign securities is another way to invest indirectly. Investors can make both of these indirect foreign securities investment transactions through a stockbroker.

To make *direct* investments in foreign companies, investors have three options. They can purchase securities on foreign exchanges, buy securities of foreign companies that trade on U.S. exchanges, or buy American Depositary Shares (ADSs).

The first way—purchasing securities on foreign exchanges—involves additional risks because foreign securities do not trade in U.S. dollars and, thus, investors must cope with currency fluctuations. This approach is not for the timid or inexperienced investor. Investors also encounter different securities exchange rules, transaction procedures, accounting standards, and tax laws in different countries. Direct transactions are best handled either through brokers at major Wall Street firms with large international operations or through major banks, such as JPMorgan Chase and Citibank, that have special units to handle foreign securities transactions. Alternatively, investors can deal with foreign broker-dealers, but such an approach is more complicated and riskier.

The second form of direct investment is to buy the securities of foreign companies that trade on both organized and over-the-counter U.S. exchanges. Transactions in foreign securities that trade on U.S. exchanges are handled in the same way as exchange-traded domestic securities. These securities are issued by large, well-known foreign companies. Stocks of companies such as Alcan (Canada), DaimlerChrysler (Germany), France Telecom (France), Head (Netherlands), Sony (Japan), and Unilever (United Kingdom) trade directly on U.S. exchanges. In addition, **Yankee bonds**, U.S. dollar–denominated debt securities issued by foreign governments or corporations and traded in U.S. securities markets, trade in both broker and dealer markets.

Finally, foreign stocks also trade on U.S. exchanges in the form of **American depositary shares (ADSs)**. These securities have been created to permit U.S. investors to hold shares of non-U.S. companies and trade them on U.S. stock exchanges. They are backed by **American depositary receipts (ADRs)**, which are U.S dollar–denominated receipts for the stocks of foreign companies that are held in the vaults of banks in the companies' home countries. Today more than 2,000 ADRs representing more than 50 home countries are traded on U.S. exchanges. About one-fourth of them are actively traded. Included are well-known companies such as Cadbury Schweppes, Hitachi, Nippon, LG Philips, Pearson, Reed Elsevier, and Siemens. ADSs, which trade in the same way as standard domestic securities, were discussed in Chapter 1.

Risks of Investing Internationally

Investing abroad is not without pitfalls. In addition to the usual risks involved in any security transaction, investors must consider the risks of doing business in a particular foreign country. Changes in trade policies, labor laws, and taxation may affect operating conditions for the country's firms. The government itself may not be stable. You must track similar environmental factors in each foreign market in which you invest. This is clearly more difficult than following your home market.

U.S. securities markets are generally viewed as highly regulated and reliable. Foreign markets, on the other hand, may lag substantially behind the United States in both operations and regulation. Additionally, some countries place various restrictions on foreign investment. In Korea and Taiwan, for example, mutual funds are the only way for foreigners to invest. Mexico has a two-tier market, with certain securities restricted from foreigners. Some countries make it difficult for foreigners to get their funds out, and many impose taxes on dividends. For example, Swiss taxes are about 35% on dividends paid to foreigners. Other difficulties include illiquid markets and an inability to obtain reliable investment information because of a lack of reporting requirements.

Furthermore, accounting standards vary from country to country. Differences in accounting practices can affect a company's apparent profitability, conceal assets (such as the hidden reserves and undervalued assets that are permitted in many countries), and facilitate failure to disclose other risks. As a result, it is difficult to compare the financial performance of firms operating in different countries. Although the accounting profession has agreed on a set of international accounting standards, it will be years until all countries have adopted them and even longer until all companies apply them.

Another concern stems from the fact that international investing involves securities denominated in foreign currencies. Trading profits and losses are affected not only by a security's price changes but also by fluctuations in currency values. The price of one currency in terms of another is called the **currency exchange rate**. The values of the world's major currencies fluctuate with respect to each other daily, and these price movements can have a significant positive or negative impact on the return that you earn on an investment in foreign securities.

For example, on January 2, 2012, the exchange rate for the European Monetary Union euro (€) and the U.S. dollar (US$) was expressed as follows:

$$US\$ = €0.7725 \qquad € = US\$1.2945$$

This means that 1 U.S. dollar was worth 0.7725 euros, or equivalently, 1 euro was worth 1.2945 U.S. dollars. On that day, if you had purchased 100 shares of Heineken, which was trading for €36.70 per share on Euronext Amsterdam, it would have cost you $4,750.81 (100 × 36.70 × 1.2945).

Four months later, value of the euro had increased relative to the dollar. On April 30, 2012, the euro/US$ exchange rate was 0.7554, which meant that during the first 4 months of 2012, the euro *appreciated* relative to the dollar (and therefore the dollar *depreciated* relative to the euro). On April 30 it took fewer euros to buy $1 (€0.7554 versus €0.7725 in January), so each euro was worth more in dollar terms ($1.3238 versus $1.2945 in January). Had the European Monetary Union euro instead *depreciated* (and the dollar *appreciated* relative to the euro), each euro would have been worth less in dollar terms.

Currency exchange risk is the risk caused by the varying exchange rates between the currencies of two countries. For example, assume that on April 30, 2012, you sold your 100 shares of Heineken, which was trading for €41.31 per share on Euronext Amsterdam; sale proceeds would have been $5,468.62.

In this example you had a win-win outcome since both the original purchase price in euros increased and the euro appreciated relative to the dollar. In dollar terms the transaction resulted in a gain of $717.81 ($5,468.62 − $4,750.81). Investors in foreign securities must be aware that the value of the foreign currency in relation to the dollar can have a profound effect on returns from foreign security transactions.

CONCEPTS IN REVIEW

Answers available at
www.pearsonhighered.com/smart

3.7   Why is globalization of securities markets an important issue today? How have international investments performed in recent years?

3.8   Describe how foreign security investments can be made, both indirectly and directly.

3.9   Describe the risks of investing internationally, particularly currency exchange risk.

Trading Hours and Regulation of Securities Markets

LG5   Understanding the structure of domestic and international securities markets is an important foundation for developing a sound investment program. Now let's look at market trading hours and the regulation of U.S. securities markets.

Trading Hours of Securities Markets

The regular trading session for organized U.S. exchanges runs from 9:30 A.M. to 4:00 P.M. eastern time. However, trading is no longer limited to these hours. Most securities exchanges and ECNs offer extended trading sessions before and after regular hours.

Most of the after-hours markets are **crossing markets,** in which orders are filled only if they can be matched. That is, buy and sell orders are filled only if they can be matched with identical opposing sell and buy orders at the desired price. These allow U.S. securities markets to compete more effectively with foreign securities markets, in which investors can execute trades when U.S. markets are closed.

The NYSE has two short electronic-trading sessions that begin after the 4:00 P.M. closing bell. One session, from 4:15 to 5:00 P.M., trades stocks at that day's closing prices via a computerized matching system. Transactions occur only if a match can be made and are handled on a first-come, first-served basis. The other session lasts from 4:00 to 6:30 P.M. and allows institutional investors to trade large blocks of stock valued at $1 million or more. Since their inception, the NYSE has experienced increased volume in both sessions.

Nasdaq has its own extended-hours electronic-trading sessions from 4:00 to 6:30 P.M. eastern time, as well as two SelectNet trading sessions, from 8:00 to 9:30 A.M. eastern time and from 4:00 to 6:30 P.M. eastern time. Regional exchanges have also moved to after-hours trading sessions. Now individual investors can participate in after-hours trading activity. Many large brokerage firms, both traditional and online, offer after-hours trading services for their individual clients.

Regulation of Securities Markets

U.S. securities laws protect investors and participants in the financial marketplace. A number of state and federal laws require that investors receive adequate and accurate disclosure of information. Such laws also regulate the activities of participants in the securities markets. State laws that control the sale of securities within state borders are commonly called *blue sky laws* because they are intended to prevent investors from being sold nothing but "blue sky." These laws typically establish procedures for regulating both security issues and sellers of securities doing business within the state. Most states have a regulatory body, such as a state securities commission, that is charged with enforcing the related state statutes. Table 3.2 (on page 106) summarizes the most important securities laws enacted by the federal government (listed in chronological order).

The intent of these federal securities laws is to protect investors. Most of these laws were passed in response to observed damaging abuses by certain market participants. In recent decades, Congress passed two major laws in response to public concern over corporate financial scandals: The *Insider Trading and Fraud Act of 1988* aims at stopping **insider trading,** the use of nonpublic information about a company to make profitable securities transactions. The *Sarbanes-Oxley Act of 2002* focuses on eliminating corporate fraud related to accounting and other information releases. Both of these acts heightened the public's awareness of **ethics**—standards of conduct or moral judgment—in business. The government and the financial community are continuing to develop and enforce ethical standards that will motivate market participants to adhere to laws and regulations. Ensuring that market participants adhere to ethical standards, whether through law enforcement or incentives, remains an ongoing challenge.

TABLE 3.2   IMPORTANT FEDERAL SECURITIES LAWS

Act	Brief Description
Securities Act of 1933	Passed to ensure full disclosure of information about new security issues. Requires the issuer of a new security to file with the Securities and Exchange Commission (SEC) a registration statement containing information about the new issue. The firm cannot sell the security until the SEC approves the registration statement, which usually takes about 20 days. Approval of the registration statement by the SEC merely indicates that the facts presented in the statement appear to reflect the firm's true position.
Securities Exchange Act of 1934	Formally established the SEC as the agency in charge of administering federal securities laws. The act gave the SEC the power to regulate the organized exchanges and the OTC market; their members, brokers, and dealers; and the securities traded in these markets. Each of these participants must file reports with the SEC and periodically update them. The 1934 act has been amended several times.
Maloney Act of 1938	An amendment to the Securities Exchange Act of 1934, it provided for the establishment of trade associations to self-regulate the securities industry. Only one such trade association, the National Association of Securities Dealers (NASD), has been formed. NASD members include nearly all of the nation's securities firms that do business with the public. The NASD, operating under SEC supervision, establishes standardized procedures for securities trading and ethical behavior, monitors and enforces compliance with these procedures, and serves as the industry spokesperson. Today any securities firms that are not members of the NASD must agree to direct SEC supervision.
Investment Company Act of 1940	Established rules and regulations for investment companies and formally authorized the SEC to regulate their practices and procedures. It required investment companies to register with the SEC and to fulfill certain disclosure requirements. An investment company obtains funds by selling its shares to investors and uses the proceeds to purchase securities. The dominant type of investment company is the mutual fund. A 1970 amendment prohibits investment companies from paying excessive fees to advisers and from charging excessive commissions to purchasers of company shares.
Investment Advisers Act of 1940	Requires investment advisers, persons hired by investors to advise them about security investments, to disclose all relevant information about their backgrounds, conflicts of interest, and any investments they recommend. Advisers must register and file periodic reports with the SEC. A 1960 amendment extended the SEC's powers to permit inspection of the records of investment advisers and to revoke the registration of advisers who violate the act's provisions.
Securities Acts Amendments of 1975	Requires the SEC and the securities industry to develop a competitive national system for trading securities. First, the SEC abolished fixed-commission schedules, thereby providing for negotiated commissions. Second, it established the Intermarket Trading System (ITS), an electronic communications network linking 9 markets and trading over 4,000 eligible issues, which allows trades to be made across these markets wherever the network shows a better price for a given issue.
Insider Trading and Fraud Act of 1988	Established penalties for insider trading, using nonpublic information to make profitable securities transactions. Insiders include anyone who obtains nonpublic information, typically a company's directors, officers, major shareholders, bankers, investment bankers, accountants, and attorneys. The SEC requires corporate insiders to file monthly reports detailing all transactions made in the company's stock. Recent legislation substantially increased the penalties for insider trading and gave the SEC greater power to investigate and prosecute claims of illegal insider-trading activity.
Sarbanes-Oxley Act of 2002	Passed to protect investors against corporate fraud, particularly accounting fraud. It created an oversight board to monitor the accounting industry, tightened audit regulations and controls, toughened penalties against executives who commit corporate fraud, strengthened accounting disclosure requirements and ethical guidelines for financial officers, established corporate board structure and membership guidelines, established guidelines for analyst conflicts of interest, and increased the SEC's authority and budgets for auditors and investigators. The act also mandated instant disclosure of stock sales by corporate executives.

3.10 How are after-hours trades typically handled? What is the outlook for after-hours trading?

3.11 Briefly describe the key requirements of the following federal securities laws:

 a. Securities Act of 1933
 b. Securities Exchange Act of 1934
 c. Maloney Act of 1938
 d. Investment Company Act of 1940
 e. Investment Advisers Act of 1940
 f. Securities Acts Amendments of 1975
 g. Insider Trading and Fraud Act of 1988
 h. Sarbanes-Oxley Act of 2002

Basic Types of Securities Transactions

LG6 An investor can make a number of basic types of security transactions. Each type is available to those who meet the requirements established by government agencies as well as by brokerage firms. Although investors can use the various types of transactions in a number of ways to meet investment objectives, we describe only the most popular use of each transaction here, as we consider the long purchase, margin trading, and short selling.

Long Purchase

The **long purchase** is a transaction in which investors buy securities in the hope that they will increase in value and can be sold at a later date for profit. The object, then, is to *buy low and sell high*. A long purchase is the most common type of transaction. Because investors generally expect the price of a security to rise over the period of time they plan to hold it, their return comes from any dividends or interest received during the ownership period, plus the difference (capital gain or loss) between the purchase and selling prices. Transaction costs, of course, reduce this return.

Ignoring dividends and transaction costs, we can illustrate the long purchase by a simple example. After studying Varner Industries, you are convinced that its common stock, which currently sells for $20 per share, will increase in value over the next few years. You expect the stock price to rise to $30 per share within 2 years. You place an order and buy 100 shares of Varner for $20 per share. If the stock price rises to, say, $40 per share, you will profit from your long purchase. If it drops below $20 per share, you will experience a loss on the transaction. Obviously, one of the major motivating factors in making a long purchase is an expected rise in the price of the security.

Margin Trading

Security purchases do not have to be made on a cash basis; investors can use funds borrowed from brokerage firms instead. This activity is referred to as **margin trading**. It is used for one basic reason: to magnify returns. As peculiar as it may sound, the term *margin* refers to the amount of equity (stated as a percentage) in an investment, or the amount that is *not* borrowed. If an investor uses 75% margin, for example, it means that 75% of the investment position is being financed with the person's own funds and the balance (25%) with borrowed money.

The Federal Reserve Board (the "Fed") sets the **margin requirement,** specifying the minimum amount of equity that must be the margin investor's own funds. The margin requirement for stocks has been at 50% for some time. By raising and lowering the margin requirement, the Fed can depress or stimulate activity in the securities markets. Brokers must approve margin purchases. The brokerage firm then lends the purchaser the needed funds and retains the purchased securities as collateral. It is important to recognize that margin purchasers must pay a specified rate of interest on the amount they borrow.

With the use of margin, you can purchase more securities than you could afford on a strictly cash basis and, thus, magnify your returns. However, the use of margin also presents substantial risks. Margin trading can only magnify returns, not produce them. One of the biggest risks is that the security may not perform as expected. If the security's return is negative, margin trading magnifies the loss. Because the security being margined is always the ultimate source of return, choosing the right securities is critical to this trading strategy. In the next section, we will look at how margin trading can magnify returns and losses.

Essentials of Margin Trading Investors can use margin trading with most kinds of securities. They regularly use it, for example, to buy common and preferred stocks, most types of bonds, mutual funds, options, warrants, and futures. It is not normally used with tax-exempt municipal bonds because the interest paid on such margin loans is not deductible for income tax purposes. It is also possible to use margin on certain foreign stocks and bonds that meet prescribed criteria and appear on the Fed's List of Foreign Margin Stocks, which is published semiannually. For simplicity, we will use common stock as the investment in our discussion of margin trading.

Magnified Profits and Losses With an investor's equity serving as a base, the idea of margin trading is to employ **financial leverage**—the use of debt financing to magnify investment returns.

Here is how it works: Suppose you have $5,000 to invest and are considering the purchase of 100 shares of stock at $50 per share. If you do not margin, you can buy exactly 100 shares of the stock (ignoring brokerage commissions). If you margin the transaction—for example, at 50%—you can acquire the same $5,000 position with only $2,500 of your own money. This leaves you with $2,500 to use for other investments or to buy on margin another 100 shares of the same stock. Either way, by margining you will reap greater benefits from the stock's price appreciation.

Table 3.3 (on page 109) illustrates the concept of margin trading. It shows a non-margined (100% equity) transaction, along with the same transaction using various margins. Remember that the margin rates (e.g., 65%) indicate the investor's equity in the investment. When the investment is nonmargined and the price of the stock goes up by $30 per share (see Table 3.3, part A), the investor enjoys a very respectable 60% rate of return. However, observe how the rate of return goes up when margin is used. The rate of return ranges from 75% to 120%, depending on the amount of equity in the investment. This occurs because the gain is the same ($3,000) *regardless of how the investor finances the transaction.* Clearly, as the investor's equity in the investment declines (with lower margins), the rate of return increases accordingly.

TABLE 3.3   THE EFFECT OF MARGIN TRADING ON SECURITY RETURNS

EXCEL with Spreadsheet

	Without Margin (100% Equity)	With Margins of		
		80%	65%	50%
Number of $50 shares purchased	100	100	100	100
Cost of investment	$ 5,000	$ 5,000	$ 5,000	$ 5,000
Less: Borrowed money	0	−1,000	−1,750	−2,500
Equity in investment	$ 5,000	$ 4,000	$ 3,250	$ 2,500
A. Investor's position if price rises by $30 to $80/share				
Value of stock	$ 8,000	$ 8,000	$ 8,000	$ 8,000
Less: Cost of investment	−5,000	−5,000	−5,000	−5,000
Capital gain	$ 3,000	$ 3,000	$ 3,000	$ 3,000
Return on investor's equity (capital gain/ equity in investment)	60%	75%	92.3%	120%
B. Investor's position if price falls by $30 to $20/share				
Value of stock	$ 2,000	$ 2,000	$ 2,000	$ 2,000
Less: Cost of investment	−5,000	−5,000	−5,000	−5,000
Capital loss*	($ 3,000)	($ 3,000)	($ 3,000)	($ 3,000)
Return on investor's equity (capital loss/ equity in investment)*	(60%)	(75%)	(92.3%)	(120%)

*Both the capital loss and the return on investor's equity are negative, as noted by the parentheses.

Three facets of margin trading become obvious from the table:

1. Movements in the stock's price are not influenced by the method used to purchase the stock.

2. The lower the amount of the investor's equity in the position, the *greater the rate of return* the investor will enjoy when the price of the security rises.

3. The *loss is also magnified* (by the same rate) when the price of the security falls (see Table 3.3, part B).

Note that Table 3.3 has an Excel with Spreadsheets icon. Throughout the text, tables with this icon indicate that the spreadsheet is available on www.myfinancelab.com. The use of electronic spreadsheets in finance and investments, as well as in all functional areas of business, is pervasive. We use spreadsheets from time to time throughout the text to demonstrate how the content has been constructed or calculated. We include Excel spreadsheet exercises at the end of most chapters to give you practice with spreadsheets and help you develop the ability to clearly set out the logic needed to solve investment problems.

Advantages and Disadvantages of Margin Trading A magnified return is the major advantage of margin trading. The size of the magnified return depends on both the price behavior of the security and the amount of margin used. Another, more modest benefit of margin trading is that it allows for greater diversification of security holdings because investors can spread their limited capital over a larger number of investments.

The major disadvantage of margin trading, of course, is the potential for magnified losses if the price of the security falls. Another disadvantage is the cost of the margin loans themselves. A **margin loan** is the official vehicle through which the borrowed funds are made available in a margin transaction. All margin loans are made at a stated interest rate, which depends on prevailing market rates and the amount of money being borrowed. This rate is usually 1% to 3% above the **prime rate**—the interest rate charged to creditworthy business borrowers. For large accounts, it may be at the prime rate. The loan cost, which investors pay, will increase daily, reducing the level of profits (or increasing losses) accordingly.

Making Margin Transactions To execute a margin transaction, an investor must establish a **margin account** with a minimum of $2,000 in equity or 100% of the purchase price, whichever is less, in the form of either cash or securities. The broker will retain any securities purchased on margin as collateral for the loan.

The margin requirement established by the Federal Reserve Board sets the minimum amount of equity for margin transactions. Investors need not execute all margin transactions by using exactly the minimum amount of margin; they can use more than the minimum if they wish. Moreover, it is not unusual for brokerage firms and the major exchanges to establish their own margin requirements, which are more restrictive than those of the Federal Reserve. Brokerage firms also may have their own lists of especially volatile stocks for which the margin requirements are higher. There are basically two types of margin requirement: initial margin and maintenance margin.

Initial Margin The minimum amount of equity that must be provided by the investor at the time of purchase is the **initial margin**. It prevents overtrading and excessive speculation. Generally, this is the margin requirement to which investors refer when discussing margin trading. All securities that can be margined have specific initial requirements, which the governing authorities can change at their discretion. Table 3.4 shows initial margin requirements for various types of securities. The more stable investments, such as U.S. government issues, generally have substantially lower margin requirements and thus offer greater opportunities to magnify returns. Stocks traded on the Nasdaq OMX markets can be margined like listed securities; OTC stocks are considered to have no collateral value and therefore cannot be margined.

TABLE 3.4	INITIAL MARGIN REQUIREMENTS FOR VARIOUS TYPES OF SECURITIES
Security	Minimum Initial Margin (Equity) Required (%)
Listed common and preferred stock	50
Nasdaq OMX stocks	50
Convertible bonds	50
Corporate bonds	30
U.S. government bills, notes, and bonds	10 of principal
U.S. government agencies	24 of principal
Options	Option premium plus 20 of market value of underlying stock
Futures	2 to 10 of the value of the contract

As long as the margin in an account remains at a level equal to or higher than prevailing initial requirements, the investor may use the account in any way he or she wants. However, if the value of the investor's holdings declines, the margin in his or her account will also drop. In this case, the investor will have what is known as a **restricted account,** one whose equity is less than the initial margin requirement. It does not mean that the investor must put up additional cash or equity. However, as long as the account is restricted, the investor may not make further margin purchases and must bring the margin back to the initial level when securities are sold.

Maintenance Margin The absolute minimum amount of margin (equity) that an investor must maintain in the margin account at all times is the **maintenance margin.** When an insufficient amount of maintenance margin exists, an investor will receive a **margin call.** This call gives the investor a short period of time (perhaps 72 hours) to bring the equity up above the maintenance margin. If this doesn't happen, the broker is authorized to sell enough of the investor's margined holdings to bring the equity in the account up to this standard.

Margin investors can be in for a surprise if markets are volatile. When the Nasdaq stock market fell 14% in one day in early April 2000, brokerages made many more margin calls than usual. Investors rushed to sell shares, often at a loss, to cover their margin calls—only to watch the market bounce back a few days later.

The maintenance margin protects both the brokerage house and investors: Brokers avoid having to absorb excessive investor losses, and investors avoid being wiped out. The maintenance margin on equity securities is currently 25%. It rarely changes, although it is often set slightly higher by brokerage firms for the added protection of brokers and customers. For straight debt securities such as government bonds, there is no official maintenance margin except that set by the brokerage firms themselves.

The Basic Margin Formula The amount of margin is always measured in terms of its relative amount of equity, which is considered the investor's collateral. A simple formula can be used with all types of long purchases to determine the amount of margin in the transaction at any given time. Basically, only two pieces of information are required: (1) the prevailing market value of the securities being margined and (2) the **debit balance,** which is the amount of money being borrowed in the margin loan. Given this information, we can compute margin according to Equation 3.1.

Equation 3.1
$$\text{Margin} = \frac{\text{Value of securities} - \text{Debit balance}}{\text{Value of securities}}$$

Equation 3.1a
$$= \frac{V - D}{V}$$

To illustrate, consider the following example. Assume you want to purchase 100 shares of stock at $40 per share at a time when the initial margin requirement is 70%. Because 70% of the transaction must be financed with equity, you can finance the (30%) balance with a margin loan. Therefore, you will borrow $0.30 \times \$4,000$, or $1,200. This amount, of course, is the *debit balance.* The remainder ($4,000 − $1,200 = $2,800) represents your equity in the transaction. In other words, equity is represented by the numerator $(V - D)$ in the margin formula.

What happens to the margin as the value of the security changes? If over time the price of the stock moves to $65, the margin is then

$$\text{Margin} = \frac{V - D}{V} = \frac{\$6,500 - \$1,200}{\$6,500} = 0.815 = \underline{81.5\%}$$

Note that the margin (equity) in this investment position has risen from 70% to 81.5%. *When the price of the security goes up, your margin also increases.*

On the other hand, *when the price of the security goes down, so does the amount of margin.* For instance, if the price of the stock in our illustration drops to $30 per share, the new margin is only 60% [($3,000 − $1,200) ÷ $3,000]. In that case, we would be dealing with a *restricted account* because the margin level would have dropped below the prevailing initial margin of 70%.

Finally, note that although our discussion has been couched largely in terms of individual transactions, the same margin formula applies to margin accounts. The only difference is that we would be dealing with input that applies to the account *as a whole*—the value of all securities held in the account and the total amount of margin loans.

Return on Invested Capital   When assessing the return on margin transactions, you must take into account the fact that you put up only part of the funds. Therefore, you are concerned with the *rate of return* earned on only the portion of the funds that you provided. Using both current income received from dividends or interest and total interest paid on the margin loan, we can apply Equation 3.2 to determine the return on invested capital from a margin transaction.

Equation 3.2

$$\begin{array}{c}\text{Return on} \\ \text{invested capital} \\ \text{from a margin} \\ \text{transaction}\end{array} = \frac{\begin{array}{c}\text{Total} \\ \text{current} \\ \text{income} \\ \text{received}\end{array} - \begin{array}{c}\text{Total} \\ \text{interest} \\ \text{paid on} \\ \text{margin loan}\end{array} + \begin{array}{c}\text{Market} \\ \text{value of} \\ \text{securities} \\ \text{at sale}\end{array} - \begin{array}{c}\text{Market} \\ \text{value of} \\ \text{securities} \\ \text{at purchase}\end{array}}{\text{Amount of equity at purchase}}$$

We can use this equation to compute either the expected or the actual return from a margin transaction. To illustrate: Assume you want to buy 100 shares of stock at $50 per share because you feel it will rise to $75 within 6 months. The stock pays $2 per share in annual dividends, and during your 6-month holding period, you will receive half of that amount, or $1 per share. You are going to buy the stock with 50% margin and will pay 10% interest on the margin loan. Therefore, you are going to put up $2,500 equity to buy $5,000 worth of stock that you hope will increase to $7,500 in 6 months. Because you will have a $2,500 margin loan outstanding at 10% for 6 months, you will pay $125 in total interest costs ($2,500 × 0.10 × 6/12 = $125). We can substitute this information into Equation 3.2 to find the expected return on invested capital from this margin transaction:

$$\begin{array}{c}\text{Return on} \\ \text{invested capital} \\ \text{from a margin} \\ \text{transaction}\end{array} = \frac{\$100 - \$125 + \$7,500 - \$5,000}{\$2,500} = \frac{\$2,475}{\$2,500} = 0.99 = \underline{99\%}$$

Keep in mind that the 99% figure represents the rate of return earned over a 6-month holding period. If you wanted to compare this rate of return to other investment opportunities, you could determine the transaction's annualized rate of return by multiplying by 2 (the number of 6-month periods in a year). This would amount to an annual rate of return of 198% ($99 \times 2 = 198$).

Uses of Margin Trading Investors most often use margin trading in one of two ways. As we have seen, one of its uses is to magnify transaction returns. The other major margin tactic is called pyramiding, which takes the concept of magnified returns to its limits. **Pyramiding** uses the paper profits in margin accounts to partly or fully finance the acquisition of additional securities. This allows investors to make such transactions at margins below prevailing initial margin levels, sometimes substantially so. In fact, with this technique it is even possible to buy securities with no new cash at all. Rather, they can all be financed entirely with margin loans. The reason is that the paper profits in the account lead to **excess margin**—more equity in the account than required. For instance, if a margin account holds $60,000 worth of securities and has a debit balance of $20,000, it is at a margin level of 66.6% [($60,000 − $20,000) ÷ $60,000]. This account would hold a substantial amount of excess margin if the prevailing initial margin requirement were only 50%.

The principle of pyramiding is to use the excess margin in the account to purchase additional securities. The only constraint—and the key to pyramiding—is that when the additional securities are purchased, your margin account must be at or above the prevailing required initial margin level. Remember that it is the account, not the individual transactions, that must meet the minimum standards. If the account has excess margin, you can use it to build up security holdings. Pyramiding can continue as long as there are additional paper profits in the margin account and as long as the margin level exceeds the initial requirement that prevailed when purchases were made. The tactic is somewhat complex but is also profitable, especially because it minimizes the amount of new capital required in the investor's account.

In general, margin trading is simple, but it is also risky. Risk is primarily associated with possible price declines in the margined securities. A decline in prices can result in a restricted account. If prices fall enough to cause the actual margin to drop below the maintenance margin, the resulting margin call will force you to deposit additional equity into the account almost immediately. In addition, losses (resulting from the price decline) are magnified in a fashion similar to that demonstrated in Table 3.3, part B. Clearly, the chance of a margin call and the magnification of losses make margin trading riskier than nonmargined transactions. Margin should be used only by investors who fully understand its operation and appreciate its pitfalls.

Short Selling

In most cases, investors buy stock hoping that the price will rise. What if you expect the price of a particular security to fall? By using short selling, you may be able to profit from falling security prices. Almost any type of security can be "shorted": common and preferred stocks, all types of bonds, convertible securities, listed mutual funds, options, and warrants. In practice, though, the short-selling activities of most investors are limited almost exclusively to common stocks and to options. (However, investors are prohibited from using short selling to protect themselves from falling security prices, a strategy called *shorting-against-the-box*.)

The Basics of Short
Selling Explained

Essentials of Short Selling Short selling is generally defined as the practice of selling borrowed securities. Unusual as it may sound, selling borrowed securities is (in most cases) legal and quite common. Short sales start when an investor borrows securities from a broker and sells these securities in the marketplace. Later, when the price of the issue has declined, the short seller buys back the securities and then returns them to the lender. A short seller must make an initial equity deposit with the broker, subject to rules similar to those for margin trading. The deposit plus the proceeds from sale of the borrowed shares assure the broker that sufficient funds are available to buy back the shorted securities at a later date, even if their price increases. Short sales, like margin transactions, require investors to work through a broker.

Making Money When Prices Fall Making money when security prices fall is what short selling is all about. Like their colleagues in the rest of the investment world, short sellers are trying to make money by buying low and selling high. The only difference is that they reverse the investment process: *They start the transaction with a sale and end it with a purchase.*

Table 3.5 shows how a short sale works and how investors can profit from such transactions. (For simplicity, we ignore transaction costs.) The transaction results in a net profit of $2,000 as a result of an initial sale of 100 shares of stock at $50 per share (step 1) and subsequent covering (purchase) of the 100 shares for $30 per share (step 2). The amount of profit or loss generated in a short sale depends on the price at which the short seller can buy back the stock. Short sellers earn profit only when the proceeds from the sale of the stock are higher than the cost of buying it back.

Who Lends the Securities? Acting through their brokers, short sellers obtain securities from the brokerage firm or from other investors. (Brokers are the principal source of borrowed securities.) As a service to their customers, brokers lend securities held in their portfolios or in *street-name* accounts. It is important to recognize that when the brokerage firm lends street-name securities, it is lending the short seller the securities of other investors. Individual investors typically do not pay fees to the broker for the privilege of borrowing the shares; in exchange, investors do not earn interest on the funds they leave on deposit with the broker.

Margin Requirements and Short Selling To make a short sale, the investor must make a deposit with the broker that is equal to the initial margin requirement (currently 50%) applied to the short-sale proceeds. In addition, the broker retains the proceeds from the short sale.

TABLE 3.5 THE MECHANICS OF A SHORT SALE	EXCEL with Spreadsheets
Step 1. Short sale initiated	
100 shares of borrowed stock are sold at $50/share:	
Proceeds from sale to investor	$5,000
Step 2. Short sale covered	
Later, 100 shares of the stock are purchased at $30/share and returned to broker from whom stock was borrowed:	
Cost to investor	−3,000
Net profit	$2,000

SEC Bans Short Selling

In September 2008, as the financial crisis grew deeper, the Securities and Exchange Commission announced a temporary ban on short sales of almost 800 financial stocks from September 19 to October 9. Research shows that the prices of stocks affected by the ban rose significantly, but those price increases were largely reversed when the ban was lifted. The vulnerability of stock markets to excessive short selling in times of crisis has led the SEC to implement rules aimed at preventing significant downward price pressure but allowing for unfettered price discovery. The alternative uptick rule (Rule 201) approved in 2010 imposes restrictions on short selling only when a stock has triggered a circuit breaker by experiencing a price decline of at least 10% in one day. At that point, short selling would be permitted if the price of the security were above the current national best bid.

To demonstrate, assume that you sell short 100 shares of Smart, Inc., at $50 per share at a time when the initial margin requirement is 50% and the maintenance margin on short sales is 30%. The values in lines 1 through 4 in column A in Table 3.6 indicate that your broker would hold a total deposit of $7,500 on this transaction. Note in columns B and C that regardless of subsequent changes in Smart's stock price, your deposit with the broker would remain at $7,500 (line 4).

By subtracting the cost of buying back the shorted stock at the given share price (line 5), you can find your equity in the account (line 6) for the current (column A) and two subsequent share prices (columns B and C). We see that at the initial short sale

TABLE 3.6 MARGIN POSITIONS ON SHORT SALES

		A	B	C
		Initial Short Sale Price ($)	Subsequent Share Prices ($)	
Line	Item			
1	Price per share	50	30	70
2	Proceeds from initial short sale [(1) × 100 shares]	5,000		
3	Initial margin deposit [0.50 × (2)]	2,500		
4	Total deposit with broker [(2) + (3)]	7,500	7,500	7,500
5	Current cost of buying back stock [(1) × 100 shares]	5,000	3,000	7,000
6	Account equity [(4) − (5)]	2,500	4,500	500
7	Actual margin [(6) ÷ (5)]	50%	150%	7.14%
8	Maintenance margin position [(7) > 30%?]	OK	OK	Margin call*

*Investor must either (a) deposit at least an additional $1,600 with the broker to bring the total deposit to $9,100 ($7,500 + $1,600), which would equal the current value of the 100 shares of $7,000 plus a 30% maintenance margin deposit of $2,100 (.30 × $7,000) or (b) buy back the 100 shares of stock and return them to the broker.

price of $50 per share, your equity would equal $2,500 (column A). If the share price subsequently drops to $30, your equity would rise to $4,500 (column B). If the share price subsequently rises to $70, your equity would fall to $500 (column C). Dividing these account equity values (line 6) by the then-current cost of buying back the stock (line 5), we can calculate the actual margins at each share price (line 7). We see that at the current $50 price the actual margin is 50%, whereas at the $30 share price it is 150%, and at the $70 share price it is 7.14%.

As indicated in line 8, given the 30% maintenance margin requirement, your margin would be okay at the current price of $50 (column A) or lower (column B). But at the $70 share price, the 7.14% actual margin would be below the 30% maintenance margin, thereby resulting in a margin call. In that case (or whenever the actual margin on a short sale falls below the maintenance margin), you must respond to the margin call either by depositing additional funds with the broker or by buying the stock and covering (i.e., closing out) the short position.

If you wished to maintain the short position when the share price has risen to $70, you would have to deposit an additional $1,600 with the broker. Those funds would increase your total deposit to $9,100 ($7,500 + $1,600)—an amount equal to the $7,000 value of the shorted stock plus the 30% maintenance margin, or $2,100 (.30 × $7,000). Buying back the stock to cover the short position would cost $7,000, thereby resulting in the return of the $500 of equity in your account from your broker. Clearly, margin requirements tend to complicate the short-sale transaction and the impact of an increase in the shorted stock's share price on required deposits with the broker.

Advantages and Disadvantages The major advantage of selling short is, of course, the chance to profit from a price decline. The key disadvantage of many short-sale transactions is that the investor faces limited return opportunities along with high-risk exposure. The price of a security can fall only so far (to zero or near zero), yet there is really no limit to how far such securities can rise in price. (Remember, a short seller is hoping for a price decline; when a security goes up in price, a short seller loses.) For example, note in Table 3.5 (on page 114) that the stock in question cannot possibly fall by more than $50, yet who is to say how high its price can go?

A less serious disadvantage is that short sellers never earn dividend (or interest) income. In fact, short sellers owe the lender of the shorted security any dividends (or interest) paid while the transaction is outstanding. That is, if a dividend is paid during the course of a short-sale transaction, the short seller must pay an equal amount to the lender of the stock. (The mechanics of these payments are taken care of automatically by the short seller's broker.)

Uses of Short Selling Investors sell short primarily to seek speculative profits when they expect the price of a security to drop. Because the short seller is betting against the market, this approach is subject to a considerable amount of risk. The actual procedure works as demonstrated in Table 3.5. Note that had you been able to sell the stock at $50 per share and later repurchase it at $30 per share, you would have generated a profit of $2,000 (ignoring dividends and brokerage commissions). However, if the market had instead moved against you, all or most of your $5,000 investment could have been lost.

3.12 What is a long purchase? What expectation underlies such a purchase? What is margin trading, and what is the key reason why investors sometimes use it as part of a long purchase?

3.13 How does margin trading magnify profits and losses? What are the key advantages and disadvantages of margin trading?

3.14 Describe the procedures and regulations associated with margin trading. Be sure to explain restricted accounts, the maintenance margin, and the margin call. Define the term *debit balance*, and describe the common uses of margin trading.

3.15 What is the primary motive for short selling? Describe the basic short-sale procedure. Why must the short seller make an initial equity deposit?

3.16 What relevance do margin requirements have in the short-selling process? What would have to happen to experience a margin call on a short-sale transaction? What two actions could be used to remedy such a call?

3.17 Describe the key advantages and disadvantages of short selling. How are short sales used to earn speculative profits?

MyFinanceLab

Here is what you should know after reading this chapter. MyFinanceLab will help you identify what you know and where to go when you need to practice.

What You Should Know	Key Terms	Where to Practice
LG1 Identify the basic types of securities markets and describe their characteristics. Short-term investment vehicles trade in the money market; longer-term securities, such as stocks and bonds, trade in the capital market. New security issues are sold in the primary market. Investors buy and sell existing securities in the secondary markets.	ask price, *p. 98* bear markets, *p. 100* bid price, *p. 98* broker market, *p. 94* bull markets, *p. 100* capital market, *p. 89* dealer market, *p. 94* designated market maker (DMM), *p. 96*	MyFinanceLab Study Plan 3.1
LG2 Explain the initial public offering process. The first public issue of a company's common stock is an IPO. The company selects an investment banker to sell the IPO. The lead investment banker may form a syndicate with other investment bankers and then create a selling group to sell the issue. The IPO process includes filing a registration statement with the Securities and Exchange Commission, getting SEC approval, promoting the offering to investors, pricing the issue, and selling the shares.	dual listing, *p. 96* electronic communications network (ECN), *p. 99* fourth market, *p. 99* initial public offering (IPO), *p. 89* investment banker, *p. 90* market makers, *p. 95* money market, *p. 89*	MyFinanceLab Study Plan 3.2

What You Should Know	Key Terms	Where to Practice
LG3 Describe broker markets and dealer markets, and discuss how they differ from alternative trading systems. In dealer markets, buy/sell orders are executed by market makers. The market makers are securities dealers who "make markets" by offering to buy or sell certain securities at stated bid/ask prices. Dealer markets also serve as primary markets for both IPOs and secondary distributions. Over-the-counter transactions in listed securities take place in the third market. Direct transactions between buyers and sellers are made in the fourth market. Market conditions are commonly classified as "bull" or "bear," depending on whether securities prices are generally rising or falling. Broker markets bring together buyers and sellers to make trades. Included are the New York Stock Exchange, the NYSE Amex, regional stock exchanges, foreign stock exchanges, options exchanges, and futures exchanges. In these markets the forces of supply and demand drive the transactions on the floor of the exchange and determine prices. These securities exchanges are secondary markets where existing securities trade.	over-the-counter (OTC) market, *p. 94* primary market, *p. 89* private placement, *p. 89* prospectus, *p. 90* public offering, *p. 89* red herring, *p. 90* rights offering, *p. 89* secondary distributions, *p. 98* secondary market, *p. 93* Securities and Exchange Commission (SEC), *p. 89* securities markets, *p. 89* selling group, *p. 91* third market, *p. 99* underwriting, *p. 91* underwriting syndicate, *p. 91*	MyFinanceLab Study Plan 3.3
LG4 Review the key aspects of the globalization of securities markets, and discuss the importance of international markets. Securities exchanges operate in over 100 countries—both large and small. Foreign security investments can be made indirectly by buying shares of a U.S.-based multinational with substantial foreign operations or by purchasing shares of a mutual fund that invests primarily in foreign securities. Direct foreign investment can be achieved by purchasing securities on foreign exchanges, by buying securities of foreign companies that are traded on U.S. exchanges, or by buying American depositary shares. International investments can enhance returns, but they entail added risk, particularly currency exchange risk.	American depositary receipts (ADRs), *p. 103* American depositary shares (ADSs), *p. 103* currency exchange rate, *p. 103* currency exchange risk, *p. 104* diversification, *p. 101* Yankee bonds, *p. 103*	MyFinanceLab Study Plan 3.4 Video Learning Aid for Problem P3.3
LG5 Discuss trading hours and the regulation of securities markets. Investors now can trade securities outside regular market hours (9:30 A.M. to 4:00 P.M., eastern time). Most after-hours markets are crossing markets, in which orders are filled only if they can be matched. Trading activity during these sessions can be quite risky. The securities markets are regulated by the federal Securities and Exchange Commission and by state commissions. The key federal laws regulating the securities industry are the Securities Act of 1933, the Securities Exchange Act of 1934, the Maloney Act of 1938, the Investment Company Act of 1940, the Investment Advisers Act of 1940, the Securities Acts Amendments of 1975, the Insider Trading and Fraud Act of 1988, and the Sarbanes-Oxley Act of 2002.	crossing markets, *p. 105* ethics, *p. 105* insider trading, *p. 105*	MyFinanceLab Study Plan 3.5

What You Should Know	Key Terms	Where to Practice
LG6 Explain long purchases, margin transactions, and short sales. Most investors make long purchases—buy low, sell high—in expectation of price increases. Many investors establish margin accounts to use borrowed funds to enhance their buying power. The Federal Reserve Board establishes the margin requirement—the minimum investor equity in a margin transaction. The return on capital in a margin transaction is magnified for both positive returns and negative returns. Paper profits can be used to pyramid a margin account by investing its excess margin. The risks of margin trading are the chance of a restricted account or margin call and the consequences of magnified losses due to price declines. Short selling is used when a decline in security prices is anticipated. It involves selling securities, typically borrowed from the broker, to earn a profit by repurchasing them at a lower price in the future. The short seller makes an initial equity deposit with the broker. If the price of a shorted stock rises, the investor may receive a margin call and must then either increase the deposit with the broker or buy back the stock to cover the short position. The major advantage of selling short is the chance to profit from a price decline. The disadvantages of selling short are the unlimited potential for loss and the fact that short sellers never earn dividend (or interest) income. Short selling is used primarily to seek speculative profits.	debit balance, *p. 111* excess margin, *p. 113* financial leverage, *p. 108* initial margin, *p. 110* long purchase, *p. 107* maintenance margin, *p. 111* margin account, *p. 110* margin call, *p. 111* margin loan, *p. 110* margin requirement, *p. 108* margin trading, *p. 107* prime rate, *p. 110* pyramiding, *p. 113* restricted account, *p. 111* short selling, *p. 114*	MyFinanceLab Study Plan 3.6 Excel Tables 3.3, 3.5 Video Learning Aid for Problem P3.19

Log into MyFinanceLab, take a chapter test, and get a personalized Study Plan that tells you which concepts you understand and which ones you need to review. From there, MyFinanceLab will give you further practice, tutorials, animations, videos, and guided solutions.
Log into **www.myfinancelab.com**

Discussion Questions

LG2 Q3.1 From 1990 to 2005, the average IPO rose by more than 20% in its first day of trading. In 1999, 117 deals doubled in price on the first day, compared to only 39 in the previous 24 years combined. Since 2000, no deals doubled on the first day. What factors might contribute to the huge first-day returns on IPOs? Some critics of the current IPO system claim that underwriters may knowingly underprice an issue. Why might they do this? Why might issuing companies accept lower IPO prices? What impact do institutional investors have on IPO pricing?

LG1 LG3 Q3.2 Why do you think some large, well-known companies such as Cisco Systems, Intel, and Microsoft prefer to trade on the Nasdaq OMX markets rather than on an organized securities exchange such as the NYSE (for which they easily meet the listing requirements)? Discuss the pros and cons of listing on an organized securities exchange.

LG1 LG2 LG4 Q3.3 On the basis of the current structure of the world's financial markets and your knowledge of the NYSE and Nasdaq OMX markets, describe the key features, functions, and problems that would be faced by a single global market (exchange) on which transactions can be made in all securities of all of the world's major companies. Discuss the likelihood of such a market developing.

LG5 Q3.4 Critics of longer trading hours believe that expanded trading sessions turn the stock market into a casino and place the emphasis more on short-term gains than on long-term investment. Do you agree? Why or why not? Is it important to have a "breathing period" to reflect on the day's market activity? Why are smaller brokerages and ECNs, more than the NYSE and Nasdaq, pushing for longer trading hours?

LG6 Q3.5 Describe how, if at all, conservative and aggressive investors might use each of the following types of transactions as part of their investment programs. Contrast these two types of investors in view of these preferences.
a. Long purchase
b. Margin trading
c. Short selling

Problems

All problems are available on www.myfinancelab.com

LG4 P3.1 The current exchange rate between the U.S. dollar and the Japanese yen is 80 (yen/$). How many dollars would you get for 1,000 Japanese yen?

LG4 P3.2 An investor recently sold some stock in a European company that was worth 20,000 euros. The U.S.$/euro exchange rate is currently 1.300. How many U.S. dollars will the investor receive?

 LG4 P3.3 In each of the following cases, calculate the price of one share of the foreign stock measured in United States dollars (US$).
a. A Belgian stock priced at 103.2 euros (€) when the exchange rate is 0.8595 €/US$.
b. A Swiss stock priced at 93.3 Swiss francs (Sf) when the exchange rate is 1.333 Sf/US$.
c. A Japanese stock priced at 1,350 yen (¥) when the exchange rate is 110 ¥/US$.

 LG4 P3.4 Erin McQueen purchased 50 shares of BMW, a German stock traded on the Frankfurt Exchange, for 64.5 euros (€) per share exactly 1 year ago when the exchange rate was 0.67 €/US$. Today the stock is trading at 71.8 (€) per share, and the exchange rate is 0.75 €/US$.
a. Did the € depreciate or appreciate relative to the US$ during the past year? Explain.
b. How much in US$ did Erin pay for her 50 shares of BMW when she purchased them a year ago?
c. For how much in US$ can Erin sell her BMW shares today?
d. Ignoring brokerage fees and taxes, how much profit (or loss) in US$ will Erin realize on her BMW stock if she sells it today?

LG5 P3.5 An investor believes that the U.S. dollar will rise in value relative to the Japanese yen. The same investor is considering two investments with identical risk and return characteristics: One is a Japanese yen investment and the other is a U.S. dollar investment. Should the investor purchase the Japanese yen investment?

LG6 P3.6 Elmo Inc.'s stock is currently selling at $60 per share. For each of the following situations (ignoring brokerage commissions), calculate the gain or loss that Courtney Schinke realizes if she makes a 100-share transaction.

a. She sells short and repurchases the borrowed shares at $70 per share.
b. She takes a long position and sells the stock at $75 per share.
c. She sells short and repurchases the borrowed shares at $45 per share.
d. She takes a long position and sells the stock at $60 per share.

LG6 P3.7 Assume that an investor buys 100 shares of stock at $50 per share, putting up a 60% margin.
a. What is the debit balance in this transaction?
b. How much equity capital must the investor provide to make this margin transaction?

LG6 P3.8 Assume that an investor buys 100 shares of stock at $50 per share, putting up a 60% margin. If the stock rises to $60 per share, what is the investor's new margin position?

LG6 P3.9 Assume that an investor buys 50 shares of stock at $45 per share, putting up a 70% margin.
a. What is the debit balance in this transaction?
b. How much equity funds must the investor provide to make this margin transaction?
c. If the stock rises to $65 per share, what is the investor's new margin position?

LG6 P3.10 Miguel Torres purchased 100 shares of CantWin.com.com for $50 per share, using as little of his own money as he could. His broker has a 50% initial margin requirement and a 30% maintenance margin requirement. The price of the stock falls to $30 per share. What does Miguel need to do?

LG6 P3.11 Jerri Kingston bought 100 shares of stock at $80 per share using an initial margin of 60%. Given a maintenance margin of 25%, how far does the stock have to drop before Jerri faces a margin call? (Assume that there are no other securities in the margin account.)

LG6 P3.12 An investor buys 200 shares of stock selling at $80 per share using a margin of 60%. The stock pays annual dividends of $1 per share. A margin loan can be obtained at an annual interest cost of 8%. Determine what return on invested capital the investor will realize if the price of the stock increases to $104 within 6 months. What is the annualized rate of return on this transaction?

LG6 P3.13 Marlene Bellamy purchased 300 shares of Writeline Communications stock at $55 per share using the prevailing minimum initial margin requirement of 50%. She held the stock for exactly 4 months and sold it without brokerage costs at the end of that period. During the 4-month holding period, the stock paid $1.50 per share in cash dividends. Marlene was charged 9% annual interest on the margin loan. The minimum maintenance margin was 25%.
a. Calculate the initial value of the transaction, the debit balance, and the equity position on Marlene's transaction.
b. For each of the following share prices, calculate the actual margin percentage, and indicate whether Marlene's margin account would have excess equity, would be restricted, or would be subject to a margin call.
   1. $45
   2. $70
   3. $35
c. Calculate the dollar amount of (1) dividends received and (2) interest paid on the margin loan during the 4-month holding period.
d. Use each of the following sale prices at the end of the 4-month holding period to calculate Marlene's annualized rate of return on the Writeline Communications stock transaction.
   1. $50
   2. $60
   3. $70

LG6 **P3.14** Not long ago, Jack Edwards bought 200 shares of Almost Anything Inc. at $45 per share; he bought the stock on margin of 60%. The stock is now trading at $60 per share, and the Federal Reserve has recently lowered *initial margin* requirements to 50%. Jack now wants to do a little pyramiding and buy another 300 shares of the stock. What is the minimum amount of equity that he'll have to put up in this transaction?

LG6 **P3.15** An investor short sells 100 shares of a stock for $20 per share. The initial margin is 50%. How much equity will be required in the account to complete this transaction?

LG6 **P3.16** An investor short sells 100 shares of a stock for $20 per share. The initial margin is 50%. Ignoring transaction costs, how much will be in the investor's account after this transaction if this is the only transaction the investor has undertaken and the investor has deposited only the required amount?

LG6 **P3.17** An investor short sells 100 shares of a stock for $20 per share. The initial margin is 50%, and the maintenance margin is 30%. The price of the stock falls to $12 per share. What is the margin, and will there be a *margin call*?

LG6 **P3.18** An investor short sells 100 shares of a stock for $20 per share. The *initial margin* is 50%, and the maintenance margin is 30%. The price of the stock rises to $28 per share. What is the margin, and will there be a margin call?

LG6 **P3.19** Calculate the profit or loss per share realized on each of the following short-sale transactions.

Transaction	Stock Sold Short at Price/Share ($)	Stock Purchased to Cover Short at Price/Share Transaction ($)
A	75	83
B	30	24
C	18	15
D	27	32
E	53	45

LG6 **P3.20** Charlene Hickman expected the price of Bio International shares to drop in the near future in response to the expected failure of its new drug to pass FDA tests. As a result, she sold short 200 shares of Bio International at $27.50. How much would Charlene earn or lose on this transaction if she repurchased the 200 shares 4 months later at each of the following prices per share?
   a. $24.75
   b. $25.13
   c. $31.25
   d. $27.00

Visit **www.myfinancelab.com** for web exercises, spreadsheets, and other online resources.

Case Problem 3.1   Dara's Dilemma: What to Buy?

LG6 Dara Simmons, a 40-year-old financial analyst and divorced mother of two teenage children, considers herself a savvy investor. She has increased her investment portfolio considerably over the past 5 years. Although she has been fairly conservative with her investments, she now feels more confident in her investment knowledge and would like to branch out into some new areas that could bring higher returns. She has between $20,000 and $25,000 to invest.

Attracted to the hot market for technology stocks, Dara was interested in purchasing a tech IPO stock and identified NewestHighTech.com, a company that makes sophisticated computer chips for wireless Internet connections, as a likely prospect. The 1-year-old company had received some favorable press when it got early-stage financing and again when its chip was accepted by a major cell phone manufacturer.

Dara also was considering an investment in 400 shares of Casinos International common stock, currently selling for $54 per share. After a discussion with a friend who is an economist with a major commercial bank, Dara believes that the long-running bull market is due to cool off and that economic activity will slow down. With the aid of her stockbroker, Dara researches Casinos International's current financial situation and finds that the future success of the company may hinge on the outcome of pending court proceedings on the firm's application to open a new floating casino on a nearby river. If the permit is granted, it seems likely that the firm's stock will experience a rapid increase in value, regardless of economic conditions. On the other hand, if the company fails to get the permit, the falling stock price will make it a good candidate for a short sale.

Dara felt that the following alternatives were open to her:

Alternative 1: Invest $20,000 in NewestHighTech.com when it goes public.

Alternative 2: Buy Casinos International now at $54 per share and follow the company closely.

Alternative 3: Sell Casinos short at $54 in anticipation that the company's fortunes will change for the worse.

Alternative 4: Wait to see what happens with the casino permit and then decide whether to buy or short sell the Casinos International stock.

Questions

a. Evaluate each of these alternatives. On the basis of the limited information presented, recommend the one you feel is best.

b. If Casinos International's stock price rises to $60, what will happen under alternatives 2 and 3? Evaluate the pros and cons of these outcomes.

c. If the stock price drops to $45, what will happen under alternatives 2 and 3? Evaluate the pros and cons of these outcomes.

Case Problem 3.2   Ravi Dumar's High-Flying Margin Account

LG6 Ravi Dumar is a stockbroker who lives with his wife, Sasha, and their five children in Milwaukee, Wisconsin. Ravi firmly believes that the only way to make money in the market is to follow an aggressive investment posture—for example, to use margin trading. In fact, Ravi has built himself a substantial margin account over the years. He currently holds $75,000 worth of stock in his margin account, though the debit balance in the account amounts to only $30,000. Recently Ravi uncovered a stock that, on the basis of extensive analysis, he feels is about to take off. The stock, Running Shoes (RS), currently trades at $20 per share. Ravi feels it should soar to at least $50 within a year. RS pays no dividends, the prevailing initial margin requirement is 50%, and margin loans are now carrying an annual interest charge of 10%. Because Ravi feels so strongly about RS, he wants to do some pyramiding by using his margin account to purchase 1,000 shares of the stock.

Questions

a. Discuss the concept of pyramiding as it applies to this investment situation.

b. What is the present margin position (in percent) of Ravi's account?

c. Ravi buys the 1,000 shares of RS through his margin account (bear in mind that this is a $20,000 transaction).

   1. What will the margin position of the account be after the RS transaction if Ravi follows the prevailing initial margin (50%) and uses $10,000 of his money to buy the stock?

   2. What if he uses only $2,500 equity and obtains a margin loan for the balance ($17,500)?

   3. How do you explain the fact that the stock can be purchased with only 12.5% margin when the prevailing initial margin requirement is 50%?

d. Assume that Ravi buys 1,000 shares of RS stock at $20 per share with a minimum cash investment of $2,500 and that the stock does take off and its price rises to $40 per share in 1 year.

   1. What is the return on invested capital for this transaction?

   2. What return would Ravi have earned if he had bought the stock without margin—that is, if he had used all his own money?

e. What do you think of Ravi's idea to pyramid? What are the risks and rewards of this strategy?

Excel with Spreadsheets

You have just learned about the mechanics of margin trading and want to take advantage of the potential benefits of financial leverage. You have decided to open a margin account with your broker and to secure a margin loan. The specifics of the account are as follows:

- Initial margin requirement is 70%.

- Maintenance margin is 30%.

- You are informed that if the value of your account falls below the maintenance margin, your account will be subject to a margin call.

You have been following the price movements of a stock over the past year and believe that it is currently undervalued and that the price will rise in the near future. You feel that the opening of a margin account is a good investment strategy. You have decided to purchase 3 round lots (i.e., 100 shares per round lot) of the stock at its current price of $25 per share.

Create a spreadsheet similar to the spreadsheet for Table 3.3, which can be viewed at www.myfinancelab.com, to model and analyze the following market transactions.

Questions

a. Calculate the value of the investment in the stock if you did not make use of margin trading. In other words, what is the value of the investment if it is funded by 100% cash equity?

b. Calculate the debit balance and the cash equity in the investment at the time of opening a margin account, adhering to the initial margin requirement.

c. If you use margin and the price of the stock rises by $15 to $40/share, calculate the capital gain earned and the return on investor's equity.

d. What is the current margin percentage based on question c?

e. If you use margin and the price of the stock falls by $15 to $10/share, calculate the capital loss and the respective return on investor's equity.

f. What is the new margin percentage based on question e, and what is the implication for you, the investor?

4

Firms and the Financial Market

LEARNING GOALS

LG1 Describe the structure and functions of financial markets.

LG2 Distinguish between commercial banks and other financial institutions in the financial marketplace.

LG3 Describe the different securities markets for bonds and stocks.

Principles P2, P4, and P5 Applied

When reading this chapter, you should keep in mind three of the basic principles of finance: **P** Principle 2: **There Is a Risk-Return Tradeoff, P** Principle 4: **Market Prices Reflect Information,** and **P** Principle 5: **Individuals Respond to Incentives.** Financial markets are organized to offer investors a wide range of investment opportunities that have different risks and different expected rates of return that reflect those risks. The goal of these markets is to provide investors with opportunities that best fit their risk and return objectives, while at the same time to provide businesses with opportunities to raise funds—to train employees, do research, and build new plants—at prices that appropriately reflect the prospects of the business.

If you have a student loan or a car loan, you have already been introduced to financial markets. You are spending more than you currently earn and have borrowed money through the financial markets to make ends meet. But once you graduate and enter the workforce, you may earn more than you spend and therefore be able to save. Once again, you will become involved in the financial markets, but this time as a saver rather than a borrower. This pattern of borrowing and saving also holds true for businesses, as they borrow money to finance their investments and as they invest their savings in the hopes of generating even more money in the future.

In this chapter we provide a preliminary overview of the U.S. financial markets. We first review some of the primary institutions that facilitate the transfer of money from investors to companies and individuals. Next, we discuss the securities markets in which different securities issued by businesses are bought and sold. The primary objective of this chapter is to provide a sense of the richness of the financial marketplace, the critical role that it plays in each of our lives, and how corporations use the financial markets to raise capital.

Defined Benefit vs. Defined Contribution Retirement Plans

When you start your first job after graduating, your employer will probably give you the option of automatically investing part of your paycheck each pay period for your retirement. Learning about the financial markets will help you analyze your options and make good selections. Twenty years ago, retirement plans were typically **defined benefit plans**. You would work for only one company, and the company would reward your loyalty and hard work by paying you a pension during your retirement based on your years of employment and the level of pay that you earned. In other words, the company set aside money to pay your pension benefit and invested it for you. Today, people change jobs often, and pension plans like the one just described are very rare. Instead, most employers now offer their employees **defined contribution plans**, such as a 401(k) savings plan. With a defined contribution pension plan, you, the employee, and your employer make periodic cash contributions to your retirement fund that you must take responsibility for investing. So, it doesn't matter whether you're a doctor, lawyer, truck driver, or salesperson, you are going to be a pension fund manager.

Your Turn: See Discussion Question 4–1.

The Basic Structure of the U.S. Financial Markets

LG1 Businesses typically opt to take on the form of a corporation when they need to raise large amounts of capital. In this chapter, we will demonstrate how a corporation raises capital using the U.S. financial markets.

A financial market is any place where money and credit are exchanged. When you take out a car loan from your bank, you participate in the financial markets. Within the financial markets there are three principal sets of players that interact:

1. **Borrowers.** Those who need money to finance their purchases. This includes businesses that need money to finance their investments or to expand their inventories as well as individuals who borrow money to purchase a new automobile or a new home.

2. **Savers (Investors).** Those who have money to invest. These are principally individuals who save money for a variety of reasons, such as accumulating a down payment for a home or saving for a return to graduate school. Firms also save when they have excess cash.

3. **Financial Institutions (Intermediaries).** The financial institutions and markets that help bring borrowers and savers together. The financial institution you are probably most familiar with is the **commercial bank,** a financial institution that accepts deposits and makes loans, such as Bank of America or Citibank, where you might have a checking account. However, as we discuss in the next section, there are many other types of financial institutions that bring together borrowers and savers.

The Financial Marketplace: Financial Institutions

LG2 The financial markets facilitate the movement of money from savers, who tend to be individuals, to borrowers, who tend to be businesses. In return for the use of the savers' money, borrowers provide the savers with a return on their investment.

As shown in Figure 4.1, the institutions that make up the financial marketplace consist of commercial banks, finance companies, insurance companies, investment banks, and investment companies. We call these institutions that help bring together individuals and businesses **financial intermediaries,** because these institutions stand between those who have money to invest and those who need money. Financial markets are often described by the maturities of the securities traded in them. For example, the **money markets** are markets for short-term debt instruments, with "short-term" meaning maturities of one year or less. On the other hand, **capital markets** are markets for long-term financial instruments. "Long-term" here means having maturities that extend beyond one year.

There are no national boundaries on financial markets. A borrower in Brazil, for example, might borrow money from a bank in London to finance a plant expansion. Furthermore, it's not just individuals and companies that raise money and invest in the global financial markets. Governments can enter the financial markets when they are experiencing a deficit and need to raise money to finance their expenditures. Governments can also enter financial markets when they have more money than they plan to spend and want to invest

FIGURE 4.1 Financial Markets, Institutions, and the Circle of Money

Financial markets consist of institutions that facilitate the transfer of savings from individuals and firms with excess cash to borrowers who have less cash than they need.

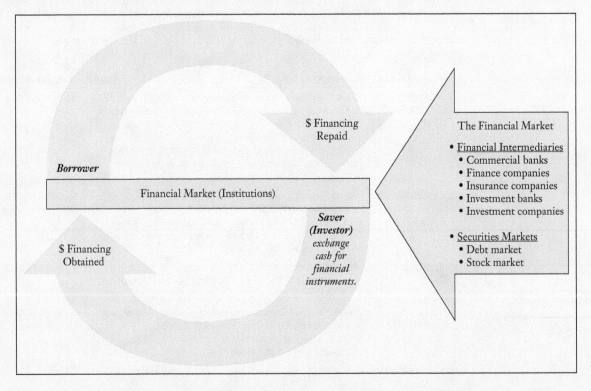

the surplus. For example, the Chinese government invests huge sums of money in U.S. Treasury bonds, which are long-term debt securities issued by the U.S. government.

Commercial Banks: Everyone's Financial Marketplace

As previously mentioned, the commercial bank is probably the first financial intermediary each of us has dealt with in the financial marketplace. And, because they provide many firms with their initial funding, commercial banks also tend to be one of the first financial intermediaries that businesses deal with. Banks collect the savings of individuals as well as businesses and then lend these pooled savings to other individuals and businesses. They make money by charging a rate of interest to borrowers that exceeds the rate they pay to savers. They are also one of the major lenders to businesses.

In the United States, although banks can loan money to industrial corporations, banks are prohibited by law from owning them. This restriction prevents banks from loaning money to the industrial firms that they own; however, this restriction is not universal around the world. For instance, in countries such as Japan and Germany, banks are among the largest owners of industrial firms. Table 4.1 lists the four largest banks in the United States and their total deposits. It is very possible that you will recognize your personal bank among this list because the very largest banks operate

TABLE 4.1	FOUR LARGEST COMMERCIAL BANKS IN THE UNITED STATES AT THE END OF THE THIRD QUARTER 2009

Commercial banks are ranked by the total dollar value of their deposits. Most large banks are owned by holding companies, which are companies that own other types of businesses in addition to the bank. However, the types of businesses that holding companies can own are restricted by federal law. Any firm that owns or controls 25 percent or more of a commercial bank is classified as a bank holding company and must register with the Federal Reserve System, which is the primary regulator of commercial banking in the United States. The financial crisis of 2008–2009 led to consolidations of weaker banks, most notably the acquisition of Wachovia by Wells Fargo.

Institution Name	Description	Total Deposits ($ in thousands)
JPMorgan Chase & Co. (JPM)	This financial holding company provides a range of financial services worldwide through six segments: Investment Banking, Retail Financial Services, Card Services, Commercial Banking, Treasury and Securities Services, and Asset Management. The company was founded in 1823 and is headquartered in New York, New York.	$1,162,998,000
Bank of America Corporation (BAC)	As of August 2, 2012, the company operated approximately 5,693 retail banking offices and 18,000 automated teller machines. Bank of America was founded in 1874 and is headquartered in Charlotte, North Carolina.	$1,062,273,625
Citigroup, Inc. (C)	As of August 3, 2012, Citigroup operated through a network of 1,036 offices. The company was founded in 1812 and is based in New York, New York.	$ 950,510,000
Wells Fargo Bank (WFC)	Wells Fargo & Company was founded in 1852 and is headquartered in San Francisco, California. The bank acquired Wachovia Corporation in 2008, resulting in 6,345 offices.	$ 921,071,000

Source: http://www.ibanknet.com/scripts/callreports/fiList.aspx?type=031

throughout the entire United States, and the 25 largest banks hold more than 50 percent of total deposits.

Non-Bank Financial Intermediaries

In addition to commercial banks, there are a number of highly specialized financial intermediaries that also provide financial services to businesses. These include:

- financial services corporations, such as General Electric's (GE) GE Capital division and CIT Corporation (CIT);

- insurance companies, such as American International Group, Inc. (AIG), and Prudential (PRU);

- investment banks, such as Goldman Sachs (GS) and Morgan Stanley (MS); and

- investment companies, including mutual funds, hedge funds, and private equity firms.

Financial Services Corporations Perhaps the best-known financial service corporation in the world is GE Capital, the finance unit of the General Electric Corporation. GE Capital provides commercial loans, financing programs, commercial insurance, equipment leasing of every kind, and other services, in over 35 countries around the world. GE provides credit services to more than 130 million customers, including consumers, retailers, auto dealers, and mortgage lenders, offering products and services ranging from credit cards to debt consolidation to home equity loans. CIT Group, Inc. is another commercial finance company that offers a wide range of financing services to businesses. The important thing to note here is that although financial services corporations are in the lending or financing business, they are not commercial banks.

Insurance Companies Insurance companies are by definition in the business of selling insurance to individuals and businesses to protect their investments. This means that they collect premiums, hold the premiums in reserves until there is an insured loss, and then pay out claims to the holders of the insurance contracts. Note that in the course of collecting and holding premiums, the insurance companies build up huge pools of reserves to pay these claims. These reserves are then used in various types of investments, including loans to individuals and businesses. American International Group, Inc. (AIG) is now a household name because of the debt market crisis of 2008 and the ensuing government bailout. However, the company's business activities serve as an example of the degree to which insurance companies have become involved in business finance. AIG not only sells insurance products but also provides financial services, including aircraft and equipment leasing, consumer finance, insurance premium financing, and debt and loan insurance. Of particular note in this listing of services is debt and loan insurance, which includes selling guarantees to lenders that reimburse them should the loans they made go into default. This type of transaction is called a **credit default swap.**

Investment Banks **Investment banks** are specialized financial intermediaries that help companies and governments raise money and provide advisory services to client firms when they enter into major transactions such as buying or merging with other firms. Prominent firms that provide investment banking services include Bank of America, Merrill Lynch, Barclays, Citigroup, Credit Suisse, Deutsche Bank, Goldman Sachs, HSBC, JPMorgan Chase, Morgan Stanley, and UBS AG.

Investment Companies

Investment companies are financial institutions that pool the savings of individual savers and invest the money, purely for investment purposes, in the securities issued by other companies.

Mutual Funds and Exchange-Traded Funds (ETFs) Perhaps the most widely known type of investment company is the **mutual fund**, a special type of intermediary through which individuals can invest in virtually all of the securities offered in the financial markets.[1] When individuals invest in a mutual fund, they receive shares in a fund that is professionally managed according to a stated investment objective or goal—for example, investing only in international stocks. Shares in the mutual fund grant ownership claim to a proportion of the mutual fund's portfolio.

A share in a mutual fund is not really like a share of stock because you can only buy and sell shares in the mutual fund directly from the mutual fund itself. The price that you pay when you buy your shares and the price you receive when you sell your shares is called the mutual fund's **net asset value** (**NAV**), which is calculated daily based on the total value of the fund divided by the number of mutual fund shares outstanding. In effect, as the value of the mutual fund investments goes up, so does the price of the mutual fund's shares.

THE BUSINESS OF LIFE

Controlling Costs in Mutual Funds

In choosing the right mutual fund, one thing is clear—costs kill. You will want to pick your fund with an eye toward keeping expenses down. In fact, the Securities and Exchange Commission has put together a website (www.sec.gov/investor/tools/mfcc/mfcc-int.htm) to show you how much damage mutual fund expenses will do to your investment. If you start with $10,000 and invest it for 30 years, achieving gross returns (before expenses) of 10.2 percent (the market average for the last three-quarters of a century), and assuming fund operating expenses of 1.4 percent (the average expense on a U.S. domestic stock fund), your $10,000 will grow to $120,713. That sounds pretty good until you notice that the cost of that 1.4 percent operating expense plus foregone earnings on your investment totals $63,554! That's over 34 percent of the gross earnings of the fund.

If you knock expenses down to 0.18 percent, your investment grows to $174,572 and your expenses drop down to $9,695!

It is possible to cut your expenses down to as little as 0.10 percent by investing in an index fund (i.e., a fund that tries to track a market index, such as the S&P 500, by buying the stocks that make up that index). In general, index funds perform better than the actively managed funds. In fact, from 1985 to 2000, 84.5 percent of U.S. actively managed stock mutual funds (as opposed to index funds) underperformed the S&P 500 index, with 77.5 percent underperforming over the entire 10 years and 81.6 percent underperforming in the most recent 5 years. According to a study from Jeremy J. Siegel's book *Stocks for the Long Run*, between 1982 and 2003, there were only three years in which more than 50 percent of mutual funds beat the S&P 500.

Your Turn: See Discussion Question 4–9.

---

[1] For a more in-depth discussion of mutual funds go to http://www.sec.gov/answers/mutfund.htm.

Mutual funds can either be *load* or *no-load* funds. A **load fund** is a mutual fund that is sold through a broker, financial advisor, or financial planner who earns a commission in the form of the load fee when he or she sells shares of the mutual fund. The term *load* refers to the sales commission you pay when acquiring ownership shares. These commissions can be quite large, typically in the 3.0 to 6.0 percent range, but in some cases they can run as high as 8.5 percent. A mutual fund that doesn't charge a commission is referred to as a **no-load fund.** When you purchase a no-load mutual fund, you generally don't deal with a broker or advisor. Instead, you deal directly with the mutual fund investment company via its website, by direct mail, or through an 800 telephone number.

An **exchange-traded fund** (or **ETF**) is very much like a mutual fund except for the fact that the ownership shares in the ETF can be bought and sold on the stock exchanges. Most ETFs track an index, such as the Dow Jones Industrial Average or the S&P 500, and generally have relatively low expenses.

Mutual funds and ETFs provide a cost-effective way to diversify, which reduces risk—a great benefit for the small investor. If you only have $10,000 to invest, it would be difficult to diversify by purchasing shares of individual companies, as you would have to pay a brokerage commission for each individual stock you purchase. For example, buying 50 different stocks is likely to cost you $500 or more in commissions, which would be 5 percent of the amount invested. By buying a mutual fund or ETF you can indirectly purchase a portfolio of 50 or more stocks with just one transaction.

Hedge Funds A **hedge fund** is very much like a mutual fund, but hedge funds are less regulated and tend to take more risk. They also tend to more actively influence the managers of the corporations that they invest in. Because of the higher risk, hedge funds are open to a limited range of investors who are deemed to be sufficiently savvy. Only an **accredited investor,** which means an individual with a net worth that exceeds $1 million, can invest in a hedge fund.

Management fees are also quite a bit higher for hedge funds; they typically run at about 2 percent of the assets and include an incentive fee (typically 20 percent of profits) based on the fund's overall performance.

Private Equity Firms A **private equity firm** is a financial intermediary that invests in equities that are not traded on the public capital markets. Two types of private equity firms dominate this group: venture capital (VC) firms and leveraged buyout (LBO) firms. **Venture capital firms** raise money from investors (wealthy people and other financial institutions), which they then use to provide financing for private start-up companies when they are first founded. For example, Sevin Rosen Funds, established in 1980, has provided venture financing to Cypress Semiconductor (CY) and Silicon Graphics (SGIC). Kleiner Perkins Caufield & Byers, or KPCB as it is commonly called, is a venture capital firm located in Silicon Valley. KPCB is perhaps best known today for its involvement in the initial financing of Google (GOOG). It has also partnered with Apple to found the iFund™, a $100 million investment initiative that will fund market-changing ideas and products that extend the iPhone and iPod Touch platform.

The second major category of private equity firms is the **leveraged buyout fund.** These funds acquire established firms that typically have not been performing very well with the objective of making them profitable again and then selling them. LBO funds have been the subject of a number of movies, including *Barbarians at the Gate, Other People's Money,* and *Wall Street.*

Prominent LBO private equity firms include Cerberus Capital Management, L.P., which purchased the Chrysler Corporation from Daimler Benz, and TPG (formerly

Texas Pacific Group), which has invested in a number of prominent firms, including Continental Airlines (CAL), Ducati (DMH.BE), Neiman Marcus, Burger King (BKC), MGM (MGM), Harrah's (HAG.HM), and Freescale Semiconductor (FSL-B). A third well-known LBO private equity firm is KKR (Kohlberg, Kravis, and Roberts), whose investment in the likes of RJR Nabisco provided the storyline for the popular movie *Barbarians at the Gate.*

The amount of money managed by private equity firms has grown dramatically over the last three decades, with new funds raised surpassing $262 billion in 2011. Three-quarters of the total is raised in North America; the majority of the remainder is raised in Europe. Of the total amount of money managed by private equity firms, roughly two-thirds is invested in the buyout or LBO category. In fact, LBO transactions grew from $7.5 billion in 1991 to $500 billion in 2006! But as you might expect, the number of deals dropped dramatically in the fourth quarter of 2008 and 2009, and is still not up to the 2006 level. However, the dollar amount of capital invested by the private equity intermediaries understates their importance to the economy. Private equity funding is largely responsible for financing the birth of new businesses and underwriting the renovation of old and faltering businesses.

CONCEPTS IN REVIEW

4.1 Explain how individuals and firms use financial intermediaries to raise money in the financial markets.

4.2 How do commercial banks differ from other non-bank financial intermediaries?

4.3 What are examples of investment companies?

4.4 What is a hedge fund, and how does it differ from a mutual fund?

4.5 What are the two principal types of private equity firms?

The Financial Marketplace: Securities Markets

LG3 A **security** is a negotiable instrument that represents a financial claim. It can take the form of ownership (stocks) or a debt agreement. The securities markets allow businesses and individual investors to trade the securities issued by public corporations. Public corporations are those whose debt and equity are traded in public markets. Securities markets are typically discussed in terms of the primary and secondary markets. A **primary market** is a market in which new, as opposed to previously issued, securities are bought and sold for the first time. In this market, firms issue new securities to raise money that they can then use to help finance their businesses. The key feature of the primary market is that the firms selling securities actually receive the money raised.

The **secondary market** is where all subsequent trading of previously issued securities takes place. In this market the issuing firm does not receive any new financing, as the securities it has sold are simply being transferred from one investor to another. The principal benefit of the secondary market for the shareholders of firms that sell their securities to the public is liquidity. That is, if you purchased some of the shares of Google when it went public, you could easily sell those shares in the secondary market if you decided you no longer wanted to hold them. This ability to sell when you want to means that your Google stock is a very liquid investment. As a result, investors are more willing to invest in these securities, which benefits the issuing firm.

How Securities Markets Bring Corporations and Investors Together

Figure 4.2 describes the role of securities markets in bringing investors together with businesses looking for financing. In this regard, the securities markets are just another component of the financial marketplace. They are unique, however, in that investors in securities markets provide money directly to the firms that need it, as opposed to making deposits in commercial banks that then loan money to those firms.

We can think of the process of raising money in the securities markets in terms of the four-step process highlighted in Figure 4.2:

Step 1.   The firm sells securities to investors. Corporations raise money in the securities markets by selling either debt or equity. When the firm initially sells the securities to the public, it is considered to take place in the primary markets. This is the only time the firm receives money in return for its securities.

Step 2.   The firm invests the funds it raises in its business. The corporation invests the cash raised in the security market in hopes that it will generate cash flows—for

FIGURE 4.2

Security Markets Provide a Link between the Corporation and Investors

Step 1: Initially, the corporation raises funds in the financial markets by selling securities (a primary market transaction). Step 2: The corporation then invests this cash in return-generating assets— new projects. Step 3: The cash flow from those assets is either reinvested in the corporation, given back to the investors, or paid to the government in the form of taxes. Step 4: Immediately after the securities have been issued, they are traded among investors in the secondary market, thereby setting their market price.

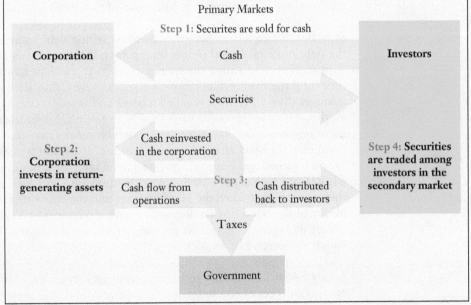

example, it may invest in a new restaurant, a new hotel, a factory expansion, or a new product line.

Step 3. **The firm distributes the cash earned from its investments.** The cash flow from the firm's investments is reinvested in the corporation, paid to the government in taxes, or distributed to the investors who own the securities issued in Step 1. In the latter case, the cash is distributed to the investors who loaned the firm money (that is, bought the firm's debt securities) through the payment of interest and principal. Cash is paid to the investors who bought equity (stock) through the payment of cash dividends or the repurchase of the shares of the firm's previously issued stock.

Step 4. **Securities trading in the secondary market.** Immediately after the securities are sold to the public, the investors who purchased them are free to resell them to other investors. These subsequent transactions take place in the secondary market.

Types of Securities

If you read the financial section of your newspaper or watch financial TV channels such as CNBC, you are already aware of the wide variety of investment alternatives to choose from. These choices fall into one of two basic categories: debt and equity.

Debt Securities Firms borrow money by selling **debt securities** in the debt market. If the debt must be repaid in less than a year, these securities are sold in the short-term debt market, also called the money market. If the debt has a **maturity** (the length of time until the debt is due) between 1 and 10 years, it is often referred to as a **note,** and if longer than 10 years it is called a **bond** and is sold in the capital market. The capital market refers to the market for long-term financial instruments. The vast majority of these bonds pay a fixed interest rate, which means that the interest the owner of the bond receives never changes over its lifetime. Bonds are generally described using fairly exotic terminology. For example, we might say that a bond has a **face** or **par value** of $1,000 and that it pays an 8 percent **coupon rate** with two payments per year. What this means is that when the bond matures and the issuer (borrower) has to repay it, the owner of the bond (the lender) will receive a payment of $1,000. In the meantime, the holder will receive an interest payment every six months equal to $40, or $80 per year, which is 8 percent of $1,000.

Equity Securities **Equity securities** represent ownership of the corporation. There are two major types of equity securities: *common stock* and *preferred stock*. When you buy equity security you are making an investment that you expect will generate a return. However, unlike a bond, which provides a promised set of interest payments and a schedule for the repayment of principal, the returns earned from an equity security are less certain. To further explore this topic, let's take a brief look at both types of equity securities.

Common Stock **Common stock** is a security that represents equity ownership in a corporation, provides voting rights, and entitles the holder to a share of the company's success in the form of dividends and any capital appreciation in the value of the security. Investors who purchase common stock are the residual owners of the firm. This means that the common stockholder's return is earned only after all other security-holder claims (debt and preferred equity) have been satisfied in full.

If you were to purchase 100 shares of Disney's common stock, you would be a part-owner in the company. In essence, you would own an interest in the firm's studios, a piece of its movies, and a piece of its theme parks, including the new park in Shanghai. The more shares you buy, the bigger the portion of Disney you own. What do you get as an owner of Disney's stock? Don't count on free tickets to Disney World or a copy of the latest *Pirates of the Caribbean* movie. As an owner of the firm, you will have voting rights that entitle you to vote for the members of the firm's board of directors who oversee the selection of the management team. But as a small-time investor, you will have limited voting rights—your 100 shares of Disney's stock give you about 0.00000556 percent of Disney's shares. So, you aren't going to have much say about who gets elected to the Disney board of directors. Nonetheless, if Disney earns a profit, you will probably receive a portion of those profits in the form of a dividend payment. *It should be noted that unlike bond payments, firms don't have to pay dividends.* For example, if a company needs money to invest in a new product or project, it can choose to retain all of its earnings within the firm and pay no dividends.

Generally, firms that earn higher profits can pay higher dividends, and this often means that investors place a higher value on that firm's stock. For example, in 1999 the stock price of Qualcomm, a high-tech communications firm, went up 2,621 percent! However, when Qualcomm's profits and dividends, and people's expectations about its future prospects, deteriorated, its stock price fell by 50 percent in 2000, another 26 percent in 2001, and then by another drop of 30 percent in 2002. Since the end of 2002 there have been ups and downs, but by 2013 the price of Qualcomm rose almost three-fold from its 2003 level. This all goes to show that stock prices can fluctuate dramatically.

Preferred Stock Preferred stock, like common stock, is an equity security. However, as the name implies, preferred stockholders take a "preferred" position relative to common shareholders. This means that preferred shareholders receive their dividends before any dividends are distributed to the common stockholders, who receive their dividends from whatever is left over. Note, however, that if the company does not earn enough to pay its interest expenses, neither preferred nor common stockholders will be paid a dividend. However, the dividends promised to the preferred stockholders will generally accrue and must be paid in full before common shareholders can receive any dividends. This feature is oftentimes referred to as a cumulative feature, and preferred stock with this feature is often referred to as cumulative preferred stock. In addition, preferred stockholders have a preferred claim on the distribution of assets of the firm in the event that the firm goes bankrupt and sells or liquidates its assets. Very simply, the firm's creditors (bondholders) get paid first, followed by the preferred stockholders, and anything left goes to the common stockholders. Of interest is that not all firms issue preferred stock.

Preferred stock is sometimes referred to as a hybrid security because it has many characteristics of both common stock and bonds. Preferred stock is similar to common stock in that (i) it has no fixed maturity date, (ii) the nonpayment of dividends does not bring on bankruptcy for the firm, and (iii) the dividends paid on these securities are not deductible for tax purposes. However, preferred stock is similar to corporate bonds in that (i) the dividends paid on the stock, like the interest payments made on bonds, are typically a fixed amount, and (ii) it does not come with any voting rights.

Stock Markets A stock market is a public market in which the stock of companies is traded. Traditionally, the stock markets are classified as either organized security exchanges or the over-the-counter markets. **Organized security exchanges** are tangible entities; that is, they physically occupy space (such as a building or part of a building), and financial instruments are traded on their premises. The **over-the-counter markets** include all security markets except the organized exchanges. In the United States, the largest public market is the New York Stock Exchange (NYSE), whose history is traced back to 1792. Because it occupies a physical space (it is located at 11 Wall Street in Manhattan), it is considered an organized exchange. The common stock of more than 4,000 listed companies is traded on this exchange, which has monthly trading volume that exceeds 20 billion shares! In addition, the total value of the shares of stock listed on the NYSE at the beginning of 2013 reached just over $14.5 trillion. As you might expect, the dramatic stock market slide in 2008 took a toll on this figure; in fact, it was down from its peak of over $18 trillion in 2007.

Today, the NYSE is a hybrid market, having qualities of both an organized exchange and an over-the-counter market, allowing for face-to-face trading between individuals on the floor of the stock exchange in addition to automated electronic trading. As a result, during times of extreme flux in the market, at the opening or close of the market, or on large trades, human judgment can be called upon to make sure that the trade is properly executed.

NASDAQ, which stands for National Association of Securities Dealers Automated Quotations, is an over-the-counter market and describes itself as a "screen-based, floor-less market." NASDAQ was formed in 1971 and is actually home to the securities of more companies than the NYSE. In 2013 some 3,200 companies were listed on NASDAQ, after reaching a peak of 5,556 in 1996. It has become highly popular as the trading mechanism of choice of several fast-growth sectors in the United States, including the high-technology sector. The common stock of computer chip maker Intel (INTC), for example, is traded via the NASDAQ, as is that of Dell (DELL), Starbucks (SBUX), Whole Foods Market (WFM), and Google (GOOG).

Reading Stock Price Quotes Figure 4.3 illustrates how to read stock price quotes from www.google.com/finance. This is just a bit of the information available on Google Finance. You'll also find stock price charts, any news items, Internet discussions, information on related companies, and analyst estimates along with the firm's financial statements and key statistics and ratios. Similar information is given at finance.yahoo.com and Wall Street Journal Online (www.wsj.com) in the "Market Data Center" under the "U.S. Stocks" link.

Other Financial Instruments So far we have touched on only the tip of the iceberg in terms of the variety of different types of financial instruments that are available to investors and firms. Table 4.2 provides a listing of a number of different financial instruments used by firms to raise money, beginning with the shortest-maturity instruments that are traded in the money market and moving through the longest-maturity securities that are traded in the capital market.

Financial Markets and the Financial Crisis Beginning in 2007 the United States experienced its most severe financial crisis since the Great Depression of the 1930s. As a result, some financial institutions collapsed while the government bailed others out, unemployment skyrocketed, the stock market plummeted, and the United States entered into a recession. Although the recession is now officially over, the economy still faces the lingering effects of the financial crisis that continue in the form of both a high rate of unemployment and a dramatic rise in our country's debt.

FIGURE 4.3 Common Stock Price Quotes

The following is typical of what you would see if you looked at www.google.com/finance.

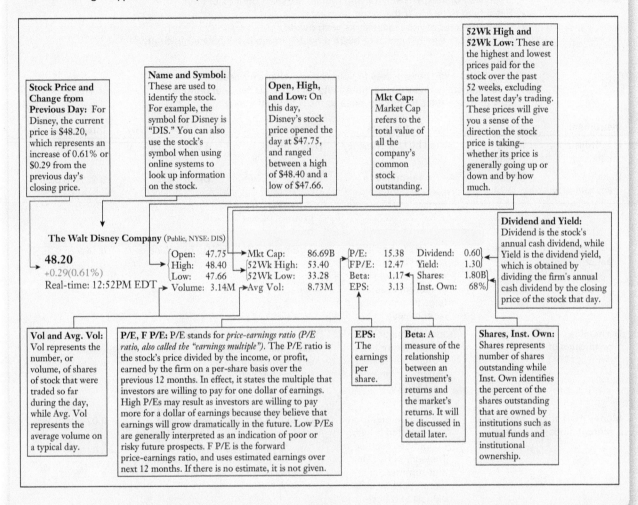

Stock Price and Change from Previous Day: For Disney, the current price is $48.20, which represents an increase of 0.61% or $0.29 from the previous day's closing price.

Name and Symbol: These are used to identify the stock. For example, the symbol for Disney is "DIS." You can also use the stock's symbol when using online systems to look up information on the stock.

Open, High, and Low: On this day, Disney's stock price opened the day at $47.75, and ranged between a high of $48.40 and a low of $47.66.

Mkt Cap: Market Cap refers to the total value of all the company's common stock outstanding.

52Wk High and 52Wk Low: These are the highest and lowest prices paid for the stock over the past 52 weeks, excluding the latest day's trading. These prices will give you a sense of the direction the stock price is taking–whether its price is generally going up or down and by how much.

The Walt Disney Company (Public, NYSE: DIS)

48.20
+0.29(0.61%)
Real-time: 12:52PM EDT

Open:	47.75	Mkt Cap:	86.69B	P/E:	15.38	Dividend:	0.60
High:	48.40	52Wk High:	53.40	FP/E:	12.47	Yield:	1.30
Low:	47.66	52Wk Low:	33.28	Beta:	1.17	Shares:	1.80B
Volume:	3.14M	Avg Vol:	8.73M	EPS:	3.13	Inst. Own:	68%

Dividend and Yield: Dividend is the stock's annual cash dividend, while Yield is the dividend yield, which is obtained by dividing the firm's annual cash dividend by the closing price of the stock that day.

Vol and Avg. Vol: Vol represents the number, or volume, of shares of stock that were traded so far during the day, while Avg. Vol represents the average volume on a typical day.

P/E, F P/E: P/E stands for *price-earnings ratio (P/E ratio, also called the "earnings multiple")*. The P/E ratio is the stock's price divided by the income, or profit, earned by the firm on a per-share basis over the previous 12 months. In effect, it states the multiple that investors are willing to pay for one dollar of earnings. High P/Es may result as investors are willing to pay more for a dollar of earnings because they believe that earnings will grow dramatically in the future. Low P/Es are generally interpreted as an indication of poor or risky future prospects. F P/E is the forward price-earnings ratio, and uses estimated earnings over next 12 months. If there is no estimate, it is not given.

EPS: The earnings per share.

Beta: A measure of the relationship between an investment's returns and the market's returns. It will be discussed in detail later.

Shares, Inst. Own: Shares represents number of shares outstanding while Inst. Own identifies the percent of the shares outstanding that are owned by institutions such as mutual funds and institutional ownership.

Although many factors contributed to the financial crisis, the most immediate cause has been attributed to the collapse of the real estate market and the resulting real estate loan (mortgage) defaults—in particular, what are commonly referred to as subprime mortgages. These were loans made to borrowers whose ability to repay them was highly doubtful. When the market for real estate began to falter in 2006, many of the homebuyers with subprime mortgages began to default. As the economy contracted during the recession, people lost their jobs and could no longer make their mortgage loan payments, resulting in even more defaults.

To complicate the problem, most real estate mortgages were packaged in portfolios and resold to investors around the world. This process of packaging mortgages is called securitization, because it takes loans that cannot be publicly traded and turns them into

TABLE 4.2 CHARACTERISTICS OF DIFFERENT FINANCIAL INSTRUMENTS

Money Market Debt

For the Borrower:
- Good way of inexpensively raising money for short periods of time.
- Rates tend to be lower than long-term rates.
- Can borrow money to match short-term needs.
- If interest rates rise, the cost of borrowing will immediately rise accordingly.

For the Investor:
- Very liquid—you have access to your money when you need it.
- Safe—generally invested in high-quality investments for brief periods.
- Low returns—rates tend to be close to the rate of inflation.

Instrument	Market	Major Participants	Riskiness	Original Maturity	Interest Rates*
U.S. Treasury bills	Money—Debt	Issued by U.S. Treasury	Default-free	4 weeks to 1 year	0.09% to 0.14%
Bankers' acceptances	Money—Debt	A firm's promise to pay, guaranteed by a bank	Low risk of default, dependent on the risk of the guaranteeing bank	Up to 180 days	0.23% to 0.38%
Commercial paper	Money—Debt	Issued by financially secure firms to fund operating expenses or current assets (e.g., inventories and receivables)	Low default risk	Up to 270 days	0.14% to 0.25%
Negotiable certificates of deposit (CDs)	Money—Debt	Issued by major money-center commercial banks with a denomination of at least $100,000 to large investors	Default risk depends on the strength of the issuing bank	2 weeks to 1 year	National average 0.30%
Money market mutual funds	Money—Debt	Issued by mutual funds and invested in debt obligations such as Treasury bills, CDs, and commercial paper; held by individuals and businesses	Low degree of risk	No specific maturity date (can be redeemed any time)	0.02% to 0.19%
Consumer credit, including credit card debt	Money—Debt	Non-mortgage consumer debt issued by banks/credit unions/finance companies	Risk is variable	Varies	Variable depending upon the risk level

Long-Term Debt and Fixed Income Securities Market

For the Borrower:
- Interest rates are locked in over the entire life of the debt.
- Has a tax advantage over common stock in that interest payments are tax deductible, whereas dividend payments are not.

For the Investor:
- Can be used to generate dependable current income.
- Some bonds produce tax-free income.
- Long-term debt tends to produce higher returns than short-term debt.
- Less risky than common stock.
- Investor can lock in an interest rate and know the future returns (assuming the issuer does not default on its payments).

TABLE 4.2   (CONTINUED)

Instrument	Market	Major Participants	Riskiness	Original Maturity	Interest Rates*
U.S. Treasury notes and bonds	Capital— Debt	Issued by the U.S. government to mutual funds, businesses, individuals, and foreign countries	No default risk but price will decline if interest rates rise	Notes have original maturities of 2, 5, and 10 years; bonds have original maturities greater than 10 years	0.17% to 2.31%
Federal agency debt	Capital— Debt	Issued by federal agencies (Fannie Mae, Ginnie Mae, and others) to businesses, individuals, and foreign countries	Close to Treasury debt, but not obligations of the federal government, still very low risk	Up to 30 years	0.14% to 2.74%
Mortgages	Capital— Debt	Borrowings from commercial banks and savings and loans (S&Ls) by individuals	Risk is variable, with subprime mortgages having a good deal of risk	Up to 30 years	2.83% (15-year fixed) to 3.41% (30-year fixed)
Municipal bonds (state and local government bonds)	Capital— Debt	Issued by state and local governments to individuals, institutional investors, and foreign countries	Riskier than U.S. government securities, with the level of risk dependent upon the issuer, but exempt from most taxes	Up to 30 years	3.41% (30-year, AAA-rated bonds)
Corporate bonds	Capital— Debt	Issued by corporations to individuals and institutional investors	Risk is dependent upon the financial strength of the issuer; riskier than U.S. government securities but less risky than preferred and common stocks	In general up to 40 years, however Walt Disney and Coca-Cola have issued 100-year bonds	2.11% (10-year, AAA bonds), 3.85% (20-year AAA bonds)

Preferred Stock	For the Insurer:

For the Insurer:
- Dividends can be omitted without the risk of bankruptcy.
- Has the disadvantage that dividends are not tax deductible for the issuer, whereas interest payments from debt are tax deductible.

For the Investor:
- To corporate investors, it has a tax advantage because at minimum, 70 percent of dividends received are tax free.

Instrument	Market	Major Participants	Riskiness	Original Maturity	Interest Rates*
Preferred stocks	Capital— Equity (Preferred Stock)	Issued by corporations to individuals, other corporations, and institutional investors	Riskier than corporate bonds, but less risky than common stock	No maturity date	Dependent upon risk, generally ranging from 4.03% to 8.47%

(continued)

TABLE 4.2 (CONTINUED)

Common Stock

For the Issuer:
- The issuing firm is not legally obligated to make payments.
- Does not have a maturity date.
- Issuance of common stock increases creditworthiness because the firm has more investor money to cushion the firm in the case of a loss.
- Has a tax disadvantage relative to debt; whereas debt interest payments are deductible for tax purposes, common stock dividends are not.

For the Investor:
- Over the long run, common stock has outperformed debt-based financial assets.
- Along with the increased expected return comes increased risk.

Instrument	Market	Major Participants	Riskiness	Original Maturity	Interest Rates
Common stocks	Capital— Equity (Common Stock)	Issued by corporations to individuals, other corporations, and institutional investors	Risky, with dividends only paid when they are declared	No maturity date	Do not pay interest

*The yields were taken from http://online.wsj.com, http://www.bloomberg.com, http://research.stlouisfed.org, http://finance. yahoo.com, and http://www.bankrate.com, retrieved November 21, 2012.

FINANCE IN A FLAT WORLD

Where's the Money Around the World

The figure shown here describes the total value of financial assets (bonds, equities, and bank assets) in the financial markets for each of the major regions of the world at the end of 2010. Although the totals change from year to year, these data provide some insight into the distribution of the value of financial assets around the world. When it comes to stock market capitalization—that is, the value of all equities—the United States clearly dominates, being the home for about one-third of equities.

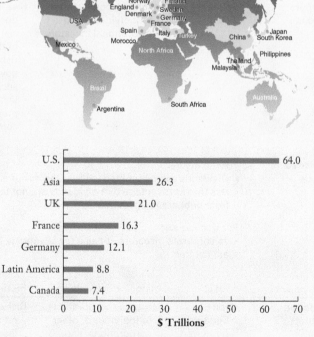

Source: International Monetary Fund, Global Financial Stability Report Statistical Appendix, April 2012, http://www.imf.org/external/pubs/ft/gfsr/2012/01/pdf/statapp.pdf

Your Turn: See Discussion Question 4–10.

securities that can be freely bought and sold by financial institutions. Here's how mortgages are securitized:

1. First, homebuyers borrow money by taking out a mortgage to finance a home purchase.

2. Second, the lender, generally a bank, savings and loan institution, or mortgage broker that made the loan, then sells the mortgage to another firm or financial institution.

3. Third, that financial institution pools together a portfolio of many different mortgages, and the purchase of that pool of mortgages is financed through the sale of securities called mortgage-backed securities, or MBSs.

4. Fourth, these MBSs are sold to investors who can hold them as an investment or resell them to other investors.

This process allows the mortgage bank or other financial institution that made the original mortgage loan to get its money back out of the loan and lend it to someone else. Thus, securitization provides liquidity to the mortgage market and makes it possible for banks to loan more money to homebuyers.

Okay, so what's the catch? As long as lenders properly screen the mortgages to make sure the borrowers are willing and able to repay their home loans and real estate values remain higher than the amount owed, everything works fine. However, if the financial institution that originates the mortgage plans on selling it rather than holding it, it may have less incentive to properly screen the borrower. Why would lenders do this? It all goes back to [P] Principle 5: **Individuals Respond to Incentives**; the lenders made their money by making the loans, and sold them almost immediately. As a result, some lenders were not concerned with whether or not the borrower could repay the loan; they were only concerned with making the loan—to them, repayment was someone else's problem.

As a result, starting around 2006, homeowners began to default on their mortgage loans. These defaults triggered losses at major banks, which in turn triggered a recession, causing people to lose their jobs and, correspondingly, the ability to make their mortgage payments. This was the scenario that played out at least through 2009. In essence, this was a perfect storm of bad loans, falling housing prices, and a contracting economy.

Unfortunately, these problems did not stay in the United States, as banks in Europe also held many of these mortgage-backed securities (MBSs), triggering a world-wide banking crisis. On top of this, European banks hold a lot of the European sovereign debt, so if countries such as Greece default on their debt, the European banking system will be in trouble. The recession that was originally sparked by the banking crisis revealed that the government budget situation in countries such as Greece was unsustainable, leading to the current European debt crisis. Many members of the European Union (EU) are experiencing severe budget problems, including Greece, Italy, Ireland, Portugal, and Spain. These nations are all unable to balance their budgets and face a very real prospect of defaulting on payments tied to government loans.

As a further result of the financial crisis, the stand-alone investment banking industry in the United States is no more. From the time of George Washington until the Great Depression in the 1930s, the U.S. economy experienced financial panics and banking crises about every 15 years. In response to the Great Depression and the failures of 4,004 banks in 1933, Congress enacted the National Banking Act of 1933, of which several sections are commonly referred to as the Glass–Steagall Act. An important component of the Glass–Steagall Act was the separation of commercial banking and the investment industry. Specifically, the act prohibited commercial banks from entering the investment industry in order to limit risks to banks. As a result, a "stand-alone" investment banking industry was created with firms like Lehman Brothers, Bear Stearns, Merrill Lynch, Goldman Sachs, and Morgan Stanley. However, in 1999 Glass–Steagall was repealed, and many commercial banks acquired investment banks, whereas others, such as JPMorgan Chase & Co. (JPM), entered the investment banking business. The advantage of this combination was that it gave investment banks access to stable funding through bank deposits along with the ability to borrow from the Federal Reserve in the case of an emergency, while the commercial bank gained access to the more lucrative, albeit more risky, investment industry.

In the wake of the 2008 financial crisis, the financial industry was again transformed. During the crisis, the major stand-alone investment banks either failed (Lehman Brothers), were acquired by commercial banks (Bear Stearns and Merrill Lynch), or were converted to commercial banks (Morgan Stanley and Goldman Sachs). Indeed, by the end of 2008, there were no major stand-alone investment banking firms left.

Then in 2010 the Dodd–Frank Wall Street Reform and Consumer Protection Act was passed. Under Dodd–Frank, banks as well as non-bank financial institutions are subject to considerably more oversight and are required to be more transparent. Another important feature of this legislation is what is known as the "Volker" rule, which prohibits banks that take deposits from **proprietary trading**, which is using the bank's capital to make speculative bets on derivatives and securities.

The hope is that these changes will increase the stability of the U.S. financial system and ensure that we will no longer be subject to financial crises that throw our economy into a severe recession. However, critics have argued that on one hand the recent legislation has not done enough to protect consumers as well as the safety of the financial system, and on the other hand that it adds unnecessary bureaucracy to our financial institutions.

CONCEPTS IN REVIEW

4.6 What are debt and equity securities, and how do they differ?

4.7 How is a primary market different from a secondary market?

4.8 How does common stock differ from preferred stock?

Applying the Principles of Finance to Chapter 4

▣ Principle 2: **There Is a Risk-Return Tradeoff** Financial markets are organized to offer investors a wide range of investment opportunities that have different risks and different expected rates of return that reflect those risks.

▣ Principle 4: **Market Prices Reflect Information** It is through the operations of the financial markets that new information is efficiently impounded in security prices.

▣ Principle 5: **Individuals Respond to Incentives** One of the reasons for the recent subprime mortgage crisis may have been in improper incentives to screen borrowers.

MyFinanceLab

Here is what you should know after reading this chapter. MyFinanceLab will help you identify what you know and where to go when you need to practice.

What You Should Know	Key Terms	
LG1 **Describe the structure and functions of financial markets.** Financial markets allocate the supply of savings in the economy to the individuals and companies that need the money. A primary market is a market in which new, as opposed to previously issued, securities are bought and sold for the first time. In this market firms issue new securities to raise money that they can then use to help finance their businesses. The key feature of the primary market is that the firms that raise money by selling securities actually receive the money.	Commercial bank, *p. 126*	A financial institution that accepts demand deposits, makes loans, and provides other services to the public.
	Defined benefit plans, *p. 126*	A company retirement plan, such as a pension plan, in which a retired employee receives a specific amount based on his or her salary history and years of service.
	Defined contribution plans, *p. 126*	A company retirement plan, such as a 401(k) plan, in which the employee elects to contribute some amount of his or her salary to the plan and the employee takes responsibility for the investment decisions.
The secondary market is where all subsequent trading of previously issued securities takes place. In this market the issuing firm does not receive any new financing, as the securities it has sold are simply being transferred from one investor to another. The principal benefit to investors of having a secondary market is the ease with which the investor can sell or liquidate investments.	Accredited investor, *p. 131*	Investor who is permitted to invest in certain types of higher-risk investments. These investors include wealthy individuals, corporations, endowments, and retirement plans.
	Capital market, *p. 127*	The market for long-term financial instruments.
	Credit default swap, *p. 129*	An insurance contract that pays off in the event of a credit event such as default or bankruptcy.
LG2 **Distinguish between commercial banks and other financial institutions in the financial marketplace** Financial institutions are intermediaries that stand in the middle between borrowers who need money and savers who have money to invest. Widely varying financial institutions have evolved over time to meet special needs for intermediation, including commercial banks that accept deposits from savers and lend to borrowers, invest-ment banks that help companies sell their securities to investors in order to raise the money they need, and many other institu-tions. Of particular interest are mutual funds that collect the investments of many small investors and invest the pool of funds in stocks, bonds, and other types of securities that are issued by businesses. In recent years, two types of investment com-panies have captured the headlines: hedge funds and private equity funds. Both of these types of investment companies accept investments from other financial institutions or wealthy individuals and invest in speculative and risky ventures.	Exchange-traded fund (ETF), *p. 131*	An investment vehicle traded on stock exchanges much like a share of stock. The entity holds investments in assets that meet the investment objective of the entity (e.g., shares of stock of companies from emerging markets).
	Financial intermediaries, *p. 127*	Institutions whose business is to bring together individuals and institutions with money to invest or lend with other firms or individuals in need of money.
	Hedge fund, *p. 131*	An investment fund that is open to a lim-ited range of investors (accredited investors) and that can undertake a wider range of investment and trading activities than other types of investment funds that are open to the general public (e.g., mutual funds).
	Investment bank, *p. 129*	A financial institution that raises capital, trades in securities, and manages corporate mergers and acquisitions.
	Investment company, *p. 130*	A firm that invests the pooled funds of retail investors for a fee.

What You Should Know	Key Terms	
LG2 (*Continued*)	Leveraged buyout fund, *p. 131*	A private equity firm that raises capital from individual investors and uses these funds along with significant amounts of debt to acquire controlling interests in operating companies.
	Load fund, *p. 131*	A mutual fund that charges investors a sales commission called a "load."
	Money market, *p. 127*	The financial market for short-term debt securities (maturing in one year or less).
	Mutual fund, *p. 130*	A professionally managed investment company that pools the investments of many individuals and invests it in stocks, bonds, and other types of securities.
	Net asset value (NAV), *p. 130*	The difference between the current market value of an entity's (such as a mutual fund) assets and the value of its liabilities.
	No-load fund, *p. 131*	A mutual fund that doesn't charge a commission.
	Private equity firm, *p. 131*	A financial intermediary that invests in equities that are not traded on the public capital markets.
	Venture capital firm, *p. 131*	An investment company that raises money from accredited investors and uses the proceeds to invest in new start-up companies.
LG3 **Describe the different securities markets for bonds and stocks.** When a corporation needs to raise large sums of money, it generally turns to the public market for bonds if it borrows or equity if it seeks funds from new owners. The buyers of these securities include individual investors and investment companies such as mutual funds. The U.S. stock and bond markets are the largest and most active in the world. In some instances these markets are physical locations where buyers and sellers interact, such as the New York Stock Exchange at 11 Wall Street, or they consist of an electronic market of interconnected computers, such as NASDAQ. Beginning in 2007, the United States experienced its most severe financial crisis since the Great Depression of the 1930s. Although there is not a single cause for the crisis, the collapse of the real estate market certainly contributed to this event.	Bond, *p. 134*	A long-term (10-year or more) promissory note issued by a borrower, promising to pay the owner of the security a predetermined amount of interest each year.
	Common stock, *p. 134*	A form of equity security that represents the residual ownership of the firm.
	Coupon rate, *p. 134*	The amount of interest paid per year expressed as a percent of the face value of the bond.
	Debt securities, *p. 134*	Financial instruments that represent loans to corporations. Long-term debt securities are called bonds and can be bought and sold in the bond market.
	Equity securities, *p. 134*	Financial instruments that represent ownership claims on a business. Equity securities for corporations are called shares of stock and can be bought and sold in the stock market.
	Face, or par value, *p. 134*	On the face of a bond, the stated amount that the firm is to repay on the maturity date.

What You Should Know	Key Terms	
LG3 (*Continued*)	Maturity, *p. 134*	The date when a debt must be repaid.
	Note, *p. 134*	Another term used to refer to indebtedness. Notes generally have a maturity between 1 and 10 years when originally issued.
	Organized security exchanges, *p. 135*	Security exchanges that physically occupy space (such as a building or part of a building) and trade financial instruments on their premises.
	Over-the-counter markets, page *p. 136*	All security markets except the organized exchanges.
	Preferred stock, *p. 135*	An equity security that holds preference over common stock in terms of the right to the distribution of cash (dividends) and the right to the distribution of proceeds in the event of the liquidation and sale of the issuing firm.
	Primary market, *p. 132*	A part of the financial market where new security issues are initially bought and sold.
	Proprietary trading, *p. 142*	Using the bank's capital to make speculative bets on derivatives and securities.
	Secondary market, *p. 132*	The financial market where previously issued securities such as stocks and bonds are bought and sold.
	Security, *p. 132*	A negotiable instrument that represents a financial claim that has value. Securities are broadly classified as debt securities (bonds) and equity securities (shares of common stock).

Discussion Questions

LG1 Q4.1 **(Related to Regardless of Your Major: Defined Benefit vs. Defined Contribution Retirement Plans on page 126)** In the *Regardless of Your Major* box feature, two types of pension plans are discussed. Describe each. Which type is now the dominant type in use?

LG1 Q4.2 What are the three principal sets of players that interact in the financial markets?

LG1 Q4.3 What is a financial intermediary? List and describe the principal types of financial intermediaries in the U.S. financial markets.

LG1 Q4.4 What do investment banks do in the financial markets?

LG1 Q4.5 Describe the difference between the primary market and the secondary market.

LG1 Q4.6 What is a mutual fund, and how does it differ from an exchange-traded fund (ETF)?

LG1   Q4.7 What is the difference between a debt security and an equity security?

LG1   Q4.8 What makes preferred stock "preferred"?

LG2   Q4.9 **(Related to The Business of Life: Controlling Costs in Mutual Funds on page 130)** In *The Business of Life: Controlling Costs in Mutual Funds* feature, the importance of keeping expenses down is discussed. The Financial Industry Regulatory Authority website provides an easy way to compare two mutual funds. Go to the website, http://apps.finra.org/fundanalyzer/1/fa.aspx, then enter Vanguard 500 Index Fund Investor Class (you will enter the ticker symbol VFINX), American Beacon Balanced Fund Class A -(ABFAX), and Quantitative Futures Strategy Fund Class C Shares (QMFCX). Now, click on "show results." Set your investment at $10,000, your return at 8%, and your period at 10 years. What is your profit or loss? Why do you think there is such a big difference? (Think expenses and fees.)

LG3   Q4.10 **(Related to Finance in a Flat World: Where's the Money around the World on page 140)** The distribution of financial assets around the world is described in the *Finance in a "Flat" World* box feature. What country dominates in terms of the stock market and total financial assets? Of the UK, Germany, and France, which country has the most in the way of financial assets and which country has the least?

LG3   Q4.11 What is a hedge fund, and how is it different from a mutual fund?

LG3   Q4.12 What are the two types of private equity funds? What does each do with the money it raises from investors?

LG3   Q4.13 Go to Yahoo! Finance (http://finance.yahoo.com) and enter the symbol for Google (GOOG) in the "Enter Symbol(s)" box at the top of the page. What price did it last trade at? What is the last trade time, and how long ago was that? What is the day's price range for the stock? What is the closing change in the price of the stock, both in dollar and percentage terms? What is the stock's 52-week price range? Now check out some of the links on the left-hand side of the page. What kind of information listed there do you find interesting?

LG3   Q4.14 Go to the CNN-Money website (http://money.cnn.com) and visit the retirement section by clicking on "Personal Finance" on the top banner. From there, click on "Retirement." You'll find all kinds of interesting articles under this link. (But be forewarned: Some are a bit scary. Saving for retirement is not an easy task.) Write up a summary of any one of the articles listed there.

LG3   Q4.15 Go to the Market Watch website (www.marketwatch.com) Personal Finance section by clicking on "Personal Finance" on the top banner. This is a great website for information and help in managing your personal finances. Find an article you like, read it, and write a summary of it. Also, consider bookmarking this website—it's one you might want to start visiting on a regular basis.

LG3   Q4.16 Calculate the value of the total shareholder wealth for Google, Inc., using the number of common shares outstanding and the current price of the firm's shares. You can obtain the necessary information from the Yahoo! Finance website.

LG3   Q4.17 Go to the Smartmoney.com website (www.smartmoney.com) and select one of the listed stories for the day; read it and prepare a brief summary to share with the class.

LG3   Q4.18 Go to the Motley Fool website (www.fool.com) and select the Retirement tab. Describe the information available here for planning for your retirement.

5

Time Value of Money
The Basics

LEARNING GOALS

LG1 Construct cash flow timelines to organize your analysis of problems involving the time value of money.

LG2 Understand compounding and calculate the future value of cash flows using mathematical formulas, a financial calculator, and an Excel spreadsheet.

LG3 Understand discounting and calculate the present value of cash flows using mathematical formulas, a financial calculator, and an Excel spreadsheet.

LG4 Understand how interest rates are quoted and know how to make them comparable.

Principle P1 Applied

Chapters 5 and 6 are dedicated to P Principle 1: **Money Has a Time Value.** This basic idea—a dollar received today, other things being the same, is worth more than a dollar received a year from now—underlies many financial decisions faced in business. In this chapter, we learn how to calculate the value today of money you will receive in the future, as well as the future value of money you have today. In Chapter 6 we extend our analysis to multiple cash flows spread out over time.

Payday Loans

Sometimes marketed to college students as quick relief for urgent expenses, a payday loan is a short-term loan to cover expenses until the next payday. As some borrowers turn to these loans during times of financial desperation, lenders can charge them extremely high rates of interest. For example, in 2012, one payday lender advertised that you could borrow $500 and repay $626.37 in eight days. This might not sound like a bad deal on the surface, but if we apply some basic rules of finance to analyze this loan, we see quite a different story. The annual interest rate for this payday loan is a whopping 2,916,780 percent! (We will examine this later in the chapter on pages 164–166.)

The very high rates of interest charged by these lenders have led some states to impose limits on the interest rates payday lenders can charge. Even so, the cost of this type of loan can be extremely high. Understanding the time value of money is an essential tool to analyzing the cost of this and other types of financing.

A Dollar Saved Is Two Dollars Earned

Suppose that you and your classmate each receive a gift of $10,000 from grandparents, but choose different ways to invest the newfound money. You immediately invest your gift until retirement, whereas your classmate carries around his gift in his wallet in the form of 100 crisp $100 bills. Then, after 15 years of carrying around a fat wallet, your classmate decides to invest his $10,000 for retirement.

If you invest your $10,000 for 46 years and earn 10 percent per year until you retire, you'll end up with over $800,000. If your classmate invests his $10,000 for 31 years (remember that he carried his money around for 15 years in his wallet) and earns the same 10 percent per year, he'll only end up with about $192,000. Knowing about the power of the time value of money provided you with an additional $600,000 at retirement. In this chapter we'll learn more about these kinds of valuation problems. For now, keep in mind that the time value of money is a concept you will want to understand, regardless of your major.

Your Turn: See Discussion Questions 5–7 and 5–8.

Using Timelines to Visualize Cash Flows

LG1 To evaluate a new project, a financial manager must be able to compare benefits and costs that occur at different times. We will use the time-value-of-money tools we develop in this chapter to make the benefits and costs comparable, allowing us to make logical decisions. We begin our study of time value analysis by introducing some basic tools. As a first step, we can construct a **timeline**, a linear representation of the timing of cash flows. A timeline identifies the timing and amount of a stream of payments—both cash received and cash spent—along with the interest rate earned. Timelines are a critical first step that financial analysts use to solve financial problems, and we will refer to timelines throughout this text.

To learn how to construct a timeline, consider the following example, where we have annual cash inflows and outflows over the course of four years. The following timeline illustrates these cash inflows and outflows from time Period 0 (the present) until the end of Year 4:

For our purposes, time periods are identified on the top of the timeline. In this example, the time periods are measured in years, indicated on the far right of the timeline. For example, time Period 0 in this example is the current year. The dollar amount of the cash flow received or spent during each time period is shown below the timeline. Positive values represent *cash inflows*. Negative values represent *cash outflows*. For example, in the timeline shown, a $100 cash outflow occurs at the beginning of the first year (at Time 0), followed by cash inflows of $30 and $20 in Years 1 and 2, a cash outflow (a negative cash flow) of $10 in Year 3, and finally a cash inflow of $50 in Year 4.

Checkpoint 5.1

Creating a Timeline

Suppose you lend a friend $10,000 today to help him finance a new Jimmy John's Sub Shop franchise and in return he promises to give you $12,155 at the end of the fourth year. How can one represent this as a timeline? Note that the interest rate is 5%.

STEP 1: Picture the problem

A timeline provides a tool for visualizing cash flows and time:

STEP 2: Decide on a solution strategy

To complete the timeline we simply record the cash flows onto the template.

STEP 3: Solve

We can input the cash flows for this investment on the timeline as shown below. Time period zero (the present) is shown at the left end of the timeline, and future time periods are shown above the timeline, moving from left to right, with the year that each cash flow occurs shown above the timeline.

Keep in mind that Year 1 represents the end of the first year as well as the beginning of the second year.

STEP 4: Analyze

Using timelines to visualize cash flows is useful in financial problem solving. From analyzing the timeline, we can see that there are two cash flows, an initial $10,000 cash outflow, and a $12,155 cash inflow at the end of Year 4.

STEP 5: Check yourself

Draw a timeline for an investment of $40,000 today that returns nothing in one year, $20,000 at the end of Year 2, nothing in Year 3, and $40,000 at the end of Year 4, where the interest rate is 13.17 percent.

ANSWER:

Timelines are typically expressed in years, but could be expressed in months, days, or, for that matter, any unit of time. For now, let's assume we're looking at cash flows that occur annually, so the distance between 0 and 1 represents the time period between today and the end of the first year. The interest rate, 10 percent in this example, is listed above the timeline.

CONCEPTS IN REVIEW

5.1   What is a timeline, and how does it help you solve problems involving the time value of money?

5.2   Does Year 5 represent the end of the fifth year, the beginning of the sixth year, or both?

Compounding and Future Value

LG2   If we assume that an investment will only earn interest on the original principal, we call this **simple interest**. Suppose that you put $100 in a savings account earning 6 percent interest annually. How much will your savings grow after one year? If you invest for one year at an interest rate of 6 percent, you will earn 6 percent simple interest on your initial deposit of $100, giving you a total of $106 in your account. What if you left your $100 in the bank for two years? In this case, you will earn interest not only on your original $100 deposit but also on the $6 in interest you earned during the first year. This process of accumulating interest on an investment over multiple time periods is called **compounding**. And, when interest is earned on both the initial principal and the reinvested interest during prior periods, the result is called **compound interest**.

Time-value-of-money calculations are essentially comparisons between what we will refer to as **present value**, what a cash flow would be worth to you today, and **future value**, what a cash flow will be worth in the future. The following is a mathematical formula that shows how these concepts relate to each other when the future value is in one year:

$$\text{Future Value in 1 Year} = \text{Present Value} \times (1 + \text{Interest Rate}) \qquad \textbf{(5–1)}$$

In the earlier example, you began with a $100 investment, so the present value is $100. The future value in one year is then given by the equation

$$\$100 \times (1 + .06) = \$106.00$$

To see how to calculate the future value in two years, let's do a timeline and a few calculations:

During the first year, your $100 deposit earns $6 in interest. Summing the interest and the original deposit gives you a balance of $106 at the end of the first year. In the second year, you earn $6.36 in interest, giving you a future value of $112.36. Why do you earn $0.36 more in interest during the second year than during the first? Because in the second year, you earn an additional 6 percent on the $6 in interest you earned in the first year. This amounts to $0.36 (or $6 × .06). Again, this result is an example of compound interest. Anyone who has ever had a savings account or purchased a government savings bond has received compound interest.

What happens to the value of your investment at the end of the third year, assuming the same interest rate of 6 percent? We can follow the same approach to calculate the future value in three years.

Using a timeline, we can calculate the future value of your $100 as follows:

Note that every time we extend the analysis for one more period, we just multiply the previous balance by (*1 + Interest Rate*). Consequently, the future value of any amount of money for any number of periods can be expressed with the following equation, where *n* = the number of periods during which the compounding occurs:

$$\text{Future Value}_{\text{Period } n} = \text{Present Value (Deposit)} \times \left(1 + \frac{\text{Interest}}{\text{Rate } (i)}\right)^n$$

or

$$\text{Future Value in Year } n\ (FV_n) = \text{Present Value } (PV) \left(1 + \frac{\text{Annual}}{\text{Interest Rate } (i)}\right)^{\text{Number of Years } (n)} \tag{5-1a}$$

Important Definitions and Concepts:

- FV_n = the future value of the investment at the end of n periods.
- i = the interest (or growth) rate per period.
- PV = the present value, or original amount invested at the beginning of the first period.

We also refer to $(1 + i)^n$ as the **future value interest factor.** To find the future value of a dollar amount, simply multiply that dollar amount by the appropriate future value interest factor,

$$FV_n = PV(1 + i)^n$$

$$FV_n = PV \times \text{Future Value Interest Factor}$$

where, Future Value Interest Factor = $(1 + i)^n$

Panel A in Figure 5.1 shows what your investment of $100 would grow to in four years if it continues to earn an annual compound interest rate of 6 percent. Notice how the amount of interest earned increases each year. In the first year, you earn only $6, but by Year 4, you earn $7.15 in interest.

Prior to the introduction of inexpensive financial calculators and Excel, future values were commonly calculated using time-value-of-money tables containing future value interest factors for different combinations of i and n. Table 5.1 provides an

FIGURE 5.1 Future Value and Compound Interest Illustrated

(Panel A) Calculating Compound Interest

This panel shows how interest compounds annually. During the first year, $100 invested at a 6% interest rate earns only $6. Because we earn 6% on the ending value for Year 1 (or $106), in Year 2 we earn $6.36 in interest. This increase in the amount of interest results from interest being earned on both the initial deposit of $100 plus the $6.00 in interest earned during Year 1. The fact that we earn interest on both principal and interest is why we refer to this as compound interest. Simple interest, on the other hand, would be earning only $6.00 in interest each and every year.

> Interest Earned = Beginning Value × Interest Rate

Year	Beginning Value	Interest Earned	Ending Value
1	$ 100.00	**$ 6.00**	$ 106.00
2	$ 106.00	**$ 6.36**	$ 112.36
3	$ 112.36	**$ 6.74**	$ 119.10
4	$ 119.10	**$ 7.15**	$ 126.25

Future value of $100 compounded at a rate of 8% per year for 15 years = $317.22 — ▪ $317.22

Future value of $100 compounded at a rate of 8% per year for 10 years = $215.89 → ▪ $215.89

Future value of $100 compounded at a rate of 0% per year equals $100 regardless of how many years it is invested.

(Panel C graph: Future value vs. Number of periods in years, 0 to 15)

(Panel B) The Power of Time

This figure illustrates the importance of time when it comes to compounding. Because interest is earned on past interest, the future value of $100 deposited in an account that earns 8% compounded annually grows over threefold in 15 years. If we were to expand this figure to 45 years (which is about how long you have until you retire, assuming you're around 20 years old right now), it would grow to over 31 times its initial value.

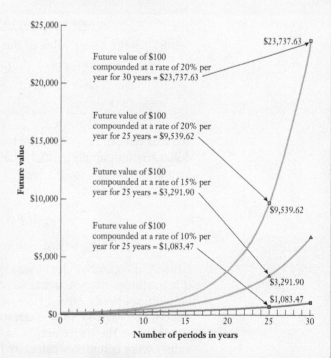

Future value of $100 compounded at a rate of 20% per year for 30 years = $23,737.63 → ▪ $23,737.63

Future value of $100 compounded at a rate of 20% per year for 25 years = $9,539.62 → ▪ $9,539.62

Future value of $100 compounded at a rate of 15% per year for 25 years = $3,291.90 → ▲ $3,291.90

Future value of $100 compounded at a rate of 10% per year for 25 years = $1,083.47 → ▪ $1,083.47

(Panel B graph: Future value vs. Number of periods in years, 0 to 30)

(Panel C) The Power of the Rate of Interest

This figure illustrates the importance of the interest rate in the power of compounding. As the interest rate climbs, so does the future value. In fact, when we change the interest rate from 10% to 20%, the future value in 25 years increases by over 8 times, jumping from $1,083.47 to $9,539.62.

TABLE 5.1 FUTURE VALUE INTEREST FACTORS

Number of Periods (n)	$i = 3\%$	$i = 6\%$	$i = 9\%$	$i = 12\%$
1	1.030	1.060	1.090	1.120
2	1.061	1.124	1.188	1.254
3	1.093	1.191	1.295	1.405
4	1.126	1.262	1.412	1.574

abbreviated future value interest factor table; you can find the expanded future value interest factor tables in Appendix B in MyFinanceLab. So, to find the value of $100 invested for four years at 6 percent, we would simply look at the intersection of the $n = 4$ row and the 6% column, finding a future value interest factor of 1.262. We would then multiply this value by $100 to find that our investment of $100 at 6 percent for four years would grow to $126.20.

Compound Interest and Time

As Panel C of Figure 5.1 shows, the future value of an investment grows with the number of periods we let it compound. For example, after five years, the future value of $100 earning 10 percent interest each year will be $161.05. However, after 25 years, the future value of that investment will be $1,083.47. Note that although we increased the number of years threefold, the future value increases by more than sixfold ($1,083.47/$161.05 = 6.7 fold). This illustrates an important point: Future value is not directly proportional to time. Instead, future value grows exponentially. This means it grows by a fixed percentage each year, which means that the dollar value grows by an increasing amount each year.

Compound Interest and the Interest Rate

Panel C of Figure 5.1 illustrates that future value increases dramatically with the level of the rate of interest. For example, the future value of $100 in 25 years, given a 10 percent interest rate, compounded annually, is $1,083.47. However, if we double the rate of interest to 20 percent, the future value increases almost ninefold in 25 years to equal $9,539.62. This illustrates another important point: The increase in future value is not directly proportional to the increase in the rate of interest. We doubled the rate of interest, and the future value of the investment increased by 8.80 times. Why did the future value jump by so much? Because there is a lot of time over 25 years for the higher interest rate to result in more interest being earned on interest.

Techniques for Moving Money through Time

In this book, we will refer to three methods for solving problems involving the time value of money: mathematical formulas, financial calculators, and spreadsheets.

- **Do the math.** You can use the mathematical formulas just as we have done in this chapter. You simply substitute the values that you know into the appropriate time-value-of-money equation to find the answer.

- **Use financial calculators.** Financial calculators have preprogrammed functions that make time-value-of-money calculations simple.

- **Use a spreadsheet on your personal computer.** Spreadsheet software such as Excel has preprogrammed functions built into it. The same inputs that are used with a financial calculator are also used as inputs to Excel. As a result, if you can correctly set a problem up to solve on your financial calculator, you can easily set it up to solve using Excel. In the business world, Excel is the spreadsheet of choice and is the most common way of moving money through time.

In Appendix A in MyFinanceLab, we will show how to solve valuation problems using each of these methods. Because the authors of this book believe that spending enough time solving problems the old-fashioned way—by doing the math—leads to a deeper understanding and better retention of the concepts found in this book, we will first demonstrate how to solve problems using the formulas; but we will also demonstrate, whenever possible, how to derive the solution using a financial calculator and Excel.

Applying Compounding to Things Other Than Money

Although this chapter focuses on moving money through time at a given interest rate, the concept of compounding applies to almost anything that grows. For example, let's suppose we're interested in knowing how big the market for wireless printers will be in five years, and assume the demand for them is expected to grow at a rate of 25 percent per year over the next five years. We can calculate the future value of the market for printers using the same formula we used to calculate the future value for a sum of money. If the market is currently 25,000 printers per year, then 25,000 would be PV, n would be 5, and i would be 25 percent. Substituting into Equation (5–1a) we would solve for FV,

$$\begin{array}{l} \text{Future Value} \\ \text{in Year } n \\ (FV_n) \end{array} = \begin{array}{c} \text{Present} \\ \text{Value } (PV) \end{array} \left(1 + \begin{array}{c} \text{Annual} \\ \text{Interest Rate } (i) \end{array} \right)^{\overset{\text{Number of}}{\underset{}{\text{Years } (n)}}} = 25,000(1+.25)^5 = 76,293$$

The power of compounding can also be illustrated through the story of a peasant who wins a chess tournament sponsored by the king. The king then asks him what he would like as his prize. The peasant answers that, for his village, he would like one grain of wheat to be placed on the first square of his chessboard, two pieces on the second square, four on the third square, eight on the fourth square, and so forth, until the board is filled up. The king, thinking he was getting off easy, pledged his word of honor that this would be done. Unfortunately for the king, by the time all 64 squares on the chessboard were filled, there were 18.5 million trillion grains of wheat on the board, because the kernels were compounding at a rate of 100 percent over the 64 squares of the chessboard. In fact, if the kernels were one-quarter inch long, they would have stretched, if laid end to end, to the sun and back 391,320 times! Needless to say, no one in the village ever went hungry. What can we conclude from this story? There is incredible power in compounding.

Compound Interest with Shorter Compounding Periods

So far, we have assumed that the compounding period is always a year in length. However, this isn't always the case. For example, banks often offer savings accounts that compound interest every day, month, or quarter. Savers prefer more frequent compounding because they earn interest on their interest sooner and more frequently. Fortunately, it's easy to adjust for different compounding periods, and later in the chapter we will examine how to compare two loans with different compounding periods in more detail.

Consider the following example: You invest $100 for five years to earn a rate of 8 percent, and the investment is compounded semiannually (twice a year). This means that

Calculating the Future Value of a Cash Flow

You are put in charge of managing your firm's working capital. Your firm has $100,000 in extra cash on hand and decides to put it in a savings account paying 7 percent interest compounded annually. How much will you have in your account in 10 years?

STEP 1: Picture the problem

We can set up a timeline to identify the cash flows from the investment as follows:

$i = 7\%$

| Time Period | 0 | 1 | 2 | 3 | 4 | 5 | 6 | 7 | 8 | 9 | 10 | Years |

Cash Flow -$100,000   Future Value = ?

STEP 2: Decide on a solution strategy

This is a simple future value problem. We can find the future value using Equation (5–1a).

STEP 3: Solve

Using the Mathematical Formulas. Substituting $PV = \$100,000$, $i = 7\%$, and $n = 10$ years into Equation (5–1a), we get

$$\text{Future Value in Year } n\ (FV_n) = \text{Present Value } (PV)\left(1 + \text{Annual Interest Rate } (i)\right)^{\text{Number of Years } (n)}$$

(5–1a)

$$FV_n = \$100,000(1 + .07)^{10}$$
$$= \$100,000(1.96715)$$
$$= \$196,715$$

At the end of 10 years, you will have $196,715 in the savings account.

Using a Financial Calculator.

Enter	10	7.0	–100,000	0	
	N	I/Y	PV	PMT	FV
Solve for					196,715

Using an Excel Spreadsheet.

= FV(rate,nper,pmt,pv) or with values entered = FV(0.07,10,0,–100000)

STEP 4: Analyze

Notice that you input the present value with a negative sign because present value represents a cash outflow. In effect, the money leaves your firm when it's first invested. In this problem your firm invested $100,000 at 7 percent and found that it will grow to $196,715 after 10 years. Put another way, given a 7 percent compound rate, your $100,000 today will be worth $196,715 in 10 years.

STEP 5: Check yourself

What is the future value of $10,000 compounded at 12 percent annually for 20 years?

ANSWER: $96,462.93.

Your Turn: For more practice, do related **Study Problems** 5–1, 5–2, 5–4, 5–6, and 5–8 through 5–11 at the end of this chapter.

interest is calculated every six months. Essentially, you are investing your money for 10 six-month periods, and in each period, you will receive 4 percent interest. In effect, we divide the annual interest rate (i) by the number of compounding periods per year (m), and we multiply the number of years (n) times the number of compounding periods per year

(m) to convert the number of years into the number of periods. So, our future value formula found in Equation (5–1a) must be adjusted as follows:

$$\begin{matrix} \text{Future Value} \\ \text{in Year } n \\ (FV_n) \end{matrix} = \begin{matrix} \text{Present} \\ \text{Value } (PV) \end{matrix} \left(1 + \cfrac{\begin{matrix}\text{Annual} \\ \text{Interest Rate } (i)\end{matrix}}{\begin{matrix}\text{Compounding} \\ \text{Periods per Year } (m)\end{matrix}} \right)^{m \times (\text{Number of Years } (n))} \qquad \textbf{(5–1b)}$$

Substituting into Equation (5–1b) gives us the following estimate of the future value in five years:

$$FV_n = \$100 \, (1 + .08/2)^{2 \times 5}$$
$$= \$100(1.4802)$$
$$= \$148.02$$

Saving for Your First House

There was a time in the early and mid-2000s when you didn't need to worry about a down payment when you bought a new house. But that all changed as the housing bubble burst and home prices fell. Today you may be able to get away with only putting down around 10 percent, but the rate on your mortgage will be lower if you can come up with 20 percent. To buy a median-priced home, which was just over $180,000 at the beginning of 2013, you'd have to come up with a 10 percent down payment of $18,000 or a 20 percent down payment of $36,000. On top of that, you'll need to furnish your new home, and that costs money too.

Putting into practice what you have learned in this chapter, you know that the sooner you start to save for your first home, the easier it will be. Once you estimate how much you'll need for that new house, you can easily calculate how much you'll need to save annually to reach your goal. All you need to do is look at two variables: n (the number of years you'll be saving the money) and i (the interest rate at which the savings will grow). You can start saving earlier, which gives you a larger value for n. Or, you can earn more on your investments—that is, invest at a higher value for i. Of course, you always prefer getting a higher i on your savings, but this is not something you can control.

First, let's take a look at a higher value for i, which translates into a higher return. For example, let's say you've just inherited $10,000, and you invest it at 6 percent annually for 10 years—after which you want to buy your first house. The calculation is easy. At the end of 10 years, you will have accumulated $17,908 on this investment. But suppose you are able to earn 12 percent annually for 10 years. What would the value of your investment be then? In this case, your investment would be worth $31,058. Needless to say, the rate of interest that you earn plays a major role in determining how quickly your investment will grow.

Now consider what happens if you wait five years before investing your $10,000. The value of n drops from 10 to 5, and, as a result, the amount you've saved also drops. In fact, if you invested your $10,000 for five years at 6 percent, you'd end up with $13,382, and even at 12 percent you'd end up with only $17,623.

The bottom line is the earlier you begin saving, the more impact every dollar you save will have.

Your Turn: See Study Problem 5–3.

Calculating Future Values Using Non-Annual Compounding Periods

You have been put in charge of managing your firm's cash position and noticed that the Plaza National Bank of Portland, Oregon, has recently decided to begin paying interest compounded semiannually instead of annually. If you deposit $1,000 with Plaza National Bank at an interest rate of 12 percent, what will your account balance be in five years?

STEP 1: Picture the problem

If you earn a 12 percent annual rate compounded semiannually for five years, you really earn 6 percent every six months for 10 six-month periods. Expressed as a timeline, this problem would look like the following:

$i = 12\% \div 2 = 6\%$ every 6 months

| Time Period | 0 | 1 | 2 | 3 | 4 | 5 | 6 | 7 | 8 | 9 | 10 | 6-Month Periods |

Cash Flow   −$1,000

Future Value of $1,000 compounded for 10 six-month periods at 12%/2 every 6 months

STEP 2: Decide on a solution strategy

In this instance we are simply solving for the future value of $1,000. The only twist is that interest is calculated on a semiannual basis. Thus, if you earn 12 percent compounded semiannually for five years, you really earn 6 percent every six months for 10 six-month periods. We can calculate the future value of the $1,000 investment using Equation (5–1b).

STEP 3: Solve

Using the Mathematical Formulas. Substituting number of years $(n) = 5$, number of compounding periods per year $(m) = 2$, annual interest rate $(i) = 12\%$, and $PV = \$1,000$ into Equation (5–1b):

$$
\begin{array}{c}
\text{Future Value} \\
\text{in Year } n \\
(FV_n)
\end{array}
=
\begin{array}{c}
\text{Present} \\
\text{Value } (PV)
\end{array}
\left(1 + \dfrac{\text{Annual Interest Rate } (i)}{\begin{array}{c}\text{Compounding} \\ \text{Period per Year } (m)\end{array}} \right)^{m \times (\text{Number of Years } (n))}
$$

$$
\text{Future Value in Year } n \ (FV_n) = \$1,000 \left(1 + \frac{12}{2} \right)^{2 \times 5} = \$1,000 \times 1.79085 = \$1,790.85
$$

Using a Financial Calculator.

Enter	10	6.0	−1,000	0	
	N	I/Y	PV	PMT	FV
Solve for					1,790.85

You will have $1,790.85 at the end of five years.

Using an Excel Spreadsheet.

= FV(rate,nper,pmt,pv) or with values entered = FV(0.06,10,0,−1000)

STEP 4: Analyze

The more often interest is compounded per year—that is, the larger m is, resulting in a larger value of *nper*—the larger the future value will be. That's because you are earning interest more often on the interest you've previously earned.

STEP 5: Check yourself

If you deposit $50,000 in an account that pays an annual interest rate of 10 percent compounded monthly, what will your account balance be in 10 years?

ANSWER: $135,352.07.

Your Turn: For more practice, do related **Study Problems** 5–5 and 5–7 at the end of this chapter.

But if the compounding had been annual rather than semiannual, the future value of the investment would have been only $146.93. Although the difference here seems modest, it can be significant when large sums of money are involved and the number of years and the number of compounding periods within those years are both large. For example, for your $100 investment, the difference is only $1.09. But if the amount were $50 million (not an unusually large bank balance for a major company), the difference would be $545,810.41.

Table 5.2 shows how shorter compounding periods lead to higher future values. For example, if you invested $100 at 15 percent for one year, and the investment was compounded daily rather than annually, you would end up with $1.18 ($116.18 − $115.00) more. However, if the period were extended to 10 years, then the difference grows to $43.47 ($448.03 − $404.56).

TABLE 5.2   THE VALUE OF $100 COMPOUNDED AT VARIOUS NON-ANNUAL PERIODS AND VARIOUS RATES

Notice that the impact of shorter compounding periods is heightened by both higher interest rates and compounding over longer time periods.

For 1 Year at i Percent	$i = 2\%$	5%	10%	15%	
Compounded annually	$102.00	$105.00	$110.00	**$115.00**	
Compounded semiannually	102.01	105.06	110.25	115.56	
Compounded quarterly	102.02	105.09	110.38	115.87	
Compounded monthly	102.02	105.12	110.47	116.08	$1.18
Compounded weekly (52)	102.02	105.12	110.51	116.16	
Compounded daily (365)	102.02	105.13	110.52	**116.18**	
For 10 Years at i Percent	$i = 2\%$	5%	10%	15%	
Compounded annually	$121.90	$162.89	$259.37	**$404.56**	
Compounded semiannually	122.02	163.86	265.33	424.79	
Compounded quarterly	122.08	164.36	268.51	436.04	$43.47
Compounded monthly	122.12	164.70	270.70	444.02	
Compounded weekly (52)	122.14	164.83	271.57	447.20	
Compounded daily (365)	122.14	164.87	271.79	**448.03**	

CONCEPTS IN REVIEW

5.3   What is compound interest, and how is it calculated?

5.4   Describe the three basic approaches that can be used to move money through time.

5.5   How does increasing the number of compounding periods affect the future value of a cash sum?

Discounting and Present Value

LG3 So far we have only been moving money forward in time; that is, we have taken a known present value of money and determined how much it will be worth at some point in the future. Financial decisions often require calculating the future value of an investment made today. However, there are many instances where we want to look at the reverse question: What is the value today of a sum of money to be received in the future? To answer this question, we now turn our attention to the analysis of a present value—the value today of a future cash flow—and the process of **discounting**, determining the present value of an expected future cash flow.

The Mechanics of Discounting Future Cash Flows

Discounting is actually the reverse of compounding. We can demonstrate the similarity between compounding and discounting by referring back to the future value formula found in Equation (5–1a):

$$\text{Future Value in Year } n\ (FV_n) = \text{Present Value } (PV)\left(1 + \text{Annual Interest Rate } (i)\right)^{\text{Number of Years } (n)} \tag{5–1a}$$

To determine the present value of a known future cash flow, we simply take Equation (5–1a) and solve for PV:

$$\text{Present Value } (PV) = \text{Future Value in Year } n\ (FV_n)\left[\frac{1}{\left(1 + \text{Annual Interest Rate } (i)\right)^{\text{Number of Years } (n)}}\right] \tag{5–2}$$

We also refer to the term in the brackets as the **present value interest factor**, which is the value that multiples the future value to calculate the present value. Thus, to find the present value of a future cash flow, we multiply the future cash flow by the present value interest factor.[1]

$$\text{Present Value } (PV) = \text{Future Value in year } n\ (FV_n) \times \left(\begin{array}{c}\text{Present Value Interest Factor}\\(PVIF)\end{array}\right)$$

$$\text{where Present Value Interest Factor } (PVIF) = \frac{1}{(1+i)^n}$$

Note that the present value of a future sum of money decreases as we increase the number of periods, n, until the payment is received, or as we increase the interest rate, i. That, of course, only makes sense because the present value interest factor is the *inverse* of the future value interest factor. Graphically, this relationship can be seen in Figure 5.2. Thus, given a **discount rate**, or interest rate at which money is being brought back to present, of 10 percent, $100 received in 10 years would be worth only $38.55 today. By contrast, if the discount rate is 5 percent, the present value would be $61.39. If the discount rate is 10 percent, but the $100 is received in 5 years instead of 10 years, the

---

[1]Related tables appear in Appendix C in MyFinanceLab.

FIGURE 5.2

The Present Value of $100 Compounded at Different Rates and for Different Time Periods

The present value of $100 to be received in the future becomes smaller as both the interest rate and number of years rise. At $i = 10\%$, notice that when the number of years goes up from 5 to 10, the present value drops from $62.09 to $38.55.

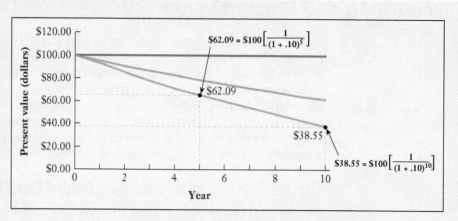

present value would be $62.09. This concept of present value plays a central role in the valuation of stocks, bonds, and new proposals. You can easily verify this calculation using any of the discounting methods we describe next.

Two Additional Types of Discounting Problems

Time-value-of-money problems do not always involve calculating either the present value or future value of a series of cash flows. There are a number problems that require that you solve for either the number of periods in the future, n, or the rate of interest, i. For example, to answer the following questions you will need to calculate the value for n:

- How many years will it be before the money I have saved will be enough to buy a second home?

- How long will it take to accumulate enough money for a down payment on a new retail outlet?

And to answer the following questions you must solve for the interest rate, i:

- What rate do I need to earn on my investment to have enough money for my new-born child's college education ($n = 18$ years)?

- If our firm introduces a new product line, what interest rate will this investment earn?

Fortunately, with the help of the mathematical formulas, a financial calculator, or an Excel spreadsheet, you can easily solve for i or n in any of these or similar situations.

Solving for the Number of Periods Suppose you want to know how many years it will take for an investment of $9,330 to grow to $20,000 if it's invested at 10 percent annually. Let's take a look at how to solve this using the mathematical formulas, a financial calculator, and an Excel spreadsheet.

Solving for the Present Value of a Future Cash Flow

Your firm has just sold a piece of property for $500,000, but under the sales agreement, it won't receive the $500,000 until 10 years from today. What is the present value of $500,000 to be received 10 years from today if the discount rate is 6 percent annually?

STEP 1: Picture the problem

Expressed as a timeline, this problem would look like the following:

STEP 2: Decide on a solution strategy

In this instance we are simply solving for the present value of $500,000 to be received at the end of 10 years. We can calculate the present value of the $500,000 using Equation (5–2).

STEP 3: Solve

Using the Mathematical Formulas. Substituting $FV_{10} = \$500,000$, $n = 10$, and $i = 6\%$ into Equation (5–2), we find

$$PV = \$500,000 \left[\frac{1}{(1+.06)^{10}} \right]$$

$$= \$500,000 \left[\frac{1}{1.79085} \right]$$

$$= \$500,000 [.558394]$$

$$= \$279,197$$

The present value of the $500,000 to be received in 10 years is $279,197. Earlier we noted that discounting is the reverse of compounding. We can easily test this calculation by considering this problem in reverse: What is the future value in 10 years of $279,197 today if the rate of interest is 6 percent? Using our *FV* Equation (5–1a), we can see that the answer is $500,000.

Using a Financial Calculator.

Enter   10   6.0   0 500,000

      N   I/Y   PV   PMT FV

Solve for   -279,197

Using an Excel Spreadsheet.

= PV(rate,nper,pmt,fv) or with values entered = PV(0.06,10,0,500000)

STEP 4: Analyze

Once you've found the present value of any future cash flow, that present value is in today's dollars and can be compared to other present values. The underlying point of this exercise is to make cash flows that occur in different time periods comparable so that we can make good decisions. Also notice that regardless of which method we use to calculate the future value—computing the formula by hand, with a calculator, or with Excel—we always arrive at the same answer.

STEP 5: Check yourself

What is the present value of $100,000 to be received at the end of 25 years given a 5 percent discount rate?

ANSWER: $29,530.

Your Turn: For more practice, do related **Study Problems** 5–12, 5–15, 5–19, and 5–28 at the end of this chapter.

Using Mathematical Formulas. Substituting for FV, PV, and i in Equation (5–1a),

$$\underset{(FV_n)}{\underset{\text{in Year } n}{\text{Future Value}}} = \underset{\text{Value } (PV)}{\text{Present}}\left(1 + \underset{\text{Interest Rate } (i)}{\text{Annual}}\right)^{\overset{\text{Number of}}{\underset{\text{Years } (n)}{}}} \qquad \textbf{(5–1a)}$$

$$\$20{,}000 = \$9{,}330(1.10)^n$$

Solving for n mathematically is tough. One way is to solve for n using a trial-and-error approach. That is, you could substitute different values of n into the equation—either increasing the value of n to make the right-hand side of the equation larger, or decreasing the value of n to make it smaller, until the two sides of the equation are equal—but that will be a bit tedious. Using the time-value-of-money features on a financial calculator or in Excel is much easier and faster.

Using a Financial Calculator. Using a financial calculator or an Excel spreadsheet, this problem becomes much easier. With a financial calculator, all you do is substitute in the values for i, PV, and FV, and solve for n:

Enter		10.0	-9,330	0	20,000
	N	I/Y	PV	PMT	FV
Solve for	8.0				

You'll notice that PV is input with a negative sign. In effect the financial calculator is programmed to assume that the $9,330 is a cash outflow (the money leaving your hands), whereas the $20,000 is money that you will receive. If you don't give one of these values a negative sign, you can't solve the problem.

Using an Excel Spreadsheet. With Excel, solving for n is straightforward. You simply use the =NPER(rate,pmt,pv,fv) or with variables entered, =NPER(0.10,0,–9330,20000).

The Rule of 72

Now you know how to determine the future value of any investment. What if all you want to know is how long it will take to double your money in that investment? One simple way to approximate how long it will take for a given sum to double in value is called the **Rule of 72**. This "rule" states that you can determine how many years it will take for a given sum to double by dividing the investment's annual growth or interest rate into 72. For example, if an investment grows at an annual rate of 9 percent per year, according to the Rule of 72 it should take 72/9 = 8 years for that sum to double.

    Keep in mind that this is not a hard-and-fast rule, just an approximation—but it's a pretty good approximation. For example, the *future value interest factor* of $(1 + i)^n$ for 8 years ($n = 8$) at 9 percent ($i = 9\%$) is 1.993, which is pretty close to the Rule of 72's approximation of 2.0.

Solving for the Rate of Interest You have just inherited $34,946 and want to use it to fund your retirement in 30 years. If you have estimated that you will need $800,000 to fund your retirement, what rate of interest would you have to earn on your $34,946 investment? Let's take a look at solving this using the mathematical formulas, a financial calculator, and an Excel spreadsheet to calculate i.

Checkpoint 5.5

Solving for the Number of Periods, *n*

Let's assume that the Toyota Corporation has guaranteed that the price of a new Prius will always be $20,000, and you'd like to buy one but currently have only $7,752. How many years will it take for your initial investment of $7,752 to grow to $20,000 if it is invested so that it earns 9 percent compounded annually?

STEP 1: Picture the problem

In this case we are solving for the number of periods:

$i = 9\%$

| Time Period | 0 | 1 | 2 | 3 | 4 | 5 | .... | ? | Years |
| Cash Flow | −$7,752 | | | | | | | $20,000 | |

STEP 2: Decide on a solution strategy

In this problem we know the interest rate, the present value, and the future value, and we want to know how many years it will take for $7,752 to grow to $20,000 at 9 percent per year. We are solving for *n*, and we can calculate it using Equation (5–1a).

STEP 3: Solve

Using a Financial Calculator.

Enter		9.0	−7,752	0	20,000
	N	I/Y	PV	PMT	FV
Solve for	11.0				

Using an Excel Spreadsheet.

= NPER(rate,pmt,pv,fv) or with values entered = NPER(0.09,0,−7752,20000)

STEP 4: Analyze

It will take about 11 years for $7,752 to grow to $20,000 at 9 percent compound interest. This is the kind of calculation that both individuals and business make in trying to plan for major expenditures.

STEP 5: Check yourself

How many years will it take for $10,000 to grow to $200,000 given a 15 percent compound growth rate?

ANSWER: 21.4 years.

Your Turn: For more practice, do related **Study Problems** 5–13 and 5–18 at the end of this chapter.

Using Mathematical Formulas. If you write this problem using our time value of money formula you get,

$$\underset{(FV_n)}{\overset{\text{Future Value}}{\text{in Year } n}} = \underset{\text{Value } (PV)}{\text{Present}} \left(1 + \underset{\text{Interest Rate } (i)}{\text{Annual}}\right)^{\overset{\text{Number of}}{\text{Years } (n)}} \qquad \text{(5–1a)}$$

$$\$800,000 = \$34,946(1 + i)^{30}$$

Once again, you could resort to a trial-and-error approach by substituting different values of i into the equation and calculating the value on the right-hand side of the equation to see if it is equal to $800,000. However, again, this would be quite cumbersome and unnecessary. Alternatively, you can solve for i directly by dividing both sides of the equation above by $34,946,

$$(1 + i)^{30} = \$800,000/\$34,946 = 22.8925$$

and then taking the 30th root of this equation to find the value of $(1 + i)$. Because taking the 30th root of something is the same as taking something to the 1/30 (or 0.033333) power, this is a relatively easy process if you have a financial calculator with a "y^n" key. In this case, you (1) enter 22.8925, (2) press the "y^n" key, (3) enter 0.033333, and (4) press the "=" key. The answer should be 1.109999, indicating that $(1 + i) = 1.109999$, and $i = 10.9999\%$ or 11%. As you might expect, it's faster and easier to use the time-value-of-money functions on a financial calculator or in Excel.

Using a Financial Calculator. Using a financial calculator or an Excel spreadsheet, this problem becomes much easier. With a financial calculator, all you do is substitute in the values for n, PV, and FV, and solve for i:

Enter	30		-34,946	0	800,000
	N	I/Y	PV	PMT	FV
Solve for		11.0			

Using an Excel Spreadsheet
= RATE(nper,pmt,pv,fv) or with values entered = RATE(30,0,–34946,800000)

CONCEPTS IN REVIEW

5.6 What does the term *discounting* mean with respect to the time value of money?

5.7 How is discounting related to compounding?

Making Interest Rates Comparable

LG4 Sometimes it's difficult to determine exactly how much you are paying or earning on a loan. That's because the loan might not be quoted as compounding annually, but rather as compounding quarterly or daily. To illustrate, let's look at two loans, one that is quoted as 8.084 percent compounded annually and another quoted as 7.85 percent compounded quarterly. Unfortunately, because on one the interest is compounded annually (you pay interest just once a year) but on the other, interest is compounded quarterly (you pay interest four times a year), they are difficult to compare. To allow borrowers to compare rates between different lenders, the U.S. Truth-in-Lending Act requires what is known as the annual percentage rate (APR) to be displayed on all consumer loan documents. The **annual percentage rate (APR)** indicates the interest rate paid or earned in one year without compounding. We can calculate APR as the interest rate per period (for example, per month or week) multiplied by the number of periods during which compounding occurs during the year (m):

$$\begin{array}{c} \text{Annual Percentage} \\ \text{Rate } (APR) \\ \text{or Simple Interest} \end{array} = \begin{pmatrix} \text{Interest Rate per} \\ \text{Period (for example} \\ \text{per month or week)} \end{pmatrix} \times \begin{array}{c} \text{Compounding} \\ \text{Periods per} \\ \text{Year } (m) \end{array} \quad \textbf{(5–3)}$$

Checkpoint 5.6

Solving for the Interest Rate, *i*

Let's go back to that Prius example in Checkpoint 5.5. Recall that the Prius always costs $20,000. In 10 years, you'd really like to have $20,000 to buy a new Prius, but you only have $11,167 now. At what rate must your $11,167 be compounded annually for it to grow to $20,000 in 10 years?

STEP 1: Picture the problem

We can visualize the problem using a timeline as follows:

i = ?%

| ■Time Period | 0 | 1 | 2 | 3 | 4 | 5 | 6 | 7 | 8 | 9 | 10 | ■Years |

| ■Cash Flow | -$11,167 | | | | | | | | | | $20,000 | |

STEP 2: Decide on a solution strategy

Here we know the number of years, the present value, and the future value, and we are solving for the interest rate. We'll use Equation (5–1a) to solve this problem.

STEP 3: Solve

Using the Mathematical Formulas.

$$\$20,000 = \$11,167 (1 + i)^{10},$$
or $1.7910 = (1 + i)^{10}$

We then take the 10th root of this equation to find the value of $(1 + i)$. Because taking the 10th root of something is the same as taking something to the 1/10 (or 0.10) power, this can be done if you have a financial calculator with a "y^n" key. In this case, you (1) enter 1.7910, (2) press the "y^n" key, (3) enter 0.10, and (4) press the "=" key. The answer should be 1.06, indicating that $(1 + i) = 1.06$, and $i = 6\%$.

Using a Financial Calculator.

Enter		10		-11,167	0	20,000
		N	I/Y	PV	PMT	FV
Solve for			6.0			

Using an Excel Spreadsheet.

= RATE(nper,pmt,pv,fv) or with values entered = RATE(10,0,–11167,20000)

STEP 4: Analyze

You can increase your future value by growing your money at a higher interest rate or by letting your money grow for a longer period of time. For most of you, when it comes to planning for your retirement, a large *n* is a real positive for you. Also, if you can earn a slightly higher return on your retirement savings, or any savings for that matter, it can make a big difference.

STEP 5: Check yourself

At what rate will $50,000 have to grow to reach $1,000,000 in 30 years?

ANSWER: 10.5 percent.

Your Turn: For more practice, do related **Study Problems** 5–14, 5–16, 5–17, 5–20 to 5–22, 5–26, and 5–27 at the end of this chapter.

Thus, if you are paying 2 percent per month, m, the number of compounding periods per year, would be 12, and the *APR* would be:

$$APR = 2\%/month \times 12\ months/year = 24\%$$

Unfortunately, the APR does not help much when the rates being compared are not compounded for the same number of periods per year. In fact, the APR is also called the **nominal or quoted (stated) interest rate** because it is the rate that the lender states you are paying. In our example, both 8.084 percent and 7.85 percent are the annual percentage rates (APRs), but they aren't comparable because the loans have different compounding periods.

To make them comparable, we calculate their equivalent rate using an annual compounding period. We do this by calculating the **effective annual rate (EAR)**, the annual compounded rate that produces the same return as the nominal, or stated, rate. The EAR can be calculated using the following equation:

$$\text{Effective Annual Rate } (EAR) = \left(1 + \frac{\text{Quoted Annual Rate}}{\text{Compouding Periods per Year } (m)}\right)^{m} - 1 \qquad \textbf{(5–4)}$$

We calculate the *EAR* for the loan that has a 7.85 percent quoted annual rate of interest compounded quarterly (i.e., $m = 4$ times per year) using Equation (5–4) as follows:

$$EAR = \left[1 + \frac{0.0785}{4}\right]^{4} - 1 = .08084\ or\ 8.084\%$$

So if your banker offers you a loan with a 7.85 percent rate that is compounded quarterly or an 8.084 percent rate with annual compounding, which should you prefer? If you didn't know how the time value of money is affected by compounding, you would have chosen the 7.85 percent rate because, on the surface, it looked like the loan with the lower cost. However, you should be indifferent because these two offers have the same cost to you—that is to say, they have the same EAR. The key point here is that to compare the two loan terms you need to convert them to the same number of compounding periods (annual in this case). Given the wide variety of compounding periods used by businesses and banks, it is important to know how to make these rates comparable so you can make logical decisions.

Now let's return to that payday loan we introduced at the chapter opening. What is its EAR? In that example, we looked at a payday lender that advertised that you could borrow $500 and repay $626.37 eight days later. On the surface, that looks like you are paying 25.274 percent ($626.37/$500 = 1.25274), but that's really what you are paying every eight days. To find the quoted annual rate we multiply the eight-day rate of 25.274 percent times the number of eight-day periods in a year (in effect, you are paying 25.274 percent every eight days, or $25.274\% \times 45.625 = 1,153.13\%$). In this case m is 45.625 because there are 45.625 eight-day periods in a year (365 days), and the annual rate is $0.25274 \times 45.625 = 11.5313$ (the eight-day rate times the number of eight-day periods in a year). Substituting into Equation (5–4), we get

$$EAR = \left[1 + \frac{11.5315}{45.625}\right]^{45.625} - 1$$

$$EAR = 29,168.80 - 1 = 29,167.80,\ or\ 2,916,780\%$$

Needless to say, you'll want to stay away from payday loans.

Checkpoint 5.7

Calculating an Effective Annual Rate or EAR

Assume that you just received your first credit card statement and the APR, or annual percentage rate, listed on the statement is 21.7 percent. When you look closer you notice that the interest is compounded daily. What is the EAR, or effective annual rate, on your credit card?

STEP 1: Picture the problem

We can visualize the problem using a timeline as follows:

If i = an annual rate of 21.7% which is compounded on a daily basis, what is the EAR?

| ■ Time Period | 0 | 1 | 2 | 3 | 4 | 5 | 6 | 7 | 8 | 9 | 10 | ■ Daily Periods |

■ Cash Flow   -$ Amount

STEP 2: Decide on a solution strategy

We'll use Equation (5–4) to solve this problem:

$$\begin{array}{l}\text{Effective}\\\text{Annual Rate}\\(EAR)\end{array} = \left(1 + \frac{\text{Quoted Annual Rate}}{\text{Compounding Periods per year } (m)}\right)^m - 1 \tag{5–4}$$

STEP 3: Solve

To calculate the EAR we can use Equation (5–4), where the quoted annual rate is 21.7 percent, or 0.217, and m is 365. Substituting in these values, we get

$$EAR = \left[1 + \frac{0.217}{365}\right]^{365} - 1$$

$EAR = 1.242264 - 1 = 0.242264$ or 24.2264%

You were right in thinking that the amount of interest you owed seemed high. In reality, the EAR, or effective annual rate, is actually 24.2264 percent. Recall that whenever interest is compounded more frequently, it accumulates faster.

STEP 4: Analyze

When you invest in a certificate of deposit, or CD, at a bank, the rate the bank will quote you is the EAR—that's because it actually is the rate that you will earn on your money—and it's also higher than the simple APR. It's important to make sure when you compare different interest rates that they are truly comparable, and the EAR allows you to make them comparable. For example, if you're talking about borrowing money at 9 percent compounded daily, although the APR is 9 percent, the EAR is actually 9.426 percent. That's a pretty big difference when you're paying the interest.

STEP 5: Check yourself

What is the EAR on a quoted or stated rate of 13 percent that is compounded monthly?

ANSWER: 13.80 percent.

Your Turn: For more practice, do related **Study Problems** 5–35 through 5–38 at the end of this chapter.

Calculating the Interest Rate and Converting It to an EAR

When you have non-annual compounding and you calculate a value for *i* using your financial calculator or Excel, you're calculating the rate per non-annual compounding period, which is referred to as the periodic rate:

$$\text{Periodic Rate} = \frac{\text{Quoted Annual Rate}}{\text{Compounding Periods per Year } (m)}$$

You can easily convert the periodic rate into an APR by multiplying it by the number of times that compounding occurs per year (*m*). However, if you're interested in the EAR, you'll have to subsequently convert the value you just calculated into an EAR. Let's look at an example.

Suppose that you've just taken out a two-year, $100,000 loan with monthly compounding and that at the end of two years you will pay $126,973 to pay the loan off. How can we find the quoted interest rate on this loan and convert it to an EAR? This problem can be solved using either a financial calculator or Excel.[2] Because the problem involves monthly compounding, *m*, the number of compounding periods per year is 12; *n*, the number of periods, becomes 24 (number of years times *m*, or 2 times 12); and the solution, *i*, will be expressed as the *monthly rate*.

Financial Calculator. Substituting in a financial calculator we find

Enter	24		-100,000	0	126,973
	N	I/Y	PV	PMT	FV
Solve for		1.0			

To determine the APR you're paying on this loan, you need to multiply the value you just calculated for *i* times 12—thus the APR on this loan is 12 percent—but that is *not* the loan's EAR. It's merely the APR. To convert the APR to an EAR, we can use Equation (5–4):

$$\text{Effective Annual Rate } (EAR) = \left(1 + \frac{\text{Quoted Annual Rate}}{\text{Compounding Periods per Year } (m)}\right)^{m} - 1 \qquad \textbf{(5–4)}$$

where the quoted annual rate is 0.12, and *m* is 12. Substituting these values into the above equation we get

$$EAR = \left[1 + \frac{0.12}{12}\right]^{12} - 1$$

$$EAR = 1.1268 - 1 = 0.126825, \text{ or } 12.68255\%$$

In reality, the EAR, or effective annual rate, is actually 12.6825 percent. In effect, if you took out a two-year loan for $100,000 at 12.6825 percent compounded annually, your payment at the end of two years would be $126,973, the same payment you had when you borrowed $100,000 at 12 percent compounded monthly.

---

[2]Using either a TI BAII-Plus or an HP 10BII calculator, there is a shortcut key that allows you to enter the number of compounding periods and the nominal rate to calculate the EAR. Those keystrokes are shown in Appendix A in MyFinanceLab.

To the Extreme: Continuous Compounding

As m (the number of compounding periods per year) increases, so does the EAR. That only makes sense because the greater the number of compounding periods, the more often interest is earned on interest. As you just saw, we can easily compute the EAR when interest is compounded daily ($m = 365$). We can just as easily calculate EAR if the interest, i, is compounded hourly ($m = 8,760$), compounded every minute ($m = 525,600$), or every second ($m = 31,536,000$). We can even calculate the EAR when interest is continuously compounded; that is, when the time intervals between interest payments are infinitely small, as

$$EAR = (e^{quoted\ annual\ rate}) - 1 \qquad \textbf{(5-5)}$$

where e is the number 2.71828, with the corresponding calculator key generally appearing as "e^x." This number e is an irrational number that is used in applications that involve things that grow continuously over time. It is similar to the number Π in geometry.[3]

Let's take another look at the credit card example we looked at in Checkpoint 5.7, but with continuous compounding. Again, the APR, or annual percentage rate, is listed at 21.7 percent. With continuous compounding, what's the EAR, or effective annual rate, on your credit card?

$$EAR = e^{.217} - 1 = 1.2423 - 1 = 0.2423, or\ 24.23\%$$

FINANCE IN A FLAT WORLD

Financial Access at Birth

Approximately half the world's population has no access to financial services such as savings, credit, and insurance. Inspired by the One-Laptop-Per-Child campaign, UCLA finance professor Bhagwan Chowdhry has a plan to take this number to zero by 2030, called the Financial Access at Birth (FAB) Campaign.

This is how FAB could work. Each child would have an online bank account opened at birth with an initial deposit of $100. The bank account would be opened together with the child's birth registration, and the deposit plus interest could be withdrawn when the child reaches 16 years of age. If the program were launched in 2011, in just 20 short years every child and young adult in the world would have access to financial services. Assuming a 5 percent annual rate of interest on the deposit, the $100 deposit would grow to about $218 when the child reaches 16. If we wait until the child reaches 21 before turning over the account, it will have grown to about $279. In many parts of the world this would be a princely sum of money. Moreover, the recipient would have a bank account!

So what's the cost of implementing FAB? Currently there are about 134 million children born annually, and assuming that a quarter of these children would not need the service, this leaves 100 million children that otherwise would not have access to a bank account. The cost of the program would then be just $10 billion per year, which is less than the amount spent per week on military expenditures around the world. If 100 million individuals would contribute just $100 per year the dream of the FAB could become a reality. Every person in the world would have access to financial services in just 20 years!

Want to learn more? Go to http://tr.im/fabcam.

CONCEPTS IN REVIEW	**5.7** How does an EAR differ from an APR?
	5.8 What is the effect of having multiple compounding periods within a year on future values?

---

[3]Like the number Π, it goes on forever. In fact, if you're interested, you can find the first 5 million digits of e at http://antwrp.gsfc.nasa.gov/htmltest/gifcity/e.5mil

Applying the Principles of Finance to Chapter 5

Principle 1: **Money Has a Time Value** This chapter begins our study of the time value of money—a dollar received today, other things being the same, is worth more than a dollar received a year from now. The concept of time value of money underlies many financial decisions faced in business. In this chapter, we learn how to calculate the value today of a sum of money received in the future and the future value of a present sum.

MyFinanceLab

Here is what you should know after reading this chapter. MyFinanceLab will help you identify what you know and where to go when you need to practice.

What You Should Know	Key Terms	
LG1 Construct cash flow timelines to organize your analysis of problems involving time value of money. Timelines can help you visualize and then solve time-value-of-money problems. Time periods—with 0 representing today, 1 the end of Period 1, and so forth—are listed on top of the timeline. Note that Period 1 represents the end of Period 1 and the beginning of Period 2. The periods can consist of years, months, days, or any unit of time. However, in general, when people analyze cash flows, they are looking at yearly periods. The cash flows appear below the timeline. Cash inflows are labeled with positive signs. Cash outflows are labeled with negative signs.	Timeline, *p. 148*	A linear representation of the timing of cash flows.
LG2 Understand compounding and calculate the future value of cash flows using mathematical formulas, a financial calculator, and an Excel spreadsheet. Compounding begins when the interest earned on an investment during a past period begins earning interest in the current period. Financial managers must compare the costs and benefits of alternatives that do not occur during the same time period. Calculating the time value of money makes all dollar values comparable; because money has a time value, it moves all dollar flows either back to the present or out to a common future date. All time value formulas presented in this chapter actually stem from the single compounding formula $FV_n = PV(1 + i)^n$. The formulas are used to deal simply with common financial situations, for example, discounting single flows or moving single flows out into the future.	Compounding, *p. 150*	The process of determining the future value of a payment or series of payments when applying the concept of compound interest.
	Compound interest, *p. 150*	The situation in which interest paid on the investment during the first period is added to the principal and, during the second period, interest is earned on the original principal plus the interest earned during the first period.
	Future value, *p. 150*	What a cash flow will be worth in the future.
	Future value interest factor, *p. 151*	The value $(1 + i)^n$ used as a multiplier to calculate an amount's future value.
	Present value, *p. 150*	The value in today's dollars of a future payment discounted back to the present at the required rate of return.
	Simple interest, *p. 150*	The interest earned on the principal.

Financial calculators are a handy and inexpensive alternative to doing the math. However, most professionals today use spreadsheet software, such as Excel.

What You Should Know	**Key Terms**

Key Equations

$$\underset{(FV_n)}{\underset{\text{in Year }n}{\text{Future Value}}} = \underset{\text{Value }(PV)}{\text{Present}} \left(1 + \frac{\text{Annual}}{\text{Interest Rate }(i)}\right)^{\text{Number of Years }(n)}$$ **(5–1a)**

$$\underset{(FV_n)}{\underset{\text{in Year }n}{\text{Future Value}}} = \underset{\text{Value }(PV)}{\text{Present}} \left(1 + \frac{\begin{array}{c}\text{Annual}\\\text{Interest Rate }(i)\end{array}}{\begin{array}{c}\text{Compounding}\\\text{Periods per Year }(m)\end{array}}\right)^{m \times (\text{Number of Years }(n))}$$ **(5–1b)**

where m is the number of compounding periods per year.

LG3 Understand discounting and calculate the present value of cash flows using mathematical formulas, a financial calculator, and an Excel spreadsheet. Previously we were solving for the future value (FV_n) of the present value (PV) of a sum of money. When we are solving for the present value, we are simply doing the reverse of solving for the future value. We can find the present value by solving for PV,

$$PV = FV_n \left[\frac{1}{(1 + i)^n}\right]$$

In addition, increasing the number of compounding periods within the year, while holding the rate of interest constant, will magnify the effects of compounding. That is, even though the rate of interest does not change, increasing the number of compounding periods means that interest gets compounded sooner than it would otherwise. This magnifies the effects of compounding.

Discount rate, *p. 159*	The interest rate used in the discounting process.
Discounting, *p. 159*	The inverse of compounding. This process is used to determine the present value of a future cash flow.
Present value interest factor, *p. 159*	The value $[1/(1 + i)^n]$ used as a multiplier to calculate a future payment's present value.
Rule of 72, *p. 162*	A method for estimating the time it takes for an amount to double in value. To determine the approximate time it takes for an amount to double in value, 72 is divided by the annual interest rate.

Key Equations

$$\underset{\text{Value }(PV)}{\text{Present}} = \left[\frac{\underset{\text{in Year }n\ (FV_n)}{\text{Future Value}}}{\left(1 + \dfrac{\text{Annual}}{\text{Interest Rate }(i)}\right)^{\substack{\text{Number of}\\\text{Years }(n)}}}\right]$$

What You Should Know	Key Terms	

LG3 *(Continued)*

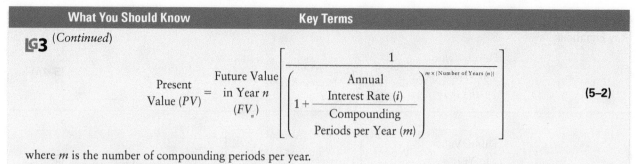

$$\text{Present Value } (PV) = \text{Future Value in Year } n \; (FV_n) \left[\frac{1}{\left(1 + \dfrac{\text{Annual Interest Rate } (i)}{\text{Compounding Periods per Year } (m)}\right)^{m \times (\text{Number of Years } (n))}} \right] \qquad (5\text{–}2)$$

where *m* is the number of compounding periods per year.

LG4 Understand how interest rates are quoted and know how to make them comparable. One way to compare different interest rates is to use the annual percentage rate (APR), which indicates the amount of interest earned in one year without compounding. The APR is the simple interest rate and is calculated as the interest rate per period multiplied by the number of periods in the year:

$$APR = \text{Interest Rate per Period} \times \text{Periods per Year} \qquad (5\text{–}3)$$

The problem with the APR is that if compounding occurs more than once a year— for example, if the interest you owe is calculated every month, then in the second month, and from then on, you will end up paying interest from the first month. The end result of this is that the actual interest rate you are paying is greater than the APR. To find out the actual amount of interest we would pay over the course of one time period, we must convert the quoted APR rate to an effective annual rate (EAR). The EAR is the annual compounded rate that produces the same cash flow as the nominal interest rate:

$$EAR = \left(1 + \frac{\text{Quoted Annual Rate}}{m}\right)^m - 1 \qquad (5\text{–}4)$$

where *EAR* is the effective annual rate, and *m* is the number of compounding periods within a year.

Annual percentage rate (APR), *p. 164*

Effective annual rate (EAR), *p. 166*

Nominal *or* quoted (stated) interest rate, *p. 166*

The interest rate paid or earned in one year without compounding. It is calculated as the interest rate per period (for example, per month or week) multiplied by the number of periods during which compounding occurs during the year (*m*).

The annual compounded rate that produces the same return as the nominal, or stated, rate.

The interest rate paid on debt securities without an adjustment for any loss in purchasing power.

What You Should Know	Key Terms

LG4 (*Continued*)

$$\text{Annual Percentage Rate } (APR) \text{ or simple interest} = \begin{pmatrix} \text{Interest} \\ \text{Rate per} \\ \text{Period} \end{pmatrix} \times \begin{matrix} \text{Compounding} \\ \text{Periods per} \\ \text{Year} \end{matrix} \qquad \textbf{(5–3)}$$

$$\text{Effective Annual Rate } (EAR) = \left(1 + \frac{\text{Quoted Annual Rate}}{\text{Compounding Periods per Year } (m)}\right)^m - 1 \qquad \textbf{(5–4)}$$

where EAR = the effective annual rate.

Discussion Questions

Q5.1 What is the time value of money? Give three examples of how the time value of money might take on importance in business decisions.

Q5.2 The processes of discounting and compounding are related. Explain this relationship.

Q5.3 What is the relationship between the number of times interest is compounded per year on an investment and the future value of that investment? What is the relationship between the number of times compounding occurs per year and the EAR?

Q5.4 How would an increase in the interest rate (i) or a decrease in the number of periods (n) affect the future value (FV_n) of a sum of money?

Q5.5 How would an increase in the interest rate (i) or a decrease in the number of periods until the payment is received (n) affect the present value (PV) of a sum of money?

Q5.6 Compare some of the different financial calculators that are available on the Internet. Look at Kiplinger Online calculators (www.kiplinger.com/tools/index.html), which include saving and investing, mutual funds, bonds, stocks, home, auto, credit cards, and budgeting online calculators. Also go to www.dinkytown.net, www.bankrate.com/calculators.aspx, and www.interest.com and click on the "Calculators" links. Which financial calculators do you find to be the most useful? Why?

Q5.7 **(Related to Chapter Introduction: Payday Loans on page 147)** The introduction to this chapter examined payday loans. Recently, Congress passed legislation limiting the interest rate charged to active military to 36 percent. Go to the Predatory Lending Association website at www.predatorylendingassociation.com and find the military base closest to you and identify the payday lenders that surround that base. Also, identify any payday lenders near you.

Q5.8 **(Related to Chapter Introduction: Payday Loans on page 147)** In the introduction to this chapter, payday loans were examined. Go to the Responsible Lending Organization website at www.responsiblelending.org/payday-lending/. How does the "debt trap" (www.responsiblelending.org/payday-lending/tools-resources/debttrap.html) associated with payday loans work?

Study Problems

Compound Interest

P5.1 **(Related to Checkpoint 5.2 on page 155)** **(Future value)** To what amount will the following investments accumulate?
  a. $5,000 invested for 10 years at 10 percent compounded annually
  b. $8,000 invested for 7 years at 8 percent compounded annually
  c. $775 invested for 12 years at 12 percent compounded annually
  d. $21,000 invested for 5 years at 5 percent compounded annually

P5.2 **(Related to Checkpoint 5.2 on page 155)** **(Future value)** Leslie Mosallam, who recently sold her Porsche, placed $10,000 in a savings account paying annual compound interest of 6 percent.
  a. Calculate the amount of money that will accumulate if Leslie leaves the money in the bank for 1, 5, and 15 years.
  b. Suppose Leslie moves her money into an account that pays 8 percent or one that pays 10 percent. Rework part (a) using 8 percent and 10 percent.
  c. What conclusions can you draw about the relationship between interest rates, time, and future sums from the calculations you just did?

P5.3 **(Related to The Business of Life: Saving for Your First House on page 158)** **(Future value)** You are hoping to buy a house in the future and recently received an inheritance of $20,000. You intend to use your inheritance as a down payment on your house.
  a. If you put your inheritance in an account that earns a 7 percent interest rate compounded annually, how many years will it be before your inheritance grows to $30,000?
  b. If you let your money grow for 10.25 years at 7 percent, how much will you have?
  c. How long will it take your money to grow to $30,000 if you move it into an account that pays 3 percent compounded annually? How long will it take your money to grow to $30,000 if you move it into an account that pays 11 percent?
  d. What does all of this tell you about the relationship among interest rates, time, and future sums?

P5.4 **(Related to Checkpoint 5.2 on page 155)** **(Future value)** Bob Terwilliger received $12,345 for his services as financial consultant to the mayor's office of his hometown of Springfield. Bob says that his consulting work was his civic duty and that he should not receive any compensation. So, he has invested his paycheck into an account paying 3.98 percent annual interest and left the account in his will to the city of Springfield on the condition that the city could not collect any money from the account for 200 years. How much money will the city receive from Bob's generosity in 200 years?

P5.5 **(Related to Checkpoint 5.3 on page 157)** **(Compound interest with non-annual periods)** Calculate the amount of money that will be in each of the following accounts at the end of the given deposit period:

Account Holder	Amount Deposited	Annual Interest Rate	Compounding Periods per Year (M)	Compounding Periods (Years)
Theodore Logan III	$ 1,000	10%	1	10
Vernell Coles	95,000	12	12	1
Tina Elliott	8,000	12	6	2
Wayne Robinson	120,000	8	4	2
Eunice Chung	30,000	10	2	4
Kelly Cravens	15,000	12	3	3

P5.6   **(Related to Checkpoint 5.2 on page 155)** (**Compound interest with non-annual periods**) You just received a $5,000 bonus.
  a. Calculate the future value of $5,000, given that it will be held in the bank for five years and earn an annual interest rate of 6 percent.
  b. Recalculate part (a) using a compounding period that is (1) semiannual and (2) bimonthly.
  c. Recalculate parts (a) and (b) using a 12 percent annual interest rate.
  d. Recalculate part (a) using a time horizon of 12 years at a 6 percent interest rate.
  e. What conclusions can you draw when you compare the answers in parts (c) and (d) with the answers in parts (a) and (b)?

P5.7   **(Related to Checkpoint 5.3 on page 157)** (**Compound interest with non-annual periods**) Your grandmother just gave you $6,000. You'd like to see what it might grow to if you invest it.
  a. Calculate the future value of $6,000, given that it will be invested for five years at an annual interest rate of 6 percent.
  b. Recalculate part (a) using a compounding period that is (1) semiannual and (2) bimonthly.
  c. Now let's look at what might happen if you can invest the money at a 12 percent rate rather than 6 percent rate; recalculate parts (a) and (b) for a 12 percent annual interest rate.
  d. Now let's see what might happen if you invest the money for 12 years rather than 5 years; recalculate part (a) using a time horizon of 12 years (annual interest rate is still 6 percent).
  e. With respect to the changes in the stated interest rate and length of time the money is invested in parts (c) and (d), what conclusions can you draw?

P5.8   **(Related to Checkpoint 5.2 on page 155)** (**Future value**) A new finance book sold 15,000 copies following the first year of its release, and was expected to increase by 20 percent per year. What sales are expected during Years 2, 3, and 4? Graph this sales trend and explain.

P5.9   **(Related to Checkpoint 5.2 on page 155)** (**Future value**) You have just introduced "must-have" headphones for the iPod. Sales of the new product are expected to be 10,000 units this year and are expected to increase by 15 percent per year in the future. What are expected sales during each of the next three years? Graph this sales trend and explain why the number of additional units sold increases every year.

P5.10   **(Related to Checkpoint 5.2 on page 155)** (**Future value**) If you deposit $3,500 today into an account earning an 11 percent annual rate of return, what would your account be worth in 35 years (assuming no further deposits)? In 40 years?

P5.11   **(Related to Checkpoint 5.2 on page 155)** (**Future value**) (**Simple and compound interest**) If you deposit $10,000 today into an account earning an 11 percent annual rate of return, in the third year how much interest would be earned? How much of the total is simple interest and how much results from compounding of interest?

Discounting and Present Value

P5–12. **(Related to Checkpoint 5.4 on page 161)** (**Present value**) Sarah Wiggum would like to make a single investment and have $2 million at the time of her retirement in 35 years. She has found a mutual fund that will earn 4 percent annually. How much will Sarah have to invest today? What if Sarah were a finance major and learned how to earn a 14 percent annual return? How soon could she then retire?

P5–13. **(Related to Checkpoint 5.5 on page 161)** (**Solving for n**) How many years will the following take?
  a. $500 to grow to $1,039.50 if it's invested at 5 percent compounded annually
  b. $35 to grow to $53.87 if it's invested at 9 percent compounded annually
  c. $100 to grow to $298.60 if it's invested at 20 percent compounded annually
  d. $53 to grow to $78.76 if it's invested at 2 percent compounded annually

P5–14. (Related to Checkpoint 5.6 on page 165) **(Solving for *i*)** At what annual interest rate would the following have to be invested?

   a. $500 to grow to $1,948.00 in 12 years
   b. $300 to grow to $422.10 in 7 years
   c. $50 to grow to $280.20 in 20 years
   d. $200 to grow to $497.60 in 5 years

P5–15. (Related to Checkpoint 5.4 on page 161) **(Present value)** What is the present value of the following future amounts?

   a. $800 to be received 10 years from now discounted back to the present at 10 percent
   b. $300 to be received 5 years from now discounted back to the present at 5 percent
   c. $1,000 to be received 8 years from now discounted back to the present at 3 percent
   d. $1,000 to be received 8 years from now discounted back to the present at 20 percent

P5–16. (Related to Checkpoint 5.6 on page 165) **(Solving for *i*)** Kirk Van Houten, who has been married for 23 years, would like to buy his wife an expensive diamond ring with a platinum setting on their 30-year wedding anniversary. Assume that the cost of the ring will be $12,000 in seven years. Kirk currently has $4,510 to invest. What annual rate of return must Kirk earn on his investment to accumulate enough money to pay for the ring?

P5–17. (Related to Checkpoint 5.6 on page 165) **(Solving for *i*)** You are considering investing in a security that will pay you $1,000 in 30 years.

   a. If the appropriate discount rate is 10 percent, what is the present value of this investment?
   b. Assume these investments sell for $365, in return for which you receive $1,000 in 30 years; what is the rate of return investors earn on this investment if they buy it for $365?

P5–18. (Related to Checkpoint 5.5 on page 163) **(Solving for *n*)** Jack asked Jill to marry him, and she has accepted under one condition: Jack must buy her a new $330,000 Rolls-Royce Phantom. Jack currently has $45,530 that he may invest. He has found a mutual fund that pays 4.5 percent annual interest in which he will place the money. How long will it take Jack to win Jill's hand in marriage?

P5–19. (Related to Checkpoint 5.4 on page 161) **(Present value)** Ronen Consulting has just realized an accounting error that has resulted in an unfunded liability of $398,930 due in 28 years. In other words, the company will need $398,930 in 28 years. Toni Flanders, the company's CEO, is scrambling to discount the liability to the present to assist in valuing the firm's stock. If the appropriate discount rate is 7 percent, what is the present value of the liability?

P5–20. (Related to Checkpoint 5.6 on page 165) **(Solving for *i*)** Seven years ago, Lance Murdock purchased a wooden statue of a Conquistador for $7,600 to put in his home office. Lance has recently married, and his home office is being converted into a sewing room. His new wife, who has far better taste than Lance, thinks the Conquistador is hideous and must go immediately. Lance decided to sell it on e-Bay and only received $5,200 for it, and so he took a loss on the investment. What was his rate of return, that is, the value of *i*?

P5–21. (Related to Checkpoint 5.6 on page 165) **(Solving for *i*)** Springfield Learning sold zero-coupon bonds (bonds that don't pay any interest—instead the bondholder gets just one payment, coming when the bond matures, from the issuer) and received $900 for each bond that will pay $20,000 when it matures in 30 years.

   a. At what rate is Springfield Learning borrowing the money from investors?
   b. If Nancy Muntz purchased a bond at the offering for $900 and sold it 10 years later for the market price of $3,500, what annual rate of return did she earn?
   c. If Barney Gumble purchased Muntz's bond at the market price of $3,500 and held it 20 years until maturity, what annual rate of return would he have earned?

P5–22. (Related to Checkpoint 5.6 on page 165) **(Solving for *i*)** If you were offered $1,079.50 ten years from now in return for an investment of $500 currently, what annual rate of interest would you earn if you took the offer?

P5–23. (**Solving for *i***) An insurance agent just offered you a new insurance product that will provide you with $2,376.50 ten years from now if you invest $700 today. What annual rate of interest would you earn if you invested in this product?

P5–24. (**Solving for *n* with non-annual periods**) Approximately how many years would it take for an investment to grow fourfold if it were invested at 16 percent compounded semiannually?

P5–25. (**Solving for n with non-annual periods**) Approximately how many years would it take for an investment to grow by sevenfold if it were invested at 10 percent compounded semiannually?

P5–26. (**Related to Checkpoint 5.6 on page 165**) (**Solving for *i***) You lend a friend $10,000, for which your friend will repay you $27,027 at the end of five years. What interest rate are you charging your "friend"?

P5–27. (**Related to Checkpoint 5.6 on page 165**) (**Solving for *i***) You've run out of money for college, and your college roommate has an idea for you. He offers to lend you $15,000, for which you will repay him $37,313 at the end of five years. If you took this loan, what interest rate would you be paying on it?

P5–28. (**Related to Checkpoint 5.4 on page 161**) (**Present-value comparison**) You are offered $100,000 today or $300,000 in 13 years. Assuming that you can earn 11 percent on your money, which should you choose?

P5–29. (**Present-value comparison**) Much to your surprise, you were selected to appear on the TV show "The Price Is Right." As a result of your prowess in identifying how many rolls of toilet paper a typical American family keeps on hand, you win the opportunity to choose one of the following: $1,000 today, $10,000 in 12 years, or $25,000 in 25 years. Assuming that you can earn 11 percent on your money, which should you choose?

P5–30. (**Related to Checkpoint 5.6 on page 165**) (**Solving for *i***) In September 1963, the first issue of the comic book *X-MEN* was issued. The original price for the issue was 12 cents. By September 2013, 50 years later, the value of this comic book had risen to $9,500. What annual rate of interest would you have earned if you had bought the comic in 1963 and sold it in 2013?

P5–31. (**Solving for *i***) In March 1963, Ironman was first introduced in issue number 39 of the comic book *Tales of Suspense*. The original price for that issue was 12 cents. By March of 2013, 50 years later, the value of this comic book had risen to $9,000. What annual rate of interest would you have earned if you had bought the comic in 1963 and sold it in 2013?

P5–32. (**Solving for *i***) A financial planner just offered you a new investment product that would require an initial investment on your part of $35,000, and then 25 years from now will be worth $250,000. What annual rate of interest would you earn if you invested in this product?

P5–33. (**Spreadsheet problem**) If you invest $900 in a bank where it will earn 8 percent compounded annually, how much will it be worth at the end of seven years? Use a spreadsheet to calculate your answer.

P5–34. (**Spreadsheet problem**) In 20 years, you would like to have $250,000 to buy a vacation home. If you have only $30,000, at what rate must it be compounded annually for it to grow to $250,000 in 20 years? Use a spreadsheet to calculate your answer.

Making Interest Rates Comparable

P5–35. (**Related to Checkpoint 5.7 on page 167**) (**Calculating an EAR**) After examining the various personal loan rates available to you, you find that you can borrow funds from a finance company at 12 percent compounded monthly or from a bank at 13 percent compounded annually. Which alternative is the most attractive?

P5–36. (**Related to Checkpoint 5.7 on page 167**) (**Calculating an EAR**) You have a choice of borrowing money from a finance company at 24 percent compounded monthly or borrowing money from a bank at 26 percent compounded annually. Which alternative is the most attractive?

P5–37. (Related to Checkpoint 5.7 on page 167) (Calculating an EAR) Your grandmother asks for your help in choosing a certificate of deposit (CD) from a bank with a one-year maturity and a fixed interest rate. The first certificate of deposit, CD #1, pays 4.95 percent APR compounded daily, and the second certificate of deposit, CD #2, pays 5.0 percent APR compounded monthly. What is the effective annual rate (the EAR) of each CD, and which CD do you recommend to your grandmother?

P5–38. (Related to Checkpoint 5.7 on page 167) (Calculating an EAR) Based on effective interest rates, would you prefer to deposit your money into Springfield National Bank, which pays 8.0 percent interest compounded annually, or into Burns National Bank, which pays 7.8 percent compounded monthly? (Hint: Calculate the EAR on each account.)

P5–39. (Calculating an EAR) Payday loans issued by banks are often referred to as "direct deposit advances." In early 2013, the average direct deposit advance charged $10 for a $100 advance and was due in 10 days. What is the effective annual rate on this type of loan?

P5–40. (Calculating an EAR) In early 2013, typical terms on a payday loan involved a $15 charge for a two-week payday loan of $100. Assuming there are twenty-six 14-day periods in a year, what is the effective annual rate on such a loan?

Mini-Case

Emily Dao, 27, just received a promotion at work that increased her annual salary to $37,000. She is eligible to participate in her employer's 401(k) retirement plan to which the employer matches, dollar for dollar, workers' contributions up to 5 percent of salary. However, Emily wants to buy a new $25,000 car in three years, and she wants to have enough money to make a $7,000 down payment on the car and finance the balance. Fortunately, she expects a sizable bonus this year that she hopes will cover that down payment in three years.

A wedding is also in her plans. Emily and her boyfriend, Paul, have set a wedding date two years in the future, after he finishes medical school. In addition, Emily and Paul want to buy a home of their own as soon as possible. This might be possible because at age 30, Emily will be eligible to access a $50,000 trust fund left to her as an inheritance by her late grandfather. Her trust fund is invested in 7 percent government bonds.

Questions

1. Justify Emily's participation in her employer's 401(k) plan using the time-value-of-money concepts by explaining how much an investment of $10,000 will grow to in 40 years if it earns 10 percent.

2. Calculate the amount of money that Emily needs to set aside from her bonus this year to cover the down payment on a new car, assuming she can earn 6 percent on her savings. What if she could earn 10 percent on her savings?

3. What will be the value of Emily's trust fund at age 60, assuming she takes possession of half of the money ($25,000 of the $50,000 trust fund) at age 30 for a house down payment, and leaves the other half of the money untouched where it is currently invested?

4. What is the relationship between discounting and compounding?

5. List at least two actions that Emily and Paul could take to accumulate more for their retirement (think about *i* and *n*)

6

The Time Value of Money
Annuities and Other Topics

LEARNING GOALS

LG1 Distinguish between an ordinary annuity and an annuity due, and calculate the present and future values of each.

LG2 Calculate the present value of a level perpetuity and a growing perpetuity.

LG3 Calculate the present and future values of complex cash flow streams.

Principles P1 and P3 Applied

In this chapter we provide tools that allow you to determine the value of a stream of cash flows, both with a limited life as well as those that continue forever and have no maturity date. Once you've mastered these tools, you'll be applying them to the valuation of stocks, bonds, and other investment opportunities, in addition to using them to determine your mortgage and car loan payments. In doing so, we will continue our examination of the first principle of finance—P Principle 1: **Money Has a Time Value.** In moving money through time, we will focus on cash flows because as we learned in P Principle 3: **Cash Flows Are the Source of Value.**

Many of you have bought a car that was financed by a bank. To repay such a loan, you make payments to the bank of a certain fixed amount each month for 48 or 60 months. Similarly, if you buy a house that you finance with a conventional mortgage, you will again face a schedule of payments due over a fixed period of time. Just like individuals, firms make loan payments that are due at regular intervals. In addition, they pay a fixed amount over a set period of time to lease equipment. And they often have investments that generate regular payments of cash. These examples all have one thing in common—they each require a fixed cash flow stream over a set period of time. As we'll see in this chapter, we call this type of cash flow stream an *annuity*.

Annuities We All Know

We encounter annuities often in our day-to-day lives. An annuity, as defined in this chapter, is simply a series of equal payments, each payable at the end of each period (month or year) and over multiple periods. For example, if you're paying off a student loan, you're paying off an annuity. In this case, the annuity represents the payment of principal and interest on your student loan. So if you have $30,000 in student loans out- standing at a 6.8 percent interest rate that you plan to repay in 10 years, you'll be making monthly payments of $345.24 over the next 10 years. We sometimes encounter annuities in which the payments are made to us. For example, if your grandparents leave you $30,000 to help pay your college expenses, you might purchase a 6 percent annuity that provides you with monthly payments of $704.55 over the next four years.

Annuities

LG1   In Chapter 5 we learned how to move single cash flows through time, calculating their future and present values. We will now extend these formulas to find the future and present values of a constant stream of cash flows. Together with what we learned in Chapter 5, the material in this chapter provides the tools to implement ▣ Principle 1: **Money Has a Time Value.** Later in the book, we will see that this principle, along with ▣ Principle 3: **Cash Flows Are the Source of Value,** provides the logic behind the valu- ation of stocks, bonds, and other investment opportunities.

Ordinary Annuities

We define an **annuity** as a series of *equal* dollar payments that are made at the end of equidistant points in time, such as monthly, quarterly, or annually, over a finite period of time, such as three years. Payments for an annuity can be made at either the begin- ning or the end of each period. If payments are made at the end of each period, the annuity is often referred to as an **ordinary annuity.** An ordinary annuity is the most common form of annuity and is oftentimes referred to simply as an annuity, without the term *ordinary* preceding it. However, some annuities have payments that are made at the beginning of each period, such as apartment rent. We'll discuss this type of annuity later in this chapter. For now, when we refer to an annuity, you should assume we are referring to an ordinary annuity where the payments are made:

- at the end of each period,
- at equidistant periods of time, such as monthly or annually, and
- for a finite period of time, such as three years.

The present and future values of an ordinary annuity can be computed using the methods described in Chapter 5 and illustrated in Figure 6.1. However, this process can

FIGURE 6.1   Future Value of a Five-Year Annuity—Saving for Grad School

The five annual annuity payments consist of $5,000 in savings that are placed in an account that earns 6% interest. This is a five-year ordinary annuity such that the first cash flow occurs at the end of the first year. This, in turn, means that this payment is only compounded until the end of year five (or for four years).

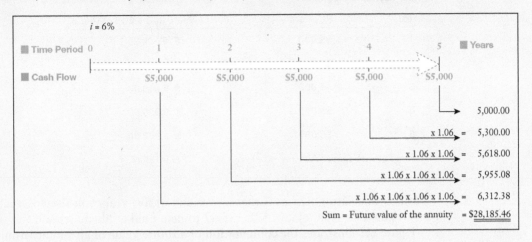

be time consuming, especially for longer annuities, so next we will discuss some simple time-value-of-money formulas for easily calculating the present value and future value of an annuity.

The Future Value of an Ordinary Annuity Let's assume that you are saving money to go to graduate school. You've taken your first job and you plan to save $5,000 each year for the next five years for your grad school fund. How much money will you accumulate by the end of Year 5?

This scenario presents a common annuity valuation problem, one we can solve by finding the future value. To answer this question, we first need to know two things: first, the rate of interest you earn on your savings, and second, for how long each of your savings deposits (the annuity payments) will earn interest. For our purposes, let's assume you save $5,000 each year for five years and that you deposit that amount in an account that earns 6 percent interest per year. A timeline depicting this is shown in Figure 6.1. We can use Equation (5–1a) from the last chapter to find the future value of each of the deposits. The future value at the end of Year 5 of the deposit made at the end of Year 1 (growing for four years) can be calculated as follows:

$$FV_n = PV(1 + i)^n \tag{5–1a}$$

$$FV_{year\ 4} = \$5,000(1 + .06)^4 = \$6,312.38$$

Note that the deposit made at the end of Year 1 has only four years to earn interest until the end of Year 5. Similarly, the deposit made at the end of Year 2 will have only three years to earn interest, and so forth. The future value of the first- through fifth-year deposits is as follows:

Interest Rate = 6%
Annuity Payment = $5,000

Year	Payment	Future Value at the End of Year 5
1	$5,000	$ 6,312.38
2	$5,000	$ 5,955.08
3	$5,000	$ 5,618.00
4	$5,000	$ 5,300.00
5	$5,000	$ 5,000.00
Sum = Future Value of Annuity =		$28,185.46

What this calculation tells us is that by the end of five years you should, if all goes as planned, have saved a total of $28,185.47 to help fund graduate school.

Figure 6.1 illustrates the computation of a future value of an annuity using a timeline. It's important to note that the future value of an annuity is simply the sum of the future values of each of the annuity payments compounded out to the end of the annuity's life—in this case the end of Year 5.

The Formula for the Future Value of an Ordinary Annuity We can solve for the future value of an ordinary annuity using the following equation:

Future value of an annuity = The sum of the future value of the individual cash flows that make up the annuity

$$\begin{array}{l} \text{Future value of} \\ \text{an annuity, } FV_n \end{array} = \begin{array}{l} \text{Annuity} \\ \text{Payment} \end{array} \left(1 + \frac{\text{Interest}}{\text{Rate}}\right)^{n-1} + \begin{array}{l} \text{Annuity} \\ \text{Payment} \end{array} \left(1 + \frac{\text{Interest}}{\text{Rate}}\right)^{n-2} + \cdots + \begin{array}{l} \text{Annuity} \\ \text{Payment} \end{array} \left(1 + \frac{\text{Interest}}{\text{Rate}}\right)^{0}$$

Note that there are n payments in the ordinary annuity. However, because the first payment is received at the end of the first period, it is compounded for only $n - 1$ periods until the end of the nth period. In addition, the last payment is received at the end of the nth period so it is compounded for $n - n$, or zero periods. Using symbols:

$$FV_n = PMT(1 + i)^{n-1} + PMT(1 + i)^{n-2} + \cdots + PMT(1 + i)^1 + PMT(1 + i)^0$$
(6–1)

Important Definitions and Concepts:

- FV_n is the future value of the annuity at the end of the nth period. Thus if periods were measured in years, the future value at the end of the third year would be FV_3.
- PMT is the annuity payment deposited or received at the end of each period.
- i is the interest (or compound) rate per period. Thus, if the periods were measured in years, it would be the annual interest rate.
- n is the number of periods for which the annuity will last.

If we just factor out the PMT term in Equation (6–1) we get the following expression:

$$FV_n = PMT\left[(1 + i)^{n-1} + (1 + i)^{n-2} + \cdots (1 + i)^1 + (1 + i)^0\right] \quad \text{(6–1a)}$$

The sum found in brackets is commonly referred to as the **annuity future value interest factor**.[1] This sum can be reduced to the following expression:

$$\text{Annuity Future Value Factor} = \left[\frac{(1 + i)^n - 1}{i}\right] \quad \text{(6–1b)}$$

So to calculate the future value of an ordinary annuity of n years where the individual payments are compounded at a rate i, we simply multiply the payment by the annuity future value interest factor:

$$FV_n = PMT\left[\frac{(1 + i)^n - 1}{i}\right] \quad \text{(6–1c)}$$

Using Mathematical Formulas. Continuing with our saving-for-grad-school example, we note that PMT is $5,000 per year, the rate of interest, i, is 6 percent annually, and n is five years. Thus,

$$FV_n = PMT\left[\frac{(1 + i)^n - 1}{i}\right] = \$5,000\left[\frac{(1 + .06)^5 - 1}{.06}\right] = \$5,000(5.63709296) = \$28,185.46$$

By simply substituting the values given above for PMT, n, and i into Equation (6–1c), we compute the future value of the level payment annuity with one computation rather than five separate future value computations that must then be summed.

Using a Financial Calculator

Enter	5	6.0	0	-5,000	
	N	I/Y	PV	PMT	FV
Solve for					28,185.46

Using an Excel Spreadsheet

$$= FV(\text{rate,nper,pmt,pv}) \text{ or with values entered} = FV(.06,5,-5000,0)$$

Solving for the PMT in an Ordinary Annuity Instead of figuring out how much money you will accumulate if you deposit a steady amount of money in a savings account each year, perhaps you would like to know how much money you *need to save* each year to accumulate a certain amount by the end of n years. In this case, we know the values of n, i, and FV_n in Equation (6–1c); what we do not know is the value of PMT, the annuity payment deposited each period.

Let's look at an example where you are trying to find out how much you must deposit annually in an account in order to reach a set goal. Suppose that you would like to have $50,000 saved 10 years from now to finance your goal of getting an MBA. If you are going to make equal annual end-of-year payments to an investment account that pays 8 percent, how big do these annual payments need to be?

---

[1]Annuity future value interest factors can be found in Appendix D in MyFinanceLab.

Here, using Equation (6–1c), we know that $n = 10$, $i = 8$, and $FV_{10} = \$50,000$, but what we do not know is the value of PMT, the annuity payment deposited each year. Substituting into Equation (6–1c), we get

$$FV_n = PMT\left[\frac{(1 + i)^n - 1}{i}\right] \tag{6–1c}$$

$$\$50,000 = PMT\left[\frac{(1 + .08)^{10} - 1}{.08}\right]$$

$$\$50,000 = PMT(14.4866)$$

$$\frac{\$50,000}{14.4866} = PMT = \$3,451$$

Checkpoint 6.1 demonstrates the calculation of an annuity payment using the mathematical formulas, a financial calculator, and Excel.

Solving for the Interest Rate in an Ordinary Annuity You may also want to calculate the *interest rate* you must earn on your investment that will allow your savings to grow to a certain amount of money by a certain future date. In this case, you will be solving for i. Consider the following example: In 15 years you hope to have $30,000 saved to buy a sports car. You are able to save $1,022 at the end of each year for the next 15 years. What rate of return must you earn on your investments in order to achieve your goal?

It is easy to solve this problem with either a financial calculator or with Excel; but, as we describe next, solving it with the mathematical formula can be somewhat difficult.

Using the Mathematical Formula. Substituting the numbers into Equation (6–1c) we get

$$FV_n = PMT\left[\frac{(1 + i)^n - 1}{i}\right] \tag{6–1c}$$

$$\$30,000 = \$1,022\left[\frac{(1 + i)^{15} - 1}{i}\right]$$

$$\frac{\$30,000}{\$1,022} = \left[\frac{(1 + i)^{15} - 1}{i}\right]$$

$$29.354 = \left[\frac{(1 + i)^{15} - 1}{i}\right]$$

The only way to solve for the interest rate at this point is by trial and error. Specifically, we substitute different numbers for i until we find the value of i that makes the right-hand side of the expression equal to 29.354.

Using a Financial Calculator. We can use a financial calculator to solve for i directly as follows:

Enter	15		0	-1,022	30,000
	N	I/Y	PV	PMT	FV
Solve for		9.0			

Solving for an Ordinary Annuity Payment

How much must you deposit at the end of each year in a savings account earning 8 percent annual interest in order to accumulate $5,000 at the end of 10 years? Let's solve this problem using the mathematical formulas, a financial calculator, and an Excel spreadsheet.

STEP 1: Picture the problem

We can use a timeline to identify the annual payments earning 8 percent that must be made in order to accumulate $5,000 at the end of 10 years as follows:

$i = 8\%$

Time Period 0   1   2   3   4   5   6   7   8   9   10   ▪ Years

Cash Flow   →PMT PMT PMT PMT PMT PMT PMT PMT PMT PMT   The Future Value of an annuity for 10 years at 8% = $5,000

We are solving for PMT

STEP 2: Decide on a solution strategy

This is a future-value-of-an-annuity problem where we know the values for n, i, and FV; and we are solving for PMT (PV is zero because there is no cash flow at time period 0). We'll use Equation (6–1c) to solve the problem.

STEP 3: Solution

Using the Mathematical Formulas. Substituting these example values in Equation (6–1c), we find

$$\$5,000 = PMT\left[\frac{(1+.08)^{10}-1}{.08}\right]$$

$$\$5,000 = PMT(14.4866)$$

$$PMT = \$5,000 \div 14.4866 = \$345.15$$

Thus, you must deposit $345.15 in the bank at the end of each year for 10 years at 8 percent interest to accumulate $5,000.

Using a Financial Calculator.

Enter   10   8.0   0   5,000

            [N]   [I/Y]   [PV]   [PMT]   [FV]

Solve for   -345.15

Using an Excel Spreadsheet.

= PMT(rate,nper,pv,fv) or with values entered = PMT(.08,10,0,5000)

STEP 4: Analyze

Notice that in a problem involving the future value of an ordinary annuity, the last payment actually occurs at the time the future value occurs. In this case, the last payment occurs at the end of Year 10, and the end of Year 10 is when you want the future value of the annuity to equal $5,000. In effect, the final payment does not have a chance to earn any interest.

STEP 5: Check yourself

If you can earn 12 percent on your investments, and you would like to accumulate $100,000 for your newborn child's education at the end of 18 years, how much must you invest annually to reach your goal?

ANSWER: $1,793.73 at the end of each year.

Your Turn: For more practice, do related **Study Problems** 6–5, 6–17, 6–19, and 6–34 at the end of this chapter.

Using an Excel Spreadsheet

= RATE(nper,pmt,pv,fv) or with values entered = RATE(15,−1022,0,30000).

Solving for the Number of Periods in an Ordinary Annuity You may also want to calculate the *number of periods* it will take for an annuity to reach a certain future value. Just as with the calculation of the interest rate in an ordinary annuity, the easiest way to do this is with a financial calculator or with a spreadsheet. For example, suppose you are investing $5,000 at the end of each year in an account that pays 7 percent. How long will it be before your account is worth $51,300?

Using a Financial Calculator. We can use a financial calculator to solve for *n* directly as follows:

Enter		7.0	0	-5,000	51,300
	N	**I/Y**	**PV**	**PMT**	**FV**
Solve for	8.0				

Thus, it will take eight years for end-of-year deposits of $5,000 every year to grow to $51,300.

Using an Excel Spreadsheet

= NPER(rate,pmt,pv,fv) or with values entered = NPER(7%,−5000,0,51300).

The Present Value of an Ordinary Annuity Let's say you just won a radio contest, and the prize is $2,500. The only catch is that you are to receive the $2,500 in the form of five $500 payments at the end of each of the next five years. Alternatively, the radio station has offered to pay you a total of $2,000 today. Which alternative should you choose?

To make this decision, you will need to calculate the present value of the $500 annuity and compare it to the $2,000 lump sum. You can do this by discounting each of the individual future cash flows back to the present and then adding all the present values together. This can be a time-consuming task, particularly when the annuity lasts for several years. Nonetheless, it can be done. If you want to know what $500 received at the end of each of the next five years is worth today, assuming you can earn 6 percent interest on your investment, you simply substitute the appropriate values into Equation (5–2), such that

$$PV = \$500\left[\frac{1}{(1+.06)^1}\right] + \$500\left[\frac{1}{(1+.06)^2}\right] + \$500\left[\frac{1}{(1+.06)^3}\right] + \$500\left[\frac{1}{(1+.06)^4}\right] + \$500\left[\frac{1}{(1+.06)^5}\right]$$

$$= \$500(0.94340) + \$500(0.89000) + \$500(0.83962) + \$500(0.79209) + \$500(0.74726)$$

$$= \$2,106.18$$

Thus, the present value of this annuity is $2,106.18. As a result, you'd be better off taking the annuity rather than the $2,000 immediately. By examining the math and the timeline presented in Figure 6.2, you can see that the present values of each cash flow are simply summed. However, many times we will be faced with a situation where *n*, the number of cash flows in the annuity, is very large. For example, a 15-year mortgage involves 180 equal monthly payments, and a 30-year mortgage involves 360 equal monthly payments—that's just too many individual cash flows to work with. For this reason, we will want to use a financial calculator, Excel, or a mathematical shortcut. Let's examine a mathematical shortcut for valuing the present value of an annuity.

FIGURE 6.2 Timeline of a Five-Year, $500 Annuity Discounted Back to the Present at 6 Percent

To find the present value of an annuity, discount each cash flow back to the present separately and then add them. In this example, we simply add up the present value of five future cash flows of $500 each to find a present value of $2,106.18.

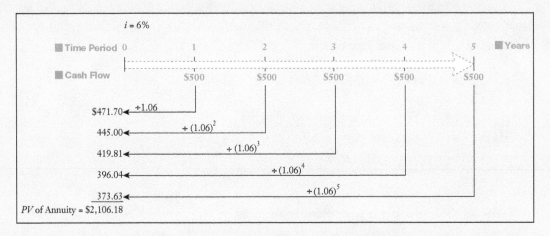

In this method for finding the present value of an annuity, we discount each cash flow separately and then add them up, as represented by the following equation:

$$PV = PMT\left[\left(\frac{1}{(1+i)^1}\right) + \left(\frac{1}{(1+i)^2}\right) + \cdots + \left(\frac{1}{(1+i)^n}\right)\right] \qquad \text{(6–2)}$$

The term in brackets is commonly referred to as the **annuity present value interest factor**. We can simplify the present value interest factor for an annuity formula as follows:

$$\text{Annuity Present Value Interest Factor} = \frac{1 - \dfrac{1}{(1+i)^n}}{i} \qquad \text{(6–2a)}$$

Thus, we can rewrite Equation (6–2) as follows:

$$\text{Present Value} = PMT\left[\frac{1 - \dfrac{1}{(1+i)^n}}{i}\right] \qquad \text{(6–2b)}$$

Important Definitions and Concepts:

- *PV* is the present value of the annuity.
- *PMT* is the annuity payment deposited or received at the end of each period.
- *i* is the discount (or interest) rate on a per-period basis. For example, if annuity payments were received annually, *i* would be expressed as an annual rate; if the payments were received monthly, it would be the monthly rate.
- *n* is the number of periods for which the annuity will last. If the annuity payments were received annually, *n* would be the number of years; if the payments were received monthly, it would be the number of months.

Checkpoint 6.2

The Present Value of an Ordinary Annuity

Your grandmother has offered to give you $1,000 per year for the next 10 years. What is the present value of this 10-year, $1,000 annuity discounted back to the present at 5 percent? Let's solve this using the mathematical formula, a financial calculator, and an Excel spreadsheet.

STEP 1: Picture the problem

We can use a timeline to identify the cash flows from the investment as follows:

$i = 5\%$

| Time Period | 0 | 1 | 2 | 3 | 4 | 5 | 6 | 7 | 8 | 9 | 10 | Years |

Cash Flow $1,000 $1,000 $1,000 $1,000 $1,000 $1,000 $1,000 $1,000 $1,000 $1,000

Sum up the present values of all the cash flows to find the present value of the annuity.

STEP 2: Decide on a solution strategy

In this case we are trying to determine the present value of an annuity, and we know the dollar value that is received at the end of each year, and the number of years the annuity lasts. We also know that the discount rate is 5 percent. We can use Equation (6–2b) to solve this problem.

STEP 3: Solution

Using the Mathematical Formulas. Substituting these example values in Equation (6–2b), we find that

$$PV = \$1,000 \left[\frac{1 - \dfrac{1}{(1+.05)^{10}}}{.05} \right] = \$1,000[(1-.6139)/.05] = \$1,000(7.722) = \$7,721.73$$

Using a Financial Calculator.

Enter	10	5.0		1,000	0
	N	I/Y	PV	PMT	FV

Solve for   -7,721.73

Using an Excel Spreadsheet.

= PV(rate,nper,pmt,fv) or with values entered = PV(0.05,10,1000,0)

STEP 4: Analyze

We will see this formula at work a bit later when we look at the value of a bond. When you buy a bond, you get the same amount of interest every year on either an annual or semiannual basis, and then at maturity you get the repayment of the bond's principal. Part of calculating the value of a bond involves calculating the present value of the bond's interest payments, which is an annuity.

STEP 5: Check yourself

What is the present value of an annuity of $10,000 to be received at the end of each year for 10 years given a 10 percent discount rate?

ANSWER: $61,446.

Your Turn: For more practice, do related **Study Problems** 6–2, 6–4, 6–28, and 6–35 at the end of this chapter.

Notice that the frequency of the payment, that is, whether payments are made on an annual, semiannual, or monthly basis, will play a role in determining the values of n and i. Moreover, it is important that n and i match; that is, if periods are expressed in terms of number of monthly payments, the interest rate must be expressed in terms of the interest rate per month. To find the present value of an annuity, all we need to do is multiply the annuity payment by the annuity present value interest factor.[2] Check-point 6.2 demonstrates the use of this formula along with the other techniques for calculating the present value of an annuity.

Amortized Loans

An **amortized loan** is a loan paid off in equal payments—consequently, the loan payments are an annuity. The present value can be thought of as the amount that has been borrowed, n is the number of periods the loan lasts, i is the interest rate per period, *future value* takes on a value of zero because the loan will be paid off after n periods, and *payment* is the loan payment that is made. Generally, the payments are made monthly, but sometimes they are made yearly. Most mortgages are amortized loans, as are almost all car loans. Suppose you plan to get a $6,000 car loan at 15 percent annual interest with annual payments that you will pay off over four years. What will your annual payments be on this loan? Let's solve this using a financial calculator.

Enter	4	15.0	6,000		0
	N	I/Y	PV	PMT	FV
Solve for				-2,101.59	

The above calculation implies that you would make annual payments of $2,101.59. Table 6.1 shows the breakdown of interest and principal over the life of the loan, which is commonly referred to as a **loan amortization schedule**.

As you can see, the interest payment declines each year as the amount owed declines and more of the principal is repaid. This is because a loan payment is made up of two parts: interest and principal. With each payment that goes toward the principal, the size of the outstanding balance goes down. And as the size of the outstanding balance goes down, the amount of interest that is due in the next period declines. Because the size of each payment remains the same and the amount of the next payment that goes toward interest declines, the amount of the next payment that goes toward principal must increase. You can see this clearly in Table 6.1. Also, if you look at Table 6.1, you'll see that the interest portion of the annuity (column 3) is calculated by multiplying the outstanding loan balance at the beginning of the year (column 1) by the interest rate of 15 percent. Thus, for the first year, the interest portion of the first year's payment is $6,000.00 × .15 = $900.00; for Year 2 it is $4,798.41 × .15 = $719.76, and so on. Of course, the amount that isn't the interest portion must be the principal portion. Thus, the repayment of the principal portion of the annuity is calculated by subtracting the interest portion of the annuity (column 3) from the annuity payment (column 2).

Amortized Loans with Monthly Payments Many loans—for example, auto and home loans—require monthly payments. As we saw before, dealing with monthly, as opposed to yearly, payments is easy. All we do is multiply the number of years by m, the number of times compounding occurs during the year, to determine n, the number of periods. Then we divide the annual interest rate, or APR, by m to find the interest rate per period.

---

[2]Related tables appear in Appendices B through E in MyFinanceLab.

TABLE 6.1 THE LOAN AMORTIZATION SCHEDULE FOR A $6,000 LOAN AT 15% TO BE REPAID IN FOUR YEARS

Year	Amount Owed on the Principal at the Beginning of the Year (1)	Annuity Payment (2)	Interest Portion of the Annuity = (1) × 15% = (3)	Repayment of the Principal Portion of the Annuity = (2) − (3) = (4)	Outstanding Loan Balance at Year End, after the Annuity Payment = (1) − (4) = (5)
1	$6,000.00	$2,101.59	$900.00	$1,201.59	$4,798.41
2	4,798.41	2,101.59	719.76	1,381.83	3,416.58
3	3,416.58	2,101.59	512.49	1,589.10	1,827.48
4	1,827.48	2,101.59	274.12	1,827.48	0.00

Let's look at an example. You've just found the perfect home. However, in order to buy it, you'll need to take out a $150,000, 30-year mortgage with monthly payments at an annual rate of 6 percent. What will your monthly mortgage payments be?

Mathematical Formulas. As we saw in the previous chapter in Equation (5–1b), in order to determine *n*, the number of periods, we multiply the number of years by *m*, where *m* is the number of times compounding occurs each year. To determine the interest rate per period, we divide the annual interest rate by *m*, where *m* is the number of times compounding occurs per year. Modifying Equation (6–2b) for non-annual compounding, we find

$$PV = PMT \left[\frac{1 - \dfrac{1}{(1 + \text{annual interest rate}/m)^{\#\,\text{years} \times m}}}{\text{annual interest rate}/m} \right] \qquad \textbf{(6–2c)}$$

Substituting *annual interest rate* = .06, *number of years* = 30, *m* = 12, and *PV* = $150,000 into Equation (6–2c), we get

$$\$150,000 = PMT \left[\frac{1 - \dfrac{1}{(1 + .06/12)^{30 \times 12}}}{.06/12} \right]$$

Notice that when you convert the annual rate of 6 percent to a monthly rate (by dividing it by 12), the monthly rate drops to 0.005, or 0.5 percent.

$$\$150,000 = PMT \left[\frac{1 - \dfrac{1}{(1 + .005)^{360}}}{.005} \right]$$

$$\$150,000 = PMT(166.7916144)$$

$$PMT = \$150,000/166.7916144 = \$899.33$$

Using a Financial Calculator. Because there are 360 monthly periods in 30 years, 360 is entered for Ⓝ, and ⓘ/ʸ becomes 0.5 (annual interest rate of 6% divided by m, which is 12).

Enter	360	0.5	150,000		0
	N	I/Y	PV	PMT	FV
Solve for				-899.33	

Using an Excel Spreadsheet

$$= \text{PMT(rate,nper,pv,fv)} \text{ or with values entered} = \text{PMT}(0.005,360,150000,0)$$

Computing Your Outstanding Balance. Let's take a look at how you might use your understanding of annuities to calculate the outstanding balance on a home mortgage loan, which is equal to the present value of your future loan payments. Remember, when you solve for your payment, the final future value of the loan is zero because after your last payment is made, the loan is paid off. The present value of the loan represents how much you originally borrowed—that is, it is the initial outstanding loan balance. What all that means is that the *remaining outstanding balance on a loan must be equal to the present value of the remaining payments on that loan*. An example of this calculation is provided in Checkpoint 6.3.

Annuities Due

Thus far, we have looked only at ordinary annuities, annuities in which payments are made at equidistant points in time at the end of a period. Now we turn our attention to valuing an **annuity due**, an annuity in which all the cash flows occur at the beginning of each period. For example, rent payments on apartments are typically annuities due because the payment for the month's rent occurs at the beginning of the month. Fortunately, compounding annuities due and determining their future and present value is actually quite simple. Let's look at how this affects our compounding calculations.

Because an annuity due merely shifts the payments from the end of the period to the beginning of the period, we can calculate its future value by compounding the cash flows for one additional period. Specifically, the compound sum, or future value, of an annuity due is simply

$$FV_n(\text{annuity due}) = PMT\left[\frac{(1 + i)^n - 1}{i}\right](1 + i) \qquad \textbf{(6–3)}$$

Recall that earlier we calculated the future value of a five-year ordinary annuity of $5,000 earning 6 percent interest to be $28,185.46. If we now assume this is a five-year annuity due, its future value increases from $28,185.46 to $29,876.59:

$$= \$5,000\left[\frac{(1 + .06)^5 - 1}{.06}\right](1 + .06) = \$28,185.46(1 + .06) = \$29,876.59$$

Because each cash flow is received one year earlier with an annuity due, its present value will be discounted back for one less period. To determine the present value of the

Determining the Outstanding Balance of a Loan

Let's say that exactly 10 years ago you took out a $200,000, 30-year mortgage with an annual interest rate of 9 percent and monthly payments of $1,609.25. But since you took out that loan, interest rates have dropped. You now have the opportunity to refinance your loan at an annual rate of 7 percent over 20 years. You need to know what the outstanding balance on your current loan is so you can take out a lower-interest-rate loan and pay it off. If you just made the 120th payment and have 240 payments remaining, what's your current loan balance?

STEP 1: Picture the problem

Because we are trying to determine how much you still owe on your loan, we need to determine the present value of your remaining payments. In this case, because we are dealing with a 30-year loan, with 240 remaining monthly payments, it's a bit difficult to draw a timeline that shows all the monthly cash flows. Still, we can mentally visualize the problem, which involves calculating the present value of 240 payments of $1,609.25 using a discount rate of 9%/12.

STEP 2: Decide on a solution strategy

Initially you took out a $200,000, 30-year mortgage with an interest rate of 9 percent, and monthly payments of $1,609.25. Because you have made 10 years worth of payments—that's 120 monthly payments—there are only 240 payments left before your mortgage will be totally paid off. We know that the outstanding balance is the present value of all the future monthly payments. To find the present value of these future monthly payments, we'll use Equation (6–2c).

STEP 3: Solve

Using the Mathematical Formulas.

Using Equation (6–2c), we'll solve for the present value of the remaining monthly payment. To find n, we multiply the number of years left until the mortgage is paid off (20) times the number of months in a year (12). Thus n becomes 240. The future value will be equal to zero because the loan will be fully paid off in 20 years. The payment will be $1,609.25, as given above. In effect, the present value of the payments you still need to make is how much you still owe.

$$PV = PMT \left[\frac{1 - \dfrac{1}{(1 + \text{annual rate of interest}/m)^{\text{\# years} \times m}}}{\text{annual rate of interest}/m} \right] \tag{6–2c}$$

where m = number of times compounding occurs per year and # years is the number of years.

Substituting annual interest rate = .09, number of years = 20, m = 12, and PMT = $1,609.25 into Equation (6–2c), we get,

$$PV = \$1{,}609.25 \left[\frac{1 - \dfrac{1}{(1 + .09/12)^{20 \times 12}}}{.09/12} \right]$$

$$PV = \$1{,}609.25(111.145)$$

$$PV = \$178{,}860.02$$

Using a Financial Calculator.

Enter

240	9.0÷12		-1,609.25	0
N	I/Y	PV	PMT	FV

Solve for 178,860.02

Using an Excel Spreadsheet.

= PV(rate,nper,pmt,fv) or with values entered = PV((9/12)%,240,-1609.25,0)

STEP 4: Analyze

To solve this problem, we began with our monthly payments. Then we determined what the present value was of the remaining payments—this is how much you still owe. Thus, after making 10 years of monthly payments on your $200,000 mortgage that originally had a maturity of 30 years and carries a 9 percent annual rate of interest with monthly payments of $1,609.25, you still owe $178,860.02.

The logic behind what was done here is that the amount you owe on a loan should be equal to the present value of the remaining loan payments. However, if interest rates dropped and you decided to refinance your mortgage, you'd find that there are some real costs associated with refinancing that we haven't touched on here. For example, there is an application fee, an appraisal fee, legal and title search fees, an origination fee for processing the loan, and a prepayment penalty, all adding to the cost of refinancing. Once you decide on a mortgage refinancing lender, make sure that you get all of your mortgage refinancing terms written down on paper.

STEP 5: Check yourself

Let's assume you took out a $300,000, 30-year mortgage with an annual interest rate of 8 percent and monthly payments of $2,201.29. Because you have made 15 years worth of payments (that's 180 monthly payments), there are another 180 payments left before your mortgage will be totally paid off. How much do you still owe on your mortgage?

ANSWER: $230,345.

Your Turn: For more practice, do related **Study Problem** 6–38 at the end of this chapter.

---

annuity due, we merely figure out what its present value would be if it were an ordinary annuity and multiply that value by $(1 + i)$. This, in effect, cancels out one year's discounting.[3]

$$PV(\text{annuity due}) = PMT\left[\frac{1 - \dfrac{1}{(1 + i)^n}}{i}\right](1 + i) \qquad \textbf{(6–4)}$$

Let's go back to our radio contest example. Suppose the radio station offered you a five-year annuity due instead of an ordinary annuity. If you were given $500 at the beginning of each of those five years and were able to invest it at an interest rate of

---

[3]Within each of the Excel functions you are given the option of identifying any cash flow as being at the beginning of a period. To solve for an annuity due in Excel, you simply change the value for "type" from 0 to 1. Recall that 0 is the default setting—the setting used to calculate an ordinary annuity. Consequently, if you don't designate a value for the variable "type," Excel will default to 0, or end-of-year payments. If you look at any of the Excel problems we have done so far, you'll notice that we have omitted entering a variable for "type," thus indicating that the cash flows occur at the end of each time period.

THE BUSINESS OF LIFE

Saving for Retirement

FIGURE 6.3 Skipping Just One Year Can Cost You Over a Quarter of a Million Dollars

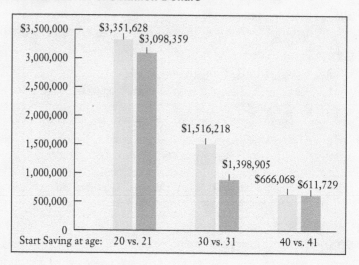

If you understand **P** Principle 1: **Money Has a Time Value**, you will have a better idea of why it's so important to begin saving for retirement as soon as possible. Putting off saving for just one year can have a big impact on the amount of money you have when you retire—in fact, it may reduce your retirement funds by over $250,000.

Individual retirement accounts, or IRAs, are personal retirement savings plans that have certain tax advantages. With a regular IRA, contributions are made on a before-tax basis. However, Roth IRA contributions are paid from earnings that have already been taxed. The difference is that after you retire and begin withdrawing money from a regular IRA, you have to pay taxes on your withdrawals. With a Roth, you don't.

Figure 6.3 assumes that at a certain age, you contribute $5,000 at the beginning of each year to a Roth IRA earning 8 percent interest per year, and you continue making contributions until age 70. For example, if at age 20 you start contributing $5,000 at the beginning of each year, you will have made 51 contributions by age 70, and you will end up with the following:

$$FV_n \text{(annuity due)} = PMT\left[\frac{(1+i)^n - 1}{i}\right](1+i)$$

$$= \$5,000\left[\frac{(1+.08)^{51} - 1}{.08}\right](1+.08) \quad \text{(6-3)}$$

$$= \$3,103,359(1+.08) = \$3,351,628$$

But what if you wait until you're 21 to start contributing? How much money would you end up with then? By waiting just one year longer to begin investing, you end up with $253,269 less in the account:

$$= \$5,000\left[\frac{(1+.08)^{50} - 1}{.08}\right](1+.08)$$

$$= \$2,868,850(1+.08) = \$3,098,359$$

As you can see, instead of accumulating $3,351,628, you would accumulate only $3,098,359.

In this example, you put $5,000 into a Roth IRA each year, but if you had only put in $2,500 each year, your total accumulation would only be half of what is listed in Figure 6.3. At present the maximum you can put into your Roth IRA per year is $5,000; and, if you're over 50, you can even put more into it. Study Problem 6–3 looks at Roth IRAs.

Your Turn: See Study Problem 6–3.

6 percent, its value would increase from $2,106.18 (the value of the ordinary annuity) to $2,232.55:

$$= \$500 \left[\frac{1 - \dfrac{1}{(1 + .06)^5}}{.06} \right] (1 + .06)$$

$$= \$2,106.18(1 + .06) = \$2,232.55$$

The result of all this is that both the future value and the present value of an annuity due are larger than that of an ordinary annuity because, in each case, all payments are received or paid earlier. Thus, when *compounding* an annuity due, the cash flows come at the beginning of the period rather than the end of the period. They are, in effect, invested one period earlier, and as a result, grow to a larger future value. By contrast, when we *discount* an annuity due, the cash flows come at the beginning of each period, in effect coming one period earlier, so their present value is larger. Although annuities due are used with some frequency in accounting, their usage is less frequent in finance. Nonetheless, an understanding of annuities due can be powerful, as you can see in the box feature *Business of Life: Saving for Retirement.*

CONCEPTS IN REVIEW	**6.1**	Define the term *annuity* as it relates to cash flows.
	6.2	Distinguish between an ordinary annuity and an annuity due.
	6.3	Describe the adjustments necessary when annuity payments occur on a monthly basis.
	6.4	How would you determine how much you currently owe on an outstanding loan?

Perpetuities

LG2 A **perpetuity** is simply an annuity that continues forever or has no maturity. It is difficult to conceptualize such a cash flow stream that goes on forever. One such example, however, is the dividend stream on a share of preferred stock. In theory, this dividend stream will go on as long as the firm continues to pay dividends, so technically the dividends on a share of preferred stock form an infinite annuity, or perpetuity.

There are two basic types of perpetuities that we will encounter in our study of finance. The first is a **level perpetuity** in which the payments are constant over time. The second is a **growing perpetuity** in which the payments grow at a constant rate from period to period over time. Let's consider each in turn.

Calculating the Present Value of a Level Perpetuity

Determining the present value of a perpetuity is simple—you merely divide the constant flow, or payment, by the discount rate. For example, the present value of a $100 perpetuity discounted back to the present at 5 percent is $100/.05 = $2,000. The equation representing the present value of a level perpetuity is as follows:

$$PV = \frac{PMT}{i} \qquad \text{(6–5)}$$

Important Definitions and Concepts:

- PV = the present value of a level perpetuity.
- PMT = the constant dollar amount provided by the perpetuity.
- i = the interest (or discount) rate per period.

Checkpoint 6.4

The Present Value of a Level Perpetuity

What is the present value of a perpetuity of $500 paid annually discounted back to the present at 8 percent?

STEP 1: Picture the problem

With a perpetuity, a timeline doesn't have an ending point but goes on forever, with the same cash flow occurring period after period, or in this case, year after year:

STEP 2: Decide on a solution strategy

Because calculating the present value of a perpetuity only involves simple division, we don't need to look at an Excel solution or any unique keystrokes with a financial calculator; instead, using Equation (6–5), we just divide the amount you received at the end of each period (forever) by the interest rate.

STEP 3: Solve

Substituting PMT = $500 and i = .08 into Equation (6–5), we find

$$PV = \frac{\$500}{.08} = \$6,250$$

Thus, the present value of this perpetuity is $6,250.

STEP 4: Analyze

Notice there is no symbol for the future value of a perpetuity. This is because there isn't a future time period when things end because a perpetuity goes on indefinitely. So, how much will this perpetuity be worth at the end of 2 years or 100 years? The answer is $6,250. That is because this perpetuity will always return $500—regardless of what the time period is, the present value of a perpetuity paying $500 at 8 percent is always $6,250.

STEP 5: Check yourself

What is the present value of stream of payments equal to $90,000 paid annually and discounted back to the present at 9 percent?

ANSWER: $1,000,000

Your Turn: For more practice, do related **Study Problem** 6–42 at the end of this chapter.

Calculating the Present Value of a Growing Perpetuity

Not all perpetuities have equal cash payments. For example, if the first payment at the end of Year 1 is $100 and the payments are assumed to grow at a rate of 5 percent per year, then the payment for Year 2 will be $100(1.05) = $105, and the payment for Year 3 will be $100(1.05)(1.05) = $110.25, and so forth.

We can calculate the present value of a growing perpetuity as follows:

$$PV = \frac{PMT_{period1}}{i-g} \qquad \text{(6–6)}$$

Checkpoint 6.5

The Present Value of a Growing Perpetuity

What is the present value of a perpetuity stream of cash flows that pays $500 at the end of Year 1 but grows at a rate of 4 percent per year indefinitely? The rate of interest used to discount the cash flows is 8 percent.

STEP 1: Picture the problem

With a growing perpetuity, a timeline doesn't have an ending point, but goes on forever, with the cash flow growing at a constant rate period after period, or in this case, year after year:

STEP 2: Decide on a solution strategy

Because calculating the present value of a growing perpetuity only involves substituting into Equation (6–6), we don't need to look at an Excel solution or any unique keystrokes with a financial calculator. Instead, we just divide the amount receive at the end of each period (forever) by the interest rate minus the growth rate.

STEP 3: Solve

Substituting $PMT_{period\ 1}$ = $500, g = .04, and i = .08 into Equation (6–6), we find

$$PV = \frac{PMT_{period\,1}}{i - g} = \frac{\$500}{.08 - .04} = \$12,500$$

Thus, the present value of the growing perpetuity is $12,500.

STEP 4: Analyze

Comparing the value of the $500 level perpetuity in Checkpoint 6.5 to the $500 perpetuity that grows at 4 percent per year, we see that adding growth to the cash flows has a dramatic effect on value. To see why this occurs, consider the Year 50 payment under both the level perpetuity and growing perpetuity. For the level perpetuity, this payment is still $500; however, for the growing perpetuity, the payment for Year 50 is the following:

$$PMT_{year\ 50} = \$500(1 + .04)^{50} = \$3,553.34$$

STEP 5: Check yourself

What is the present value of a stream of payments where the Year 1 payment is $90,000 and the future payments grow at a rate of 5 percent per year? The interest rate used to discount the payments is 9 percent.

ANSWER: $2,250,000

Your Turn: For more practice, do related **Study Problem** 6–44 at the end of this chapter.

Important Definitions and Concepts:

- PV = the present value of a growing perpetuity.
- $PMT_{period\,1}$ = the amount of the payment made at the end of the first period (e.g., this was $100 in the example used above).
- i = the rate of interest used to discount the growing perpetuity's cash flows.
- g = the rate of growth in the payment cash flows from period to period.

The growth rate, g, must be less than the rate of interest used to discount the cash flows, i. If g is greater than i, then the present value becomes infinitely large because the cash flows are growing at a faster rate than they are being discounted.

CONCEPTS IN REVIEW	**6.5** Define the term *perpetuity* as it relates to cash flows.
	6.6 What is a growing perpetuity, and how is it calculated?

Complex Cash Flow Streams

LG3 Actual investment cash flows are often more complicated than the examples we have considered thus far. They often consist of multiple sets of annuities or different cash flow amounts mixed in with annuities. In general they will involve spending money today in the hopes of receiving more in the future, and once we bring all the future cash flows back to the present, they can be compared. For example, Marriott recently decided to build timeshare resorts in Dubai, United Arab Emirates. The resorts are close to Dubailand, a giant entertainment complex that, when finished, will be twice the size of the entire Disneyland and Disney World resorts put together.

The resorts' cash flows are a mixture of both positive and negative cash flows, as shown in Figure 6.4. The early cash flows are negative as Marriott begins construction on the various phases of the project and later become positive as the development makes money. Because of this mixture of positive and negative cash flows, we cannot use the annuities formulas that we described earlier. Instead, we calculate the present value of the investment project by summing the present values of all the individual cash flows.

Assuming a 6 percent discount rate, we can calculate the present value of all 10 years of cash flows by discounting each back to the present and adding the positive flows and subtracting the negative ones. Note that the cash flows for Years 1 through 3 are different, so we will have to find their present values by discounting each cash flow back to the present. The present values of the payments (in millions of $) received in Years 1 through 3 are $471.70 = \$500/(1 + .06)$, $178.00 = \$200/(1 + .06)^2$, and $-\$335.85 = -\$400/(1 + .06)^3$.

Next, we see that in Years 4 through 10 the cash flows correspond to an ordinary annuity of $500 per year. Because these cash flows are all equal and are received annually, they are a seven-year annuity. The unique feature of the annuity is that the first cash flow comes at the end of Year 4. To find the present value of the seven-year annuity, we follow a two-step process:

- First, we consolidate the seven-year annuity into a single cash flow that is equal to its present value. In effect, we are consolidating the $500 million payments that occur at the end of Years 4 through 10 into an equivalent single cash flow at the beginning of Year 4 (or the end of Period 3). Recall that we can find the present

The Present Value of a Complex Cash Flow Stream

What is the present value of cash flows of $500 at the end of Years 1 through 3, a cash flow of a negative $800 at the end of Year 4, and cash flows of $800 at the end of Years 5 through 10 if the appropriate discount rate is 5 percent?

STEP 1: Picture the problem

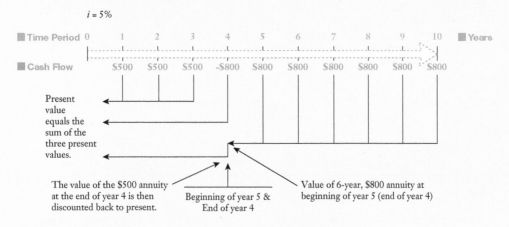

STEP 2: Decide on a solution strategy

This problem involves two annuities and the single (negative) cash flow. Once their present value is determined they will be added together. The $500 annuity over Years 1 through 3 can be discounted directly to the present using Equation (6–2b), and the $800 cash outflow at the end of Year 4 can be discounted back to present using Equation (5–2) . Because it is an outflow, it will carry a negative sign and be subtracted from the present value of the inflows. To determine the present value of the six-year, $800 annuity over Years 5 through 10, we must first consolidate the six-year annuity that runs from Years 5 through 10 into an equivalent single cash flow at the beginning of Year 5, which is the same as the end of Year 4, using Equation (6–2b). We now have an equivalent single cash flow at the end of Year 4 that we can bring directly back to the present using Equation (5–2). Once everything is in today's dollars, we simply add the values together.

STEP 3: Solve

Using the Mathematical Formulas.

Here we have two annuities. One of them, an annuity of $500 over Years 1 through 3, can be discounted directly back to the present by multiplying it by the annuity present value interest factor, or

$$\left[\frac{1 - \dfrac{1}{(1+.05)^3}}{.05} \right]$$

for a value of $1,361.62. The second annuity, which is a six-year annuity of $800 per year over Years 5 through 10, must be discounted twice—once to find the value of the annuity at the beginning of Year 5, which is also the end of Year 4, and then again to bring that value back to the present. The value of the second annuity at the end of Year 4 is found by multiplying it ($800) by the annuity present value interest factor, or

$$\left[\frac{1 - \dfrac{1}{(1+.05)^6}}{.05} \right]$$

resulting in a value $4,060.55. In effect, we have now consolidated the annuity into an equivalent single cash flow at the end of Year 4. This equivalent single cash flow is then discounted back to the present by multiplying it by the value of $1/(1.05)^4$, for a value of $3,340.62. Because cash flows in the same time period can be added and subtracted from each other, to arrive at the total present value of this investment, we subtract the present

(6.6 CONTINUED >> ON NEXT PAGE)

value of the $800 cash outflow at the end of Year 4 (which is $658.16) from the sum of the present value of the two annuities ($1,361.62 and $3,340.62). Thus, the present value of this series of cash flows is $4,044.08. Remember, once the cash flows from an investment have been brought back to the present, they can be combined by adding and subtracting to determine the project's total present value.

Using a Financial Calculator. Using a financial calculator, we can arrive at the same answer:

(a) The present value of the first annuity, Years 1 through 3 (give it a positive sign because it is an inflow) = **$1,361.62**.

Enter	3	5		500	0
	N	I/Y	PV	PMT	FV
Solve for			-1,361.62		

(b) The present value of the $800 cash **outflow** (thus it is given a negative sign because it is an outflow) = **−$658.16**.

Enter	4	5		0	-800
	N	I/Y	PV	PMT	FV
Solve for			658.16		

(c) (Part 1) The value at end of Year 4 of the second annuity (which is a six-year annuity), Years 5 through 10 (give it a positive sign because it is an inflow) = $4,060.55,

Enter	6	5		800	0
	N	I/Y	PV	PMT	FV
Solve for			-4,060.55		

and then,

(Part 2) The present value (give it a positive sign because it is an inflow) of the $4,060.55 (which was calculated in c: part 1 and is received at the end of Year 4) = **$3,340.62**.

Enter	4	5		0	4,060.55
	N	I/Y	PV	PMT	FV
Solve for			-3,340.62		

(d) Summing the present values together, the total present value = **$4,044.08**.

Using an Excel Spreadsheet. Using Excel, the cash flows are brought back to the present using the =PV function, keeping in mind that inflows will take on positive signs and outflows negative signs.

STEP 4: Analyze

When cash flows from different time periods are expressed in the same time period's dollars, they can be added in the case of an inflow or subtracted in the case of an outflow to come up with a total value at some point in time. In fact, we will combine P Principle 1: **Money Has a Time Value** with P Principle 3: **Cash Flows Are the Source of Value** later in the book to value stocks, bonds, and investment proposals. The bottom line is that understanding the time value of money is a key to making good decisions.

STEP 5: Check yourself

What is the present value of cash flows of $300 at the end of Years 1 through 5, a cash flow of negative $600 at the end of Year 6, and cash flows of $800 at the end of Years 7 through 10 if the appropriate discount rate is 10 percent?

ANSWER: $2,230.

Your Turn: For more practice, do related **Study Problem** 6–48 at the end of this chapter.

FIGURE 6.4 **Present Value of Single Cash Flows and an Annuity ($ value in millions)**

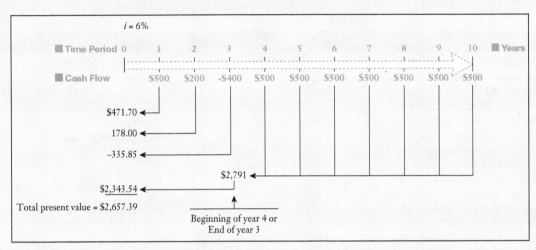

value of the annuity by multiplying the annual payment of $500 by the annuity present value interest factor:

$$\frac{1 - \dfrac{1}{(1 + i)^n}}{i}$$. In Figure 6.4 we see that the present value of this annuity at the end of Year 3 is $2,791 million.

- Second, we discount the $2,791 million present value of the annuity cash flows back three years to the present, which is the beginning of Year 1. The present value of this sum (in millions), then, is $2,343.54 = $2,791/(1 + .06)^3.

Finally, we can calculate the present value of the complex set of future cash flows by adding up the individual present values of each of the future cash flows. The result is a present value of $2,657.39 million. We would then compare the present value of all the future cash flows with what the project costs. It should now be apparent that drawing out a timeline is a critical first step when trying to solve any complex problem involving the time value of money.

CONCEPTS IN REVIEW

6.7 When are cash flows comparable—that is, when can they be added together or subtracted from each other?

6.8 Why would you want to be able to compare cash flows that occur in different time periods with each other?

Applying the Principles of Finance to Chapter 6

P Principle 1: **Money Has a Time Value** This chapter continues our study of the time value of money—a dollar received today, other things being the same, is worth more than a dollar received a year from now. In this chapter, we expand upon what we learned in the previous chapter by applying the time value of money to annuities, perpetuities, and complex cash flows.

P Principle 3: **Cash Flows Are the Source of Value** In this chapter we introduced the idea that we will use **Principle 1** in combination with **Principle 3** to value stocks, bonds, and investment proposals.

MyFinanceLab

Here is what you should know after reading this chapter. MyFinanceLab will help you identify what you know and where to go when you need to practice.

What You Should Know	Key Terms	
LG1 **Distinguish between an ordinary annuity and an annuity due, and calculate the present and future values of each.** An annuity is a series of equal dollar payments, where the periods between the payments are of equal length, such as monthly or annually. An ordinary annuity involves cash payments made at the end of each period, whereas an annuity due involves payments at the beginning of each period. Appendices B through E in MyFinanceLab contain tables with future value interest factors, present value interest factors, annuity future value interest factors, and annuity present value interest factors for various combinations of i and n.	Amortized loan, *p. 189*	A loan that is paid off in equal periodic payments.
	Annuity, *p. 180*	A series of equal dollar payments for a specified period of time.
	Annuity due, *p. 191*	An annuity in which the payments occur at the beginning of each period.
	Annuity future value interest factor, *p. 183*	The value, $\left[\dfrac{(1 + i)^n - 1}{i}\right]$, used as a multiplier to calculate the future value of an annuity.
	Annuity present value interest factor, *p. 187*	The value, $\left[\dfrac{1 - \dfrac{1}{(1 + i)^n}}{i}\right]$, used as a multiplier to calculate the present value of an annuity.
	Loan amortization schedule, *p. 189*	A breakdown of the interest and principal payments on an amortized loan.
	Ordinary annuity, *p. 180*	A series of equal dollar payments for a specified number of periods with the payments occurring at the end of each period.

Key Equations

$$FV_n = PMT\left[\frac{(1 + i)^n - 1}{i}\right] \qquad (6\text{–}1c)$$

$$PV = PMT\left[\frac{1 - \dfrac{1}{(1 + i)^n}}{i}\right] \qquad (6\text{–}2b)$$

$$PV = PMT\left[\frac{1 - \dfrac{1}{(1 + \text{annual interest rate}/m)^{\#\,years \times m}}}{\text{annual interest rate}/m}\right] \qquad (6\text{–}2c)$$

$$FV_n = PMT\left[\frac{(1 + \text{annual interest rate}/m)^{\#\,years \times m} - 1}{\text{annual interest rate}/m}\right]$$

$$FV_n(\text{annuity due}) = PMT\left[\frac{(1 + i)^n - 1}{i}\right](1 + i) \qquad (6\text{–}3)$$

$$PV(\text{annuity due}) = PMT\left[\frac{1 - \dfrac{1}{(1 + i)^n}}{i}\right](1 + i) \qquad (6\text{–}4)$$

What You Should Know	Key Terms	
LG2 Calculate the present value of a level perpetuity and a growing perpetuity. A perpetuity is an annuity that continues forever. That is, every period it pays the same dollar amount. With a growing perpetuity, rather than receiving the same amount each period, the periodic payment increases at a constant rate every period.	Growing perpetuity, *p. 195*	A perpetuity in which the payments grow at a constant rate from period to period over time.
	Level perpetuity, *p. 195*	An annuity with a constant level of payments with an infinite life.
	Perpetuity, *p. 195*	An annuity with an infinite life.

Key Equations

$$PV = \frac{PMT}{i} \qquad\qquad (6\text{–}5)$$

$$PV = \frac{PMT_{period1}}{i-g} \qquad\qquad (6\text{–}6)$$

LG3 Calculate the present and future values of complex cash flow streams. Understanding how to make cash flows that occur in different time periods comparable is essential to understanding finance. All time value formulas presented in this chapter and in the previous chapter stem from the single compounding formula $FV_n = PV(1 + i)^n$. The formulas are used to deal simply with common financial situations, such as, for example, discounting single flows, compounding annuities, and discounting annuities.

Discussion Questions

Q6–1. What is an annuity? Give some examples of annuities.

Q6–2. How do you calculate the future value of an annuity?

Q6–3. What is the relationship between the present value interest factor (from Chapter 5) and the annuity present value interest factor (from Equation [6–2])?

Q6–4. Assume you bought a home and took out a 30-year mortgage on it 10 years ago. How would you determine how much principal on your mortgage you still have to pay off?

Q6–5. Distinguish between an ordinary annuity and an annuity due.

Q6–6. What is a level perpetuity? A growing perpetuity?

Q6–7. How do you calculate the present value of an annuity? A perpetuity? A growing perpetuity?

Q6–8. With an uneven stream of future cash flows, the present value is determined by discounting all of the cash flows back to the present and then adding the present values up. Is there ever a time when you can treat some of the cash flows as annuities and apply the annuity techniques you learned in this chapter?

Study Problems

MyFinanceLab **Annuities**

Go to www.myfinancelab.com
to complete these exercises online
and get instant feedback.

P6–1. **(Future value of an ordinary annuity)** What is the future value of each of the following streams of payments?
   a. $500 a year for 10 years compounded annually at 5 percent
   b. $100 a year for 5 years compounded annually at 10 percent
   c. $35 a year for 7 years compounded annually at 7 percent
   d. $25 a year for 3 years compounded annually at 2 percent

P6–2. **(Related to Checkpoint 6.2 on page 188)** **(Present value of an ordinary annuity)** What is the present value of the following annuities?
   a. $2,500 a year for 10 years discounted back to the present at 7 percent
   b. $70 a year for 3 years discounted back to the present at 3 percent
   c. $280 a year for 7 years discounted back to the present at 6 percent
   d. $500 a year for 10 years discounted back to the present at 10 percent

P6–3. **(Related to The Business of Life: Saving for Retirement on page 194)** **(Future value of an ordinary annuity)** You are graduating from college at the end of this semester and after reading the *The Business of Life* box in this chapter, you have decided to invest $5,000 at the end of each year into a Roth IRA for the next 45 years. If you earn 8 percent compounded annually on your investment, how much will you have when you retire in 45 years? How much will you have if you wait 10 years before beginning to save and only make 35 payments into your retirement account?

P6–4. **(Related to Checkpoint 6.2 on page 188)** **(Present value of an ordinary annuity)** Nicki Johnson, a sophomore mechanical engineering student, received a call from an insurance agent who believes that Nicki is an older woman who is ready to retire from teaching. He talks to her about several annuities that she could buy that would guarantee her a fixed annual income. The annuities are as follows:

Annuity	Purchase Price of the Annuity	Amount of Money Received Per Year	Duration of the Annuity (Years)
A	$50,000	$8,500	12
B	$60,000	$7,000	25
C	$70,000	$8,000	20

Nicki could earn 11 percent on her money by placing it in a savings account. Alternatively, she could place it in any of the above annuities. Which annuities in the table above, if any, will earn Nicki a higher return than investing in the savings account earning 11 percent?

P6–5. **(Related to Checkpoint 6.1 on page 185)** **(Annuity payments)** Mr. Bill S. Preston, Esq., purchased a new house for $80,000. He paid $20,000 up front on the down payment and agreed to pay the rest over the next 25 years in 25 equal annual payments that include principal payments plus 9 percent compound interest on the unpaid balance. What will these equal payments be?

P6–6. **(Annuity payments)** Emily Morrison purchased a new house for $150,000. She paid $30,000 up front and agreed to pay the rest over the next 25 years in 25 equal annual payments that include principal payments plus 10 percent compound interest on the unpaid balance. What will these equal payments be?

P6–7. **(Annuity payments)** To pay for your education, you've taken out $25,000 in student loans. If you make monthly payments over 15 years at 7 percent compounded monthly, how much are your monthly student loan payments?

P6–8. (**Annuity payments**) To pay for your child's education, you wish to have accumulated $15,000 at the end of 15 years. To do this, you plan to deposit an equal amount into the bank at the end of each year. If the bank is willing to pay 6 percent compounded annually, how much must you deposit each year to obtain your goal?

P6–9. (**Annuity payments**) You plan to retire in 10 years and buy a house in Oviedo, Florida. The house you are looking at currently costs $100,000 and is expected to increase in value each year at a rate of 5 percent. Assuming you can earn 10 percent annually on your investments, how much must you invest at the end of each of the next 10 years to be able to buy your dream home when you retire?

P6–10. (**Annuity payments**) The Aggarwal Corporation needs to save $10 million to retire a $10 million mortgage that matures in 10 years. To retire this mortgage, the company plans to put a fixed amount into an account at the end of each year for 10 years. The Aggarwal Corporation expects to earn 9 percent annually on the money in this account. What equal annual contribution must the firm make to this account to accumulate the $10 million by the end of 10 years?

P6–11. (**Annuity payments**) The Knutson Corporation needs to save $15 million to retire a $15 million mortgage that matures in 10 years. To retire this mortgage, the company plans to put a fixed amount into an account at the end of each year for 10 years. The Knutson Corporation expects to earn 10 percent annually on the money in this account. What equal annual contribution must the firm make to this account to accumulate the $15 million by the end of 10 years?

P6–12. (**Future value of an annuity**) Upon graduating from college 35 years ago, Dr. Nick Riviera was already planning for his retirement. Since then, he has made deposits into a retirement fund on a quarterly basis in the amount of $300. Nick has just completed his final payment and is at last ready to retire. His retirement fund has earned 9 percent compounded quarterly.
   a. How much has Nick accumulated in his retirement account?
   b. In addition to this, 15 years ago Nick received an inheritance check for $20,000 from his beloved uncle. He decided to deposit the entire amount into his retirement fund. What is his current balance in the fund?

P6–13. (**Annuity number of periods**) How long will it take to pay off a loan of $50,000 at an annual rate of 10 percent compounded monthly if you make monthly payments of $600?

P6–14. (**Annuity number of periods**) Alex Karev has taken out a $200,000 loan with an annual rate of 8 percent compounded monthly to pay off hospital bills from his wife Izzy's illness. If the most Alex can afford to pay is $1,500 per month, how long will it take to pay the loan off? How long will it take for him to pay off the loan if he can pay $2,000 per month?

P6–15. (**Present value of an annuity**) What is the present value of a 10-year annuity that pays $1,000 annually, given a 10 percent discount rate?

P6–16. (**Annuity interest rate**) Your folks just called and would like some advice from you. An insurance agent just called them and offered them the opportunity to purchase an annuity for $21,074.25 that will pay them $3,000 per year for 20 years. They don't have the slightest idea what return they would be making on their investment of $21,074.25. What rate of return would they be earning?

P6–17. (**Related to Checkpoint 6.1 on page 185**) (**Annuity payments**) On December 31, Beth Klemkosky bought a yacht for $50,000. She paid $10,000 down and agreed to pay the balance in 10 equal annual installments that include both the principal and 10 percent interest on the declining balance. How big will the annual payments be?

P6–18. (**Annuity interest rate**) You've been offered a loan of $30,000, which you will have to repay in five equal annual payments of $10,000, with the first payment to be received one year from now. What interest rate would you be paying on that loan?

P6–19. (Related to Checkpoint 6.1 on page 185) (Annuity payments) A firm borrows $25,000 from the bank at 12 percent compounded annually to purchase some new machinery. This loan is to be repaid in equal annual installments at the end of each year over the next five years. How much will each annual payment be?

P6–20. (Annuity payments) You plan to buy some property in Florida five years from today. To do this, you estimate that you will need $20,000 at that time. You would like to accumulate these funds by making equal annual deposits in your savings account, which pays 12 percent annually. If you make your first deposit at the end of this year, and you would like your account to reach $20,000 when the final deposit is made, how much will you have to deposit in the account annually?

P6–21. (Annuity number of periods) You've just bought a new flat-screen TV for $3,000 and the store you bought it from offers to let you finance the entire purchase at an annual rate of 14 percent compounded monthly. If you take the financing and make monthly payments of $100, how long will it take to pay the loan off? How much will you pay in interest over the life of the loan?

P6–22. (Comprehensive problem) You would like to have $75,000 in 15 years. To accumulate this amount, you plan to deposit an equal sum in the bank each year that will earn 8 percent interest compounded annually. Your first payment will be made at the end of the year.
   a. How much must you deposit annually to accumulate this amount?
   b. If you decide to make a large lump-sum deposit today instead of the annual deposits, how large should the lump-sum deposit be? (Assume you can earn 8 percent on this deposit.)
   c. At the end of five years, you will receive $20,000 and deposit it in the bank in an effort to reach your goal of $75,000 at the end of 15 years. In addition to the deposit, how much must you deposit in equal annual deposits to reach your goal? (Again, assume you can earn 8 percent on this deposit.)

P6–23. (Annuity payments) You plan to buy property in Florida five years from today. To do this, you estimate that you will need $30,000 at that time for the purchase. You would like to accumulate these funds by making equal annual deposits in your savings account, which pays 10 percent annually. If you make your first deposit at the end of this year, and you would like your account to reach $30,000 when the final deposit is made, what amount do you need to deposit annually?

P6–24. (Future value of an annuity and annuity payments) You are trying to plan for retirement in 10 years and currently you have $150,000 in a savings account and $250,000 in stocks. In addition, you plan to deposit $8,000 per year into your savings account at the end of each of the next five years, and then $10,000 per year at the end of each year for the final five years until you retire.
   a. Assuming your savings account returns 8 percent compounded annually, and your investment in stocks will return 12 percent compounded annually, how much will you have at the end of 10 years?
   b. If you expect to live for 20 years after you retire, and at retirement you deposit all of your savings in a bank account paying 11 percent, how much can you withdraw each year after you retire (making 20 equal withdrawals beginning one year after you retire) so that you end up with a zero balance at death?

P6–25. (Annuity payments) On December 31, Son-Nan Chen borrowed $100,000, agreeing to repay this sum in 20 equal annual installments that include both principal and 15 percent interest on the declining balance. How large will the annual payments be?

P6–26. (Annuity payments) To buy a new house, you must borrow $150,000. To do this, you take out a $150,000, 30-year, 10 percent mortgage. Your mortgage payments, which are made at the end of each year (one payment each year), include both principal and 10 percent interest on the declining balance. How large will your annual payments be?

P6–27. (Components of annuity payments) You've just taken on a 20-year, $150,000 mortgage with a quoted interest rate of 6 percent calling for payments semiannually. How much of your first year's loan payments (the initial two payments, with the first coming after six months have passed, and the second one coming at the end of the first year) goes toward paying *interest*, rather than principal?

P6–28. (Related to Checkpoint 6.2 on page 188) (**Present value of annuity payments**) The state lottery's million-dollar payout provides for $1 million to be paid over the course of 19 years in amounts of $50,000. The first $50,000 payment is made immediately, and the 19 remaining $50,000 payments occur at the end of each of the next 19 years. If 10 percent is the discount rate, what is the present value of this stream of cash flows? If 20 percent is the discount rate, what is the present value of the cash flows?

P6–29. (Future value of an annuity) Find the future value at the end of Year 10 of an annuity that pays $1,000 per year for 10 years compounded annually at 10 percent. What would be the future value of this annuity if it were compounded annually at 15 percent?

P6–30. (Present value of an annuity due) Determine the present value of an annuity due of $1,000 per year for 10 years discounted back to the present at an annual rate of 10 percent. What would be the present value of this annuity due if it were discounted at an annual rate of 15 percent?

P6–31. (Present value of an annuity) Determine the present value of an ordinary annuity of $1,000 per year for 10 years, assuming it earns 10 percent. Assume that the first cash flow from the annuity comes at the end of Year 8 and the final payment at the end of Year 17. That is, no payments are made on the annuity at the end of Years 1 through 7. Instead, annual payments are made at the end of Years 8 through 17.

P6–32. (Components of an annuity payment) You take out a 25-year mortgage for $300,000 to buy a new house. What will your monthly payments be if the interest rate on your mortgage is 8 percent? Use a spreadsheet to calculate your answer. Now, calculate the portion of the 48th monthly payment that goes toward interest and principal.

P6–33. (Comprehensive problem) Over the past few years, Microsoft founder Bill Gates's net worth has fluctuated between $20 and $130 billion. In early 2006, it was about $26 billion—after he reduced his stake in Microsoft from 21 percent to around 14 percent by moving billions into his charitable foundation. Let's see what Bill Gates can do with his money in the following problems.

    a. Manhattan's native tribe sold Manhattan Island to Peter Minuit for $24 in 1626. Now, 387 years later in 2013, Bill Gates wants to buy the island from the "current natives." How much would Bill have to pay for Manhattan if the "current natives" want a 6 percent annual return on the original $24 purchase price?

    b. Bill Gates decides to pass on Manhattan and instead plans to buy the city of Seattle, Washington, for $50 billion in 10 years. How much would Bill have to invest today at 10 percent compounded annually in order to purchase Seattle in 10 years?

    c. Now assume Bill Gates only wants to invest half his net worth today, $13 billion, in order to buy Seattle for $50 billion in 10 years. What annual rate of return would he have to earn in order to complete his purchase in 10 years?

    d. Instead of buying and running large cities, Bill Gates is considering quitting the rigors of the business world and retiring to work on his golf game. To fund his retirement, Bill would invest his $20 billion fortune in safe investments with an expected annual rate of return of 7 percent. He also wants to make 40 equal annual withdrawals from this retirement fund beginning a year from today, running his retirement fund to $0 at the end of 40 years. How much can his annual withdrawal be in this case?

P6–34. (Related to Checkpoint 6.1 on page 185) (**Annuity payments**) Lisa Simpson wants to have $1,000,000 in 45 years by making equal annual end-of-the-year deposits into a tax-deferred account paying 8.75 percent annually. What must Lisa's annual deposit be?

P6–35. (Related to Checkpoint 6.2 on page 188) (**Present value of an annuity**) Imagine that Homer Simpson actually invested the $100,000 he earned providing Mr. Burns entertainment five years ago at 7.5 percent annual interest and that he starts investing an additional $1,500 a year today and at the beginning of each year for 20 years at the same 7.5 percent annual rate. How much money will Homer have 20 years from today?

P6–36. (Annuity payments) Prof. Finance is thinking about trading cars. She estimates she will still have to borrow $25,000 to pay for her new car. How large will Prof. Finance's monthly car loan payment be if she can get a five-year (60 equal monthly payments) car loan from the VTech Credit Union at 6.2 percent APR?

P6–37. (Annuity payments) Ford Motor Company's current incentives include 4.9 percent APR financing for 60 months or $1,000 cash back on a Mustang. Let's assume Suzie Student wants to buy the premium Mustang convertible, which costs $25,000, and she has no down payment other than the cash back from Ford. If she chooses the $1,000 cash back, Suzie can borrow from the VTech Credit Union at 6.9 percent APR for 60 months (Suzie's credit isn't as good as that of Prof. Finance). What will Suzie Student's monthly payment be under each option? Which option should she choose?

P6–38. (Related to Checkpoint 6.3 on page 192) (Determining the outstanding balance of a loan) Five years ago you took out a $300,000, 25-year mortgage with an annual interest rate of 7 percent and monthly payments of $2,120.34. What is the outstanding balance on your current loan if you just made the 60th payment?

P6–39. (Annuity payments) Calvin Johnson has a $5,000 debt balance on his Visa card that charges 12.9 percent APR compounded monthly. In 2005, Calvin's minimum monthly payment is 3 percent of his debt balance, which is $150. How many months (round up) will it take Calvin Johnson to pay off his credit card if he pays the current minimum payment of $150 at the end of each month? In 2006, as the result of a federal mandate, the minimum monthly payment on credit cards rose to 4 percent. If Calvin made monthly payments of $200 at the end of each month, how long would it take to pay off his credit card?

P6–40. (Future value of an annuity) Let's say you deposited $160,000 in a 529 plan (a tax-advantaged college savings plan) hoping to have $420,000 available 12 years later when your first child starts college. However, you didn't invest very well, and two years later the account's balance dropped to $140,000. Let's look at what you need to do to get the college savings plan back on track.

    a. What was the original annual rate of return needed to reach your goal when you started the fund two years ago?

    b. With only $140,000 in the fund and 10 years remaining until your first child starts college, what annual rate of return would the fund have to make to reach your $420,000 goal if you add nothing to the account?

    c. Shocked by your experience of the past two years, you feel the college fund has invested too much in stocks, and you want a low-risk fund in order to ensure you have the necessary $420,000 in 10 years. You are willing to make end-of-the-month deposits to the fund as well. You find you can get a fund that promises to pay a guaranteed annual return of 6 percent that is compounded monthly. You decide to transfer the $140,000 to this new fund and make the necessary monthly deposits. How large of a monthly deposit must you make into this new fund each month?

    d. After seeing how large the monthly deposit would be (in part c of this problem), you decide to invest the $140,000 today and $500 at the end of each month for the next 10 years into a fund consisting of 50 percent stock and 50 percent bonds and hope for the best. What APR would the fund have to earn in order to reach your $420,000 goal?

P6–41. (Saving for retirement—future value of an annuity) Selma and Patty Bouvier are twins and both work at the Springfield DMV. Selma and Patty Bouvier decide to save for retirement, which is 35 years away. They'll both receive an 8 percent annual return on their investment over the next 35 years. Selma invests $2,000 per year at the end of each year *only* for the first 10 years of the 35-year period—for a total of $20,000 saved. Patty doesn't start saving for 10 years and then saves $2,000 per year at the end of each year for the remaining 25 years—for a total of $50,000 saved. How much will each of them have when they retire?

Perpetuities

P6–42. (Related to Checkpoint 6.4 on page 196) **(Present value of a perpetuity)** What is the present value of the following?
- a. A $300 perpetuity discounted back to the present at 8 percent
- b. A $1,000 perpetuity discounted back to the present at 12 percent
- c. A $100 perpetuity discounted back to the present at 9 percent
- d. A $95 perpetuity discounted back to the present at 5 percent

P6–43. (Present value of a perpetuity) At a discount rate of 8.5 percent, find the present value of a perpetual payment of $1,000 per year. If the discount rate were lowered to half the size (4.25 percent), what would be the value of the perpetuity?

P6–44. (Related to Checkpoint 6.5 on page 197) **(Present value of a growing perpetuity)** What is the present value of a perpetuity stream of cash flows that pays $1,000 at the end of Year 1, and the annual cash flows grow at a rate of 4 percent per year indefinitely, if the appropriate discount rate is 8 percent? What if the appropriate discount rate is 6 percent?

P6–45. (Present value of a growing perpetuity) What is the present value of a perpetuity stream of cash flows that pays $50,000 at the end of Year 1 and then grows at a rate of 6 percent per year indefinitely? The rate of interest used to discount the cash flows is 10 percent.

P6–46. (Present value of a growing perpetuity) As a result of winning the Gates Energy Innovation Award, you are awarded a growing perpetuity. The first payment will occur in a year and will be for $20,000. You will continue receiving monetary awards annually, with each award increasing by 5 percent over the previous award, and these monetary awards will continue forever. If the appropriate interest rate is 10 percent, what is the present value of this award?

P6–47. (Present value of a growing perpetuity) Your firm has taken on cost-saving measures that will provide a benefit of $10,000 in the first year. These cost savings will decrease each year at a rate of 3 percent forever. If the appropriate interest rate is 6 percent, what is the present value of these savings?

Complex Cash Flow Streams

P6–48. (Related to Checkpoint 6.6 on page 199) **(Present value of annuities and complex cash flows)** You are given three investment alternatives to analyze. The cash flows from these three investments are as follows:

Investment Alternatives

End of Year	A	B	C
1	$10,000		$10,000
2	10,000		
3	10,000		
4	10,000		
5	10,000	$10,000	
6		10,000	50,000
7		10,000	
8		10,000	
9		10,000	
10		10,000	10,000

Assuming a 20 percent discount rate, find the present value of each investment.

P6–49. (Present value of annuities and complex cash flows) You are given three investment alternatives to analyze. The cash flows from these three investments are as follows:

Investment

End of Year	A	B	C
1	$15,000		$20,000
2	15,000		
3	15,000		
4	15,000		
5	15,000	$15,000	
6		15,000	60,000
7		15,000	
8		15,000	
9		15,000	
10		15,000	20,000

Assuming a 20 percent interest rate, find the present value of each investment.

P6–50. (Present value of an uneven stream of payments) You are given three investment alternatives to analyze. The cash flows from these three investments are as follows:

Investment

End of Year	A	B	C
1	$2,000	$2,000	$ 5,000
2	3,000	2,000	5,000
3	4,000	2,000	(5,000)
4	(5,000)	2,000	(5,000)
5	5,000	5,000	15,000

What is the present value of each of these three investments if the appropriate discount rate is 10 percent?

P6–51. (Present value of complex cash flows) You have an opportunity to make an investment that will pay $100 at the end of the first year, $400 at the end of the second year, $400 at the end of the third year, $400 at the end of the fourth year, and $300 at the end of the fifth year.

    a. Find the present value if the interest rate is 8 percent. (Hint: You can simply bring each cash flow back to the present and then add them up. Another way to work this problem is to either use the =NPV function in Excel or to use the CF key on your financial calculator—but you'll want to check your calculator's manual before you use this key. Keep in mind that with the =NPV function in Excel, there is no initial outlay. That is, all this function does is bring all of the future cash flows back to the present. With a financial calculator, you should keep in mind that CF_0 is the initial outlay or cash flow at time 0, and, because there is no cash flow at time 0, $CF_0 = 0$.)

    b. What would happen to the present value of this stream of cash flows if the interest rate were 0 percent?

P6–52. (Present value of complex cash flows) How much do you have to deposit today so that beginning 11 years from now you can withdraw $10,000 a year for the next five years (Periods 11 through 15) plus an *additional* amount of $20,000 in the last year (Period 15)? Assume an interest rate of 6 percent.

P6–53. (Comprehensive problem) You would like to have $50,000 in 15 years. To accumulate this amount, you plan to deposit an equal sum in the bank each year that will earn 7 percent interest compounded annually. Your first payment will be made at the end of the year.

    a. How much must you deposit annually to accumulate this amount?

    b. If you decide to make a large lump-sum deposit today instead of the annual deposits, how large should this lump-sum deposit be? (Assume you can earn 7 percent on this deposit.)

    c. At the end of five years, you will receive $10,000 and deposit this in the bank toward your goal of $50,000 at the end of 15 years. In addition to this deposit, how much must you deposit in equal annual deposits to reach your goal? (Again, assume you can earn 7 percent on this deposit.)

P6–54. (Complex annuity payments) Milhouse, 22, is about to begin his career as a rocket scientist for a NASA contractor. Being a rocket scientist, Milhouse knows that he should begin saving for retirement immediately. Part of his inspiration came from reading an article on Social Security in *Time*. The article indicated that the ratio of workers paying taxes to retirees collecting checks will drop dramatically in the future. In fact, the number will drop to two workers for every retiree in 2040. Milhouse's retirement plan allows him to make equal yearly contributions, and it pays 9 percent interest annually. Upon retirement, Milhouse plans to buy a new boat, which he estimates will cost him $300,000 in 43 years, which is when he plans to retire (at age 65). He also estimates that in order to live comfortably he will require a yearly income of $80,000 for each year after he retires. Based on his family history, Milhouse expects to live until age 80 (that is, he would like to receive 15 payments of $80,000 at the end of each year). When he retires, Milhouse will purchase his boat in one lump sum and place the remaining balance into an account that pays 6 percent interest, from which he will withdraw his $80,000 per year. If Milhouse's first contribution is made one year from today, and his last is made the day he retires, how much money must he contribute each year to his retirement fund?

P6–55. (Comprehensive problem) Having just inherited a large sum of money, you are trying to determine how much you should save for retirement and how much you can spend now. For retirement, you will deposit today (January 1, 2013) a lump sum in a bank account paying 10 percent compounded annually. You don't plan on touching this deposit until you retire in five years (January 1, 2018), and you plan on living for 20 additional years. During your retirement, you would like to receive income of $50,000 per year to be received the first day of each year, with the first payment on January 1, 2018, and the last payment on January 1, 2037. Complicating this objective is your desire to have one final three-year fling during which time you'd like to track down all the original members of *Hey Dude* and *Saved by the Bell* and get their autographs. To finance this, you want to receive $250,000 on January 1, 2033, and *nothing* on January 1, 2034, and January 1, 2035, because you will be on the road. In addition, after you pass on (January 1, 2038), you would like to have a total of $100,000 to leave to your children.

    a. How much must you deposit in the bank at 10 percent interest on January 1, 2013, to achieve your goal? (Use a timeline to answer this question. Keep in mind that the last second of December 31st is equivalent to the first second of January 1st.)

    b. What kinds of problems are associated with this analysis and its assumptions?

P6–56. (Future value of a complex annuity) Springfield mogul Montgomery Burns, age 80, wants to retire at age 100 so he can steal candy from babies full time. Once Mr. Burns retires, he wants to withdraw $1 billion at the beginning of each year for 10 years from a special offshore account that will pay 20 percent annually. In order to fund his retirement, Mr. Burns will make 20 equal end-of-the-year deposits in this same special account that will pay 20 percent annually. How much money will Mr. Burns need at age 100, and how large of an annual deposit must he make to fund this retirement amount?

P6–57. (Comprehensive problem) Suppose that you are in the fall of your senior year and are faced with the choice of either getting a job when you graduate or going to law school. Of course, your choice is not purely financial. However, to make an informed decision you would like to know the financial implications of the two alternatives. Let's assume that your opportunities are as follows:

If you take the "get a job" route you expect to start off with a salary of $40,000 per year. There is no way to predict what will happen in the future, your best guess is that your salary will grow at 5 percent per year until you retire in 40 years. As a law student, you will be paying $25,000 per year tuition for each of the three years you are in graduate school. However, you can then expect a job with a starting salary of $70,000 per year. Moreover, you expect your salary to grow by 7 percent per year until you retire 35 years later.

Clearly, your total expected lifetime salary will be higher if you become a lawyer. However, the additional future salary is not free. You will be paying $25,000 in tuition at the beginning of each of the three years of law school. In addition, you will be giving up a little more than $126,000 in lost income over the three years of law school: $40,000 the first year, $42,000 the second year, and $44,100 the third year.

    a. To start your analysis of whether to go to law school, calculate the present value of the future earnings that you will realize by going directly to work, assuming a 3 percent discount rate.

    b. What is the present value today of your future earnings if you decide to attend law school, assuming a 3 percent discount rate? Remember that you will be in law school for three years before you start to work as a lawyer. (Hint: Assume that you are paid at the end of each year so that your first salary payment if you decide to go to law school occurs four years from now.)

    c. If you pay your law school tuition at the beginning of each year, what is the present value of your tuition, assuming a 3 percent discount rate?

P6–58. (Present value of a complex stream) Don Draper has signed a contract that will pay him $80,000 at the end of each year for the next six years, plus an additional $100,000 at the end of Year 6. If 8 percent is the appropriate discount rate, what is the present value of this contract?

P6–59. (Present value of a complex stream) Don Draper has signed a contract that will pay him $80,000 at the *beginning* of each year for the next six years, plus an additional $100,000 at the end of Year 6. If 8 percent is the appropriate discount rate, what is the present value of this contract?

P6–60. (Complex stream of cash flows) Roger Sterling has decided to buy an ad agency and is going to finance the purchase with seller financing—that is, a loan from the current owners of the agency. The loan will be for $2,000,000 financed at a 7 percent nominal annual interest rate. This loan will be paid off over five years with end-of-month payments along with a $500,000 lump-sum payment at the end of Year 5. That is, the $2 million loan will be paid off with monthly payments and there will also be a final payment of $500,000 at the end of the final month. How much will the monthly payments be?

Mini-Case

Bill Petty, 56, just retired after 31 years of teaching. He is a husband and father of two children who are still dependent. He received a $150,000 lump-sum retirement bonus and will receive $2,800 per month from his retirement annuity. He has saved $150,000 in a 403(b) retirement plan and another $100,000 in other accounts. His 403(b) plan is invested in mutual funds, but most of his other investments are in bank accounts earning 2 or 3 percent annually. Bill has asked your advice in deciding where to invest his lump-sum bonus and other accounts now that he has retired. He also wants to know how much he can withdraw per month, considering he has two children and a nonworking spouse. Because he has children, his current monthly expenses total $5,800. He is not eligible for Social Security until age 62, when he will draw approximately $1,200 per month; however, he would rather defer drawing on Social Security until age 67 to increase his monthly benefit amount to $1,550.

Questions

1. Bill has an emergency fund already set aside, so he can use his $400,000 of savings for retirement. How much can he withdraw on a monthly basis to supplement his retirement annuity if his investments return 5 percent annually and he expects to live 30 more years?

2. Ignoring his Social Security benefit, is the amount determined in question 1 sufficient to meet his current monthly expenses (keep in mind that he will receive a pension of $2,800 per month)? If not, how long will his retirement last if his current expenses remain the same? What if his expenses are reduced to $4,500 per month?

3. Considering the information obtained in question 2, should Bill wait until age 67 for his Social Security benefits? If he waits until age 67, how will his monthly Social Security benefit change the answers to question 2? (*Hint*: Calculate his portfolio value as of age 67 and then calculate how long that amount will last if it earns 5 percent annually.)

4. If the inflation rate averages 3.5 percent during Bill's retirement, how old will he be when prices have doubled from current levels? How much will a soda cost when Bill dies, if he lives the full 30 years and the soda costs $1 today?

7

Market Efficiency and Behavioral Finance

LEARNING GOALS

After studying this chapter, you should be able to:

LG1 Describe the characteristics of an efficient market, explain what market anomalies are, and note some of the challenges that investors face when markets are efficient.

LG2 Summarize the evidence which indicates that the stock market is efficient.

LG3 List four "decision traps" that may lead investors to make systematic errors in their investment decisions.

LG4 Explain how behavioral finance links market anomalies to investors' cognitive biases.

LG5 Describe some of the approaches to technical analysis.

LG6 Compute and use technical trading rules for individual stocks and the market as a whole.

In the TV show *Who Wants to Be a Millionaire?* contestants answer a series of trivia questions for a $1 million prize. One wrong answer sends the contestant home with a small consolation prize, but when contestants are unsure of the answer to a question, they may use one of several "lifelines." In an early version of the game, one lifeline permitted a phone call to a friend for help. The success rate of these "phone a friend" calls was about 65%.

That success rate pales in comparison to the 91% success rate achieved by another of the show's lifelines—a simple poll of the audience. The poll works because members of the audience who do not know the answer simply guess, spreading their answers randomly across the 4 options to answer the question. The responses of audience members who know the answer cluster on the correct choice, which causes the correct response to receive the greatest number of votes. Thus, it is a rare contestant who ignores the wisdom of the audience and survives in the game.

What does this have to do with investments? Estimating the value of a company's stock is more difficult than answering a trivia question. Many variables affect a stock's value, and relevant information about those variables becomes available to different investors at different times. Moreover, thousands of professional investors follow the stock market, ferreting out information to gain an advantage over other investors. According to a famous theory, known as the efficient markets hypothesis, the end result of all this analysis is that the market price is right, just as the audience poll tends to be right most of the time. The market price of a stock reflects everything that investors know about that security, and the collective information known to the market is greater than what any single investor can replicate. Thus, when an investor buys a stock, thinking that the market price doesn't reflect the stock's true value, it's equivalent to a contestant on *Who Wants to Be a Millionaire?* rejecting the results of the audience poll. The evidence is clear that such a strategy succeeds a very small percentage of the time, and if markets are efficient, investors would be wise to think twice before betting that the market has overvalued or undervalued a particular stock.

(Source: James Surowiecki, *The Wisdom of Crowds*, www.randomhouse.com)

Efficient Markets

LG1 LG2 To some observers, the stock market is little more than a form of legalized gambling. They argue that stock prices move almost at random and have no real connection to what is happening in the economy or to the financial results produced by specific companies. In the eyes of people who hold this view, large swings in the market are driven by emotions like greed and fear rather than by business fundamentals. In this chapter, we study the connection between prices in the stock market (and other financial markets) and real business conditions, and we ask whether and how stock prices might be affected by human emotions.

To begin, consider Figure 7.1, which shows quarterly revenues reported by Walmart from 2000 to 2012. A quick glance at the figure reveals 2 obvious patterns. First, Walmart's revenues have grown over time. In early 2012, the company reported first-quarter revenues of $113 billion, more than double the revenue that they generated in the same quarter in 2000. Perhaps an even more striking pattern is that there is clearly one quarter each year in which Walmart earns higher revenues than any other quarter. Those quarterly revenue peaks are marked by red dots in Figure 7.1, and they correspond to Walmart's fourth-quarter revenues. In other words, in every year since 2000, Walmart has sold more goods in the last 3 months of the year than in any other quarter, a remarkably stable pattern. When you think about this pattern a little, it should come as no surprise. Nearly every retail company in the United States sells more in the last 3 months of the year because of the Christmas season, and Walmart is no exception. Although Figure 7.1 plots Walmart's revenues, a plot of the company's net income would show similar patterns.

Walmart is a huge corporation, and nearly 10% of U.S. retail sales (not counting automobiles) occur in Walmart stores. Partly because it is so large and partly because much of its business focuses on life's necessities, Walmart's financial results are not terribly difficult to predict. This is another lesson from Figure 7.1. The persistence of the

FIGURE 7.1

Walmart Quarterly Revenues

From 2000 to 2012, Walmart steadily increased its revenues from $43 billion to more than $113 billion. The long-term upward trend is marked by a distinct seasonal pattern in which Walmart's revenue peaks in the fourth quarter each year, marked by red dots in the figure. The fourth-quarter peak in revenues is due to the Christmas shopping season and is common in retail companies.

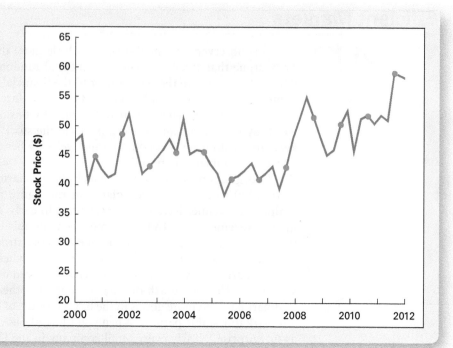

FIGURE 7.2

Walmart's Stock Price

From 2000 to 2012, Walmart's stock price rose, but it did not follow a predictable upward trend. Furthermore, the seasonal pattern in Walmart's revenues does not appear in its stock price. The stock price in the fourth quarter of each year is marked by a red dot, and those red dots show no discernible pattern over the past 12 years.

patterns in Walmart's revenues over a long period of time suggests that forecasts of Walmart's future performance, at least in the not-too-distant future, are likely to be fairly accurate. Is Walmart's stock price just as predictable?

Figure 7.2 plots Walmart's stock price at the end of each quarter from 2000 to 2012, the same period covered in Figure 7.1. Like the company's revenues, Walmart's stock price was higher in 2012 than it was in 2000, but it hardly followed the relatively smooth upward trend that revenues did. The striking difference between Figures 7.1 and 7.2 is the seemingly random movements in Walmart's stock price, which stand in sharp contrast to the predictable movements in Walmart's revenues. Clearly there was no tendency for Walmart's stock to peak at the same time that its revenues did (i.e., at the end of each year, marked by the red dots in Figure 7.2). Does this mean that there is no connection between Walmart's financial performance and the behavior of its stock?

Naturally our answer to that question is a firm no. To understand why, it may be helpful to think about what would happen if Walmart's stock price moved in sync with its revenues, showing a seasonal peak at the end of each year. Suppose that over many years, Walmart stock displayed a regular, predictable tendency to shoot up every year in the fourth quarter. If that pattern persisted and investors came to expect the pattern to continue, what would they do? Smart investors would buy Walmart's stock in the third quarter each year, hoping to profit from the fourth quarter run-up. But if investors rushed to buy Walmart shares in the third quarter each year, that would put upward pressure on the stock price in the third quarter rather than the fourth. In other words, the pattern of fourth-quarter peaks in the stock price would change to a pattern of third-quarter peaks. Pretty soon, investors would see that pattern and begin buying even sooner, perhaps in the second quarter each year. Eventually, the actions of investors trying to buy ahead of any peak in the stock price would cause the seasonal pattern to disappear. So the lesson here is that even if a company's financial results follow a highly predictable pattern, its stock price will not follow the same pattern (or perhaps even any pattern). If stock prices do exhibit predictable patterns, the actions of investors will tend to eliminate those patterns over time.

A second line of argument helps explain why the seemingly random behavior of Walmart's stock price (or any stock price) does not imply that there is a disconnect between the stock market and Walmart's financial performance. A stock's price depends on investors' expectations about the future performance of the company that issued the stock. Prices move up when investors' expectations become brighter, and prices move down when the opposite occurs. Investors who bought Walmart's stock way back in 2000 probably expected that over the next 12 years the company's revenues would grow and that they would peak in the fourth quarter every year. After all, by the year 2000, Walmart had already established a long history of growth, and the seasonal pattern in revenues was well known to the investment community. In other words, much of the performance displayed in Figure 7.1 would not have surprised investors and therefore would not have moved Walmart's stock a great deal. What would cause a sudden and potentially large change in Walmart's stock price is any sign that the firm's future financial performance would deviate from what investors expected. For example, suppose that in 2008 Walmart's revenues were not only high in the fourth quarter (as usual) but that they were even higher than investors had anticipated they would be. In that case, investors would likely raise their expectations about Walmart's future performance, and the company's stock price would go up as a result. If Walmart reported financial results that failed to match investors' expectations, then its stock price would probably fall as investors revised their views about how the company would perform in the future.

The main point here is that stock prices respond to new information. By definition, new information is something that people do not already know and that they do not anticipate. That Walmart's revenues peak at the end of each year is not new information, so when the peak occurs each year it does not tend to boost the company's stock price. Only if fourth-quarter revenues are surprising (better or worse than expected) would Walmart's stock price respond. Because new information is unpredictable, stock price movements are also largely unpredictable. This is the central idea of the **random walk hypothesis**, which says that predicting stock price movements is very difficult, if not impossible. We must emphasize here that if stock prices move at random, it is not a sign that the stock market is a casino that is disconnected from the real business world. Just the opposite is true. The seemingly random behavior of stock prices is a sign that the stock market is processing information quickly and efficiently. In fact, economists say that a market that rapidly and fully incorporates all new information is an **efficient market**.

The Efficient Markets Hypothesis

The notion that stock prices (and prices in other financial markets) rapidly incorporate new information is known formally as the **efficient markets hypothesis (EMH)**. An implication of this idea is that it is very difficult for investors, even professional investors, to earn abnormally high returns by identifying undervalued stocks and buying them (or identifying overvalued stocks and selling them). Spotting bargains in the stock market is difficult because if the market is indeed efficient, by the time you have processed the information that leads you to believe that a stock is a good buy, the market has already incorporated that information, and the information is reflected in the stock's price.

The EMH says that investors should not expect to earn abnormal returns consistently. What constitutes an abnormal return? In Chapter 5 you learned that there is a positive relation between risk and return. Investments that tend to earn higher returns also tend to be riskier. Therefore, an investment's expected return is directly related to its risk. An **abnormal return** is the difference between an investment's actual return and its expected return (i.e., the return that it should earn given its risk).

Equation 7.1   Abnormal return = Actual return − Expected return

In Chapter 11 you will learn that one way that investors can estimate the expected return on a stock is to use the capital asset pricing model, or CAPM. That model says that the expected return on a stock ($E(r_j)$) is equal to the risk-free rate (r_{rf}) plus the product of the stock's beta (b_j) and the risk premium on the overall market ($r_m - r_{rf}$).

Equation 7.2 $E(r_j) = r_{rf} + b_j(r_m - r_{rf})$

Example

Suppose that a particular stock has a beta of 1.0. This means that the stock has average risk and should earn a return that is on average equal to the return on the overall market. Suppose that in a particular year the risk-free rate is 2%, and the return on the overall stock market is 10%. The equation above tells us that the return that we should expect on this stock is 10%:

$$E(r) = 2\% + 1.0(10\% - 2\%) = 10\%$$

Suppose instead that the stock earned a 12% return. In this case it earns an abnormal positive return of 2%:

$$\text{Abnormal return} = \text{Actual return} - \text{Expected return}$$
$$= 12\% - 10\%$$
$$= 2\%$$

The EMH says that spotting stocks like this (i.e., stocks that earn positive abnormal returns) on a consistent basis over time is nearly impossible, even for highly sophisticated investors with extensive training.

The efficient markets hypothesis focuses on the extent to which markets incorporate information into prices. The more information that is incorporated into stock prices and the more rapidly that information becomes incorporated into prices, the more efficient the market becomes. One way of characterizing the extent to which markets are efficient is to define different levels of efficiency corresponding to different types of information that prices may reflect. These levels of market efficiency are known as the weak form, the semi-strong form, and the strong form.

Weak Form The **weak form of the EMH** holds that stock prices fully reflect any relevant information that can be obtained from an analysis of past price movements. If investors study the historical record of stock prices and spot some kind of pattern that seems to repeat, their attempts to exploit that pattern through trading will cause the pattern to disappear over time. We have already described this idea to explain why Walmart's stock price does not exhibit predictable patterns, even though its revenues show distinct seasonal peaks. In short, the weak form of the EMH says that past data on stock prices are of no use in predicting future price changes. According to this hypothesis, prices follow a random walk, meaning that tomorrow's price change is unrelated to today's, yesterday's, or that of any other day.

The earliest research on the weak form of market efficiency appeared to confirm the prediction that prices moved at random. Using databases that contained the past prices of listed stocks in the United States, researchers constructed a variety of "trading rules," such as buying a stock when it hit a 52-week low, and then tested these rules using historical information to see what returns investors following these rules might have earned. The results were encouraging to theorists but not to traders—none of the trading rules earned abnormal returns, but they did generate significant transactions costs. The researchers concluded that investors would do better by purchasing a diversified portfolio and holding it.

Semi-Strong Form The **semi-strong form of the EMH** asserts that stock prices fully reflect all relevant information that investors can obtain from any public source. This means that investors cannot consistently earn abnormally high returns using publicly available information such as annual reports and other required filings, analyst recommendations, product reviews, and so on. To illustrate the idea, suppose that you see that a particular firm has just posted its latest financial results online. You read the report and see that the company reported an unexpected surge in profits in the most recent quarter. Should you call your broker and buy some shares? The semi-strong form of the EMH says that by the time you download the annual report, read it, and call your broker, the market price of the stock will have already increased, reflecting the company's latest good news.

Figure 7.3 comes from a recent research study that tested this form of the EMH. The researchers gathered data on a large number of earnings announced by different companies and tracked the companies' stock price behavior before and after the earnings announcements. The common factor in all of these announcements was that the

FIGURE 7.3 **Daily Stock Price Reactions Surrounding Positive Earnings News**

The figure shows that for a group of companies reporting favorable earnings news, abnormal returns are close to 0 leading up to the announcement and beyond 2 days after the announcement. The market responds fully to the new information in 1 or at most 2 days. Source: Andreas Neuhierl, Anna Scherbina, and Bernd Schlusche. "Market Reaction to Corporate Press Releases," forthcoming in the *Journal of Financial and Quantitative Analysis*.

companies were reporting good news in the sense that their earnings were higher than analysts had expected. In a sense, the question that the researchers were asking was, is it smart to buy the stock of a company that announces this kind of good news?

The horizontal axis of Figure 7.3 measures time relative to the earnings announcement day. The earnings announcement day is day 0, so day −1 is one day before the announcement and day +1 is one day after the announcement. Keep in mind that many firms release their financial information after the market has closed. This means that the first opportunity for the stock market to incorporate the new information occurs the day after the announcement, on day +1. The vertical axis in the figure measures the average abnormal return exhibited by companies in the sample. The behavior of stock prices exhibited in Figure 7.3 is very close to what the semi-strong form of the EMH would predict. Observe that leading up to the earnings announcements, the companies in the sample earn returns that are essentially normal (i.e., the abnormal return is 0, so the actual return matches the expected return). However, from day 0 to day +1, the average company in the sample earned an abnormal return of about 2.5%, with an additional 1% abnormal return occurring from day +1 to day +2. Beyond that point, however, abnormal returns quickly revert to 0%. In other words, the market quickly (in a day or at most 2 days) incorporates the good news from earnings announcements.

Many tests of semi-strong efficiency have examined how stock prices respond before and after particular types of news events. One study looked at 4 companies that were major contractors in the space shuttle program. When the shuttle *Challenger* exploded shortly after liftoff in 1986, the stock prices of all 4 companies fell, but the one that fell the most was Morton Thiokol. That company made the booster rockets that lifted the shuttle into orbit, and months after the accident occurred, an investigation concluded that a problem with the O-rings in these rockets had caused the accident. In other words, the market's initial reaction within minutes of the accident seemed to point to the same conclusion as the subsequent investigation.

Numerous studies have examined the investment performance of professional investors such as mutual fund managers. Some people argue that although the stock market may be efficient enough to prevent individual investors from earning abnormally high returns, surely professional investors who have advanced training in investments and who spend their entire professional lives thinking about investments can perform better. The conclusions from research in this area are not unanimous, but most studies find that even professional investors struggle to earn abnormal returns on a consistent basis. On average, mutual fund managers do not earn returns that beat the market average by a sufficient degree to cover the fees that they charge investors. Furthermore, there is not much persistence in mutual fund returns. In other words, fund managers who have above-average returns one year do not have a very high likelihood of generating above-average returns the next year.

The overwhelming evidence indicates that stock prices react very rapidly to any important new information, which makes it very hard for investors (individuals or professionals) to "beat the market." Unless you hear about an event almost as soon as it happens, the stock price will adjust to the news before you can trade the stock.

Strong Form The **strong form of the EMH** holds that the stock market can rapidly incorporate new information even if it is not disseminated through public sources. It states that stock prices rapidly adjust to any information, even if it isn't available to every investor.

One type of private information is the kind obtained by corporate insiders, such as officers or directors of a corporation. They have access to valuable information about major strategic and tactical decisions the company makes. They also have detailed information about the financial state of the firm that may not be available to other shareholders. Insiders are generally prohibited from trading the shares of their employer prior to major news releases. However, at other times corporate insiders may legally trade shares of stock in their company, if they report the transactions to the Securities and Exchange Commission (SEC). When insiders file the required forms with the SEC, they are quickly made available to the public via the Internet. Several studies of corporate insiders find that their trades are particularly well timed, meaning that they tend to buy before significant price increases and sell prior to big declines. This, of course, is contrary to what you'd expect to find if the strong form of the EMH were true.

Insiders and other market participants occasionally have inside—nonpublic—information that they obtained or traded on illegally. With this information, they can gain an unfair advantage that permits them to earn an abnormal return. Clearly, those who violate the law when they trade have an unfair advantage. Empirical research has confirmed that those with such inside information do indeed have an opportunity to earn an abnormal return—but there might be an awfully high price attached, such as spending time in prison, if they're caught.

Market Anomalies

Despite considerable evidence in support of the EMH, researchers have uncovered some patterns that seem inconsistent with the theory. Collectively, this body of puzzling evidence is known as **market anomalies**, a name that itself suggests that there is less evidence contradicting the EMH than there is in support of it. What all of these anomalies have in common is that they reveal patterns or trading strategies that, at least in hindsight, earned higher returns than would be expected in efficient markets.

Calendar Effects One widely cited anomaly is the so-called *calendar effect*, which holds that stock returns may be closely tied to the time of the year or the time of the week. That is, certain months or days of the week may produce better investment results than others. The most famous of the calendar anomalies is the *January effect,* which is a tendency for small-cap stocks to outperform large-cap stocks by an unusually wide margin in the month of January. One possible explanation for this pattern has to do with taxes. Under certain conditions, investors can deduct investment losses when calculating their federal income taxes. Thus, there is an incentive for investors to sell stocks that have gone down in value during the year, and investors who recognize that incentive are particularly likely to sell in December as the tax year comes to a close. Think about what happens to the market capitalization of a firm when its stock falls during the year—the market cap gets smaller. Thus, if investors have a tax incentive to sell their loser stocks in December, and if these stocks by definition tend to be smaller than average, then their prices may be temporarily depressed due to December tax selling, and they may rebound in January. As plausible as this explanation may sound, there is at best mixed evidence that it can account for the puzzling behavior of small stocks in January.

Small-Firm Effect Another anomaly is the *small-firm effect*, or size effect, which states that small firms tend to earn positive abnormal returns. Indeed, several studies have shown that small firms (or small-cap stocks) earn higher returns than large-cap stocks (and not just in January), even after taking into account the higher betas typical of most small firms. This tendency has been documented in the United States as well as in many stock markets around the world.

Post Earnings Announcement Drift (or Momentum) Another market anomaly has to do with how stock prices react to earnings announcements. In Figure 7.3 we showed the results of a study that tracked stock returns around earnings announcements. In that study, stocks reporting good earnings exhibited abnormal returns for a day or two, but those abnormal returns quickly dissipated. However, several older studies reported a tendency for stocks to "drift" after earnings announcements in the same direction as the initial reaction. In other words, when companies reported better-than-expected earnings, their stock prices jumped immediately, earning positive abnormal returns. But surprisingly, these firms' stock prices continued to earn positive abnormal returns for weeks or even months after the earnings announcements. Similarly, firms reporting bad earnings earned negative abnormal returns that continued for several months beyond the initial announcement. This seems to indicate that investors underreact to the information in earnings announcements. When firms report good news, investors don't realize just how good the news is, and similarly, when bad news comes, investors don't fully appreciate how bad the news is, and stock prices take a long time to fully adjust to a new level. This pattern seems to create an opportunity for investors to earn abnormal returns by purchasing stocks that have recently issued good earnings news or by short selling stocks that have recently delivered poor earnings results.

Figure 7.4 illustrates the post earnings announcement drift pattern. The horizontal axis marks time, measured in weeks relative to an earnings announcement, and the vertical axis measures the cumulative abnormal return from 52 weeks prior to the earnings announcement to 52 weeks after the announcement. The earnings announcement occurs at week 0. Two types of companies are tracked in the figure—companies that announce better-than-expected earnings and companies that announce worse-than-expected earnings.

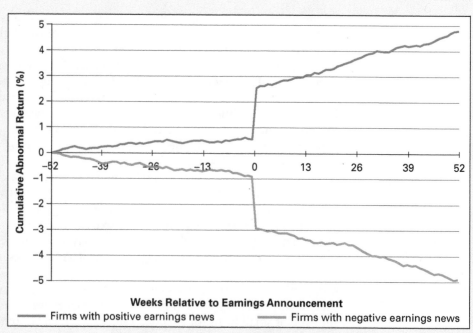

FIGURE 7.4

Post Earnings Announcement Drift

When firms announce better-than-expected earnings, their stock prices jump quickly as the EMH would predict, but contrary to the EMH, stock prices continue to drift upward at an abnormally rapid clip over the next year or so. The same thing happens in reverse when firms announce poor earnings.

Weeks Relative to Earnings Announcement

— Firms with positive earnings news   — Firms with negative earnings news

The blue line in the figure plots cumulative abnormal returns (i.e., the abnormal return over the entire period) earned by the sample of "good news" stocks, and the red line tracks abnormal returns for the "bad news" stocks. Notice that when firms announce good news, their stock prices react quickly, as indicated by the jump in the blue line at week 0. Similarly, when firms reveal that their earnings are below investors' expectations, their stock prices move down almost immediately, as shown by the drop in the red line at week 0. That rapid initial reaction is exactly the pattern that an efficient market should produce.

However, it appears that investors underreact to the news contained in earnings announcements. Observe that after the initial reaction to the earnings announcement, both the blue and red lines exhibit trends, with the blue line slowly rising and the red line slowly falling. This means that the initial reaction to the earnings announcement was not large enough, and stock prices are adjusting slowly to the information contained in the earnings announcement. The slow adjustment process creates an opportunity for investors. For example, after a company announces positive earnings news (i.e., investors do not have to anticipate what the content of the announcement will be), investors who buy the stock earn significant abnormal returns. Looking at the blue line in Figure 7.4, you can see that the amount of drift is roughly 2% over the 52 weeks following the earnings announcement. In other words, Figure 7.4 suggests that investors who closely monitor earnings announcements and buy stocks after firms announce better-than-expected returns will earn a return that is about 2% above normal (i.e., 2% greater than one would expect given the risk of the stocks being purchased). Investors can also make money by short selling the shares of companies that announce poor earnings results. The drift in stock prices following the earnings announcement is not consistent with the predictions of the EMH.

A slight variation on this story is known as the momentum anomaly. In physics, *momentum* refers to the tendency of an object in motion to continue moving or the tendency of an object at rest to remain at rest. Applied to stocks, momentum refers to the tendency for stocks that have gone up recently to keep going up, or the tendency for stocks that have gone down recently to continue going down. The connection to earnings announcement drift is easy to see. When a company has a particularly good quarter, it is common for some of the good news to leak out into the market before the official earnings announcement. So leading up to the earnings release, it is common to see the stock price moving up, just as the blue line in Figure 7.4 rises ahead of the earnings news. As we've already discussed, when the firm releases the news that it has had a very strong quarter, the price goes up more, but then it continues to drift up for weeks. Taking the entire pattern into account, we observe that before a company releases very good earnings news, its stock price has gone up, and then it keeps going up after the earnings announcement. Hence, these stocks display positive momentum. The same thing happens in reverse for companies that have particularly bad quarters. Some of the bad news leaks out early, and the stock goes down (see the red line in Figure 7.4), but then the stock continues to go down after the announcement.

The Value Effect According to the *value effect*, the best way to make money in the market is to buy stocks that have relatively low prices relative to some measure of fundamental value such as book value or earnings. An investor following a value strategy might calculate the P/E ratio or the ratio of market value to book value for many stocks, and then buy the stocks with the lowest ratios (and perhaps short-sell the stocks with high P/E or market-to-book ratios). Studies have shown that, on average, value stocks outperform stocks with high P/E or market-to-book ratios (so-called growth stocks). This pattern has repeated itself decade after decade in the United States and in most stock markets around the world.

Possible Explanations

Each new discovery of an anomaly that appears to violate the EMH prompts a flurry of research that offers rational explanations for the pattern observed. The most common explanation for market anomalies is that the stocks that earn abnormally high returns are simply riskier than other stocks, so the higher returns on these stocks reflect a risk premium rather than mispricing by the market. For example, most academics and practitioners would agree that small firms are riskier than large firms, so it is not surprising that small stocks earn higher returns. The real question is, how much riskier are small firms, and how large should the risk premium be on those securities? According to the CAPM, if a small stock has a beta of 2.0 and a large stock has a beta of 1.0, the small stock should earn roughly twice the risk premium (over Treasury bills) that the large stock earns. The reason that the small firm effect is known as an anomaly is that small stocks seem to earn higher returns than their betas can justify. Believers in the EMH argue that beta is an imperfect measure of risk and that if a better risk measure were available, the difference in returns between small and large stocks could be fully attributed to differences in risk.

Another explanation for market anomalies is that even in an efficient market where prices move essentially at random, some trading rules may appear to earn abnormally high returns simply as a matter of chance. For example, one of the more amusing market anomalies is known as the Super Bowl anomaly. This anomaly says that if the team winning the Super Bowl in a particular year is one of the original National Football League teams (prior to the merger with the old American Football League), then the stock market will rise. Otherwise, the stock market will fall. This "trading rule" correctly predicted the direction of the market more than 80% of the time in the last 40 years. But should investors rely on it in the future? Most people would agree that the connection between the Super Bowl winner and the stock market is purely a matter of chance and is unlikely to exhibit a similar track record in the next 40 years. Some EMH advocates believe that most market anomalies are similarly just an artifact of random chance. However, this explanation is less persuasive in the face of evidence that anomalies such as the small firm effect, momentum, and the value effect appear in most markets around the world.

The discovery of these and other anomalies led to the development of an entirely new way of viewing the workings of financial markets that has come to be known as **behavioral finance**. In contrast to traditional finance, which starts with the assumption that investors, managers, and other actors in financial markets are rational, behavioral finance posits that market participants make systematic mistakes, and that those mistakes are inextricably linked to cognitive biases that are hard-wired into human nature. We now turn to a discussion of the basic tenets of behavioral finance and how they may help explain market anomalies.

CONCEPTS IN REVIEW
Answers available at www.pearsonhighered.com/smart

7.1 What is the random walk hypothesis, and how does it apply to stocks? What is an efficient market? How can a market be efficient if its prices behave in a random fashion?

7.2 Explain why it is difficult, if not impossible, to consistently outperform an efficient market.
   a. Does this mean that high rates of return are not available in the stock market?
   b. How can an investor earn a high rate of return in an efficient market?

7.3 What are market anomalies and how do they come about? Do they support or refute the EMH? Briefly describe each of the following:
   a. The January effect
   b. The size effect
   c. The value effect

Behavioral Finance: A Challenge to the Efficient Markets Hypothesis

LG3 LG4 For more than 30 years, the efficient markets hypothesis has been an influential force in financial markets. The notion that asset prices fully reflect all available information is supported by a large body of academic research. In practitioner circles, supporters of market efficiency include John Bogle of Vanguard, who helped pioneer the development of a special type of mutual fund known as an index fund. Managers of index funds don't try to pick individual stocks or bonds because they assume that the market is efficient. They recognize that any time and energy spent researching individual securities will merely serve to increase the fund's expenses, which will drag down investors' returns.

Although considerable evidence supports the concept of market efficiency, an increasing number of academic studies have begun to cast doubt on the EMH. This research documents various anomalies and draws from research on cognitive psychology to offer explanations for the anomalies. One notable event that acknowledged the importance of this field was the awarding of the 2002 Nobel Prize in economics to Daniel Kahneman, whose work integrated insights from psychology and economics. In addition to academic studies, some professional money managers are also incorporating concepts from behavioral finance into their construction and management of portfolios.

Investor Behavior and Security Prices

Researchers in behavioral finance believe that investors' decisions are affected by a number of psychological biases that lead investors to make systematic, predictable mistakes in certain decision-making situations. These mistakes, in turn, may lead to predictable patterns in asset prices that create opportunities for other investors to earn abnormally high profits without accepting abnormally high risk. Let's now take a look at some of the behavioral factors that might influence the actions of investors.

Overconfidence and Self-Attribution Bias Research in psychology provides overwhelming evidence that, on average, people tend to exhibit **overconfidence**, putting too much faith in their own ability to perform complex tasks. Try this experiment. The next time you are in a large group, ask people to indicate whether they believe they have above average, average, or below average skill in driving a car. What you will probably find is that a majority of the group believes that they have above-average ability, and almost no one will lay claim to having below-average skill. But simply by the definition of average, some people have to be above average and some must be below average. Therefore, at least some people in the group are overconfident in their driving ability.

Closely linked to overconfidence is a phenomenon known as self-attribution bias. **Self-attribution bias** roughly means that when something good happens, individuals attribute that outcome to actions that they have taken, but when something bad happens, they attribute it to bad luck or external factors beyond their control. The connection to overconfidence is straightforward. An individual takes an action or makes a decision that leads to a favorable outcome. Self-attribution bias causes the individual to discount the role that chance may have played in determining the outcome and to put too much emphasis on his or her actions as the cause. This causes the individual to become overconfident.

What effects do overconfidence and self-attribution bias have in the investments realm? Consider an individual investor, or even a professional money manager, who analyzes stocks to determine which ones are overvalued and which are bargains. Suppose in a particular year the investor's portfolio earns very high returns. Perhaps the high returns are largely due to a booming stock market, but perhaps in addition the investor's stock picks performed even better than the overall market. Is this the result of good fortune or good analysis? It's not easy to separate the roles of skill and luck, but most investors would probably attribute the favorable outcome to their own investing prowess. What is the consequence if investors mistakenly attribute investment success to their own skill? One study found that investors whose portfolios had outperformed the market in the past subsequently increased their trading activity. After beating the overall market average by 2% per year for several years, these investors increased their trading activity more than 70%. The increase in trading led to much higher transactions costs and much lower returns. The same group of investors trailed the market by 3% per year after increasing their trading activity.

This tendency is not confined to individual investors. A recent study found that CEOs exhibit similar behavior when they undertake acquisitions of other firms. When a CEO acquires another firm and the acquisition target performs well, the CEO is more likely to acquire another firm. The CEO is also more likely to buy more shares in his or her employer's stock prior to the next acquisition. But these second acquisitions actually destroy shareholder value on average. In other words, it appears that CEOs become overconfident regarding their ability to acquire other firms and run them profitably.

Loss Aversion Here's an interesting series of questions. Suppose you have just won $8,500 in a game of chance. You can walk away with your winnings or you can risk them. If you take the risk, there is a 90% chance that you will win an additional $1,500, but there is a 10% chance that you will lose everything. Would you walk away or gamble? Most people who are asked this question say that they would take the $8,500—the sure thing. They say this even though the expected value from the additional gamble is $500. That is,

$$\text{Expected value} = (\text{Probability of gain}) \times (\text{Amount of gain}) - (\text{Probability of loss})$$
$$\times (\text{Amount of loss}) = 0.90 \times \$1,500 - 0.10 \times \$8,500 = \underline{\$500}$$

In this case, the decision to take the $8,500 indicates that the individual making that choice is risk averse. The risk of losing $8,500 isn't worth the expected $500 gain.

However, if we reframe the question, most people respond differently. Suppose you have already lost $8,500 in a game of chance. You can walk away and cut your losses or you can gamble again. If you gamble, there is a 90% chance that you will lose $1,500 more, but there is a 10% chance that you will win $8,500, thus entirely reversing your initial loss. When confronted with this choice, most people say that they will take the risk to try to "get even," even though the expected value of this gamble is −$500.

$$\text{Expected value} = 0.10 \times \$8,500 - 0.90 - \$1,500 = \underline{-\$500}$$

In this case, people are exhibiting risk-seeking behavior. They are accepting a risk that they do not have to take, and it is a risk that has a negative expected return.

In behavioral finance, the tendency to exhibit risk-averse behavior when confronting gains and risk-seeking behavior when confronting losses is called **loss aversion**. Loss

Loss Aversion and Trading Volume

When people are loss averse, they are reluctant to sell investments that have lost value because doing so forces them to realize the loss. But if investors are reluctant to sell when prices are falling, trading activity can dry up. That was a finding from a study of residential real estate activity over several market cycles in Boston. Researchers found that when market prices were rising, homeowners were generally willing to sell their properties at market value. But when price declines left homeowners in a position such that the market value of their home was less than what they had paid for it, homeowners exhibited a tendency to set asking prices above the true market value. As a consequence, homes sat on the market month after month, with very few transactions taking place.

(Source: David Genesove and Christopher Mayer. 2001. "Loss Aversion and Seller Behavior: Evidence from the Housing Market." *Quarterly Journal of Economics.*)

aversion simply means that people feel the pain of loss more acutely than the pleasure of gain. In an investments context, loss aversion can lead people to hold onto investments that have lost money longer than they should. In fact, numerous studies have documented that when investors want to sell a stock in their portfolio, they are much more likely to sell a stock that has gone up in value than one that has fallen.

Representativeness

Overreaction In an interesting experiment, 6 people were asked to flip a coin 20 times and count the number of heads that came up. Another group of 6 was asked to imagine flipping a coin 20 times and write down the sequence of heads and tails that might occur. The table below shows the results reported by each group.

Group	Subject	Number of Heads	Group	Subject	Number of Heads
A	1	10	B	1	6
	2	10		2	13
	3	8		3	7
	4	10		4	11
	5	10		5	8
	6	10		6	14

Looking at the responses from individuals in each group, which group do you think actually flipped coins, and which imagined doing so?

The answer is that Group A only imagined flipping coins. Notice that almost everyone in the group said they expected to obtain 10 heads in 20 flips, but in the group that actually tossed the coins, the number of heads varied widely, from 6 to 14. What accounts for the differences between the two groups?

Representativeness refers to cognitive biases that occur because people have difficulty thinking about randomness in outcomes. Subjects in Group A assume (correctly) that the probability of obtaining a heads on any single flip of a coin is 50%, but they also assume (incorrectly) that this means that in 20 flips of a coin, it is very likely that heads will come up exactly 10 times. In other words, when people know the probability of a particular event occurring, they assume that a series of events will mirror that probability. As the results of Group B's coin flips clearly show, it is rather unusual to obtain exactly 10 heads in 20 flips. Lots of other outcomes are quite likely.

A similar problem occurs when people do not know whether or to what extent randomness influences the outcomes of a series of events. That is, when people observe what appears to be a systematic pattern in a series of numbers or outcomes, they under-

estimate the likelihood that such a pattern might be the outcome of random chance, and they overestimate the likelihood that some underlying force will cause the pattern to repeat. In other words, they overreact to a series of similar events. For example, suppose a particular mutual fund outperforms the S&P 500 index 3 years in a row. According to the EMH, earning above-average returns is more a matter of luck than of skill, so any particular investor (individual or professional) has roughly a 50% chance of beating the market in a particular year. With so many mutual funds available, it would hardly be surprising to see some of these beat the market 3 years in a row, even if doing so is purely due to good luck as the EMH would suggest. In fact, there is a great deal of evidence indicating that most professional mutual fund managers fail to outperform the market average over long periods.

Even so, what do you think happens when one fund does well for 3 consecutive years? Research shows that investors overreact and pour money into successful funds, enriching the fund managers but not necessarily the fund investors. Apparently, many investors see a string of good performance and overestimate the likelihood that the trend will continue. Investors overreact to the past performance of funds, even though there is little objective evidence that past performance is a good predictor of future success.

This logic may provide a behavioral explanation for the value phenomenon cited earlier. Recall that value stocks are stocks that have low prices relative to earnings or book value. These stocks generally display rather poor past performance—several years of declining prices is what puts these stocks in the value category. Similarly, growth stocks, firms with high prices relative to earnings or book value, generally have very good past performance. One of the earliest studies of the value effect studied the results of a very simple trading rule. Each year, researchers sorted all stocks based on their cumulative performance in the previous 3 years. The trading rule was to buy the stocks that had performed worst (the value stocks) and sell short the stocks that had performed best (the growth stocks). Researchers discovered that this strategy earned returns that beat the market by 8% per year! Why would such a simple trading rule that anyone could follow work so well?

The researchers argued that it was due to representativeness. To be specific, they proposed that investors who watched particular stocks decline in value for 3 years in a row eventually decided that the trend would continue indefinitely, so they bid the prices of these stocks below their true values. Similarly, after watching other stocks do very well several years in a row, investors naively assumed that this excellent performance would continue, and they bid up the prices of these stocks above their true values. Over time, the firms that had been performing poorly surprised investors by rebounding, and the firms that had been earning spectacular returns failed to sustain that performance. As a result, past price trends reversed themselves, and value investors made money.

As before, individual investors are not the only participants in markets likely to be affected by representativeness. Consider a firm that is looking to make an acquisition. What makes an acquisition target attractive? One criterion might be a firm with recent increases in sales and earnings. Would acquirers be wise to pay a premium to acquire a firm that has been growing faster than its competitors in recent years? The research evidence says no. There is almost no correlation between how fast firms have grown in the past and how fast they will grow in the future. In fact, that is a fundamental prediction of basic economic theory. When one firm enjoys great success in a particular market, other firms will enter the industry. Competition makes it more difficult for firms to sustain the high growth that attracted new entrants in the first place. Yet there is ample evidence that managers do pay a larger premium when they acquire firms that experienced rapid growth prior to the acquisition, even though the prospect of sustaining the growth is low.

Underreaction In certain instances, representativeness can cause investors to underreact to new information. Consider this problem from statistics. On a table are 100 sacks, each of which contains 1,000 poker chips. Forty-five of these sacks contain 70% black chips and 30% red chips. The other 55 bags hold 70% red chips and 30% black chips. If you pick one bag at random, what is the likelihood that it will contain mostly black chips?

Most people get this answer right. If 45 out of 100 bags contain mostly black chips, then the probability of picking a bag at random that has mostly black chips is 45%. Here is a much harder problem. Suppose you choose one bag at random and then take out 12 chips, without looking at the others. Of the 12 chips that you pull out, 8 are black and 4 are red. What is the probability that the bag you picked contains mostly black chips?

Intuitively, people know that if the sample of 12 chips taken from the bag has a majority of black chips, then that means the probability that the bag has mostly black chips is higher than in the first problem where we simply select a bag at random. But how much higher? Few people come close to guessing that the probability is over 95%! In other words, people tend to underreact to the new information they obtain in the second version of the question.

Let's make an analogy between drawing poker chips out of a bag and reading firms' earnings announcements. Earnings announcements contain a mix of good and bad news that varies over time. When a company announces particularly good (or bad) news, representativeness may cause investors to underreact to the new information. That next quarter has gone up (and vice versa for bad news this quarter). That could explain the post-earnings announcement drift (or momentum) phenomenon discussed earlier.

A careful reader may object that we have asserted that representativeness can lead to both overreaction (in the case of value stocks) and underreaction (in the case of momentum). Keep in mind that there are important differences in the nature of the information that investors are reacting to in each case. In the value phenomenon, investors see a common string of information—several good years or several bad years in a row. This causes them to discount the role of chance in the outcome and overreact to the series of events. In the case of earnings announcement drift, investors are responding to a single new piece of information that is extreme—particularly good or particularly bad. In that case, representativeness may lead investors to underreact to the new information they've received.

Narrow Framing Many people tend to analyze a situation in isolation, while ignoring the larger context. This behavior is called **narrow framing**. A common example in investments relates to the asset allocation decisions that investors make in their retirement plans. The table below summarizes the retirement savings plans offered to employees of 2 firms. Firm A offers its employees 2 options for investing retirement savings—a stock fund and a bond fund. Firm B also offer two options—a stock fund and a blended fund that holds 50% stocks and 50% bonds.

Fund Offered	Company A	Company B
Stock fund (100% stocks)	Yes	Yes
Bond fund (100% bonds)	Yes	Not available
Blended fund (50% stocks, 50% bonds)	Not available	Yes

Research shows that many investors view this decision through the narrow frame of 2 choices, and they follow a simple guideline—put 50% into one fund and 50% into the other. It is as if investors know that they should diversify, so they divide their investments equally between the available options. However, investors seemingly fail to recognize how the asset allocation of the individual funds influences the resulting composition of their overall portfolios. The narrow frame (splitting money evenly between 2 funds) combined with the options offered by each company produces an odd outcome. Employees of Firm A who divide their money between the stock fund and the bond fund will wind up with portfolios containing 50% stocks and 50% bonds. Employees of Firm B also divide their money equally between the 2 funds, but in this case the 2 funds are the stock fund and the blended fund. Splitting money equally between those options results in an overall portfolio allocation of 75% stocks and 25% bonds. The retirement portfolios held by employees of Firm B are much riskier than those held by workers at Firm A, but not necessarily because Firm B's employees prefer to take more risk. Instead, the risk of their portfolios is influenced by framing effects.

Belief Perseverance People typically ignore information that conflicts with their existing beliefs, a phenomenon called **belief perseverance**. If they believe a stock is good and purchase it, for example, they later tend to discount any signs of trouble. In many cases, they even avoid gathering new information for fear it will contradict their initial opinion. It would be better to view each stock owned as a "new" stock when periodically reviewing a portfolio and to ask whether the information available at that time would cause you to buy or sell the stock.

Familiarity Bias In this text we have discussed a number of analytical methods that investors can use to decide whether they want to purchase a particular investment. It turns out that in many cases people simply invest in things that are familiar to them, a behavior called **familiarity bias**. Research has shown that investors tend to invest in stocks located close to their homes. Even professional investors are not immune to this bias. A recent study found that mutual fund managers tend to invest more heavily in stocks located in their home states.

Investing in something familiar is not necessarily a bad thing. Perhaps being more familiar with a company helps investors determine whether that company's stock is a good buy. However, if familiarity helps give investors an information edge, then investors should earn higher returns on the investments that they make based on familiarity (e.g., investments in companies located nearby). Even among professional investors, the evidence on this question is mixed. One study found that mutual fund managers earned unusually high returns on their investments in nearby firms, but other studies found that investing in companies based on familiarity influenced fund managers to form portfolios that were not fully diversified. As a result, those funds did not earn higher returns, but they did experience higher risk.

TABLE 7.1 **USING BEHAVIORAL FINANCE TO IMPROVE INVESTMENT RESULTS**

Studies have documented a number of behavioral factors that appear to influence investors' decisions and adversely affect their returns. By following some simple guidelines, you can avoid making mistakes and improve your portfolio's performance. A little common sense goes a long way in the financial markets!

- **Don't hesitate to sell a losing stock.** If you buy a stock at $20 and its price drops to $10, ask yourself whether you would buy that same stock if you came into the market today with $10 in cash. If the answer is yes, then hang onto it. If not, sell the stock and buy something else.
- **Don't chase performance.** The evidence suggests that there are no "hot hands" in investment management. Don't buy last year's hottest mutual fund if it doesn't make sense for you. Always keep your personal investment objectives and constraints in mind.
- **Be humble and open-minded.** Many investment professionals, some of whom are extremely well paid, are frequently wrong in their predictions. Admit your mistakes and don't be afraid to take corrective action. The fact is, reviewing your mistakes can be a very rewarding exercise—all investors make mistakes, but the smart ones learn from them. Winning in the market is often about not losing, and one way to avoid loss is to learn from your mistakes.
- **Review the performance of your investments on a periodic basis.** Remember the old saying, "Out of sight, out of mind." Don't be afraid to face the music and to make changes as your situation changes. Nothing runs on "autopilot" forever—including investment portfolios.
- **Don't trade too much.** Investment returns are uncertain, but transaction costs are guaranteed. Considerable evidence indicates that investors who trade frequently perform poorly.

Implications of Behavioral Finance for Security Analysis

Our discussion of the psychological factors that affect financial decisions suggests that behavioral finance can play an important role in investing. Naturally, the debate on the efficiency of markets rages on and will continue to do so for many years. The contribution of behavioral finance is to identify particular psychological factors that can lead investors to make systematic mistakes, and to determine whether those mistakes may contribute to predictable patterns in stock prices. If that's the case, the mistakes of some investors may be the profit opportunities for others. See Table 7.1 for our advice on how to keep your own mistakes to a minimum.

CONCEPTS IN REVIEW

Answers available at www.pearsonhighered.com/smart

7.4 How can behavioral finance have any bearing on investor returns? Do supporters of behavioral finance believe in efficient markets? Explain.

7.5 Briefly explain how behavioral finance can affect each of the following:

   a. The trading activity of investors
   b. The tendency of value stocks to outperform growth stocks
   c. The tendency of stock prices to drift up (down) after unusually good (bad) earnings news

Technical Analysis

LG5 **LG6** In the first section of this chapter we introduced the idea of market efficiency and suggested that there are many good reasons to believe that stock prices (and prices in other financial markets) are inherently unpredictable. The second section presented the behavioral finance challenge to market efficiency and discussed the evidence that there is at least some predictability in stock returns. In this section we introduce **technical analysis,** which is the practice of searching the historical record of stock prices and returns for patterns. If these patterns repeat, investors who know about them and can spot them early may have an opportunity to earn better-than-average returns.

Because it focuses on using past price movements to predict future returns, technical analysis is fundamentally at odds with even the weak form of market efficiency. For this reason, the practice of technical analysis remains controversial. For some investors, it's another piece of information to use when deciding whether to buy, hold, or sell a stock. For others, it's the only input they use in their investment decisions. Still others regard technical analysis as a waste of time.

Analyzing market behavior dates back to the 1800s, when there was no such thing as industry or company analysis. Detailed financial information about individual companies simply was not made available to stockholders, let alone the general public. About the only thing investors could study was the market itself. Some investors used detailed charts to monitor what large market operators were doing. These charts were intended to show when major buyers were moving into or out of particular stocks and to provide information useful for profitable buy-and-sell decisions. The charts centered on stock price movements. These movements were said to produce certain "formations," indicating when the time was right to buy or sell a particular stock. The same principle is still applied today: Technical analysts argue that internal market factors, such as trading volume and price movements, often reveal the market's future direction long before it is evident in financial statistics.

Measuring the Market

If using technical analysis to assess the overall market is a worthwhile endeavor, then we need some sort of tool or measure to do it. Charts are popular with many investors because they provide a visual summary of the behavior of the market and the price movements of individual stocks. As an alternative or supplement to charting, some investors prefer to study various market statistics. They might look at trends in market indexes or track other aspects of market behavior such as trading volume, short selling, or trading behavior of small investors (e.g., odd-lot transactions).

Technical analysis addresses those factors in the marketplace that can (or may) have an effect on the price movements of stocks in general. The idea is to get a handle on the general condition (or "tone") of the market and to gain some insights into where the market may be headed over the next few months. Several approaches try to do just that, and we summarize some of the more common approaches below.

The Confidence Index One measure that attempts to capture the tone of the market is the **confidence index**, which deals not with the stock market but with bond returns. Computed and published by *Barron's*, the confidence index is a ratio that reflects the spread between the average yield on high-grade corporate bonds relative to the yield on average- or intermediate-grade corporate bonds. Technically, the index is computed by relating the average yield on 10 high-grade corporate bonds to the yield on 10 intermediate-grade bonds. The formula is as follows:

Equation 7.3
$$\frac{\text{Confidence}}{\text{index}} = \frac{\text{Average yield on 10 high-grade corporate bonds}}{\text{Average yield on 10 intermediate-grade bonds}}$$

Thus, the index measures the yield spread between high-grade bonds and intermediate-grade bonds. Because the yield on high-grade bonds should always be lower than the average yield on a sample of intermediate-grade bonds, the confidence index should never exceed 1.0. Indeed, as the measure approaches 1.0 (or 100%), the spread between the two sets of bonds will get smaller and smaller, which, according to the theory, is a positive sign. The idea is that as investors become more confident about the economy, they will be willing to invest in riskier bonds, driving down their yields and pushing up the confidence index. Those who follow the confidence index interpret a rise in the index as a positive sign for future stock returns.

Consider, for example, a point in time where high-grade bonds are yielding 4.50%, while intermediate-grade bonds, on average, are yielding 5.15%. This would amount to a yield spread of 65 "basis points," or 65/100 of 1% (i.e., 5.15% − 4.50% = 0.65%), and a confidence index of 4.50 ÷ 5.15 = 87.38%. Now, look what happens when yields (and yield spreads) fall or rise:

	Yields (Yield Spreads)	
	Fall	Rise
Yields on high-grade bonds	4.25%	5.25%
Yields on average bonds	4.50%	6.35%
Yield spread	0.25%	1.10%
Confidence index	94.44%	82.68%

Lower-yield spreads, in effect, lead to higher confidence indexes. These, in turn, indicate that investors are demanding a lower premium in yield for the lower-rated (riskier) bonds, and in so doing are showing more confidence in the economy. This theory implies that the trend of "smart money" is usually revealed in the bond market before it shows up in the stock market, meaning that a rise in the confidence index today foreshadows a future rise in the stock market.

Market Volume Market volume is an obvious reflection of the amount of investor interest in stocks. As a rule, technical analysts who follow market volume say that increasing volume during a rising market is a positive sign that the upward movement in stocks will continue. On the other hand, when stocks are falling, a decline in volume may suggest that the decline in stock prices is approaching an end. In a similar vein, when stocks have been moving up and volume begins to drop off, that may signal the end of the bull market. Numerous financial periodicals and websites report total market volume daily, so it is an easy statistic to track.

Breadth of the Market Each trading day, some stocks go up in price and others go down. In market terminology, some stocks advance and others decline. Breadth of the market deals with these advances and declines. The principle behind this indicator is that the number of advances and declines reflects the underlying sentiment of investors.

Analysts who use market breadth to help guide their investment decisions interpret the numbers as follows. As long as the number of stocks that advance in price on a given day exceeds the number that decline, the market is strong. The extent of that strength depends on the spread between the number of advances and declines. For example, if the spread narrows (the number of declines starts to approach the number of advances), market strength deteriorates. Similarly, the market is weak when the number of declines repeatedly exceeds the number of advances. When the mood is optimistic, advances outnumber declines. Again, data on advances and declines are widely available. Figure 7.5 (on page 234) illustrates data on market volume, advances, and declines taken from Yahoo! Finance.

FIGURE 7.5 Basic Market Statistics

Here is an example of the kind of information on market volume, advances, and declines that is easily accessible on the web. (Source: http://finance.yahoo.com/advances, accessed August 12, 2012.)

Advances & Declines

	NYSE	AMEX	NASDAQ	BB
Advancing Issues	1,659 (52%)	688 (49%)	1,093 (42%)	206 (41%)
Declining Issues	1,392 (44%)	658 (47%)	1,366 (53%)	176 (35%)
Unchanged Issues	125 (4%)	50 (4%)	124 (5%)	122 (24%)
Total Issues	**3,176**	**1,396**	**2,583**	**504**
New Highs	**109**	**26**	**48**	**10**
New Lows	**7**	**29**	**38**	**51**
Up Volume	1,680,443,020 (61%)	123,480,477 (42%)	808,471,279 (51%)	40,718,961 (20%)
Down Volume	1,036,423,723 (38%)	167,711,649 (57%)	723,518,165 (45%)	145,902,309 (70%)
Unchanged Volume	24,923,884 (1%)	3,055,557 (1%)	62,973,654 (4%)	20,497,090 (10%)
Total Volume	**2,741,790,627[1]**	**294,247,683[1]**	**1,594,963,098[1]**	**207,118,360[1]**

Short Interest When investors anticipate a market decline, they sometimes sell a stock short. That is, they sell borrowed stock. The number of shares of stocks sold short in the market at any point in time is known as the **short interest**. The more stocks are sold short, the higher the short interest. Because all short sales must eventually be "covered" (the borrowed shares must be returned), a short sale in effect ensures future demand for the stock. Thus, the market is viewed optimistically when the level of short interest becomes relatively high by historical standards. The logic is that as shares are bought back to cover outstanding short sales, the additional demand will push stock prices up. The amount of short interest on the NYSE, the Amex, and Nasdaq's National Market is published in the *Wall Street Journal*, *Barron's*, and other sources.

Keeping track of the level of short interest can indicate future market demand, but it can also reveal present market optimism or pessimism. Short selling is usually done by knowledgeable investors, and a significant buildup or decline in the level of short interest hints at the sentiment of sophisticated investors about the current state of the market or a company. For example, a significant shift upward in short interest might indicate pessimism concerning the current state of the market, even though it may signal optimism with regard to future levels of demand.

Odd-Lot Trading A rather cynical saying on Wall Street suggests that the best thing to do is just the opposite of whatever the small investor is doing. The reasoning behind this is that as a group, small investors exhibit notoriously bad timing. The investing public usually does not come into the market in force until after a bull market has pretty much run its course, and it does not get out until late in a bear market. Although its validity is debatable, this is the premise behind a widely followed technical indicator and is the basis for the **theory of contrary opinion**. This theory uses the amount and type of odd-lot trading as an indicator of the current state of the market and pending changes.

Because many individual investors deal in transactions of less than 100 shares, their combined sentiments are supposedly captured in odd-lot figures.

The idea is to see what odd-lot investors "on balance" are doing. So long as there is little or no difference in the spread between the volume of odd-lot purchases and sales, the theory of contrary opinion holds that the market will probably continue pretty much along its current line (either up or down). A dramatic change in the balance of odd-lot purchases and sales may be a signal that a bull or bear market is about to end. For example, if the amount of odd-lot purchases starts to exceed odd-lot sales by an ever-widening margin, speculation on the part of small investors may be starting to get out of control—an ominous signal that the final stages of a bull market may be at hand.

Trading Rules and Measures

Market technicians—analysts who believe it is chiefly (or solely) supply and demand that drive stock prices—use a variety of mathematical equations and measures to assess the underlying condition of the market. These analysts often use computers to produce the measures, plotting them on a daily basis. They then use those measures as indicators of when to get into or out of the market or a particular stock. In essence, they develop trading rules based on these market measures. Technical analysts almost always use several of these market measures, rather than just one (or two), because one measure rarely works the same way for all stocks. Moreover, they generally look for confirmation of one measure by another. In other words, market analysts like to see 3 or 4 of these ratios and measures all pointing in the same direction.

Although dozens of these market measures and trading rules exist, we'll confine our discussion here to some of the more widely used technical indicators: (1) advance-decline lines, (2) new highs and lows, (3) the arms index, (4) the mutual fund cash ratio, (5) on-balance volume, and (6) the relative strength index (RSI).

Advance-Decline Line Each trading day, the NYSE, Amex, and Nasdaq publish statistics on how many of their stocks closed higher on the day (i.e., advanced in price) and how many closed lower (declined in price). The *advance-decline (A/D) line* is simply the difference between these two numbers. To calculate it, you take the number of stocks that have risen in price and subtract the number that have declined, usually for the previous day. For example, if 1,000 issues advanced on a day when 450 issues declined, the day's net number would be 550 (i.e., $1,000 - 450$). If 450 advanced and 1,000 declined, the net number would be -550 ($450 - 1,000$). Each day's net number is then added to (or subtracted from) the running total, and the results are plotted on a graph.

If the graph is rising, the advancing issues are dominating the declining issues, and the technical analysts conclude that the market is strong. When declining issues start to dominate, the graph will turn down as the market begins to soften. Technicians use the A/D line as a signal for when to buy or sell stocks.

New Highs–New Lows This measure is similar to the advance-decline line but looks at price movements over a longer period of time. A stock is defined as reaching a "new high" if its current price is at the highest level it has been over the past year (sometimes referred to as the "52-week high"). Conversely, a stock reaches a "new low" if its current price is at the lowest level it has been over the past year.

The *new highs–new lows (NH-NL) indicator* equals the number of stocks reaching new 52-week highs minus the number reaching new lows. Thus, you end up with a net number, which can be either positive (when new highs dominate) or negative (when new lows exceed new highs), just like with the advance-decline line. To smooth out the daily fluctuations, the net number is often added to (or subtracted from) a 10-day moving average and then plotted on a graph.

As you might have guessed, a graph that's increasing over time indicates a strong market, where new highs are dominating. A declining graph indicates a weak market, where new lows are more common than new highs. Technicians following a momentum-based strategy will buy stocks when new highs dominate and sell them when there are more new lows than new highs. Alternatively, they might use the indicator to rotate money into stocks when the market looks strong and to rotate out of stocks and into cash or bonds when the market looks weak.

The Arms Index This indicator, also known as the TRIN, for *trading index*, builds on the advance-decline line by considering the volume in advancing and declining stocks in addition to the number of stocks rising or falling in price. The formula is

Equation 7.4

$$\text{TRIN} = \frac{\text{Number of up stocks}}{\text{Number of down stocks}} \div \frac{\text{Volume in up stocks}}{\text{Volume in down stocks}}$$

For example, suppose we are analyzing the S&P 500. Assume on a given day 300 of these stocks rose in price and 200 fell in price. Also assume that the total trading volume in the rising ("up") stocks was 400 million shares, and the total trading volume in the falling ("down") stocks was 800 million shares. The value of the TRIN for the day would be

$$\text{TRIN} = \frac{300}{200} \div \frac{400 \text{ million}}{800 \text{ million}} = 3.0$$

Alternatively, suppose the volume in up stocks was 700 million shares, and the volume in down stocks was 300 million. The value of the TRIN then would be

$$\text{TRIN} = \frac{300}{200} \div \frac{700 \text{ million}}{300 \text{ million}} = 0.64$$

Higher TRIN values are interpreted as being bad for the market because even though more stocks rose than fell, the trading volume in the falling stocks was much greater. The underlying idea is that a strong market is characterized by more stocks rising in price than falling, along with greater volume in the rising stocks than in the falling ones, as in the second example.

Mutual Fund Cash Ratio This indicator looks at the cash position of mutual funds as an indicator of future market performance. The *mutual fund cash ratio* (*MFCR*) measures the percentage of mutual fund assets that are held in cash. It is computed as follows:

Equation 7.5

MFCR = Mutual fund cash position ÷ Total assets under management

The assumption is that the higher the MFCR, the stronger the market. Indeed, the ratio is considered very bullish when it moves to abnormally high levels (i.e., when mutual fund cash exceeds 10% to 12% of assets). It is seen as bearish when the ratio drops to very low levels (e.g., less than 5% of assets). The logic goes as follows: When fund managers hold a lot of cash (when the MFCR is high), that's good news for the market because they will eventually have to invest that cash, buying stocks and causing prices to rise. If fund managers hold very little cash, investors might be concerned for two reasons. First, there is less demand for stocks if most of the cash is already invested. Second, if the market takes a downturn, investors might want to withdraw their money. Fund managers will then have to sell some of their stocks to accommodate these redemptions, putting additional downward pressure on prices.

On-Balance Volume Technical analysts usually consider stock prices to be the key measure of market activity. However, they also consider trading volume as a secondary indicator. *On-balance volume (OBV)* is a momentum indicator that relates volume to price change. It uses trading volume in addition to price and tracks trading volume as a running total. In this way, OBV indicates whether volume is flowing into or out of a security. When the security closes higher than its previous close, all the day's volume is considered "up-volume," all of which is added to the running total. In contrast, when a stock closes lower, all the day's volume is considered "down-volume," which is then subtracted from the running total.

The OBV indicator is used to confirm price trends. According to this measure, you want to see a lot of volume when a stock's price is rising because that would suggest that the stock will go even higher. On the other hand, if prices are rising but OBV is falling, technical analysts would describe the situation as a divergence and interpret it as a sign of possible weakness.

When analyzing OBV, it is the direction or trend that is important, not the actual value. To begin the computation of OBV, you can start with an arbitrary number, such as 50,000. Suppose you are calculating the OBV for a stock that closed yesterday at a price of $50 per share, and you start with an OBV value of 50,000. Assume that the stock trades 80,000 shares today and closes at $49. Because the stock declined in price, we would subtract the full 80,000 shares from the previous balance (our starting point of 50,000); now the OBV is 50,000 − 80,000 = −30,000. (Note that the OBV is simply the trading volume running total.) If the stock trades 120,000 shares on the following day and closes up at $52 per share, we would then add all of those 120,000 shares to the previous day's OBV: −30,000 + 120,000 = +90,000. This process would continue day after day. The normal procedure is to plot these daily OBVs on a graph. As long as the graph is moving up, it's bullish; when the graph starts moving down, it's bearish.

Relative Strength One of the most widely used technical indicators is the *relative strength index (RSI)*, an index measuring a security's strength of advances and declines over time. The RSI indicates a security's momentum and gives the best results when used for short trading periods. It also helps identify market extremes, signaling that a security is approaching its price top or bottom and may soon reverse trend. The RSI is the ratio of average price change on "up days" to the average price change on "down days" during the same period. The index formula is

Equation 7.6

$$RSI = 100 - \left[100 \div \left(1 + \frac{\text{Average price change on up days}}{\text{Average price change on down days}} \right) \right]$$

The RSI can cover various periods of time (days, weeks, or months). The most common RSIs are 9-, 14-, and 25-day periods.

The RSI ranges between 0 and 100, with most RSIs falling between 30 and 70. Generally, values above 70 or 80 indicate an *overbought* condition (more and stronger buying than fundamentals would justify). RSI values below 30 indicate a possible *oversold* condition (more selling than fundamentals may indicate). When the RSI crosses these points, it signals a possible trend reversal. The wider 80–20 range is often used with the 9-day RSI, which tends to be more volatile than longer-period RSIs. In bull markets, 80 may be a better upper indicator than 70; in bear markets, 20 is a more accurate lower level. Different sectors and industries may have varying RSI threshold levels.

To use the RSI in their own trading, investors set buy and sell ranges—such as sell when the RSI crosses above 70 and buy when it moves below 30. Another strategy is to

Smart's Tour of the Web
To watch author Scott Smart discuss key websites for this chapter, visit www.myfinancelab.com

compare RSIs with stock charts. Most of the time both move in the same direction, but a divergence between RSI and a price chart can be a strong predictor of a changing trend.

Charting

Practice Your Charting Skills

Charting is perhaps the best-known activity of the technical analyst. Indeed, technical analysts use various types of charts to plot the behavior of everything from the Dow Jones Industrial Average and share price movements of individual stocks to moving averages (see below) and advance-decline lines. In fact, as noted above, just about every type of technical indicator is charted in one form or another.

Charts are popular because they provide a visual summary of activity over time. Perhaps more important (in the eyes of technicians, at least), they contain valuable information about developing trends and the future behavior of the market or individual stocks. Chartists believe price patterns evolve into chart formations that provide signals about the future course of the market or a stock.

Chart Formations A chart by itself tells you little more than where the market or a stock has been. But to chartists, those price patterns yield formations that tell them what to expect in the future. Chartists believe that history repeats itself, so they study the historical reactions of stocks (or the market) to various formations, and they devise trading rules based on these observations. It makes no difference to chartists whether they are following the market or an individual stock. It is the formation that matters, not the issue being plotted. If you know how to interpret charts (which is no easy task), you can see formations building and recognize buy and sell signals. These chart formations are often given exotic names, such as *head and shoulders*, *falling wedge*, *scallop and saucer*, *ascending triangle*, and *island reversal*, to name just a few.

Figure 7.6 (on page 239) shows 6 of these formations. The patterns form "support levels" and "resistance lines" that, when combined with the basic formations, yield buy and sell signals. Panel A is an example of a buy signal that occurs when prices break out above a resistance line in a particular pattern. In contrast, when prices break out below a support level, as they do at the end of the formation in panel B, a sell signal is said to occur. Supposedly, a sell signal means everything is in place for a major drop in the market (or in the price of a share of stock). A buy signal indicates that the opposite is about to occur.

Unfortunately, one of the major problems with charting is that the formations rarely appear as neatly and cleanly as those in Figure 7.6. Rather, identifying and interpreting them often demands considerable imagination.

Moving Averages One problem with daily price charts is that they may contain a lot of often meaningless short-term price swings that mask the overall trend in prices. As a result, technical analysts often use moving averages not only to eliminate those minor blips but also to highlight underlying trends. A **moving average (MA)** is a mathematical procedure that records the average value of a series of prices, or other data, over time. Because they incorporate a stream of these average values, MAs will smooth out a data series and make it easier to spot trends. The moving average is one of the oldest and most popular technical indicators. It can, in fact, be used not only with share prices but also with market indexes and even other technical measures.

Moving averages are computed over periods ranging from 10 to 200 days—meaning that from 10 to 200 data points are used in each calculation. For example, a series of 15 data points is used in a 15-day moving average. The length of the time period has a bearing on how the MA will behave. Shorter periods (10 to 30 days) are

FIGURE 7.6

Some Popular Chart Formations

To chartists, each of these formations has meaning about the future course of events.

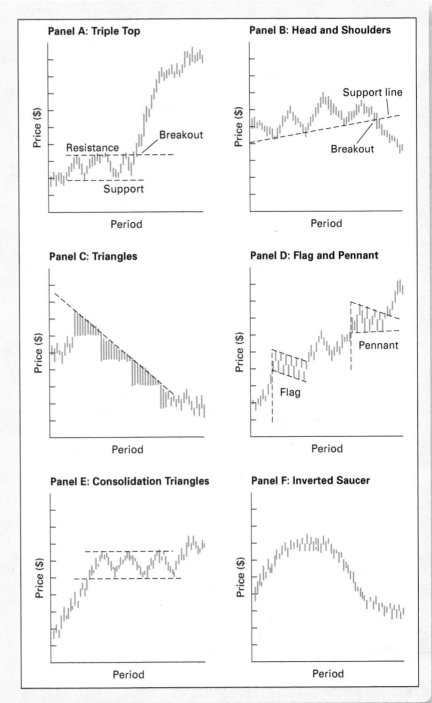

Panel A: Triple Top

Panel B: Head and Shoulders

Panel C: Triangles

Panel D: Flag and Pennant

Panel E: Consolidation Triangles

Panel F: Inverted Saucer

more sensitive and tend to more closely track actual daily behavior. Longer periods (say, 100 to 200 days) are smoother and do a better job of picking up the major trends. Several types of moving averages exist, with the most common (and the one we'll use here) being the *simple average*, which gives equal weight to each observation. In contrast, there are other procedures that give more weight to the most recent data points (e.g., the "exponential" and "weighted" averages) or apply more weight to the middle of the time period (e.g., "triangular" averages).

Using closing share prices as the basis of discussion, we can calculate the simple moving average by adding up the closing prices over a given time period (e.g., 10 days) and then dividing this total by the length of the time period. Thus, the simple moving average is nothing more than the arithmetic mean. To illustrate, consider the following stream of closing share prices:

Day:	1	2	3	4	5	6	7	8	9	10	11	12	13	...
Price:	$4	$5	$6	$6	$7	$5	$3	$5	$8	$9	$6	$2	$4	...

Using a 10-day moving average, we add up the closing prices for days 1 through 10 ($\$4 + \$5 + \cdots + \$8 + \$9 = \$58$) and then divide this total by 10 ($\$58 \div 10 = \$5.8$). Thus, the average closing price for this 10-day period was \$5.80. The next day, the process is repeated once again for days 2 through 11; that turns out to be $\$60 \div 10 = \$6.00$. This procedure is repeated each day, so that over time we have a series of these individual averages that, when linked together, form a moving-average line. This line is then plotted on a chart, either by itself or along with other market information.

Figure 7.7 shows a 100-day moving average (the red line) plotted against the daily closing prices for ExxonMobil (the blue line). In contrast to the actual closing prices, the moving average provides a much smoother line, without all the short-term fluctuations; it clearly reveals the general trend in prices for this stock.

Technicians will often use charts like the one in Figure 7.7 to help them make buy and sell decisions about a stock. Specifically, if the security's price starts moving above

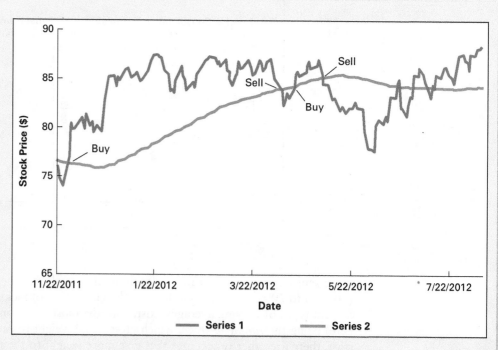

FIGURE 7.7

A 100-Day Moving-Average Line

Moving-average lines are often plotted along with the actual daily (or weekly) closing prices for a stock. They're also widely used with market indexes, such as the S&P 500, and a variety of technical indicators, including the advance-decline line.

the moving average, they read that situation as a good time to buy because prices should be drifting up (see the buy signals on the chart). In contrast, a sell signal occurs when the security's price moves below the moving-average line (see the sell signals). A problem arises when volatility in the stock prices leads to repeated buy and sell signals, which occurs several times in Figure 7.7. Acting on every buy and sell signal leads to high transactions costs without necessarily generating superior returns.

CONCEPTS IN REVIEW

Answers available at www.pearsonhighered.com/smart

7.6 What is the purpose of technical analysis? Explain how and why it is used by technicians; note how it can be helpful in timing investment decisions.

7.7 Can the market really have a measurable effect on the price behavior of individual securities? Explain.

7.8 Describe the confidence index, and note the feature that makes it unique.

7.9 Briefly describe each of the following and explain how it is used in technical analysis:

    a. Breadth of the market
    b. Short interest
    c. Odd-lot trading

7.10 Briefly describe each of the following and note how it is computed and how it is used by technicians:

    a. Advance-decline lines
    b. Arms index
    c. On-balance volume
    d. Relative strength index
    e. Moving averages

7.11 What is a stock chart? What kind of information can be put on charts, and what is the purpose of charting?

MyFinanceLab

Here is what you should know after reading this chapter. MyFinanceLab will help you identify what you know and where to go when you need to practice.

What You Should Know	Key Terms	Where to Practice
LG1 **Describe the characteristics of an efficient market, explain what market anomalies are, and note** some of the challenges that investors face when markets are efficient. An efficient market is one in which prices fully reflect all available information, and in an efficient market, price movements are nearly random. If markets are efficient, then investors should not expect to earn above-average returns consistently by using either technical or fundamental analysis.	abnormal return, *p. 218* behavioral finance, *p. 224* efficient market, *p. 217* efficient markets hypothesis (EMH), *p. 217* market anomalies, *p. 221* random walk hypothesis, *p. 217* semi-strong form (EMH), *p. 219* strong form (EMH), *p. 220* weak form (EMH), *p. 218*	MyFinanceLab Study Plan 7.1
LG2 **Summarize the evidence which suggests that the stock market is efficient.** Early research on the market efficiency question found that stock prices were essentially unpredictable and moved at random. Other studies found that even professional investors did not consistently earn returns that beat market averages.		MyFinanceLab Study Plan 7.2

What You Should Know	Key Terms	Where to Practice
LG3 **List four "decision traps" that may lead investors to make systematic errors in their investment decisions.** Behavioral finance asserts that investors are subject to a variety of decision traps, which include overconfidence, loss aversion, representativeness, narrow framing, and belief perseverance. If investors do indeed make systematic errors in their investment decisions, then those errors may influence prices in financial markets.	belief perseverance, *p. 230* familiarity bias, *p. 230* loss aversion, *p. 226* narrow framing, *p. 229* overconfidence, *p. 225* representativeness, *p. 227* self-attribution bias, *p. 225*	MyFinanceLab Study Plan 7.3
LG4 **Explain how behavioral finance links market anomalies to investors' cognitive biases.** A market anomaly represents a pattern in stock prices that would appear to present investors with an opportunity to earn above-average returns without taking above-average risk. Behavioral finance suggests that some market anomalies exist because investors make systematic errors, such as undervaluing stocks that have performed poorly in recent years.		MyFinanceLab Study Plan 7.4
LG5 **Describe some of the approaches to technical analysis, including, among others, moving averages, charting, and various indicators of the technical condition of the market.** Market analysts look at those factors in the marketplace that can affect the price behavior of stocks in general. This analysis can be done by assessing the overall condition of the market, by informally or formally studying various internal market statistics (e.g., short interest or advance-decline lines), or by charting various aspects of the market (including the use of moving averages).	confidence index, *p. 232* market technician, *p. 235* short interest, *p. 234* technical analysis, *p. 231* theory of contrary opinion, *p. 234*	MyFinanceLab Study Plan 7.5 Video Learning Aid for Problems P7.2, P7.6
LG6 **Compute and use technical trading rules for individual stocks and the market as a whole.** Technical analysts use a number of mathematical equations and measures to gauge the direction of the market, including advance-decline lines, new highs and lows, the trading index, the mutual fund cash ratio, on-balance volume, and the relative strength index. They test different indicators using historical price data to find those that generate profitable trading strategies, which then are developed into trading rules used to guide buy and sell decisions.	charting, *p. 238* moving average (MA), *p. 238*	MyFinanceLab Study Plan 7.6

Log into MyFinanceLab, take a chapter test, and get a personalized Study Plan that tells you which concepts you understand and which ones you need to review. From there, MyFinanceLab will give you further practice, tutorials, animations, videos, and guided solutions.
Log into **www.myfinancelab.com**

Discussion Questions

LG1 Q7.1 Much has been written about the concept of an efficient market. It's probably safe to say that some of your classmates believe the markets are efficient and others believe they are not. Have a debate to see whether you can resolve this issue (at least among you and your classmates). Pick a side, either for or against efficient markets, and then develop your "ammunition." Be prepared to discuss these three aspects:

    a. What is an efficient market? Do such markets really exist?

    b. Are stock prices always (or nearly always) correctly set in the market? If so, does that mean little opportunity exists to find undervalued stocks?

    c. Can you cite any reasons to use fundamental or technical analysis in your stock selection process? If not, how would you go about selecting stocks?

LG1 LG2 Q7.2 Each year financial periodicals like the *Wall Street Journal* and *Money Magazine* publish a list of the top performing mutual fund managers. And every year there are some fund managers who earn much higher returns than the market average, and in some cases they do so without taking above-average risk. Is this inconsistent with the efficient markets hypothesis?

LG3 LG4 Q7.3 Briefly define each of the following terms and describe how it can affect investors' decisions.

    a. Loss aversion

    b. Representativeness

    c. Narrow framing

    d. Overconfidence

    e. Biased self-attribution

LG3 LG4 Q7.4 Describe how representativeness may lead to biases in stock valuation.

LG5 Q7.5 Briefly describe how technical analysis is used as part of the stock valuation process. What role does it play in an investor's decision to buy or sell a stock?

LG5 Q7.6 Describe each of the following approaches to technical analysis and note how it would be used by investors.

    a. Confidence index

    b. Arms index

    c. Trading action

    d. Odd-lot trading

    e. Charting

    f. Moving averages

    g. On-balance volume

Which of these approaches is likely to involve some type of mathematical equation or ratio?

LG5 Q7.7 Briefly define each of the following and note the conditions that would suggest the market is technically strong.

    a. Breadth of the market

    b. Short interest

    c. Relative strength index

    d. Theory of contrary opinion

    e. Head and shoulders

Problems

All problems are available on www.myfinancelab.com

LG5 LG6 P7.1 Compute the Arms index for the S&P 500 over the following 3 days:

Day	Number of Stocks Rising in Price	Number of Stocks Falling in Price	Volume for Stocks Rising in Price	Volume for Stocks Falling in Price
1	350	150	850 million shares	420 million shares
2	275	225	450 million shares	725 million shares
3	260	240	850 million shares	420 million shares

Which of the 3 days would be considered the most bullish? Explain why.

LG5 LG6 P7.2 Listed below are data that pertain to the corporate bond market. (*Note:* Each "period" below covers a span of 6 months.)

	Period 1	Period 2	Period 3	Period 4
Average yield on 10 high-grade corporate bonds	5.30%	5.70%	5.10%	?
Yield on the Dow Jones average of 40 corporate bonds	6.50%	?	6.00%	4.90%
Yield spread (in basis points)	?	155	?	25
Confidence index	____	____	____	____

a. Compute the confidence index for each of the 4 periods listed above.
b. Assume that the latest confidence index (for period 0, in effect) amounts to 86.83%, while the yield spread between high- and average-grade corporate bonds is 85 basis points. Based on your calculations, what's happening to bond yield spreads and the confidence index over the period of time covered in the problem (i.e., from period 0 through period 4)?
c. Based on the confidence index measures you computed, what would be your overall assessment of the stock market? In which one or more of the periods (1 through 4) is the confidence index bullish? In which one(s) is it bearish?

LG5 LG6 P7.3 Compute the level of on-balance volume (OBV) for the following 3-day period for a stock, if the beginning level of OBV is 50,000 and the stock closed yesterday at $25.

Day	Closing Price ($)	Trading Volume (shares)
1	27	70,000
2	26	45,000
3	29	120,000

Does the movement in OBV appear to confirm the rising trend in prices? Explain.

LG5 **LG6**   P7.4   Below are figures representing the number of stocks making new highs and new lows for each month over a six-month period:

Month	New Highs	New Lows
July	117	22
August	95	34
September	84	41
October	64	79
November	53	98
December	19	101

Would a technical analyst consider the trend to be bullish or bearish over this period? Explain.

LG5 **LG6**   P7.5   You hear a market analyst on television say that the advance/decline ratio for the session was 1.2. What does that mean?

LG5 **LG6**   P7.6   At the end of a trading day you find that on the NYSE 2,200 stocks advanced and 1,000 stocks declined. What is the value of the advance-decline line for that day?

LG5 **LG6**   P7.7   You are given the following information:

Day	New Highs	New Lows
1 (yesterday)	117	22
2	95	34
3	84	41
4	64	79
5	53	98
6	19	101
7	19	105
8	18	110
9	19	90
10	22	88

a. Calculate the 10-day moving-average NH-NL indicator.
b. If there are 120 new highs and 20 new lows today, what is the new 10-day moving-average NH-NL indicator?

LG5 **LG6**   P7.8   You have collected the following NH-NL indicator data:

Day	NH-NL Indicator
1 (yesterday)	100
2	95
3	61
4	43
5	−15
6	−45
7	−82
8	−86
9	−92
10	−71

If you are a technician following a momentum-based strategy, are you buying or selling today?

LG5 **LG6**   P7.9   You are presented with the following data:

Week	Mutual Fund Cash Position ($)	Mutual Fund Total Assets ($)
Most recent	281,478,000.00	2,345,650,000.00
2	258,500,000.00	2,350,000,000.00
3	234,800,000.00	2,348,000,000.00
4	211,950,000.00	2,355,000,000.00
5	188,480,000.00	2,356,000,000.00

Calculate the MFCR for each week. Based on the result, are you bullish or bearish?

LG5 **LG6**   P7.10   You find the closing prices for a stock you own. You want to use a 10-day moving average to monitor the stock. Calculate the 10-day moving average for days 11 through 20. Based on the data in the table below, are there any signals you should act on? Explain.

Day	Closing Price ($)	Day	Closing Price ($)
1	25.25	11	30.00
2	26.00	12	30.00
3	27.00	13	31.00
4	28.00	14	31.50
5	27.00	15	31.00
6	28.00	16	32.00
7	27.50	17	29.00
8	29.00	18	29.00
9	27.00	19	28.00
10	28.00	20	27.00

Visit **www.myfinancelab.com** for web exercises, spreadsheets, and other online resources.

Case Problem 7.1   Brett Runs Some Technical Measures on a Stock

LG5   Brett Daly is an active stock trader and an avid market technician. He got into technical analysis about 10 years ago, and although he now uses the Internet for much of his analytical work, he still enjoys running some of the numbers and doing some of the charting himself. Brett likes to describe himself as a serious stock trader who relies on technical analysis for some—but certainly not all—of the information he uses to make an investment decision; unlike some market technicians, he does not totally ignore a stock's fundamentals. Right now he's got his eye on a stock that he's been tracking for the past 3 or 4 months.

The stock is Nautilus Navigation, a mid-sized high-tech company that's been around for a number of years and has a demonstrated ability to generate profits year-in and year-out. The problem is that the earnings are a bit erratic, tending to bounce up and down from year to year, which causes the price of the stock to be a bit erratic as well. And that's exactly why Brett likes the stock—as a trader, the volatile prices enable him to move in and out of the stock over relatively short (3- to 6-month) periods of time.

Brett has already determined that the stock has "decent" fundamentals, so he does not worry about its basic soundness. Hence, he can concentrate on the technical side of the stock. In particular, he wants to run some technical measures on the market price behavior of the security. He's obtained recent closing prices on the stock, which are shown in the table below.

Recent Price Behavior: Nautilus Navigation			
14 (8/15/13)	18.55	20	17.50
14.25	17.50	20.21	18.55
14.79	17.50	20.25	19.80
15.50	17.25	20.16	19.50
16	17	20	19.25
16	16.75	20.25	20
16.50	16.50	20.50	20.90
17	16.55	20.80	21
17.25	16.15	20	21.75
17.20	16.80	20	22.50
18	17.15	20.25	23.25
18 (9/30/13)	17.22	20	24
18.55	17.31 (10/31/13)	19.45	24.25
18.65	17.77	19.20	24.15
18.80	18.23	18.25 (11/30/13)	24.75
19	19.22	17.50	25
19.10	20.51	16.75	25.50
18.92	20.15	17	25.55 (12/31/13)

Nautilus shares are actively traded on the Nasdaq Global Market and enjoy considerable market interest.

Questions

a. Use the closing share prices in the table above to compute the stock's relative strength index for (1) the 20-day period from 9/30/13 to 10/31/13; and (2) the 22-day period from 11/30/13 to 12/31/13. [*Hint:* Use a simple (unweighted) average to compute the numerator (average price change on up days) and the denominator (average price change on down days) of the RSI formula shown on page 237.]

    1. Contrast the two RSI measures you computed. Is the index getting bigger or smaller, and is that good or bad?

    2. Is the latest RSI measure giving a buy or a sell signal? Explain.

b. Based on the above closing share prices, prepare a moving-average line covering the period shown in the table; use a 10-day time frame to calculate the individual average values.

    1. Plot the daily closing prices for Nautilus from 8/15/13 through 12/31/13 on a graph/chart.

    2. On the same graph/chart, plot a moving-average line using the individual average values computed earlier. Identify any buy or sell signals.

    3. As of 12/31/13, was the moving-average line giving a buy, hold, or sell signal? Explain. How does that result compare to what you found with the RSI in part a? Explain.

c. Based on the technical measures and charts you've prepared, what course of action would you recommend that Brett take with regard to Nautilus Navigation? Explain.

Case Problem 7.2   Deb Takes Measure of the Market

LG5   Several months ago, Deb Forrester received a substantial sum of money from the estate of her late aunt. Deb initially placed the money in a savings account because she was not sure what to do with it. Since then, however, she has taken a course in investments at the local university. The textbook for the course was, in fact, this one, and the class just completed this chapter. Excited about what she has learned in class, Deb has decided that she definitely wants to invest in stocks. But before she does, she wants to use her newfound knowledge in technical analysis to determine whether now would be a good time to enter the market.

Deb has decided to use all of the following measures to help her determine if now is, indeed, a good time to start putting money into the stock market:

- Advance-decline line
- New highs-new lows indicator (Assume the current 10-day moving average is 0 and the last 10 periods were each 0.)
- Arms index
- Mutual fund cash ratio

Deb goes to the Internet and, after considerable effort, is able to put together the accompanying table of data.

Questions

a. Based on the data presented in the table, calculate a value (where appropriate) for periods 1 through 5, for each of the 4 measures listed above. Chart your results, where applicable.

b. Discuss each measure individually and note what it indicates for the market, as it now stands. Taken collectively, what do these 4 measures indicate about the current state of the market? According to these measures, is this a good time for Deb to consider getting into the market, or should she wait a while? Explain.

c. Comment on the time periods used in the table, which are not defined here. What if they were relatively long intervals of time? What if they were relatively short? Explain how the length of the time periods can affect the measures.

	Period 1	Period 2	Period 3	Period 4	Period 5
Dow Jones Industrial Average	8,300	7,250	8,000	9,000	9,400
Dow Transportation Average	2,375	2,000	2,000	2,850	3,250
New highs	68	85	85	120	200
New lows	75	60	80	75	20
Volume up	600,000,000	836,254,123	275,637,497	875,365,980	1,159,534,297
Volume down	600,000,000	263,745,877	824,362,503	424,634,020	313,365,599
Mutual fund cash (trillions of dollars)	$0.31	$0.32	$0.47	$0.61	$0.74
Total assets managed (trillions of dollars)	$6.94	$6.40	$6.78	$6.73	$7.42
Advancing issues (NYSE)	1,120	1,278	1,270	1,916	1,929
Declining issues (NYSE)	2,130	1,972	1,980	1,334	1,321

Excel with Spreadsheets

Technical analysis looks at the demand and supply for securities based on trading volumes and price studies. Charting is a common method used to identify and project price trends in a security. A well-known technical indicator is the Bollinger Band. It creates two bands, one above and one below the price performance of a stock. The upper band is a resistance level and represents the level above which the stock is unlikely to rise. The bottom forms a support level and shows the price that a stock is unlikely to fall below.

According to technicians, if you see a significant "break" in the upper band, the expectation is that the stock price will fall in the immediate future. A "break" in the lower band signals that the security is about to rise in value. Either of these occurrences will dictate a unique investment strategy.

Replicate the following technical analysis for Amazon.com **(AMZN)**

- Go to money.msn.com.

- Symbol(s): **AMZN**

- In the left-hand column, click on Interactive Chart.

- Select a 5-year chart.

- Click on Technical Indicators.

- Choose Bollinger Bands.

- The price performance graph for Amazon stock with an upper and lower red Bollinger Band should appear.

- Make sure that the graph covers, at a minimum, the first 6 months of 2012.

Questions

a. On approximately April 27, 2012, what happened to the upper band (resistance level) of Amazon stock?

b. During the following 9 days, how did the price of the stock behave?

c. Is this in line with what a technician would predict?

d. What strategy would a technician have undertaken on April 27?

e. At around the same time, what happened to the lower band (support level) of Amazon stock?

f. How did the stock behave through the month of May 2012?

CFA Exam Questions

Investing in Common Stocks

Following is a sample of 11 Level-I CFA exam questions that deal with many topics covered in Chapters 1, 7, and 12 of this text, including the use of financial ratios, various stock valuation models, and efficient market concepts. (*Note*: When answering some of the questions, remember: "Forward P/E" is the same as a P/E based on estimated earnings 1 year out.) When answering the questions, give yourself 1½ minutes for each question; the objective is to correctly answer 8 of the 11 questions in a period of 16½ minutes.

1. Holding constant all other variables and excluding any interactions among the determinants of value, which of the following would most likely increase a firm's price-to-earnings multiple?
   a. The risk premium increases.
   b. The retention rate increases.
   c. The beta of the stock increases.

2. A rationale for the use of the price-to-sales (P/S) approach is:
   a. Sales are more volatile than earnings.
   b. P/S ratios assess cost structures accurately.
   c. Revenues are less subject to accounting manipulation than earnings.

3. A cyclical company tends to
   a. have earnings that track the overall economy.
   b. have a high price-to-earnings ratio.
   c. have less volatile earnings than the overall market.

4. Consider a company that earned $4.00 per share last year and paid a dividend of $1.00. The firm has maintained a consistent payout ratio over the years and analysts expect this to continue. The firm is expected to earn $4.40 per share next year, and the stock is expected to sell for $30.00. The required rate of return is 12%. What is the best estimate of the stock's current value?
   a. $44.00
   b. $22.67
   c. $27.77

5. A stock's current dividend is $1 and its expected dividend is $1.10 next year. If the investor's required rate of return is 15% and the stock is currently trading at $20.00, what is the implied expected price in one year?
   a. $21.90
   b. $22.00
   c. $23.00

6. A firm has total revenues of $187,500, net income of $15,000, total current liabilities of $50,000, total common equity of $75,000, and total assets of $150,000. What is the firm's ROE?
   a. 15%
   b. 20%
   c. 24%

7. A stock currently pays a dividend of $2.00 per share. Expected dividend growth is 20% for the next 3 years and then is expected to revert to 7% thereafter indefinitely. The required rate of return on this stock is 15%. The stock's current intrinsic value is
   a. $6.54
   b. $165.63
   c. $36.93

8. The required rate of return used in equity valuation is influenced most by which of the following?
   a. Expected inflation
   b. Actual inflation
   c. The ability to sell short

9. Confirmation bias is the tendency for investors to
   a. focus on information that confirms prior opinions and actions.
   b. be overconfident in forecasting future growth.
   c. feel responsible for poor investments and do even worse.

10. Which of the following would provide the most compelling evidence contradicting the semi-strong form of the efficient markets hypothesis?
    a. Transactions costs are high.
    b. Low P/E stocks have positive long-term abnormal returns.
    c. Approximately half of professionally managed funds outperform the overall market.

11. The strong-form efficient market hypothesis
    a. assumes that no one has an informational advantage.
    b. assumes that certain groups have access to privileged information.
    c. directly challenges the methods of technical analysis.

Answers: 1. b; 2. c; 3. a; 4. c; 5. a; 6. b; 7. c; 8. a; 9. a; 10. b; 11. a.

8

Bond Valuation

LEARNING GOALS

After studying this chapter, you should be able to:

LG1 Explain the behavior of market interest rates and identify the forces that cause interest rates to change.

LG2 Describe the term structure of interest rates and note how yield curves can be used by investors.

LG3 Understand how bonds are valued in the marketplace.

LG4 Describe the various measures of yield and return and explain how these standards of performance are used in bond valuation.

LG5 Understand the basic concept of duration, how it can be measured, and its use in the management of bond portfolios.

LG6 Discuss various bond investment strategies and the different ways these securities can be used by investors.

Money market investors made very little money during the Great Recession due to historically low interest rates on the short-term debt securities that comprise the U.S. money market. At the start of 2007, U.S. Treasury bills, which account for the majority of money market securities, with 6-month maturities were earning yields slightly better than 5%. Over the next two years, Treasury bill yields would tumble to record lows. By the end of 2009, investors who purchased a 6-month bill at the Treasury auction could expect to earn only one-fifth of 1 percent (0.20%) on their money. Even worse, at the start of 2012 investors in 6-month bills could only expect a yield of 6 basis points (0.06%).

Interest rates on other money market securities also fell, in large part due to the falling Treasury rates. The net effect for U.S. money market investors was an average annual return of less than one-tenth of 1 percent (0.10%) from 2010 to 2012. At that rate, a $1 million investment in the money market earned just $1,000 a year in interest.

The low interest rates were a result of actions by the U.S. Federal Reserve, which was trying to stimulate the economy to help pull the country out of recession. Central banks in other countries were doing much the same, and in Europe extremely low rates on corporate bonds sparked a borrowing binge.

In this chapter we'll learn about the forces that move market interest rates up and down and how those movements affect bonds and the investors who buy them.

(Sources: Paul Armstrong and Esteban Duarte, "Corporate Bond Market on Fire in Europe as New Issues Jump," September 8, 2009, Bloomberg.com; Forbes, "Low Interest Rates Are Killing Money Market Funds," July 9, 2012, www.forbes.com/sites/kenkam/2012/07/09/low-interest-rates-are-killing-money-market-funds-2/; U.S. Department of the Treasury, Data and Charts Center, July 18, 2012, www.treasury.gov/)

The Behavior of Market Interest Rates

LG1 **LG2** Rational investors try to earn a return that fully compensates them for risk. In the case of bondholders, that required return (r_i) has 3 components: the real rate of return (r^*), an expected inflation premium (IP), and a risk premium (RP). Thus, the required return on a bond can be expressed by the following equation:

Equation 8.1

$$r_i = r^* + IP + RP$$

The real rate of return and inflation premium are external economic factors, which together equal the risk-free rate (r_f). To find the required return, we need to consider the unique features and properties of the bond issue itself that influence its risk. After we do this, we add a risk premium to the risk-free rate to obtain the required rate of return. A bond's risk premium (RP) will take into account key issue and issuer characteristics, including such variables as the type of bond, the issue's term to maturity, its call features, and bond rating.

Together, the 3 components in Equation 8.1 (r^*, IP, and RP) drive the required return on a bond. Recall in Chapter 2 that we identified 5 types of risks to which bonds are exposed. All of these risks are embedded in a bond's required rate of return. That is, the bond's risk premium addresses, among other things, the business and financial (credit) risk characteristics of an issue, along with its liquidity and call risks, whereas the risk-free rate (r_f) takes into account interest rate and purchasing power risks.

Because these interest rates have a significant bearing on bond prices and yields, investors watch them closely. For example, more conservative investors watch interest rates because one of their major objectives is to lock in high yields. Aggressive traders also have a stake in interest rates because their investment programs are often built on the capital gains opportunities that accompany major swings in rates.

Keeping Tabs on Market Interest Rates

The bond market is not a single market. Rather, it consists of many different sectors. Similarly, there is no single interest rate that applies to all segments of the bond market. Instead, different interest rates apply to different segments. Granted, the various rates do tend to drift in the same direction over time, but it is also common for **yield spreads** (interest rate differentials) to exist among the various market sectors. Some important factors to keep in mind when you think about interest rates on bonds are as follows:

- Municipal bonds usually offer the lowest market rates because of their tax-exempt feature. As a rule, their market yields are about 20% to 30% lower than corporate bond yields.

- In the municipal sector, revenue bonds pay higher rates than general obligation bonds.

- In the taxable sector, Treasury securities have the lowest yields (because they have the least risk), followed by agency bonds and then corporate bonds, which provide the highest returns.

- Issues that normally carry bond ratings (e.g., municipals or corporates) generally display the same behavior: the lower the rating, the higher the yield.

Signs of a Recession

When short-term interest rates on treasury bills exceed the rates on long-term treasury bonds, watch out. That is often the precursor to a recession. This "inversion" in the relationship between short-term and long-term rates has occurred prior to each of the last 5 U.S. recessions. Just as important, this indicator has rarely issued a false-positive signal.

- As a rule, bonds with long maturities tend to yield more than short issues. However, this rule does not always hold; short-term yields, which equal or exceed the yields on long-term bonds, may be an early signal that a recession is coming, as they were in February 2006.

- Bonds that are freely callable generally pay the highest interest rates, at least at date of issue. These are followed by deferred call obligations and then by noncallable bonds, which yield the least.

The preceding list can be used as a general guide to the higher-yielding segments of the market.

As an investor, you should pay close attention to interest rates and yield spreads. Try to stay abreast of both the current state of the market and the future direction of market rates. Thus, if you are a conservative (income-oriented) investor and think that rates have just about peaked, that should be a signal to try to lock in the prevailing high yields with some form of call protection. (For example, buy bonds, such as Treasuries or AA-rated utilities that are noncallable or still have lengthy call deferments.) In contrast, if you're an aggressive bond trader who thinks rates have peaked (and are about to drop), that should be a clue to buy bonds that offer maximum price appreciation potential (low-coupon bonds that still have a long time before they mature).

But how do you formulate such expectations? Unless you have considerable training in economics, you will probably need to rely on various published sources. Fortunately, a wealth of such information is available. Your broker is an excellent source for such reports, as are investor services like Moody's and Standard & Poor's. Also, of course, there are numerous online sources. Finally, there are widely circulated business and financial publications (like the *Wall Street Journal*, *Forbes*, *Business Week*, and *Fortune*) that regularly address the current state and future direction of market interest rates. Predicting the direction of interest rates is not easy. However, by taking the time to read some of these publications and reports regularly and carefully, you can at least get a handle on what experts predict is likely to occur in the near future.

What Causes Rates to Move?

Although the determination of interest rates is a complex economic issue, we do know that certain forces are especially important in influencing rate movements. Serious bond investors should make it a point to become familiar with the major determinants of interest rates and try to monitor those variables, at least informally.

Money Illusion—An investment that offers a high interest rate may seem attractive, but remember it's the real return, after inflation, that matters. Although interest rates were very high in the late 1970s, so was the inflation rate, and many bond investors earned negative real returns during that period.

In that regard, perhaps no variable is more important than inflation. Changes in the inflation rate, or to be more precise, changes in the expected inflation rate, have a direct and profound effect on market interest rates. When investors expect inflation to slow down, market interest rates generally fall as well. To gain an appreciation of the extent to which interest rates are linked to inflation, look at Figure 8.1. The figure plots the behavior of the interest rate on a 10-year Treasury bond and the inflation rate from 1963 to 2011. The red line in the figure tracks the actual inflation rate over time, although as we have already noted, the expected inflation rate has a more direct effect on interest rates. Even so, there is a clear link between actual inflation and interest rates. Note that, in general, as inflation drifts up, so do interest rates. On the other hand, a decline in inflation is matched by a similar decline in interest rates. Most of the time, the rate on the 10-year bond exceeded the inflation rate, which is exactly what you should expect. When that is not the case, such as in the mid-1970s and more recently in 2011, investors in the 10-year Treasury bond did not earn enough interest to keep up with inflation. On average, the 10-year Treasury yield exceeded the inflation rate by about 2.4 percentage points per year.

FIGURE 8.1 **The Impact of Inflation on the Behavior of Interest Rates**

The behavior of interest rates has always been closely tied to the movements in the rate of inflation. Since 1963 the average spread between the U.S. 10-year Treasury rate and inflation is 2.4 percentage points. This spread fluctuates quite a bit over time. Some extreme examples occurred in 1974 when the rate of inflation exceeded the 10-year Treasury rate by 4.7 percentage points and in 1983 when 10-year Treasury rates outpaced inflation by 8 percentage points.

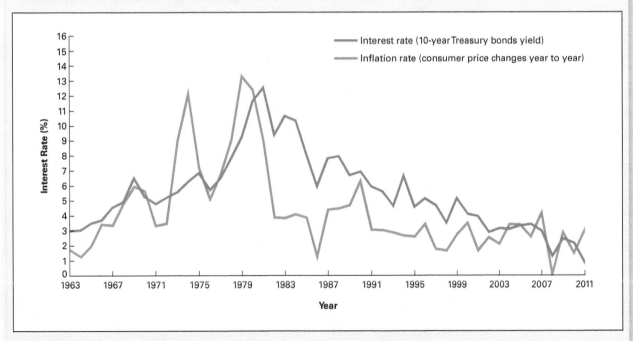

In addition to inflation, 5 other important economic variables can significantly affect the level of interest rates:

- *Changes in the money supply.* An increase in the money supply pushes rates down (as it makes more funds available for loans), and vice versa. This is true only up to a point, however. If the growth in the money supply becomes excessive, it can lead to inflation, which, of course, means higher interest rates.

- *The size of the federal budget deficit.* When the U.S. Treasury has to borrow large amounts to cover the budget deficit, the increased demand for funds exerts an upward pressure on interest rates. That's why bond market participants become so concerned when the budget deficit gets bigger and bigger—other things being equal, that means more upward pressure on market interest rates.

- *The level of economic activity.* Businesses need more capital when the economy expands. This need increases the demand for funds, and rates tend to rise. During a recession, economic activity contracts, and rates typically fall.

- *Policies of the Federal Reserve.* Actions of the Federal Reserve to control inflation also have a major effect on market interest rates. When the Fed wants to slow actual (or anticipated) inflation, it usually does so by driving up interest rates, as it did repeatedly in the mid- and late 1970s. Unfortunately, such actions sometimes have the side effect of slowing down business activity as well. Likewise, when the Federal Reserve wants to stimulate the economy, it takes action to push interest rates down, as it did repeatedly during and after the 2008-2009 recession.

- *The level of interest rates in major foreign markets.* Today, investors look beyond national borders for investment opportunities. Rising rates in major foreign markets put pressure on rates in the United States to rise as well; if U.S. rates don't keep pace, foreign investors may be tempted to dump their dollars to buy higher-yielding foreign securities.

The Term Structure of Interest Rates and Yield Curves

Living Yield Curve

Bonds having different maturities typically have different interest rates. The relationship between interest rates (yield) and time to maturity for any class of similar-risk securities is called the **term structure of interest rates**. This relationship can be depicted graphically by a **yield curve**, which relates a bond's term to maturity to its yield to maturity at a given point in time. The yield curve constantly changes as market forces push bond yields at different maturities up and down.

Types of Yield Curves Two types of yield curves are illustrated in Figure 8.2 (on page 257). By far, the most common type is curve 1, the upward-sloping curve. It indicates that yields tend to increase with longer maturities. That's partly because the longer a bond has to maturity, the greater the potential for price volatility. Investors, therefore, require higher risk premiums to induce them to buy the longer, riskier bonds. Long-term rates may also exceed short-term rates if investors believe short-term rates will rise. In that case, rates on long-term bonds might have to be higher than short-term rates to attract investors. That is, if investors think short-term rates are rising, they will not want to tie up their money for long at today's lower rates. Instead, they would prefer to invest in a short-term security so that they can reinvest that money quickly after rates have risen. To induce investors to purchase a long-term bond, the bond must offer a higher rate than a short-term bond provides.

FIGURE 8.2

Two Types of Yield Curves
A yield curve plots the relation between term to maturity and yield to maturity for a series of bonds that are similar in terms of risk. Although yield curves come in many shapes and forms, the most common is the upward-sloping curve. It shows that investor returns (yields) increase with longer maturities.

Historical Yield Curves

Occasionally, the yield curve becomes inverted, or downward sloping, as shown in curve 2, which occurs when short-term rates are higher than long-term rates. This curve sometimes results from actions by the Federal Reserve to curtail inflation by driving short-term interest rates way up. An inverted yield curve may also occur when firms are very hesitant to borrow long-term (such as when they expect a recession). With very low demand for long-term loans, long-term interest rates fall. In addition to these two common yield curves, two other types appear from time to time: the *flat* yield curve, when rates for short- and long-term debt are essentially the same, and the *humped* yield curve, when intermediate-term rates are the highest.

Plotting Your Own Curves Yield curves are constructed by plotting the yields for a group of bonds that are similar in all respects but maturity. Treasury securities (bills, notes, and bonds) are typically used to construct yield curves. There are several reasons for this: Their yields are easily found in financial publications, they have no risk of default, and they are homogeneous with regard to quality and other issue characteristics. Investors can also construct yield curves for other classes of debt securities, such as A-rated municipal bonds, Aa-rated corporate bonds, and even certificates of deposit.

Figure 8.3 (on page 258) shows the yield curves for Treasury securities on July 17, 2009, and July 17, 2012. To draw these curves, you need Treasury quotes from the U.S. Department of the Treasury or some other similar source. (Note that actual quoted yields for curve 2 are provided in the boxed information below the graph.) Given the required quotes, select the yields for the Treasury bills, notes, and bonds maturing in approximately 1 month, 3 months, 6 months, and 1, 2, 3, 5, 7, 10, 20, and 30 years. The yields used for curve 2 are highlighted in Figure 8.3. Next, plot the points on a graph whose horizontal (*x*) axis represents time to maturity in years and whose vertical (*y*) axis represents yield to maturity. Now, just connect the points to create the curves shown in

FIGURE 8.3

Yield Curves on U.S. Treasury Issues

Here we see two yield curves constructed from actual market data (quotes). Although both yield curves are upward sloping, they are based on considerably different yields. Curve 2 comprises yields that on average are about 60% less than those that comprise curve 1. In fact, the yields that make up curve 2 are very near U.S. record low levels. (Source: U.S. Department of the Treasury, July 17, 2012.)

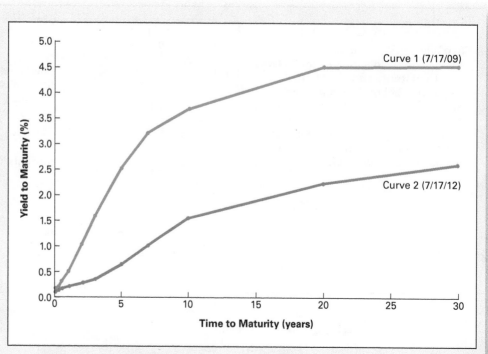

Date	1 mo	3 mo	6 mo	1 yr	2 yr	3 yr	5 yr	7 yr	10 yr	20 yr	30 yr
07/02/12	0.06	0.10	0.15	0.21	0.30	0.39	0.67	1.04	1.61	2.30	2.69
07/03/12	0.08	0.09	0.15	0.21	0.30	0.39	0.69	1.08	1.65	2.36	2.74
07/05/12	0.07	0.08	0.15	0.19	0.28	0.39	0.68	1.05	1.62	2.34	2.72
07/06/12	0.06	0.08	0.15	0.20	0.27	0.37	0.64	1.01	1.57	2.28	2.66
07/09/12	0.06	0.09	0.14	0.20	0.27	0.36	0.63	0.98	1.53	2.24	2.62
07/10/12	0.07	0.09	0.15	0.20	0.27	0.37	0.63	0.98	1.53	2.22	2.60
07/11/12	0.07	0.10	0.15	0.20	0.27	0.36	0.64	0.99	1.54	2.22	2.60
07/12/12	0.08	0.10	0.15	0.20	0.25	0.35	0.63	0.98	1.50	2.18	2.57
07/13/12	0.08	0.10	0.15	0.20	0.25	0.34	0.63	0.99	1.52	2.20	2.58
07/16/12	0.04	0.10	0.14	0.18	0.24	0.31	0.60	0.97	1.50	2.18	2.56
07/17/12	0.08	0.10	0.14	0.18	0.25	0.32	0.62	0.99	1.53	2.22	2.59

Figure 8.3. You'll notice that both curves are upward sloping, but the yields on curve 1 are higher than those on curve 2 for every maturity. Curve 2 reflects the historically low interest rates that prevailed when the U.S. economy was struggling to emerge from a deep recession.

Explanations of the Term Structure of Interest Rates As we noted earlier, the shape of the yield curve can change over time. Three commonly cited theories—the expectations hypothesis, the liquidity preference theory, and the market segmentation theory—explain more fully the reasons for the general shape of the yield curve.

Expectations Hypothesis The **expectations hypothesis** suggests that the yield curve reflects investor expectations about the future behavior of interest rates. This theory argues that the relationship between short-term and long-term interest rates today reflects investors' expectations about how interest rates will change in the future. When the yield curve slopes upward, and long-term rates are higher than short-term rates, the expectations hypothesis interprets this as a sign that investors expect short-term rates to rise in the future. That's why long-term bonds pay a premium compared to short-term bonds. People will not lock their money away in a long-term investment when they think interest rates are going to rise unless the rate on the long-term investment is higher than the current rate on short-term investments.

For example, suppose the current interest rate on a 1-year Treasury bill is 5%, and the current rate on a 2-year Treasury note is 6%. The expectations hypothesis says that this pattern of interest rates reveals that investors believe that the rate on a 1-year Treasury bill will go up to 7% next year. Why? That's the rate that makes investors today indifferent between locking their money away for 2 years and earning 6% on the 2-year note versus investing in the 1-year T-bill today at 5% and then next year reinvesting the money from that instrument into another 1-year T-bill paying 7%.

Investment Strategy	(1) Rate Earned This Year (%)	(2) Rate Earned Next Year (%)	(3) Return over 2 Years [(1) + (2)] (%)
Buy 2-year note today	6	6	12
Buy 1-year T-bill, then reinvest in another T-bill next year	5	7	12

Only if the rate on a 1-year T-bill rises from 5% this year to 7% next year will investors be indifferent between these 2 strategies. Thus, according to the expectations hypothesis, an upward-sloping yield curve means that investors expect interest rates to rise, and a downward-sloping yield curve means that investors expect interest rates to fall.

Example

Suppose the yield curve is inverted, and 1-year bonds offer a 5% yield while 2-year bonds pay a 4.5% yield. According to the expectations hypothesis, what do investors expect the 1-year bond yield to be 1 year from now? Remember that the expectations hypothesis says today's short-term and long-term interest rates are set at a level which makes investors indifferent between short-term and long-term bonds, given their beliefs about where interest rates are headed. Therefore, to determine the expected 1-year bond yield next year, you must determine what return in the second year would make investors just as happy to buy two 1-year bonds as they are to buy one 2-year bond.

Return on a 2-year bond	4.5% + 4.5%
Return on two 1-year bonds	5.0% + x

The x in the second equation represents the expected rate on the 1-year bond next year. The top equation shows that an investor earns 9% over 2 years by purchasing a 2-year bond, so to achieve the same return on a series of two 1-year bonds, the return in the second year must be 4%.

Liquidity Preference Theory More often than not, yield curves have an upward slope. The expectations hypothesis would interpret this as a sign that investors *usually* expect rates to rise. That seems somewhat illogical. Why would investors expect interest rates to rise more often than they expect rates to fall? Put differently, why would investors expect interest rates to trend up over time? There is certainly no historical pattern to lead one to hold that view. One explanation for the frequency of upward-sloping yield curves is the **liquidity preference theory**. This theory states that long-term bond rates should be higher than short-term rates because of the added risks involved with the longer maturities. In other words, because of the risk differential between long- and short-term debt securities, rational investors will prefer the less risky, short-term obligations unless they can be motivated, via higher interest rates, to invest in longer bonds.

Actually, there are a number of reasons why rational investors should prefer short-term securities. To begin with, they are more liquid (more easily converted to cash) and less sensitive to changing market rates, which means there is less price volatility. For a given change in market rates, the prices of longer-term bonds will show considerably more movement than the prices of short-term bonds. In addition, just as investors tend to require a premium for tying up funds for longer periods, borrowers will also pay a premium in order to obtain long-term funds. Borrowers thus assure themselves that funds will be available, and they avoid having to roll over short-term debt at unknown and possibly unfavorable rates. All of these preferences explain why higher rates of interest should be associated with longer maturities and why it's perfectly rational to expect upward-sloping yield curves.

Market Segmentation Theory Another often-cited theory, the **market segmentation theory**, suggests that the market for debt is segmented on the basis of the maturity preferences of different financial institutions and investors. According to this theory, the yield curve changes as the supply and demand for funds within each maturity segment determines its prevailing interest rate. The equilibrium between the financial institutions that supply the funds for short-term maturities (e.g., banks) and the borrowers of those short-term funds (e.g., businesses with seasonal loan requirements) establishes interest rates in the short-term markets. Similarly, the equilibrium between suppliers and demanders in such long-term markets as life insurance and real estate determines the prevailing long-term interest rates.

The shape of the yield curve can slope either upward or downward, as determined by the general relationship between rates in each market segment. When supply outstrips demand for short-term loans, short-term rates are relatively low. If, at the same time, the demand for long-term loans is higher than the available supply of funds, then long-term rates will move up, and the yield curve will have an upward slope. If supply and demand conditions are reversed—with excess demand for borrowing in the short-term market and an excess supply of funds in the long-term market—the yield curve could slope down.

Which Theory Is Right? All 3 theories of the term structure have at least some merit in explaining the shape of the yield curve. These theories tell us that, at any time, the slope of the yield curve is affected by the interaction of (1) expectations regarding future interest rates, (2) liquidity preferences, and (3) the supply and demand conditions in the short- and long-term market segments. Upward-sloping yield curves result from expectations of rising interest rates, lender preferences for shorter-maturity loans, and a greater supply of short- than of long-term loans relative to the respective demand in each market segment. The opposite conditions lead to a downward-sloping yield curve.

More about the
Yield Curve

Using the Yield Curve in Investment Decisions Bond investors often use yield curves in making investment decisions. Analyzing the changes in yield curves provides investors with information about future interest rate movements, which in turn affect the prices and returns on different types of bonds. For example, if the entire yield curve begins to move upward, it usually means that inflation is starting to heat up or is expected to do so in the near future. In that case, investors can expect that interest rates, too, will rise. Under these conditions, most seasoned bond investors will turn to short or intermediate (3 to 5 years) maturities, which provide reasonable returns and at the same time minimize exposure to capital loss when interest rates go up. A downward-sloping yield curve signals that rates have peaked and are about to fall and that the economy is slowing down.

Another factor to consider is the difference in yields on different maturities—the "steepness" of the curve. For example, a steep yield curve is one where long-term rates are much higher than short-term rates. This shape is often seen as an indication that the spread between long-term and short-term rates is about to fall, either because long-term rates will fall or short-term rates will rise. Steep yield curves are generally viewed as a bullish sign. For aggressive bond investors, they could be the signal to start moving into long-term securities. Flatter yield curves, on the other hand, sharply reduce the incentive for going long-term since the difference in yield between the 5- and 30-year maturities can be quite small. Under these conditions, investors would be well advised to just stick with the 5- to 10-year maturities, which will generate about the same yield as long bonds but without the risks.

CONCEPTS IN REVIEW

Answers available at
www.pearsonhighered.com/
smart

8.1 Is there a single market rate of interest applicable to all segments of the bond market, or are there a series of market yields? Explain and note the investment implications of such a market environment.

8.2 Explain why interest rates are important to both conservative and aggressive bond investors. What causes interest rates to move, and how can you monitor such movements?

8.3 What is the term structure of interest rates and how is it related to the yield curve? What information is required to plot a yield curve? Describe an upward-sloping yield curve and explain what it has to say about the behavior of interest rates. Do the same for a flat yield curve.

8.4 How might you, as a bond investor, use information about the term structure of interest rates and yield curves when making investment decisions?

The Pricing of Bonds

LG3 No matter who the issuer is, what kind of bond it is, or whether it's fully taxable or tax-free, all bonds are priced pretty much the same. That is, all bonds (including notes with maturities of more than 1 year) are priced according to the present value of their future cash flow streams. Indeed, once the prevailing or expected market yield is known, the whole process becomes rather mechanical.

Market yields largely determine bond prices. That's because in the marketplace, investors first decide what yield is appropriate for a particular bond, given its risk, and then they use that yield to find the bond's price (or market value). As we saw earlier, the appropriate yield on a bond is a function of certain market and economic forces (e.g., the risk-free rate of return and inflation), as well as key issue and issuer characteristics (like years to maturity and the issue's bond rating). Together these forces combine to form the required rate of return, which is the rate of return the investor would like to earn in order to justify an investment in a given fixed-income security. The required return defines the yield at which the bond should be trading and serves as the discount rate in the bond valuation process.

The Basic Bond Valuation Model

Generally speaking, when you buy a bond you receive 2 distinct types of cash flows: (1) periodic interest income (i.e., coupon payments) and (2) the principal (or par value) at the end of the bond's life. Thus, in valuing a bond, you're dealing with an annuity of coupon payments for a specified number of periods plus a large single cash flow at maturity. You can use these cash flows, along with the required rate of return on the investment, in a present value–based bond valuation model to find the dollar value, or price, of a bond. Using annual compounding, you can calculate the price of a particular bond (BP_i) using the following equation:

Equation 8.2

$$BP_i = \sum_{t=1}^{N} \frac{C}{(1 + r_i)^t} + \frac{PV_N}{(1 + r_i)^N}$$

$$= \underset{\text{coupon payments}}{\text{Present value of}} + \underset{\text{bond's par value}}{\text{Present value of}}$$

where

BP_i = current price (or value) of a particular bond i
C = annual coupon (interest) payment
PV_N = par value of the bond, at maturity
N = number of years to maturity
r_i = prevailing market yield, or required annual return on bonds similar to bond i

In this form, you can compute the current value of the bond, or what you would be willing to pay for it, given that you want to generate a certain rate of return, as defined by r_i. Alternatively, if you already know the bond's price, you can solve for r_i in the equation, in which case you'd be looking for the yield embedded in the current market price of the bond.

In the discussion that follows, we will demonstrate the bond valuation process in 2 ways. First, we'll use annual compounding—that is, because of its computational simplicity, we'll assume we are dealing with coupons that are paid once a year. Second, we'll examine bond valuation under conditions of semiannual compounding, which is the way most bonds actually pay their interest.

Annual Compounding

You need the following information to value a bond: (1) the annual coupon payment, (2) the par value (usually $1,000), and (3) the number of years (i.e., time periods) remaining to maturity. You then use the prevailing market yield as the discount rate to compute the bond's price, as follows:

Equation 8.3

$$\text{Bond price} = \frac{\text{Present value of the annuity}}{\text{of annual coupon payments}} + \frac{\text{Present value of the}}{\text{bond's par value}}$$

Equation 8.3a

$$BP_i = \frac{C}{(1 + r_i)^1} + \frac{C}{(1 + r_i)^2} + \ldots + \frac{C}{(1 + r_i)^N} + \frac{\$1,000}{(1 + r_i)^N}$$

where, in this case,
C = annual coupon payment
N = number of years to maturity

Example

To illustrate this bond price formula in action, consider a 20-year, 9.5% bond priced to yield 10%. That is, the bond pays an annual coupon of 9.5% (or $95), has 20 years left to maturity, and should be priced to provide a market yield of 10%. We can now use Equation 8.3 to find the price of our bond.

$$BP_i = \frac{\$95}{(1 + 0.10)^1} + \frac{\$95}{(1 + 0.10)^2} + \ldots + \frac{\$95}{(1 + 0.10)^{20}} + \frac{\$1,000}{(1 + 0.10)^{20}} = \$957.43$$

Note that because this is a coupon-bearing bond, we have an annuity of coupon payments of $95 a year for 20 years, plus a single cash flow of $1,000 that occurs at the end of year 20. Thus, we find the present value of the coupon annuity and then add that amount to the present value of the recovery of principal at maturity. In this particular case, you should be willing to pay about $958 for this bond, so long as you're satisfied with earning 10% on your money.

Notice that this bond trades at a discount of $42.57 ($1,000 – $957.43). It trades at a discount because its coupon rate (9.5%) is below the market's required return (10%). You can directly link the size of the discount on this bond to the present value of the difference between the coupons that it pays ($95) and the coupons that would be required if the bond matched the market's 10% required return ($100). In other words, this bond's coupon payment is $5 less than what the market requires, so if you take the present value of that difference over the bond's life, you will calculate the size of the bond's discount:

$$\frac{\$5}{(1 + 0.10)^1} + \frac{\$5}{(1 + 0.10)^2} + \ldots + \frac{\$5}{(1 + 0.10)^{20}} = \$42.57$$

In a similar vein, for a bond that trades at a premium, the size of that premium equals the present value of the difference between the coupon that the bond pays and the (lower) coupon that the market requires.

Bonds initially sell for a price close to par value because bond issuers generally set the bond's coupon rate equal or close to the market's required return at the time the bonds are issued. If market interest rates change during the life of the bond, then the bond's price will adjust up or down to reflect any differences between the bond's stated interest rate and the market interest rate. Although bonds can sell at premiums or discounts over their lives, as the maturity date arrives, bond prices will converge to par value. This happens because as time passes and a bond's maturity date approaches,

Input	Function
20	N
10.0	I
95	PMT
1000	FV
	CPT
	PV

Solution
(−957.43)

Financial Calculator
Tutorials

there are fewer interest payments remaining (so any premium or discount is diminishing) and the principal to be repaid at maturity is becoming an ever bigger portion of the bond's price since the periods over which it is being discounted are disappearing.

CALCULATOR USE For annual compounding, to price a 20-year, 9.5% bond to yield 10%, use the keystrokes shown in the margin, where:

$$N = \text{number of years to maturity}$$
$$I = \text{required annual return on the bond (what the bond is being priced to yield)}$$
$$PMT = \text{annual coupon payment}$$
$$FV = \text{par value of the bond}$$
$$PV = \text{computed price of the bond}$$

Recall that the calculator result shows the bond's price as a negative value, which indicates that the price is a cash outflow for an investor when buying the bond's cash flows.

Semiannual Compounding

Although using annual compounding simplifies the valuation process a bit, it's not the way most bonds are actually valued in the marketplace. In practice, most bonds pay interest every 6 months, so it is appropriate to use semiannual compounding to value bonds. Fortunately, it's relatively easy to go from annual to semiannual compounding: All you need to do is cut the annual interest income and the required rate of return in half and double the number of periods until maturity. In other words, rather than one compounding and payment interval per year, there are two (i.e., two 6-month periods per year). Given these changes, finding the price of a bond under conditions of semiannual compounding is much like pricing a bond using annual compounding. That is,

Equation 8.4

$$\begin{matrix}\text{Bond price (with semi-} \\ \text{annual compounding)}\end{matrix} = \begin{matrix}\text{Present value of the annuity of} \\ \text{semiannual coupon payments}\end{matrix} + \begin{matrix}\text{Present value of the} \\ \text{bond's par value}\end{matrix}$$

Equation 8.4a

$$BP_i = \frac{C/2}{\left(1+\dfrac{r_i}{2}\right)^1} + \frac{C/2}{\left(1+\dfrac{r_i}{2}\right)^2} + \cdots + \frac{C/2}{\left(1+\dfrac{r_i}{2}\right)^{2N}} + \frac{\$1{,}000}{\left(1+\dfrac{r_i}{2}\right)^{2N}}$$

where, in this case,

$$C/2 = \text{semiannual coupon payment, or the amount of interest paid every 6 months}$$
$$r_i/2 = \text{the required rate of return per 6-month period}$$

Example

In the previous bond-pricing example, you priced a 20-year bond to yield 10%, assuming annual interest payments of $95. Suppose the bond makes semiannual interest payments instead. With semiannual payments of $47.50, you adjust the semiannual return to 5% and the number of periods to 40. Using Equation 8.4, you'd have:

$$BP_i = \frac{\$95/2}{\left(1+\dfrac{0.10}{2}\right)^1} + \frac{\$95/2}{\left(1+\dfrac{0.10}{2}\right)^2} + \cdots + \frac{\$95/2}{\left(1+\dfrac{0.10}{2}\right)^{40}} + \frac{1{,}000}{\left(1+\dfrac{0.10}{2}\right)^{40}} = \$957.10$$

The price of the bond in this case ($957.10) is slightly less than the price we obtained with annual compounding ($957.43).

Input	Function
40	N
5.0	I
47.50	PMT
1000	FV
	CPT
	PV

Solution
(−957.10)

CALCULATOR USE For *semiannual compounding*, to price a 20-year, 9.5% semiannual-pay bond to yield 10%, use the keystrokes shown in the margin, where:

N = number of 6-month periods to maturity ($20 \times 2 = 40$)
I = yield on the bond, adjusted for semiannual compounding ($10\% \div 2 = 5\%$)
PMT = semiannual coupon payment ($\$95.00 \div 2 = \$47.50$)
FV = par value of the bond
PV = computed price of the bond

Accrued Interest

Most bonds pay interest every 6 months, but you can trade them any time that the market is open. Suppose you own a bond that makes interest payments on January 15 and July 15 each year. What happens if you sell this bond at some time between the scheduled coupon payment dates? For example, suppose you sell the bond on October 15, a date that is roughly halfway between two payment dates. Fortunately, interest accrues on bonds between coupon payments, so selling the bond prior to a coupon payment does not mean that you sacrifice any interest that you earned. **Accrued interest** is the amount of interest earned on a bond since the last coupon payment. When you sell a bond in between coupon dates, the bond buyer adds accrued interest to the bond's price (the price calculated using Equation 8.3 or 8.4 depending on whether coupons arrive annually or semiannually).

Example

Suppose you purchase a $1,000 par value bond that pays a 6% coupon in semi-annual installments of $30. You received a coupon payment 2 months ago, and now you are ready to sell the bond. Contacting a broker, you learn that the bond's current market price is $1,010. If you sell the bond, you will receive not only the market price, but also accrued interest. Because you are about one-third of the way between the last coupon payment and the next one, you receive accrued interest of $10 (1/3 × $30), so the total cash that you receive in exchange for your bond is $1,020.

Traders in the bond market sometimes refer to the price of a bond as being either clean or dirty. The **clean price** of a bond equals the present value of its cash flows, as in Equations 8.3 and 8.4. As a matter of practice, bond price quotations that you may find in financial periodicals or online are nearly always clean prices. The **dirty price** of a bond is the clean price plus accrued interest. In the example above, the clean price is $1,010, and the dirty price is $1,020.

CONCEPTS IN REVIEW

Answers available at
www.pearsonhighered.com/
smart

8.5 Explain how market yield affects the price of a bond. Could you price a bond without knowing its market yield? Explain.

8.6 Why are bonds generally priced using semiannual compounding? Does it make much difference if you use annual compounding?

Measures of Yield and Return

LG4 In the bond market, investors focus as much on a bond's yield as on its price. As you have seen, the yield helps determine the price at which a bond trades, but it also measures the rate of return on the bond. When you can observe the price of a bond that is trading in the market, you can simply reverse the bond valuation process described above to solve for the bond's yield rather than its price. That gives you a pretty good idea of the return that you might earn if you purchased the bond at its current market price. Actually, there are 3 widely used metrics to assess the return on a bond: the current yield, the yield to maturity, and the yield to call (for bonds that are callable). We'll look at all 3 measures here, along with a concept known as the *expected return*, which measures the expected (or actual) rate of return earned over a specific holding period.

Current Yield

The **current yield** is the simplest of all bond return measures, but it also has the most limited application. This measure looks at just one source of return: a bond's annual interest income. In particular, it indicates the amount of current income a bond provides relative to its prevailing market price. The current yield equals:

Equation 8.5
$$\text{Current yield} = \frac{\text{Annual interest income}}{\text{Current market price of the bond}}$$

Example

An 8% bond would pay $80 per year in interest for every $1,000 of principal. However, if the bond was currently priced at $800, it would have a current yield of 10% ($80 ÷ $800 = 0.10). The current yield measures a bond's annual interest income, so it is of interest primarily to investors seeking high levels of current income, such as endowments or retirees.

Yield to Maturity

The **yield to maturity (YTM)** is the most important and most widely used measure of the return provided by a bond. It evaluates the bond's interest income and any gain or loss that results from differences between the price that an investor pays for a bond and the par value that the investor receives at maturity. The YTM takes into account all of the cash flow received over a bond's life. Also known as the **promised yield**, the YTM shows the fully compounded rate of return earned by an investor, given that the bond is held to maturity and all principal and interest payments are made in a prompt and timely fashion. In addition, the YTM calculation implicitly assumes that the investor can reinvest all the coupon payments at an interest rate equal to the bond's yield to maturity. This "reinvestment assumption" plays a vital role in the YTM, which we will discuss in more detail later in this chapter (see the section entitled Yield Properties).

The yield to maturity is used not only to gauge the return on a single issue but also to track the behavior of the market in general. In other words, market interest rates are basically a reflection of the average promised yields that exist in a given segment of the market. The yield to maturity provides valuable insights into an issue's investment merits that investors can use to assess the attractiveness of different bonds. Other things being equal, the higher the promised yield of an issue, the more attractive it is.

Although there are a couple of ways to compute the YTM, the best and most accurate procedure is derived directly from the bond valuation model described above. That is, you can use Equations 8.3 and 8.4 to determine the YTM for a bond. The difference is that now, instead of trying to determine the price of the bond, you know its price and are trying to find the discount rate that will equate the present value of the bond's cash flow (coupon and principal payments) to its current market price. The YTM is basically the internal rate of return on a bond. When you find that, you have the bond's yield to maturity.

Using Annual Compounding Finding yield to maturity is a matter of trial and error. In other words, you try different values for YTM until you find the one that solves the equation. Let's say you want to find the YTM for a 7.5% ($1,000 par value) annual-coupon-paying bond that has 15 years remaining to maturity and is currently trading in the market at $809.50. From Equation 8.3, we know that

$$BP_i = \$809.50 = \frac{\$75}{(1 + r_i)^1} + \frac{\$75}{(1 + r_i)^2} + \ldots + \frac{\$75}{(1 + r_i)^{15}} + \frac{\$1,000}{(1 + r_i)^{15}}$$

Notice that this bond sells below par (i.e., it sells at a discount). What do we know about the relationship between the required return on a bond and its coupon rate when the bond sells at a discount? Bonds sell at a discount when the required return (or yield to maturity) is higher than the coupon rate, so the yield to maturity on this bond must be higher than 7.5%.

Through trial and error, we might initially try a discount rate of 8% or 9% (or, since it sells at a discount, any value above the bond's coupon). Sooner or later, we'll try a discount rate of 10%. And look what happens at that point: Using Equation 8.3 to price this bond at a discount rate of 10%, we see that the price equals $809.85.

The computed price of $809.85 is reasonably close to the bond's current market price of $809.50. As a result, the 10% rate represents the yield to maturity on this bond. That is, 10% is the discount rate that leads to a computed bond price that's equal (or very close) to the bond's current market price. In this case, if you were to pay $809.50 for the bond and hold it to maturity, you would expect to earn a YTM of 10.0%. Doing trial and error by hand can be time consuming, so you can use a handheld calculator or computer software to calculate the YTM.

Input	Function
15	N
−809.50	PV
75	PMT
1000	FV
	CPT
	I
Solution	
10.00	

CALCULATOR USE For annual compounding, to find the YTM of a 15-year, 7.5% bond that is currently priced in the market at $809.50, use the keystrokes shown in the margin. The present value (PV) key represents the current market price of the bond, and all other keystrokes are as defined earlier.

Using Semiannual Compounding Given some fairly simple modifications, it's also possible to find the YTM using semiannual compounding. To do so, we cut the annual coupon and discount rate in half and double the number of periods to maturity. Returning to the 7.5%, 15-year bond, let's see what happens when you use Equation 8.4 and try an initial discount rate of 10%.

$$BP_i = \frac{\$75.00/2}{\left(1 + \dfrac{0.10}{2}\right)^1} + \frac{\$75.00/2}{\left(1 + \dfrac{0.10}{2}\right)^2} + \ldots + \frac{\$75.00/2}{\left(1 + \dfrac{0.10}{2}\right)^{30}} + \frac{\$1,000}{\left(1 + \dfrac{0.10}{2}\right)^{30}} = \$807.85$$

As you can see, a semiannual discount rate of 5% results in a computed bond value that's well short of the market price of $809.50. Given the inverse relationship between price and yield, it follows that if you need a higher price, you have to try a lower YTM (discount rate). Therefore, you know the semiannual yield on this bond has to be something less than 5%. By trial and error, you would determine that the yield to maturity on this bond is just a shade under 5% per half year—4.987% to be more precise. Remember, however, that this is the yield expressed over a 6-month period. The market convention is to simply state the annual yield as twice the semiannual yield. This practice produces what the market refers to as the **bond-equivalent yield**. Returning to the YTM problem started above, you know that the issue has a semiannual yield of 4.987%. According to the bond-equivalent yield convention, you double the semiannual rate to obtain the annual rate of return on this bond. Doing this results in an annualized yield to maturity (or promised yield) of 4.987% × 2 = 9.97%. This is the annual rate of return you will earn on the bond if you hold it to maturity.

CALCULATOR USE For semiannual compounding, to find the YTM of a 15-year, 7.5% bond that is currently priced in the market at $809.50, use the keystrokes shown here. As before, the *PV* key is the current market price of the bond, and all other keystrokes are as defined earlier. Remember that to find the bond-equivalent yield, you must double the computed value of *I*. That is, 4.987% × 2 = 9.974%.

Yield Properties Actually, in addition to holding the bond to maturity, there are several other critical assumptions embedded in any yield to maturity figure. The promised yield measure—whether computed with annual or semiannual compounding—is based on present value concepts and therefore contains important reinvestment assumptions. To be specific, the YTM calculation assumes that when each coupon payment arrives, you can reinvest it for the remainder of the bond's life at a rate that is equal to the YTM. When this assumption holds, the return that you earn over a bond's life is in fact equal to the YTM. In essence, the calculated yield to maturity figure is the return "promised" only so long as the issuer meets all interest and principal obligations on a timely basis and the investor reinvests all interest income at a rate equal to the computed promised yield. In our example above, you would need to reinvest each of the coupon payments and earn a 10% return on those reinvested funds. Failure to do so would result in a realized yield of less than the 10% YTM. If you made no attempt to reinvest the coupons, you would earn a realized yield over the 15-year investment horizon of just over 6.5%—far short of the 10% promised return. On the other hand, if you could reinvest coupons at a rate that exceeded 10%, the actual yield on your bond over the 15 years would be higher than its 10% YTM. The bottom line is that unless you are dealing with a zero-coupon bond, a significant portion of the bond's total return over time comes from reinvested coupons.

When we use present value–based measures of return, such as the YTM, there are actually 3 components of return: (1) coupon/interest income, (2) capital gains (or losses), and (3) interest on interest. Whereas current income and capital gains make up the profits from an investment, interest on interest is a measure of what *you* do with those profits. In the context of a bond's yield to maturity, the computed YTM defines the required, or minimum, reinvestment rate. Put your investment profits (i.e., interest income) to work at this rate and you'll earn a rate of return equal to YTM. This rule applies to any coupon-bearing bond—so long as there's an annual or semiannual flow of interest income, the reinvestment of that income and interest on interest are matters that you must deal with. Also, keep in mind that the bigger the coupon and/or the longer the maturity, the more important the reinvestment assumption. Indeed, for many long-term, high-coupon bond investments, interest on interest alone can account for well over half the cash flow.

Finding the Yield on a Zero You can also use the same procedures described above (Equation 8.3 with annual compounding or Equation 8.4 with semiannual compounding) to find the yield to maturity on a zero-coupon bond. The only difference is that you can ignore the coupon portion of the equation because it will, of course, equal 0. All you need to do to find the promised yield on a zero-coupon bond is to solve the following expression:

$$\text{Yield} = \left(\frac{\$1{,}000}{\text{Price}}\right)^{\frac{1}{N}} - 1$$

Suppose that today you could buy a 15-year zero-coupon bond for $315. If you purchase the bond at that price and hold it to maturity, what is your YTM?

$$\text{Yield} = \left(\frac{\$1{,}000}{\$315}\right)^{\frac{1}{15}} - 1 = 0.08 = 8\%$$

Example

The zero-coupon bond pays an annual compound return of 8%. Had we been using semiannual compounding, we'd use the same equation except we'd substitute 30 for 15 (because there are 30 semiannual periods in 15 years). The yield would change to 3.926% per half year, or 7.845% per year.

Input	Function
30	N
−315	PV
1000	FV
0	PMT
	CPT
	I

Solution
3.926

CALCULATOR USE For semiannual compounding, to find the YTM of a 15-year zero-coupon bond that is currently priced in the market at $315, use the keystrokes shown in the margin. *PV* is the current market price of the bond, and all other keystrokes are as defined earlier. To find the bond-equivalent yield, double the computed value of *I*. That is, 3.926% × 2 = 7.85%.

Yield to Call

Bonds can be either noncallable or callable. Recall from Chapter 2 that a noncallable bond prohibits the issuer from calling the bond prior to maturity. Because such issues will remain outstanding to maturity, you can value them by using the standard yield to maturity measure. In contrast, a callable bond gives the issuer the right to retire the bond prematurely, so the issue may or may not remain outstanding to maturity. As a result, the YTM may not always provide a good measure of the return that you can expect if you purchase a callable bond. Instead, you should consider the impact of the bond being called away prior to maturity. A common way to do that is to use a measure known as the **yield to call (YTC)**, which shows the yield on a bond if the issue remains outstanding not to maturity but rather until its first (or some other specified) call date.

The YTC is commonly used with bonds that carry deferred-call provisions. Remember that such issues start out as noncallable bonds and then, after a call deferment period (of 5 to 10 years), become freely callable. Under these conditions, the YTC would measure the expected yield on a deferred-call bond assuming that the issue is retired at the end of the call deferment period (that is, when the bond first becomes freely callable). You can find the YTC by making two simple modifications to the standard YTM equation (Equation 8.3 or 8.4). First, define the length of the investment horizon (N) as the number of years to the first call date, not the number of years to maturity. Second, instead of using the bond's par value ($1,000), use the bond's call price (which is stated in the indenture and is nearly always greater than the bond's par value).

For example, assume you want to find YTC on a 20-year, 10.5% deferred-call bond that is currently trading in the market at $1,204, but has 5 years to go to first call (that is, before it becomes freely callable), at which time it can be called in at a price of $1,085. Rather than using the bond's maturity of 20 years in the valuation equation (Equation 8.3 or 8.4), you use the number of years to first call (5 years), and rather than the bond's par value, $1,000, you use the issue's call price, $1,085. Note, however, you still use the bond's coupon (10.5%) and its current market price ($1,204). Thus, for annual compounding, you would have:

Equation 8.6

$$BP_i = \$1,204 = \frac{\$105}{(1 + r_i)^1} + \frac{\$105}{(1 + r_i)^2} + \frac{\$105}{(1 + r_i)^3} + \frac{\$105}{(1 + r_i)^4} + \frac{\$105}{(1 + r_i)^5} + \frac{\$1,085}{(1 + r_i)^5}$$

Through trial and error, you could determine that at a discount rate of 7%, the present value of the future cash flows (coupons over the next 5 years, plus call price) will exactly (or very nearly) equal the bond's current market price of $1,204.

Thus, the YTC on this bond is 7%. In contrast, the bond's YTM is 8.37%. In practice, bond investors normally compute both YTM and YTC for deferred-call bonds that are trading at a premium. They do this to find which yield is lower; the market convention is *to use the lower, more conservative measure of yield (YTM or YTC) as the appropriate indicator of the bond's return.* As a result, the premium bond in our example would be valued relative to its yield to call. The assumption is that because interest rates have dropped so much (the YTM is 2 percentage points below the coupon rate), it will be called in the first chance the issuer gets. However, the situation is totally different when this or any bond trades at a discount. Why? Because YTM on any discount bond, whether callable or not, will always be less than YTC. Thus, YTC is a totally irrelevant measure for discount bonds—it's used only with premium bonds.

Input	Function
5	N
−1204	PV
105	PMT
1085	FV
	CPT
	I
Solution	
7.00	

Calculator Use For annual compounding, to find the YTC of a 20-year, 10.5% bond that is currently trading at $1,204 but can be called in 5 years at a call price of $1,085, use the keystrokes shown in the margin. In this computation, N is the number of years to first call date, and FV represents the bond's call price. All other keystrokes are as defined earlier.

Expected Return

Rather than just buying and holding bonds, some investors prefer to actively trade in and out of these securities over fairly short investment horizons. As a result, measures such as yield to maturity and yield to call have relatively little meaning, other than as indicators of the rate of return used to price the bond. These investors obviously need an alternative measure of return that they can use to assess the investment appeal of those bonds they intend to trade. Such an alternative measure is the **expected return**. It indicates the rate of return an investor can expect to earn by holding a bond over a period of time that's less than the life of the issue. (Expected return is also known as **realized yield** because it shows the return an investor would realize by trading in and out of bonds over short holding periods.)

The expected return lacks the precision of the yield to maturity (and YTC), because the major cash flow variables are largely the product of investor estimates. In particular, going into the investment, both the length of the holding period and the future selling price of the bond are pure estimates and therefore subject to uncertainty. Even so, you can use essentially the same procedure to find a bond's realized yield as you did to find the promised yield. That is, with some simple modifications to the standard bond-pricing formula, you can use the following equation to find the expected return on a bond:

Equation 8.7

$$\text{Bond price} = \begin{array}{c} \text{Present value of the bond's} \\ \text{annual coupon payments} \\ \text{over the holding period} \end{array} + \begin{array}{c} \text{Present value of the bond's} \\ \text{future price at the} \\ \text{end of the holding period} \end{array}$$

Equation 8.7a

$$BP_i = \frac{C}{(1 + r_i)^1} + \frac{C}{(1 + r_i)^2} + \ldots + \frac{C}{(1 + r_i)^N} + \frac{FV}{(1 + r_i)^N}$$

where this time N represents the length of the holding period (not years to maturity), and FV is the expected future price of the bond.

As indicated above, you must determine the future price of the bond when computing its expected return. This is done by using the standard bond price formula, as described earlier. The most difficult part of deriving a reliable future price is, of course, coming up with future market interest rates that you feel will exist when the bond is sold. By evaluating current and expected market interest rate conditions, you can estimate the YTM that you expect the issue to provide at the date of sale and then use that yield to calculate the bond's future price.

To illustrate, take one more look at our 7.5%, 15-year bond. This time, let's assume that you feel the price of the bond, which is now trading at a discount, will rise sharply as interest rates fall over the next few years. In particular, assume the bond is currently priced at $809.50 (to yield 10%) and you anticipate holding the bond for 3 years. Over that time, you expect market rates to drop to 8%. With that assumption in place, and recognizing that 3 years from now the bond will have 12 remaining coupon payments, you can use Equation 8.3 to estimate that the bond's price will be $960 in 3 years. Thus, you are assuming that you will buy the bond today at a market price of $809.50 and sell it 3 years later—after interest rates have declined to 8%—at a price of $960. Given these assumptions, the expected return (realized yield) on this bond is 14.6%, which is the discount rate in the following equation that will produce a current market price of $809.50.

$$BP_i = \$809.50 = \frac{\$75}{(1 + r_i)^1} + \frac{\$75}{(1 + r_i)^2} + \frac{\$75}{(1 + r_i)^3} + \frac{\$960}{(1 + r_i)^3}$$

where $r_i = 0.146 = 14.6\%$.

The better-than-14.5% return on this investment is fairly substantial, but keep in mind that this is only a measure of expected return. It is, of course, subject to variation if things do not turn out as anticipated, particularly with regard to the market yield expected at the end of the holding period. This example uses annual compounding, but you could just as easily have used semiannual compounding, which, everything else being the same, would have resulted in an expected yield of 14.4% rather than the 14.6% found with annual compounding.

CALCULATOR USE For semiannual compounding, to find the expected return on a 7.5% bond that is currently priced in the market at $809.50 but is expected to rise to $960 within a 3-year holding period, use the keystrokes shown in the margin. In this computation, *PV* is the current price of the bond, and *FV* is the expected price of the bond at the end of the (3-year) holding period. All other keystrokes are as defined earlier. To find the bond-equivalent yield, double the computed value of *I*: 7.217% $\times$ 2 = 14.43%.

Valuing a Bond

Depending on their objectives, investors can estimate the return that they will earn on a bond by calculating either its yield to maturity or its expected return. Conservative, income-oriented investors focus on the YTM. Earning interest income over extended periods of time is their principal objective, not earning a quick capital gain if interest rates fall. Because these investors intend to hold most of the bonds that they buy to maturity, the YTM (or the YTC) is a reliable measure of the returns that they can expect over time—assuming, of course, the reinvestment assumptions embedded in the yield measure are reasonable. More aggressive bond traders, who hope to profit from swings in market interest rates, calculate the expected return to estimate the return that they will earn on a bond. Earning capital gains by purchasing and selling bonds over relatively short holding periods is their chief concern, so the expected return is more important to them than the YTM.

In either case, the promised or expected yield provides a *measure of return* that can be used to determine the relative attractiveness of fixed-income securities. But to evaluate the merits of different bonds, we must evaluate their returns and their risks. Bonds are no different from stocks in that the return (promised or expected) that they provide should be sufficient to compensate investors for the risks that they take. Thus, the greater the risk, the greater the return the bond should generate.

CONCEPTS IN REVIEW

Answers available at www.pearsonhighered.com/smart

8.7 What's the difference between current yield and yield to maturity? Between promised yield and realized yield? How does YTC differ from YTM?

8.8 Briefly describe the term *bond-equivalent yield.* Is there any difference between promised yield and bond-equivalent yield? Explain.

8.9 Why is the reinvestment of interest income so important to bond investors?

Duration and Immunization

LG5 One of the problems with the yield to maturity is that it assumes you can reinvest the bond's periodic coupon payments at the same rate over time. If you reinvest this interest income at a lower rate (or if you spend it), your actual return will be lower than the YTM. Another flaw is that YTM assumes the investor will hold the bond to maturity. If you sell a bond prior to its maturity, the price that you receive will reflect prevailing interest rates, which means that the return that you will earn will probably differ from the YTM. If rates have moved up since you purchased the bond, the bond will sell at a discount, and your return will be less than the YTM. If interest rates have dropped, the opposite will happen.

The problem with yield to maturity, then, is that it fails to take into account the effects of reinvestment risk and price (or market) risk. To see how reinvestment and price risks behave relative to one another, consider a situation in which market interest rates have undergone a sharp decline. Under such conditions, bond prices will rise. You might be tempted to cash out your holdings and take some gains (i.e., do a little "profit taking"). Indeed, selling before maturity is the only way to take advantage of falling interest rates because a bond will pay its par value at maturity, regardless of prevailing interest rates. That's the good news about falling rates, but there is a downside: When interest rates fall, so do the opportunities to reinvest at high rates. Therefore, although you gain on the price side, you lose on the reinvestment side. Even if you don't sell out, you are faced with increased reinvestment risk. In order to earn the YTM promised on your bonds, you must reinvest each coupon payment at the same YTM rate. Obviously, as rates fall, you'll find it increasingly difficult to reinvest the stream of coupon payments at that rate. When market rates rise, just the opposite happens: The price of the bond falls, but your reinvestment opportunities improve.

Bond investors need a measure that helps them judge just how significant these risks are for a particular bond. Such a yardstick is provided by something called **duration**. It captures in a single measure the extent to which the price of a bond will react to different interest rate environments. Because duration gauges the price volatility of a bond, it gives you a better idea of how likely you are to earn the return (YTM) you expect. That, in turn, will help you tailor your holdings to your expectations of interest rate movements.

The Concept of Duration

The concept of duration was first developed in 1938 by actuary Frederick Macaulay to help insurance companies match their cash inflows with payments. When applied to bonds, duration recognizes that the amount and frequency of interest payments, the yield to maturity, and the term to maturity all affect the interest rate risk of a particular bond. Term to maturity is important because it influences how much a bond's price will rise or fall as interest rates change. In general, when rates move, bonds with longer maturities fluctuate more than shorter issues. On the other hand, while the amount of price risk embedded in a bond is related to the issue's term to maturity, the amount of reinvestment risk is directly related to the size of a bond's coupon. Bonds that pay high coupons have greater reinvestment risk simply because there's more to reinvest.

As it turns out, both price and reinvestment risk are related in one way or another to interest rates, and therein lies the conflict. Any change in interest rates (whether up or down) will cause price risk and reinvestment risk to push and pull bonds in opposite directions. An increase in rates will produce a drop in price but will lessen reinvestment risk. Declining rates, in contrast, will boost prices but increase reinvestment risk. At some point in time, these two forces should exactly offset each other. That point in time is a bond's duration.

In general, bond duration possesses the following properties:

- Higher *coupons* result in shorter durations.

- Longer *maturities* mean longer durations.

- Higher *yields* (YTMs) lead to shorter durations.

Together, these variables—coupon, maturity, and yield—interact to determine an issue's duration. Knowing a bond's duration is helpful because it captures the bond's underlying price volatility. That is, since a bond's duration and volatility are directly related, it follows that the shorter the duration, the less volatility in bond prices—and vice versa, of course.

Measuring Duration

Duration is a measure of the average maturity of a fixed-income security. The term *average maturity* may be confusing because bonds have only one final maturity date. An alternative definition of average maturity might be that it captures the average timing of the bond's cash flow. For a zero-coupon bond that makes only one cash payment on the final maturity date, the bond's duration equals its maturity. But because coupon-paying bonds make periodic interest payments, the average timing of these payments (i.e., the average maturity) is different from the actual maturity date. For instance, a 10-year bond that pays a 5% coupon each year distributes a small cash flow in year 1, in year 2, and so on up until the last and largest cash flow in year 10. Duration is a measure that puts some weight on these intermediate payments, so that the "average maturity" is a little less than 10 years.

You can think of duration as the *weighted-average life of a bond*, where the weights are the fractions of the bond's total value accounted for by each cash payment that the bond makes over its life. Mathematically, we can find the duration of a bond as follows:

Equation 8.8

$$\text{Duration} = \sum_{t=1}^{N} \left[\frac{PV(C_t)}{BP} \times t \right]$$

where

$PV(C_t)$ = present value of a future coupon or principal payment
BP = current market price of the bond
t = year in which the cash flow (coupon or principal) payment is received
N = number of years to maturity

The duration measure obtained from Equation 8.8 is commonly referred to as *Macaulay duration*—named after the actuary who developed the concept.

Although duration is often computed using semiannual compounding, Equation 8.8 uses annual coupons and annual compounding to keep the ensuing discussion and calculations as simple as possible. Even so, the formula looks more formidable than it really is. If you follow the basic steps noted below, you'll find that duration is not tough to calculate.

Step 1. Find the present value of each annual coupon or principal payment [$PV(C_t)$]. Use the prevailing YTM on the bond as the discount rate.

Step 2. Divide this present value by the current market price of the bond (BP). This is the weight, or the fraction of the bond's total value accounted for by each individual payment. Because a bond's value is just the sum of the present values of its cash payments, these weights must sum to 1.0.

Step 3. Multiply this weight by the year in which the cash flow is to be received (t).

Step 4. Repeat steps 1 through 3 for each year in the life of the bond, and then add up the values computed in step 3.

Duration for a Single Bond Table 8.1 (on page 275) illustrates the four-step procedure for calculating the duration of a 7.5%, 15-year bond priced at $957.20 to yield 8%.

TABLE 8.1   DURATION CALCULATION FOR A 7.5%, 15-YEAR BOND PRICED TO YIELD 8%

(1) Year (t)	(2) Annual Cash Flow (C_t)	(3) Present Value at 8% of Annual Cash Flows [$PV(C_t)$] (2) × [$1/(1.08)^t$]	(4) $PV(C_t)$ Divided by Current Market Price of the Bond* (3) ÷ $957.20	(5) Time-Weighted Relative Cash Flow (1) × (4)
1	$ 75	$ 69.44	.0725	.0725
2	75	64.30	.0672	.1344
3	75	59.54	.0622	.1866
4	75	55.13	.0576	.2304
5	75	51.04	.0533	.2666
6	75	47.26	.0494	.2963
7	75	43.76	.0457	.3200
8	75	40.52	.0423	.3387
9	75	37.52	.0392	.3528
10	75	34.74	.0363	.3629
11	75	32.17	.0336	.3696
12	75	29.78	.0311	.3734
13	75	27.58	.0288	.3745
14	75	25.53	.0267	.3735
15	1,075	338.88	.3540	5.3106

Duration: 9.36 yr

*If this bond is priced to yield 8%, it will be quoted in the market at $957.20.

INVESTOR FACTS

Different Bonds, Same Durations—Sometimes, you really can't judge a book—or a bond, for that matter—by its cover. Here are 3 bonds that, on the surface, appear to be totally different:

- An 8-year, zero-coupon bond priced to yield 6%
- A 12-year, 8.5% bond that trades at a yield of 8%
- An 18-year, 10.5% bond priced to yield 13%

Although these bonds have different coupons and different maturities, they have one thing in common: they all have identical durations of 8 years. Thus, if interest rates went up or down by 50 to 100 basis points, the market prices of these bonds would all behave pretty much the same!

Table 8.1 provides the basic input data: Column (1) shows the year (t) in which each cash payment arrives. Column (2) provides the dollar amount of each cash payment (coupons and principal) made by the bond. Column (3) lists the present value of each cash flow, given an 8% discount rate (which is equal to the prevailing YTM on the bond). For example, in row 1 of Table 8.1, we see that in year 1 the bond makes a $75 coupon payment, and discounting that to the present at 8% reveals that the first coupon payment has a present value of $69.44.

Next, in column 4 we divide the present value in column 3 by the current market price of the bond. If the present value of this bond's first coupon payment is $69.45 and the total price of the bond is $957.20, then that first payment accounts for 7.25% of the bond's total value ($69.45 ÷ $957.20 = 0.0725). Therefore, 7.25% is the "weight" given to the cash payment made in year 1. If you sum the weights in column 4, you will see that they add to 1.0. Multiplying the weights from column 4 by the year (t) in which the cash flow arrives results in a time-weighted value for each of the annual cash flow streams shown in column 5. Adding up all the values in column 5 yields the duration of the bond. As you can see, the duration of this bond is a lot less than its maturity. In addition, keep in mind that the duration on any bond will change over time as YTM and term to maturity change. For example, the duration on this 7.5%, 15-year bond will fall as the bond nears maturity and/or as the market yield (YTM) on the bond increases.

Duration for a Portfolio of Bonds The concept of duration is not confined to individual bonds only. It can also be applied to whole portfolios of fixed-income securities. The duration of an entire portfolio is fairly easy to calculate. All we need are the durations of the individual securities in the portfolio and their weights (i.e., the proportion that each security contributes to the overall value of the portfolio). Given this, the duration of a portfolio is the weighted average of the durations of the individual securities in the portfolio. Actually, this weighted-average approach provides only an approximate measure of duration. But it is a reasonably close approximation and, as such, is widely used in practice—so we'll use it, too.

To see how to measure duration using this approach, consider the following 5-bond portfolio:

Bond	Amount Invested*	Weight	×	Bond Duration	=	Portfolio Duration
Government bonds	$ 270,000	0.15		6.25		0.9375
Aaa corporates	180,000	0.10		8.90		0.8900
Aa utilities	450,000	0.25		10.61		2.6525
Agency issues	360,000	0.20		11.03		2.2060
Baa industrials	540,000	0.30		12.55		3.7650
	$1,800.000	1.00				10.4510

*Amount invested = Current market price × Par value of the bonds. That is, if the government bonds are quoted at 90 and the investor holds $300,000 in these bonds, then 0.90 × $300,000 = $270,000.

In this case, the $1.8 million bond portfolio has an average duration of approximately 10.5 years.

If you want to change the duration of the portfolio, you can do so by (1) changing the asset mix of the portfolio (shift the weight of the portfolio to longer- or shorter-duration bonds, as desired) and/or (2) adding new bonds to the portfolio with the desired duration characteristics. As we will see below, this approach is often used in a bond portfolio strategy known as *bond immunization*.

Bond Duration and Price Volatility

A bond's price volatility is, in part, a function of its term to maturity and, in part, a function of its coupon. Unfortunately, there is no exact relationship between bond maturities and bond price volatilities with respect to interest rate changes. There is, however, a fairly close relationship between bond duration and price volatility—as long as the market doesn't experience wide swings in interest rates. A bond's duration can be used as a viable predictor of its price volatility only so long as the yield swings are relatively small (no more than 50 to 100 basis points, or so). That's because as interest rates change, bond prices change in a nonlinear (convex) fashion. For example, when interest rates fall, bond prices rise at an increasing rate. When interest rates rise, bond prices fall at a decreasing rate. The duration measure essentially predicts that as interest rates change, bond prices will move in the opposite direction in a linear fashion. This means that when interest rates fall, bond prices will rise a bit faster than the duration measure would predict, and when interest rates rise, bond prices will fall at a slightly slower rate than the duration measure would predict. The bottom line is that the duration measure helps investors understand how bond prices will respond to changes in market rates, as long as those changes are not too large.

The mathematical link between changes in interest rates and changes in bond prices involves the concept of *modified duration*. To find modified duration, we simply take the (Macaulay) duration for a bond (as found from Equation 8.8) and adjust it for the bond's yield to maturity.

Equation 8.9

$$\text{Modified duration} = \frac{\text{(Macaulay) Duration in years}}{1 + \text{Yield to maturity}}$$

Thus, the modified duration for the 15-year bond discussed above is

$$\text{Modified duration} = \frac{9.36}{1 + 0.08} = \underline{\underline{8.67}}$$

Note that here we use the bond's computed (Macaulay) duration of 9.36 years and the same YTM we used to compute duration in Equation 8.8; in this case, the bond was priced to yield 8%, so we use a yield to maturity of 8%.

To determine, in percentage terms, how much the price of this bond would change as market interest rates increased by 50 basis points from 8% to 8.5%, we multiply the modified duration value calculated above first by –1 (because of the inverse relationship between bond prices and interest rates) and then by the change in market interest rates. That is,

Equation 8.10

$$\begin{aligned}\text{Percent change in bond price} &= -1 \times \text{Modified duration} \times \text{Change in interest rates} \\ &= -1 \times 8.67 \times 0.5\% = \underline{\underline{-4.33}}\end{aligned}$$

Thus, a 50-basis-point (or ½ of 1%) increase in market interest rates will lead to an approximate 4.33% drop in the price of this 15-year bond. Such information is useful to bond investors seeking—or trying to avoid—price volatility.

Effective Duration

One problem with the duration measures that we've studied so far is that they do not always work well for bonds with embedded options such as callable bonds. That is, the duration measures we've been using assume that the bond's future cash flows are paid as originally scheduled through maturity, but that may not be the case with callable bonds (or convertible bonds or bonds with other types of options attached to them). An alternative duration measure that is used for these types of bonds is the effective duration. To calculate effective duration (ED), you use Equation 8.11:

Equation 8.11

$$\text{ED} = \frac{BP(r_i\downarrow) - BP(r_i\uparrow)}{2 \times BP \times \Delta r_i}$$

where

$BP(r_i\uparrow)$ = the new price of the bond if market interest rates go up
$BP(r_i\downarrow)$ = the new price of the bond if market interest rates go down
BP = the original price of the bond
Δr_i = the change in market interest rates

Example

> Suppose you want to know the effective duration of a 25-year bond that pays a 6% coupon semiannually. The bond is currently priced at $882.72 for a yield of 7%. Now suppose the bond's yield goes up by 0.5% to 7.5%. At that yield the new price would be $831.74 (using a calculator, N = 50, I = 3.75, PMT = 30, and PV = 1,000). What if the yield drops by 0.5% to 6.5%? In that case, the price rises to $938.62 (N = 50, I = 3.25, PMT = 30, PV = 1,000). Now we can use Equation 8.11 to calculate the bond's effective duration.
>
> Effective duration = ($938.62 − $831.74) ÷ (2 × $882.72 × 0.005) = 12.11

This means that if interest rates rise or fall by a full percentage point, the price of the bond would fall or rise by approximately 12.11%. Note that you can use effective duration in place of modified duration in Equation 8.10 to find the percent change in the price of a bond when interest rates move by more or less than 1.0%. When calculating the effective duration of a callable bond, one modification may be necessary. If the calculated price of the bond when interest rates fall is greater than the bond's call price, then use the call price in the equation rather than $BP(r_i\downarrow)$ and proceed as before.

Uses of Bond Duration Measures

You can use duration analysis in many ways to guide your decisions about investing in bonds. For example, as we saw earlier, you can use modified duration or effective duration to measure the potential price volatility of a particular issue. Another equally important use of duration is in the *structuring of bond portfolios*. That is, if you thought that interest rates were about to increase, you could reduce the overall duration of the portfolio by selling higher-duration bonds and buying shorter-duration bonds. Such a strategy could prove useful because shorter-duration bonds do not decline in value to the same degree as longer-duration bonds. On the other hand, if you felt that interest rates were about to decline, the opposite strategy would be appropriate.

Active, short-term investors frequently use duration analysis in their day-to-day operations. Longer-term investors also employ it in planning their investment decisions. Indeed, a strategy known as *bond portfolio immunization* represents one of the most important uses of duration.

Bond Immunization Some investors hold portfolios of bonds not for the purpose of "beating the market," but rather to accumulate a specified level of wealth by the end of a given investment horizon. For these investors, bond portfolio **immunization** often proves to be of great value. Immunization allows you to derive a specified rate of return from bond investments over a given investment interval regardless of what happens to market interest rates over the course of the holding period. In essence, you are able to "immunize" your portfolio from the effects of changes in market interest rates over a given investment horizon.

To understand how and why bond portfolio immunization is possible, you will recall from our earlier discussion that changes in market interest rates will lead to 2 distinct and opposite changes in bond valuation. The first effect is known as the *price effect*, and the second is known as the *reinvestment effect*. Whereas an increase in rates has a negative effect on a bond's price, it has a positive effect on the reinvestment of coupons. Therefore, when interest rate changes do occur, the price and reinvestment effects work against each other from the standpoint of the investor's wealth.

When the average duration of the portfolio just equals the investment horizon, these counteracting effects offset each other and leave your position unchanged. This should not come as much of a surprise because such a property is already embedded in the duration measure itself. If that relationship applies to a single bond, it should also apply to the weighted-average duration of a whole bond portfolio. When such a condition (of offsetting price and reinvestment effects) exists, a bond portfolio is said to be immunized. More specifically, your wealth is immunized from the effects of interest rate changes when the weighted-average duration of the bond portfolio exactly equals your desired investment horizon. Table 8.2 provides an example of bond immunization using a 10-year, 8% coupon bond with a duration of 8 years. Here, we assume that your desired investment horizon is also 8 years.

The example in Table 8.2 assumes that you originally purchased the 8% coupon bond at par. It further assumes that market interest rates for bonds of this quality drop from 8% to 6% at the end of the fifth year. Because you had an investment horizon of exactly 8 years and desire to lock in an interest rate return of exactly 8%, it follows that you expect to have a terminal value of $1,850.93 [i.e., $1,000 invested at 8% for 8 years = $1,000 $\times$ (1.08)^8. = $1,850.93], regardless of interest rate changes in the interim. As can be seen from the results in Table 8.2, the immunization strategy netted you a total of $1,850.31—just 62 cents short of your desired goal. Note that in this case, although reinvestment opportunities declined in years 5, 6, and 7 (when market interest rates dropped to 6%), that same lower rate led to a higher market price for the bond. That higher price, in turn, provided enough capital gains to offset the loss in reinvested income. This remarkable result clearly demonstrates the power of bond immunization and the versatility of bond duration. And note that even though the table uses a single bond for purposes of illustration, the same results can be obtained from a bond portfolio that is maintained at the proper weighted-average duration.

TABLE 8.2	BOND IMMUNIZATION							EXCEL with Spreadsheets
Year	Cash Flow from Bond ($)							Terminal Value of Reinvested Cash Flow
1	80	$\times$	(1.08)^4	$\times$	(1.06)^3		=	$ 129.63
2	80	$\times$	(1.08)^3	$\times$	(1.06)^3		=	120.03
3	80	$\times$	(1.08)^2	$\times$	(1.06)^3		=	111.14
4	80	$\times$	(1.08)	$\times$	(1.06)^3		=	102.90
5	80	$\times$	(1.06)^3				=	95.28
6	80	$\times$	(1.06)^2				=	89.89
7	80	$\times$	(1.06)				=	84.80
8	80						=	80.00
8	1,036.64*							1,036.64
					Total			$1,850.31
					Investor's required wealth at 8%			1,850.93
					Difference			$ .62

*The bond could be sold at a market price of $1,036.64, which is the value of an 8% bond with 2 years to maturity that is priced to yield 6%.

Note: Bond interest coupons are assumed to be paid at year-end. Therefore, there are 4 years of reinvestment at 8% and 3 years at 6% for the first year's $80 coupon.

Maintaining a fully immunized portfolio (of more than one bond) requires continual portfolio rebalancing. Indeed, every time interest rates change, the duration of a portfolio changes. Because effective immunization requires that the portfolio have a duration value equal in length to the remaining investment horizon, the composition of the portfolio must be rebalanced each time interest rates change. Further, even in the absence of interest rate changes, a bond's duration declines more slowly than its term to maturity. This, of course, means that the mere passage of time will dictate changes in portfolio composition. Such changes will ensure that the duration of the portfolio continues to match the remaining time in the investment horizon. In summary, portfolio immunization strategies can be extremely effective, but immunization is not a passive strategy and is not without potential problems, the most notable of which are associated with portfolio rebalancing.

CONCEPTS IN REVIEW
Answers available at
www.pearsonhighered.com/
smart

8.10 What does the term *duration* mean to bond investors and how does the duration of a bond differ from its maturity? What is modified duration, and how is it used? What is effective duration, and how does it differ from modified duration?

8.11 Describe the process of bond portfolio immunization, and explain why an investor would want to immunize a portfolio. Would you consider portfolio immunization a passive investment strategy comparable to, say, a buy-and-hold approach? Explain.

Bond Investment Strategies

LG6 Generally speaking, bond investors tend to follow 1 of 3 kinds of investment programs. First, there are those who live off the income. They are conservative, quality-conscious, income-oriented investors who seek to maximize current income. Second, there are the speculators (bond traders). Their investment objective is to maximize capital gains, often within a short time span. Finally, there are the serious long-term investors. Their objective is to maximize total return—from both current income and capital gains—over fairly long holding periods.

In order to achieve the objectives of any of these programs, you need to adopt a strategy that is compatible with your goals. Professional money managers use a variety of techniques to manage the multimillion- (or multibillion-) dollar bond portfolios under their direction. These range from passive approaches, to semiactive strategies, to active, fully managed strategies using interest rate forecasting and yield spread analysis. Most of these strategies are fairly complex and require substantial computer support. Even so, we can look briefly at some of the more basic strategies to gain an appreciation of the different ways in which you can use fixed-income securities to reach different investment objectives.

Passive Strategies

The bond immunization strategies we discussed earlier are considered to be primarily passive in nature. Investors using these tools typically are not attempting to beat the market but to lock in specified rates of return (or terminal values) that they deem acceptable, given the risks involved. As a rule, passive investment strategies are characterized by a lack of input regarding investor expectations of changes in interest rates and/or bond prices. Further, these strategies typically do not generate significant transaction costs. A buy-and-hold strategy is perhaps the most passive of all investment strategies. All that is required is that the investor replace bonds that have deteriorating credit ratings, have matured, or have been called. Although buy-and-hold investors restrict their ability to earn above-average returns, they also minimize the losses that transaction costs represent.

One popular approach that is a bit more active than buy-and-hold is the use of **bond ladders**. In this strategy, equal amounts are invested in a series of bonds with staggered maturities. Here's how a bond ladder works. Suppose you want to confine your investing to fixed-income securities with maturities of 10 years or less. Given that maturity constraint, you could set up a ladder by investing (roughly) equal amounts in, say, 3-, 5-, 7-, and 10-year issues. When the 3-year issue matures, you would put the money from it (along with any new capital) into a new 10-year note. You would continue this rolling-over process so that eventually you would hold a full ladder of staggered 10-year notes. By rolling into new 10-year issues every 2 or 3 years, you can do a kind of dollar-cost averaging and thereby lessen the impact of swings in market rates. The laddered approach is a safe, simple, and almost automatic way of investing for the long haul. A key ingredient of this or any other passive strategy is, of course, the use of high-quality investments that possess attractive features, maturities, and yields.

Trading on Forecasted Interest Rate Behavior

In contrast to passive strategies, a more risky approach to bond investing is the *forecasted interest rate* approach. Here, the investor seeks attractive capital gains when interest rates are expected to decline and preservation of capital when an increase in interest rates is anticipated. It's risky because it relies on the imperfect forecast of future interest rates. The idea is to increase the return on a bond portfolio by making strategic moves in anticipation of interest rate changes. Such a strategy is essentially *market timing*. An unusual feature of this tactic is that most of the trading is done with investment-grade securities because these securities are the most sensitive to interest rate movements, and that sensitivity is what active traders hope to profit from.

This strategy rests largely on technical matters. For example, when a decline in rates is anticipated, aggressive bond investors often seek to lengthen the maturity (or duration) of their bonds (or bond portfolios) because longer-term bonds rise more in price than shorter-term issues. At the same time, investors look for low-coupon and/or moderately discounted bonds because these bonds have higher durations, and their prices will rise more when interest rates fall. These interest swings are usually short-lived, so bond traders try to earn as much as possible in as short a time as possible. When rates start to level off and move up, these investors begin to shift their money out of long, discounted bonds and into high-yielding issues with short maturities. In other words, they do a complete reversal. During those periods when bond prices are dropping, investors are more concerned about preservation of capital, so they take steps to protect their money from capital losses. Thus, they tend to use such short-term obligations as Treasury bills, money funds, short-term (2- to 5-year) notes, or even variable-rate notes.

Bond Swaps

In a **bond swap**, an investor simultaneously liquidates one position and buys a different issue to take its place. Swaps can be executed to increase current yield or yield to maturity, to take advantage of shifts in interest rates, to improve the quality of a portfolio, or for tax purposes. Although some swaps are highly sophisticated, most are fairly simple transactions. They go by a variety of colorful names, such as "profit takeout," "substitution swap," and "tax swap," but they are all used for one basic reason: portfolio improvement. We will briefly review 2 types of bond swaps that are fairly simple and hold considerable appeal: the yield pickup swap and the tax swap.

In a **yield pickup swap,** an investor switches out of a low-coupon bond into a comparable higher-coupon issue in order to realize an instantaneous pickup of current yield and yield to maturity. For example, you would be executing a yield pickup swap if you sold 20-year, A-rated, 6.5% bonds (which were yielding 8% at the time) and replaced them with an equal amount of 20-year, A-rated, 7% bonds that were priced to yield 8.5%. By executing the swap, you would improve your current yield (your interest income would increase from $65 a year to $70 a year) as well as your yield to maturity (from 8% to 8.5%). Such swap opportunities arise because of the yield spreads that normally exist between different types of bonds. You can execute such swaps simply by watching for swap candidates and asking your broker to do so. In fact, the only thing you must be careful of is that transaction costs do not eat up all the profits.

Another popular type of swap is the **tax swap,** which is also relatively simple and involves few risks. You can use this technique whenever you have a substantial tax liability as a result of selling some security holdings at a profit. The objective is to execute a swap to eliminate or substantially reduce the tax liability accompanying the capital gains. This is done by selling an issue that has undergone a capital loss and replacing it with a comparable obligation.

For example, assume that you had $10,000 worth of corporate bonds that you sold (in the current year) for $15,000, resulting in a capital gain of $5,000. You can eliminate the tax liability accompanying the capital gain by selling securities that have capital losses of $5,000. Let's assume you find you hold a 20-year, 4.75% municipal bond that has undergone a $5,000 drop in value. Thus, you have the required tax shield in your portfolio. Now you need to find a viable swap candidate. Suppose you find a comparable 20-year, 5% municipal issue currently trading at about the same price as the issue being sold. By selling the 4.75s and simultaneously buying a comparable amount of the 5s, you will not only increase your tax-free yields (from 4.75% to 5%) but also eliminate the capital gains tax liability.

The only precaution in doing tax swaps is that you cannot use identical issues in the swap transactions. The IRS would consider that a "wash sale" and disallow the loss. Moreover, the capital loss must occur in the same taxable year as the capital gain. Typically, at year-end, tax loss sales and tax swaps multiply as knowledgeable investors hurry to establish capital losses.

CONCEPTS IN REVIEW

Answers available at
www.pearsonhighered.com/
smart

8.12 Briefly describe a bond ladder and note how and why an investor would use this investment strategy. What is a tax swap and why would it be used?

8.13 What strategy would you expect an aggressive bond investor (someone who's looking for capital gains) to employ?

8.14 Why is interest sensitivity important to bond speculators? Does the need for interest sensitivity explain why active bond traders tend to use high-grade issues? Explain.

MyFinanceLab

Here is what you should know after reading this chapter. MyFinanceLab will help you identify what you know and where to go when you need to practice.

What You Should Know	Key Terms	Where to Practice
LG1 Explain the behavior of market interest rates and identify the forces that cause interest rates to change. The behavior of interest rates is the most important force in the bond market. It determines not only the amount of current income an investor will receive but also the investor's capital gains (or losses). Changes in market interest rates can have a dramatic impact on the total returns obtained from bonds over time.	yield spreads, *p. 253*	MyFinanceLab Study Plan 8.1
LG2 Describe the term structure of interest rates and note how yield curves can be used by investors. Many forces drive the behavior of interest rates over time, including inflation, the cost and availability of funds, and the level of interest rates in major foreign markets. One particularly important force is the term structure of interest rates, which relates yield to maturity to term to maturity. Yield curves essentially plot the term structure and are often used by investors as a way to get a handle on the future behavior of interest rates.	expectations hypothesis, *p. 259* liquidity preference theory, *p. 260* market segmentation theory, *p. 260* term structure of interest rates, *p. 256* yield curve, *p. 256*	MyFinanceLab Study Plan 8.2
LG3 Understand how bonds are valued in the marketplace. Bonds are valued (priced) in the marketplace on the basis of their required rates of return (or market yields). The process of pricing a bond begins with the yield it should provide. Once that piece of information is known (or estimated), a standard, present value–based model is used to find the dollar price of a bond.	accrued interest, *p. 265* clean price, *p. 265* dirty price, *p. 265*	MyFinanceLab Study Plan 8.3 Video Learning Aid for Problems P8.1, P8.2
LG4 Describe the various measures of yield and return and explain how these standards of performance are used in bond valuation. Four types of yields are important to investors: current yield, promised yield, yield to call, and expected yield (or return). Promised yield (yield to maturity) is the most widely used bond valuation measure. It captures both the current income and the price appreciation of an issue. Yield to call, which assumes the bond will be outstanding only until its first (or some other) call date, also captures both current income and price appreciation. The expected return, in contrast, is a valuation measure used by aggressive bond traders to show the total return that can be earned from trading in and out of a bond long before it matures.	bond-equivalent yield, *p. 268* current yield, *p. 266* expected return, *p. 270* promised yield, *p. 266* realized yield, *p. 270* yield to call (YTC), *p. 269* yield to maturity (YTM), *p. 266*	MyFinanceLab Study Plan 8.4

What You Should Know	Key Terms	Where to Practice
LG5 **Understand the basic concept of duration, how it can be measured, and its use in the management of bond portfolios.** Bond duration takes into account the effects of both reinvestment and price (or market) risks. It captures in a single measure the extent to which the price of a bond will react to different interest rate environments. Equally important, duration can be used to immunize whole bond portfolios from the often-devastating forces of changing market interest rates.	duration, *p. 273* immunization, *p. 278*	MyFinanceLab Study Plan 8.5 Excel Tables 8.1, 8.2
LG6 **Discuss various bond investment strategies and the different ways these securities can be used by investors.** Bonds can be used as a source of income, as a way to seek capital gains by speculating on interest rate movement, or as a way to earn long-term returns. Investors often employ one or more of the following strategies: passive strategies such as buy-and-hold, bond ladders, and portfolio immunization; bond trading based on forecasted interest rate behavior; and bond swaps.	bond ladders, *p. 281* bond swap, *p. 281* tax swap, *p. 282* yield pickup swap, *p. 282*	MyFinanceLab Study Plan 8.6

Log into MyFinanceLab, take a chapter test, and get a personalized Study Plan
that tells you which concepts you understand and which ones you need to
review. From there, MyFinanceLab will give you further practice, tutorials,
animations, videos, and guided solutions.
Log into **www.myfinancelab.com**

Discussion Questions

LG1   Q8.1 Briefly describe each of the following theories of the term structure of interest rates.
a. Expectations hypothesis
b. Liquidity preference theory
c. Market segmentation theory

According to these theories, what conditions would result in a downward-sloping yield curve? What conditions would result in an upward-sloping yield curve? Which theory do you think is most valid, and why?

LG2   Q8.2 Using the *Wall Street Journal* or *Barron's*, find the bond yields for Treasury securities with the following maturities: 3 months, 6 months, 1 year, 3 years, 5 years, 10 years, 15 years, and 20 years. Construct a yield curve based on these reported yields, putting term to maturity on the horizontal (*x*) axis and yield to maturity on the vertical (*y*) axis. Briefly discuss the general shape of your yield curve. What conclusions might you draw about future interest rate movements from this yield curve?

LG5   Q8.3 Briefly explain what will happen to a bond's duration measure if each of the following events occur.
a. The yield to maturity on the bond falls from 8.5% to 8%.
b. The bond gets 1 year closer to its maturity.
c. Market interest rates go from 8% to 9%.
d. The bond's modified duration falls by half a year.

LG6 Q8.4 Assume that an investor comes to you looking for advice. She has $200,000 to invest and wants to put it all into bonds.

a. If she considers herself a fairly aggressive investor who is willing to take the risks necessary to generate the big returns, what kind of investment strategy (or strategies) would you suggest? Be specific.

b. What kind of investment strategies would you recommend if your client were a very conservative investor who could not tolerate market losses?

c. What kind of investor do you think is most likely to use

1. an immunized bond portfolio?

2. a yield pickup swap?

3. a bond ladder?

4. a long-term zero-coupon bond when interest rates fall?

LG4 LG5 Q8.5 Using the resources at your campus or public library (or on the Internet), select any 6 bonds you like, consisting of 2 Treasury bonds, 2 corporate bonds, and 2 agency issues. Determine the latest current yield and promised yield for each. (For promised yield, use annual compounding.) In addition, find the duration and modified duration for each bond.

a. Assuming that you put an equal amount of money into each of the 6 bonds you selected, find the duration for this 6-bond portfolio.

b. What would happen to your bond portfolio if market interest rates fell by 100 basis points?

c. Assuming that you have $100,000 to invest, use at least 4 of these bonds to develop a bond portfolio that emphasizes either the potential for capital gains or the preservation of capital. Briefly explain your logic.

Problems

All problems are available on **www.myfinancelab.com**

LG3 P8.1 An investor is considering the purchase of a $1,000 par value bond with an 8% coupon rate (with interest paid semiannually) that matures in 5 years. If the bond is priced to yield 6%, what is the bond's current price?

LG3 P8.2 Two bonds have par values of $1,000. One is a 5%, 15-year bond priced to yield 8%. The other is a 7.5%, 20-year bond priced to yield 6%. Which of these has the lower price? (Assume annual compounding in both cases.)

LG3 P8.3 Using semiannual compounding, find the prices of the following bonds.

a. A 10.5%, 15-year bond priced to yield 8%
b. A 7%, 10-year bond priced to yield 8%
c. A 12%, 20-year bond priced at 10%

Repeat the problem using annual compounding. Then comment on the differences you found in the prices of the bonds.

LG3 P8.4 A 15-year bond has an annual-pay coupon of 7.5% and is priced to yield 9%. Calculate the price per $1,000 par value.

LG3 P8.5 A $1,000 par value bond has a current price of $800 and a maturity value of $1,000 and matures in 5 years. If interest is paid semiannually and the bond is priced to yield 8%, what is the bond's annual coupon rate?

LG3 P8.6 A 20-year bond has a coupon of 10% and is priced to yield 8%. Calculate the price per $1,000 par value using semiannual compounding. If an investor purchases this bond 2 months before a scheduled coupon payment, how much accrued interest must be paid to the seller?

LG4 P8.7 An investor buys a 10% bond for $900 and sells it in 1 year for $950. What is the investor's holding period return?

LG4   **P8.8** A bond is priced in the market at $1,150 and has a coupon of 8%. Calculate the bond's current yield.

LG4   **P8.9** A $1,000 par value bond with an 8% coupon rate (semiannual interest) matures in 5 years and currently sells for $1,200. What is the bond's yield to maturity?

LG4   **P8.10** What is the current yield for a $1,000 par value bond that pays interest semiannually, has 9 years to maturity, and is currently selling for $937 with a bond equivalent yield of 12%?

LG3   **P8.11** An investor is considering the purchase of an 8%, 18-year corporate bond that's being priced to yield 10%. She thinks that in a year, this bond will be priced in the market to yield 9%. Using annual compounding, find the price of the bond today and in 1 year. Next, find the holding period return on this investment, assuming that the investor's expectations are borne out. (If necessary, see Chapter 4 for the holding period return formula.)

LG4   **P8.12** A bond is currently selling in the market for $1,170.68. It has a coupon of 12% and a 20-year maturity. Using annual compounding, calculate the promised yield on this bond.

LG4   **P8.13** A bond is currently selling in the market for $1,098.62. It has a coupon of 9% and a 20-year maturity. Using annual compounding, calculate the yield to maturity on this bond.

LG4   **P8.14** Compute the current yield of a 10%, 25-year bond that is currently priced in the market at $1,200. Use annual compounding to find the promised yield on this bond. Repeat the promised yield calculation, but this time use semiannual compounding to find yield to maturity.

LG4   **P8.15** You are evaluating an outstanding issue of $1,000 par value bonds with a 12% coupon rate that mature in 30 years and make quarterly interest payments. If the current market price for the bonds is $1,065, what is the quoted annual yield to maturity for the bonds?

LG4   **P8.16** A 10%, 25-year bond has a par value of $1,000 and a call price of $1,075. (The bond's first call date is in 5 years.) Coupon payments are made semiannually (so use semiannual compounding where appropriate).
    a. Find the current yield, YTM, and YTC on this issue, given that it is currently being priced in the market at $1,200. Which of these 3 yields is the highest? Which is the lowest? Which yield would you use to value this bond? Explain.
    b. Repeat the 3 calculations above, given that the bond is being priced at $850. Now which yield is the highest? Which is the lowest? Which yield would you use to value this bond? Explain.

LG4   **P8.17** Assume that an investor is looking at 2 bonds: Bond A is a 20-year, 9% (semiannual pay) bond that is priced to yield 10.5%. Bond B is a 20-year, 8% (annual pay) bond that is priced to yield 7.5%. Both bonds carry 5-year call deferments and call prices (in five years) of $1,050.
    a. Which bond has the higher current yield?
    b. Which bond has the higher YTM?
    c. Which bond has the higher YTC?

LG4   **P8.18** A zero-coupon bond that matures in 15 years is currently selling for $209 per $1,000 par value. What is the promised yield on this bond?

LG4   **P8.19** A zero-coupon ($1,000 par value) bond that matures in 10 years has a promised yield of 9%. What is the bond's price?

LG4   **P8.20** A 25-year, zero-coupon bond was recently being quoted at 11.625% of par. Find the current yield and the promised yield of this issue, given that the bond has a par value of $1,000. Using semiannual compounding, determine how much an investor would have to pay for this bond if it were priced to yield 12%.

LG4   **P8.21** Assume that an investor pays $800 for a long-term bond that carries an 8% coupon. In 3 years, he hopes to sell the issue for $950. If his expectations come true, what yield will this investor realize? (Use annual compounding.) What would the holding period return be if he were able to sell the bond (at $950) after only 9 months?

LG4 P8.22 Using annual compounding, find the yield to maturity for each of the following bonds.
    a. A 9.5%, 20-year bond priced at $957.43
    b. A 16%, 15-year bond priced at $1,684.76
    c. A 5.5%, 18-year bond priced at $510.65

Now assume that each of the above bonds is callable as follows: Bond a is callable in 7 years at a call price of $1,095; bond b is callable in 5 years at $1,250; and bond c is callable in 3 years at $1,050. Use annual compounding to find the yield to call for each bond.

LG5 P8.23 A bond has a Macaulay duration equal to 9.5 and a yield to maturity of 7.5%. What is the modified duration of this bond?

LG5 P8.24 A bond has a Macaulay duration of 8.62 and is priced to yield 8%. If interest rates go up so that the yield goes to 8.5%, what will be the percentage change in the price of the bond? Now, if the yield on this bond goes down to 7.5%, what will be the bond's percentage change in price? Comment on your findings.

LG5 P8.25 An investor wants to find the duration of a 25-year, 6% semiannual-pay, noncallable bond that's currently priced in the market at $882.72, to yield 7%. Using a 50 basis point change in yield, find the effective duration of this bond. (Hint: Use Equation 8.11.)

LG5 P8.26 Find the Macaulay duration and the modified duration of a 20-year, 10% corporate bond priced to yield 8%. According to the modified duration of this bond, how much of a price change would this bond incur if market yields rose to 9%? Using annual compounding, calculate the price of this bond in one year if rates do rise to 9%. How does this price change compare to that predicted by the modified duration? Explain the difference.

LG5 P8.27 Which one of the following bonds would you select if you thought market interest rates were going to fall by 50 basis points over the next 6 months?
    a. A bond with a Macaulay duration of 8.46 years that's currently being priced to yield 7.5%
    b. A bond with a Macaulay duration of 9.30 years that's priced to yield 10%
    c. A bond with a Macaulay duration of 8.75 years that's priced to yield 5.75%

LG5 LG6 P8.28 Stacy Picone is an aggressive bond trader who likes to speculate on interest rate swings. Market interest rates are currently at 9%, but she expects them to fall to 7% within a year. As a result, Stacy is thinking about buying either a 25-year, zero-coupon bond or a 20-year, 7.5% bond. (Both bonds have $1,000 par values and carry the same agency rating.) Assuming that Stacy wants to maximize capital gains, which of the 2 issues should she select? What if she wants to maximize the total return (interest income and capital gains) from her investment? Why did one issue provide better capital gains than the other? Based on the duration of each bond, which one should be more price volatile?

LG5 LG6 P8.29 Elliot Karlin is a 35-year-old bank executive who has just inherited a large sum of money. Having spent several years in the bank's investments department, he's well aware of the concept of duration and decides to apply it to his bond portfolio. In particular, Elliot intends to use $1 million of his inheritance to purchase 4 U.S. Treasury bonds:
    a. An 8.5%, 13-year bond that's priced at $1,045 to yield 7.47%
    b. A 7.875%, 15-year bond that's priced at $1,020 to yield 7.60%
    c. A 20-year stripped Treasury that's priced at $202 to yield 8.22%
    d. A 24-year, 7.5% bond that's priced at $955 to yield 7.90%

    1. Find the duration and the modified duration of each bond.

    2. Find the duration of the whole bond portfolio if Elliot puts $250,000 into each of the 4 U.S. Treasury bonds.

    3. Find the duration of the portfolio if Elliot puts $360,000 each into bonds a and c and $140,000 each into bonds b and d.

4. Which portfolio—**b** or **c**—should Elliot select if he thinks rates are about to head up and he wants to avoid as much price volatility as possible? Explain. From which portfolio does he stand to make more in annual interest income? Which portfolio would you recommend, and why?

Visit **www.myfinancelab.com** for web exercises, spreadsheets, and other online resources.

Case Problem 8.1   The Bond Investment Decisions of Dave and Marlene Carter

LG3 LG4 LG6   Dave and Marlene Carter live in the Boston area, where Dave has a successful orthodontics practice. Dave and Marlene have built up a sizable investment portfolio and have always had a major portion of their investments in fixed-income securities. They adhere to a fairly aggressive investment posture and actively go after both attractive current income and substantial capital gains. Assume that it is now 2013 and Marlene is currently evaluating 2 investment decisions: one involves an addition to their portfolio, the other a revision to it.

The Carters' first investment decision involves a short-term trading opportunity. In particular, Marlene has a chance to buy a 7.5%, 25-year bond that is currently priced at $852 to yield 9%; she feels that in 2 years the promised yield of the issue should drop to 8%.

The second is a bond swap. The Carters hold some Beta Corporation 7%, 2026 bonds that are currently priced at $785. They want to improve both current income and yield to maturity and are considering 1 of 3 issues as a possible swap candidate: (a) Dental Floss, Inc., 7.5%, 2038, currently priced at $780; (b) Root Canal Products of America, 6.5%, 2026, selling at $885; and (c) Kansas City Dental Insurance, 8%, 2027, priced at $950. All of the swap candidates are of comparable quality and have comparable issue characteristics.

Questions

a. Regarding the short-term trading opportunity:
   1. What basic trading principle is involved in this situation?
   2. If Marlene's expectations are correct, what will the price of this bond be in 2 years?
   3. What is the expected return on this investment?
   4. Should this investment be made? Why?

b. Regarding the bond swap opportunity:
   1. Compute the current yield and the promised yield (use semiannual compounding) for the bond the Carters currently hold and for each of the 3 swap candidates.
   2. Do any of the swap candidates provide better current income and/or current yield than the Beta Corporation bonds the Carters now hold? If so, which one(s)?
   3. Do you see any reason why Marlene should switch from her present bond holding into one of the other issues? If so, which swap candidate would be the best choice? Why?

Case Problem 8.2   Grace Decides to Immunize Her Portfolio

LG4 LG5 LG6   Grace Hesketh is the owner of an extremely successful dress boutique in downtown Chicago. Although high fashion is Grace's first love, she's also interested in investments, particularly bonds and other fixed-income securities. She actively manages her own investments and over time has built up a substantial portfolio of securities. She's well versed on the latest investment techniques and is not afraid to apply those procedures to her own investments.

Grace has been playing with the idea of trying to immunize a big chunk of her bond portfolio. She'd like to cash out this part of her portfolio in 7 years and use the proceeds to buy a vacation home in her home state of Oregon. To do this, she intends to use the $200,000 she now has invested in the following 4 corporate bonds (she currently has $50,000 invested in each one).

1. A 12-year, 7.5% bond that's currently priced at $895
2. A 10-year, zero-coupon bond priced at $405
3. A 10-year, 10% bond priced at $1,080
4. A 15-year, 9.25% bond priced at $980

   (*Note:* These are all noncallable, investment-grade, nonconvertible/straight bonds.)

Questions

a. Given the information provided, find the current yield and the promised yield for each bond in the portfolio. (Use annual compounding.)

b. Calculate the Macaulay and modified durations of each bond in the portfolio and indicate how the price of each bond would change if interest rates were to rise by 75 basis points. How would the price change if interest rates were to fall by 75 basis points?

c. Find the duration of the current 4-bond portfolio. Given the 7-year target that Grace has set, would you consider this an immunized portfolio? Explain.

d. How could you lengthen or shorten the duration of this portfolio? What's the shortest portfolio duration you can achieve? What's the longest?

e. Using 1 or more of the 4 bonds described above, is it possible to come up with a $200,000 bond portfolio that will exhibit the duration characteristics Grace is looking for? Explain.

f. Using 1 or more of the 4 bonds, put together a $200,000 immunized portfolio for Grace. Because this portfolio will now be immunized, will Grace be able to treat it as a buy-and-hold portfolio—one she can put away and forget about? Explain.

Excel with Spreadsheets

All bonds are priced according to the present value of their future cash flow streams. The key components of bond valuation are par value, coupon interest rate, term to maturity, and market yield. It is market yield that drives bond prices. In the market for bonds, the appropriate yield at which the bond should sell is determined first, and then that yield is used to find the market value of the bond. The market yield can also be referred to as the required rate of return. It implies that this is the rate of return that a rational investor requires before he or she will invest in a given fixed-income security.

Create a spreadsheet to model and answer the following bond valuation questions.

Questions

a. One of the bond issues outstanding by H&W Corporation has an annual-pay coupon of 5.625% plus a par value of $1,000 at maturity. This bond has a remaining maturity of 23 years. The required rate of return on securities of similar-risk grade is 6.76%. What is the value of this corporate bond today?

b. What is the current yield for the H&W bond?

c. In the case of the H&W bond issue from question **a,** if the coupon interest payment is compounded on a semiannual basis, what would be the value of this security today?

d. How would the price of the H&W bond react to changing market interest rates? To find out, determine how the price of the issue reacts to changes in the bond's yield to maturity. Find the value of the security when the YTM is (1) 5.625%, (2) 8.0%, and (3) 4.5%. Label your findings as being a premium, par, or discount bond; comment on your findings.

e. The Jay & Austin Company has a bond issue outstanding with the following characteristics: par of $1,000, a semiannual-pay coupon of 6.5%, remaining maturity of 22 years, and a current price of $878.74. What is the bond's YTM?

CFA Exam Questions

Investing in Fixed-Income Securities

Following is a sample of 10 Level-I CFA exam questions that deal with many of the topics covered in Chapters 2 and 8 of this text, including bond prices and yields, interest rates and risks, bond price volatility, and bond redemption provisions. (When answering the questions, give yourself 1½ minutes for each question; the objective is to correctly answer 7 of the 10 questions in 15 minutes.)

1. Sinking funds are most likely to
   a. reduce credit risk (default risk).
   b. never allow issuers to retire more than the sinking fund requirement.
   c. always reduce the outstanding balance of the bond issue to 0 prior to maturity.

2. An analyst stated that a callable bond has less reinvestment risk and more price appreciation potential than an otherwise identical option-free bond. The analyst's statement most likely is
   a. incorrect with respect to both reinvestment risk and price appreciation potential.
   b. incorrect with respect to reinvestment risk but correct with respect to price appreciation potential.
   c. correct with respect to reinvestment risk but incorrect with respect to price appreciation potential.

3. A bond portfolio manager gathered the following information about a bond issue:

Par value	$10,000,000
Current market value	$9,850,000
Duration	4.8

   If yields are expected to decline by 75 basis points, which of the following would provide the most appropriate estimate of the price change for the bond issue?
   a. 3.6% of $9,850,000
   b. 3.6% of $10,000,000
   c. 4.8% of $9,850,000

4. A U.S. Treasury note with exactly 4 years to maturity most likely can be broken into as many as
   a. 4 Treasury STRIPS.
   b. 8 Treasury STRIPS.
   c. 9 Treasury STRIPS.

5. Frieda Wannamaker is a taxable investor who is currently in the 28% income-tax bracket. She is considering purchasing a tax-exempt bond with a yield of 3.75%. The taxable equivalent yield on this bond is closest to
   a. 1.46%.
   b. 5.21%.
   c. 7.47%.

6. The present value of a $1,000 par value, zero-coupon bond with a 3-year maturity assuming an annual discount rate of 6% compounded semiannually is closest to
   a. $837.48.
   b. $839.62.
   c. $943.40.

7. A bond with 14 years to maturity and a coupon rate of 6.375% has a yield to maturity of 4.5%. Assuming the bond's YTM remains constant, the bond's value as it approaches maturity will most likely
   a. increase.
   b. decrease.
   c. remain constant.

8. A coupon-bearing bond purchased when issued at par value was held until maturity during which time interest rates rose. The ex-post realized return of the bond investment most likely was
   a. above the YTM at the time of issue.
   b. below the YTM at the time of issue.
   c. equal to the YTM at the time of issue because the bond was held until maturity.

9. An analyst accurately calculates that the price of an option-free bond with a 9% coupon would experience a 12% change if market yields increase 100 basis points. If market yields decrease 100 basis points, the bond's price would most likely
   a. increase by 12%.
   b. increase by less than 12%.
   c. increase by more than 12%.

10. A bond with a par value of $1,000 has a duration of 6.2. If the yield on the bond is expected to change from 8.80% to 8.95%, the estimated new price for the bond following the expected change in yield is best described as being
    a. 0.93% lower than the bond's current price.
    b. 1.70% lower than the bond's current price.
    c. 10.57% lower than the bond's current price.

Answers: 1. a; 2. a; 3. a; 4. c; 5. b; 6. a; 7. b; 8. a; 9. c; 10. a.

9

Stock Valuation

LEARNING GOALS

After studying this chapter, you should be able to:

LG1 Explain the role that a company's future plays in the stock valuation process.

LG2 Develop a forecast of a stock's expected cash flow, starting with corporate sales and earnings, and then moving to expected dividends and share price.

LG3 Discuss the concepts of intrinsic value and required rates of return, and note how they are used.

LG4 Determine the underlying value of a stock using the zero-growth, constant-growth, and variable-growth dividend valuation models.

LG5 Use other types of present value–based models to derive the value of a stock, as well as alternative price-relative procedures.

LG6 Gain a basic appreciation of the procedures used to value different types of stocks, from traditional dividend-paying shares to more growth-oriented stocks.

What drives a stock's value? Many factors come into play, including how much profit the company earns, how its new products fare in the marketplace, and the overall state of the economy. But what matters most is what investors believe about the company's future.

Nothing illustrates this principle better than the behavior of Bed Bath & Beyond stock (ticker symbol BBBY) around the firm's earnings announcement on June 20, 2012. After business hours on that day, the company released its quarterly earnings figures. Bed Bath & Beyond earned a profit of $0.89 per share, which was considerably higher than the $0.72 earnings per share from the same quarter in 2011 and higher than the $0.85 figure that analysts had expected. That was good news, but the next day BBBY moved down almost 17%. The reason for the stock's slide was that in its quarterly earnings report, the company projected that in the following quarter it would earn somewhere between $0.97 and $1.03 per share, but analysts had anticipated that the coming quarter would be even better, with earnings per share at $1.08. Investors seemed to believe that BBBY's earnings would continue to disappoint for more than just one quarter, so they sold the stock and sent its price into a steep decline.

How do you determine a stock's true value? This chapter explains how to determine a stock's intrinsic value by using dividends, dividends and earnings, price/earnings, and other valuation models.

(Source: "Bed Bath & Beyond (BBBY) Is Sharply Lower on Weak Q2 Forecast," RTT News, http://www.rttnews.com/1910352/bed-bath-beyond-bbby-is-sharply-lower-on-weak-q2-forecast.aspx?utm_source=google&utm_campaign=sitemap, accessed on July 8, 2012.)

Valuation: Obtaining a Standard of Performance

LG1 LG2 LG3 A performance estimate of a stock's intrinsic value that can be used to judge the investment merits of a share of stock is the underlying purpose of **stock valuation**. Investors attempt to resolve the question of whether and to what extent a stock is under- or overvalued by comparing its current market price to its intrinsic value. At any given time, the price of a share of common stock depends on investors' expectations about the future performance of the company that issued the stock. When the outlook for the company improves, the stock price will probably go up. If investors' expectations become less rosy, the price of the stock will probably go down. Let's look now at the most important issue in the stock valuation process: the future.

Valuing a Company and Its Future

Thus far we have examined several aspects of security analysis: macroeconomic factors, industry factors, and company-specific factors. But as we've said, it's not the past that's important but the future. The primary reason for looking at past performance is to gain insight about the firm's future direction. Although past performance provides no guarantees about future returns, it can give us a good idea of a company's strengths and weaknesses. For example, history can tell us how well the company's products have done in the marketplace, how the company's fiscal health shapes up, and how management tends to respond to difficult situations. In short, the past can reveal how well the company is positioned to take advantage of the things that may occur in the future.

Because the value of a share of stock depends on the company's future performance, your task is to use historical data to project key financial variables into the future. In this way, you can judge whether a stock's market price aligns well with the company's prospects.

Forecasted Sales and Profits The key to your forecast is, of course, the future behavior of the company, and the most important aspects to consider in this regard are the outlook for sales and profits. One way to develop a sales forecast is to assume that the company will continue to perform as it has in the past and simply extend the historical trend. For example, if a firm's sales have been growing at a rate of 10% per year, then you might assume they will continue at that rate. Of course, if there is some evidence about the economy, industry, or company that suggests a faster or slower rate of growth, you would want to adjust the forecast accordingly. Often, this "naive" approach will be about as effective as more complex techniques.

Once you have produced a sales forecast, you can shift your attention to the net profit margin. We want to know what profit the firm will earn on the sales that it achieves. One of the best ways of doing that is to use what is known as a **common-size income statement**. Basically, a common-size statement takes every entry found on an ordinary income statement or balance sheet and converts it to a percentage. To create a common-size income statement, you divide every item on the statement by *net sales*—which, in effect, is the common denominator. An example of this appears in Table 9.1 (on page 294), which shows the 2013 dollar-based and common-size income statements for Universal Office Furnishings.

TABLE 9.1 COMPARATIVE DOLLAR-BASED AND COMMON-SIZE INCOME STATEMENTS FOR UNIVERSAL OFFICE FURNISHINGS, INC. 2013 INCOME STATEMENTS

EXCEL with Spreadsheets

	$ (in millions)	% (common-size)*
Net sales	1,938.0	100.0
Cost of goods sold	1,128.5	58.2
Gross profit	**809.5**	**41.8**
Selling, administrative, and other operating expenses	496.7	25.6
Depreciation & amortization	77.1	4.0
Other expenses	0.5	0.1
Total operating expenses	**574.3**	**29.7**
Earnings before interest & taxes (EBIT)	235.2	12.1
Interest expense	13.4	0.7
Income taxes	82.1	4.2
Net profit after taxes	**139.7**	**7.2**

*Common-size figures are found by using net sales as the common denominator, and then dividing all entries by net sales. For example, cost of goods sold = $1,128.5 ÷ $1,938.0 = 58.2%; EBIT = $235.20 ÷ $1,938.0 = 12.1%.

Example

To understand how to construct these statements, let's use the gross profit margin (of 41.8%) as an illustration. In this case, you divide the gross operating profit of $809.5 million by net sales of $1,938.0 million:

$$\$809.5 \div \$1,938.0 = 0.4177 = 41.8\%$$

Using net sales of $1,938.0 million, use the same procedure for every other entry on the income statement. Note that a common-size statement adds up, just like its dollar-based counterpart. For example, net sales of 100.0% minus costs of goods sold of 58.2% equals a gross profit margin of 41.8%. (You can also work up common-size balance sheets, using total assets as the common denominator.)

Securities analysts and investors use common-size income statements to compare operating results from one year to the next. The common-size format helps investors identify changes in profit margins and highlights possible causes of those changes. For example, a common-size income statement can quickly reveal whether a decline in a firm's net profit margin is caused by a reduction in the gross profit margin or a rise in other expenses. That information also helps analysts make projections of future profits. For example, analysts might use the most recent common-size statement (or perhaps an average of the statements that have prevailed for the past few years) combined with a sales forecast to create a forecasted income statement a year or two ahead. Analysts can make adjustments to specific line items to sharpen their projections. For example, if analysts know that a firm has accumulated an unusually large amount of inventory this year, it is likely that the firm will cut prices next year to reduce its inventory holdings, and that will put downward pressure on profit margins. Adjustments like these (hopefully) improve the accuracy of forecasts of future profits.

Given a satisfactory sales forecast and estimate of the future net profit margin, we can combine these two pieces of information to arrive at future earnings (i.e., profits).

Equation 9.1

$$\frac{\text{Future after-tax}}{\text{earnings in year } t} = \frac{\text{Estimated sales}}{\text{for year } t} \times \frac{\text{Net profit margin}}{\text{expected in year } t}$$

The *year t* notation in this equation simply denotes a future calendar or fiscal year. Suppose that in the year just completed, a company reported sales of $100 million. Based on the company's past growth rate and on industry trends, you estimate that revenues will grow at an 8% annual rate, and you think that the net profit margin will be about 6%. Thus, your forecast for next year's sales is $108 million ($100 million × 1.08), and next year's profits will be $6.5 million:

$$\text{Future after-tax earnings next year} = \$108 \text{ million} \times 0.06 = \underline{\$6.5 \text{ million}}$$

Using this same process, you could estimate sales and earnings for other years in the forecast period.

Forecasted Dividends and Prices At this point you have an idea of the future earnings performance of the company. The next step is to evaluate how these results will influence the company's stock price. Given a corporate earnings forecast, you need three additional pieces of information:

- An estimate of future dividend payout ratios

- The number of common shares that will be outstanding over the forecast period

- A future price-to-earnings (P/E) ratio

For the first 2 pieces of information, unless you have evidence to the contrary, you can simply project the firm's recent experience into the future. Payout ratios are usually fairly stable, so recent experience is a fairly good indicator of what the future will bring. Similarly, the number of shares outstanding does not usually change a great deal from one year to the next, so using the current number in a forecast will usually not lead to significant errors.

Getting a Handle on the P/E Ratio The most difficult issue in this process is coming up with an estimate of the future P/E ratio—a figure that has considerable bearing on the stock's future price behavior. Generally speaking, the P/E ratio (also called the P/E multiple) is a function of several variables, including the following:

- The growth rate in earnings

- The general state of the market

- The amount of debt in a company's capital structure

- The current and projected rate of inflation

- The level of dividends

As a rule, higher P/E ratios are associated with higher rates of growth in earnings, an optimistic market outlook, and lower debt levels (less debt means less financial risk).

The link between the inflation rate and P/E multiples, however, is a bit more complex. Generally speaking, as inflation rates rise, so do the interest rates offered by bonds. As returns on bonds increase, investors demand higher returns on stocks because they are riskier than bonds. Future returns on stocks can increase if companies earn higher profits and pay higher dividends, but if earnings and profits remain fixed, investors will only earn higher future returns if stock prices are lower today. Thus, inflation often puts downward pressure on stock prices and P/E multiples. On the other hand, declining inflation (and interest) rates normally have positive effects on the economy

What Is a P/E Ratio?

and business conditions, and that translates into higher P/E ratios and stock prices. Holding all other factors constant, a higher dividend payout ratio leads to a higher P/E ratio. In practice, however, most companies with high P/E ratios have *low* dividend payouts because firms that have the opportunity to grow rapidly tend to reinvest most of their earnings. In that case, the prospect of earnings growth drives up the P/E more than it offsets the low dividend payout ratio.

A Relative Price-to-Earnings Multiple A useful starting point for evaluating the P/E ratio is the *average market multiple*. This is simply the average P/E ratio of all the stocks in a given market index, like the S&P 500 or the DJIA. The average market multiple indicates the general state of the market. It gives us an idea of how aggressively the market, in general, is pricing stocks. Other things being equal, the higher the P/E ratio, the more optimistic the market, though there are exceptions to that general rule. Figure 9.1 plots the S&P 500 price-to-earnings multiple from 1940 to 2012. This figure calculates the market P/E ratio by dividing prices at the beginning of the year by earnings over the previous 12 months. The figure shows that market multiples move over a fairly wide range. For example, in 2009, the market P/E ratio was at an all-time high of more than 70, but just one year later the ratio had fallen to just under 21. It is worth noting that the extremely high P/E ratio in 2009 was not primarily the result of stock prices hitting all-time highs. Instead, the P/E ratio at the time was high because earnings over the preceding 12 months had been extraordinarily low due to a severe recession. This illustrates that you must be cautious when interpreting P/E ratios as a sign of the health of individual stocks or of the overall market.

FIGURE 9.1 **Average P/E Ratio of S&P 500 Stocks**

The average price-to-earnings ratio for stocks in the S&P 500 fluctuated around a mean of 13 from 1940 to 1990 before starting an upward climb. Increases in the P/E ratio do not necessarily indicate a bull market. The P/E ratio spiked in 2009, not because prices were high, but because earnings were very low due to the recession.

P/E Ratios Can Be Misleading

The most recent spike in the S&P 500 P/E ratio cannot be explained by a booming economy or a rising stock market. Recall that in 2008 stock prices fell dramatically, with the overall market declining by more than 30%. Yet, as 2009 began the average P/E ratio stood at an extraordinarily high level. The reason is that with the deep recession of 2008, corporate earnings declined even more sharply than stock prices did. So, in the market P/E ratio, the denominator (last year's earnings) declined more rapidly than the numerator (prices), and the overall P/E ratio jumped. In fact, in mid-2009 the average S&P 500 P/E ratio reached an all-time high of 144!

Looking at Figure 9.1, you can see that the market's P/E ratio has increased in recent years. From 1940 to 1990, the market P/E averaged about 13, but since then its average value has been above 24 (or more than 22 if you exclude the peak in 2009). At least during the 1990s, that upward trend could easily be explained by the very favorable state of the economy. Business was booming and new technologies were emerging at a rapid pace. There were no recessions from 1991 to 2000. If investors believed that the good times would continue indefinitely, then it's easy to understand why they might be willing to pay higher and higher P/E ratios over time.

With the market multiple as a benchmark, you can evaluate a stock's P/E performance relative to the market. That is, you can calculate a **relative P/E multiple** by dividing a stock's P/E by a market multiple. For example, if a stock currently has a P/E of 35 and the market multiple for the S&P 500 is, say, 25, the stock's relative P/E is 35/25 = 1.4. Looking at the relative P/E, you can quickly get a feel for how aggressively the stock has been priced in the market and what kind of relative P/E is normal for the stock.

Other things being equal, a high relative P/E is desirable—up to a point, at least. For just as abnormally high P/Es can spell trouble (i.e., the stock may be overpriced and headed for a fall), so too can abnormally high relative P/Es. Given that caveat, it follows that the higher the relative P/E measure, the higher the stock will be priced in the market. But watch out for the downside: High relative P/E multiples can also mean lots of price volatility, which means that both large gains and large losses are possible. (Similarly, you can use average industry multiples to get a feel for the kind of P/E multiples that are standard for a given industry. You can then use that information, along with market multiples, to assess or project the P/E for a particular stock.)

Next, you can generate a forecast of the stock's future P/E over the anticipated *investment horizon* (the period of time over which you expect to hold the stock). For example, with the existing P/E multiple as a base, an increase might be justified if you believe the market multiple will increase (as the market becomes more bullish) even if you do not expect the relative P/E to change. Of course, if you believe the stock's relative P/E will increase as well, that would result in an even more bullish forecast.

Estimating Earnings per Share So far you've been able to come up with an estimate for the dividend payout ratio, the number of shares outstanding, and the price-to-earnings multiple. You're now ready to forecast the stock's future earnings per share (EPS) as follows:

Equation 9.2

$$\text{Estimated EPS in year } t = \frac{\text{Future after-tax earnings in year } t}{\text{Number of shares of common stock outstanding in year } t}$$

Earnings per share is a critical part of the valuation process, for once you have EPS, you can combine it with (1) the dividend payout ratio to obtain (future) dividends per share and (2) the price-to-earnings multiple to project the (future) price of the stock.

Equation 9.2 simply converts aggregate or total corporate earnings to a per-share basis by relating forecasted company profits to the expected number of shares outstanding. Although this approach works quite effectively, some investors would rather bypass the projection of aggregate sales and earnings and instead concentrate on earnings per share right from the start. You can do that by looking at the major forces that drive earnings per share: ROE and book value. Quite simply, by using these two variables, earnings per share could be expressed as follows:

Equation 9.3

$$ EPS = \frac{\text{After-tax earnings}}{\text{Book value of equity}} \times \frac{\text{Book value of equity}}{\text{Shares outstanding}} = ROE \times \text{Book value per share} $$

This formula will produce the same results as the standard EPS equation shown first in Chapter 1 (Equation 1). The major advantage of this form of the equation is that it allows you to assess the extent to which EPS is influenced by the company's book value and (especially) its ROE. As we saw in the previous chapter, ROE is a key financial measure because it captures the amount of success the firm is having in managing its assets, operations, and capital structure. And as we see here, ROE not only is important in defining overall corporate profitability, but it also plays a crucial role in defining a stock's EPS.

To produce an estimated EPS using Equation 9.3, you would go directly to the two basic components of the formula and try to get a handle on their future behavior. In particular, what kind of growth is expected in the firm's book value per share, and what's likely to happen to the company's ROE? In the vast majority of cases, ROE is really the driving force, so it's important to produce a good estimate of that variable. Investors often do that by breaking ROE into its component parts— net profit margin, total asset turnover, and the equity multiplier.

Once you have projected ROE and book value per share, you can plug these figures into Equation 9.3 to produce estimated EPS. The bottom line is that, one way or another (using the approach reflected in Equation 9.2 or that in Equation 9.3), you have to arrive at a forecasted EPS number that you are comfortable with. When you've done that, it's a simple matter to use the forecasted payout ratio to estimate dividends per share:

Equation 9.4

$$ \frac{\text{Estimated dividends}}{\text{per share in year } t} = \frac{\text{Estimated EPS}}{\text{for year } t} \times \frac{\text{Estimated}}{\text{payout ratio}} $$

And then the future price of the stock, which can be determined as

Equation 9.5

$$ \frac{\text{Estimated share price}}{\text{at end of year } t} = \frac{\text{Estimated EPS}}{\text{in year } t} \times \frac{\text{Estimated P/E}}{\text{ratio}} $$

Pulling It All Together You've seen the various components that go into estimates of future dividends and share prices. Now, to see how they all fit together, let's continue with the example we started above. Using the aggregate sales and earnings approach, if the company had 2 million shares of common stock outstanding and you expected that to remain constant, then given the estimated earnings of $6.5 million that you computed earlier, the firm should generate earnings per share next year of

$$\text{Estimated EPS next year} = \frac{\$6.5 \text{ million}}{2 \text{ million}} = \underline{\$3.25}$$

You could obtain the same figure if you had forecasts of the firm's ROE and its book value per share. For instance, suppose you estimate that the firm will have an ROE of 15% and a book value per share of $21.67. According to Equation 9.3, those conditions would also produce an estimated EPS of $3.25 (i.e., 0.15 × $21.67). Using this EPS figure, along with an estimated payout ratio of 40%, dividends per share next year should equal

$$\text{Estimated dividends per share next year} = \$3.25 \times .40 = \underline{\$1.30}$$

If the firm adheres to a fixed-dividend policy, you may have to adjust this estimate to reflect the steady dividend payment. For example, if the company has been paying annual dividends at the rate of $1.25 per share and you expect it to continue doing so, then you would adjust estimated dividends accordingly (i.e., use $1.25/share). Finally, if it has been estimated that the stock should sell at 17.5 times earnings, then a share of stock in this company should be trading at $56.88 by the end of next year.

$$\text{Estimated share price at the end of next year} = \$3.25 \times 17.5 = \underline{\$56.88}$$

Actually, you are interested in the price of the stock at the end of the anticipated investment horizon. Thus, the $56.88 figure would be appropriate if you had a 1-year horizon. However, if you had a 3-year holding period, you would have to extend the EPS figure for 2 more years and repeat your calculations with the new data. The bottom line is that the estimated share price is important because it has embedded in it the capital gains portion of the stock's total return.

Developing an Estimate of Future Behavior

Using information obtained from Universal Office Furnishings (UVRS), we can illustrate the forecasting procedures we discussed above. An assessment of the economy and the office equipment industry was positive and that the company's operating results and financial condition looked strong, both historically and relative to industry standards. Because everything looks favorable for Universal, we decide to take a look at the future prospects of the company and its stock.

Assume we have chosen a 3-year investment horizon because we believe (from earlier studies of economic and industry factors) that the economy and the market for office equipment stocks will start running out of steam near the end of 2016 or early 2017. (Some investors prefer to use 1-year investment horizons because they believe that trying to forecast out any further involves too many uncertainties. We use a 3-year investment horizon here primarily for illustration—and because we feel comfortable forecasting the numbers out that far. Should that not be the case, then by all means use a shorter investment horizon.)

Table 9.2 (on page 300) provides selected historical financial data for the company, covering a 5-year period (ending with the latest fiscal year) and

TABLE 9.2	SELECTED HISTORICAL FINANCIAL DATA, UNIVERSAL OFFICE FURNISHINGS				
	2009	2010	2011	2012	2013
Total assets (millions)	$554.2	$694.9	$755.6	$761.5	$941.2
Total asset turnover	1.72×	1.96×	2.12×	2.32×	2.06×
Net sales (millions)	$953.2	$1,283.9	$1,495.9	$1,766.2	$1,938.0
Annual rate of growth in sales*	11.5%	34.7%	16.5%	18.1%	9.7%
Net profit margin	4.2%	6.6%	7.5%	8.0%	7.2%
Payout ratio	6.8%	5.2%	5.5%	6.0%	6.6%
Price/earnings ratio	13.5×	16.2×	13.9×	15.8×	18.4×
Number of common shares outstanding (millions)	77.7	78.0	72.8	65.3	61.8

*Annual rate of growth in sales = Change in sales from one year to the next ÷ Level of sales in the base (or earliest) years. For 2010, the annual rate of growth in sales equaled 34.7% = (2010 sales − 2009 sales)/2009 sales = ($1,283.9 − $953.2)/$953.2 = 0.3469.

provides the basis for much of our forecast. The data reveal that, with one or two exceptions, the company has performed at a fairly steady pace and has been able to maintain a very attractive rate of growth. Our economic analysis suggests that the economy is about to pick up, and research indicates that the industry and company are well situated to take advantage of the upswing. Therefore, we conclude that the rate of growth in sales should pick up dramatically from the abnormally low level of 2013, attaining a growth rate of over 20% in 2014—more in line with the firm's 5-year average. After a modest amount of pent-up demand is worked off, the rate of growth in sales should drop to about 19% in 2015 and to 15% in 2016.

The essential elements of the financial forecast for 2014 through 2016 are provided in Table 9.3 (on page 300). Highlights of the key assumptions and the reasoning behind them are as follows:

- *Net profit margin.* Various published industry and company reports suggest a comfortable improvement in earnings, so we decide to use a profit margin of 8.0% in 2014 (up a bit from the latest margin of 7.2% recorded in 2013). We're projecting even better profit margins (8.5%) in 2015 and 2016, as some cost improvements start to take hold.

- *Common shares outstanding.* We believe the company will continue to pursue its share buyback program, but at a substantially slower pace than in the 2010–2013 period. From a current level of 61.8 million shares, we project that the number of shares outstanding will drop to 61.5 million in 2014, to 60.5 million in 2015, and to 59.0 million in 2016.

- *Payout ratio.* We assume that the dividend payout ratio will hold at a steady 6% of earnings, as it has for most of the recent past.

- *P/E ratio.* Primarily on the basis of expectations for improved growth in revenues and earnings, we are projecting a P/E multiple that will rise from its present level of 18.4 times earnings to roughly 20 times earnings in 2014. Although this is a fairly conservative increase in the P/E, when it is coupled with the hefty growth in EPS, the net effect will be a big jump in the projected price of Universal stock.

TABLE 9.3   SUMMARY FORECAST STATISTICS, UNIVERSAL OFFICE FURNISHINGS

	Latest Actual Figure (Fiscal 2013)	Average for the Past 5 Years (2009–2013)	Forecasted Figures		
			2014	2015	2016
Annual rate of growth in sales	9.7%	18.1%	22%	19%	15%
Net sales (millions)	$1,938.0	N/A*	$2,364.4**	$2,813.6**	$3,235.6**
× Net profit margin	7.2%	5.6%	8.0%	8.5%	8.5%
= Net after-tax earnings (millions)	$ 139.7	N/A	$ 189.2	$ 239.2	$ 275.0
÷ Common shares outstanding (millions)	61.8	71.1	61.5	60.5	59.0
= Earnings per share	$ 2.26	N/A	$ 3.08	$ 3.95	$ 4.66
× Payout ratio	6.6%	6.2%	6.0%	6.0%	6.0%
= Dividends per share	$ 0.15	$0.08	$ 0.18	$ 0.24	$ 0.28
Earnings per share	$ 2.26	N/A	$ 3.08	$ 3.95	$ 4.66
× P/E ratio	18.4	16.8	20.0	19.0	20.0
= Share price at year end	$ 41.58	N/A	$ 61.60	$ 75.05	$ 93.20

*N/A: Not applicable.

**Forecasted sales figures: Sales from preceding year × Growth rate in sales = Growth in sales; then Growth in sales + Sales from preceding year = Forecast sales for the year. For example, for 2014: $1,938.0 × 0.22 = $426.4 + $1938.0 = $2,364.4.

Table 9.3 also shows the sequence involved in arriving at forecasted dividends and share price behavior; that is:

1. The company dimensions of the forecast are handled first. These include sales and revenue estimates, net profit margins, net earnings, and the number of shares of common stock outstanding. Note that we derive after-tax earnings according to the procedure described earlier in this chapter.

2. Next we estimate earnings per share, following the procedures established earlier.

3. The bottom line of the forecast is, of course, the returns in the form of dividends and capital gains expected from a share of Universal stock, given that the assumptions about net sales, profit margins, earnings per share, and so forth hold up. We see in Table 9.3 that dividends should go up to 28 cents per share, which is a big jump from where they are now (15 cents per share). Even so, with annual dividends of a little over 25 cents per share, it's clear that dividends still won't account for much of the stock's return. In fact, our projections indicate that the dividend yield in 2016 will fall to just 0.3%. Clearly, the returns from this stock are going to come from capital gains, not dividends. That's obvious when we look at year-end share prices, which we expect to more than double over the next 3 years. That is, if our projections are valid, the price of a share of stock should rise from around $41.50 to more than $93.00 by year-end 2016.

We now have an idea of what the future cash flows of the investment are likely to be. We can now use that information to establish an intrinsic value for Universal Office Furnishings stock.

The Valuation Process

Valuation is a process by which an investor determines the worth of a security using the risk and return concepts that will be introduced in Chapters 10 and 11. This process can be applied to any asset that produces a stream of cash—a share of stock, a bond, a piece of real estate, or an oil well. To establish the value of an asset, the investor must determine certain key inputs, including the amount of future cash flows, the timing of these cash flows, and the rate of return required on the investment.

In terms of common stock, the essence of valuation is to determine what the stock ought to be worth, given estimated returns to stockholders (future dividends and price behavior) and the amount of potential risk. Toward that end we employ various types of stock valuation models, the end product of which represents the elusive intrinsic value we have been seeking. That is, the stock valuation models determine either an expected rate of return or the intrinsic worth of a share of stock, which in effect represents the stock's "justified price." In this way, we obtain a standard of performance, based on forecasted stock behavior, which we can use to judge the investment merits of a particular security.

Either of two conditions would make us consider a stock a worthwhile investment candidate: (1) the computed rate of return equals or exceeds the yield we feel is warranted, or (2) the justified price (intrinsic worth) is equal to or greater than the current market price. Note that a security is considered acceptable even if its yield simply equals the required rate of return or if its intrinsic value simply equals the current market price of the stock. There is nothing irrational about purchasing a security in those circumstances. In either case, the security meets your minimum standards to the extent that it is giving you the rate of return you wanted.

Remember this, however, about the valuation process: Even though valuation plays an important part in the investment process, there is absolutely no assurance that the actual outcome will be even remotely similar to the projections. The stock is still subject to economic, industry, company, and market risks, any one of which could negate **all** your assumptions about the future. Security analysis and stock valuation models are used not to guarantee success but to help you better understand the return and risk dimensions of a potential transaction.

Required Rate of Return One of the key ingredients in the stock valuation process is the **required rate of return**. Generally speaking, the amount of return required by an investor should be related to the level of risk that must be assumed to generate that return. In essence, the required return establishes a level of compensation compatible with the amount of risk involved. Such a standard helps you determine whether the expected return on a stock (or any other security) is satisfactory. Because you don't know for sure what the cash flow of an investment will be, you should expect to earn a rate of return that reflects this uncertainty. Thus, the greater the perceived risk, the more you should expect to earn. As we will see in Chapter 11, this is basically the notion behind the capital asset pricing model (CAPM).

Recall that using the CAPM, we can define a stock's required return as

Equation 9.6
$$\begin{array}{c}\text{Required}\\\text{rate of return}\end{array} = \begin{array}{c}\text{Risk-free}\\\text{rate}\end{array} + \left[\begin{array}{c}\text{Stock's}\\\text{beta}\end{array} \times \left(\begin{array}{c}\text{Market}\\\text{return}\end{array} - \begin{array}{c}\text{Risk-free}\\\text{rate}\end{array} \right) \right]$$

The required inputs for this equation are readily available. You can obtain a stock's beta from many different online sites or print sources. The risk-free rate is basically the return on Treasury bills, and a good proxy for the market return is the long-run average

Rod Holloway
Equity Portfolio Manager, **CFCI**

"The higher the beta, the more that stock will move up if the market is going up."

MyFinanceLab

INVESTOR FACTS

How to Spot an Undervalued (or Overvalued) Market—Just as shares of common stock can become over- or undervalued, so can the market as a whole. How can you tell if the market is overvalued? Some market observers suggest you look at comparative yields. That is, compare the so-called earnings yield on stocks with the yields on 10-year Treasuries. The earnings yield on stocks is the inverse of the market's P/E ratio—if the market P/E is 18 times earnings, the earnings yield would be 5.56% (1/18). If the earnings yield is above the yield on 10-year Treasuries, stocks are undervalued (cheap), especially compared to bonds. In contrast, you'd normally expect the earnings yield on stocks to be less than 10-year Treasury yields; as that spread continues to widen, the market is becoming more and more overvalued—definitely not a good thing.

return on the stock market. This average return may, of course, have to be adjusted up or down a bit based on what you expect the market to do over the next year or so.

In the CAPM, the risk of a stock is captured by its beta. For that reason, the required return on a stock increases (or decreases) with increases (or decreases) in its beta. As an illustration of the CAPM at work, consider Universal's stock, which we'll assume has a beta of 1.30. If the risk-free rate is 5.5% and the expected market return is 15%, according to the CAPM model, this stock would have a required return of

$$\text{Required return} = 5.5\% + [1.30 \times (15.0\% - 5.5\%)] = \underline{17.85\%}$$

This return—let's round it to 18%—can now be used in a stock valuation model to assess the investment merits of a share of stock.

As an alternative, or perhaps even in conjunction with the CAPM, you could take a more subjective approach to finding the required return. For example, if your assessment of the historical performance of the company had uncovered some volatility in sales and earnings, you could conclude that the stock is subject to a good deal of business risk. Also important is market risk, as measured by a stock's beta. A valuable reference point in arriving at a measure of risk is the rate of return available on less risky but competitive investments. Thus, you could use the rate of return on long-term Treasury bonds or high-grade corporate issues as a starting point in defining your desired rate of return. That is, starting with yields on long-term bonds, you could adjust those returns for the levels of business and market risk to which you believe the common stock is exposed.

To see how these elements make up the desired rate of return, let's go back to Universal Office Furnishings. Assume that it is now early 2014 and rates on high-grade corporate bonds are hovering around 9%. Given that our analysis thus far has indicated that the office equipment industry in general, and Universal in particular, is subject to a "fair" amount of business risk, we would want to adjust that figure upward—probably by around 2 or 3 points. In addition, with its beta of 1.30, we can conclude that the stock carries a good deal of market risk. Thus, we should increase our base rate of return even more—say, by another 4 or 5 points. That is, starting from a base (high-grade corporate bond) rate of 9%, we tack on, say, 3% for the company's added business risk and another 4.5% or 5% for the stock's market risk. Adding these up, we find that an appropriate required rate of return for Universal's common stock is around 17% or 17.5%. This figure is reasonably close to what we would obtain with CAPM using a beta of 1.30, a risk-free rate of 5.5%, and an expected market return of 15% (as in Equation 9.6). The fact that the two numbers are close shouldn't be surprising. If they're carefully (and honestly) done, the CAPM and the subjective approach should yield similar results. Whichever procedure you use, the required rate of return stipulates the minimum return you should expect to receive from an investment. To accept anything less means you'll fail to be fully compensated for the risk you must assume.

9.1 What is the purpose of stock valuation? What role does intrinsic value play in the stock valuation process?

9.2 Are the expected future earnings of the firm important in determining a stock's investment suitability? Discuss how these and other future estimates fit into the stock valuation framework.

9.3 Can the growth prospects of a company affect its price-to-earnings multiple? Explain. How about the amount of debt a firm uses? Are there any other variables that affect the level of a firm's P/E ratio?

9.4 What is the market multiple and how can it help in evaluating a stock's P/E ratio? Is a stock's relative P/E the same thing as the market multiple? Explain.

9.5 In the stock valuation framework, how can you tell whether a particular security is a worthwhile investment candidate? What roles does the required rate of return play in this process? Would you invest in a stock if all you could earn was a rate of return that just equaled your required return? Explain.

Stock Valuation Models

Investors employ several different stock valuation models. Although they may all be aimed at a security's future cash benefits, their approaches to valuation are nonetheless considerably different. Some investors, for example, search for value in a company's financials—by keying in on such factors as book value, debt load, return on equity, and cash flow. These so-called value investors rely as much on historical performance as on earnings projections to identify undervalued stock. Then there are the growth investors, who concentrate primarily on growth in earnings. To them, though past growth is important, the real key lies in projected earnings—in finding companies that will produce big earnings, along with big P/E multiples.

AN ADVISER'S PERSPECTIVE

Rod Holloway
Equity Portfolio Manager, CFCI

"The stock valuation model that I prefer depends on the type of stock that I'm looking for."

MyFinanceLab

There are still other stock valuation models in use—models that employ such variables as dividend yield, abnormally low P/E multiples, relative price performance over time, and even company size or market cap as key elements in the decision-making process. For purposes of our discussion, we'll focus on several stock valuation models that derive value from the fundamental performance of the company. We'll look first at stocks that pay dividends and at a procedure known as the dividend valuation model. From there, we'll look at several valuation procedures that can be used with companies that pay little or nothing in dividends. Finally, we'll move on to procedures that set the price of a stock based on how it behaves relative to earnings, cash flow, sales, or book value. The stock valuation procedures that we'll examine in this chapter are the same as those used by many professional security analysts, and are, in fact, found throughout the "Equity Investments" portion of the CFA exam, especially at Level-I. And, of course, as more fully discussed in the Ethics in Investing box on page 305), an understanding of these valuation models will enable you to better evaluate analysts' recommendations.

The Dividend Valuation Model

In the valuation process, the intrinsic value of any investment equals the present value of its expected cash benefits. For common stock, this amounts to the cash dividends received each year plus the future sale price of the stock. One way to view the cash flow benefits from common stock is to assume that the dividends will be received over an infinite time horizon—an assumption that is appropriate so long as the firm is considered a "going concern." Seen from this perspective, the value of a share of stock is equal to the present value of all the future dividends it is expected to provide over an infinite time horizon.

When an investor sells a stock, from a strictly theoretical point of view, what he or she is really selling is the right to all future dividends. Thus, just as the current value of a share of stock is a function of future dividends, the future price of the stock is also a function of future dividends. In this framework, the future price of the stock will rise or fall as the outlook for dividends (and the required rate of return) changes. This approach, which holds that the value of a share of stock is a function of its future dividends, is known as **dividend valuation model (DVM)**.

There are three versions of the dividend valuation model, each based on different assumptions about the future rate of growth in dividends:

1. *The zero-growth model* assumes that dividends will not grow over time.

2. *The constant-growth model*, which is the basic version of the dividend valuation model, assumes that dividends will grow by a constant rate over time.

3. *The variable-growth model* assumes that the rate of growth in dividends will vary over time.

In one form or another, the DVM is widely used in practice to value many of the larger, more mature companies.

ETHICS IN INVESTING   Stock Analysts: Don't Always Believe the Hype

Buy, sell, or hold? Unfortunately, many investors have learned the hard way not to trust these recommendations.

Consider the late 1990s stock market bubble. As the market began to fall in 2000, 95% of publicly traded stocks were free of sell recommendations, according to investment research firm Zacks, and 5% of stocks that did have a sell rating had exactly that: a sell rating from a single analyst. When the market began its climb back up, analysts missed the boat again: From 2000 to 2004, stocks that analysts told investors to sell rose 19% per annum on average, while their "buys" and "holds" rose just 7%.

Why were the all-star analysts wrong so often? Conflict of interest is one explanation. Analysts are handsomely rewarded for generating investment banking business. They often felt pressure to make positive comments to please current or prospective investment banking clients. Also, analysts are expected to generate commissions for their firms by making buy and sell recommendations.

Analyst hype is a real problem for both Wall Street and Main Street, and the securities industry has taken steps to correct it. The SEC's Regulation Fair Disclosure requires that all company information must be released to the public rather than quietly disseminated to analysts. Some brokerages ban analysts from owning stocks they cover. In 2003 the SEC ruled that compensation for analyst research must be separated from investment banking fees, so that the analyst's job is to research stock rather than solicit clients.

Most important, investors must learn how to read between the lines of analysts' reports. In early 2012 there were 10 times as many stocks in the S&P 500 rated as "buys" than rated as "sells." If analysts were really unbiased, it seems very unlikely that their recommendations would be so heavily tilted toward the buy side. What should investors do? To start, they should probably lower analysts' ratings by one notch. A strong buy could be interpreted as a buy, a buy as a hold, and a hold or neutral as a sell. Also, investors should give more weight to negative ratings than to positive ones. Downgrades and those rare sell recommendations may signal future problems. Investors should also pay attention to forecasts in which a ratings change is accompanied by an earnings forecast revision in the same direction. That is, if an analyst moves a stock from sell to buy and simultaneously raises the earnings forecast for the stock, that is more credible than a report that simply changes the rating to "buy." Finally, when in doubt, investors should do their own homework, using the techniques taught in this book.

Critical Thinking Question Do you agree with the policies forbidding analysts to own stock of the companies they cover?

(Sources: Jack Hough, "How to Make Money off Analysts' Stock Recommendations," *Smart Money*, January 19, 2012, http://www.smartmoney.com/invest/stocks/how-to-make-money-off-analysts-stock-recommendations-1326759491635/; Rich Smith, "Analysts Running Scared," *The Motley Fool*, April 5, 2006, www.fool.com.)

Zero Growth The simplest way to picture the dividend valuation model is to assume the stock has a fixed stream of dividends. In other words, dividends stay the same year in and year out, and they're expected to do so in the future. Under such conditions, the value of a zero-growth stock is simply the capitalized value of its annual dividends. To find the capitalized value, just divide annual dividends by the required rate of return, which in effect acts as the capitalization rate. That is,

Equation 9.7

$$\frac{\text{Value of a}}{\text{share of stock}} = \frac{\text{Annual dividends}}{\text{Required rate of return}}$$

Example

Suppose a stock pays a dividend of $3 per share each year, and you don't expect that dividend to change. If you want a 10% return on your investment, how much should you be willing to pay for the stock?

Value of stock = $3 ÷ 0.10 = $30

If you paid a higher price, you would earn a rate of return less than 10%, and likewise if you could acquire the stock for less, your rate of return would exceed 10%.

As you can see, the only cash flow variable that's used in this model is the fixed annual dividend. Given that the annual dividend on this stock never changes, does that mean the price of the stock never changes? Absolutely not! For as the required rate of return (capitalization rate) changes, so will the price of the stock. Thus, if the required rate of return goes up to, say, 15%, the price of the stock will fall to $20 ($3 ÷ 0.15). Although this may be a very simplified view of the valuation model, it's actually not as far-fetched as it may appear, for this is basically the procedure used to price preferred stocks in the marketplace.

Constant Growth The zero-growth model is a good beginning, but it does not take into account a growing stream of dividends. The standard and more widely recognized version of the dividend valuation model assumes that dividends will grow over time at a specified rate. In this version, the value of a share of stock is still considered to be a function of its future dividends, but such dividends are expected to grow forever at a constant rate of growth, *g*. Accordingly, we can find the value of a share of stock as follows:

Equation 9.8

$$\frac{\text{Value of a}}{\text{share of stock}} = \frac{\text{Next year's dividends}}{\text{Required rate} - \text{Constant rate of}}$$
$$\frac{\quad}{\text{of return} \quad \text{growth in dividends}}$$

Equation 9.8a

$$V = \frac{D_1}{r - g}$$

where
D_1 = annual dividends expected next year (the first year in the forecast period)
r = the capitalization rate, or discount rate (which defines the required rate of return on the investment)
g = the annual rate of growth in dividends

Even though this version of the model assumes that dividends will grow at a constant rate forever, it is important to understand that doesn't mean we assume the

Smart's Tour of the Web
To watch author Scott Smart discuss key websites for this chapter, visit www.myfinancelab.com

investor will hold the stock forever. Indeed, the DVM makes no assumptions about how long the investor will hold the stock, for the simple reason that the investment horizon has no bearing on the computed value of a stock. Thus, with the constant-growth DVM, it is irrelevant whether the investor has a 1-year, 5-year, or 10-year expected holding period. The computed value of the stock will be the same under all circumstances. So long as the input assumptions (r, g, and D_1) are the same, the value of the stock will be the same regardless of the intended holding period.

You'll also note that as simple as this model is, it nonetheless succinctly captures the very essence of stock valuation. Increase the cash flow (through D or g) or decrease the required rate of return (r), and the stock value will increase. Also note that in the DVM, r defines the total return to the stockholder, and g represents the expected capital gains on the investments. We know that, in practice, there are potentially two components that make up the total return to a stockholder: dividends and capital gains. As it turns out, the returns from both dividends and capital gains are captured in the DVM. That is, because r represents total returns and g defines the amount of capital gains embedded in r, it follows that if you subtract g from r, you'll have the expected dividend yield on the stock ($r - g$). Thus, the expected total return on a stock (r) equals the returns from capital gains (g) plus the returns from dividends ($r - g$).

The constant-growth DVM should not be used with just any stock. Rather, it is best suited to the valuation of mature, dividend-paying companies. These are companies with strong track records that have reached the "mature" stage of growth. They are probably large-cap (or perhaps even some mature mid-cap) companies that have demonstrated an ability to generate steady—although perhaps not spectacular—rates of growth year in and year out. The growth rates may not be identical from year to year, but they tend to move within a relatively narrow range. These are companies that have established dividend policies and fairly predictable growth rates in earnings and dividends.

Example

In the 20 years between 1992 and 2012, the food company General Mills increased its dividend payments by about 6% per year. The food industry is not one where we would expect explosive growth. Food consumption is closely tied to population growth, so profits in this business should grow relatively slowly over time. Traditionally, General Mills increases its dividend every summer, so in the summer of 2012, investors were expecting a modest increase in General Mills dividends over the coming year to $1.34 per share. If the required return on General Mills stock is 10%, the investors should have been willing to pay $33.50 for the stock ($1.34 ÷ (0.10 − 0.06)). In fact, General Mills stock traded in a range between $38 and $39 in July 2012, so the constant growth model seems to work fairly well for that company.

In addition to its use in valuing mature, dividend-paying companies, the constant-growth DVM is also widely used to value the market as a whole. That is, using something like the DJIA or the S&P 500, analysts will often employ the DVM to determine the expected return on the market for the coming year—in other words, they'll use it to find the r_m in the capital asset pricing model (CAPM).

Applying the Constant-Growth DVM Use of the constant-growth DVM requires some basic information about the stock's required rate of return, its current level of dividends, and the expected rate of growth in dividends. A fairly simple, albeit naïve, way to find the dividend growth rate, *g*, is to look at the historical behavior of dividends. If they are growing at a relatively constant rate, you can assume they will continue to grow at (or near) that average rate in the future. You can get historical dividend data in a company's annual report, from various online sources, or from publications like *Value Line*.

With the help of a calculator or spreadsheet, we can use basic present value arithmetic to find the growth rate embedded in a stream of dividends. Here's how: Take the level of dividends, say, 10 years ago, and the level that's being paid today. Presumably, dividends today will be (much) higher than they were 10 years ago, so, using your calculator, find the discount rate that equates the present value of today's dividend to the dividend paid 10 years earlier. When you find that rate, you've found the growth rate. In this case, the discount rate is the average rate of growth in dividends. (See Chapter 4 for a detailed discussion of how to calculate growth rates.) Finding the appropriate growth rate, *g*, is a critical element in the DVM. Accordingly, we'll examine another method for finding the growth rate later in this chapter. For now, we will assume that the naïve approach (above) does an adequate job in defining the growth rate, so let's proceed with our illustration of the DVM.

Growth Rate Calculator

Once you've determined the dividend growth rate, you can find next year's dividend, D_1, as $D_0 \times (1 + g)$, where D_0 equals the current dividend. Let's say that in the latest year, Amalgamated Anything paid $2.50 a share in dividends. If you expect those dividends to grow at the rate of 6% a year, you can find next year's dividends as follows: $D_1 = D_0(1 + g) = \$2.50 (1 + 0.06) = \$2.50(1.06) = \$2.65$. The only other information you need is the required rate of return (capitalization rate), *r*. (Note that *r* must be greater than *g* for the constant-growth model to be mathematically operative.)

> Consider a stock that currently pays an annual dividend of $1.75 a share. Suppose that by using the present value approach described above, you find that dividends are growing at a rate of 8% per year, and you expect they will continue to do so. In addition, based on the CAPM, you determine that this investment should carry a required rate of return of 12%. Given this information, you can use Equation 9.8 to value the stock. That is, given $D_0 = \$1.75$, $g = 0.08$, and $r = 0.12$, it follows that
>
> **Example**
>
> $$\frac{\text{Value of a}}{\text{share of stock}} = \frac{D_0(1 + g)}{r - g} = \frac{\$1.75(1.08)}{0.12 - 0.08} = \frac{\$1.89}{0.04} = \$47.25$$
>
> Thus, if you want to earn a 12% return on this investment—made up of 8% in capital gains (*g*), plus 4% in dividend yield (i.e., $1.89 ÷ $47.25 = 0.04)—then according to the constant-growth dividend valuation model, you should pay no more than $47.25 a share for this stock.

With this version of the DVM, the price of the stock will increase over time so long as *r* and *g* don't change. In fact, as we noted earlier, the growth rate (*g*) defines the amount of (expected) capital gains embedded in the future price of the stock. So, if *g* = 8%, then we can expect the future price of the stock to go up around 8% per year.

This will occur because the cash flow from the investment will increase as dividends grow. To see how this happens, let's carry our example a little further. Recall that we determined that $47.25 was an appropriate price for the stock today given that next year's dividend was $1.89, that dividends would grow at 8%, and that the required return was 12%. We can extend Equation 9.8a to estimate the stock's price 1 year from today. To do that, we must first estimate the dividend in year 2. If next year's dividend is $1.89, then the year after that the dividend should increase by 8% to $2.04. Plugging this value into Equation 9.8a, we find that the value of the stock next year should be $51:

$$\$51 = \frac{\$2.04}{0.12 - 0.08}$$

Observe that next year's price of $51 is about 8% higher than this year's price of $47.25. As we stated earlier, in the DVM, g represents not only the growth rate in dividends but also the expected capital gain on the stock. The table below shows that the stock price increases by 8% year after year as long as r and g remain unchanged.

Year	Dividend ($)	Stock Price* ($)
(Current year) 0	1.75	47.25
1	1.89	51.00
2	2.04	55.00
3	2.20	59.50
4	2.38	64.25
5	2.57	69.50

*As determined by the dividend valuation model, given $g = 0.08$, $r = 0.12$.

Just as we can use this version of the DVM to value a stock today, so too can we find the expected price of the stock in the future by using the same valuation model. To do this, we simply redefine the appropriate level of dividends. For example, to find the price of the stock in year 3, we use the expected dividend in the third year, $2.20, and increase it by the factor $(1 + g)$. Thus, the stock price in year 3 should be $D_3 \times (1 + g) \div (r - g) =$ $2.20 \times (1 + 0.08) \div (0.12 - 0.08) = \$2.38 \div 0.04 = \$59.50$. Of course, if future expectations about r or g do change, the future price of the stock will change accordingly. Should that occur, you could use the new information to decide whether to continue to hold the stock.

Variable Growth Although the constant-growth dividend valuation model is an improvement over the zero-growth model, it still has some shortcomings. The most obvious is the fact that it does not allow for changes in expected growth rates. To overcome this problem, we can use a form of the DVM that allows for variable rates of growth over time. Essentially, the variable-growth dividend valuation model calculates a stock price in two stages. In the first stage, dividends grow rapidly, and not necessarily at a single rate. The dividend growth rate can rise or fall during this initial stage. After the initial stage (i.e., in the second stage), the company matures and dividend growth settles down to some long-run, sustainable rate. At that point, it is possible to value the stock using the constant-growth version of the DVM. The variable-growth version of the model finds the value of a share of stock as follows:

Equation 9.9

$$\begin{array}{ccc} \text{Value of a share} \\ \text{of stock} \end{array} = \begin{array}{c} \text{Present value of} \\ \text{future dividends} \\ \text{during the initial} \\ \text{variable-growth period} \end{array} + \begin{array}{c} \text{Present value of the price} \\ \text{of the stock at the end of} \\ \text{the variable-growth period} \end{array}$$

Equation 9.9a

$$V = \frac{D_1}{(1+r)^1} + \frac{D_2}{(1+r)^2} + \cdots \frac{D_v}{(1+r)^v} + \frac{\dfrac{D_v(1+g)}{(r-g)}}{(1+r)^v}$$

where

D_1, D_2, etc. = future annual dividends

v = number of years in the initial variable-growth period

Note that the last element in this equation is the standard constant-growth dividend valuation model, which is used to find the price of the stock at the end of the initial variable-growth period, discounted back v periods.

This form of the DVM is appropriate for companies that are expected to experience rapid or variable rates of growth for a period of time—perhaps for the first 3 to 5 years—and then settle down to a more stable growth rate thereafter. This, in fact, is the growth pattern of many companies, so the model has considerable application in practice. (It also overcomes one of the operational shortcomings of the constant-growth DVM in that r does not have to be greater than g during the initial stage. That is, during the variable-growth period, the rate of growth, g, can be greater than the required rate of return, r, and the model will still be fully operational.)

Finding the value of a stock using Equation 9.9 is actually a lot easier than it looks. To do so, follow these steps:

1. Estimate annual dividends during the initial variable-growth period and then specify the constant rate, g, at which dividends will grow after the initial period.

2. Find the present value of the dividends expected during the initial variable-growth period.

3. Using the constant-growth DVM, find the price of the stock at the end of the initial growth period.

4. Find the present value of the price of the stock (as determined in step 3). Note that the price of the stock is discounted for the same length of time as the last dividend payment in the initial growth period because the stock is being priced (per step 3) at the end of this initial period.

5. Add the 2 present value components (from steps 2 and 4) to find the value of a stock.

Applying the Variable-Growth DVM To see how this works, let's apply the variable-growth model to one of our favorite companies: Sweatmore Industries. Let's assume that dividends will grow at a variable rate for the first 3 years (2013, 2014, and 2015). After that, the annual rate of growth in dividends is expected to settle down to 8% and stay there for the foreseeable future. Starting with the latest (2012) annual dividend of

TABLE 9.4	USING THE VARIABLE-GROWTH DVM TO VALUE SWEATMORE STOCK	EXCEL with Spreadsheets

Step

1. Projected annual dividends:

	2013	$2.65
	2014	3.08
	2015	3.48

Estimated annual rate of growth in dividends, g, for 2016 and beyond: 8%

2. Present value of dividends, using a required rate of return, r, of 14%, during the initial variable-growth period:

Year	Dividends ($)	Present Value ($)
2013	2.65	2.32
2014	3.08	2.37
2015	3.48	2.35
	Total	$7.04 (to step 5)

3. Price of the stock at the end of the initial growth period:

$$P_{2015} = \frac{D_{2016}}{r - g} = \frac{D_{2015} \times (1 - g)}{r - g} = \frac{\$3.48 \times (1.08)}{0.14 - 0.08} = \frac{\$3.76}{0.06} = \underline{\$62.67}$$

4. Discount the price of the stock (as computed above) back to its present value, at r, of 14%:

$$\$62.67 \div (1.14)^3 = \$42.30 \text{ (to step 5)}$$

5. Add the present value of the initial dividend stream (step 2) to the present value of the price of the stock at the end of the initial growth period (step 4):

Value of Sweatmore stock: $7.04 + $4.30 = \underline{\$49.34}$

$2.21 a share, we estimate that Sweatmore's dividends should grow by 20% next year (in 2013), by 16% in 2014, and then by 13% in 2015 before dropping to an 8% rate.

Using these (initial) growth rates, we project that dividends in 2013 will amount to $2.65 a share ($2.21 × 1.20), and will rise to $3.08 ($2.65 × 1.16) in 2014 and to $3.48 ($3.08 × 1.13) in 2015. In addition, using CAPM, we figure that Sweatmore's stock should produce a minimum (required) rate of return (r) of at least 14%. We now have all the input we need and are ready to put a value on Sweatmore Industries. Table 9.4 shows the variable-growth DVM in action. The value of Sweatmore stock, according to the variable-growth DVM, is just under $49.34 a share. In essence, that's the maximum price you should be willing to pay for the stock if you want to earn a 14% rate of return.

Defining the Expected Growth Rate Mechanically, application of the DVM is really quite simple. It relies on just 3 key pieces of information: future dividends, future growth in dividends, and a required rate of return. But this model is not without its difficulties. One of the most difficult (and most important) aspects of the DVM is specifying the appropriate growth rate, g, over an extended period of time. Whether you are using the constant-growth or the variable-growth version of the dividend valuation model, the growth rate, g, has an enormous impact on the value derived from the model. Indeed, the DVM is very sensitive to the growth rate being used because that rate affects both the model's numerator and its denominator. As a result, in practice analysts spend a good deal of time trying to come up with a growth rate, *g*, for a given company and its stock.

As we saw earlier in this chapter, we can define the growth rate from a strictly historical perspective (by using present value to find the past rate of growth) and then use it (or something close) in the DVM. While that approach might work in some cases, it does have some serious shortcomings. What's needed is a procedure that looks at the key forces that actually drive the growth rate. Fortunately, we have such an approach, one that's widely used in practice; it defines the growth rate, *g*, as follows:

Equation 9.10 $g = \text{ROE} \times \text{The firm's retention rate}, rr$

where

Equation 9.10a $rr = 1 - \text{Dividend payout ratio}$

Both variables in Equation 9.10 (ROE and *rr*) are directly related to the firm's rate of growth, and both play key roles in defining a firm's future growth. The retention rate represents the percentage of its profits that the firm plows back into the company. Thus, if the firm pays out 35% of its earnings in dividends (i.e., it has a dividend payout ratio of 35%), then it has a retention rate of 65%: $rr = 1 - 0.35 = 0.65$. The retention rate, in effect, indicates the amount of capital that is flowing back into the company to finance growth. Other things being equal, the more money being retained in the company, the higher the growth rate.

The other component of Equation 9.10 is the familiar return on equity (ROE). Clearly, the more the company can earn on its retained capital, the higher the growth rate. Remember that ROE is made up of the net profit margin, total asset turnover, and equity multiplier (see Equation 7.13, page 273), so if you want to get a handle on how ROE is impacting the firm's growth rate, look to those 3 components.

Example

Consider a situation where a company retains, on average, about 80% of its earnings and generates an ROE of around 18%. (Driving the firm's ROE is a net profit margin of 7.5%, a total asset turnover of 1.20, and an equity multiplier of 2.0.) Under these circumstances, we would expect the firm to have a growth rate of around 14.5%:

$$g = \text{ROE} \times rr = 0.18 \times 0.80 = 14.4\%$$

Actually, the growth rate will probably be a bit more than 14.5%, because Equation 9.10 ignores financial leverage, which in itself will magnify growth. But at least the equation gives you a good idea of what to expect. Similarly, Equation 9.10 can serve as a starting point in assessing past and future growth. You can use it to compute expected growth and then assess the 2 key components of the formula (ROE and *rr*) to see whether they're likely to undergo major changes in the future. If so, then what impact is the change in ROE or *rr* likely to have on the growth rate, *g*? The idea is to take the time to study the forces (ROE and *rr*) that drive the growth rate because the DVM itself is so sensitive to the rate of growth being used. Employ a growth rate that's too high and you'll end up with an intrinsic value that's way too high also. The downside, of course, is that you may end up buying a stock that you really shouldn't.

Other Approaches to Stock Valuation

In addition to the DVM, the market has developed other ways of valuing stock. Some are simply variations of the DVM, while others are alternatives to it. One motivation for using these approaches is to find techniques that allow investors to estimate the values of non-dividend-paying stocks. In addition, for a variety of reasons, some investors prefer to use procedures that don't rely on corporate earnings as the basis of valuation. For these investors, it's not earnings that matter, but instead things like cash flow, sales, or book value.

One valuation procedure that is popular with many investors is the so-called *dividends-and-earnings approach*, which directly uses future dividends and the future selling price of the stock as the relevant cash flows. Another is the *P/E approach*, which builds the stock valuation process around the stock's price-to-earnings ratio. One of the major advantages of these procedures is that they don't rely on dividends as the only input. Accordingly, investors can use these methods to value stocks that are more growth-oriented and that pay little or nothing in dividends. Let's take a closer look at both of these approaches, as well as a technique that arrives at the expected return on the stock (in percentage terms) rather than a (dollar-based) "justified price."

A Dividends-and-Earnings Approach As we saw earlier, the value of a share of stock is a function of the amount and timing of future cash flows and the level of risk that must be taken on to generate that return. The **dividends-and-earnings (D&E) approach** (also known as the *discounted cash flow*, or *DCF*, *approach*) conveniently captures the essential elements of expected risk and return and does so in a present value context. The model is as follows:

Equation 9.11

$$\text{Value of a share of stock} = \text{Present value of future dividends} + \text{Present value of the price of the stock at the date of sale}$$

Equation 9.11a

$$V = \frac{D_1}{(1 + r)^1} + \frac{D_2}{(1 + r)^2} + \cdots + \frac{D_N}{(1 + r)^N} + \frac{SP_N}{(1 + r)^N}$$

where

D_t = future annual dividend in year t
SP_N = estimated share price of the stock at date of sale, year N
N = number of years in the investment horizon

Note the similarities here to the variable-growth DVM. Equation 9.11a is present value–based, and its value is derived from future dividends and the expected future price of the stock. The big difference between the two procedures revolves around the role that dividends play in determining the future price of the stock. That is, the D&E approach does not estimate the future price of the stock by calculating the present value of a dividend stream that is growing at a constant rate. Instead, the D&E estimates the future stock price by multiplying future earnings times a P/E ratio. Because the D&E calculation does not require a long-run estimate of a stock's dividend stream, it works just as well with companies that pay little or nothing in dividends as it does with stocks that pay out a lot in dividends. Thus, the D&E approach is more flexible than the DVM. Using the D&E valuation approach, we focus on projecting future dividends and share price behavior over a defined, finite investment horizon, much as we did for Universal Office Furnishings in Table 9.3 (on page 301).

Especially important in the D&E approach is finding a viable P/E multiple that you can use to project the future price of the stock. This is a critical part of this valuation process because of the major role that capital gains (and therefore the estimated price of the stock at its date of sale) play in defining the level of security returns. Using market or industry P/E ratios as benchmarks, you should establish a multiple that you feel the stock will trade at in the future. Like the growth rate, g, in the DVM, the P/E multiple is the most important (and most difficult) variable to project in the D&E approach.

Using this input, along with estimated future dividends and earnings per share, this present value–based model generates a justified price based on estimated returns. This value represents the price you should be willing to pay for the stock, given its expected dividend and price behavior and assuming you want to generate a return that is equal to or greater than your required rate of return.

Example

To see how this procedure works, consider once again the case of Universal Office Furnishings. Let's return to our original 3-year investment horizon. Given the forecasted annual dividends and share price from Table 9.3, along with a required rate of return of 18% (as computed earlier using Equation 9.6 on page 302), we can see that the value of Universal's stock is

$$V = \frac{\$0.18}{1.18} + \frac{\$0.24}{1.18^2} + \frac{\$0.28}{1.18^3} + \frac{\$93.20}{1.18^3} = \$0.15 + \$0.17 + \$0.17 + \$56.72 = \$57.22$$

According to the D&E approach, Universal's stock should be valued at about $57 a share. That assumes, of course, that our projections hold up—particularly with regard to our forecasted EPS and P/E multiple in 2016. For example, if the P/E drops from 20 to 17 times earnings, then the value of a share of stock will drop to less than $50 (to around $48.75/share). Given that we have confidence in our projections, the present value figure computed here means that we would realize our desired rate of return of 18% so long as we can buy the stock at no more than $57 a share. Because UVRS is currently trading around $41.50, we can conclude that the stock at present is an attractive investment. That is, because we can buy the stock at less than its computed intrinsic value, we'll be able to earn our required rate of return, and then some.

Note that by most standards, Universal would be considered a highly risky investment, if for no other reason than the fact that nearly all the return is derived from capital gains. Indeed, dividends alone account for less than 1% of the value of the stock. That is, only 49 cents of the $57.22 comes from dividends. Clearly, if we're wrong about EPS or the P/E multiple, the future price of the stock in 2013 could be way off the mark, and so, too, would our projected return.

Actually, the D&E approach to stock valuation is really a variation of the DVM model. That is, regardless of what holding period you use in the D&E approach, the computed value will be the same as that obtained with the constant-growth (or even variable-growth) DVM, so long as the input assumptions regarding g and D_0 are the same. Need proof? Consider the constant-growth DVM example we used earlier (see Example on page 308). Recall that we used a stock that had a current annual dividend (D_0) of $1.75 a share, a growth rate (g) of 8%, and a required return (r) of 12%. Let's use this same stock, with the same assumptions, but this time we'll use the D&E approach to value the stock, assuming a 3-year investment horizon. Under these conditions, with an 8% growth rate, dividends would grow to $1.89 next year ($1.75 × 1.08), $2.04 in the second year, and $2.20 a share in year 3. Also, at an 8% appreciation rate, the price of the stock would go up to $59.50 by the end of year 3. Using this information in the D&E model, the value of the stock would be:

$$Value = \frac{\$1.89}{1.12^1} + \frac{\$2.04}{1.12^2} + \frac{\$2.20}{1.12^3} + \frac{\$59.50}{1.12^3} = \$1.69 + \$1.63 + \$1.56 + \$42.35 = \$47.23$$

Note that we end up with the same value here as we did using the DVM (see page 308). So no matter what holding period or which procedure we use, D&E or DVM, so long as the input assumptions are the same, the computed share values will be the same.

Finding the Value of Non–Dividend-Paying Stocks

What about the value of a stock that does not pay dividends—and is not expected to do so for the foreseeable future? That's not a problem with the D&E approach. Using Equation 9.11, simply set all dividends to 0, so the computed value of the stock would come solely from its projected future price. In other words, the value of the stock will equal the present value of its price at the end of the holding period.

Input	Function
70	FV
2	N
15	I
	CPT
	PV

Solution
-52.93

Consider, for example, an investor who's looking at a stock that pays no dividends; she estimates that at the end of a 2-year holding period, this stock should be trading at around $70 a share. Using a 15% required rate of return, this stock would have a present value of $70 ÷ 1.15^2 = $52.93. This value is, of course, the intrinsic value, or justified price of the stock. So long as it's trading for around $53 or less, it would be a worthwhile investment candidate. (*Note:* As shown at the left, you can just as easily use a calculator to find the value of this stock.)

Determining Expected Return

Sometimes investors find it more convenient to deal in terms of expected return than a dollar-based justified price. This is no problem, nor is it necessary to sacrifice the present value dimension of the stock valuation model to achieve such an end. You can find the expected return by using the (present-value–based) internal rate of return (IRR) procedure in Chapter 10. This approach to stock valuation uses forecasted dividend and price behavior, along with the current market price, to arrive at the fully compounded rate of return you can expect to earn from a given investment.

To see how a stock's expected return is computed, look once again at Universal Office Furnishings. Using 2014–2016 data from Table 9.3 (on page 301), along with the stock's current price of $41.58, you can determine Universal's expected return. To do so, you must find the discount rate that equates the future stream of benefits (i.e., the future annual dividends and future price of the stock) to the stock's current market price. In other words, find the discount rate that produces a present value of future benefits equal to the price of the stock, and you have the IRR, or expected return on that stock.

Here's how it works. From the Universal example, you know that the stock is expected to pay per-share dividends of $0.18, $0.24, and $0.28 over the next 3 years. At the end of that time, you hope to sell the stock for $93.20. Given that the stock is currently trading at $41.58, you're looking for the discount rate, r, that will produce a present value (of the future annual dividends and stock price) equal to $41.58. That is,

$$\frac{\$0.18}{(1 + r)^1} + \frac{\$0.24}{(1 + r)^2} + \frac{\$0.28}{(1 + r)^3} + \frac{\$93.20}{(1 + r)^3} = \$41.58$$

You need to solve for the discount rate (the present value interest factors) in this equation. Through a process of "hit and miss" (or with the help of a spreadsheet or calculator), you'll find that with an interest factor of 31.3%, the present value of the future cash benefits from this investment will equal exactly $41.58. That, of course, is your expected return. Thus, you can expect Universal to earn a fully compounded annual return of about 31%, assuming that you buy the stock at $41.58, hold it for 3 years (during which time you receive the indicated annual dividends), and then sell it for $93.20 at the end of the 3-year period. When compared to its 18% required rate of return, the 31.3% expected return makes Universal look like a very attractive investment candidate.

It's even easier to determine the return on stocks that don't pay dividends. Just find the discount rate that equates the projected future price of the stock to its current share price. For example, if Universal didn't pay dividends, then all we'd have to do is find the discount rate that equates the projected share price of $93.20 (3 years from now) to the stock's current price of $41.58. Using a calculator as shown at the left, we arrive at an expected rate of return of about 30.9%. Given the return of 31.3% with dividends versus the 30.9% without, the cash flow from dividends clearly doesn't play much of a role in defining the potential return on this stock.

Input	Function
−41.58	PV
93.20	FV
3	N
	CPT
	I

Solution
30.87

The Price-to-Earnings (P/E) Approach One of the problems with the stock valuation procedures we've looked at so far is that they are fairly mechanical. They involve a good deal of "number crunching." Although such approaches are fine with some stocks, they do not work well with others. Fortunately, there is a more intuitive approach. That alternative is the **price-to-earnings (P/E) approach** to stock valuation.

The P/E approach is a favorite of professional security analysts and is widely used in practice. It's relatively simple to use; it's based on the standard P/E formula. There we showed that a stock's P/E ratio is equal to its market price divided by the stock's EPS. Using this equation and solving for the market price of the stock, we have

Equation 9.12   Stock price = EPS × P/E ratio

Equation 9.12 basically captures the P/E approach to stock valuation. That is, given an estimated EPS figure, you decide on a P/E ratio that you feel is appropriate for the stock. Then you use it in Equation 9.12 to see what kind of price you come up with and how that compares to the stock's current price.

Actually, this approach is no different from what's used in the market every day. Look at the stock quotes in the *Wall Street Journal* or online at Yahoo! Finance. They include the stock's P/E ratio and show what investors are willing to pay for 1 dollar of earnings. Essentially, this ratio relates the company's earnings per share for the last 12 months (known as *trailing earnings*) to the latest price of the stock. In practice, however, investors buy stocks not for their past earnings but for their expected future earnings. Thus, in Equation 9.12, it's customary to use forecasted EPS for next year—that is, to use projected earnings 1 year out.

The first thing you have to do to implement the P/E approach is to come up with an expected EPS figure for next year. In the early part of this chapter, we saw how this might be done (see, for instance, Equations 9.2 and 9.3 on pages 297 and 298). Given the forecasted EPS, the next step is to evaluate the variables that drive the P/E ratio. Most of that assessment is intuitive. For example, you might look at the stock's expected rate of growth in earnings, any potential major changes in the firm's capital structure or dividends, and any other factors such as relative market or industry P/E multiples that might affect the stock's multiple. You could use such inputs to come up with a base P/E ratio. Then adjust that base, as necessary, to account for the perceived state of the market and/or anticipated changes in the rate of inflation.

Along with estimated EPS, we now have the P/E ratio we need to compute (via Equation 9.12) the price at which the stock should be trading. Take, for example, a stock that's currently trading at $37.80. One year from now, it's estimated that this stock should have an EPS of $2.25 a share. If you feel that the stock should be trading at a P/E ratio of 20 times projected earnings, then it should be valued at $45 a share (i.e., $2.25 × 20). By comparing this targeted price to the current market price of the stock, you can decide whether the stock is a good buy. In this case, you would consider the stock undervalued and therefore a good buy, since the computed price of the stock of $45 is more than its market price of $37.80.

While this is the principal application of the P/E approach, you'll find that a variation of this procedure is also used with the D&E and IRR approaches. That is, by using estimated figures for both EPS and the P/E multiple, you can come up with the share price that's expected to prevail at the end of a given investment horizon. Throw in any dividends that may be received, discount that cash flow (of dividends and future share price) back to the present, and you have either the justified price, as in the D&E approach, or the expected rate of return, as in the IRR approach.

Other Price-Relative Procedures

As we saw with the P/E approach, price-relative procedures base their valuations on the assumptions that the value of a share of stock should be directly linked to a given performance characteristic of the firm, such as earnings per share. These procedures involve a good deal of judgment and intuition, and they rely heavily on the market expertise of the analysts. Besides the P/E approach, there are several other price-relative procedures that are used by investors who, for one reason or another, want to use some measure other than earnings to value stocks. They include:

- The price-to-cash-flow (P/CF) ratio

- The price-to-sales (P/S) ratio

- The price-to-book-value (P/BV) ratio

Like the P/E multiple, these procedures determine the value of a stock by relating share price to cash flow, sales, or book value. Let's look at each of these in turn to see how they're used in stock valuation.

A Price-to-Cash-Flow (P/CF) Procedure This measure has long been popular with investors who believe that cash flow provides a more accurate picture of a company's true value than do net earnings. When used in stock valuation, the procedure is almost identical to the P/E approach. That is, analysts use a P/CF ratio along with projected cash flow per share to estimate the stock's value.

Although it is quite straightforward, this procedure nonetheless has one problem—defining the appropriate cash flow measure. While some investors use cash flow from operating activities, as obtained from the statement of cash flows, others use *free cash flow*. The one measure that seems to be the most popular with professional analysts is EBITDA (earnings before interest, taxes, depreciation, and amortization), which we'll use here. EBITDA represents "cash earnings" to the extent that the major noncash expenditures (depreciation and amortization) are added back to operating earnings (EBIT).

The price-to-cash-flow ratio is computed as follows:

Equation 9.13
$$\text{P/CF ratio} = \frac{\text{Market price of common stock}}{\text{Cash flow per share}}$$

where cash flow per share = EBITDA ÷ number of common shares outstanding.

Before you can use the P/CF procedure to assess the current market price of a stock, you first have to come up with a forecasted cash flow per share 1 year out and then define an appropriate P/CF multiple to use. For most firms, it is very likely that the cash flow (EBITDA) figure will be larger than net earnings available to stockholders. As a result, the cash flow multiple will probably be lower than the P/E multiple. In any event, once you determine an appropriate P/CF multiple (subjectively and with the help of any historical market information), simply multiply it by the expected cash flow per share 1 year from now to find the price at which the stock should be trading. That is, the computed price of a share of stock = cash flow per share × P/CF ratio.

Example

Assume a company currently is generating an EBITDA of $325 million, which is expected to increase by some 12% to around $364 million ($325 million × 1.12) over the course of the next 12 months. Suppose the company has 5.6 million shares of stock outstanding. On a per-share basis, the company's projected cash flow per share is $6.50. If we feel this stock should be trading at about 8 times its projected cash flow per share, then it should be valued at around $52 a share. Thus, if it is currently trading in the market at $45.50 (or at 7 times its projected cash flow per share), we can conclude, once again, that the stock is undervalued and, therefore, should be considered a viable investment candidate.

Price-to-Sales (P/S) and Price-to-Book-Value (P/BV) Ratios Some companies, like high-tech startups, have little, if any, earnings. Or if they do have earnings, they tend to be quite volatile and therefore highly unpredictable. In these cases, valuation procedures based on earnings (and even cash flows) aren't much help. So investors turn to other procedures—those based on sales or book value, for example. While companies may not have much in the way of profits, they almost always have sales and, ideally, some book value. *Book value* is simply another term for equity, or net worth.

Investors use the P/S and P/BV ratios exactly like the P/E and P/CF procedures. We defined the P/BV ratio as follows:

$$\text{P/BV ratio} = \frac{\text{Market price of common stock}}{\text{Book value per share}}$$

We can define the P/S ratio in a similar fashion:

Equation 9.14

$$\text{P/S ratio} = \frac{\text{Market price of common stock}}{\text{Sales per share}}$$

where sales per share equals net annual sales (or revenues) divided by the number of common shares outstanding.

INVESTOR FACTS

Fender Tender—In July 2012 Fender Musical Instruments Corp., the famous guitar maker, announced its intention to go public in an IPO that would value the company at almost $400 million. At the time, the company's revenues were roughly $700 million, which implied that Fender's P/S ratio was 1.75, a very low multiple compared to the high-flying tech companies that tend to dominate the IPO market.

INVESTOR MISTAKES

Short-Lived Growth—So-called value stocks are stocks that have low price-to-book ratios, and growth stocks are stocks that have relatively high price-to-book ratios. Many studies demonstrate that value stocks outperform growth stocks, perhaps because investors overestimate the odds that a firm that has grown rapidly in the past will continue to do so.

Many bargain-hunting investors look for stocks with P/S ratios of 2.0 or less. They believe that these securities offer the most potential for future price appreciation. Especially attractive to these investors are very low P/S multiples of 1.0 or less. Think about it: With a P/S ratio of, say, 0.9, you can buy $1 in sales for only 90 cents! So long as the company isn't a basket case, such low P/S multiples may well be worth pursuing.

Keep in mind that while the emphasis may be on low multiples, high P/S ratios aren't necessarily bad. To determine if a high multiple—more than 3.0 or 4.0, for example—is justified, look at the company's net profit margin. Companies that can consistently generate high net profit margins often have high P/S ratios. Here's a valuation rule to remember: High profit margins should go hand-in-hand with high P/S multiples. That makes sense, too, because a company with a high profit margin brings more of its sales down to the bottom line in the form of profits.

You would also expect the price-to-book-value measure to be low, but probably not as low as the P/S ratio. Indeed, unless the market becomes grossly overvalued (think about what happened in 1999 and 2000), most stocks are likely to trade at multiples of less than 3 to 5 times their book values. And in this case, unlike with the P/S multiple, there's usually little justification for abnormally high price-to-book-value ratios—except perhaps for firms that have abnormally low levels of equity in their capital structures. Other than that, high P/BV multiples are almost always caused by "excess exuberance." As a rule, when stocks start trading at 7 or 8 times their book values, or more, they are becoming overvalued.

CONCEPTS IN REVIEW

Answers available at www.pearsonhighered.com/smart

9.6 Briefly describe the dividend valuation model and the three versions of this model. Explain how CAPM fits into the DVM.

9.7 What is the difference between the variable-growth dividend valuation model and the dividends-and-earnings approach to stock valuation? Which procedure would work better if you were trying to value a growth stock that pays little or no dividends? Explain.

9.8 How would you go about finding the expected return on a stock? Note how such information would be used in the stock selection process.

9.9 Briefly describe the P/E approach to stock valuation and note how this approach differs from the variable-growth DVM. Describe the P/CF approach and note how it is used in the stock valuation process. Compare the P/CF approach to the P/E approach, noting the relative strengths and weaknesses of each.

9.10 Briefly describe the price-to-sales ratio and explain how it is used to value stocks. Why not just use the P/E multiple? How does the P/S ratio differ from the P/BV measure?

MyFinanceLab

Here is what you should know after reading this chapter. MyFinanceLab will help you identify what you know and where to go when you need to practice.

What You Should Know	Key Terms	Where to Practice
LG1 **Explain the role that a company's future plays in the stock valuation process.** The final phase of security analysis involves an assessment of the investment merits of a specific company and its stock. The focus here is on formulating expectations about the company's prospects and the risk and return behavior of the stock. In particular, we would want some idea of the stock's future earnings, dividends, and share prices, which are ultimately the basis of return.	common-size income statement, *p. 293* relative P/E multiple, *p. 297* stock valuation, *p. 293* target price, *p. 299*	MyFinanceLab Study Plan 9.1 Excel Table 9.1
LG2 **Develop a forecast of a stock's expected cash flow, starting with corporate sales and earnings, and then moving to expected dividends and share price.** Because the value of a share of stock is a function of its future returns, investors must try to formulate expectations about what the future holds for the company. Look first at the company's projected sales and earnings, and then translate those data into forecasted dividends and share prices. These variables define an investment's future cash flow and, therefore, investor returns.	valuation, *p. 302*	MyFinanceLab Study Plan 9.2 Excel Table 9.3
LG3 **Discuss the concepts of intrinsic value and required rates of return, and note how they are used.** Information such as projected sales, forecasted earnings, and estimated dividends are important in establishing intrinsic value. This is a measure, based on expected return and risk exposure, of what the stock ought to be worth. A key element is the investor's required rate of return, which is used to define the amount of return that should be earned given the stock's perceived exposure to risk.	required rate of return, *p. 302*	MyFinanceLab Study Plan 9.3 Video Learning Aid for Problem P9.18
LG4 **Determine the underlying value of a stock using the zero-growth, constant-growth, and variable-growth dividend valuation models.** The dividend valuation model (DVM) derives the value of a share of stock from the stock's future growth in dividends. There are 3 versions of the DVM. Zero-growth valuation assumes that dividends are fixed and won't change. Constant-growth valuation assumes that dividends will grow at a constant rate into the future. Variable-growth valuation assumes that dividends will initially grow at varying (or abnormally high) rates before eventually settling down to a constant rate of growth.	dividend valuation model (DVM), *p. 305*	MyFinanceLab Study Plan 9.4 Excel Table 9.4 Video Learning Aid for Problem P9.9

What You Should Know	Key Terms	Where to Practice
LG5 Use other types of present value–based models to derive the value of a stock, as well as alternative price-relative procedures. The DVM works well with some types of stocks but not so well with others. Investors may turn to other stock-valuation approaches, including the D&E and IRR approaches, as well as certain price-relative procedures, like the P/E, P/CF, P/S, and P/BV methods. The dividends-and-earnings approach uses a finite investment horizon to derive a present value–based "justified price." Or investors can determine the expected return on a stock (via IRR) by finding the discount rate that equates the stock's future cash flows to its current market price. Several price-relative procedures exist as well, such as the price-to-earnings approach, which uses projected EPS and the stock's P/E ratio to determine whether a stock is fairly valued.	dividends-and-earnings (D&E) approach, *p. 313* price-to-earnings (P/E) approach, *p. 316*	MyFinanceLab Study Plan 9.5 Video Learning Aid for Problem P9.18
LG6 Gain a basic appreciation of the procedures used to value different types of stocks, from traditional dividend-paying shares to more growth-oriented stocks. All sorts of stock valuation models are used in the market; this chapter examined 9 widely used procedures. One thing that becomes apparent in stock evaluation is that one approach definitely does not fit all situations. Some approaches (like the DVM) work well with mature, dividend-paying companies. Others (like the D&E, IRR, P/E, and P/CF approaches) are more suited to growth-oriented firms, which may not pay dividends. Other price-relative procedures (like P/S and P/BV) are often used to value companies that have little or nothing in earnings or whose earnings records are sporadic.		MyFinanceLab Study Plan 9.6

Log into MyFinanceLab, take a chapter test, and get a personalized study plan
that tells you which concepts you understand and which ones you need to
review. From there, MyFinanceLab will give you further practice, tutorials,
animations, videos, and guided solutions.
Log into **www.myfinancelab.com**

Discussion Questions

LG1 Q9.1 Using the resources available at your campus or public library, select a company from *Value Line* that would be of interest to you. (*Hint*: Pick a company that's been publicly traded for at least 10 years and avoid public utilities, banks, and other financial institutions.) Obtain a copy of the latest *Value Line* report on your chosen company. Using the historical and forecasted data reported in *Value Line*, along with one of the valuation techniques described in this chapter, calculate the maximum (i.e., justified) price you'd be willing to pay for this stock. Use the CAPM to find the required rate of return on your stock. (For this problem, use a market rate of return of 12%, and for the risk-free rate, use the latest 3-month Treasury bill rate.)

a. How does the justified price you computed compare to the latest market price of the stock?

b. Would you consider this stock to be a worthwhile investment candidate? Explain.

LG5 LG6 Q9.2 In this chapter, we examined 9 stock valuation procedures:
- Zero-growth DVM
- Constant-growth DVM
- Variable-growth DVM
- Dividends-and-earnings (D&E) approach
- Expected return (IRR) approach
- P/E approach
- Price-to-cash-flow ratio
- Price-to-sales ratio
- Price-to-book-value ratio

a. Which one (or more) of these procedures would be appropriate when trying to put a value on:

1. A growth stock that pays little or nothing in dividends?

2. The S&P 500?

3. A relatively new company that has only a brief history of earnings?

4. A large, mature, dividend-paying company?

5. A preferred stock that pays a fixed dividend?

6. A company that has a large amount of depreciation and amortization?

b. Of the 9 procedures listed above, which 3 do you think are the best? Explain.

c. If you had to choose just one procedure to use in practice, which would it be? Explain. (*Note:* Confine your selection to the list above.)

LG1 LG3 Q9.3 Explain the role that the future plays in the stock valuation process. Why not just base the valuation on historical information? Explain how the intrinsic value of a stock is related to its required rate of return. Illustrate what happens to the value of a stock when the required rate of return increases.

LG4 Q9.4 Assume an investor uses the constant-growth DVM to value a stock. Listed below are various situations that could affect the computed value of a stock. Look at each one of these individually and indicate whether it would cause the computed value of a stock to go up, go down, or stay the same. Briefly explain your answers.

a. Dividend payout ratio goes up.

b. Stock's beta rises.

c. Equity multiplier goes down.

d. T-bill rates fall.

e. Net profit margin goes up.

f. Total asset turnover falls.

g. Market return increases.

Assume throughout that the current dividend (D_0) remains the same and that all other variables in the model are unchanged.

Problems

LG2 **P9.1** An investor estimates that next year's sales for Dursley's Hotels Inc. should amount to about $100 million. The company has 5.0 million shares outstanding, generates a net profit margin of about 10%, and has a payout ratio of 50%. All figures are expected to hold for next year. Given this information, compute the following.
  a. Estimated net earnings for next year
  b. Next year's dividends per share
  c. The expected price of the stock (assuming the P/E ratio is 24.5 times earnings)
  d. The expected holding period return (latest stock price: $40 per share)

LG2 **P9.2** GrowthCo had sales of $55 million in 2011 and is expected to have sales of $83,650,000 for 2014. The company's net profit margin was 5% in 2011 and is expected to increase to 8% by 2014. Estimate the company's net profit for 2014.

LG2 **P9.3** Granger Toothpaste Corp. has total equity of $400 million and 100 million shares outstanding. Its ROE is 20%. Calculate the company's EPS.

LG2 **P9.4** Goodstuff Corporation has total equity of $500 million and 100 million shares outstanding. Its ROE is 15%. The dividend payout ratio is 33.3%. Calculate the company's dividends per share (round to the nearest penny).

LG2 **P9.5** HighTeck has an ROE of 15%. Its earnings per share are $2.00, and its dividends per share are $0.20. Estimate HighTeck's growth rate.

LG2 **P9.6** Last year, InDebt Company paid $75 million of interest expense, and its average rate of interest for the year was 10%. The company's ROE is 15%, and it pays no dividends. Estimate next year's interest expense assuming that interest rates will fall by 25% and the company keeps a constant equity multiplier of 20%.

LG2 **P9.7** Melissa Popp is thinking about buying some shares of R. H. Lawncare Equipment, at $48 per share. She expects the price of the stock to rise to $60 over the next 3 years. During that time she also expects to receive annual dividends of $4 per share.
  a. What is the intrinsic worth of this stock, given a 12% required rate of return?
  b. What is its expected return?

LG4 **P9.8** Amalgamated Aircraft Parts, Inc., is expected to pays a dividend of $1.50 in the coming year. The required rate of return is 16%, and dividends are expected to grow at 7% per year. Using the dividend valuation model, find the intrinsic value of the company's common shares.

LG4 **P9.9** Danny is considering a stock purchase. The stock pays a constant annual dividend of $2.00 per share and is currently trading at $20. Danny's required rate of return for this stock is 12%. Should he buy this stock?

LG4 **LG5** **P9.10** Larry, Moe, and Curley are brothers. They're all serious investors, but each has a different approach to valuing stocks. Larry, the oldest, likes to use a 1-year holding period to value common shares. Moe, the middle brother, likes to use multiyear holding periods. Curley, the youngest of the three, prefers the dividend valuation model.
  As it turns out, right now, all three of them are looking at the same stock—American Home Care Products, Inc. (AHCP). The company has been listed on the NYSE for over 50 years and is

widely regarded as a mature, rock-solid, dividend-paying stock. The brothers have gathered the following information about AHCP's stock:

Current dividend (D_0) = $2.50/share

Expected growth rate (g) = 9.0%

Required rate of return (r) = 12.0%

All of them agree that these variables are appropriate, and they will use them in valuing the stock. Larry and Moe intend to use the D&E approach; Curley is going to use the constant-growth DVM. Larry will use a 1-year holding period; he estimates that with a 9% growth rate, the price of the stock will increase to $98.80 by the end of the year. Moe will use a 3-year holding period; with the same 9% growth rate, he projects the future price of the stock will be $117.40 by the end of his investment horizon. Curley will use the constant-growth DVM, so his holding period isn't needed.

    a. Use the information provided above to value the stocks first for Larry, then for Moe, and then for Curley.

    b. Comment on your findings. Which approach seems to make the most sense?

LG5   **P9.11** Assume you've generated the following information about the stock of Bufford's Burger Barns: The company's latest dividends of $4 a share are expected to grow to $4.32 next year, to $4.67 the year after that, and to $5.04 in year 3. In addition, the price of the stock is expected to rise from $56.50 (its current price) to $77.75 in 3 years.

    a. Use the dividends-and-earnings model and a required return of 15% to find the value of the stock.

    b. Use the IRR procedure to find the stock's expected return.

    c. Given that dividends are expected to grow indefinitely at 8%, use a 15% required rate of return and the dividend valuation model to find the value of the stock.

    d. Assume dividends in year 3 actually amount to $5.04, the dividend growth rate stays at 8%, and the required rate of return stays at 15%. Use the dividend valuation model to find the price of the stock at the end of year 3. [*Hint:* In this case, the value of the stock will depend on dividends in year 4, which equal $D_3 \times (1 + g)$.] Do you note any similarity between your answer here and the forecasted price of the stock ($77.75) given in the problem? Explain.

LG6   **P9.12** Let's assume that you're thinking about buying stock in West Coast Electronics. So far in your analysis, you've uncovered the following information: The stock pays annual dividends of $2.50 a share (and that's not expected to change within the next few years—nor are any of the other variables). It trades at a P/E of 18 times earnings and has a beta of 1.15. In addition, you plan on using a risk-free rate of 7% in the CAPM, along with a market return of 14%. You would like to hold the stock for 3 years, at the end of which time you think EPS will peak at about $7 a share. Given that the stock currently trades at $70, use the IRR approach to find this security's expected return. Now use the present value (dividends-and-earnings) model to put a price on this stock. Does this look like a good investment to you? Explain.

LG6   **P9.13** The price of Myrtle's Plumbing Supply Co. is now $80. The company pays no dividends. Ms. Bossard expects the price 4 years from now to be $110 per share. Should she buy Myrtle's Plumbing stock if she desires a 10% rate of return? Explain.

LG5   **P9.14** This year, Shoreline Light and Gas (SL&G) paid its stockholders an annual dividend of $3 a share. A major brokerage firm recently put out a report on SL&G stating that, in its opinion, the company's annual dividends should grow at the rate of 10% per year for each of the next 5 years and then level off and grow at the rate of 6% a year thereafter.

    a. Use the variable-growth DVM and a required rate of return of 12% to find the maximum price you should be willing to pay for this stock.

    b. Redo the SL&G problem in part **a**, this time assuming that after year 5, dividends stop growing altogether (for year 6 and beyond, $g = 0$). Use all the other information given to find the stock's intrinsic value.

    c. Contrast your two answers and comment on your findings. How important is growth to this valuation model?

LG5 **P9.15** Assume there are 3 companies that in the past year paid exactly the same annual dividend of $2.25 a share. In addition, the future annual rate of growth in dividends for each of the 3 companies has been estimated as follows:

Buggies-Are-Us	Steady Freddie, Inc.	Gang Buster Group	
$g = 0$	$g = 6\%$	Year 1	$2.53
(i.e., dividends	(for the	2	$2.85
are expected	foreseeable	3	$3.20
to remain at	future)	4	$3.60
$2.25/share)		Year 5 and beyond: $g = 6\%$	

Assume also that as the result of a strange set of circumstances, these 3 companies all have the same required rate of return ($r = 10\%$).

    a. Use the appropriate DVM to value each of these companies.

    b. Comment briefly on the comparative values of these 3 companies. What is the major cause of the differences among these 3 valuations?

LG6 **P9.16** New Millennium Company's stock sells at a P/E ratio of 21 times earnings. It is expected to pay dividends of $2 per share in each of the next 5 years and to generate an EPS of $5 in year 5. Using the dividends-and-earnings model and a 12% discount rate, compute the stock's justified price.

LG6 **P9.17** A particular company currently has sales of $250 million; sales are expected to grow by 20% next year (year 1). For the year after next (year 2), the growth rate in sales is expected to equal 10%. Over each of the next 2 years, the company is expected to have a net profit margin of 8% and a payout ratio of 50% and to maintain the common stock outstanding at 15 million shares. The stock always trades at a P/E of 15 times earnings, and the investor has a required rate of return of 20%. Given this information,

    a. Find the stock's intrinsic value (its justified price).

    b. Use the IRR approach to determine the stock's expected return, given that it is currently trading at $15 per share.

    c. Find the holding period returns for this stock for year 1 and for year 2.

LG3 LG5 **P9.18** Assume a major investment service has just given Oasis Electronics its highest investment rating, along with a strong buy recommendation. As a result, you decide to take a look for yourself and to place a value on the company's stock. Here's what you find: This year Oasis paid its stockholders an annual dividend of $3 a share, but because of its high rate of growth in earnings, its dividends are expected to grow at the rate of 12% a year for the next 4 years and then to level out at 9% a year. So far, you've learned that the stock has a beta of 1.80, the risk-free rate of return is 6%, and the expected return on the market is 11%. Using the CAPM to find the required rate of return, put a value on this stock.

LG5 **P9.19** Consolidated Software doesn't currently pay any dividends but is expected to start doing so in 4 years. That is, Consolidated will go 3 more years without paying dividends and then is expected to pay its first dividend (of $3 per share) in the fourth year. Once the company starts paying dividends, it's expected to continue to do so. The company is expected to have a dividend payout ratio of 40% and to maintain a return on equity of 20%. Based on the DVM, and given a required rate of return of 15%, what is the maximum price you should be willing to pay for this stock today?

LG5   **P9.20** Assume you obtain the following information about a certain company:

Total assets	$50,000,000
Total equity	$25,000,000
Net income	$3,750,000
EPS	$5.00 per share
Dividend payout ratio	40%
Required return	12%

Use the constant-growth DVM to place a value on this company's stock.

LG6   **P9.21** You're thinking about buying some stock in Affiliated Computer Corporation and want to use the P/E approach to value the shares. You've estimated that next year's earnings should come in at about $4.00 a share. In addition, although the stock normally trades at a relative P/E of 1.15 times the market, you believe that the relative P/E will rise to 1.25, whereas the market P/E should be around 18.5 times earnings. Given this information, what is the maximum price you should be willing to pay for this stock? If you buy this stock today at $87.50, what rate of return will you earn over the next 12 months if the price of the stock rises to $110.00 by the end of the year? (Assume that the stock doesn't pay dividends.)

LG5   **P9.22** AviBank Plastics generated an EPS of $2.75 over the last 12 months. The company's earnings are expected to grow by 25% next year, and because there will be no significant change in the number of shares outstanding, EPS should grow at about the same rate. You feel the stock should trade at a P/E of around 30 times earnings. Use the P/E approach to set a value on this stock.

LG6   **P9.23** Newco is a young company that has yet to make a profit. You are trying to place a value on the stock, but it pays no dividends and you obviously cannot calculate a P/E ratio. As a result, you decide to look at other stocks in the same industry as Newco to see if you can find a way to value this company. You find the following information:

	Per-Share Data ($)			
	Newco	Adolescentco	Middle-Ageco	Oldco
Sales	10	200	800	800
Profit	–10	10	60	80
Book value	–2	2	5	8
Market value	?	20	80	75

Estimate a market value for Newco. Discuss how your estimate could change if Newco was expected to grow much faster than the other companies.

LG4   **P9.24** World Wide Web Wares (4W, for short) is an online retailer of small kitchen appliances and utensils. The firm has been around for a few years and has created a nice market niche for itself. In fact, it actually turned a profit last year, albeit a fairly small one. After doing some basic research on the company, you've decided to take a closer look. You plan to use the price-to-sales ratio to value the stock, and you have collected P/S multiples on the following Internet retailer stocks:

Company	P/S Multiples
Amazing.com	4.5
ReallyCooking.com	4.1
Fixtures & Appliances Online	3.8

Find the average P/S ratio for these 3 firms. Given that 4W is expected to generate $40 million in sales next year and will have 10 million shares of stock outstanding, use the average P/S ratio you computed above to put a value on 4W's stock.

Case Problem 9.1   Chris Looks for a Way to Invest His Newfound Wealth

LG1 LG2 LG4   Chris Norton is a young Hollywood writer who is well on his way to television superstardom. After writing several successful television specials, he was recently named the head writer for one of TV's top-rated sitcoms. Chris fully realizes that his business is a fickle one and, on the advice of his dad and manager, has decided to set up an investment program. Chris will earn about a half-million dollars this year. Because of his age, income level, and desire to get as big a bang as possible from his investment dollars, he has decided to invest in speculative, high-growth stocks.

Chris is currently working with a respected Beverly Hills broker and is in the process of building up a diversified portfolio of speculative stocks. The broker recently sent him information on a hot new issue. She advised Chris to study the numbers and, if he likes them, to buy as many as 1,000 shares of the stock. Among other things, corporate sales for the next 3 years have been forecasted as follows:

Year	Sales ($ in millions)
1	22.5
2	35.0
3	50.0

The firm has 2.5 million shares of common stock outstanding. They are currently being traded at $70 a share and pay no dividends. The company has a net profit rate of 20%, and its stock has been trading at a P/E of around 40 times earnings. All these operating characteristics are expected to hold in the future.

Questions

a. Looking first at the stock:
   1. Compute the company's net profits and EPS for each of the next 3 years.
   2. Compute the price of the stock 3 years from now.
   3. Assuming that all expectations hold up and that Chris buys the stock at $70, determine his expected return on this investment.
   4. What risks is he facing by buying this stock? Be specific.
   5. Should he consider the stock a worthwhile investment candidate? Explain.

b. Looking at Chris's investment program in general:
   1. What do you think of his investment program? What do you see as its strengths and weaknesses?
   2. Are there any suggestions you would make?
   3. Do you think Chris should consider adding foreign stocks to his portfolio? Explain.

Case Problem 9.2   An Analysis of a High-Flying Stock

LG2 LG6   Marc Dodier is a recent university graduate and a security analyst with the Kansas City brokerage firm of Lippman, Brickbats, and Shaft. Marc has been following one of the hottest issues on Wall Street, C&I Medical Supplies, a company that has turned in an outstanding performance lately and, even more important, has exhibited excellent growth potential. It has 5 million shares outstanding and pays a nominal annual dividend of 5 cents per share. Marc has decided to take a closer look at C&I to see whether it still has any investment play left. Assume the company's sales for the past five years have been as follows:

Year	Sales ($ in millions)
2009	10.0
2010	12.5
2011	16.2
2012	22.0
2013	28.5

Marc is concerned with the future prospects of the company, not its past. As a result, he pores over the numbers and generates the following estimates of future performance:

Expected net profit margin	12%
Estimated annual dividends per share	5¢
Number of common shares outstanding	No change
P/E ratio at the end of 2014	35
P/E ratio at the end of 2015	50

Questions

a. Determine the average annual rate of growth in sales over the past 5 years. (Assume sales in 2008 amounted to $7.5 million.)

1. Use this average growth rate to forecast revenues for next year (2014) and the year after that (2015).
2. Now determine the company's net earnings and EPS for each of the next 2 years (2014 and 2015).
3. Finally, determine the expected future price of the stock at the end of this 2-year period.

b. Because of several intrinsic and market factors, Marc feels that 25% is a viable figure to use for a desired rate of return.

1. Using the 25% rate of return and the forecasted figures you came up with in question a, compute the stock's justified price.
2. If C&I is currently trading at $32.50 per share, should Marc consider the stock a worthwhile investment candidate? Explain.

Excel with Spreadsheets

Fundamental to the valuation process is the determination of the intrinsic value of a security, where an investor calculates the present value of the expected future cash benefits of the investment. Specifically, in the case of common stock, these future cash flows are defined by expected future dividend payments and future potential price appreciation. A simple but useful way to view stock value is that it is equal to the present value of all expected future dividends it may provide over an infinite time horizon.

Based on this latter concept, the dividend valuation model (DVM) has evolved. It can take on any one of 3 versions—the zero-growth model, the constant-growth model, and the variable-growth model.

Create a spreadsheet that applies the variable-growth model to predict the intrinsic value of the Rhyhorn Company common stock. Assume that dividends will grow at a variable rate for the next 3 years (2013, 2014, and 2015). After that, the annual rate of growth in dividends is expected to be 7% and stay there for the foreseeable future. Starting with the latest (2012) annual dividend of $2.00 per share, Rhyhorn's earnings and dividends are estimated to grow by 18% in 2013, by 14% in 2014, and by 9% in 2015 before dropping to a 7% rate. Given the risk profile of the firm, assume a minimum required rate of return of at least 12%. The spreadsheet for Table 9.4, which you can view on www.myfinance.lab.com, is a good reference for solving this problem.

Questions

a. Calculate the projected annual dividends over the years 2013, 2014, and 2015.

b. Determine the present value of dividends during the initial variable-growth period.

c. What do you believe the price of Rhyhorn stock will be at the end of the initial growth period (2015)?

d. Having determined the expected future price of Rhyhorn stock in part c, discount the price of the stock back to its present value.

e. Determine the total intrinsic value of Rhyhorn stock based on your calculations above.

Chapter-Opening Problem

At the beginning of this chapter you read about a 2012 earnings announcement from Bed Bath & Beyond in which earnings per share were reported as $0.89 for the quarter. Let's make a simple assumption and say that earnings for the year were 4 times as much, or $3.56 per share. At the time of that announcement, the average P/E for stocks in the U.S. was close to 15.

a. If you use the market's P/E and BBBY's current earnings to estimate the stock's intrinsic value, what value do you obtain?

b. The actual price of BBBY after the earnings announcement was about $60. What does this tell you about your answer to part a?

c. Suppose BBBY paid out all of its earnings as a dividend. Suppose also that investors expected the firm to continue doing that forever, and because the company was not reinvesting any earnings, investors expected no growth in dividends. If the required return on BBBY stock is 9%, what is the stock price?

d. Comment on your answer to part c in light of BBBY's market price at the time.

10

Return and Risk

LEARNING GOALS

After studying this chapter, you should be able to:

LG1 Review the concept of return, its components, the forces that affect the level of return, and historical returns.

LG2 Discuss the role of time value of money in measuring return and defining a satisfactory investment.

LG3 Describe real, risk-free, and required returns and the calculation and application of holding period return.

LG4 Explain the concept and the calculation of yield and how to find growth rates.

LG5 Discuss the key sources of risk that might affect potential investments.

LG6 Understand the risk of a single asset, risk assessment, and the steps that combine return and risk.

An old saying often attributed to Mark Twain advises, "Buy land—they're not making it anymore." That bit of folk wisdom gained enormous popularity during the U.S. real estate boom. According to the S&P/Case-Shiller Index, which tracks home prices in 20 large cities, U.S. homeowners saw their property values increase almost 70% from 2002 to 2005. Over the same 4 years, the U.S. stock market eked out a meager 16% gain.

Moreover, the tantalizing returns on real estate seemed to come without much risk. The average home price rose every single month from July 1996 to May 2006. No wonder, then, that investing in real estate became fashionable, as evidenced by the introduction of television shows such as A&E's *Flip This House*.

Unfortunately, home prices declined in the summer of 2006, and their fall continued through March 2012. Over that period, average home prices dropped 34% and 3.6 million properties were lost to foreclosure, reminding homeowners that investing in real estate had both rewards and risks. Foreclosures slowed during 2011, with 34% fewer properties than in 2010, but in 2012 foreclosures are expect to spike again as banks make up for foreclosure processing delays in 2011 caused by a flurry of investigations into banks' foreclosure practices. From boom to bust, the housing market is a great example of the inextricable link between return and risk.

(Source: S&P/Case-Shiller price indexes downloaded from standardandpoors.com and RealtyTrac.com "Year-End 2011 U.S. Foreclosure Market Report.")

The Concept of Return

LG1 **LG2** People are motivated to invest in a given asset by its expected return. The **return** is the level of profit from an investment—that is, the reward for investing. Suppose you have $1,000 in an insured savings account paying 2% annual interest, and a business associate asks you to lend her that much money. If you lend her the money for 1 year, at the end of which she pays you back, your return will depend on the amount of interest you charge. If you make an interest-free loan, your return will be 0. If you charge 2% interest, your return will be $20 (0.02 × $1,000). Because you are already earning a safe 2% on the $1,000, it seems clear that to equal that return you should charge your associate a minimum of 2% interest.

Some investments guarantee a return, but most do not. The return on a bank deposit insured by the federal government is virtually certain. The return earned on a loan to your business associate might be less certain. The size and the certainty of the expected return are important factors in choosing a suitable investment.

> **INVESTOR FACTS**
>
> **Dividend—An Easy Pill to Swallow**—On the first trading day of 2011, the stock of the pharmaceutical giant Merck & Co. sold for $33.66 per share, just 1.6% higher than its price exactly 1 year earlier ($33.16). Though it might seem that 2011 was a poor year for Merck's shareholders, the stock paid dividends during the year totaling $1.52, and those dividends raised the total return on Merck stock in 2011 to 6.2%.

Components of Return

The return on an investment may come from more than one source. The most common source is periodic payments, such as dividends and interest. The other source of return is the change in the investment's price. We call these two sources of return *current income* and *capital gains* (or *capital losses*), respectively.

Income Income may take the form of dividends from stocks or mutual funds or interest received on bonds. To be considered income, it must be in the form of cash or be readily convertible into cash. For our purposes, an investment's **income** is usually cash that investors periodically receive as a result of owning an investment.

Using the data in Table 10.1, we can calculate the income from investments A and B, both purchased for $1,000, over a 1-year period of ownership. Investment A provides income of $80, and investment B pays $120. Solely on the basis of the income received over the 1 year, investment B seems preferable.

TABLE 10.1   PROFILES OF TWO INVESTMENTS

	Investment	
	A	B
Purchase price (beginning of year)	$1,000	$1,000
Cash received		
1st quarter	10	0
2nd quarter	20	0
3rd quarter	20	0
4th quarter	30	120
Total income (for year)	$ 80	$ 120
Sale price (end of year)	$1,100	$ 960

TABLE 10.2 TOTAL RETURNS OF TWO INVESTMENTS

Return	Investment A	Investment B
Income	$ 80	$120
Capital gain (loss)	100	(40)
Total return	$180	$ 80

Capital Gains (or Losses) The second dimension of return focuses on the change in an investment's market value. As noted in Chapter 1, the amount by which the proceeds from the sale of an investment exceed its original purchase price is a *capital gain*. If an investment sells for less than its original purchase price, a *capital loss* results.

We can calculate the capital gain or loss of the investments shown in Table 10.1. Investment A experiences a capital gain of $100 ($1,100 sale price − $1,000 purchase price) over the 1-year period. For investment B, a $40 capital loss results ($960 sale price − $1,000 purchase price).

Combining the capital gain (or loss) with the income (calculated in the preceding section) gives the **total return**. Table 10.2 shows the total return for investments A and B over the year. Investment A earns a $180 total return, compared to just $80 earned by investment B.

It is generally preferable to use *percentage returns* rather than dollar returns. Percentages allow direct comparison of different sizes and types of investments. Investment A earned an 18% return ($180 ÷ $1,000); B produced only an 8% return ($80 ÷ $1,000). At this point investment A appears preferable, but as we'll see, differences in risk might cause some investors to prefer B.

Why Return Is Important

An asset's return is a key variable in the investment decision because it indicates how rapidly an investor can build wealth. Naturally, because most people prefer to have more wealth rather than less, they prefer investments that offer high returns rather than low returns if all else is equal. However, we've already said that the returns on most investments are uncertain, so how do investors distinguish assets that offer high returns from those likely to produce low returns? One way to make this kind of assessment is to examine the returns that different types of investments have produced in the past.

Historical Performance Most people recognize that future performance is not guaranteed by past performance, but past data often provide a meaningful basis for future expectations. A common practice in the investment world is to look closely at the historical record when formulating expectations about the future.

Interest rates and other measures of financial return are most often cited on an annual basis. Evaluation of past investment returns is typically done on the same basis. Consider the data for ExxonMobil Corporation presented in Table 10.3 (on page 334). ExxonMobil paid dividends every year from 2002 through 2011. ExxonMobil's stock price generally rose during this decade, starting at $39.30 and ending at $84.76. Despite the overall upward trend, the company's stock fell slightly in 2002 (largely due to the September 11 terrorist attack and the recession that followed), and it declined again in 2008 and 2009 (as oil prices plunged from over $140 per barrel to less than $40 in response to the Great Recession).

TABLE 10.3   HISTORICAL INVESTMENT DATA FOR EXXONMOBIL CORP. (XOM)

| | Market Value (Price) | | | | Total Return | |
Year	(1) Dividend Income	(2) Beginning of Year	(3) End of Year	(4) (3) − (2) Capital Gain	(5) (1) + (4)	(6) (5) / (2)
2002	$0.92	$39.30	$34.94	−$4.36	−$3.44	−8.8%
2003	0.98	34.94	41.00	6.06	7.04	20.1
2004	1.06	41.00	51.26	10.26	11.32	27.6
2005	1.14	51.26	56.17	4.91	6.05	11.8
2006	1.28	56.17	76.63	20.46	21.74	38.7
2007	1.37	76.63	93.69	17.06	18.43	24.1
2008	1.55	93.69	79.83	−13.86	−12.31	−13.1
2009	1.66	79.83	68.19	−11.64	−9.98	−12.5
2010	1.74	68.19	73.12	4.93	6.67	9.8
2011	1.85	73.12	84.76	11.64	13.49	18.4
Average	$1.36			$4.55	$5.90	11.6%

(Source: Dividends and end-of-year closing prices were obtained from Yahoo! Finance.)

Two aspects of these data are important. First, we can determine the *average level of return* generated by this investment over the past 10 years. The total return earned by ExxonMobil's shareholders (column 6) over this period averaged 11.6%, performance that put ExxonMobil well ahead of most other stocks for the same period. Second, observe that there was considerable variation in ExxonMobil's return from one year to the next. The firm's best year was 2006, during which its investors earned a total return of 38.7%. But in 2008, ExxonMobil's worst year, shareholders lost 13.1%.

Expected Return   In the final analysis, of course, it's the future that matters when we make investment decisions. Therefore, **expected return** is a vital measure of performance. It's what you think the investment will earn in the future that determines what you should be willing to pay for it.

To demonstrate, let's return to the data in Table 10.3. A naive investor might estimate ExxonMobil's expected return to be the same as its average return from the prior decade, 11.6%. That's not necessarily a bad starting point, but it would be wise to ask, "What contributed to ExxonMobil's past success, and is it likely that the same factors will occur in the future?" Central to ExxonMobil's success in the recent past was a generally upward trend in oil prices. In early 2002, crude oil traded for around $20 per barrel, but prices rose steadily until they peaked at more than $140 per barrel in June 2008. An investor who believed that oil prices would not continue to move up indefinitely but rather would stabilize might estimate ExxonMobil's expected return by looking at its historical performance during a period of relatively stable oil prices.

Level of Return

The level of return achieved or expected from an investment will depend on a variety of factors. The key factors are internal characteristics and external forces.

Recession Pushes Prices Down

For most of your lifetime, prices of most goods and services have been rising. There are important exceptions, such as the prices of consumer electronics and computers, but from one year to the next, the overall price level rose continuously in the United States from 1955 through 2007. However, as the recession deepened in 2008, consumer prices in the United States began to decline, falling in each of the last 5 months that year. The year-over-year change in consumer prices was negative for March through October of 2009 and bottomed out in July at –2.1%, the largest 12-month drop in nearly 60 years. The news raised fears among some investors that the recession might turn into a depression like the one that had brought about a price decline of –27% from November 1929 to March 1933. Fortunately, prices began to rise again, increasing a modest 4.9% over the next 2 years.

Internal Characteristics Certain characteristics of an investment affect its return. For investments issued by companies, the important characteristics include things such as the type of investment (e.g., stocks or bonds), the quality of the firm's management, and whether the firm finances its operations with debt or equity. For example, investors might expect a different return on the common stock of a large, well-managed, completely equity-financed plastics manufacturer than they would anticipate from the common stock of a small, poorly managed, largely debt-financed clothing manufacturer. As we will see in later chapters, assessing internal factors and their impact on return is one important step in analyzing potential investments.

External Forces External forces such as Federal Reserve actions, shortages, war, price controls, and political events may also affect an investment's return. None of these are under the control of the issuer of the investment, and investments react differently to these forces. For example, if investors expect oil prices to rise, they may raise their expected return for ExxonMobil stock and lower it for the stock of an automobile manufacturer that specializes in gas guzzlers. Likewise, the economies of various countries respond to external forces in different ways.

Another external force is the *general level of price changes*, either up—**inflation**—or down—**deflation**. Inflation tends to have a positive impact on investments such as real estate and a negative impact on stocks and fixed-income securities. Rising interest rates, which normally accompany increasing rates of inflation, can significantly affect returns. The actions, if any, the Federal Reserve takes to control inflation can also have significant effects on investments. Furthermore, the return on each type of investment exhibits its unique response to inflation.

What Is Inflation?

Historical Returns

Returns vary both over time and among types of investments. By averaging historical returns over a long period of time, it is possible to observe the differences in returns earned by various types of investments. Table 10.4 shows the average annual rates of return for a number of popular security investments (and inflation) in 19 countries over the 112-year period from 1900 to 2011. With more than 100 years of data to draw on, some clear patterns emerge. You can see that significant differences exist

TABLE 10.4   HISTORICAL RETURNS FOR SELECT ASSET CLASSES (1900–2011)

	Average Annual Return			
	Stocks (%)	Long-Term Government Bonds (%)	Short-Term Government Bills (%)	Inflation (%)
Australia	11.3	5.5	4.6	3.9
Belgium	7.8	5.2	4.9	5.3
Canada	8.9	5.3	4.6	3.0
Denmark	8.9	7.2	6.2	4.0
Finland	12.6	7.1	6.7	7.2
France	10.2	7.1	4.1	6.9
Germany	8.1	2.9	2.2	4.6
Ireland	8.1	5.2	4.9	4.2
Italy	10.2	6.5	4.5	8.1
Japan	10.8	5.8	4.9	6.8
Netherlands	7.9	4.5	3.6	2.9
New Zealand	9.7	5.9	5.5	3.8
Norway	7.9	5.6	4.9	3.7
South Africa	12.5	6.8	6.0	5.0
Spain	9.4	7.2	6.1	5.8
Sweden	9.9	6.2	5.5	3.7
Switzerland	6.5	4.5	3.1	2.3
United Kingdom	9.4	5.5	5.0	4.0
United States	9.3	5.0	3.9	2.9

(Source: Elroy Dimson, Paul Marsh, and Mike Staunton, Credit Suisse Global Investment Returns Sourcebook 2012.)

among the average annual rates of return realized on stocks, long-term government bonds, and short-term government bills. In all 19 countries, stocks earn higher returns than government bonds, which in turn earn higher average returns than short-term government bills. Later in this chapter, we will see how we can link these differences in return to differences in the risk of each of these investments.

We now turn our attention to the role that time value of money principles play in determining investment returns.

Time Value of Money and Returns

The phrase *the time value of money* refers to the fact that it is generally better to receive cash sooner rather than later. For example, consider two investments, A and B. Investment A will pay you $100 next year and $100 the year after that. Investment B pays you $200 in 2 years. Assume that neither investment has any risk, meaning that you are certain that you will receive these cash payments. Clearly both investments pay $200 over 2 years, but investment A is preferable because you can reinvest the $100 you receive in the first year to earn more interest the second year. You should always consider time value money principles when making investment decisions.

We now review the key computational aids available for streamlining time value of money calculations, and then we demonstrate the application of time value of money techniques to determine an acceptable investment.

Computational Aids for Use in Time Value Calculations The often time-consuming calculations involved in applying time value of money techniques can be simplified with a number of computational aids. Throughout this book we will demonstrate the use of hand-held financial calculators and electronic spreadsheets. Financial calculators include numerous preprogrammed financial routines. To demonstrate the calculator keystrokes for various financial computations, we show a keypad, with the keys defined below. *Electronic spreadsheet* use has become a prime skill for today's investors. Like financial calculators, electronic spreadsheets have built-in routines that simplify time value calculations. For most time value calculations in the book, we show spreadsheet solutions that identify cell entries.

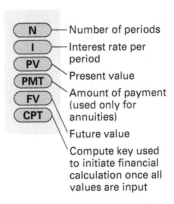

Determining a Satisfactory Investment Time value of money techniques can be used to determine whether an investment's return is satisfactory given the investment's cost. Ignoring risk at this point, a **satisfactory investment** would be one for which the present value of benefits (discounted at the appropriate discount rate) equals or exceeds its cost. The three possible cost–benefit relationships and their interpretations follow:

1. If the present value of the benefits equals the cost, you would earn a rate of return equal to the discount rate.

2. If the present value of benefits exceeds the cost, you would earn a rate of return greater than the discount rate.

3. If the present value of benefits is less than the cost, you would earn a rate of return less than the discount rate.

You would prefer only those investments for which the present value of benefits equals or exceeds its cost—situations 1 and 2. In these cases, the rate of return would be equal to or greater than the discount rate.

The information in Table 10.5 (on page 338) demonstrates the application of present value to investment decision making. (*Note:* You can use a financial calculator or an Excel spreadsheet to convert the algebraic expression in column 2 to the numeric value in column 3.) This investment is expected to make a series of payments over the next 7 years. Because the payments arrive at different times, we calculate the present value of

End of Year	(1) Income ($)	(2) Present Value Calculation at 8% ($)	(3) Present Value at 8% ($)
1	90	$90/(1.08)^1$	83.33
2	100	$100/(1.08)^2$	85.73
3	110	$110/(1.08)^3$	87.32
4	120	$120/(1.08)^4$	88.20
5	100	$100/(1.08)^5$	68.06
6	100	$100/(1.08)^6$	63.02
7	1,200	$1,200/(1.08)^7$	700.19
		Total Present Value	$1,175.85

TABLE 10.5 PRESENT VALUE APPLIED TO AN INVESTMENT — EXCEL with Spreadsheets

Time Is Money

each payment to determine how much each payment is worth in today's dollars. The present value of the benefits (i.e., the income) provided by this investment over its 7-year life is $1,175.85. If the cost of the investment today is $1,175.85 or less, then the investment is acceptable. At that cost, an investor would earn a rate of return equal to at least 8%. At a cost above the $1,175.85 present value, the investment would not be acceptable because the rate of return would be less than 8%. In that case it would be preferable to find an alternative investment with a present value of benefits that equals or exceeds its cost.

CONCEPTS IN REVIEW

Answers available at
www.pearsonhighered.com/
smart

10.1 Explain what is meant by the return on an investment. Differentiate between the two components of return—income and capital gains (or losses).

10.2 What role do historical performance data play in estimating an investment's expected return? Discuss the key factors affecting investment returns—internal characteristics and external forces.

10.3 What is a satisfactory investment? When the present value of benefits exceeds the cost of an investment, what can you conclude about the rate of return earned by the investor relative to the discount rate?

Measuring Return

Thus far, we have discussed the concept of return in terms of its two components (income and capital gains) and the key factors that affect the level of return (internal characteristics and external forces). These discussions intentionally oversimplified the computations involved in determining the historical or expected return. To compare returns from different investments, we need to incorporate time value of money concepts that explicitly consider differences in the timing of investment income and capital gains. We must also be able to calculate the present value of future benefits. Here we will look at several measures that enable us to compare alternative investments. First, we must define and consider the relationships among various rates of return.

Real, Risk-Free, and Required Returns

Inflation and Returns Glance back at Table 10.4 (on page 336) which reports that in the United States, the average annual return on a short-term government Treasury bill was 3.9% between 1900 and 2011. The table also shows that the average annual inflation rate was about 2.9%. It's no coincidence that the T-bill rate of return exceeds the inflation rate because investors want to earn returns that exceed the inflation rate. Inflation erodes the purchasing power of money. For example, if prices of most goods and services rise by 3% in a year, $1 buys 3% fewer goods and services at the end of the year than at the beginning. Thus, if investors seek to increase their purchasing power over time, they must earn returns that exceed the inflation rate.

The **nominal rate of return** on an investment is the return that the investment earns expressed in current dollars. For example, if you put $50 into an investment that promises to pay 3% interest, at the end of the year you will have $51.50 (the initial $50 plus a $1.50 return). Your nominal return is 3%, but this does not necessarily mean that you are better off financially at the end of the year because the nominal return does not take into account the effects of inflation.

To continue the example, assume that at the beginning of the year, one bag of groceries costs $50. During the year, suppose grocery prices rise by 3%. This means that by the end of the year one bag of groceries costs $51.50. In other words, at the beginning of the year you could have used your $50 either to buy one bag of groceries or to make the investment that promised a 3% return. If you invested your money rather than spending it on groceries, by the end of 1 year you would have had $51.50, still just enough to buy one bag of groceries. In other words, your purchasing power did not increase at all during the year. The **real rate of return** on an investment measures the increase in purchasing power that the investment provides. In our continuing example, the real rate of return is 0% even though the nominal rate of return is 3%. In dollar terms, by investing $50 you increased your wealth by 3% to $51.50, but in terms of purchasing power you are no better off because your money is only enough to buy the same amount of goods that it could have bought before you made the investment. In mathematical terms, the real rate of return is approximately equal to the nominal rate of return minus the inflation rate.

Example

Suppose you have $50 today and are trying to decide whether to invest that money or spend it. If you invest it, you believe that you can earn a nominal return of 10%, so after 1 year your money will grow to $55. If you spend the money today, you plan to feed your caffeine habit by purchasing 20 lattes at your favorite coffee shop at $2.50 each. You decide to save and invest your money, so a year later you have $55. Unfortunately, during that time inflation caused the price of a latte to increase by 4.8% from $2.50 to $2.62. At the new price, you can just about afford to buy 21 lattes (21 × $2.62 = $55.02). That extra latte represents an increase in your purchasing power of 5% (i.e., 21 is 5% more than 20), so your real return on the investment is 5% because it enabled you to buy 5% more than you could before you invested. Notice that the real return is approximately equal to the difference between the investment's nominal return (10%) and the inflation rate (4.8%):

$$\text{Real return} \approx \text{Nominal return} - \text{inflation rate}$$

$$5\% \approx 10\% - 4.8\%$$

Risk and Returns Investors are generally *risk averse*, meaning that they do not like risk and will only take risk when they expect compensation for doing so. The greater the risk associated with any particular investment, the greater the return that investors will require to make that investment. The rate of return that fully compensates for an investment's risk is called the **required return**. Note that the required return is a kind of forecast. If an investor expects an investment to earn a return equal to or greater than the required return, the investor will want to buy the investment. However, the return that an investment actually earns can be quite different from the investor's required return.

The required return on any investment *j* consists of 3 basic components: the real rate of return, an expected inflation premium, and a risk premium, as noted in Equation 10.1.

Equation 10.1

$$\text{Required return on investment } j = \text{Real rate of return} + \text{Expected inflation premium} + \text{Risk premium for investment } j$$

Equation 10.1a

$$r_j = r^* + IP + RP_j$$

The **expected inflation premium** represents the rate of inflation expected over an investment's life. Although the historical average inflation rate in the United States has been close to 3.0%, investors' expectations may deviate from the historical norm for many reasons. For instance, most inflation forecasts for 2012 projected very low inflation due to the lingering effects of the global recession. By adding the first 2 terms in Equation 10.1, we obtain the **risk-free rate**. This is the rate of return that can be earned on a risk-free investment, such as a short-term U.S. Treasury bill. The formula for this rate appears in Equation 10.2.

Equation 10.2

$$\text{Risk-free rate} = \text{Real rate of return} + \text{Expected inflation premium}$$

Equation 10.2a

$$r_f = r^* + IP$$

The required return can be found by adding to the risk-free rate a **risk premium**, which varies depending on specific issue and issuer characteristics. *Issue characteristics* are the type of investment (stock, bond, etc.), its maturity (2 years, 5 years, infinity, etc.), and its features (voting/nonvoting, callable/noncallable, etc.). *Issuer characteristics* are industry and company factors such as the line of business and financial condition of the issuer. Together, the issue and issuer factors contribute to the overall risk of an investment and cause investors to require a risk premium above the risk-free rate.

Substituting the risk-free rate, r_f, from Equation 10.2a into Equation 10.1a for the first 2 terms to the right of the equal signs ($r^* + IP$), we get Equation 10.3.

Equation 10.3

$$\text{Required return on investment } j = \text{Risk-free rate} + \text{Risk premium for investment } j$$

Equation 10.3a

$$r_j = r_f + RP_j$$

For example, if the required return on Nike common stock is 11% when the risk-free rate is 6%, investors require a 5% risk premium (11% – 6%) as compensation for the risk associated with common stock (the issue) and Nike (the issuer). Notice also that if investors expect 3% inflation, then the real required rate on Nike is 8% (11% – 3%). Later, in Chapter 11, we will explore further the relationship between the risk premium and required returns.

Next, we consider the specifics of return measurement. We look at 2 return measures—one used primarily for short-term investments and the other for longer-term investments.

Holding Period Return

The return to a *saver* is the amount of interest earned on a given deposit. Of course, the amount "invested" in a savings account does not change in value, as does the amount invested in stocks, bonds, and mutual funds. Because we are concerned with a broad range of investments, we need a measure of return that captures both periodic income and changes in value. One such measure is the *holding period return*.

The **holding period** is the period of time over which one wishes to measure the return on an investment. When comparing returns, be sure to use holding periods of the same length. For example, comparing the return on a stock over a 6-month period with the return on a bond over a 1-year period could result in a poor investment decision. To avoid this problem, be sure you define the holding period. It is common practice to annualize the holding period and use that as a standard.

Understanding Return Components Earlier in this chapter we identified the 2 components of investment return: income and capital gains (or losses). The income received by the investor during the investment period is a **realized return**. Capital gains and losses, on the other hand, are realized only when the investor sells an asset at the end of the investment period. Until the sale occurs, the capital gain or loss is merely a **paper return**.

Smart's Tour of the Web

To watch author Scott Smart discuss key websites for this chapter, visit www.myfinancelab.com

For example, the capital gain return on an investment that increases in market value from $50 to $70 during a year is $20. For that capital gain to be realized, you would sell the investment for $70 at the end of that year. An investor who purchased the same investment but plans to hold it for another 3 years would also experience the $20 capital gain return during the first year, but he or she would not have realized the gain by collecting the $20 profit in cash. However, even if the capital gain is not realized, it must be included in the total return calculation.

A second point to recognize about returns is that both the income and the capital gains components can have a negative value. Occasionally, an investment may have negative income. That is, you may be required to pay out cash to meet certain obligations. (This situation is most likely to occur in various types of property investments that require periodic maintenance.) A capital loss can occur on any investment: Stocks, bonds, mutual funds, options, futures, real estate, and gold can all decline in value.

Computing the Holding Period Return The **holding period return (HPR)** is the total return earned from holding an investment for a specified time (the holding period). Analysts typically use the HPR with holding periods of 1 year or less. (We'll explain why later.) It represents the sum of income and capital gains (or losses) achieved over the holding period, divided by the beginning investment value (market price). The equation for HPR is

Equation 10.4

$$\text{Holding period return} = \frac{\begin{array}{c}\text{Income} \\ \text{during period}\end{array} + \begin{array}{c}\text{Capital gain (or loss)} \\ \text{during period}\end{array}}{\text{Beginning investment value}}$$

Equation 10.4a

$$\text{HPR} = \frac{\text{Inc} + \text{CG}}{V_0}$$

where

Equation 10.5

$$\begin{array}{c}\text{Capital gain (or loss)} \\ \text{during period}\end{array} = \begin{array}{c}\text{Ending} \\ \text{investment value}\end{array} - \begin{array}{c}\text{Beginning} \\ \text{investment value}\end{array}$$

Equation 10.5a

$$CG = V_n - V_0$$

The HPR equation provides a convenient method for either measuring the total return realized or estimating the total return expected. For example, Table 10.6 summarizes the key financial variables for 4 investments over the past year. The total income and capital gain or loss during the investment period appear in the lines labeled (1) and (3), respectively. The total return over the year is calculated, as shown in line (4), by adding these 2 sources of return. Dividing the total return value [line (4)] by the beginning-of-year investment value [line (2)], we find the holding period return, given in line (5). Over the 1-year holding period the common stock had the highest HPR (12.25%). The savings account had the lowest (6%).

As these calculations show, to find the HPR we need the beginning-of-period and end-of-period investment values, along with income received during the period. Note that if the current income and capital gain (or loss) values in lines (1) and (3) of Table 10.6 had been drawn from a 6-month rather than a 1-year period, the HPR values calculated in line 5 would have been the same.

TABLE 10.6   KEY FINANCIAL VARIABLES FOR FOUR INVESTMENTS   EXCEL with Spreadsheets

	Investment			
	Savings Account	Common Stock	Bond	Real Estate
Cash Received				
1st quarter	$ 15	$ 10	$ 0	$ 0
2nd quarter	15	10	70	0
3rd quarter	15	10	0	0
4th quarter	15	15	70	0
(1) Total current income	$ 60	$ 45	$ 140	$ 0
Investment Value				
End-of-year	$1,000	$2,200	$ 970	$3,300
(2) Beginning-of-year	1,000	2,000	1,000	3,000
(3) Capital gain (loss)	$ 0	$ 200	($ 30)	$ 300
(4) Total return [(1) + (3)]	$ 60	$ 245	$ 110	$ 300
(5) Holding period return [(4) ÷ (2)]	6.00%	12.25%	11.00%	10.00%

An investment's holding period return can be negative or positive. You can use Equation 10.4 to calculate HPRs using either historical data (as in the preceding example) or forecast data.

Using the HPR in Investment Decisions The holding period return is easy to use in making investment decisions. It measures an investment's return (including both the income and capital gains components) relative to the investment's initial cost, and in so doing makes it easier to compare the performance of investments that may differ greatly in terms of the amount of money required from an investor.

If we look only at the total returns calculated for each of the investments in Table 10.6 [line (4)], the real estate investment appears best because it has the highest total return. However, the real estate investment would require the largest dollar outlay ($3,000). The holding period return offers a *relative comparison*, by dividing the total return by the amount of the investment. Comparing HPRs [line (5)], we find the investment alternative with the highest return per invested dollar to be the common stock's HPR of 12.25%. Because the return per invested dollar reflects the efficiency of the investment, the HPR provides a logical method for evaluating and comparing investment returns, particularly for holding periods of 1 year or less.

Yield: The Internal Rate of Return

An alternative way to define a satisfactory investment is in terms of the compound annual rate of return it earns. Why do we need an alternative to the HPR? Because HPR fails to fully account for the time value of money. Although the holding period return is useful with investments held for 1 year or less, it is generally inappropriate for longer holding periods. Sophisticated investors typically do not use HPR when the time period is greater than 1 year. Instead, they use a present value–based measure, called **yield** (or **internal rate of return**), to determine the compound annual rate of return earned on investments held for longer than 1 year. An investment's yield is the discount rate that equates the investment's cost to the present value of the benefits that it provides for the investor.

Once you know the yield, you can decide whether an investment is acceptable. If the yield on an investment is equal to or greater than the required return, then the investment is acceptable. An investment with a yield below the required return is unacceptable.

The yield on an investment providing a single future cash flow is relatively easy to calculate. The yield on an investment providing a stream of future cash flows generally involves more complex calculations. Hand-held financial calculators or Excel spreadsheets simplify these calculations.

Yield for a Single Cash Flow Some investments, such as U.S. savings bonds, stocks paying no dividends, and zero-coupon bonds, provide no periodic income. Instead, investors pay a lump sum up front to purchases these investments, and in return investors expect to receive a single, future cash flow at maturity or when the investments are sold. The yield on such an investment is easy to calculate using a financial calculator or an Excel spreadsheet.

CALCULATOR USE Assume you wish to find the yield on an investment that costs $1,000 today and will pay you $1,400 at the end of 5 years. To compute the yield for this investment on a financial calculator, you treat the investment's cost as a present value, PV, and the investment's payoff as a future value, FV. (*Note:* Most calculators require you to enter either the PV or FV as a negative number to calculate an unknown yield.

Generally, the PV is entered as a negative value since it represents the initial cost of an investment.) Using the inputs shown at the left, you can verify that the yield is 6.96%.

SPREADSHEET USE The yield for the single cash flow also can be calculated as shown on the following Excel spreadsheet.

◇	A	B
1	YIELD FOR A SINGLE CASH FLOW	
2	Investment	Cash Flow
3	Cost (PV)	−$1,000
4	Payoff (FV)	$1,400
5	Number of Years	5
6	Yield	6.96%
7	Entry in Cell B6 is =Rate(B5,0,B3,B4,0). The minus sign appears before the 1,000 in B3 because the cost of the investment is treated as a cash outflow.	

Yield for a Stream of Income Investments such as income-oriented stocks and bonds typically provide the investor with a stream of income. The yield (or internal rate of return) on an investment that pays income periodically is the discount rate that equates the present value of the investment's cash flows to its current price.

Consider once more the investment presented in Table 10.5 (on page 338). The table illustrates that the present value of the investment's cash flows given a discount rate of 8% is $1,175.85. If the market price of the investment is also $1,175.85 (equal to the present value), then 8% is its internal rate of return, because at that discount rate the present value and the market price are the same. Suppose that the price of this investment falls to $1,100. At that price, what yield does the investment offer? Table 10.7 uses a trial-and-error approach in an attempt to find the answer. If we discount the investment's cash flows at 9%, the present value of those cash flows is $1,117.75. That's above the investment's market price, so the yield must be above 9%. Table 10.7 shows that at a 10% discount rate, the present value of the cash flows is $1,063.40, so the investment's yield must be below 10%. Therefore, you need to keep searching for the exact discount rate at which the investment's cash flows equal $1,100. You can do that using a financial calculator or an Excel spreadsheet.

Example

TABLE 10.7   PRESENT VALUE APPLIED TO AN INVESTMENT   EXCEL with Spreadsheets

End of Year	(1) Income	(2) Present Value Calculation at 9%	(3) Present Value at 9%	(4) Present Value Calculation at 10%	(5) Present Value at 10%
1	$ 90	$ 90/(1 + 0.09)^1	$ 82.57	$ 90/(1 + 0.1)^1	$ 81.82
2	100	100/(1 + 0.09)^2	84.17	100/(1 + 0.1)^2	82.64
3	110	110/(1 + 0.09)^3	84.94	110/(1 + 0.1)^3	82.64
4	120	120/(1 + 0.09)^4	85.01	120/(1 + 0.1)^4	81.96
5	100	100/(1 + 0.09)^5	64.99	100/(1 + 0.1)^5	62.09
6	100	100/(1 + 0.09)^6	59.63	100/(1 + 0.1)^6	56.45
7	1,200	1,200/(1 + 0.09)^7	656.44	1,200/(1 + 0.1)^7	615.79
Total Present Value			$1,117.75		$1,063.40

CALCULATOR USE Using a financial calculator to find an investment's yield typically involves three steps: (1) Enter the cost of the investment (typically referred to as the *cash outflow* at time 0). (2) Enter all of the income expected each period (typically referred to as the *cash inflow* in year *x*). (3) Calculate the yield (typically referred to as the *internal rate of return, IRR*).

SPREADSHEET USE We can also calculate the yield for a stream of income as shown on the following Excel spreadsheet.

	A	B
1	YIELD FOR A STREAM OF INCOME	
2	Year	Cash Flow
3	0	−$1,100
4	1	$90
5	2	$100
6	3	$110
7	4	$120
8	5	$100
9	6	$100
10	7	$1,200
11	Yield	9.32%
12	Entry in Cell B11 is =IRR(B3:B10). The minus sign appears before the 1,100 in B3 because the cost of the investment is treated as a cash outflow.	

Interest on Interest: The Critical Assumption The yield is a measure of the return that an investment provides, but the yield calculation contains a subtle assumption. That assumption is that the investor can reinvest all of the income that the investment provides, and that the return earned on reinvested income equals the return on the original investment. This concept can best be illustrated with a simple example. Suppose you buy a $1,000 U.S. Treasury bond that pays 8% annual interest ($80) over its 20-year life. Each year you receive $80, and at maturity you get the $1,000 principal back. All payments arrive right on time. But in order to earn 8% on this investment, you must be able to reinvest the $80 annual interest receipts and earn 8% on them.

Figure 10.1 (on page 346) shows the elements of return on this investment to demonstrate the point. If you don't *reinvest* the interest income of $80 per year, you'll end up on the 5% line. You'll have $2,600—the $1,000 principal plus $1,600 interest income ($80/year × 20 years)—at the end of 20 years. (The yield on a single cash flow of $1,000 today that will be worth $2,600 in 20 years is about 5%.) To move to the 8% line, you must earn 8% on the annual interest receipts. If you do, at the end of 20 years you'll have $4,661—the $1,000 principal plus the $3,661 future value of the 20-year $80 annuity of interest receipts invested at 8%. (The yield on a single cash flow of $1,000 today that will be worth $4,661 in 20 years is 8%.) The future value of the investment would be $2,061 greater ($4,661 − $2,600) with interest on interest than without reinvestment of the interest receipts. Even though we used a bond in this illustration, the same principle applies to many other investments.

It should be clear to you that if you start out with an 8% investment, you must earn that same rate of return when reinvesting your income. The rate of return you start with is the required, or minimum, **reinvestment rate**. This is the rate of return earned on interest or other income received over the relevant investment horizon. By putting your income to work at this rate, you'll earn the rate of return you set out to earn. If you must reinvest income at a lower rate, your return will decline accordingly.

FIGURE 10.1

Earning Interest on Interest

If you invested in a $1,000, 20-year bond with an 8% coupon, you would have only $2,600 at the end of 20 years if you did not reinvest the $80 annual interest receipts. That is roughly equivalent to investing $1,000 today and letting it grow at 5% for 20 years.

If you reinvested the interest at 8%, you would have $4,661 at the end of 20 years. That's about the same amount that you would have by investing $1,000 today and letting that grow at 8% per year. To achieve the calculated yield of 8%, you must therefore be able to earn interest on interest at that rate.

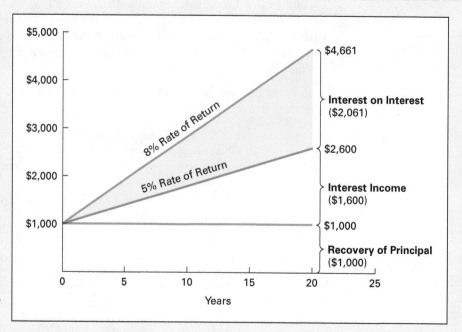

Because the yield calculation assumes that you can earn interest on the periodic income that you receive, financial experts say that the yield (or internal rate of return) is a **fully compounded rate of return**. It's an important concept: You can't start reaping the full potential from your investments until you start earning a fully compounded rate of return on them.

Interest on interest is a particularly important element of return for investment programs that involve a lot of income. You must actively reinvest income. (With capital gains, the money is automatically reinvested unless you sell the asset to realize the gain.) It follows, therefore, that for investment programs that lean toward income-oriented securities, the continued reinvestment of income plays an important role in investment success.

Finding Growth Rates

In addition to finding compound annual rates of return, we frequently need to find the **rate of growth**. This is the compound annual *rate of change* in some financial quantity, such as the price of a stock or the size of its dividend. Here we use an example to demonstrate a simple technique for estimating growth rates using a financial calculator and an Excel spreadsheet.

CALCULATOR USE Imagine that you wish to determine the rate at which ExxonMobil Corp. dividends grew from 2002 to 2011. Exxon's dividends appear in Table 10.3 (on page 334). The table presents 10 years of dividend payments, which means that the dividend had 9 years to grow from its 2002 value through 2011.

To use a financial calculator to find the growth rate for ExxonMobil dividends shown in Table 10.3, you treat the earliest (2002) value as a present value, PV, and the

Input	Function
−0.92	PV
1.85	FV
9	N
	CPT
	I

Solution
8.07

latest (2011) value as a future value, FV. (*Note:* Most calculators require you to key in either the PV or the FV as a negative number to calculate an unknown growth rate.) As noted above, although 10 years of dividends are shown in Table 10.3, there are only 9 years of growth (N = 9) because the earliest year (2002) must be defined as the base year (year 0). Using the inputs shown at the left, we calculate the growth rate to be 8.07%.

SPREADSHEET USE You can also calculate the growth rate using an Excel spreadsheet as shown below. Like the calculator, the spreadsheet equation simply calculates the annualized rate of change from the first dividend paid in 2002 to the last dividend paid in 2011. (Notice that only the first and last dividends and the 9 years between them were necessary to find the annual growth rate.)

In Chapter 9 we explored in greater detail the use of growth rates, which are often an important input to the common stock valuation process.

	A	B
1	GROWTH RATE FOR A DIVIDEND STREAM	
2	Year	Dividend
3	2002	$0.92
4	2003	$0.98
5	2004	$1.06
6	2005	$1.14
7	2006	$1.28
8	2007	$1.37
9	2008	$1.55
10	2009	$1.66
11	2010	$1.74
12	2011	$1.85
13	Annual Growth Rate	8.07%
14	Entry in Cell B13 is =RATE((A12-A3),0,-B3,B12,0). The expression (A12-A3) in the entry calculates the number of years of growth. The minus sign in front of B3 in the RATE formula is required because the dividend in 2002 is treated as a cash outflow.	

10.4 Define the following terms and explain how they are used to find the risk-free rate of return and the required rate of return for a given investment.

    a. *Real rate of return*

    b. *Expected inflation premium*

    c. *Risk premium* for a given investment

10.5 What is meant by the holding period, and why is it advisable to use holding periods of equal length when comparing alternative investments? Define the *holding period return*, and explain for what length holding periods it is typically used.

10.6 Define *yield* (*internal rate of return*). When is it appropriate to use yield rather than the HPR to measure the return on an investment?

10.7 Explain why you must earn 10% on all income received from an investment during its holding period in order for its yield actually to equal the 10% value you've calculated.

10.8 Explain how either the present value (of benefits versus cost) or the yield measure can be used to find a satisfactory investment. Given the following data, indicate which, if any, of these investments is acceptable. Explain your findings.

	Investment		
	A	B	C
Cost	$200	$160	$500
Required return	7%	10%	9%
Present value of income	—	$150	—
Yield	8%	—	8%

Risk: The Other Side of the Coin

LG5 LG6 Thus far, our primary concern in this chapter has been return. However, we cannot consider return without also looking at risk. *Risk* is the uncertainty surrounding the actual return that an investment will generate.

The risk associated with a given investment is directly related to its expected return. In general, the greater the investment's risk, the higher the expected return it must offer to attract investors. Riskier investments should provide higher returns. Otherwise, what incentive is there for an investor to risk his or her capital?

This relationship between risk and return is called the **risk-return tradeoff**. In general, investors want to obtain the highest possible return for the level of risk that they are willing to take. We introduce the risk-return tradeoff here and discuss it in greater detail in Chapter 11. We begin by examining the key sources of risk. We then consider the measurement and assessment of risk: the risk of a single asset, the assessment of risk associated with a potential investment, and the steps by which return and risk can be combined in the decision process.

How Are Risk and Return Related?

Sources of Risk

The risk associated with an investment may come from many different sources. A prudent investor considers how the major sources of risk might affect potential investments. The combined effect of different risks will be reflected in the investment's *risk premium*. As discussed earlier in the chapter and shown in Equation 10.3, you can find the required return on an investment by adding its risk premium to the risk-free rate. This premium in a broad sense results from the sources of risk, which derive from characteristics of both the issue and the issuer.

Business Risk In general, **business risk** is the degree of uncertainty associated with an investment's earnings and the investment's ability to pay the returns (interest, principal, dividends) owed investors. For example, business owners may receive no return if the firm's earnings are not adequate to meet obligations. Debt holders, on the other hand, are likely to receive some (but not necessarily all) of the amount owed them because of the preferential treatment legally accorded to debt.

The business risk associated with an investment is tied to the firm's industry. For example, the business risk in a public utility common stock differs from the risk in the stock of a high-fashion clothing manufacturer or an Internet start-up. Generally, investments in similar kinds of firms have similar business risk, although differences in management, costs, and location can cause varying risk levels.

Financial Risk Many firms raise money both by issuing common stock to investors and by borrowing money. When firms borrow money, they commit themselves to make future interest and principal payments, and those payments are generally not linked to a firm's profits but are instead fixed according to a contract between the firm and its lender. Therefore, when business conditions are good and profits are high, shareholders benefit from the use of debt because payments to lenders do not rise with profits, leaving more for shareholders. All other things being equal, a firm that uses debt will generate higher profits for its shareholders compared to a firm that uses no debt, but only when business conditions are good. When business conditions are poor, firms must repay their debts even if they are not making a profit. In that case, debt magnifies the losses that shareholders must endure, so a firm that uses debt will experience greater losses compared to a firm that has no debt. If a firm using debt has higher profits in good times and steeper losses in bad times (compared to a firm that borrows no money), we can say that debt magnifies a firm's business risk. Firms in all industries are subject to the ups and downs that we refer to as business risk, but firms that use debt take even more risk. That is why debt is also referred to as *leverage*. The increased uncertainty that results when a firm borrows money is called **financial risk**. The more debt used to finance a firm, the greater its financial risk.

Purchasing Power Risk The chance that unanticipated changes in price levels (inflation or deflation) will adversely affect investment returns is **purchasing power risk**. Specifically, this risk is the chance that an unexpected increase in prices (inflation) will reduce purchasing power (the goods and services that can be purchased with a dollar).

In general, investments whose values move with general price levels have low purchasing power risk and are most profitable during periods of rising prices. Those that provide fixed returns have high purchasing power risk, and they are most profitable during periods of low inflation or declining price levels. The returns on stocks of durable-goods manufacturers, for example, tend to move with the general price level, whereas returns from deposit accounts and bonds do not.

Interest Rate Risk Securities are especially affected by interest rate risk. This is particularly true for those securities that offer purchasers a fixed periodic return. **Interest rate risk** is the chance that changes in interest rates will adversely affect a security's value. The interest rate changes themselves result from changes in the general relationship between the supply of and the demand for money.

As interest rates change, the prices of many securities fluctuate. As we saw in greater detail in Chapters 2 and 8, the prices of fixed-income securities (bonds and preferred stock) typically drop when interest rates rise. As interest rates rise, new securities become available in the market, and those new securities pay the new, higher rates. Securities that are already outstanding make cash payments that reflect lower market rates from the past, so they are not competitive in the higher rate environment. Investors sell them, and their prices fall. The opposite occurs when interest rates fall: Prices of outstanding securities that make cash payments above the current market become more attractive, and their prices rise.

A second, more subtle aspect of interest rate risk is associated with reinvestment of income. As noted earlier, only if you can earn the initial rate of return on income received from an investment can you achieve a fully compounded rate of return equal to the initial rate of return. In other words, if a bond pays 8% annual interest, you must be able to earn 8% on the interest received during the bond's holding period in order to earn a fully compounded 8% rate of return over that period. This same aspect of interest rate risk applies to reinvestment of the proceeds received from an investment at its maturity or sale.

A final aspect of interest rate risk is related to investing in short-term securities such as U.S. Treasury bills and certificates of deposit. Investors face the risk that when short-term securities mature, they may have to invest those proceeds in lower-yielding, new short-term securities. By initially making a long-term investment, you can lock in a return for a period of years rather than face the risk of declines in short-term interest rates. Clearly, when interest rates are declining, the returns from investing in short-term securities are adversely affected. (On the other hand, interest rate increases have a positive impact on such a strategy.) The chance that interest rates will decline is therefore the interest rate risk of a strategy of investing in short-term securities.

Most investments are subject to interest rate risk. Although interest rate movements most directly affect fixed-income securities, they also affect other long-term investments such as common stock and mutual funds. Generally, the higher the interest rate, the lower the value of an investment, and vice versa.

Liquidity Risk The risk of not being able to sell (or liquidate) an investment quickly and at a reasonable price is called **liquidity risk**. One can generally sell an investment by significantly cutting its price. However, a liquid investment is one that investors can sell quickly without having an adverse impact on its price. For example, a security recently purchased for $1,000 would not be viewed as highly liquid if it could be quickly sold only at a greatly reduced price, such as $500.

An investment's liquidity is an important consideration. In general, investments traded in thin markets, where transaction volume is low, tend to be less liquid than those traded in broad markets. Assets such as stocks and bonds of major companies listed on the New York Stock Exchange are generally highly liquid; others, such as artwork and antique furniture, are relatively illiquid.

Tax Risk The chance that Congress will make unfavorable changes in tax laws is known as **tax risk**. The greater the chance that such changes will drive down the after-tax returns and market values of certain investments, the greater the tax risk. Unfavorable changes in tax laws include elimination of tax exemptions, limitation of deductions, and increases in tax rates.

Congress has passed numerous changes in tax laws through the years. One of the most significant, the Tax Reform Act of 1986, contained provisions that affected the attractiveness of many investments. In one of these provisions, the act mandated that capital gains would be taxed at the same rate as ordinary income (subject to a maximum rate of 28%). The Taxpayer Relief Act of 1997 reduced the maximum capital gains rate to 21.2%. More recently, the Jobs and Growth Tax Relief Reconciliation Act of 2003 temporarily reduced the capital gains rate to 15% (5% for individuals in the lowest two income tax brackets). The 15% rate on qualified dividends and long-term capital gains was initially scheduled to expire in 2008 but was extended through 2010 as a result of the Tax Increase Prevention and Reconciliation Act of 2005 signed into law by President Bush. The reduced rate was extended through 2012 in legislation passed by Congress and signed by President Barack Obama in December 2010. As a result, (1) from 2008 to 2012, the tax rate on qualified dividends and long-term capital gains is 0% for those in the 10% and 15% income tax brackets; (2) after 2012, dividends will be taxed at the taxpayer's ordinary income tax rate, regardless of his or her tax bracket; (3) after 2012, the long-term capital gains tax rate will be 20% (10% for taxpayers in the 15% tax bracket); and (4) after 2012, the qualified 5-year 18% capital gains rate (8% for taxpayers in the 15% tax bracket) will be reinstated (qualified 5-year gains are gains from the sale of certain properties held for 5 years or more).

Although virtually all investments are vulnerable to increases in tax rates, certain tax-advantaged investments, such as municipal and other bonds, real estate, and natural resources, generally have greater tax risk.

Event Risk **Event risk** occurs when something happens to a company that has a sudden and substantial impact on its financial condition. Event risk goes beyond business and financial risk. It does not necessarily mean the company or market is doing poorly. Instead, it involves an unexpected event that has a significant and usually immediate effect on the underlying value of an investment. An example of event risk is the February 2012 death of the chairman and CEO of Micron Technology, Inc. On the day he was killed, when an experimental plane he was piloting crashed, trading in Micron stock was halted on Nasdaq. When Micron stock opened for trading the following Monday morning, it was down 3.2%.

Event risk can take many forms and can affect all types of investments. Fortunately, its impact tends to be isolated in most cases.

Market Risk **Market risk** is the risk that investment returns will decline because of market factors independent of the given investment. Examples include political, economic, and social events, as well as changes in investor tastes and preferences. Market risk actually embodies a number of different risks including purchasing power risk, interest rate risk, and tax risk.

The impact of market factors on investment returns is not uniform. Both the degree and the direction of change in return differ among investments. For example, legislation placing restrictive import quotas on Japanese goods may result in a significant increase in the value (and therefore the return) of domestic companies that face direct competition from Japanese manufacturers. Essentially, market risk is reflected in a stock's sensitivity to these broad market forces. In other words, if a stock tends to move up or down sharply when the overall market moves, that stock has a high degree of market risk.

Risk of a Single Asset

Most people have at some time in their lives asked themselves how risky some anticipated course of action is. In such cases, the answer is usually a subjective judgment. In finance, we are able to quantify risk, which improves comparisons between investments and enhances decision making.

We can use statistical concepts to measure the risk of both single assets and portfolios of assets. First, we focus solely on the risk of single assets, and we show how the concept of standard deviation provides insights regarding an investment's risk. We will consider the risk and return of portfolios of assets later in Chapter 11.

Standard Deviation: An Absolute Measure of Risk The most common single indicator of an asset's risk is the **standard deviation, *s*.** It measures the dispersion (variation) of returns around an asset's average or expected return. The formula is

Equation 10.6

$$\text{Standard deviation} = \sqrt{\dfrac{\displaystyle\sum_{t=1}^{n} \left(\begin{array}{cc}\text{Return for} & \text{Average or} \\ \text{outcome } t & \text{expected return}\end{array}\right)^2}{\begin{array}{c}\text{Total number} \\ \text{of outcomes}\end{array} - 1}}$$

Equation 10.6a

$$s = \sqrt{\dfrac{\displaystyle\sum_{t=1}^{n}(r_t - \bar{r})^2}{n-1}}$$

Consider two competing investments—shares of stock in Target Corporation (TGT) and American Eagle Outfitters, Inc. (AEO)—described in Table 10.8. From 2002 to 2011, Target earned an average return of 6.4%, but American Eagle Outfitters achieved a considerably superior average return of 26.4%. Looking at the returns each year, you can see that American Eagle Outfitters returns fluctuated over a much wider range (from −53.5% to 187.8%) than did Target returns (from −30.0% to 42.5%).

The standard deviation provides a quantitative tool for comparing investment risk. Table 10.9 (on page 353) demonstrates the calculation of the standard deviations for Target and American Eagle Outfitters. We can see that the standard deviation of 26.2% for the returns on Target is, not surprisingly, considerably below the standard deviation of 77.2% for American Eagle Outfitters. The fact that American Eagle Outfitters stock returns fluctuate over a very wide range is reflected in its larger standard deviation and indicates that American Eagle Outfitters is a more volatile investment than Target. Of course, these figures are based on historical data. There is no assurance that the risks of these two investments will remain the same in the future.

TABLE 10.8 HISTORICAL ANNUAL RETURNS FOR TARGET AND AMERICAN EAGLE OUTFITTERS | EXCEL with Spreadsheets

Year (*t*)	Annual Rate of Return* (r_t)%	
	Target	American Eagle Outfitters
2002	−26.5	−47.3
2003	29.0	19.1
2004	36.2	187.8
2005	6.6	−1.3
2006	4.7	105.8
2007	−11.6	−32.4
2008	−30.0	−53.5
2009	42.5	86.4
2010	26.3	−8.5
2011	−13.0	8.0
Average ($\bar{r}$)	**6.4**	**26.4**

*Annual rate of return is calculated based on end-of-year closing prices.

(Source: End-of-year closing prices are obtained from Yahoo! Finance and are adjusted for dividends and stock splits.)

TABLE 10.9 **CALCULATION OF STANDARD DEVIATIONS OF RETURNS FOR TARGET AND AMERICAN EAGLE OUTFITTERS**

EXCEL
with Spreadsheets

Target

Year (t)	(1) Return r_t (%)	(2) Average Return $\bar{r}$ (%)	(3) (1) − (2) $r_t - \bar{r}$ (%)	(4) $(3)^2$ $(r_t - \bar{r})^2$ (%)
2002	−26.5	6.4	−32.9	1080.8
2003	29.0	6.4	22.6	508.8
2004	36.2	6.4	29.8	885.1
2005	6.6	6.4	0.2	0.0
2006	4.7	6.4	−1.8	3.1
2007	−11.6	6.4	−18.0	323.5
2008	−30.0	6.4	−36.4	1326.4
2009	42.5	6.4	36.1	1299.7
2010	26.3	6.4	19.9	395.9
2011	−13.0	6.4	−19.4	375.8
			Sum	6199.0
		Variance %^{2}	$s^2_{TGT} =$	688.8
		Standard deviation %	$s_{TGT} =$	26.2

$$s_{TGT} = \sqrt{\frac{\sum_{t=1}^{10}(r_t - \bar{r})^2}{n-1}} = \sqrt{\frac{6,199.0}{10-1}} = \sqrt{688.8} = 26.2\%$$

American Eagle Outfitters

Year (t)	(1) Return r_t (%)	(2) Average Return $\bar{r}$ (%)	(3) (1) − (2) $r_t - \bar{r}$ (%)	(4) $(3)^2$ $(r_t - \bar{r})^2$ (%)
2002	−47.3	26.4	−73.7	5438.8
2003	19.1	26.4	−7.3	53.3
2004	187.8	26.4	161.3	26033.5
2005	−1.3	26.4	−27.7	768.2
2006	105.8	26.4	79.4	6304.7
2007	−32.4	26.4	−58.8	3461.3
2008	−53.5	26.4	−79.9	6388.3
2009	86.4	26.4	60.0	3600.8
2010	−8.5	26.4	−34.9	1215.6
2011	8.0	26.4	−18.4	337.3
			Sum	53601.7
		Variance %^{2}	$s^2_{AOE} =$	5955.7
		Standard deviation %	$s_{AEO} =$	77.2

$$s_{AEO} = \sqrt{\frac{\sum_{t=1}^{10}(r_t - \bar{r})^2}{n-1}} = \sqrt{\frac{53,601.7}{10-1}} = \sqrt{5,955.7} = 77.2\%$$

Historical Returns and Risk We can now use the standard deviation as a measure of risk to assess the historical (1900–2011) investment return data in Table 10.4. Table 10.10 reports the average return and the standard deviation associated with each investment. Within each country, a close relationship exists between the average return and the standard deviation of different types of investments. Stocks earn higher returns than bonds, and bonds earn higher returns than bills. Similarly, stock returns are more volatile than bond returns, with bill returns displaying the least volatility (i.e., the lowest standard deviation). Regardless of the country, the general pattern is clear: Investments with higher average returns have higher standard deviations. Because higher standard deviations are associated with greater risk, the historical data confirm the existence of a positive relationship between risk and return. That relationship reflects the fact that market participants require higher returns as compensation for greater risk.

Assessing Risk

Techniques for quantifying the risk of an investment are quite useful. However, they will be of little value if you are unaware of your feelings toward risk. Individual investors typically seek answers to these questions: "Is the amount of perceived risk worth taking to get the expected return?" "Can I get a higher return for the same level of risk,

TABLE 10.10   HISTORICAL RETURNS AND STANDARD DEVIATIONS FOR SELECT ASSET CLASSES (1900–2011)

	Stocks		Long-Term Government Bonds		Short-Term Government Bills	
	Average Annual Return (%)	Standard Deviation of Returns (%)	Average Annual Return (%)	Standard Deviation of Returns (%)	Average Annual Return (%)	Standard Deviation of Returns (%)
Australia	11.3	18.2	5.5	13.2	4.6	5.4
Belgium	7.8	23.6	5.2	11.9	4.9	8.0
Canada	8.9	17.2	5.3	10.4	4.6	4.9
Denmark	8.9	20.9	7.2	11.7	6.2	6.0
Finland	12.6	30.4	7.1	13.6	6.7	11.8
France	10.2	23.5	7.1	13.0	4.1	9.5
Germany	8.1	32.2	2.9	15.6	2.2	13.3
Ireland	8.1	23.1	5.2	14.8	4.9	6.6
Italy	10.2	29.0	6.5	14.0	4.5	11.5
Japan	10.8	29.8	5.8	20.0	4.9	13.9
Netherlands	7.9	21.8	4.5	9.4	3.6	4.9
New Zealand	9.7	19.7	5.9	9.1	5.5	4.7
Norway	7.9	27.3	5.6	12.2	4.9	7.1
South Africa	12.5	22.5	6.8	10.3	6.0	6.2
Spain	9.4	22.2	7.2	11.7	6.1	5.8
Sweden	9.9	22.9	6.2	12.4	5.5	6.8
Switzerland	6.5	19.7	4.5	9.3	3.1	5.0
United Kingdom	9.4	19.9	5.5	13.8	5.0	6.4
United States	9.3	20.2	5.0	10.3	3.9	4.7

(Source: Elroy Dimson, Paul Marsh, and Mike Staunton, Credit Suisse Global Investment Returns Sourcebook 2012.)

FIGURE 10.2

Risk-Return Tradeoffs for Various Investments

A risk-return tradeoff exists such that for a higher risk one expects a higher return, and vice versa. In general, low-risk/low-return investments include U.S. government securities and deposit accounts. High-risk/high-return investments include real estate and other tangible investments, common stocks, options, and futures.

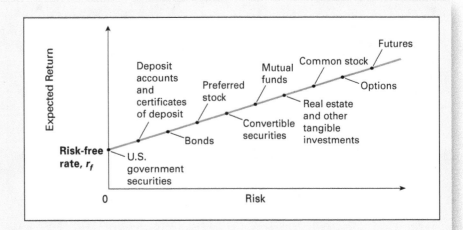

or can I earn the same return while taking less risk?" A look at the general risk-return characteristics of alternative investments and at the question of an acceptable level of risk will shed light on how to evaluate risk.

Risk-Return Characteristics of Alternative Investments A very rough generalization of the risk-return characteristics of the major types of investments appears in Figure 10.2. Of course, within each category, specific investments can vary dramatically in terms of their risk and return characteristics. For instance, some common stocks offer low returns and low risk, while others offer high returns and high risk. In other words, once you have selected the appropriate type of investment, you must still decide which specific security to acquire.

An Acceptable Level of Risk Individuals differ in the amount of risk that they are willing to bear and the return that they require as compensation for bearing that risk. Broadly speaking, we can talk about investors' attitudes toward risk by defining three distinct categories of investors whose preferences regarding risk vary in fundamental ways, as depicted in Figure 10.3 (on page 356). The figure shows how the required return on an investment is related to risk for investors with different preferences. The three categories are risk-indifferent, risk-averse, and risk-seeking investors.

- For **risk-indifferent** (or risk-neutral) investors, the required return does not change as risk changes. For example, in Figure 10.3, the horizontal blue line indicates that the risk-indifferent investor will accept the same return even if an investment's risk increases from x_1 to x_2.

- For **risk-averse** investors, the required return increases with risk. Because they do not like risk, these investors require higher expected returns to compensate them for taking greater risk. In Figure 10.3, the preferences of risk-averse investors are depicted by the upward sloping green line.

- For the **risk-seeking** investor, the required return decreases as risk increases. These investors simply enjoy the thrill of taking a risk, so they willingly give up some return to take more risk, as indicated by the downward sloping red line in Figure 10.3.

FIGURE 10.3

Risk Preferences

The risk-indifferent investor requires no change in return for a given increase in risk. The risk-averse investor requires an increase in return for a given risk increase. The risk-seeking investor gives up some return for more risk. The majority of investors are risk averse.

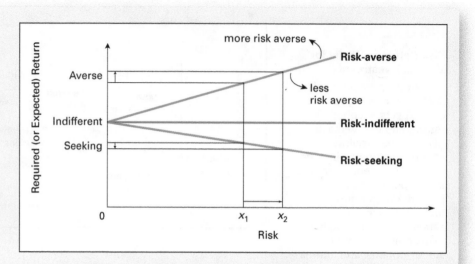

We have already seen historical data on the risk and return of different investments from all over the world, and that data indicate that riskier investments tend to pay higher returns. This simply reflects the fact that most investors are risk averse, so riskier investments must offer higher returns to attract buyers.

How much additional return is required to convince an investor to purchase a riskier investment? The answer to that question varies from one person to another depending on the investor's degree of risk aversion. A very risk-averse investor requires a great deal of compensation to take on additional risk, meaning that the green line in Figure 10.3 would be very steep for such a person. Someone who is less risk averse does not require as much compensation to be persuaded to accept risk, so for that sort of person the green line would be flatter (but still upward sloping).

Steps in the Decision Process: Combining Return and Risk

When you are deciding among alternative investments, you should take the following steps to combine return and risk.

1. Using historical or projected return data, estimate the expected return over a given holding period. Be sure that your estimate of an investment's expected return takes into account the time value of money.

2. Using historical or projected return data, assess the risk associated with the investment. You can assess an investment's risk by making a subjective judgment, by calculating the standard deviation of an investment's returns, or by using a more sophisticated method (developed in Chapter 11).

3. Evaluate the risk-return characteristics of each investment option to make sure that the return that you expect is reasonable given the risk that you are taking. If other investments with lower levels of risk provide equal or greater expected returns, the investment is not acceptable.

4. Select the investments that offer the highest returns associated with the level of risk you are willing to take. As long as you get the highest expected return for your acceptable level of risk, you have made a "good investment."

Probably the most difficult step in this process is assessing risk. Aside from return and risk considerations, other factors such as taxes and liquidity affect the investment decision. You will learn more about assessing these other factors in subsequent chapters.

CONCEPTS IN REVIEW

Answers available at www.pearsonhighered.com/smart

10.9 Define *risk*. Explain what we mean by the *risk-return tradeoff*. What happens to the required return as risk increases? Explain.

10.10 Define and briefly discuss each of the following sources of risk.

a. Business risk
b. Financial risk
c. Purchasing power risk
d. Interest rate risk

e. Liquidity risk
f. Tax risk
g Event risk
h. Market risk

10.11 Briefly describe standard deviation as a measure of risk or variability.

10.12 Differentiate among the three basic risk preferences: risk-indifferent, risk-averse, and risk-seeking. Which of these attitudes toward risk best describes most investors?

10.13 Describe the steps involved in the investment decision process. Be sure to mention how returns and risks can be evaluated together to determine acceptable investments.

MyFinanceLab

Here is what you should know after reading this chapter. MyFinanceLab will help you identify what you know and where to go when you need to practice.

What You Should Know	Key Terms	Where to Practice
LG1 Review the concept of return, its components, the forces that affect the level of return, and historical returns. Return is the reward for investing. The total return provided by an investment includes income and capital gains (or losses). Return is commonly calculated on a historical basis and then used to project expected returns. The level of return depends on internal characteristics and external forces, which include the general level of price changes. Significant differences exist among the average annual rates of return realized over time on various types of security investments.	deflation, *p. 335* expected return, *p. 334* income, *p. 332* inflation, *p. 335* return, *p. 332* total return, *p. 333*	MyFinanceLab Study Plan 10.1 Excel Table 10.3
LG2 Discuss the role of time value of money in measuring return and defining a satisfactory investment. Because investors have opportunities to earn interest on their funds, money has a time value. Time value concepts should be considered when making investment decisions. Financial calculators and electronic spreadsheets can be used to streamline time value calculations. A satisfactory investment is one for which the present value of its benefits equals or exceeds the present value of its costs.	satisfactory investment, *p. 337*	MyFinanceLab Study Plan 10.2 Excel Table 10.5

What You Should Know	Key Terms	Where to Practice
LG3 **Describe real, risk-free, and required returns and the calculation and application of holding period return.** The required return is the rate of return an investor must earn to be fully compensated for an investment's risk. It represents the sum of the real rate of return and the expected inflation premium (which together represent the risk-free rate), plus the risk premium. The risk premium varies depending on issue and issuer characteristics. The holding period return (HPR) is the return earned over a specified period of time. It is frequently used to compare returns earned in periods of 1 year or less.	expected inflation premium, *p. 340* holding period, *p. 341* holding period return (HPR), *p. 341* nominal rate of return, *p. 339* paper return, *p. 341* real rate of return, *p. 339* realized return, *p. 341* required return, *p. 340* risk-free rate, *p. 340* risk premium, *p. 340*	MyFinanceLab Study Plan 10.3 Excel Table 10.6 Video Learning Aid for Problem P10.10
LG4 **Explain the concept and the calculation of yield and how to find growth rates.** Yield (or internal rate of return) is the compound annual rate of return earned on investments held for more than one year. If the yield is greater than or equal to the required return, the investment is acceptable. The concept of yield assumes that the investor will be able to earn interest at the calculated yield rate on all income from the investment. Present value techniques can be used to find a rate of growth, which is the compound annual rate of change in the value of a stream of income, particularly dividends or earnings.	fully compounded rate of return, *p. 346* rate of growth, *p. 346* reinvestment rate, *p. 345* yield (internal rate of return), *p. 343*	MyFinanceLab Study Plan 10.4 Excel Table 10.7
LG5 **Discuss the key sources of risk that might affect potential investments.** Risk is uncertainty surrounding the actual return that an investment will generate. Risk results from a combination of sources: business, financial, purchasing power, interest rate, liquidity, tax, market, and event risk. These risks have varying effects on different types of investments. The combined impact of any of the sources of risk in a given investment would be reflected in its risk premium.	business risk, *p. 348* financial risk, *p. 349* interest rate risk, *p. 349* liquidity risk, *p. 350* purchasing power risk, *p. 349* risk-return tradeoff, *p. 348* tax risk, *p. 350*	MyFinanceLab Study Plan 10.5
LG6 **Understand the risk of a single asset, risk assessment, and the steps that combine return and risk.** The standard deviation measures the volatility of both single assets and portfolios of assets. Investors require higher returns as compensation for greater risk. Generally, each type of investment displays certain risk-return characteristics. Most investors are risk averse: For a given increase in risk, they require an increase in expected return. Investors estimate the return and risk of each alternative and then select investments that offer the highest returns for the level of acceptable risk.	event risk, *p. 351* market risk, *p. 351* risk-averse, *p. 355* risk-indifferent, *p. 355* risk-seeking, *p. 355* standard deviation, *s*, *p. 352*	MyFinanceLab Study Plan 10.6 Excel Table 10.9

Log into MyFinanceLab, take a chapter test, and get a personalized Study Plan that tells you which concepts you understand and which ones you need to review. From there, MyFinanceLab will give you further practice, tutorials, animations, videos, and guided solutions.
Log into **www.myfinancelab.com**

Discussion Questions

G1 **Q10.1** Choose a publicly traded company that has been listed on a major exchange or in the over-the-counter market for at least 5 years. Use any data source of your choice to find the annual cash dividend, if any, paid by the company in each of the past 5 calendar years. Also find the closing price of the stock at the end of each of the preceding 6 years.

   a. Calculate the return for each of the five 1-year periods.

   b. Create a graph that shows the return that the investment earned on the y-axis and the year in which the return was earn on the x-axis.

   c. On the basis of the graph in part **b**, estimate the return for the coming year, and explain your answer.

G2 **Q10.2** Two investments offer a series of cash payments over the next 4 years, as shown in the following table:

Investment	Year 1	Year 2	Year 3	Year 4
1	$100	$200	$300	$400
2	$250	$250	$250	$250

   a. What is the total amount of money paid by each investment over the 4 years?

   b. From a time value of money perspective, which of these investments is more attractive?

   c. Can you think of a reason why investors might prefer Investment 1?

G4 **Q10.3** Access appropriate estimates of the expected inflation rate over the next year, and the current yield on 1-year, risk-free securities (the yield on these securities is referred to as the *nominal* rate of interest). Use the data to estimate the current risk-free *real* rate of interest.

G3 G6 **Q10.4** Choose 3 NYSE-listed stocks and maintain a record of their dividend payments, if any, and closing prices each week over the next 6 weeks.

   a. At the end of the 6-week period, calculate the 1-week HPRs for each stock for each of the 6 weeks.

   b. For each stock, average the 6 weekly HPRs calculated in part **a** and compare them.

   c. Use the averages you computed in part **b** and compute the standard deviation of the six HPRs for each stock. Discuss the stocks' relative risk and return behavior. Did the stocks with the highest risk earn the greatest return?

Problems

All problems are available on **www.myfinancelab.com**

G1 **P10.1** How much would an investor earn on a stock purchased 1 year ago for $45 if it paid an annual cash dividend of $2.25 and had just been sold for $52.50? Would the investor have experienced a capital gain? Explain.

G1 **P10.2** An investor buys a bond for $10,000. The bond pays $300 interest every 6 months. After 18 months, the investor sells the bond for $9,500. Describe the types of income and/or loss the investor had.

G1 **P10.3** Assuming you purchased a share of stock for $50 one year ago, sold it today for $60, and during the year received 3 dividend payments totaling $2.70, calculate the following.

   a. Income

   b. Capital gain (or loss)

   c. Total return

      (1) In dollars

      (2) As a percentage of the initial investment

LG1   P10.4   Assume you purchased a bond for $9,500. The bond pays $300 interest every 6 months. You sell the bond after 18 months for $10,000. Calculate the following:
  a. Income
  b. Capital gain or loss
  c. Total return in dollars and as a percentage of the original investment

LG1   P10.5   Consider the historical data for an investment given in the accompanying table.
  a. Calculate the total return (in dollars) for each year.
  b. Indicate the level of return you would expect in 2015 and in 2016.
  c. Comment on your forecast.

| Year | Income ($) | Market Value (Price $) | |
		Beginning	Ending
2010	1.00	30.00	32.50
2011	1.20	32.50	35.00
2012	1.30	35.00	33.00
2013	1.60	33.00	40.00
2014	1.75	40.00	45.00

LG1   P10.6   Refer to the table in Problem 10.5. What is the total return in dollars and as a percentage of your original investment if you purchased 100 shares of the investment at the beginning of 2010 and sold it at the end of 2012?

LG3   P10.7   Given a real rate of interest of 2%, an expected inflation premium of 3%, and risk premiums for investments A and B of 4% and 6%, respectively, find the following.
  a. The risk-free rate of return, r_f
  b. The required returns for investments A and B

LG3   P10.8   The risk-free rate is 7%, and expected inflation is 4.5%. If inflation expectations change such that future expected inflation rises to 5.5%, what will the new risk-free rate be?

LG3   P10.9   Calculate the holding period return for the following two investment alternatives. Which, if any, of the return components is likely not to be realized if you continue to hold each of the investments beyond 1 year? Which investment would you prefer, assuming they are of equal risk? Explain.

| | Investment | |
	X	Y
Cash received		
1st quarter	$ 1.00	$ 0
2nd quarter	1.20	0
3rd quarter	0	0
4th quarter	2.30	2.00
Investment value		
Beginning of year	$30.00	$50.00
End of year	29.00	56.00

LG3   P10.10   You are considering 2 investment alternatives. The first is a stock that pays quarterly dividends of $0.25 per share and is trading at $30 per share; you expect to sell the stock in 6 months for $34. The second is a stock that pays quarterly dividends of $0.50 per share and is trading at $27 per share; you expect to sell the stock in 1 year for $30. Which stock will provide the better annualized holding period return?

LG3   **P10.11**   You are considering purchasing a bond that pays annual interest of $50 per $1,000 of par value. The bond matures in 1 year, when you will collect the par value and the interest payment. If you can purchase this bond for $950, what is the holding period return?

LG4   **P10.12**   Assume you invest $5,000 today in an investment that promises to return $9,000 in exactly 10 years.
      a. Use the present value technique to estimate the yield on this investment.
      b. If a minimum return of 9% is required, would you recommend this investment?

LG4   **P10.13**   You invest $7,000 in stock and receive $65, $70, $70, and $65 in dividends over the following 4 years. At the end of the 4 years, you sell the stock for $7,900. What was the yield on this investment?

LG4   **P10.14**   Your friend asks you to invest $10,000 in a business venture. Based on your estimates, you would receive nothing for 4 years, at the end of year 5 you would receive $4,690, and at the end of year 6 you would receive $14,500. If your estimates are correct, what would be the yield on this investment?

LG4   **P10.15**   Use a financial calculator or an Excel spreadsheet to estimate the yield each of the following investments.

Investment	Initial Investment ($)	Future Value ($)	End of Year
A	1,000	1,200	5
B	10,000	20,000	7
C	400	2,000	20
D	3,000	4,000	6
E	5,500	25,000	30

LG4   **P10.16**   Sara Holliday must earn a return of 10% on an investment that requires an initial outlay of $2,500 and promises to return $6,000 in 8 years.
      a. Use present value techniques to estimate the yield on this investment.
      b. On the basis of your finding in part a, should Sara make the proposed investment? Explain.

LG4   **P10.17**   Use a financial calculator or an Excel spreadsheet to estimate the yield for each of the following investments.

	Investment	
	A	B
Initial Investment	$8,500	$9,500
End of Year	Income ($)	
1	2,500	2,000
2	2,500	2,500
3	2,500	3,000
4	2,500	3,500
5	2,500	4,000

LG4   P10.18   Elliott Dumack must earn a minimum rate of return of 11% to be adequately compensated for the risk of the following investment.

Initial Investment	$14,000
End of Year	Income ($)
1	6,000
2	3,000
3	5,000
4	2,000
5	1,000

a. Use present value techniques to estimate the yield on this investment.
b. On the basis of your finding in part a, should Elliott make the proposed investment? Explain.

LG4   P10.19   Assume that an investment generates the following income stream and can be purchased at the beginning of 2014 for $1,000 and sold at the end of 2020 for $1,200. Estimate the yield for this investment. If a minimum return of 9% is required, would you recommend this investment? Explain.

End of Year	Income Stream ($)
2014	140
2015	120
2016	100
2017	80
2018	60
2019	40
2020	20

LG4   P10.20   For each of the following streams of dividends, estimate the compound annual rate of growth between the earliest year for which a value is given and 2014.

	Dividend Stream		
Year	A	B	C
2005		$1.50	
2006		1.55	
2007		1.61	
2008		1.68	$2.50
2009		1.76	2.60
2010	$5.00	1.85	2.65
2011	5.60	1.95	2.65
2012	6.40	2.06	2.80
2013	7.20	2.17	2.85
2014	8.00	2.28	2.90

LG4   P10.21   A company paid dividends of $1.00 per share in 2006 and just announced that it will pay $2.21 in 2013. Estimate the compound annual growth rate of the dividends.

LG4   P10.22   A company reported net income in 2009 of $350 million. In 2013 the company expects net income to be $441.7 million. Estimate the annual compound growth rate of net income.

LG4   P10.23   The historical returns for 2 investments—A and B—are summarized in the table below for the period 2010 to 2014. Use the data to answer the questions that follow.

	A	B
Year	Rate of Return (%)	
2010	19	8
2011	1	10
2012	10	12
2013	26	14
2014	4	16
Average	12	12

a. On the basis of a review of the return data, which investment appears to be more risky? Why?

b. Calculate the standard deviation for each investment's returns.

c. On the basis of your calculations in part **b**, which investment is more risky? Compare this conclusion to your observation in part **a**.

Visit **www.myfinancelab.com** for web exercises, spreadsheets, and other online resources.

Case Problem 10.1   Coates's Decision

LG2 LG4   On January 1, 2014, Dave Coates, a 23-year-old mathematics teacher at Xavier High School, received a tax refund of $1,100. Because Dave didn't need this money for his current living expenses, he decided to make a long-term investment. After surveying a number of alternative investments costing no more than $1,100, Dave isolated 2 that seemed most suitable to his needs.

Each of the investments cost $1,050 and was expected to provide income over a 10-year period. Investment A provided a relatively certain stream of income. Dave was a little less certain of the income provided by investment B. From his search for suitable alternatives, Dave found that the appropriate discount rate for a relatively certain investment was 12%. Because he felt a bit uncomfortable with an investment like B, he estimated that such an investment would have to provide a return at least 4% higher than investment A. Although Dave planned to reinvest funds returned from the investments in other vehicles providing similar returns, he wished to keep the extra $50 ($1,100 − $1,050) invested for the full 10 years in a savings account paying 5% interest compounded annually.

As he makes his investment decision, Dave has asked for your help in answering the questions that follow the expected return data for these investments.

	Expected Returns	
End of Year	A	B
2014	$150	$100
2015	150	150
2016	150	200
2017	150	250
2018	150	300
2019	150	350
2020	150	300
2021	150	250
2022	150	200
2023	1,150	150

Questions

a. Assuming that investments A and B are equally risky and using the 12% discount rate, apply the present value technique to assess the acceptability of each investment and to determine the preferred investment. Explain your findings.

b. Recognizing that investment B is more risky than investment A, reassess the 2 alternatives, adding the 4% risk premium to the 12% discount rate for investment A and therefore applying a 16% discount rate to investment B. Compare your findings relative to acceptability and preference to those found for question a.

c. From your findings in questions a and b, indicate whether the yield for investment A is above or below 12% and whether that for investment B is above or below 16%. Explain.

d. Use the present value technique to estimate the yield on each investment. Compare your findings and contrast them with your response to question c.

e. From the information given, which, if either, of the 2 investments would you recommend that Dave make? Explain your answer.

f. Indicate to Dave how much money the extra $50 will have grown to by the end of 2023, assuming he makes no withdrawals from the savings account.

Case Problem 10.2   The Risk-Return Tradeoff: Molly O'Rourke's Stock Purchase Decision

LG3 LG6   Over the past 10 years, Molly O'Rourke has slowly built a diversified portfolio of common stock. Currently her portfolio includes 20 different common stock issues and has a total market value of $82,500.

Molly is at present considering the addition of 50 shares of either of 2 common stock issues—X or Y. To assess the return and risk of each of these issues, she has gathered dividend income and share price data for both over the last 10 years (2004–2013). Molly's investigation of the outlook for these issues suggests that each will, on average, tend to behave in the future just as it has in the past. She therefore believes that the expected return can be estimated by finding the average HPR over the past 10 years for each of the stocks. The historical dividend income and stock price data collected by Molly are given in the accompanying table.

		Stock X				Stock Y	
		Share Price				Share Price	
Year	Dividend Income	Beginning	Ending	Dividend Income	Beginning	Ending
2004	$1.00	$20.00	$22.00	$1.50	$20.00	$20.00
2005	1.50	22.00	21.00	1.60	20.00	20.00
2006	1.40	21.00	24.00	1.70	20.00	21.00
2007	1.70	24.00	22.00	1.80	21.00	21.00
2008	1.90	22.00	23.00	1.90	21.00	22.00
2009	1.60	23.00	26.00	2.00	22.00	23.00
2010	1.70	26.00	25.00	2.10	23.00	23.00
2011	2.00	25.00	24.00	2.20	23.00	24.00
2012	2.10	24.00	27.00	2.30	24.00	25.00
2013	2.20	27.00	30.00	2.40	25.00	25.00

Questions

a. Determine the HPR for each stock in each of the preceding 10 years. Find the expected return for each stock, using the approach specified by Molly.

b. Use the HPRs and expected return calculated in question a to find the standard deviation of the HPRs for each stock over the 10-year period.

c. Use your findings to evaluate and discuss the return and risk associated with stocks X and Y. Which stock seems preferable? Explain.

d. Ignoring her existing portfolio, what recommendations would you give Molly with regard to stocks X and Y?

Excel with Spreadsheets

From her Investment Analysis class, Laura has been given an assignment to evaluate several securities on a risk-return tradeoff basis. The specific securities to be researched are International Business Machines, Helmerich & Payne, Inc., and the S&P 500 Index. The respective ticker symbols for the stocks are IBM and HP. She finds the following data on the securities in question.

Year	2006	2007	2008	2009	2010	2011
Price$_{IBM}$	$ 97.15	$ 108.10	$ 84.16	$ 130.90	$ 146.76	$ 183.88
Dividend$_{IBM}$	1.10	1.50	1.90	2.15	2.50	2.90
Price$_{HP}$	24.47	40.07	22.75	39.88	48.48	58.36
Dividend$_{HP}$	0.17	0.18	0.19	0.20	0.22	0.26
Value$_{S\&P}$	1,418.30	1,468.40	903.30	1,115.10	1,257.60	1,257.60

Note: The value of the S&P 500 index includes dividends.

Questions

Part One

a. Use the data that Laura has found on the 3 securities and create a spreadsheet to calculate the holding period return for each year and the average return over a 5-year period. Specifically, the HPR will be based upon 5 unique periods of 1 year (i.e., 2006 to 2007, 2007 to 2008, 2008 to 2009, 2009 to 2010, 2010 to 2011). Use the following formula:

$$HPR = [Inc + (V_n - V_0)]/V_0$$

Where

Inc = income during period

V_n = ending investment value

V_0 = beginning investment value

Part Two

Create a spreadsheet similar to the spreadsheet for Table 10.9 (on page 353), which can be viewed at www.myfinancelab.com, in order to evaluate the risk-return tradeoff.

b. Calculate the standard deviations of the returns for IBM, HP, and the S&P 500 Index.

c. What industries are associated with IBM and HP?

d. Based on your answer in part c and your results for the average return and the standard deviation, what conclusions can Laura make about investing in either IBM or HP?

Chapter-Opening Problem

The table below shows the annual change in the average U.S. home price from 2002 to 2011 according to the S&P/Case-Shiller Index. Calculate the average annual return and its standard deviation. Compare this to the average return and standard deviation for Target Corporation and American Eagle Outfitters, Inc., shown in Table 10.9 (on page 353). In terms of average return and standard deviation, how does residential real estate compare as an investment relative to those 2 common stocks?

Year	% Change
2002	12.2
2003	11.4
2004	16.2
2005	15.5
2006	0.7
2007	−9.0
2008	−18.6
2009	−3.1
2010	−2.4
2011	−4.1

11

Modern Portfolio Concepts

LEARNING GOALS

After studying this chapter, you should be able to:

LG1 Understand portfolio objectives and the procedures used to calculate portfolio return and standard deviation.

LG2 Discuss the concepts of correlation and diversification and the key aspects of international diversification.

LG3 Describe the components of risk and the use of beta to measure risk.

LG4 Explain the capital asset pricing model (CAPM) conceptually, mathematically, and graphically.

LG5 Review the traditional and modern approaches to portfolio management.

LG6 Describe portfolio betas, the risk-return tradeoff, and reconciliation of the two approaches to portfolio management.

United Rentals Inc. (URI) rents construction and industrial equipment to contractors, businesses, governments, and individuals. The company specializes in heavy equipment such as earth-moving machines and forklifts. During the recession that began in 2007, many companies found that they did not have enough work to do to keep the machines they already owned running, so naturally the demand for rental equipment suffered. URI stock reached a 2007 peak of just over $35 per share in May, but after that began a long slide, hitting bottom at $2.52 in March 2009.

That spring, the economy began to show signs of life, and URI stock surged, rising nearly 200% from its low point by August 2009. Heiko Ihle, a stock analyst for the Gabelli & Co. money management firm, issued a "buy" rating on URI despite the fact that the company had high leverage (meaning that it borrowed a lot of money to finance its operations). Ihle noted that URI stock had a high beta, meaning that it moved sharply when the broader market shifted.

Mr. Ihle's recommendation proved to be a good one. From the end of August 2009 to the end of April 2012, the value of URI stock climbed more than 400% and was trading above $46 per share. Over that same period of time, the S&P 500 Index, a widely used indicator of the overall stock market, rose by a less dramatic 38%.

In this chapter we continue to explore the tradeoff between risk and return, and we'll see that a stock's beta—it's sensitivity to movements in the overall stock market—has a big effect on both the stock's risk and the return that it offers investors.

(Sources: Yahoo! Finance; "U.S. Hot Stocks: Legg Mason, JDA Software Active in Late Trading," July 20, 2009; The Wall Street Journal Digital Network, online.wsj.com/article/BT-CO-20090720-713541.html)

Principles of Portfolio Planning

LG1 LG2 Investors benefit from holding portfolios of investments rather than single investments. Without necessarily sacrificing returns, investors who hold portfolios can reduce risk. Surprisingly, the volatility of a portfolio may be less than the volatilities of the individual assets that make up the portfolio. In other words, when it comes to portfolios and risk, the whole is less than the sum of its parts!

A *portfolio* is a collection of investments assembled to meet one or more investment goals. Of course, different investors have different objectives for their portfolios. The primary goal of a **growth-oriented portfolio** is long-term price appreciation. An **income-oriented portfolio** is designed to produce regular dividends and interest payments.

Portfolio Objectives

Setting portfolio objectives involves definite tradeoffs, such as the tradeoff between risk and return or between potential price appreciation and income. How you evaluate these tradeoffs will depend on your tax bracket, current income needs, and ability to bear risk. The key point is that your portfolio objectives must be established *before* you begin to invest.

The ultimate goal of an investor is an **efficient portfolio**, one that provides the highest return for a given level of risk. Efficient portfolios aren't necessarily easy to identify. You usually must search out investment alternatives to get the best combinations of risk and return.

Portfolio Return and Standard Deviation

The first step in forming a portfolio is to analyze the characteristics of the securities that an investor might include in the portfolio. Two of the most important characteristics to examine are the returns that each asset might be expected to earn and the uncertainty surrounding that expected return. As a starting point, we will examine historical data to see what returns stocks have earned in the past and how much those returns have fluctuated to get a feel for what the future might hold.

The return on a portfolio is calculated as a weighted average of returns on the assets (i.e., the investments) that make up the portfolio. You can calculate the portfolio return, r_p, by using Equation 11.1. The portfolio return depends on the returns of each asset in the portfolio and on the fraction invested in each asset, w_j.

Equation 11.1

$$
\begin{aligned}
\begin{matrix}\text{Return} \\ \text{on} \\ \text{portfolio}\end{matrix} &=
\left(\begin{matrix}\text{Proportion of} \\ \text{portfolio's total} \\ \text{dollar value} \\ \text{invested in} \\ \text{asset 1}\end{matrix} \times \begin{matrix}\text{Return} \\ \text{on asset} \\ 1\end{matrix}\right) +
\left(\begin{matrix}\text{Proportion of} \\ \text{portfolio's total} \\ \text{dollar value} \\ \text{invested in} \\ \text{asset 2}\end{matrix} \times \begin{matrix}\text{Return} \\ \text{on asset} \\ 2\end{matrix}\right) + \cdots + \\[2em]
&\left(\begin{matrix}\text{Proportion of} \\ \text{portfolio's total} \\ \text{dollar value} \\ \text{invested in} \\ \text{asset } n\end{matrix} \times \begin{matrix}\text{Return} \\ \text{on asset} \\ n\end{matrix}\right) =
\sum_{j=1}^{n}\left(\begin{matrix}\text{Proportion of} \\ \text{portfolio's total} \\ \text{dollar value} \\ \text{invested in} \\ \text{asset } j\end{matrix} \times \begin{matrix}\text{Return} \\ \text{on asset} \\ j\end{matrix}\right)
\end{aligned}
$$

Equation 11.1a

$$r_p = (w_1 \times r_1) + (w_2 \times r_2) + \cdots + (w_n \times r_n) = \sum_{j=1}^{n}(w_j \times r_j)$$

Of course, $\sum_{j=1}^{n} w_j = 1$, which means that 100% of the portfolio's assets must be included in this computation.

Panel A of Table 11.1 shows the historical annual returns on two stocks, International Business Machines Corp. (IBM) and Celgene Corp. (CELG), from 2001 through 2010. Over that period, IBM earned an average annual return of 10.4%, which is close to the average annual return on the U.S. stock market during the past century. In contrast, Celgene Corp. earned a spectacular 32.1% annual return. Although Celgene is unlikely to repeat that kind of performance over the next decade, it is still instructive to examine the historical figures.

Now suppose we want to calculate the return on a portfolio containing investments in both IBM and Celgene. The first step in that calculation is to determine how much of each stock to hold. In other words, we must to decide what weight each stock should receive in the portfolio. Let's assume that we want to invest 86% of our money in IBM and 14% in CELG. What kind of return would such a portfolio earn?

TABLE 11.1	INDIVIDUAL AND PORTFOLIO RETURNS AND STANDARD DEVIATION OF RETURNS FOR INTERNATIONAL BUSINESS MACHINES (IBM) AND CELGENE (CELG)	EXCEL with Spreadsheets

A. Individual and Portfolio Returns

Year (t)	(1) $r_{IBM}\%$	(2) $r_{CELG}\%$	(3) Portfolio Weights		(4) Portfolio Return $r_p\%$
	Historical Returns*		$W_{IBM} = 0.86$	$W_{CELG} = 0.14$	
2001	43.0	−1.7	$(0.86 \times 43.0\%) + (0.14 \times -1.7\%) =$		36.7
2002	−35.5	−32.7	$(0.86 \times -35.5\%) + (0.14 \times -32.7\%) =$		−35.1
2003	20.5	108.9	$(0.86 \times 20.5\%) + (0.14 \times 108.9\%) =$		32.9
2004	7.2	18.2	$(0.86 \times 7.2\%) + (0.14 \times 18.2\%) =$		8.7
2005	−15.8	144.3	$(0.86 \times -15.8\%) + (0.14 \times 144.3\%) =$		6.6
2006	19.8	77.6	$(0.86 \times 19.8\%) + (0.14 \times 77.6\%) =$		27.9
2007	12.8	−19.7	$(0.86 \times 12.8\%) + (0.14 \times -19.7\%) =$		8.3
2008	−20.8	19.6	$(0.86 \times -20.8\%) + (0.14 \times 19.6\%) =$		−15.1
2009	58.6	0.7	$(0.86 \times 58.6\%) + (0.14 \times 0.7\%) =$		50.5
2010	14.3	6.2	$(0.86 \times 14.3\%) + (0.14 \times 6.2\%) =$		13.1
Average Return	10.4	32.1			13.5

B. Individual and Portfolio Standard Deviations

Standard Deviation Calculation for IBM:

$$s_{IBM} = \sqrt{\frac{\sum_{t=1}^{10}(r_t - \bar{r})^2}{n-1}} = \sqrt{\frac{(43.0\% - 10.4\%)^2 + \ldots + (14.3\% - 10.4\%)^2}{10-1}} = \sqrt{\frac{7,375.2\%^2}{10-1}} = 28.6\%$$

Standard Deviation Calculation for CELG:

$$s_{CELG} = \sqrt{\frac{\sum_{t=1}^{10}(r_t - \bar{r})^2}{n-1}} = \sqrt{\frac{(-1.7\% - 32.1\%)^2 + \ldots + (6.2\% - 32.1\%)^2}{10-1}} = \sqrt{\frac{30,598.2\%^2}{10-1}} = 58.3\%$$

Standard Deviation Calculation for Portfolio:

$$s_p = \sqrt{\frac{\sum_{t=1}^{10}(r_t - \bar{r})^2}{n-1}} = \sqrt{\frac{(36.7\% - 13.5\%)^2 + \ldots + (13.1\% - 13.5\%)^2}{10-1}} = \sqrt{\frac{5,770.7\%^2}{10-1}} = 25.3\%$$

*Historical return is calculated based on end-of-year prices.

(Source: End-of-year prices are obtained from Yahoo! Finance. Prices are adjusted for dividends and stock splits.)

We know that over this period, Celgene earned much higher returns than IBM, so intuitively we might expect that a portfolio containing both stocks would earn a return higher than IBM's but lower than Celgene's. Furthermore, because most (86%) of the portfolio is invested in IBM, you might guess that the portfolio's return would be closer to IBM's than to Celgene's.

Columns 3 and 4 in Panel A show the portfolio's return each year. The average annual return on this portfolio was 13.5%. As expected, that return is a little higher than the return on IBM stock. By investing a little in Celgene, an investor could earn a higher return than he or she would achieve by holding IBM stock in isolation.

What about the portfolio's risk? One measure of a portfolio's risk is its standard deviation. The standard deviation of a portfolio's returns is found by applying the same equation that we used in Chapter 10 to find the standard deviation of a single asset. Panel B of Table 11.1 reproduces this formula and applies it to calculate the standard deviation of returns on IBM and Celgene stock. Or, if you prefer, rather than using the formulas in Table 11.1 to find the standard deviation of returns for IBM and CELG, you can construct an Excel spreadsheet to do the calculations as shown below. The standard deviation of IBM's returns is 28.6%, and for Celgene's stock returns the standard deviation is 58.3%. Here again we see evidence of the tradeoff between risk and return. Celgene's stock earned much higher returns than IBM's stock, but Celgene returns fluctuate a great deal more as well.

The final calculation in Panel B inserts the IBM-Celgene portfolio return data from column 4 in Panel A into the standard deviation formula to calculate the portfolio standard deviation. Intuitively, because the portfolio contains a lot of IBM stock and a little of Celgene, you might expect the portfolio standard deviation to be slightly higher than the standard deviation of IBM's returns. In fact, Panel B shows the surprising result that the portfolio returns are less volatile than are the returns of either stock in the portfolio! The portfolio consisting of 86% IBM and 14% Celgene displays a standard deviation of 25.3%. This is great news for investors. An investor who held only IBM shares would have earned an average return of only 10.4%, but to achieve that return the investor would have had to endure IBM's 28.6% standard deviation. By selling a few IBM shares and using the proceeds to buy a few Celgene shares (resulting in the 0.86 and 0.14 portfolio weights shown in Table 11.1), an investor could have simultaneously increased his or her return to 13.5% and reduced the standard deviation to 25.3%. In other words, the investor could have had more return and less risk at the same time. This means that an investor who owns nothing but IBM shares holds an

◇	A	B	C	D
1	STANDARD DEVIATION OF RETURNS FOR IBM, CELG, PORTFOLIO			
2	Year (t)	r_{IBM}%	r_{CELG}%	r_p%
3	2001	43.0	-1.7	36.7
4	2002	-35.5	-32.7	-35.1
5	2003	20.5	108.9	32.9
6	2004	7.2	18.2	8.7
7	2005	-15.8	144.3	6.6
8	2006	19.8	77.6	27.9
9	2007	12.8	-19.7	8.3
10	2008	-20.8	19.6	-15.1
11	2009	58.6	0.7	50.5
12	2010	14.3	6.2	13.1
13	Standard deviation	28.6	58.3	25.3
14	Entries in Cells B13, C13, and D13 are =STDEV(B3:B12), =STDEV(C3:C12), and =STDEV(D3:D12), respectively.			
15				

inefficient portfolio—an alternative portfolio exists that has a better return-to-risk tradeoff. That's the power of diversification. Next, we will see that the key factor in making this possible is a low correlation between IBM and Celgene returns.

Correlation and Diversification

As noted in Chapter 3, diversification involves the inclusion of a number of different investments in a portfolio. It is an important aspect of creating an efficient portfolio. Underlying the intuitive appeal of diversification is the statistical concept of **correlation**. For effective portfolio planning, you need to understand the concepts of correlation and diversification and their relationship to a portfolio's total risk and return.

Correlation **Correlation** is a statistical measure of the relationship between two series of numbers. If two series move in the same direction, they are **positively correlated**. For instance, if each day we record the number of hours of sunshine and the average daily temperature, we would expect those two series to display positive correlation. Days with more sunshine tend to be days with higher temperatures. If the series move in opposite directions, they are **negatively correlated**. For example, if each day we record the number of hours of sunshine and the amount of rainfall, we would expect those two series to display negative correlation because, on average, rainfall is lower on days with lots of sunshine. Finally, if two series bear no relationship to each other, then they are **uncorrelated**. For example, we would probably expect no correlation between the number of hours of sunshine on a particular day and the change in the value of the U.S. dollar against other world currencies on the same day. There is no obvious connection between sunshine and world currency markets.

The degree of correlation—whether positive or negative—is measured by the **correlation coefficient**, which is generally represented by the Greek symbol rho (ρ). It's easy to use Excel to calculate the correlation coefficient between IBM and Celgene stock returns as shown in the following spreadsheet.

Excel will quickly tell you that the correlation coefficient between IBM and Celgene during the 2001–2010 period was −0.08. The (slightly) negative figure means that there was a modest tendency over this period for the two stocks to move in opposite directions. A negative correlation between two stocks is somewhat unusual because most stocks are affected in the same way by large, macroeconomic forces. In other words, most stocks tend to move in the same direction as the overall economy, which means

◇	A	B	C
1	CORRELATION COEFFICIENT OF RETURNS FOR IBM AND CELG		
2	Year (t)	r_{IBM}%	r_{CELG}%
3	2001	43.0	-1.7
4	2002	-35.5	-32.7
5	2003	20.5	108.9
6	2004	7.2	18.2
7	2005	-15.8	144.3
8	2006	19.8	77.6
9	2007	12.8	-19.7
10	2008	-20.8	19.6
11	2009	58.6	0.7
12	2010	14.3	6.2
13		Correlation coefficient	-0.08
14		Entry in Cell C13 is	
15		=CORREL(B3:B12,C3:C12).	

FIGURE 11.1

The Correlations of Series M, N, and P

The perfectly positively correlated series M and P in the graph on the left move exactly together. The perfectly negatively correlated series M and N in the graph on the right move in exactly opposite directions.

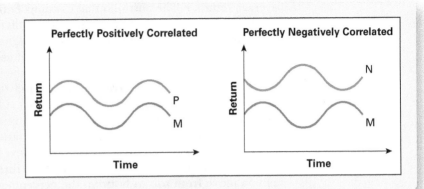

Perfectly Positively Correlated

Perfectly Negatively Correlated

What's the Correlation?

that most stocks will display at least some positive correlation with each other. In this case, the correlation between IBM and Celgene is so close to zero that there was very little relationship between the two stocks over this period. It's not too surprising that returns on IBM and Celgene shares display a relatively low correlation. IBM is a major provider of information technology services, and Celgene is a biopharmaceutical manufacturer. The companies compete in entirely different industries, have different customers and suppliers, and operate within very different regulatory constraints. Many of the factors that have a large impact on IBM's profitability have little relevance for Celgene's business, and vice versa.

The correlation coefficient ranges from +1 for **perfectly positively correlated** series to −1 for **perfectly negatively correlated** series. These two extremes are depicted in Figure 11.1 for series M, N, and P. The perfectly positively correlated series (M and P) move exactly together. The perfectly negatively correlated series (M and N) move in exactly opposite directions. While these two extreme cases can be illustrative, the correlations between most asset returns exhibit some degree (ranging from high to low) of positive correlation. Negative correlation is the exception.

Diversification   As a general rule, the lower the correlation between any two assets, the greater the risk reduction that can be achieved by combining those assets in a portfolio. Figure 11.2 shows negatively correlated assets F and G, both having the same

FIGURE 11.2

Combining Negatively Correlated Assets to Diversify Risk

The risk or variability of returns, resulting from combining negatively correlated assets F and G, both having the same average return, $\bar{r}$, results in a portfolio (shown in the rightmost graph) with the same level of average return but less risk.

average return, $\bar{r}$. The portfolio that contains both F and G has the same return, $\bar{r}$, but has less risk (variability) than either of the individual assets because some of the fluctuations in asset F cancel out fluctuations in G. As a result, the combination of F and G is less volatile than either F or G alone. Even if assets are not negatively correlated, the lower the positive correlation between them, the lower the resulting risk.

Table 11.2 shows the average return and the standard deviation of returns for many combinations of IBM and Celgene stock. Columns 1 and 2 show the percentage of the portfolio invested in IBM and Celgene, respectively, and columns 3 and 4 show the portfolio average return and standard deviation. Notice that as you move from the top of the table to the bottom (i.e., from investing all of the portfolio in IBM to investing all of it in Celgene), the portfolio return goes up. That makes sense because as you move from top to bottom, the percentage invested in Celgene increases, and Celgene's average return is higher than IBM's. The general conclusion from column 3 is that when a portfolio contains two stocks, with one having a higher average return than the other, the portfolio's return rises the more you invest in the stock with the higher return.

Column 4 shows the standard deviation of returns for different portfolios of IBM and Celgene. Here again we see a surprising result. A portfolio invested entirely in IBM has a standard deviation of 28.6%. Intuitively, it might seem that reducing the investment in IBM slightly and increasing the investment in Celgene would increase the portfolio's standard deviation because Celgene stock is so much more volatile than IBM stock. However, the opposite is true, at least up to a point. The portfolio standard

			EXCEL with Spreadsheets
TABLE 11.2	**PORTFOLIO RETURNS AND STANDARD DEVIATIONS FOR INTERNATIONAL BUSINESS MACHINES (IBM) AND CELGENE (CELG)**		

(1) (2) Portfolio Weights		(3) Portfolio Average Return		(4) Portfolio Standard Deviation
W_{IBM}	W_{CELG}	$\bar{r}_{IBM} = 10.4\%$	$\bar{r}_{CELG} = 32.1\%$	
1.0	0.0	$(1.0 \times 10.4\%) + (0.0 \times 32.1\%) = 10.4\%$		28.6%
0.9	0.1	$(0.9 \times 10.4\%) + (0.1 \times 32.1\%) = 12.6\%$		26.0%
0.8	0.2	$(0.8 \times 10.4\%) + (0.2 \times 32.1\%) = 14.8\%$		24.9%
0.7	0.3	$(0.7 \times 10.4\%) + (0.3 \times 32.1\%) = 16.9\%$		25.5%
0.6	0.4	$(0.6 \times 10.4\%) + (0.4 \times 32.1\%) = 19.1\%$		27.9%
0.5	0.5	$(0.5 \times 10.4\%) + (0.5 \times 32.1\%) = 21.3\%$		31.5%
0.4	0.6	$(0.4 \times 10.4\%) + (0.6 \times 32.1\%) = 23.5\%$		35.9%
0.3	0.7	$(0.3 \times 10.4\%) + (0.7 \times 32.1\%) = 25.6\%$		41.0%
0.2	0.8	$(0.2 \times 10.4\%) + (0.8 \times 32.1\%) = 27.8\%$		46.5%
0.1	0.9	$(0.1 \times 10.4\%) + (0.9 \times 32.1\%) = 30.0\%$		52.3%
0.0	1.0	$(0.0 \times 10.4\%) + (1.0 \times 32.1\%) = 32.1\%$		58.3%

Example: Calculation of the Standard Deviation for the Equally Weighted Portfolio

$s_{IBM} = 28.6\%$

$s_{CELG} = 58.3\%$

$\rho_{IBM,\ CELG} = -0.08$

$s_p = \sqrt{w_i^2 s_i^2 + w_j^2 s_j^2 + 2w_i w_j \rho_{i,j} s_i s_j}$

$s_p = \sqrt{0.5^2 \times 28.6\%^2 + 0.5^2 \times 58.3\%^2 + 2(0.5 \times 0.5 \times -0.08 \times 28.6\% \times 58.3\%)} = 31.5\%$

FIGURE 11.3

Portfolios of IBM and Celgene

Because the returns of IBM and Celgene are not highly correlated, investors who hold only IBM shares can simultaneously increase their portfolio return and reduce its standard deviation by holding at least some Celgene shares. At some point, however, investing more in Celgene does increase the portfolio volatility while also increasing its expected return.

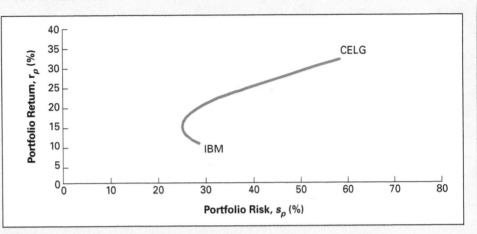

deviation initially falls as the percentage invested in Celgene rises. Eventually, however, increasing the amount invested in Celgene does increase the portfolio's standard deviation. So the general conclusion from column 4 is that when a portfolio contains two stocks, with one having a higher standard deviation than the other, the portfolio's standard deviation may rise or fall the more you invest in the stock with the higher standard deviation.

Figure 11.3 illustrates the two lessons emerging from Table 11.2. The curve plots the average return (*y*-axis) and standard deviation (*x*-axis) for each portfolio listed in Table 11.2. As the portfolio composition moves from 100% IBM to a mix of IBM and Celgene, the average return rises, but the standard deviation initially falls. Therefore, portfolios of IBM and Celgene trace out a backward-bending arc. Clearly no investor should place all of his or her money in IBM because a higher return and lower standard deviation can be achieved by holding at least some stock in Celgene. However, investors who want to earn the highest possible returns, and who therefore will invest heavily in Celgene, have to accept a higher standard deviation.

The relationship between IBM and Celgene is obviously a special case, so let's look at the more general patterns that investors encounter in the markets. In addition, let's shift our focus from historical to expected returns. Table 11.3 (on page 376) presents the expected returns from three assets—X, Y, and Z—over the next 5 years (2015–2019), along with their average expected returns and standard deviations. Asset X has an average expected return of 12% and a standard deviation of 3.2%. Assets Y and Z each have an average expected return of 16% and a standard deviation of 6.3%. Thus, we can view asset X as having a low-return, low-risk profile while assets Y and Z are high-return, high-risk stocks. The returns of assets X and Y are perfectly negatively correlated—they move in exactly opposite directions over time. The returns of assets X and Z are perfectly positively correlated—they move in precisely the same direction.

TABLE 11.3 **EXPECTED RETURNS, AVERAGE RETURNS, AND STANDARD DEVIATIONS FOR ASSETS X, Y, AND Z AND PORTFOLIOS XY AND XZ**

Year (t)	Asset's Expected Returns			Portfolio's Expected Returns	
	$E(r_X\%)$	$E(r_Y\%)$	$E(r_Z\%)$	$E(r_{xy})$ $[2/3 \times E(r_X\%) + 1/3 \times E(r_Y\%)]$	$E(r_{xz})$ $[2/3 \times E(r_X\%) + 1/3 \times E(r_Z\%)]$
2015	8.0	24.0	8.0	13.3	8.0
2016	10.0	20.0	12.0	13.3	10.7
2017	12.0	16.0	16.0	13.3	13.3
2018	14.0	12.0	20.0	13.3	16.0
2019	16.0	8.0	24.0	13.3	18.7
Average Expected Return	12.0	16.0	16.0	13.3	13.3
Standard Deviation	3.2	6.3	6.3	0.0	4.2

Portfolio XY (shown in Table 11.3) is constructed by investing $\frac{2}{3}$ in asset X and $\frac{1}{3}$ in asset Y. The expected return on this portfolio, 13.3%, is a weighted average of the expected returns of assets X and Y $\left(\frac{2}{3} \times 12\% + \frac{1}{3} \times 16\%\right)$. To calculate the portfolio's standard deviation, use the equation shown in Table 11.2 (on page 374) with a value of −1.0 for the correlation between X and Y. Notice that portfolio XY generates a predictable 13.3% return every year. In other words, the portfolio is risk-free and has a standard deviation of 0.

Portfolio XZ uses the same proportions: $\frac{2}{3}$ invested in X and $\frac{1}{3}$ invested in Z. Like portfolio XY, portfolio XZ has an expected return of 13.3% and a standard deviation of 0.0%. But unlike portfolio XY, portfolio XZ is risky. Its returns fluctuate between 8% and 18.7% and its standard deviation is 4.2%.

To summarize, the two portfolios, XY and XZ, have identical expected returns, but they differ in terms of risk. The reason for that difference is correlation. Movements in X are offset by movements in Y, so by combining the two assets in a portfolio, the investor can reduce or eliminate risk. Assets X and Z move together, so movements in one cannot offset movements in the other, and the standard deviation of portfolio XZ cannot be reduced below the standard deviation of asset X.

Figure 11.4 illustrates the relation between a portfolio's expected return and standard deviation and the correlation between the assets in the portfolio. The black line illustrates a case like portfolio XY where the correlation coefficient is −1.0. In that case, it is possible to combine two risky assets in just the right proportions so that the

FIGURE 11.4

Risk and Return for Combinations of Two Assets with Various Correlation Coefficients

This graph illustrates how a low-return, low-risk asset can be combined with a high-return, high-risk asset in a portfolio, and how the performance of that portfolio depends on the correlation between the two assets. In general, as an investor shifts the portfolio weight from the low-return to the high-return investment, the portfolio return will rise. But the portfolio's standard deviation may rise or fall depending on the correlation. In general, the lower the correlation, the greater the risk reduction that can be achieved through diversification.

portfolio return is completely predictable (i.e., has no risk). Notice that in this situation, it would be very unwise for an investor to hold an undiversified position in the least risky asset. By holding a portfolio of assets rather than just one, the investor moves up and to the left along the black line to earn a higher return while taking less risk. Beyond some point, however, increasing the investment in the more risky asset pushes both the portfolio return and risk higher, so the investor's portfolio moves up and to the right along the second segment of the black line.

The red line in Figure 11.4 illustrates a situation like portfolio XZ in which the correlation coefficient is +1.0. In that instance, when an investor decreases their investment in the low-risk asset to hold more of the high-risk asset, the portfolio's expected return rises, but so does its standard deviation. The investor moves up and to the right along the red line. An investor might choose to invest in both assets, but making that decision is a matter of one's risk tolerance, and not all investors will make that choice. In other words, when the correlation between two assets is −1.0, diversifying is definitely the right move, but when the correlation is +1.0, whether to diversify or not is less obvious.

The blue line in Figure 11.4 illustrates an intermediate case in which the correlation coefficient is between −1.0 and +1.0. This is what investors encounter in real markets most of the time—assets are neither perfectly negatively correlated, nor are they perfectly positively correlated. When the correlation coefficient is between the extremes, portfolios of two assets lie along an arc (i.e., the blue line). When two assets have very low correlation, that arc may bend back upon itself, as was the case with IBM and Celgene. When the correlation is higher, but still below 1.0, the arc merely curves up and to the right. Even then, the benefits of diversification are better than when the correlation is 1.0, meaning that portfolios along the blue arc earn higher returns for the same risk compared to portfolios along the red line.

International Diversification

Diversification is clearly a primary consideration when constructing an investment portfolio. As noted earlier, many opportunities for international diversification are now available. Here we consider three aspects of international diversification: effectiveness, methods, and costs.

Effectiveness of International Diversification Investing internationally offers greater diversification than investing only domestically. That is true for U.S. investors as well as for investors from countries with capital markets that offer much more limited diversification opportunities than are available in the United States. Broadly speaking, the diversification benefits from investing internationally come from two sources. The first source is that returns in different markets around the world do not move exactly in sync, that is, the correlation between markets is less than +1.0. As you have already seen, the lower the correlation is between investments, the larger are the benefits from diversification. Unfortunately, as globalization has brought about greater integration of markets (both financial markets and markets for goods and services) around the world, the correlation in returns across national markets has risen. This trend reduces the benefit of international diversification.

However, the second source of the benefits of international diversification has been on the rise for many years. Over time, the number of stock markets around the world has been increasing. For example, at the beginning of the 20th century there were fewer than 40 countries in the world with active stock markets, but by the end of the century the number of stock markets had more than doubled. Just as someone who invests only in domestic stocks will generally have a more diversified portfolio if there are more stocks in the portfolio, so it is for investors who can diversify across many different stock markets around the world rather than just a few.

On net, there is little question that it benefits investors to diversify internationally, even if the rising correlation across markets (especially the larger, more developed markets) limits these benefits to an extent. Next, we discuss how investors can access international markets to diversify their portfolios.

Methods of International Diversification In later chapters we will examine a wide range of alternatives for international portfolio diversification. We will see that investors can make investments in bonds and other debt instruments in U.S. dollars or in foreign currencies—either directly or via foreign mutual funds. Foreign currency investment, however, brings currency exchange risk. This risk can be hedged with contracts such as currency forwards, futures, and options. Even if there is little or no currency exchange risk, investing abroad is generally less convenient, more expensive, and riskier than investing domestically. When making direct investments abroad, you must know what you're doing. You should have a clear idea of the benefits being sought and enough time to monitor foreign markets.

U.S. investors can capture at least some of the benefits of international diversification without having to send money abroad. Investors can buy stock of foreign companies listed on U.S. exchanges. Many foreign issuers, both corporate and government, sell their bonds (called *Yankee bonds*) in the United States. The stocks of more than 2,000 foreign companies, from more than 50 countries, trade in the United States in the form of American depositary shares (ADSs). Finally, international mutual funds provide foreign investment opportunities.

You might wonder whether it is possible to achieve the benefits of international diversification by investing in a portfolio of U.S.-based multinational corporations. The answer is yes and no. Yes, a portfolio of U.S. multinationals is more diversified than a portfolio of wholly domestic firms. Multinationals generate revenues, costs, and profits in many markets and currencies, so when one part of the world is doing poorly, another part may be doing well.

Investors who invest only in U.S.-based multinationals will still not enjoy the full benefits of international diversification. That's because a disproportionate share of the revenues and costs generated by these firms *is* still in the United States. Thus, to fully realize the benefits of international diversification, it is necessary to invest in firms located outside the United States.

Costs of International Diversification You can find greater returns overseas than in the United States, and you can reduce a portfolio's risk by including foreign investments. Still, you should not jump to the conclusion that it is wise to invest all of your money in overseas assets. A successful global investment strategy depends on many things, just as a purely domestic strategy does. The percentage of your portfolio that you should allocate to foreign investments depends on your overall investment goals and risk preferences. Many investment advisers suggest allocations to foreign investments of about 20% to 30%, with two-thirds of this allocation in established foreign markets and the other one-third in emerging markets.

In general, investing directly in foreign-currency-denominated instruments is very costly. Unless you have hundreds of thousands of dollars to invest, the transaction costs of buying securities directly on foreign markets will tend to be high. A less costly approach to international diversification is to invest in international mutual funds, which offer diversified foreign investments and the professional expertise of fund managers. You could also purchase ADSs to make foreign investments in individual stocks. With either mutual funds or ADSs, you can obtain international diversification along with low cost, convenience, transactions in U.S. dollars, and protection under U.S. security laws.

CONCEPTS IN REVIEW

Answers available at www.pearsonhighered.com/ smart

11.1 What is an efficient portfolio, and what role should such a portfolio play in investing?

11.2 How can the return and standard deviation of a portfolio be determined? Compare the calculation of a portfolio's standard deviation to that for a single asset.

11.3 What is correlation, and why is it important with respect to asset returns? Describe the characteristics of returns that are (a) positively correlated, (b) negatively correlated, and (c) uncorrelated. Differentiate between perfect positive correlation and perfect negative correlation.

11.4 What is diversification? How does the diversification of risk affect the risk of the portfolio compared to the risk of the individual assets it contains?

11.5 Discuss how the correlation between asset returns affects the risk and return behavior of the resulting portfolio. Describe the potential range of risk and return when the correlation between two assets is (a) perfectly positive, (b) uncorrelated, and (c) perfectly negative.

11.6 What benefit, if any, does international diversification offer the individual investor? Compare and contrast the methods of achieving international diversification by investing abroad versus investing domestically.

The Capital Asset Pricing Model

LG3 **LG4** Intuitively we would expect that any risky investment should offer a return that exceeds what investors can earn on a risk-free investment. In other words, the return that investors expect to earn on a risky asset equals the risk-free rate plus a risk premium. But what determines the magnitude of the risk premium? In the previous section we learned that investors can reduce or eliminate many types of risk simply by diversifying their portfolios, a process that is neither particularly time consuming nor expensive. However, diversification can't eliminate risk entirely. Therefore, from an investor's perspective, the most worrisome risk is *undiversifiable risk*—the risk that can't be eliminated through diversification. The more undiversifiable risk that a particular investment entails, the higher the risk premium it must offer to attract investors.

That logic provides the underpinning for a theory that links return and risk for all assets. The theory is called the *capital asset pricing model*, or the *CAPM*. The CAPM says that the expected return on a risky asset equals the risk-free rate plus a risk premium, and the risk premium depends on how much of the asset's risk is undiversifiable. In this section, we introduce the concept of undiversifiable risk, and we explain how the CAPM quantifies that risk and links it to investment returns.

Components of Risk

The risk of an investment consists of two components: diversifiable and undiversifiable risk. **Diversifiable risk**, sometimes called **unsystematic risk**, results from factors that are firm-specific, such as whether a new product succeeds or fails, the performance of senior managers, or a firm's relationships with its customers and suppliers. Unsystematic risk is the portion of an investment's risk that can be eliminated through diversification. **Undiversifiable risk**, also called **systematic risk** or **market risk**, is the inescapable portion of an investment's risk. In other words, it's the risk that remains even if a portfolio is well diversified. Systematic risk is associated with broad forces such as economic growth, inflation, interest rates, and political events that affect all investments and therefore are not unique to any single investment. The sum of undiversifiable risk and diversifiable risk is called **total risk**.

Equation 11.2   Total risk = Undiversifiable risk + Diversifiable risk

Any careful investor can reduce or virtually eliminate diversifiable risk by holding a diversified portfolio of securities. Studies have shown that investors can eliminate most diversifiable risk by carefully selecting a portfolio of as few as 8 to 15 securities, and most investors hold many more securities than that through investments such as mutual funds and pension funds. Because it is relatively easy to eliminate unsystematic risk through diversification, there is no reason for investors to expect a reward (i.e., higher returns) for bearing this kind of risk. Investors who fail to diversify are simply bearing more risk than they have to without getting a reward for doing so.

But no matter how many securities are in a portfolio, some systematic risk will remain. Remember, undiversifiable risk refers to the broad forces that tend to affect most stocks simultaneously, such as whether the economy is booming or in recession. Some stocks are more sensitive to these forces than others. For example, companies that produce luxury goods tend to do very well when the economy is surging, but when a recession hits, these companies struggle to find customers. On the other hand, some stocks are relatively insulated from swings in the business cycle. Companies that produce food and other basic necessities do not see their revenues and profits rise and fall sharply with the ups and downs of the economy. This discussion implies that systematic risk varies from one stock to another, and stocks with greater systematic risk must offer higher returns to attract investors. To identify these stocks, we need a way to measure the undiversifiable risk associated with any particular stock. The CAPM provides just such a measure called the stock's *beta*.

Beta: A Measure of Undiversifiable Risk

During the past 50 years, the finance discipline has developed much theory on the measurement of risk and its use in assessing returns. The two key components of this theory are beta, which is a measure of systematic risk, and the capital asset pricing model, which links an investment's beta to its return.

First we will look at **beta**, a number that quantifies undiversifiable risk. A security's beta indicates how the security's return responds to fluctuations in **market returns**, which is why *market risk* is synonymous with undiversifiable risk. The more sensitive the return of a security is to changes in market returns, the higher that security's beta. When we speak of returns on the overall market, what we have in mind is something like the return on a broad portfolio of stocks or on a stock index. Analysts commonly use changes in the value of the Standard & Poor's 500 Index or some other broad stock index to measure market returns. To calculate a security's beta, you gather historical returns on the security and on the overall market to see how they relate to each other. You don't have to calculate betas yourself; you can easily obtain them for actively traded securities from a variety of published and online sources. But you should understand how betas are derived, how to interpret them, and how to apply them to portfolios.

Deriving Beta We can demonstrate graphically the relationship between a security's return and the market return. Figure 11.5 plots the relationship between the returns of two securities, C and D, and the market return. Note that the horizontal (*x*) axis measures the historical market returns, and the vertical (*y*) axis measures the individual security's historical returns.

The first step in deriving beta is plotting the coordinates for the market return and the security return at various points in time. Figure 11.5 shows such annual market-return and security-return coordinates *for security D* for the years 2005 to 2012 (the years are noted in parentheses). For example, in 2010, security D's return was 20% when the market return was 10%.

By use of statistical techniques, the "characteristic line" that best explains the relationship between security-return and market-return coordinates is fit to the data points. The slope of this line is beta. The beta for security D is 1.30. In comparison to a beta of 0.80 for security C (also shown in Figure 11.5), security D's higher beta—steeper characteristic line—indicates that its return is more responsive to changing market returns. Therefore, security D is more risky than security C.

Interpreting Beta The beta for the overall market is equal to 1.0. That also implies that the beta of the "average" stock is 1.0. All other betas are viewed in relation to this value.

FIGURE 11.5

Graphical Derivation of Beta for Securities C and D*

Betas can be derived graphically by plotting the coordinates for the market return and security return at various points in time and using statistical techniques to fit the "characteristic line" to the data points. The slope of the characteristic line is beta. For securities C and D, the betas are 0.80 and 1.30, respectively.

*All data points shown are associated with security D. No data points are shown for security C.

TABLE 11.4   SELECTED BETAS AND ASSOCIATED INTERPRETATIONS

Beta	Comment	Interpretation
2.0	Move in same direction as the market	Twice as responsive as the market
1.0		Same response as the market
0.5		One half as responsive as the market
0.0		Unaffected by market movement
−0.5	Move in opposite direction of the market	One-half as responsive as the market
−1.0		Same response as the market
−2.0		Twice as responsive as the market

Table 11.4 shows some selected beta values and their associated interpretations. As you can see, betas can, in principle, be positive or negative, although nearly all betas are positive. The positive or negative sign preceding the beta number merely indicates whether the stock's return moves in the same direction as the general market (*positive beta*) or in the opposite direction (*negative beta*).

Most stocks have betas that fall between 0.50 and 1.75. The return of a stock that is half as responsive as the market ($b = 0.5$) will, on average, change by ½ of 1% for each 1% change in the return of the market portfolio. A stock that is twice as responsive as the market ($b = 2$) will, on average, experience a 2% change in its return for each 1% change in the return of the market portfolio. Listed here, for illustration purposes, are the actual betas for some popular stocks, as reported on Yahoo! Finance on May 7, 2012:

Stock	Beta	Stock	Beta
Amazon.com Inc.	0.64	Int'l Business Machines Corp.	0.62
Molson Coors Brewing Co.	0.75	Goldman Sachs Inc.	1.62
Bank of America Corp.	1.96	Microsoft Corp.	1.00
Procter & Gamble Co.	0.35	Nike Inc.	0.99
Walt Disney Co.	1.29	Celgene Corp.	0.81
eBay Inc.	1.11	Qualcomm Inc.	1.18
ExxonMobil Corp.	0.69	Sempra Energy	0.40
Gap Inc.	1.26	Walmart Stores Inc.	0.52
Ford Motor Co.	1.84	Xerox Corp.	1.79
INTEL Corp.	1.01	YAHOO! Inc.	0.99

How to Estimate a Beta

Many large brokerage firms, as well as subscription services like Value Line, publish betas for a broad range of securities. You can also find them online at sites such as Yahoo! Finance (http://finance.yahoo.com/). Later in this chapter we discuss the importance of beta in planning and building portfolios of securities.

Applying Beta Individual investors will find beta useful. It can help in assessing the risk of a particular investment and in understanding the impact the market can have on the return expected from a share of stock. In short, beta reveals how a security responds to market forces. For example, if the market is expected to experience a 10% increase

Bulging Betas

Ford Motor Company has always been considered a cyclical stock whose fortunes rise and fall with the state of the economy as illustrated by its beta of 1.84 reported in the table on page 382. Ford's beta was as high as 2.80 during the financial crisis, which hit auto manufacturers particularly hard and resulted in the bankruptcy of Ford's major competitor, General Motors. Notice that Bank of America, another firm in an industry hit hard by the recession, had a beta of 1.96, indicating that it too was extremely sensitive to movements in the overall economy.

in its rate of return over the next period, we would expect a stock with a beta of 1.5 to experience an increase in return of about 15% (1.5 × 10%).

For stocks with positive betas, increases in market returns result in increases in security returns. Unfortunately, decreases in market returns are translated into decreasing security returns. In the preceding example, if the market is expected to experience a 10% decrease in its rate of return, then a stock with a beta of 1.5 should experience a 15% decrease in its return. Because the stock has a beta greater than 1.0, it is riskier than an average stock and will tend to experience dramatic swings when the overall market moves.

Stocks that have betas less than 1.0 are, of course, less responsive to changing returns in the market and are therefore less risky. For example, a stock with a beta of 0.50 will increase or decrease its return by about half that of the market as a whole. Thus, if the market return went down by 8%, such a stock's return would probably experience only about a 4% (0.50 × 8%) decline.

Here are some important points to remember about beta:

- Beta measures the undiversifiable (or market) risk of a security.

- The beta for the market as a whole, and for the average stock, is 1.0.

- In theory, stocks may have positive or negative betas, but most stocks have positive betas.

- Stocks with betas greater than 1.0 are more responsive than average to market fluctuations and therefore are more risky than average. Stocks with betas less than 1.0 are less risky than the average stock.

- Because greater risk is generally linked to higher returns, the higher a stock's beta, the greater its expected return.

The CAPM: Using Beta to Estimate Return

About 50 years ago, finance professors William F. Sharpe and John Lintner developed a model that uses beta to formally link the notions of risk and return. Called the **capital asset pricing model (CAPM)**, it attempts to explain the behavior of security prices. It also provides a mechanism whereby investors can assess the impact of a proposed security investment on their portfolio's risk and return. The CAPM predicts that a stock's expected return depends on three things: the risk-free rate, the expected return on the overall market, and the stock's beta.

The Equation With beta, b, as the measure of undiversifiable risk, the capital asset pricing model defines the required return on an investment as follows.

Equation 11.3

$$\begin{matrix} \text{Required return} \\ \text{on investment } j \end{matrix} = \begin{matrix} \text{Risk-free} \\ \text{rate} \end{matrix} + \left[\begin{matrix} \text{Beta for} \\ \text{investment } j \end{matrix} \times \left(\begin{matrix} \text{Expected market} \\ \text{return} \end{matrix} - \begin{matrix} \text{Risk-free} \\ \text{rate} \end{matrix} \right) \right]$$

Equation 11.3a

$$r_j = r_{rf} + [b_j \times (r_m - r_{rf})]$$

where

r_j = the required return on investment j, given its risk as measured by beta
r_{rf} = the risk-free rate of return; the return that can be earned on a risk-free investment
b_j = beta coefficient, or index of undiversifiable risk for investment j
r_m = the expected market return; the average return on all securities (typically measured by the average return on all securities in the Standard & Poor's 500 Composite Index or some other broad stock market index)

The CAPM can be divided into two parts: (1) the risk-free rate of return, r_{rf}, and (2) the *risk premium*, $b_j \times (r_m - r_{rf})$. The risk premium is the return investors demand beyond the risk-free rate to compensate for the investment's undiversifiable risk as measured by beta. The equation shows that as beta increases, the stock's risk premium increases, thereby causing the required return to increase.

Example

We can demonstrate use of the CAPM with the following example. Assume you are considering security Z with a beta (b_Z) of 1.25. The risk-free rate (r_{rf}) is 6% and the market return (r_m) is 10%. Substituting these data into the CAPM equation, Equation 11.3a, we get:

$$r_z = 6\% + [1.25 \times (10\% - 6\%)] = 6\% + [1.25 \times 4\%]$$
$$= 6\% + 5\% = \underline{11\%}$$

You should therefore expect—indeed, require—an 11% return on this investment as compensation for the risk you have to assume, given the security's beta of 1.25.

If the beta were lower, say, 1.00, the required return would be lower. In fact, in this case the required return on the stock is the same as the expected (or required) return on the market.

$$r_z = 6\% + [1.0 \times (10\% - 6\%)] = 6\% + 4\% = \underline{10\%}$$

If the beta were higher, say 1.50, the required return would be higher:

$$r_z = 6\% + [1.5 \times (10\% - 6\%)] = 6\% + 6\% = \underline{12\%}$$

Clearly, the CAPM reflects the positive tradeoff between risk and return: The higher the risk (beta), the higher the risk premium, and therefore the higher the required return.

Smart's Tour of the Web

To watch author Scott Smart discuss key websites for this chapter, visit www.myfinancelab.com

The Graph: The Security Market Line When the capital asset pricing model is depicted graphically, it is called the **security market line** (**SML**). Plotting the CAPM, we would find that the SML is, in fact, a straight line. For each level of undiversifiable risk (beta), the SML reflects the required return the investor should earn in the marketplace.

We can plot the CAPM by simply calculating the required return for a variety of betas. For example, as we saw earlier, using a 6% risk-free rate and a 10% market return, the required return is 11% when the beta is 1.25. Increase the beta to 2.00, and the required return equals 14% $[6\% + 2.0 \times (10\% - 6\%)]$. Similarly, we can find the required return for a number of betas and end up with the following combinations of risk (beta) and required return.

Risk (beta)	Required Return (%)
0.0	6
0.5	8
1.0	10
1.5	12
2.0	14
2.5	16

Plotting these values on a graph (with beta on the horizontal axis and required return on the vertical axis) would yield a straight line like the one in Figure 11.6. The shaded area shows the amount by which the required return exceeds the risk-free rate. It represents the risk premiums. It is clear from the SML that as risk (beta) increases, so do the risk premium and required return, and vice versa.

Some Closing Comments The capital asset pricing model generally relies on historical data. The betas may or may not actually reflect the future variability of returns. Therefore, the required returns specified by the model can be viewed only as rough approximations. Analysts who use betas commonly make subjective adjustments to the historically determined betas to reflect their expectations of the future.

Despite its limitations, the CAPM provides a useful conceptual framework for evaluating and linking risk and return. Its simplicity and practical appeal cause beta

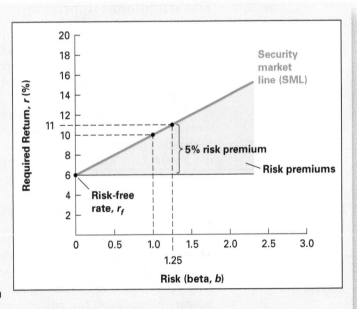

FIGURE 11.6

The Security Market Line (SML)

The security market line clearly depicts the tradeoff between risk and return. At a beta of 0, the required return is the risk-free rate of 6%. At a beta of 1.0, the required return is the market return of 10%. Given these data, the required return on an investment with a beta of 1.25 is 11% and its risk premium is 5% (11% − 6%).

and CAPM to remain important tools for investors who seek to measure risk and link it to required returns in security markets. The CAPM also sees widespread use in corporate finance. Before they spend large sums of money on big investment projects, companies need to know what returns their shareholders require. Many surveys show that the primary method that companies use to determine the required rate of return on their stock is the CAPM.

CONCEPTS IN REVIEW

Answers available at www.pearsonhighered.com/smart

11.7 Briefly define and give examples of each of the following components of total risk. Which type of risk matters, and why?

    a. Diversifiable risk   b. Undiversifiable risk

11.8 Explain what is meant by beta. What type of risk does beta measure? What is the market return? How is the interpretation of beta related to the market return?

11.9 What range of values does beta typically exhibit? Are positive or negative betas more common? Explain.

11.10 What is the capital asset pricing model (CAPM)? What role does beta play in the model? What is the risk premium? How is the security market line (SML) related to the CAPM?

11.11 Is the CAPM a predictive model? Why do beta and the CAPM remain important to investors?

Traditional Versus Modern Portfolio Management

LG5 LG6 Individual and institutional investors currently use two approaches to plan and construct their portfolios. The traditional approach refers to the less quantitative methods that investors have been using since the evolution of the public securities markets. Modern portfolio theory (MPT) is a more recent, more mathematical development that relies on quantitative analysis to guide investment decisions.

The Traditional Approach

Traditional portfolio management emphasizes "balancing" the portfolio by assembling a wide variety of stocks and/or bonds. The typical emphasis is *interindustry diversification*. This produces a portfolio with securities of companies from a broad range of industries. Traditional portfolios are constructed using the security analysis techniques discussed in Chapter 9.

Table 11.5 presents some of the industry groupings and the percentages invested in them by a typical mutual fund that is managed by professionals using the traditional approach. This fund, American Funds' Growth Fund of America (AGTHX), is an open-end mutual fund with a net asset value of $126.2 billion as of April 2012. Its objective is to invest in a wide range of companies that appear to offer superior opportunities for growth of capital. The Growth Fund of America holds shares of more than 300 different stocks from a wide range of industries as well as short-term securities of several dozen issuers.

Analyzing the stock position of The Growth Fund of America, which accounts for 94.3% of the fund's assets, we observe the traditional approach to portfolio management at work. This fund holds numerous stocks from a broad cross-section of the universe of available stocks. The stocks are a mix of large and small companies. The largest industry group is oil, gas, and consumable fuels, representing 8.9% of the portfolio. The fund's largest individual holding is Apple Inc., which accounts for 5.5% of the

TABLE 11.5 THE GROWTH FUND OF AMERICA (AGTHX) INVESTMENTS IN SELECT INDUSTRY GROUPS AS OF MARCH 31, 2012

The Growth Fund of America appears to adhere to the traditional approach to portfolio management. Its total portfolio value is $126.2 billion, of which 78.4% ($120 billion) is U.S. equities, 15.9% ($20 billion) is non-U.S. equities, and 5.7% ($20 billion) is short-term securities from several dozen issuers.

Select Industry Group	Percentage
Oil, gas, & consumable fuels	8.9
Media	6.7
Computers & peripherals	6.6
Semiconductors & semiconductor equipment	5.2
Biotechnology	4.9
Software	3.6
Internet & catalog retail	3.1
Hotels, restaurants, & leisure	3.0
Chemicals	2.9
Pharmaceuticals	2.9

(Source: Data from The Growth Fund of America, Class A Shares, Prospectus, March 31, 2012.)

portfolio. Amazon.com Inc., one of the largest online retailers in the world, ranks second, at about 2.5%. The third largest holding—2.4%—is Comcast Corporation. Although many of the fund's stocks are those of large, recognizable companies, its portfolio does include stocks of smaller, less recognizable firms.

Those who manage traditional portfolios want to invest in well-known companies for three reasons. First, because these are known as successful enterprises, investing in them is perceived as less risky than investing in lesser-known firms. Second, the securities of large firms are more liquid and are available in large quantities. Third, institutional investors prefer successful, well-known companies because it is easier to convince clients to invest in them. Called *window dressing*, this practice of loading up a portfolio with successful, well-known stocks makes it easier for institutional investors to sell their services.

One tendency often attributed to institutional investors during recent years is that of "herding"—investing in securities similar to those held by their competitors. These institutional investors effectively mimic the actions of their competitors. In the case of The Growth Fund of America, for example, its managers would buy stocks in companies that are held by other large, growth-oriented mutual funds. While we don't know for certain why The Growth Fund of America's managers bought specific stocks, it is clear that most funds with similar objectives hold many of the same well-known stocks.

Modern Portfolio Theory

During the 1950s, Harry Markowitz, a trained mathematician, first developed the theories that form the basis of modern portfolio theory. In the years since Markowitz's pioneering work, many other scholars and investment experts have contributed to the theory. **Modern portfolio theory (MPT)** uses several basic statistical measures to develop a portfolio plan. Included are expected returns and standard deviations of returns for both securities and portfolios, and the correlation between returns. According to MPT, diversification is achieved by combining securities in a portfolio in such a way that individual securities have negative (or low-positive) correlations between each other's rates of return. Thus, the statistical diversification is the deciding factor in choosing securities for an MPT portfolio. Two important aspects of MPT are the efficient frontier and portfolio betas.

The Efficient Frontier   At any point in time, you are faced with hundreds of investments from which to choose. You can form any number of possible portfolios. In fact, using only, say, 10 different assets, you could create hundreds of portfolios by changing the proportion of each asset in the portfolio.

If we were to create all possible portfolios, calculate the return and risk of each, and plot each risk-return combination on a graph, we would have the *feasible*, or *attainable*, *set* of possible portfolios. This set is represented by the shaded area in Figure 11.7. It is the area bounded by ABYOZCDEF. As defined earlier, an *efficient portfolio* is a portfolio that provides the highest return for a given level of risk. For example, let's compare portfolio T to portfolios B and Y shown in Figure 11.7. Portfolio Y appears preferable to portfolio T because it has a higher return for the same level of risk. Portfolio B also "dominates" portfolio T because it has lower risk for the same level of return.

The boundary BYOZC of the feasible set of portfolios represents all efficient portfolios—those portfolios that provide the best tradeoff between risk and return. This boundary is the **efficient frontier**. All portfolios on the efficient frontier are preferable to all other portfolios in the feasible set. Any portfolios that would fall to the left of the

FIGURE 11.7

The Feasible, or Attainable, Set and the Efficient Frontier

The feasible, or attainable, set (shaded area) represents the risk-return combinations attainable with all possible portfolios; the efficient frontier is the locus of all efficient portfolios. The point O, where the investor's highest possible indifference curve is tangent to the efficient frontier, is the optimal portfolio. It represents the highest level of satisfaction the investor can achieve given the available set of portfolios.

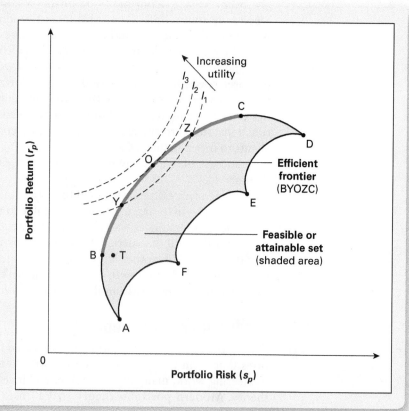

efficient frontier are not available for investment because they fall outside of the attainable set. Portfolios that fall to the right of the efficient frontier are not desirable because their risk-return tradeoffs are inferior to those of portfolios on the efficient frontier.

We can, in theory, use the efficient frontier to find the highest level of satisfaction the investor can achieve given the available set of portfolios. To do this, we would plot on the graph an *investor's utility function*, or *risk-indifference curves*. These curves indicate, for a given level of utility (satisfaction), the set of risk-return combinations about which an investor would be indifferent. These curves, labeled I_1, I_2, and I_3 in Figure 11.7, reflect increasing satisfaction as we move from I_1 to I_2 to I_3. The optimal portfolio, O, is the point at which indifference curve I_2 meets the efficient frontier. The investor cannot achieve the higher utility provided by I_3 because there is no investment available that offers a combination of risk and return falling on the curve I_3.

If we introduced a risk-free investment-paying return r_f into Figure 11.7, we could eventually derive the equation for the capital asset pricing model introduced previously. Rather than focus further on theory, let's shift our attention to the more practical aspects of the efficient frontier and its extensions.

Portfolio Betas As we have noted, investors strive to diversify their portfolios by including a variety of noncomplementary investments that allow investors to reduce risk while meeting their return objectives. Remember that investments embody two basic types of risk: (1) diversifiable risk, the risk unique to a particular investment, and (2) undiversifiable risk, the risk possessed, at least to some degree, by every investment.

A great deal of research has been conducted on the topic of risk as it relates to security investments. The results show that, in general, to earn a higher return, you must bear more risk. More startling, however, are research results showing that the positive relation between risk and return holds only for undiversifiable risk. High levels of diversifiable risk do not result in correspondingly high levels of return. Because there is no reward for bearing diversifiable risk, investors should minimize this form of risk by diversifying the portfolio so that only undiversifiable risk remains.

Risk Diversification As we've seen, diversification minimizes diversifiable risk by offsetting the below-average return on one investment with the above-average return on another. Minimizing diversifiable risk through careful selection of investments requires that the investments chosen for the portfolio come from a wide range of industries.

To better understand how diversification benefits investors, let's examine what happens when we begin with a single asset (security) in a portfolio and then expand the portfolio by randomly selecting additional securities. Using the standard deviation, s_p, to measure the portfolio's total risk, we can depict the behavior of the total portfolio risk as more securities are added, as done in Figure 11.8 (on page 390). As we add securities to the portfolio (x-axis), the total portfolio risk (y-axis) declines because of the effects of diversification, but there is a limit to how much risk reduction can be achieved.

On average, most of the risk-reduction benefits of diversification can be gained by forming portfolios containing 8 to 15 carefully selected securities, but our recommendation is to hold 40 or more securities to achieve efficient diversification. This suggestion tends to support the popularity of investment in mutual funds.

Because any investor can create a portfolio of assets that will eliminate virtually all diversifiable risk, the only **relevant risk** is that which is undiversifiable. You must therefore be concerned solely with undiversifiable risk. The measurement of undiversifiable risk is thus of primary importance.

FIGURE 11.8

Portfolio Risk and Diversification

As more securities are combined to create a portfolio, the total risk of the portfolio (measured by its standard deviation, s_p) declines. The portion of the risk eliminated is the diversifiable risk; the remaining portion is the undiversifiable, or relevant, risk.

Calculating Portfolio Betas As we saw earlier, beta measures the undiversifiable, or relevant, risk of a security. The beta for the market is equal to 1.0. Securities with betas greater than 1.0 are more risky than the market, and those with betas less than 1.0 are less risky than the market. The beta for the risk-free asset is 0.

The **portfolio beta**, b_p, is merely the weighted average of the betas of the individual assets it includes. You can easily calculate a portfolio's beta by using the betas of the component assets. To find the portfolio beta, b_p, calculate a weighted average of the betas of the individual stocks in the portfolio, where the weights represent the percentage of the portfolio's value invested in each security as shown in Equation 11.4.

Equation 11.4

$$\text{Portfolio beta} = \begin{pmatrix} \text{Proportion of} \\ \text{portfolio's total} \\ \text{dollar value} \\ \text{in asset 1} \end{pmatrix} \times \begin{pmatrix} \text{Beta} \\ \text{for} \\ \text{asset 1} \end{pmatrix} + \begin{pmatrix} \text{Proportion of} \\ \text{portfolio's total} \\ \text{dollar value} \\ \text{in asset 2} \end{pmatrix} \times \begin{pmatrix} \text{Beta} \\ \text{for} \\ \text{asset 2} \end{pmatrix} + \cdots +$$

$$\begin{pmatrix} \text{Proportion of} \\ \text{portfolio's total} \\ \text{dollar value} \\ \text{in asset } n \end{pmatrix} \times \begin{pmatrix} \text{Beta} \\ \text{for} \\ \text{asset } n \end{pmatrix} = \sum_{j=1}^{n} \begin{pmatrix} \text{Proportion of} \\ \text{portfolio's total} \\ \text{dollar value} \\ \text{in asset } j \end{pmatrix} \times \begin{pmatrix} \text{Beta} \\ \text{for} \\ \text{asset } j \end{pmatrix}$$

Equation 11.4a

$$b_p = (w_1 \times b_1) + (w_2 \times b_2) + \cdots + (w_n \times b_n) = \sum_{j=1}^{n} (w_j \times b_j)$$

Of course, $\sum_{j=1}^{n} w_j = 1$, which means that 100% of the portfolio's assets must be included in this computation.

Portfolio betas are interpreted in exactly the same way as individual asset betas. They indicate the degree of responsiveness of the portfolio's return to changes in the market return. For example, when the market return increases by 10%, a portfolio with a beta of 0.75 will experience a 7.5% increase in its return ($0.75 \times 10\%$). A

TABLE 11.6 AUSTIN FUND'S PORTFOLIOS V AND W

Asset	Portfolio V		Portfolio W	
	Proportion	Beta	Proportion	Beta
1	0.10	1.65	0.10	0.80
2	0.30	1.00	0.10	1.00
3	0.20	1.30	0.20	0.65
4	0.20	1.10	0.10	0.75
5	0.20	1.25	0.50	1.05
Total	1.00		1.00	

portfolio with a beta of 1.25 will experience a 12.5% increase in its return (1.25 × 10%). Low-beta portfolios are less responsive, and therefore less risky, than high-beta portfolios. Clearly, a portfolio containing mostly low-beta assets will have a low beta, and vice versa.

To demonstrate, consider the Austin Fund, a large investment company that wishes to assess the risk of 2 portfolios, V and W. Both portfolios contain 5 assets, with the proportions and betas shown in Table 11.6. We can calculate the betas for portfolios V and W, b_v and b_w, by substituting the appropriate data from the table into Equation 11.4, as follows.

$$b_v = (0.10 \times 1.65) + (0.30 \times 1.00) + (0.20 \times 1.30) + (0.20 \times 1.10) + (0.20 \times 1.25)$$
$$= 0.165 + 0.300 + 0.260 + 0.220 + 0.250 = 1.195 \approx \underline{1.20}$$
$$b_w = (0.10 \times 0.80) + (0.10 \times 1.00) + (0.20 \times 0.65) + (0.10 \times 0.75) + (0.50 \times 1.05)$$
$$= 0.080 + 0.100 + 0.130 + 0.075 + 0.525 = \underline{0.91}$$

Portfolio V's beta is 1.20, and portfolio W's is 0.91. These values make sense because portfolio V contains relatively high-beta assets and portfolio W contains relatively low-beta assets. Clearly, portfolio V's returns are more responsive to changes in market returns—and therefore more risky—than portfolio W's.

Interpreting Portfolio Betas If a portfolio has a beta of 1.0, the portfolio experiences changes in its rate of return equal to changes in the market's rate of return. The 1.0 beta portfolio would tend to experience a 10% increase in return if the stock market as a whole experienced a 10% increase in return. Conversely, if the market return fell by 6%, the return on the 1.0 beta portfolio would also fall by 6%.

Table 11.7 (on page 392) lists the expected returns for three portfolio betas in two situations: an increase in market return of 10% and a decrease in market return of 10%. The portfolio with a beta of 2.0 moves twice as much (on average) as the market does. When the market return increases by 10%, the portfolio return increases by 20%. When the market return declines by 10%, the portfolio's return will fall by 20%. This portfolio would be considered a high-risk, high-return portfolio.

The middle, 0.5 beta portfolio is considered a low-risk, low-return portfolio. This would be a conservative portfolio for investors who wish to maintain a low-risk investment posture. The 0.5 beta portfolio is half as volatile as the market.

A portfolio with a beta of −1.0 moves in the opposite direction from the market. A bearish investor would probably want to own a negative-beta portfolio because this

TABLE 11.7   PORTFOLIO BETAS AND ASSOCIATED CHANGES IN RETURNS

Portfolio Beta	Changes in Market Return (%)	Change in Expected Portfolio Return (%)
+ 2.0	+ 10.0	+ 20.0
	− 10.0	− 20.0
+ 0.5	+ 10.0	+ 5.0
	− 10.0	− 5.0
− 1.0	+ 10.0	− 10.0
	− 10.0	+ 10.0

type of investment tends to rise in value when the stock market declines, and vice versa. Finding securities with negative betas is difficult, however. Most securities have positive betas because they tend to experience return movements in the same direction as changes in the stock market.

The Risk-Return Tradeoff: Some Closing Comments Another valuable outgrowth of modern portfolio theory is the specific link between undiversifiable risk and investment return. The basic premise is that an investor must have a portfolio of relatively risky investments to earn a relatively high rate of return. That relationship is illustrated in Figure 11.9. The upward-sloping line shows the **risk-return tradeoff**. The point where the risk-return line crosses the return axis is called the **risk-free rate, r_f.** This is the return an investor can earn on a risk-free investment such as a U.S. Treasury bill or an insured money market deposit account.

As we proceed upward along the risk-return tradeoff line, portfolios of risky investments appear, as depicted by four investment portfolios, A through D. Portfolios A and B are investment opportunities that provide a level of return commensurate with their respective risk levels. Portfolio C provides a high return at a relatively low risk level—and therefore would be an excellent investment. Portfolio D, in contrast, offers high risk but low return—an investment to avoid.

FIGURE 11.9

The Portfolio Risk-Return Tradeoff

As the risk of an investment portfolio increases from 0, the return provided should increase above the risk-free rate, r_f. Portfolios A and B offer returns commensurate with their risk, portfolio C provides a high return at a low-risk level, and portfolio D provides a low return for high risk. Portfolio C is highly desirable; portfolio D should be avoided.

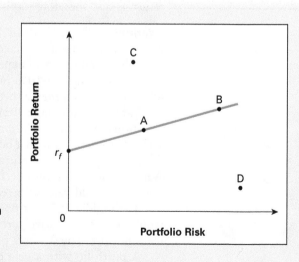

Reconciling the Traditional Approach and MPT

We have reviewed two fairly different approaches to portfolio management: the traditional approach and MPT. The question that naturally arises is which technique should you use? There is no definite answer; the question must be resolved by the judgment of each investor. However, we can offer a few useful ideas.

The average individual investor does not have the resources, computers, and mathematical acumen to implement a total MPT portfolio strategy. But most individual investors can extract and use ideas from both the traditional and MPT approaches. The traditional approach stresses security selection, which was discussed in Chapter 9. It also emphasizes diversification of the portfolio across industry lines. MPT stresses reducing correlations among rates of return for the securities within the portfolio. This approach calls for diversification to minimize diversifiable risk. Thus, diversification must be accomplished to ensure satisfactory performance with either strategy. Also, beta is a useful tool for determining the level of a portfolio's undiversifiable risk and should be part of the decision-making process.

We recommend the following portfolio management policy, which uses aspects of both approaches:

- Determine how much risk you are willing to bear.

- Seek diversification among types of securities and across industry lines, and pay attention to how the return from one security is related to that from another.

- Consider how a security responds to the market, and use beta in diversifying your portfolio to keep the portfolio in line with your acceptable level of risk.

- Evaluate alternative portfolios to make sure that the portfolio selected provides the highest return for the acceptable level of risk.

CONCEPTS IN REVIEW

Answers available at www.pearsonhighered.com/ smart

11.12 Describe traditional portfolio management. Give three reasons why traditional portfolio managers like to invest in well-established companies.

11.13 What is modern portfolio theory (MPT)? What is the feasible or attainable set of all possible portfolios? How is it derived for a given group of investments?

11.14 What is the efficient frontier? How is it related to the attainable set of all possible portfolios? How can it be used with an investor's utility function to find the optimal portfolio?

11.15 Define and differentiate among the diversifiable, undiversifiable, and total risk of a portfolio. Which is considered the relevant risk? How is it measured?

11.16 Define beta. How can you find the beta of a portfolio when you know the beta for each of the assets included within it?

11.17 Explain how you can reconcile the traditional and modern portfolio approaches.

MyFinanceLab

Here is what you should know after reading this chapter. MyFinanceLab will help you identify what you know and where to go when you need to practice.

What You Should Know	Key Terms	Where to Practice
LG1 **Understand portfolio objectives and the procedures used to calculate portfolio return and standard deviation.** A portfolio is a collection of investments assembled to achieve one or more investment goals. It produces potential price appreciation and current income, subject to a tradeoff between risk and return. The return on a portfolio is calculated as a weighted average of the returns of the assets from which it is formed. The standard deviation of a portfolio's returns is found by applying the same formula that is used to find the standard deviation of a single asset.	efficient portfolio, *p. 369* growth-oriented portfolio, *p. 369* income-oriented portfolio, *p. 369*	MyFinanceLab Study Plan 11.1 Excel Table 11.1 Video Learning Aid for Problem P11.5
LG2 **Discuss the concepts of correlation and diversification and the key aspects of international diversification.** Correlation is a statistic used to measure the relationship between the returns on assets. To diversify, it is best to add assets with negatively correlated returns. In general, the less positive and more negative the correlation between asset returns, the more effectively a portfolio can be diversified to reduce its risk. Diversification can reduce the risk (standard deviation) of a portfolio below the risk of the least risky asset (sometimes to 0). The return of the resulting portfolio will be no lower than the smallest return of its component assets. For any two-asset portfolio, the ability to reduce risk depends on both the degree of correlation and the proportion of each asset in the portfolio. International diversification may allow an investor to reduce portfolio risk without necessarily imposing a corresponding reduction in return. It can be achieved by investing abroad or through domestic investment in foreign companies or funds, but it typically cannot be achieved by investing in U.S. multinationals. The preferred method of international diversification for individual investors is the use of ADSs or international mutual funds available in the United States. Although opportunities to earn "excess" returns in international investments are diminishing over time, international investments continue to provide an effective way to diversify.	correlation, *p. 372* correlation coefficient, *p. 372* negatively correlated, *p. 372* perfectly negatively correlated, *p. 373* perfectly positively correlated, *p. 373* positively correlated, *p. 372* uncorrelated, *p. 372*	MyFinanceLab Study Plan 11.2 Excel Tables 11.2, 11.3

What You Should Know	Key Terms	Where to Practice
LG3 Describe the components of risk and the use of beta to measure risk. The two basic components of total risk are diversifiable (unsystematic) and undiversifiable (systematic) risk. Undiversifiable risk is the relevant risk. Beta measures the undiversifiable, or market, risk associated with a security investment. It is derived from the historical relationship between a security's return and the market return.	beta, *p. 380* diversifiable (unsystematic) risk, *p. 379* market return, *p. 380* undiversifiable (systematic) risk, *p. 380* total risk, *p. 380*	MyFinanceLab Study Plan 11.3 Video Learning Aid for Problem P11.22
LG4 Explain the capital asset pricing model (CAPM) conceptually, mathematically, and graphically. The CAPM relates risk (as measured by beta) to return. It can be divided into (1) the risk-free rate of return, r_{rf}, and (2) the risk premium, $b \times (r_m - r_{rf})$. The graphic depiction of the CAPM is the security market line (SML). The CAPM reflects increasing required returns for increasing risk.	capital asset pricing model (CAPM), *p. 383* security market line (SML), *p. 384*	MyFinanceLab Study Plan 11.4
LG5 Review the traditional and modern approaches to portfolio management. The traditional approach constructs portfolios by combining a large number of securities issued by companies from a broad cross-section of industries. Modern portfolio theory (MPT) uses statistical diversification to develop efficient portfolios. To determine the optimal portfolio, MPT finds the efficient frontier and couples it with an investor's risk-indifference curves.	efficient frontier, *p. 388* modern portfolio theory (MPT), *p. 387* portfolio beta, b_p, *p. 390* relevant risk, *p. 389* risk-return tradeoff, *p. 392* risk-free rate, r_{rf}, *p. 392* traditional portfolio management, *p. 386*	MyFinanceLab Study Plan 11.5
LG6 Describe portfolio betas, the risk-return tradeoff, and reconciliation of the two approaches to portfolio management. Portfolio betas can be used to develop efficient portfolios consistent with the investor's risk-return preferences. Portfolio betas are merely a weighted average of the betas of the individual assets in the portfolio. Generally, investors use elements of both the traditional approach and MPT to create portfolios. This approach involves determining how much risk you are willing to bear, seeking diversification, using beta to diversify your portfolio, and evaluating alternative portfolios to select the one that offers the highest return for an acceptable level of risk.		MyFinanceLab Study Plan 11.6 Video Learning Aid for Problem P11.22

Log into MyFinanceLab, take a chapter test, and get a personalized Study Plan
that tells you which concepts you understand and which ones you need
to review. From there, MyFinanceLab will give you further practice,
tutorials, animations, videos, and guided solutions.
Log into **www.myfinancelab.com**

Discussion Questions

LG1 **Q11.1** State your portfolio objectives. Then construct a 10-stock portfolio that you feel is consistent with your objectives. (Use companies that have been public for at least 5 years.) Obtain annual dividend and price data for each of the past 5 years.

    a. Calculate the historical return for each stock for each year.

    b. Using your findings in part a, calculate the historical portfolio return for each of the 5 years.

    c. Use your findings in part b to calculate the average portfolio return over the 5 years.

    d. Use your findings in parts b and c to find the standard deviation of the portfolio's returns over the 5-year period.

    e. Use the historical average return from part c and the standard deviation from part d to evaluate the portfolio's return and risk in light of your stated portfolio objectives.

LG2 **Q11.2** Using the following guidelines, choose the stocks—A, B, and C—of 3 firms that have been public for at least 10 years. Stock A should be one you are interested in buying. Stock B should be a stock, possibly in the same line of business or industry, that you feel will have the highest possible return correlation with stock A. Stock C should be one you feel will have the lowest possible return correlation with stock A.

    a. Calculate the annual rates of return for each of the past 10 years for each stock.

    b. Plot the 10 annual return values for each stock on the same set of axes, where the x-axis is the year and the y-axis is the annual return in percentage terms.

    c. Join the points for the returns for each stock on the graph. Evaluate and describe the returns of stocks A and B in the graph. Do they exhibit the expected positive correlation? Why or why not?

    d. Evaluate and describe the relationship between the returns of stocks A and C in the graph. Do they exhibit negative correlation? Why or why not?

    e. Compare and contrast your findings in parts c and d to the expected relationships among stocks A, B, and C. Discuss your findings.

LG3 **Q11.3** From the *Wall Street Journal*, a website such as Yahoo! Finance, or some other source, obtain a current estimate of the risk-free rate (use a 10-year Treasury bond). Use the *Value Line Investment Survey* or Yahoo! Finance to obtain the beta for each of the following stocks:

Ford (autos)
Dell (computers)
Sempra Energy (utilities)
Kroger (groceries)
Bank of America (financial services)

Use the information you gathered along with the market risk premium on large stocks given in the chapter to find the required return for each stock with the capital asset pricing model.

LG3 **LG4** **Q11.4** From the *Wall Street Journal*, a website such as Yahoo! Finance, or some other source, obtain a current estimate of the risk-free rate (use a 10-year Treasury bond). Use the *Value Line Investment Survey* or Yahoo! Finance to obtain the beta for each of the companies listed on page *180*.

    a. Compare the current betas to the May 7, 2012, betas given in the chapter for each of the companies.

    b. What might cause betas to change over time, even in a stable economic environment?

    c. Use the current betas, along with a market risk premium on stocks of 8.5%, to find the required return for each stock with the CAPM.

    d. Compare and discuss your findings in part c with regard to the specific business of each company.

LG2 LG5 LG6   Q11.5   Obtain a prospectus and an annual report for a major mutual fund that includes some international securities. Carefully read the prospectus and annual report and study the portfolio's composition in light of the fund's stated objectives.

     a. Evaluate the amount of diversification and the types of industries and companies held. Is the portfolio well diversified?

     b. Discuss the additional risks faced by an investor in this fund compared to an investor in a domestic stock portfolio such as the S&P 500.

LG6   Q11.6   Use *Value Line Investment Survey* or some other source to select 4 stocks with betas ranging from about 0.50 to 1.50. Record the current market prices of each of these stocks. Assume you wish to create a portfolio that combines all 4 stocks in such a way that the resulting portfolio beta is about 1.10.

     a. Through trial and error, use all 4 stocks to create a portfolio with the target beta of 1.10.

     b. If you have $100,000 to invest in this portfolio, on the basis of the weightings determined in part **a**, what dollar amounts would you invest in each stock?

     c. Approximately how many shares of each of the 4 stocks would you buy given the dollar amounts calculated in part **b**?

     d. Repeat parts **a**, **b**, and **c** with a different set of weightings that still result in a portfolio beta of 1.10. Can only one unique portfolio with a given beta be created from a given set of stocks?

Problems

All problems are available on www.myfinancelab.com

LG1   P11.1 Your portfolio had the values in the following table for the 4 years listed. Calculate your average return over the 4-year period.

Year	Beginning Value ($)	Ending Value ($)
2010	50,000.00	55,000.00
2011	55,000.00	58,000.00
2012	58,000.00	65,000.00
2013	65,000.00	70,000.00

LG1   P11.2 Using your data from Problem 11.1, calculate the portfolio standard deviation.

LG1 LG2   P11.3 Assume you are considering a portfolio containing 2 assets, L and M. Asset L will represent 40% of the dollar value of the portfolio, and asset M will account for the other 60%. The expected returns over the next 6 years, 2015–2020, for each of these assets are summarized in the following table.

	Expected Return (%)	
Year	Asset L	Asset M
2015	14	20
2016	14	18
2017	16	16
2018	17	14
2019	17	12
2020	19	10

     a. Calculate the expected portfolio return, $\bar{r}_p$, for each of the 6 years.

     b. Calculate the average expected portfolio return, $\bar{r}_p$, over the 6-year period.

c. Calculate the standard deviation of expected portfolio returns, s_p, over the 6-year period.
d. How would you characterize the correlation of returns of the assets L and M?
e. Discuss any benefits of diversification achieved through creation of the portfolio.

LG1 LG2 P11.4 Refer to Problem 11.3. Assume that asset L represents 60% of the portfolio and asset M is 40%. Calculate the average expected return and standard deviation of expected portfolio returns over the 6-year period. Compare your answers to the answers from Problem 11.3.

LG1 LG2 P11.5 You have been given the following return data on 3 assets—F, G, and H—over the period 2015–2018.

	Expected Return (%)		
Year	Asset F	Asset G	Asset H
2015	16	17	14
2016	17	16	15
2017	18	15	16
2018	19	14	17

Using these assets, you have isolated 3 investment alternatives:

Alternative	Investment
1	100% of asset F
2	50% of asset F and 50% of asset G
3	50% of asset F and 50% of asset H

a. Calculate the portfolio return over the 4-year period for each of the 3 alternatives.
b. Calculate the standard deviation of returns over the 4-year period for each of the 3 alternatives.
c. On the basis of your findings in parts a and b, which of the 3 investment alternatives would you recommend? Why?

LG1 LG2 P11.6 You have been asked for your advice in selecting a portfolio of assets and have been supplied with the following data.

	Expected Return (%)		
Year	Asset A	Asset B	Asset C
2015	12	16	12
2016	14	14	14
2017	16	12	16

You have been told that you can create 2 portfolios—one consisting of assets A and B and the other consisting of assets A and C—by investing equal proportions (50%) in each of the 2 component assets.
a. What is the average expected return, $\bar{r}$, for each asset over the 3-year period?
b. What is the standard deviation, s, for each asset's expected return?
c. What is the average expected return, $\bar{r}_p$, for each of the portfolios?
d. How would you characterize the correlations of returns of the 2 assets in each of the portfolios identified in part c?
e. What is the standard deviation of expected returns, s_p, for each portfolio?
f. Which portfolio do you recommend? Why?

LG1 LG2   P11.7 Referring to Problem 11.6 earlier, what would happen if you constructed a portfolio consisting of assets A, B, and C, equally weighted? Would this reduce risk or enhance return?

LG1 LG2   P11.8 Assume you wish to evaluate the risk and return behaviors associated with various combinations of assets V and W under 3 assumed degrees of correlation: perfect positive, uncorrelated, and perfect negative. The following average return and risk values were calculated for these assets.

Asset	Average Return, $\bar{r}$ (%)	Risk (Standard Asset Deviation), s (%)
V	8	5
W	13	10

a. If the returns of assets V and W are perfectly positively correlated (correlation coefficient = +1), describe the range of (1) return and (2) risk associated with all possible portfolio combinations.
b. If the returns of assets V and W are uncorrelated (correlation coefficient = 0), describe the approximate range of (1) return and (2) risk associated with all possible portfolio combinations.
c. If the returns of assets V and W are perfectly negatively correlated (correlation coefficient = −1), describe the range of (1) return and (2) risk associated with all possible portfolio combinations.

LG1   P11.9 The following table contains annual returns for the stocks of Home Depot (HD) and Lowe's (LOW). The returns are calculated using end-of-year prices (adjusted for dividends and stock splits) retrieved from http://finance.yahoo.com/. Use Excel to create a spreadsheet that calculates annual portfolio returns for an equally weighted portfolio of HD and LOW. Also, calculate the average annual return for both stocks and the portfolio. (Hint: review panel A of Table 11.1.)

Year	HD Returns (%)	LOW Returns (%)
2002	−52.6	−19.1
2003	49.0	48.0
2004	21.5	4.2
2005	−4.3	16.1
2006	1.0	−6.0
2007	−31.2	−26.8
2008	−11.4	−3.3
2009	30.6	10.6
2010	24.9	9.2
2011	23.5	3.4

LG1 LG2   P11.10 Use the table of annual returns in Problem 11.9 for Home Depot (HD) and Lowe's (LOW) to create an Excel spreadsheet that calculates the standard deviation of annual returns for HD, LOW, and the equally weighted portfolio of HD and LOW. (Hint: review the Excel screenshot on page *371*.)

LG1 LG2   P11.11 Use the table of annual returns in Problem 11.9 for Home Depot (HD) and Lowe's (LOW) to create an Excel spreadsheet that calculates the correlation coefficient for HD and LOW annual returns. (Hint: review the Excel screenshot on page *372*.)

LG1 LG2   P11.12 Use the table of annual returns in Problem 11.9 for Home Depot (HD) and Lowe's (LOW) to create an Excel spreadsheet that calculates returns for portfolios comprised of HD and LOW using the following, respective, weightings: (1.0, 0.0), (0.9, 0.1), (0.8, 0.2), (0.7, 0.3), (0.6, 0.4), (0.5, 0.5), (0.4, 0.6), (0.3, 0.7), (0.2, 0.8), (0.1, 0.9), and (0.0, 1.0). Also, calculate the portfolio standard deviation associated with each portfolio composition. You will need to use the standard deviations found previously for HD and LOW and their correlation coefficient. (Hint: review Table 11.2.)

LG1 LG2   P11.13 Create an Excel spreadsheet that graphs the portfolio return and standard deviation combinations found in Problem 11.12 for Home Depot and Lowe's. (Hint: review Figure 11.3.)

LG3   P11.14 Imagine you wish to estimate the betas for 2 investments, A and B. You have gathered the following return data for the market and for each of the investments over the past 10 years, 2005–2014.

	Historical Returns		
		Investment (%)	
Year	Market	A	B
2005	6	11	16
2006	2	8	11
2007	−13	−4	10
2008	−4	3	3
2009	−8	0	3
2010	16	19	30
2011	10	14	22
2012	15	18	29
2013	8	12	19
2014	13	17	26

a. On a set of market return (x-axis)–investment return (y-axis) axes, use the data to draw the characteristic lines for investments A and B on the same graph.
b. Use the characteristic lines from part a to estimate the betas for investments A and B.
c. Use the betas found in part b to comment on the relative risks of investments A and B.

LG3   P11.15 You are evaluating 2 possible stock investments, Buyme Co. and Getit Corp. Buyme Co. has an expected return of 14% and a beta of 1. Getit Corp. has an expected return of 14% and a beta of 1.2. Based only on this data, which stock should you buy and why?

LG3   P11.16 Referring to Problem 11.15, if you expected a significant market rally, would your decision be altered? Explain.

LG3   P11.17 A security has a beta of 1.2. Is this security more or less risky than the market? Explain. Assess the impact on the required return of this security in each of the following cases.
a. The market return increases by 15%.
b. The market return decreases by 8%.
c. The market return remains unchanged.

LG3   P11.18 Assume the betas for securities A, B, and C are as shown here.

Security	Beta
A	1.4
B	0.8
C	−0.9

a. Calculate the change in return for each security if the market experiences an increase in its rate of return of 13.2% over the next period.
b. Calculate the change in return for each security if the market experiences a decrease in its rate of return of 10.8% over the next period.
c. Rank and discuss the relative risk of each security on the basis of your findings. Which security might perform best during an economic downturn? Explain.

LG3 LG6 P11.19 Referring to Problem 11.18, assume you have a portfolio with $20,000 invested in each of investments A, B, and C. What is your portfolio beta?

LG3 LG6 P11.20 Referring to Problem 11.19, using the portfolio beta, what would you expect the value of your portfolio to be if the market rallied 20%? Declined 20%?

LG4 P11.21 Use the capital asset pricing model to find the required return for each of the following securities in light of the data given.

Security	Risk-Free Rate (%)	Market Return (%)	Beta
A	5	8	1.3
B	8	13	0.9
C	9	12	0.2
D	10	15	1.0
E	6	10	0.6

LG4 P11.22 Jay is reviewing his portfolio of investments, which include certain stocks and bonds. He has a large amount tied up in U.S. Treasury bills paying 3%. He is considering moving some of his funds from the T-bills into a stock. The stock has a beta of 1.25. If Jay expects a return of 14% from the stock (a little better than the current market return of 13%), should he buy the stock or leave his funds in the T-bill?

LG4 P11.23 The risk-free rate is currently 7%, and the market return is 12%. Assume you are considering the following investments.

Investment	Beta
A	1.5
B	1.0
C	0.75
D	0.0
E	2.0

a. Which investment is most risky? Least risky?
b. Use the capital asset pricing model to find the required return on each of the investments.
c. Using your findings in part **b**, draw the security market line.
d. On the basis of your findings in part **c**, what relationship exists between risk and return? Explain.

LG5 LG6 P11.24 Portfolios A through J, which are listed in the following table along with their returns (r_p) and risk (measured by the standard deviation, s_p), represent all currently available portfolios in the feasible or attainable set.

Portfolio	Return, r_p (%)	Risk, s_p (%)
A	9	8
B	3	3
C	14	10
D	12	14
E	7	11
F	11	6
G	10	12
H	16	16
I	5	7
J	8	4

a. Plot the feasible, or attainable, set represented by these data on a graph showing portfolio risk, s_p (x-axis), and portfolio return, r_p (y-axis).

b. Draw the efficient frontier on the graph in part a.

c. Which portfolios lie on the efficient frontier? Why do these portfolios dominate all others in the feasible set?

d. How would an investor's utility function or risk-indifference curves be used with the efficient frontier to find the optimal portfolio?

LG5 LG6   P11.25 For his portfolio, Jack Cashman randomly selected securities from all those listed on the New York Stock Exchange. He began with one security and added securities one by one until a total of 20 securities were held in the portfolio. After each security was added, Jack calculated the portfolio standard deviation, s_p. The calculated values follow.

Number of Securities	Portfolio Risk, s_p (%)	Number of Securities	Portfolio Risk, s_p (%)
1	14.5	11	7.00
2	13.3	12	6.80
3	12.2	13	6.70
4	11.2	14	6.65
5	10.3	15	6.60
6	9.5	16	6.56
7	8.8	17	6.52
8	8.2	18	6.5
9	7.7	19	6.48
10	7.3	20	6.47

a. On a graph showing the number of securities in the portfolio (x-axis) and portfolio risk, s_p (y-axis), plot the portfolio risk given the data in the preceding table.

b. Divide the portfolio risk in the graph into its undiversifiable and diversifiable risk components, and label each of these on the graph.

c. Describe which of the two risk components is the relevant risk, and explain why it is relevant. How much of this risk exists in Jack Cashman's portfolio?

LG3 LG6   P11.26 If portfolio A has a beta of 1.5 and portfolio Z has a beta of −1.5, what do the two values indicate? If the return on the market rises by 20%, what impact, if any, would this have on the returns from portfolios A and Z? Explain.

LG3 LG6   P11.27 Stock A has a beta of 0.8, stock B has a beta of 1.4, and stock C has a beta of −0.3.

a. Rank these stocks from the most risky to the least risky.

b. If the return on the market portfolio increases by 12%, what change in the return for each of the stocks would you expect?

c. If the return on the market portfolio declines by 5%, what change in the return for each of the stocks would you expect?

d. If you felt the stock market was about to experience a significant decline, which stock would you be most likely to add to your portfolio? Why?

e. If you anticipated a major stock market rally, which stock would you be most likely to add to your portfolio? Why?

LG6   P11.28 Jeanne Lewis is attempting to evaluate 2 possible portfolios consisting of the same 5 assets but held in different proportions. She is particularly interested in using beta to compare the risk of the portfolios and, in this regard, has gathered the following data:

		Portfolio Weights (%)	
Asset	Asset Beta	Portfolio A	Portfolio B
1	1.3	10	30
2	0.7	30	10
3	1.25	10	20
4	1.1	10	20
5	0.9	40	20
Total		100	100

a. Calculate the betas for portfolios A and B.

b. Compare the risk of each portfolio to the market as well as to each other. Which portfolio is more risky?

LG4 P11.29 Referring to Problem 11.28, if the risk-free rate is 2% and the market return is 12%, calculate the required return for each portfolio using the CAPM.

LG5 LG6 P11.30 Referring to Problem 11.28, assume that each of the 5 assets has an expected return as shown in the table below. Based on these figures and the weights in Problem 11.28, calculate the expected return on Portfolios A and B. Which portfolio would you invest in and why?

Asset	Returns (%)
1	16.5
2	12.0
3	15.0
4	13.0
5	7.0

Visit **www.myfinancelab.com** for web exercises, spreadsheets, and other online resources.

Case Problem 11.1   Traditional Versus Modern Portfolio Theory: Who's Right?

LG5 LG6 Walt Davies and Shane O'Brien are district managers for Lee, Inc. Over the years, as they moved through the firm's sales organization, they became (and still remain) close friends. Walt, who is 33 years old, currently lives in Princeton, New Jersey. Shane, who is 35, lives in Houston, Texas. Recently, at the national sales meeting, they were discussing various company matters, as well as bringing each other up to date on their families, when the subject of investments came up. Each had always been fascinated by the stock market, and now that they had achieved some degree of financial success, they had begun actively investing.

As they discussed their investments, Walt said he thought the only way an individual who does not have hundreds of thousands of dollars can invest safely is to buy mutual fund shares. He emphasized that to be safe, a person needs to hold a broadly diversified portfolio and that only those with a lot of money and time can achieve independently the diversification that can be readily obtained by purchasing mutual fund shares.

Shane totally disagreed. He said, "Diversification! Who needs it?" He thought that what one must do is look carefully at stocks possessing desired risk-return characteristics and then invest all one's money in the single best stock. Walt told him he was crazy. He said, "There is no way to measure risk conveniently—you're just gambling." Shane disagreed. He explained how his stock-broker had acquainted him with beta, which is a measure of risk. Shane said that the higher the beta, the more risky the stock, and therefore the higher its return. By looking up the betas for potential stock investments on the Internet, he can pick stocks that have an acceptable risk level for him. Shane explained that with beta, one does not need to diversify; one merely needs to be willing to accept the risk reflected by beta and then hope for the best.

The conversation continued, with Walt indicating that although he knew nothing about beta, he didn't believe one could safely invest in a single stock. Shane continued to argue that his broker had explained to him that betas can be calculated not just for a single stock but also for a portfolio of stocks, such as a mutual fund. He said, "What's the difference between a stock with a beta of, say, 1.2 and a mutual fund with a beta of 1.2? They have the same risk and should therefore provide similar returns."

As Walt and Shane continued to discuss their differing opinions relative to investment strategy, they began to get angry with each other. Neither was able to convince the other that he was right. The level of their voices now raised, they attracted the attention of the company's vice president of finance, Elinor Green, who was standing nearby. She came over and indicated she had overheard their argument about investments and thought that, given her expertise on financial matters, she might be able to resolve their disagreement. She asked them to explain the crux of their disagreement, and each reviewed his own viewpoint. After hearing their views, Elinor responded, "I have some good news and some bad news for each of you. There is some validity to what each of you says, but there also are some errors in each of your explanations. Walt tends to support the traditional approach to portfolio management. Shane's views are more supportive of modern portfolio theory." Just then, the company president interrupted them, needing to talk to Elinor immediately. Elinor apologized for having to leave and offered to continue their discussion later that evening.

Questions

a. Analyze Walt's argument and explain why a mutual fund investment may be overdiversified. Also explain why one does not necessarily have to have hundreds of thousands of dollars to diversify adequately.

b. Analyze Shane's argument and explain the major error in his logic relative to the use of beta as a substitute for diversification. Explain the key assumption underlying the use of beta as a risk measure.

c. Briefly describe the traditional approach to portfolio management and relate it to the approaches supported by Walt and Shane.

d. Briefly describe modern portfolio theory and relate it to the approaches supported by Walt and Shane. Be sure to mention diversifiable risk, undiversifiable risk, and total risk, along with the role of beta.

e. Explain how the traditional approach and modern portfolio theory can be blended into an approach to portfolio management that might prove useful to the individual investor. Relate this to reconciling Walt's and Shane's differing points of view.

Case Problem 11.2   Susan Lussier's Inherited Portfolio: Does It Meet Her Needs?

LG3 LG4
LG5 LG6

Susan Lussier is 35 years old and employed as a tax accountant for a major oil and gas exploration company. She earns nearly $135,000 a year from her salary and from participation in the company's drilling activities. An expert on oil and gas taxation, she is not worried about job security—she is content with her income and finds it adequate to allow her to buy and do whatever she wishes. Her current philosophy is to live each day to its fullest, not concerning herself with retirement, which is too far in the future to require her current attention.

A month ago, Susan's only surviving parent, her father, was killed in a sailing accident. He had retired in La Jolla, California, 2 years earlier and had spent most of his time sailing. Prior to retirement, he managed a children's clothing manufacturing firm in South Carolina. Upon retirement he sold his stock in the firm and invested the proceeds in a security portfolio that provided him with supplemental retirement income of over $30,000 per year. In his will, he left his entire estate to Susan. The estate was structured in such a way that in addition to a few family heir-looms, Susan received a security portfolio having a market value of nearly $350,000 and about $10,000 in cash.

Susan's father's portfolio contained 10 securities: 5 bonds, 2 common stocks, and 3 mutual funds. The following table lists the securities and their key characteristics. The common stocks were issued by large, mature, well-known firms that had exhibited continuing patterns of dividend payment over the past 5 years. The stocks offered only moderate growth potential—probably no more than 2% to 3% appreciation per year. The mutual funds in the portfolio were income funds invested in diversified portfolios of income-oriented stocks and bonds. They provided stable streams of dividend income but offered little opportunity for capital appreciation.

The Securities Portfolio That Susan Lussier Inherited

Bonds

Par Value ($)	Issue	S&P Rating	Interest Income ($)	Quoted Price ($)	Total Cost ($)	Current Yield (%)
40,000	Delta Power and Light 10.125% due 2029	AA	4,050	98.000	39,200	10.33
30,000	Mountain Water 9.750% due 2021	A	2,925	102.000	30,600	9.56
50,000	California Gas 9.500% due 2016	AAA	4,750	97.000	48,500	9.79
20,000	Trans-Pacific Gas 10.000% due 2027	AAA	2,000	99.000	19,800	10.10
20,000	Public Service 9.875% due 2017	AA	1,975	100.000	20,000	9.88

Common Stocks

Number of Shares	Company	Dividend per Share ($)	Dividend Income ($)	Price per Share ($)	Total Cost ($)	Beta	Dividend Yield (%)
2,000	International Supply	2.40	4,800	22	44,900	0.97	10.91
3,000	Black Motor	1.50	4,500	17	52,000	0.85	8.82

Mutual Funds

Number of Shares	Fund	Dividend per Share Income ($)	Dividend Income ($)	Price per Share ($)	Total Cost	Beta	Dividend Yield (%)
2,000	International Capital Income A Fund	0.80	1,600	10	20,000	1.02	8.00
1,000	Grimner Special Income Fund	2.00	2,000	15	15,000	1.10	7.50
4,000	Ellis Diversified Income Fund	1.20	4,800	12	48,000	0.90	10.00

Total annual income: $33,400   Portfolio value: $338,000   Portfolio current yield: 9.88%

Now that Susan owns the portfolio, she wishes to determine whether it is suitable for her situation. She realizes that the high level of income provided by the portfolio will be taxed at a rate (federal plus state) of about 40%. Because she does not currently need it, Susan plans to invest the after-tax income primarily in common stocks offering high capital gain potential. During the coming years she clearly needs to avoid generating taxable income. (Susan is already paying out a sizable portion of her income in taxes.) She feels fortunate to have received the portfolio and wants to make certain it provides her with the maximum benefits, given her financial situation. The $10,000 cash left to her will be especially useful in paying brokers' commissions associated with making portfolio adjustments.

Questions

a. Briefly assess Susan's financial situation and develop a portfolio objective for her that is consistent with her needs.

b. Evaluate the portfolio left to Susan by her father. Assess its apparent objective and evaluate how well it may be doing in fulfilling this objective. Use the total cost values to describe the asset allocation scheme reflected in the portfolio. Comment on the risk, return, and tax implications of this portfolio.

c. If Susan decided to invest in a security portfolio consistent with her needs—indicated in response to question **a**—describe the nature and mix, if any, of securities you would recommend she purchase. Discuss the risk, return, and tax implications of such a portfolio.

d. From the response to question **b**, compare the nature of the security portfolio inherited by Susan with what you believe would be an appropriate security portfolio for her, based on the response to question **c**.

e. What recommendations would you give Susan about the inherited portfolio? Explain the steps she should take to adjust the portfolio to her needs.

Excel with Spreadsheets

Katie plans to form a portfolio consisting of two securities, Intel (INTC) and Procter & Gamble (PG), and she wonders how the portfolio's return will depend on the amount that she invests in each stock. Katie's professor suggests that she use the capital asset pricing model to define the required returns for the 2 companies. (Refer to Equations 11.3 and 11.3a.)

$$r_j = r_{rf} + [b_j \times (r_m - r_{rf})]$$

Katie measures r_{rf} using the current long-term Treasury bond return of 5%. Katie determines that the average return on the S&P 500 index over the last several years is 6.1%, so she uses that figure to measure r_m. She researches a source for the beta information and follows these steps:

*   Go to money.msn.com

*   In the Get Quote box, type INTC and press Get Quote.

*   On the next page, look for the stock's beta.

*   Repeat the steps for the PG stock.

Questions

a. What are the beta values for INTC and PG? Using the CAPM, create a spreadsheet to determine the required rates of return for both INTC and PG.

b. Katie has decided that the portfolio will be distributed between INTC and PG in a 60% and 40% split, respectively. Hence, a weighted average can be calculated for both the returns and betas of the portfolio. This concept is shown in the spreadsheet for Table 11.2, which can be viewed at www.myfinancelab.com. **Create a spreadsheet** using the following models for the calculations:

$$war = (w_i \times r_i) + (w_j \times r_j)$$

where:

war = weighted average required rate of return for the portfolio

w_i = weight of security i in the portfolio

r_i = required return of security i in the portfolio

w_j = weight of security j in the portfolio

r_j = required return of security j in the portfolio

$$wab = (w_i \times b_i) + (w_j \times b_j)$$

where:

wab = weighted average beta for the portfolio

w_i = weight of security i in the portfolio

b_i = beta for security i

w_j = weight of security j in the portfolio

b_j = beta for security j

Chapter-Opening Problem

In this problem we will visit United Rentals Inc. (URI), which was introduced at the beginning of the chapter. The following table shows the monthly return on URI stock and on the S&P 500 stock index from May 2007 to April 2012.

Month/Year	S&P 500 Return (%)	United Rentals Return (%)	Month/Year	S&P 500 Return (%)	United Rentals Return (%)
5/1/2007	3.3	0.1	6/1/2009	0.0	36.6
6/1/2007	−1.8	−3.0	7/1/2009	7.4	15.1
7/2/2007	−3.2	−1.2	8/3/2009	3.4	23.0
8/1/2007	1.3	1.4	9/1/2009	3.6	12.1
9/4/2007	3.6	−1.3	10/1/2009	−2.0	−7.9
10/1/2007	1.5	6.3	11/2/2009	5.7	−2.8
11/1/2007	−4.4	−31.9	12/1/2009	1.8	6.4
12/3/2007	−0.9	−21.1	1/4/2010	−3.7	−18.3
1/2/2008	−6.1	−0.7	2/1/2010	2.9	−5.7
2/1/2008	−3.5	10.3	3/1/2010	5.9	24.2
3/3/2008	−0.6	−6.3	4/1/2010	1.5	53.1
4/1/2008	4.8	0.0	5/3/2010	−8.2	−15.4
5/1/2008	1.1	9.3	6/1/2010	−5.4	−23.3
6/2/2008	−8.6	−4.8	7/1/2010	6.9	41.4
7/1/2008	−1.0	−17.5	8/2/2010	−4.7	−14.6
8/1/2008	1.2	0.1	9/1/2010	8.8	31.9
9/2/2008	−9.1	−5.9	10/1/2010	3.7	26.6
10/1/2008	−16.9	−32.7	11/1/2010	−0.2	4.4
11/3/2008	−7.5	−21.3	12/1/2010	6.5	16.0
12/1/2008	0.8	13.0	1/3/2011	2.3	17.1
1/2/2009	−8.6	−38.8	2/1/2011	3.2	16.2
2/2/2009	−11.0	−27.4	3/1/2011	−0.1	7.4
3/2/2009	8.5	4.0	4/1/2011	2.8	−11.6
4/1/2009	9.4	43.9	5/2/2011	−1.4	−7.1
5/1/2009	5.3	−21.6	6/1/2011	−1.8	−7.1

Month/Year	S&P 500 Return (%)	United Rentals Return (%)	Month/Year	S&P 500 Return (%)	United Rentals Return (%)
7/1/2011	−2.1	−9.4	12/1/2011	0.9	5.0
8/1/2011	−5.7	−27.5	1/3/2012	4.4	29.4
9/1/2011	−7.2	1.0	2/1/2012	4.1	9.0
10/3/2011	10.8	39.0	3/1/2012	3.1	2.9
11/1/2011	−0.5	20.2	4/2/2012	−0.7	8.8

Questions

a. Calculate the average monthly return on URI stock and on the S&P 500.

b. Calculate the standard deviation of monthly returns for URI and the S&P 500. What do your answers tell you about diversifiable risk, undiversifiable risk, and total risk?

c. Plot the returns of URI on the vertical axis and the returns of the S&P 500 on the horizontal axis of a graph. Does it appear that URI and the S&P 500 are correlated? If so, are they correlated positively or negatively?

d. Draw a line that you think best fits the scatterplot of points that you created in part c. What is the slope of this line? How can you interpret the slope? What does it say about the risk of URI compared to the risk of the S&P 500?

CFA Exam Questions

Being certified as a Chartered Financial Analyst (CFA) is globally recognized as the highest professional designation you can receive in the field of professional money management. The CFA charter is awarded to those candidates who successfully pass a series of 3 levels of exams, with each exam lasting 6 hours and covering a full range of investment topics. The CFA program is administered by the CFA Institute in Charlottesville, VA. (For more information about the CFA program, go to www.cfainstitute.org.)

Starting with this Part (2) of the text, and at the end of each part hereafter, you will find a small sample of questions similar to those that you might encounter on the Level I exam.

The Investment Environment and Conceptual Tools

Following is a sample of questions similar to ones that you might find on the CFA exam, Level 1. These questions deal with many of the topics covered earlier in this text, including the time value of money, measures of risk and return, securities markets, and portfolio management. (When answering the questions, give yourself 1½ minutes for each question; the objective is to correctly answer 8 of the 11 questions in 16½ minutes.)

1. Liquidity is best described as:
   a. wanting a portfolio to grow over time in real terms to meet future needs.
   b. converting an asset into cash without much of a price concession.
   c. wanting to minimize the risk of loss and maintain purchasing power.

2. A portfolio consists of 75% invested in Security A with an expected return of 35% and 25% invested in Security B with an expected return of 7%. Compute the expected return on the portfolio.

3. Stocks A and B have standard deviations of 8% and 15%, respectively. The correlation between the two stocks' returns has historically been 0.35. What is the standard deviation of a portfolio consisting of 60% invested in Stock A and 40% invested in Stock B?

4. Which of the following portfolios would be off the efficient frontier?

Portfolio	Expected Return (%)	Risk (%)
A	13	17
B	12	18
C	18	30

5. As the correlation coefficient between 2 securities changes in a portfolio,
   a. both expected return and risk change.
   b. neither expected return nor risk changes.
   c. only risk changes.

6. Portfolio risk is
   a. equal to the sum of the standard deviations of each of the securities in the portfolio.
   b. not dependent on the relative weights of the securities in the portfolio.
   c. not equal to the weighted average of the risks of the individual securities in the portfolio.

7. Faced with an efficient set of portfolios, an investor would
   a. choose the one with the highest expected return.
   b. always select portfolios on the left end of the efficient frontier.
   c. choose the portfolio at the point of tangency between the investor's highest indifference curve and the efficient frontier.

8. Both Portfolio Y and Portfolio Z are well diversified. The risk-free rate is 6%, the expected return on the market is 15%, and the portfolios have these characteristics:

Portfolio	Expected Return (%)	Beta
Y	17	1.20
Z	14	1.00

   Which of the following best characterizes the valuations of Portfolio Y and Portfolio Z?

	Portfolio Y	Portfolio Z
a.	Undervalued	Correctly valued
b.	Correctly valued	Overvalued
c.	Undervalued	Overvalued

9. For a stock with a margin requirement of 40%, how much cash is required, expressed as a percentage of the purchase cost?
   a. 0%
   b. 40%
   c. 50%

10. Which of the following is not a weighting scheme commonly used in creating equity market indexes?
    a. Price-weighted
    b. Industry-weighted
    c. Value-weighted

11. iCorporation has a relative systematic risk level that is 40% greater than the overall market. The expected return on the market is 16%, and the risk-free rate is 7%. Using the CAPM, the required rate of return for iCorporation is closest to
    a. 16.0%
    b. 19.6%
    c. 22.4%

Answers: 1. b; 2. 28%; 3. approximately 8.9%; 4. Portfolio B; 5. c; 6. c; 7. c; 8. c; 9. b; 10. b; 11. b

12

More on Risk and Return
Capital Market Theory

LEARNING GOALS

LG1 Calculate the expected rate of return and volatility for a portfolio of investments and describe how diversification affects the returns to a portfolio of investments.

LG2 Understand the concept of systematic risk for an individual investment and calculate portfolio systematic risk (beta).

LG3 Estimate the investor's expected rate of return using the Capital Asset Pricing Model.

Principles **P2** and **P4** Applied

In this chapter we will continue our discussion of **P** Principle 2: **There Is a Risk–Return Tradeoff**. In particular, we will extend our analysis of risk and return to consider portfolios of risky investments and the beneficial effects of portfolio diversification on risk. In addition, we will learn more about what types of risk are associated with both higher and lower expected rates of return. To do this we first develop the tools needed to calculate both the expected rate of return and the variance of the return of a portfolio consisting of many investments. Having developed these tools, we then investigate the concept of diversification and define what is meant by an investment's diversifiable and non-diversifiable risks. Finally, we describe the Capital Asset Pricing Model (CAPM), which helps us understand how the risk of an individual investment should be measured. In addition, as **P** Principle 4: **Market Prices Reflect Information** states, as new information arrives and changes investors' risk and return expectations, prices will change.

Good News Plus Bad News Equals No News

On Monday, April 28, 2008, Veeco Instruments Inc. (VECO) reported quarterly earnings that exceeded analysts' expectations for the quarter by 200 percent. The surprise earnings performance was greeted by a 6 percent rise in the company's share price for the day. On the same day, Travelzoo Inc. (TZOO) reported quarterly earnings that were dramatically below the level that was expected, and the company's stock price declined by more than 7 percent. Taken individually, Veeco's shareholders would be very happy at the end of the day, but Travelzoo's stockholders would not. Yet if you held a portfolio that included both company's shares, its value may not have changed much at all.

This example illustrates how diversification can reduce risk. **Diversification** is simply "not putting all your eggs in one basket." For example, if your portfolio consists only of stocks of oil companies such as ExxonMobil (XOM) and ConocoPhillips (COP), you would lose a substantial amount of money if the price of oil fell. Similarly, if your portfolio consists entirely of banking stocks such as that of Bank of America (BAC) and JPMorgan Chase (JPM), you are likely to lose a lot of money when the default rate on loans increases. On the other hand, if you were to invest half your money in oil stocks and the other half in banking stocks, the ups and downs of these investments would tend to offset one another, which would reduce the extreme returns on the downside as well as the upside. This is diversification.

Risk and Your Personal Investment Plan

Vanguard, one of the leading mutual fund families, identifies four key guidelines you should consider when making personal investment decisions:

1. Select investment products suited to your objective.
2. Find a comfortable balance between risk and return.
3. Diversify wisely to help manage risks.
4. Evaluate your portfolio periodically.

Notice that two of these four common-sense suggestions deal with risk. When you set up your own personal investment plan, which you might create for a variety of reasons—a rainy day fund, a down payment on a home, an education fund for your children, or simply retirement—you will need to determine your comfort level with risk and adjust your investments accordingly.

Some people can live with the substantial ups and downs of very risky investments. Others reach for the antacid when the value of their investments takes a plunge.

Your Turn: See Discussion Question 12–1.

Portfolio Returns and Portfolio Risk

LG1 The most important thing that we learn in this chapter is that with appropriate diversification, you can lower the risk of your portfolio without lowering the portfolio's expected rate of return. How does this concept of diversification relate to **P** Principle 2: **There Is a Risk–Return Tradeoff?** What we learn in this chapter is that some risk can be eliminated by diversification, and that those risks that can be eliminated are not necessarily rewarded in the financial marketplace. To understand this, we must delve into the computation of portfolio expected return and portfolio risk.

Calculating the Expected Return of a Portfolio

The expected rate of return for a portfolio of investments is simply a weighted average of the expected rates of return of the individual investments in that portfolio. To calculate a portfolio's expected rate of return we *weight* each individual investment's expected rate of return using the fraction of the portfolio invested in that particular investment. For instance, if you put half your money in the stock of ExxonMobil, with an expected rate of return of 12 percent, and the other half in General Electric (GE) stock, with an expected rate of return of 8 percent, then we can calculate the expected rate of return of the portfolio as follows: $(1/2 \times 12\%) + (1/2 \times 8\%) = 10\%$.

In general, we calculate the expected rate of return of a portfolio that includes n different assets as follows:

$$
\begin{aligned}
\text{Expected Portfolio} \atop \text{Return} =\ & \left(\begin{array}{c} \text{Fraction of Portfolio} \\ \text{Invested in Asset 1} \end{array} \times \begin{array}{c} \text{Expected Rate of} \\ \text{Return on Asset 1} \end{array} \right) \\
+\ & \left(\begin{array}{c} \text{Fraction of Portfolio} \\ \text{Invested in Asset 2} \end{array} \times \begin{array}{c} \text{Expected Rate of} \\ \text{Return on Asset 2} \end{array} \right) \\
+\ & \left(\begin{array}{c} \text{Fraction of Portfolio} \\ \text{Invested in Asset 3} \end{array} \times \begin{array}{c} \text{Expected Rate of} \\ \text{Return on Asset 3} \end{array} \right) \\
+\ \cdots\ +\ & \left(\begin{array}{c} \text{Fraction of Portfolio} \\ \text{Invested in Asset } n \end{array} \times \begin{array}{c} \text{Expected Rate of} \\ \text{Return on Asset } n \end{array} \right)
\end{aligned}
$$

Because the number of elements used to calculate the portfolio expected return is somewhat lengthy, we generally abbreviate the formula using symbols as follows:

Portfolio Expected Rate of Return

$$
E(r_{portfolio}) = [W_1 \times E(r_1)] + [W_2 \times E(r_2)] + [W_3 \times E(r_3)] + \cdots + [W_n \times E(r_n)] \tag{12-1}
$$

Important Definitions and Concepts:

- $E(r_{portfolio})$ = the expected rate of return on a portfolio of n assets.
- W_i = the portfolio weight for asset i.
- $E(r_i)$ = the expected rate of return earned by asset i. Recall that we can estimate the expected rate of return for a risky asset. In this chapter we will assume that this calculation has already been made and that the expected rate of return for risky assets is known.
- $[W_1 \times E(r_1)]$ = the contribution of asset 1 to the portfolio expected return.
- Note that the expected rate of return on a portfolio of n assets is simply a weighted average of the expected rates of return on each of the n assets.

Evaluating Portfolio Risk

In the last section we showed that the expected rate of return of a portfolio is simply the weighted average of the expected rates of returns of the individual investments that make up the portfolio. Next we calculate the risk of a portfolio using the standard deviation of portfolio returns. However, as we will illustrate in this section, the standard deviation of a portfolio's return is generally *not* equal to the weighted average of the standard deviations of the returns of the individual investments held in the portfolio. To understand why this is the case, we must look deeper into the concept of diversification.

Portfolio Diversification In most cases, combining investments in a portfolio leads to risk reduction. This effect of reducing risks by including a large number of investments in a portfolio is called **diversification**. As a consequence of diversification, the standard deviation of a portfolio's return is typically less than the average of the standard deviations of the returns of each of the portfolio's individual investments.

To illustrate this, suppose you open a shop to cater to the tourist trade on a beautiful Caribbean island. The two products that you consider selling are sunglasses and umbrellas. Sunglasses generate a 20 percent rate of return during the sunny season and a 0 percent return during the rainy season. In contrast, umbrellas generate a 0 percent rate of return during the sunny season, but during the rainy season the umbrella business will generate a 20 percent return. So if the probability of a rainy year is 50 percent and the probability of a mostly sunny year is 50 percent, then the expected rate of return from each of these items is 10 percent. The problem comes into play when rainy and sunny seasons vary in length. For example, if you only sold sunglasses and the sunny season only lasted for 2 months, you wouldn't do very well at all; likewise, if you only invested in umbrellas and the sunny season lasted for 10 months, you would likewise do poorly.

In this example the revenues from both products, when viewed in isolation, are quite risky. However, if you invest half of your money in sunglasses and the other half in umbrellas, you will earn 10 percent on your total investment regardless of how long the sunny season lasts because at all times one of your products will be returning 20 percent while the other will be returning 0 percent. In effect, when you combine sunglasses and umbrellas, you completely eliminate risk.

Do you always get this diversification benefit when two investments are combined? Not necessarily. For example, if you were currently selling sunglasses and added sunscreen, which also returns 20 percent in the sunny season and 0 percent in the rainy season, there would be no benefit to diversification because the returns of the sunscreen and sunglasses investments are perfectly *correlated*. As a result, if the rainy season lasted for three-quarters of the year, you would only earn 5 percent that year. Moreover, your return would be the same whether you only invested in sunglasses or you invested half your money in sunglasses and half in sunscreen. In effect, you will achieve no diversification gains when investments are perfectly correlated.

The concept of correlation is critical to our understanding of portfolio diversification. We measure the degree to which the returns on two investments are correlated using the **correlation coefficient**, a measure of the relationship of the return earned by one investment to another. The correlation coefficient can range from –1.0 (perfect negative correlation), meaning that two variables move in perfectly opposite directions (e.g., the sales of umbrellas and sunglasses), to +1.0 (perfect positive correlation), meaning that two assets move exactly together (e.g., the sales of sunglasses and sunscreen increase and decrease simultaneously). A correlation coefficient of 0.0 means that there is no relationship between the returns earned by the two assets.

In the previous example, sunglasses and sunscreen sales are perfectly *positively* correlated with one another. This means that their returns move up and down exactly in unison. The sale of umbrellas, on the other hand, goes up when sunscreen and sunglass sales fall, and vice versa. So umbrella sales are perfectly *negatively* correlated with sunscreen and sunglass sales. In most cases, the returns of two different investments will neither be perfectly correlated positively nor perfectly correlated negatively. However, there will be a tendency for most investment returns to move together, that is, in positive correlation. As long as the investment returns are not perfectly positively correlated, there will be diversification benefits. However, the diversification benefits will be greater when the correlations are low or negative.

Checkpoint 12.1

Calculating a Portfolio's Expected Rate of Return

Penny Simpson has her first full-time job and is considering how to invest her savings. Her dad suggested she invest no more than 25 percent of her savings in the stock of her employer, Emerson Electric (EMR), so she is considering investing the remaining 75 percent in a combination of a risk-free investment in U.S. Treasury bills, currently paying 4 percent, and Starbucks (SBUX) common stock. Penny's father has invested in the stock market for many years and suggested that Penny might expect to earn 8 percent on the Emerson shares and 12 percent from the Starbucks shares. Penny decides to put 25 percent in Emerson, 25 percent in Starbucks, and the remaining 50 percent in Treasury bills. Given Penny's portfolio allocation, what rate of return should she expect to receive on her investment?

STEP 1: Picture the problem

The following figure shows the expected rates of return for each investment in Penny's portfolio.

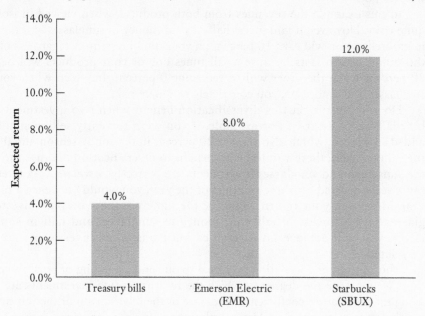

The expected rate of return for Penny's portfolio can be calculated as a weighted average of these expected rates of return, where the weights are the proportions of each investment.

STEP 2: Decide on a solution strategy

The portfolio expected rate of return is simply a weighted average of the expected rates of return of the investments in the portfolio. So we use Equation (12–1) to calculate the expected rate of return for Penny's portfolio. Fill in the *shaded cells* under the "Product" column in the following table to calculate a weighted average.

	E(Return) ×	Weight =	Product
U.S. Treasury bills	4.0%	0.50	
Emerson Electric (EMR)	8.0%	0.25	
Starbucks (SBUX)	12.0%	0.25	
Portfolio E(Return) = Sum of product column			

STEP 3: Solve

We can use Equation (12–1) to calculate the expected rate of return for the portfolio as follows:

$$E(r_{portfolio}) = W_{Treasury\ Bills}E(r_{Treasury\ Bills}) + W_{EMR}E(r_{EMR}) + W_{SBUX}E(r_{SBUX})$$

$$= (1/2 \times .04) + (1/4 \times .08) + (1/4 \times .12) = .07 \text{ or } 7\%$$

Alternatively, by filling out the table described above we get the same result.

	E(Return)	Weight	Product
Treasury bills	4.0%	0.50	2.0%
Emerson Electric (EMR)	8.0%	0.25	2.0%
Starbucks (SBUX)	12.0%	0.25	3.0%
		Portfolio E(Return) =	7.0%

STEP 4: Analyze

The expected rate of return for the portfolio composed of 50 percent invested in Treasury bills, 25 percent in Emerson Electric stock, and the remaining 25 percent in Starbucks stock is 7 percent. Note that we have referred to the Treasury bill rate as its expected rate of return. This is technically accurate because this return is assumed to be risk-free. That is, if you purchase a Treasury bill that promises to pay you 4 percent, because this security is risk-free, this is the only possible outcome. This is not the case for either of the other investment alternatives. We can calculate the expected rate of return for the portfolio in exactly the same way regardless of the risk of the investments contained in the portfolio. However, as we learn next, the risk of the portfolio is affected by the riskiness of the returns of the individual investments contained in the portfolio.

STEP 5: Check yourself

Evaluate the expected return for Penny's portfolio in which she places a quarter of her money in Treasury bills, half in Starbucks stock, and the remainder in Emerson Electric stock.

ANSWER: 9 percent.

Your Turn: For more practice, do related **Study Problems** 12–1 and 12–5 at the end of this chapter.

Diversification Lessons We can take away two key lessons from this initial look at portfolio risk and diversification:

- First, a portfolio can be less risky than the average risk of its individual investments in the portfolio.

- Second, the key to reducing risk through diversification is to combine investments whose returns do not move together and thus are not perfectly positively correlated (such as the sales of sunglasses and umbrellas).

Calculating the Standard Deviation of a Portfolio's Returns

Consider the problem faced by Patty. Patty just received $20,000 from her Aunt Gladys, who suggests she invest the money in the stock market. Patty told her aunt that she is considering the possibility of investing the money in the common stock of either Apple (AAPL) or Coca-Cola (KO). When she hears this, Aunt Gladys advises Patty to put half the money in Apple stock and half in Coca-Cola stock.

To analyze Aunt Gladys's suggested investment strategy, let's calculate the expected return and standard deviation of a portfolio that includes both Apple and Coca-Cola stocks. We saw from Equation (12–1) that the expected return is simply the weighted average of the expected returns of the individual securities in the portfolio. So if we assume that individually, Apple and Coca-Cola stocks have the same expected rate of return of 14 percent, and Patty invests in each equally, then the portfolio consisting of both stocks will have the same expected rate of return as the individual stocks, or 14 percent:

$$E(r_{portfolio}) = W_{Apple}E(r_{Apple}) + W_{CocaCola}E(r_{CocaCola}) = (1/2 \times .14) + (1/2 \times .14) = .14 \text{ or } 14\%$$

Now let's consider the riskiness of Patty's portfolio. To measure the portfolio's risk, we use the standard deviation of the portfolio. As we noted earlier, the standard deviation of the portfolio is *not* simply a weighted average of the respective standard deviations of the two stock investments. Indeed, if the returns on investing in Apple stock are less than perfectly correlated with the returns on Coca-Cola stock, the standard deviation of the portfolio that combines the two firms' shares will be less than this simple weighted average of the two firms' standard deviations. This reduction in portfolio standard deviation is due to the effects of diversification. The magnitude of the reduction in the portfolio's standard deviation resulting from diversification will depend on the extent to which the returns are correlated. This can be understood by looking at the mathematics for calculating the standard deviation of a portfolio with two stocks. The mathematics may look forbidding at first, but it offers a useful key to understanding how diversification works.

We learned that the standard deviation is the square root of the variance, so we first calculate the variance and then take the square root of the result. In the following formula, we will substitute Apple stock for asset 1 and Coca-Cola stock for asset 2. To illustrate, consider the following formula for the variance of a two-asset portfolio comprised of asset 1 and asset 2:

$$\sigma_{portfolio} = \sqrt{W_1^2\sigma_1^2 + W_2^2\sigma_2^2 + 2W_1W_2\rho_{1,2}\sigma_1\sigma_2} \qquad \textbf{(12–2)}$$

Important Definitions and Concepts:

- $\sigma_{portfolio}$ = the standard deviation in portfolio returns,
- W_i = the proportion of the portfolio that is invested in asset i,
- σ_i = the standard deviation in the rate of return earned by asset i, and
- $\rho_{i,j}$ = correlation between the rates of return earned by assets i and j. The symbol $\rho_{i,j}$ (pronounced "rho") represents correlation between the rates of return for asset 1 and asset 2.

Once again, correlation tells us the strength of the linear relationship between two assets. It can take on a value that ranges from 1.0, meaning these two assets move in a perfectly opposite linear manner as in the sunglasses and umbrellas example, to +1.0, which means that these two assets move in a perfectly linear manner together as in the sunglasses and sunscreen example. A value of 0.0 would mean that there is no linear relationship between the movements of the two assets. The amount of risk reduction that takes place as a result of diversification is a function of correlation. The higher correlation between two assets, the less benefit, or risk reduction, there is from diversification.[1]

Now, let's look at the calculation of the standard deviation of this two-asset portfolio and let the correlation coefficient vary between –1.0 and +1.0. Let's also assume the following:

- Patty invests half of her money in each of the two company's shares.

- The standard deviation for both Apple and Coca-Cola's individual stock returns is .20.

- Correlation between the stock returns of Apple and Coca-Cola is .75.

Substituting into Equation (12–2) we get the following result:

$$\sigma_{portfolio} = \sqrt{W_{Apple}^2 \sigma_{Apple}^2 + W_{Coke}^2 \sigma_{Coke}^2 + 2W_{Apple}W_{Coke}\rho_{Apple,Coke}\sigma_{Apple}\sigma_{Coke}}$$

$$= \sqrt{(.5^2 \times .20^2) + (.5^2 \times .20^2) + (2 \times .5 \times .5 \times .75 \times .20 \times .20)}$$

$$= \sqrt{.035} = .187$$

> Correlation coefficient of +0.75 indicates the stock returns of the two firms move together but not in perfect unison.

Because the standard deviation of each of the stocks is equal to .20, a simple weighted average of the standard deviations of the Apple and Coca-Cola stock returns would produce a portfolio standard deviation of .20. However, a correlation coefficient of .75 indicates that the stocks are not perfectly correlated and produces a portfolio standard deviation of 0.187. To see how the correlation between the investments influences the portfolio standard deviation, let's look at what happens when we substitute a correlation coefficient of 1.0 into Equation (12–2):

$$\sigma_{portfolio} = \sqrt{W_{Apple}^2 \sigma_{Apple}^2 + W_{Coke}^2 \sigma_{Coke}^2 + 2W_{Apple}W_{Coke}\rho_{Apple,Coke}\sigma_{Apple}\sigma_{Coke}}$$

$$= \sqrt{(.5^2 \times .20^2) + (.5^2 \times .20^2) + (2 \times .5 \times .5 \times 1.00 \times .20 \times .20)}$$

$$= \sqrt{.040} = .20$$

> Correlation coefficient of +1.0 indicates the stock returns of the two firms move in exact unison.

When the two stocks' rates of return are perfectly positively correlated (move in unison), the standard deviation of the portfolio is simply the weighted average of their individual standard deviations. When this is the case, there is no benefit to diversification. However, when the correlation coefficient is less than +1.0, the standard deviation of the portfolio is less than the weighted average of the individual stock standard deviations, indicating a benefit from diversification.

Figure 12.1 illustrates the importance of the correlation coefficient as a determinant of the portfolio standard deviation. Note that the lower the correlation between the returns of the investments in the portfolio, the greater the benefit of diversification.

---

[1]The correlation coefficient is actually a standardized covariance. The covariance provides an absolute measure of how two securities move over time; however, because it depends upon the volatility of the two series of returns, it can be hard to interpret. For this reason we generally standardize the covariance by the variability of the two series of returns, and that way it varies between 1.0 and +1.0.

FIGURE 12.1 Diversification and the Correlation Coefficient—Apple and Coca-Cola

The effects of diversification on the risk of the portfolio are contingent on the degree of correlation between the assets included in the portfolio. If the correlation is +1 (meaning the two assets are perfectly correlated and move together in lockstep, as was the case with sunglasses and sunscreen), then there is no benefit to diversification. However, if the correlation is –1 (meaning the two assets move in lockstep in opposite directions, as was the case with sunglasses and umbrellas), it will be possible to construct a portfolio that completely eliminates risk.

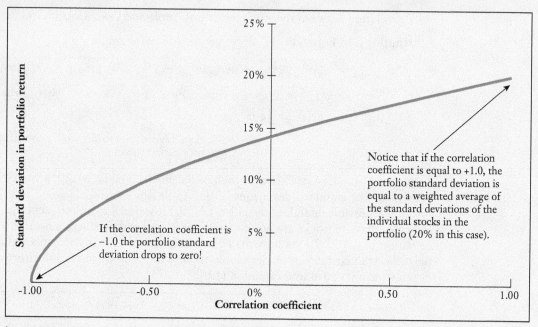

Notice that if the correlation coefficient is equal to +1.0, the portfolio standard deviation is equal to a weighted average of the standard deviations of the individual stocks in the portfolio (20% in this case).

If the correlation coefficient is –1.0 the portfolio standard deviation drops to zero!

Legend:

Correlation	E(Return)	Standard Deviation
–1.00	0.14	0%
–0.80	0.14	6%
–0.60	0.14	9%
–0.40	0.14	11%
–0.20	0.14	13%
0.0	0.14	14%
0.20	0.14	15%
0.40	0.14	17%
0.60	0.14	18%
0.80	0.14	19%
1.00	0.14	20%

All portfolios are comprised of equal investments in Apple and Coca-Cola shares.

For example, consider the diversification benefits derived from combining two investments whose returns are perfectly positively correlated (+1), uncorrelated (0), and perfectly negatively correlated (−1):

Correlation between Investment Returns	Diversification Benefits
+1	None. No risk has been eliminated because there is no diversification realized by combining the investments because they move together perfectly. This is exactly the case we saw earlier in this chapter when we combined the sunglasses product line with the sunscreen lotion—no elimination of risk.
0.0	There is substantial value to diversification.
−1	Diversification is extremely effective in reducing portfolio risk. In fact, it is possible to select the portfolio weights for two investments whose returns are perfectly negatively correlated, such that all variability is eliminated from the portfolio return and the portfolio standard deviation is zero. Earlier, we encountered a correlation of −1.0 when we considered the sunglasses and umbrellas example.

FINANCE IN A FLAT WORLD

International Diversification

One of the great things about diversification is that it reduces risk without reducing expected return. That is, whereas returns are simply the weighted average of the returns on the investments that make up your portfolio, the portfolio's risk, as measured by its standard deviation, is less than the weighted average of the standard deviations of these investments. In effect, the less closely the returns of the investments move together over time, the greater the benefit of diversification. The key, then, is to include stocks in your portfolio that are not too highly correlated with each other.

One way to do this is to include more international stocks in your portfolio. International and domestic securities tend to react differently to the same economic or market information. For example, historically, when the price of oil rises, the prices of U.S. auto companies react differently than those of their Japanese counterparts because Japanese consumers prefer fuel-efficient economy cars to gas-guzzling SUVs that are a mainstay of the U.S. automakers. Thus, the price increase for oil may be bad for the economy in general, but it is worse news for domestic automakers than for Toyota and Nissan. Because of this, a portfolio that includes Japanese as well as U.S. auto stocks will be less risky than a portfolio that includes only U.S. auto stocks.

Unfortunately, international diversification appears to be less effective than it used to be. Over the past 20 years, the returns of U.S. stocks and foreign stocks have become more highly correlated. This is one of the side effects of economic globalization. Only time will tell the full extent of this trend, but it still makes sense to invest beyond the U.S. borders as part of an effort to effectively diversify.

Checkpoint 12.2

Evaluating a Portfolio's Risk and Return

Sarah Marshall Tipton is considering her 401(k) retirement portfolio and wonders if she should move some of her money into international investments. To this point in her short working life (she graduated just four years ago), she has simply put her retirement savings into a mutual fund with an investment strategy that mimicked the returns of the S&P 500 stock index (large company stocks). This fund has historically earned a return averaging 12 percent over the last 80 or so years, but recently the returns were depressed somewhat, as the economy was languishing in a mild recession. Sarah is considering an international mutual fund that diversifies its holdings around the industrialized economies of the world and has averaged a 14 percent annual rate of return. The international fund's higher average return is offset by the fact that the standard deviation in its returns is 30 percent compared to only 20 percent for the domestic index fund. Upon closer investigation, Sarah learned that the domestic and international funds tend to earn high returns and low returns at about the same times in the business cycle, such that correlation is .75. Suppose Sarah moves half her money into the international fund and leaves the remainder in the domestic fund. What is the expected return and standard deviation of the combined portfolio?

STEP 1: Picture the problem

We can visualize the expected rates of return and corresponding standard deviations as follows:

Investment Fund	Expected Return	Standard Deviation	Investment Proportion
S&P 500 Fund	12%	20%	50%
International Fund	14%	30%	50%
Portfolio			100%

The challenge Sarah faces is estimating the portfolio's expected return and standard deviation when she places half her money in each of the two mutual funds. She needs answers to place in the shaded squares in the grid.

STEP 2: Decide on a solution strategy

The portfolio expected rate of return is simply a weighted average of the expected rates of return of the investments in the portfolio. However, the standard deviation is a bit more complicated, as diversification can lead to a reduction in the standard deviation below the weighted average of the standard deviations of the investments in the portfolio. We use Equations (12–1) and (12–2) to calculate the expected rate of return and standard deviation for the portfolio.

STEP 3: Solve

Calculating the Expected Return for the Portfolio.

We use Equation (12–1) to calculate the expected rate of return for the portfolio as follows:

$$E(r_{portfolio}) = W_{S\&P500}E(r_{S\&P500}) + W_{International}E(r_{International})$$
$$= (1/2 \times .12) + (1/2 \times .14) = .13 \text{ or } 13\%$$

Calculating the Standard Deviation for the Portfolio.

The standard deviation can be calculated using Equation (12–2) as follows:

$$\sigma_{portfolio} = \sqrt{W_1^2\sigma_1^2 + W_2^2\sigma_2^2 + 2W_1W_2\rho_{1,2}\sigma_1\sigma_2}$$
$$= \sqrt{(.5^2 \times .20^2) + (.5^2 \times .30^2) + (2 \times .5 \times .5 \times .75 \times .20 \times .30)}$$
$$= .235 \text{ or } 23.5\%$$

STEP 4: Analyze

The expected rate of return for the portfolio comprised of 50 percent in the S&P 500 fund and 50 percent in the international fund is 13 percent, which plots exactly halfway between the two investments' expected returns on the following graph:

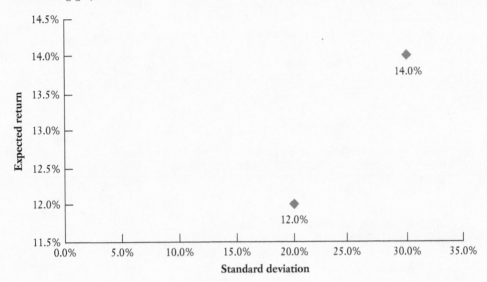

However, the standard deviation of the portfolio is not equal to 25 percent, the midpoint between the standard deviations of 20 percent and 30 percent (i.e., the weighted average of the two investments' standard deviations). It is, instead, equal to only 23.5 percent, which shows that we gain something from diversifying between the international and domestic markets. The returns in these two markets are not perfectly positively correlated, so there is some reduction in the standard deviation of the portfolio that is gained by putting the two investment alternatives together.

STEP 5: Check yourself

Evaluate the expected return and standard deviation of the portfolio of the S&P 500 and international fund where correlation is estimated to be .20 and Sarah still places half of her money in each of the funds.

ANSWER: Expected return = 13 percent and standard deviation = 19.6 percent.

Your Turn: For more practice, do related **Study Problem** 12–2 at the end of this chapter.

Tools of Financial Analysis—Portfolio Mean and Variance

Name of Tool	Formula	What It Tells You
Expected Portfolio Return, $E(r_{portfolio})$	$[W_1 \times E(r_1)] + [W_2 \times E(r_2)] + \ldots + [W_n \times E(r_n)]$ • $E(r_{portfolio})$ = the expected rate of return for a portfolio of n assets. • W_i = the proportion of the portfolio that is invested in asset i. • $E(r_i)$ = the expected rate of return earned by asset i.	• Measures the expected rate of return from investing in a portfolio of n different assets or securities • The portfolio return is simply an average of the rates of return expected from each security in the portfolio, where the weights reflect the relative amount of funds invested in each security.
Portfolio Variance, $\sigma_{Portfolio}$	$\sqrt{W_1\sigma_1^2 + W_2\sigma_2^2 + 2W_1\sigma_2^2 + 2W_1 W_2 \rho_{1,2}\sigma_1\sigma_1}$ • $\sigma_{portfolio}$ = the standard deviation in portfolio returns, • W_i = the proportion of the portfolio that is invested in asset i, • σ_i = the standard deviation in the rate of return earned by asset i, and • $\rho_{i,j}$ = correlation between the rate of return earned by assets i and j. The symbol $\rho_{i,j}$ (pronounced "rho") represents correlation between the rates of return for asset 1 and asset 2.	• Measures the return from investing in a security as a percent of the dollars invested • A higher rate of return means a greater return earned by the investment (measured as a percent of the initial investment).

CONCEPTS IN REVIEW

12.1 How is the expected rate of return on a portfolio related to the expected rates of return of the individual assets contained in the portfolio?

12.2 When the returns of two risky investments are perfectly negatively correlated, how does combining them in a portfolio affect the overall riskiness of the portfolio?

12.3 When the returns of two risky investments are perfectly positively correlated, how does combining them in a portfolio affect the overall riskiness of the portfolio?

Systematic Risk and the Market Portfolio

LG2 In the last section, we showed that the correlation between the returns of two stocks in a portfolio plays a key role in determining the overall risk of the portfolio. The intuition that combining imperfectly correlated investments into a portfolio reduces risk also applies to portfolios that include many different investments. In particular, those investments whose returns have low correlations with other investments in the portfolio contribute less to the overall riskiness of a diversified portfolio than those investments whose returns are highly correlated with the other investments in the portfolio.

This logic implies that we cannot simply say that the standard deviation of an individual investment is the relevant measure of the investment's risk. The standard deviation ignores how the investment's returns are correlated with the returns of other investments, and thus cannot tell us how the investment would contribute to the overall risk of an investor's portfolio. However, because there are thousands of possible investments, it is impractical to calculate all of the correlations of each investment's returns with all other investments, so coming up with a simple measure of the riskiness of an investment is clearly a challenge.

Fortunately, we have a theory, known as the **Capital Asset Pricing Model (CAPM)**, that provides a relatively simple measure of risk. This theory, which was recognized in 1990 in the Nobel Memorial Prize in Economics for Harry Markowitz and William Sharpe, assumes that investors choose to hold the optimally diversified portfolio that includes *all* risky investments. This optimally diversified portfolio that includes all of the economy's assets is generally referred to as the **market portfolio**. According to the CAPM, the relevant risk of an investment relates to how the investment contributes to the risk of this market portfolio.

To understand how an investment contributes to the risk of the market portfolio, it is useful to categorize the risks of the individual investments into two categories— *systematic* and *unsystematic*. The **systematic risk** component measures the contribution of the investment to the risk of the market portfolio. In contrast, the **unsystematic risk** component is the element of risk that does not contribute to the risk of the market portfolio. This component is effectively diversified away when the investment is combined with other investments. In summary, we can think of the total risk of an investment as follows:

$$\text{Total risk} = \text{Systematic risk} + \text{Unsystematic risk} \qquad \textbf{(12–3)}$$

Intuitively, systematic risk refers to those risks that affect the returns of almost all investments. This is the common element of investment returns that causes the returns to be correlated. For example, if the economy were to slip into a recession, virtually all investments would experience negative returns. Alternatively, if all wars in the world were suddenly ended, it is likely that all stocks (with the exception of the firms that supply armaments and weapons of war) would experience positive returns.

The returns of some investments are more sensitive to systematic (or market-wide) risk than those of other investments. The returns of these investments will tend to be more highly correlated with the returns of most of the other stocks in a portfolio, and will thus make a substantial contribution to the portfolio's overall risk. Unsystematic risk is simply the variability in the returns of an investment that is due to events that are specific to the investment. For example, variation in the stock returns of a particular company can result from the death of the firm's CEO, a product recall, a major fire at a manufacturing plant, or perhaps an event that helps one industry at the expense of other industries. If the risk of an investment comes mainly from unsystematic risk, the investment will tend to have a low correlation with the returns of most of the other stocks in the portfolio, and will thus make only a minor contribution to the portfolio's overall risk. Thus, an investment's systematic risk is far more important than its unsystematic risk.

Diversification and Unsystematic Risk

A more descriptive term for systematic risk is **non-diversifiable risk**. Likewise, unsystematic risk is **diversifiable risk**. The idea here is that large diversified portfolios are still subject to systematic risk—in other words, systematic risk is non-diversifiable. However, unsystematic risk contributes almost nothing to the standard deviation of large diversified portfolios—in other words, unsystematic risk can be diversified away. We illustrate in Figure 12.2 that as the number of securities in a portfolio increases, the contribution of unsystematic risk to the standard deviation of the portfolio declines. This happens because the unsystematic risk of the individual stocks is uncorrelated, so the unsystematic components of the individual stock returns tend to offset one another. If a portfolio consists of stocks in different industries with very different characteristics,

FIGURE 12.2

Portfolio Risk and the Number of Investments in the Portfolio

Adding more investments to a portfolio that are not highly correlated with the other assets in the portfolio can dramatically reduce the portfolio's risk. In fact, for randomly selected shares of common stock, the benefits of diversification can be virtually fully achieved with a portfolio of about 50 stocks (assuming equal investment in each stock).

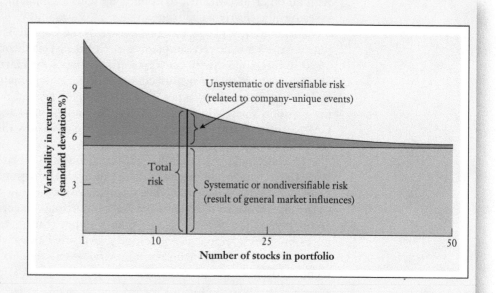

then as the number of stocks gets large, virtually all of the variation of the portfolio will come from systematic risk, and virtually none will come from unsystematic risk. The unsystematic component of risk has been diversified away and portfolio risk is comprised almost entirely of the systematic risk of the portfolio stocks.

Diversification and Systematic Risk

Diversification leads to the reduction and eventual elimination of unsystematic risk (the dark green area in Figure 12.2), but this does not hold true for systematic risk. Because systematic risk is common to most investments, it is a source of correlation between the returns. Indeed, by definition, the systematic sources of risk are perfectly correlated. As we learned earlier, when the returns of two investments are perfectly positively correlated, there is no risk reduction benefit to be gained by diversifying. This means that very large and diversified portfolios are likely to be influenced by the risks associated with interest rates, inflation, wars, and all other factors that affect all companies' stock returns.

Systematic Risk and Beta

Up to this point, we have examined the basic intuition behind systematic risk and why it is important to any investor. In this section, we will describe how systematic risk is measured. Recall that we have defined systematic risk as that portion of an asset's return variation that is shared with many other investments. Because investments with a high level of systematic risk tend to be highly correlated with the returns of many other investments, they are also highly correlated with the returns of a broad market portfolio that includes all investments. This suggests that we can measure the systematic risk of an investment using the extent to which the returns of the investment correlate with the returns on the overall market portfolio.

To measure the systematic risk of an investment, we estimate what is referred to as the investment's **beta coefficient**, often simply called beta. The beta of an investment, which is referenced using the Greek letter β, measures the extent to which a particular investment's returns vary with the returns of the market portfolio. Specifically, our measure of systematic risk is referred to as the investment's beta because in practice it is estimated as the slope of a straight line such as the one found in Figure 12.3. Note that the figure contains historical monthly rates of return earned by Home Depot (HD) and a market index (the S&P 500) for the period November 2010 through October 2012. The beta for Home Depot is simply the slope of the straight line that best fits the market and Home Depot stock return pattern. In this case the slope is .67, which means that if the market increases by 10 percent over the year, Home Depot would only increase by 6.7 percent. In other words, the systematic risk of Home Depot's shares is less than the average for all stocks (the index, which has a beta of 1.00). This may seem a bit odd, but remember that we are talking about only that portion of Home Depot's return volatility that is shared with the market portfolio, or its systematic risk. The rest of the volatility in Home Depot's stock returns is unsystematic and can be diversified away by simply investing in a diversified portfolio.

Although we could estimate betas ourselves, this is generally not necessary because these estimates are readily available from a wide variety of sources. Table 12.1 contains beta estimates for several well-known companies. Note that the beta estimates vary between Yahoo Finance and MoneyCentral.com. The difference reflects differences in the time intervals of data used in the estimate. To get some perspective on the size of these beta coefficients, we can compare them to the beta of a risk-free bond, which is zero, and the beta of the overall market portfolio, which is 1. Moreover, it appears that the beta coefficients of the computer and software companies are much higher than those of the utilities companies. For example, a 10 percent rise or fall in the overall market would lead to a smaller than 10 percent change in the utility stock returns, whereas the change would be much larger for the computer and software companies. In fact, for Apple the increase or decrease would be almost 30 percent.

Calculating Portfolio Beta

The **portfolio beta** measures the systematic risk of the portfolio, just like a beta for an individual stock measures its systematic risk. The portfolio beta is straightforward to calculate because it is simply a weighted average of the betas for the individual investments contained in the portfolio. Therefore, for a portfolio that contains n different risky assets, the portfolio beta can be calculated as follows:

Portfolio Beta

$$\begin{matrix} \text{Portfolio} \\ \text{Beta} \end{matrix} = \left(\begin{matrix} \text{Proportion of} & \text{Beta for} \\ \text{Portfolio Invested} \times \text{Asset 1} \\ \text{in Asset 1 } (W_1) & (\beta_1) \end{matrix} \right) + \left(\begin{matrix} \text{Proportion of} & \text{Beta for} \\ \text{Portfolio Invested} \times \text{Asset 2} \\ \text{in Asset 2 } (W_2) & (\beta_2) \end{matrix} \right)$$
$$+ \cdots + \left(\begin{matrix} \text{Proportion of} & \text{Beta for} \\ \text{Portfolio Invested} \times \text{Asset } n \\ \text{in Asset } n \ (W_n) & (\beta_n) \end{matrix} \right) \qquad \textbf{(12–4)}$$

Or, written using symbols, the beta for a portfolio is simply the weighted average of the betas of individual assets that are held in the portfolio, that is,

$$\beta_{portfolio} = W_1\beta_1 + W_2\beta_2 + \cdots + W_n\beta_n$$

FIGURE 12.3

Estimating Home Depot's (HD) Beta Coefficient

A firm's beta coefficient is the slope of a straight line that fits the relationship between the firm's stock returns and those of a broad market index. In the following graph, the market index used is the Standard and Poor's (S&P) 500 index.

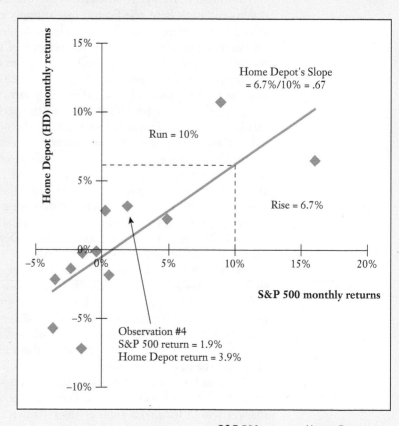

Calculating beta:

1. Visual—the slope of a straight line can be estimated visually by drawing a straight line that best "fits" the scatter of Home Depot's stock returns and those of the market index. The beta coefficient then is the "rise over the run." The blue dots on the graph correspond to values indicated on the chart.

2. Financial calculator—financial calculators have built-in functions for computing the beta coefficient. However, because the procedure varies from one calculator to another we do not present it here.

3. Excel—Excel's Slope function can be used to calculate the slope as follows: =slope(C2:C12,B2:B12)

4. Internet—there are a number of resources that can be used to obtain beta estimates on the Internet, including Yahoo! Finance and Google finance. The estimates can differ depending on the time period used to make the estimate.

Observation	Date	S&P 500 Returns	Home Depot Stock Returns
1	Nov-10	−0.23%	−1.47%
2	Dec-10	6.53%	16.05%
3	Jan-11	2.26%	4.88%
4	Feb-11	3.90%	1.90%
5	Mar-11	−0.10%	−0.43%
6	Apr-11	2.85%	0.24%
7	May-12	−1.35%	−2.34%
8	Jun-12	−1.83%	0.52%
9	Jul-12	−2.15%	−3.56%
10	Aug-12	−5.68%	−3.72%
11	Sep-12	−7.18%	−1.53%
12	Oct-12	10.77%	8.91%

TABLE 12.1   BETA COEFFICIENTS FOR SELECTED COMPANIES

This table contains two sources of beta estimates (Yahoo.com and MSN.com). These estimates were accessed on the same day and can vary over time because historical stock and market returns are used to calculate the beta estimates.

Company	Yahoo Finance (Yahoo.com)	Microsoft Money Central (MSN.com)
Computers and Software		
Apple Inc. (AAPL)	2.90	2.58
Dell Inc. (DELL)	1.81	1.37
Hewlett Packard (HPQ)	1.27	1.47
Utilities		
American Electric Power Co. (AEP)	0.74	0.73
Duke Energy Corp. (DUK)	0.40	0.56
Centerpoint Energy (CNP)	0.82	0.91

Important Definitions and Concepts:

- W_i = the proportion of the portfolio that is invested in asset i,
- β_i = the beta coefficient for asset i, and
- $\beta_{portfolio}$ = the portfolio beta, which is a weighted average of the betas for the individual assets contained in the portfolio.

For example, consider the following portfolio that is comprised of three investments with betas equal to 1.20, .70, and .25. If half of the portfolio is invested in the first investment and one-fourth in each of the remaining investments, we can calculate the portfolio beta using Equation (12–4) as follows:

$$\beta_{portfolio} = W_1\beta_1 + W_2\beta_2 + W_3\beta_3$$
$$= (.50 \times 1.20) + (.25 \times .70) + (.25 \times .25) = .8375$$

The beta for the three-investment portfolio is therefore .8375.

What if the first asset in the preceding example is a risk-free Treasury bond, which by definition has a zero beta? In this case, the portfolio beta calculation would be as follows:

$$\beta_{portfolio} = W_1\beta_1 + W_2\beta_2 + W_3\beta_3$$
$$= (.50 \times 0.00) + (.25 \times .70) + (.25 \times .25) = .2375$$

Tools of Financial Analysis—Portfolio Beta

Name of Tool	Formula	What It Tells You
Portfolio Beta, $\beta_{portfolio}$	$(W_1 \times \beta_1) + (W_2 \times \beta_2) + \cdots + (W_n \times \beta_n)$ • $\beta_{portfolio}$ = the weighted average beta for the portfolio. • W_i = the weight of the ith security's beta, which reflects the proportion of the portfolio invested in that security.	• Measures the systematic risk of a portfolio of securities • The average is weighted by the fraction of the portfolio invested in each security.

CONCEPTS IN REVIEW

12.4 What are some factors that influence the returns of a company such as Home Depot that would constitute a source of systematic risk? Unsystematic risk?

12.5 How many different stocks are required to essentially diversify away unsystematic risk?

The Security Market Line and the CAPM

LG3 In addition to suggesting that an investment's beta is the appropriate measure of its risk, the Capital Asset Pricing Model (or the CAPM) describes how these betas relate to the expected rates of return that investors require on their investments. *The key insights of the CAPM are that investments with the same beta have the same expected rate of return and that investors will require a higher rate of return on investments with higher betas.*

To understand the CAPM expected return equation that comes from this theory, recall that the beta of a portfolio equals the average beta of the investments in the portfolio, and the expected return of a portfolio equals the average expected return of the investments in the portfolio. For example, let's consider the relation between the beta and expected return of a portfolio invested 80 percent in the market portfolio, W_M equals 80 percent, and 20 percent in a risk-free security. The market portfolio has a beta of 1.0 and, for purposes of this example, we will assume that the expected return for the market portfolio, $E(r_M)$ is 11 percent. The risk-free security has a beta of 0, and we will assume it offers a 6 percent risk-free return, r_f equals 6 percent. The expected rate of return using Equation (12–1) for this two-investment portfolio is then:

$$E(r_{portfolio}) = \begin{pmatrix} \text{Percent of} \\ \text{Funds Invested} \\ \text{in the Market} \\ \text{Portfolio } (W_M) \end{pmatrix} \begin{pmatrix} \text{Expected Return} \\ \text{on the Market} \\ \text{Portfolio } [E(r_m)] \end{pmatrix} + \begin{bmatrix} 1 - \begin{pmatrix} \text{Percent of} \\ \text{Funds Invested} \\ \text{in the Market} \\ \text{Portfolio } (W_M) \end{pmatrix} \end{bmatrix} \begin{pmatrix} \text{Risk-free} \\ \text{Rate } (r_f) \end{pmatrix}$$

> Because all money is invested in either the market portfolio or the risk-free security, the proportion invested in the risk-free security is equal to $(1 - W_M)$.

$$E(r_{portfolio}) = W_M[E(r_M)] + (1 - W_M)r_f = 0.8 \times 11\% + (1 - 0.8) \times 6\% = 9.3\%$$

If we rearrange the terms in this equation slightly we have,

$$E(r_{portfolio}) = r_f + W_M[E(r_M) - r_f] \tag{12-5}$$

Similarly, we can calculate the portfolio beta using Equation (12–4), which says that a portfolio beta should be equal to the weighted average of the individual assets' betas that make up the portfolio. For this two-investment portfolio:

> The beta coefficient for the risk-free security, β_{rf}, is equal to 0.0 because it has zero systematic risk.

$$\beta_{portfolio} = W_M \times \beta_M + (1 - W_M)\beta_f = 0.8 \times 1.0 + (1 - 0.8) \times 0.0 = 0.80$$

Figure 12.4 provides the expected returns and betas for a variety of portfolios comprised of the market portfolio and the risk-free asset. However, because the CAPM specifies that all investments with the same betas have the same expected returns, the expected return and beta combinations illustrated in this figure apply to all investments, not just to portfolios consisting of the market and the risk-free rate.

The straight-line relationship between the betas and expected returns in Figure 12.4 is called the **security market line**, and its slope is often referred to as the reward-to-risk ratio. Note that the security market line is simply a graphical representation of the Capital Asset Pricing Model. We can measure the slope of the security market line by computing the ratio of the change in expected rate of return measured along the vertical axis divided by the corresponding change in the beta for the portfolios with these two expected returns. To illustrate how this is done we compare the expected rates of return for a portfolio with zero beta (the risk-free security, which earns 6 percent) and a portfolio that has an expected rate of return of 9 percent and has a beta of 0.60. The slope then is calculated as follows:

$$\text{Slope} = \frac{\text{Rise}}{\text{Run}} = \frac{.09 - .06}{0.60 - 0.0} = \frac{.03}{.60} = 0.05 \text{ or } 5\%$$

The security market line can be expressed as the following equation, which is often referred to as the CAPM pricing equation:

$$\begin{array}{c}\text{Expected Return on} \\ \text{Risky Asset } j\end{array} = \begin{array}{c}\text{Risk-free} \\ \text{Rate of Return}\end{array} + \begin{array}{c}\text{Beta for} \\ \text{Asset } j\end{array} \times \left(\begin{array}{c}\text{Expected Return} \\ \text{on the Market Portfolio}\end{array} - \begin{array}{c}\text{Risk-free} \\ \text{Rate of Return}\end{array} \right)$$

$$E(r_{Asset\,j}) = r_f + \beta_{Asset\,j}[E(r_{Market}) - r_f] \qquad \textbf{(12–6)}$$

Note that Equation (12–6) looks very much like Equation (12–5). The weight associated with the market portfolio, W_M, in Equation (12–5) is equal to the portfolio beta in Equation (12–6). In other words, if we substitute beta for W_M in Equation (12–5), we get Equation (12–6). Hence, according to the CAPM, low-beta investments are equivalent to portfolios that are mostly invested in the risk-free investment and just slightly invested in the market portfolio. These portfolios are less risky and thus require lower rates of return. In contrast, higher-beta investments are equivalent to portfolios that are more heavily invested in the market portfolio, and hence require a higher expected rate of return. Of course, most investments cannot be viewed as simply a combination of the market and the risk-free investment. They also contain unsystematic risk. However, because unsystematic risk can be eliminated in a diversified portfolio, it is does not affect the investment's expected rate of return.

A critically important learning point here is that because systematic risk cannot be eliminated through diversification and must be borne by the investor, this is the source of risk that is reflected in expected returns. The higher the systematic risk of an investment, other things remaining the same, the higher will be the expected rate of return an investor would require to invest in the asset. This is a simple restatement of 🅿 Principle 2: **There Is a Risk–Return Tradeoff.**

Using the CAPM to Estimate Expected Rates of Return

The CAPM provides a theory of how risk and expected return are connected or traded off in the capital markets. For example, earlier we estimated the beta for Home Depot to be .92. If the risk-free rate of interest in the economy is currently about 3 percent, and if the **market risk premium,** which is the difference between the expected return on the market portfolio and the risk-free rate of return, is estimated to be 5 percent, we can estimate the expected rate of return on Home Depot's common stock using the CAPM from Equation (12–6) as follows:

$$E(r_{Home\,Depot}) = r_{risk\text{-}free} + \beta_{Home\,Depot}[E(r_{market}) - r_{risk\text{-}free}]$$
$$E(r_{Home\,Depot}) = .03 + .92[.05] = .076 \text{ or } 7.6\%$$

The systematic risk of Home Depot's shares is reflected in the beta, which was only .92, suggesting that the shares have very nearly the same systematic risk as the market portfolio which has a beta of 1.0.

FIGURE 12.4

Risk and Return for Portfolios Containing the Market and the Risk-Free Security

The following graph depicts the systematic risk and expected rate of return for portfolios comprised of the risk-free security (with beta of zero) plus the market portfolio of all risky assets (with a beta of 1). In the most extreme case, we invest 120 percent in the market portfolio by borrowing 20 percent of the funds and paying the risk-free rate. The risk-free rate is assumed to be 6 percent, and the market risk premium (difference in the expected rate of return on the market portfolio and the risk-free rate) is 5 percent.

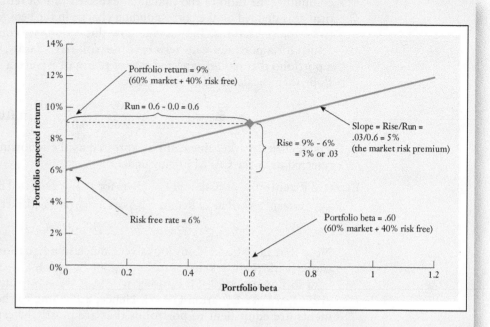

Legend:

% Market Portfolio, W_{Market}	% Risk-Free Asset, $W_{Risk-free}$	Portfolio Beta, $\beta_{Portfolio}$	Expected Portfolio Return, $E(r_{Portfolio})$
0%	100%	0.0	6.0%
20%	80%	0.2	7.0%
40%	60%	0.4	8.0%
60%	**40%**	**0.6**	**9.0%**
80%	20%	0.8	10.0%
100%	0%	1.0	11.0%
120%	−20%	1.2	12.0%

Checkpoint 12.3

Estimating the Expected Rate of Return Using the CAPM

Jerry Allen graduated from the University of Texas with a finance degree in the spring of 2013 and took a job with a Houston-based investment banking firm as a financial analyst. One of his first assignments is to investigate the investor-expected rates of return for three technology firms: Apple (APPL), Dell (DELL), and Hewlett Packard (HPQ). Jerry's supervisor suggests that he make his estimates using the CAPM, where the risk-free rate is 4.5 percent, the expected return on the market is 10.5 percent, and the risk premium for the market as a whole (the difference between the expected return on the market and the risk-free rate) is 6 percent. Use the two estimates of beta provided for these firms in Table 12.1 to calculate two estimates of the investor-expected rates of return for the sample firms.

STEP 1: Picture the problem

Calculating the expected rates of return using the CAPM can be viewed graphically using the security market line, where the intercept of the line equals the risk-free rate (4.5 percent in this case) and the slope is equal to the market risk premium (6 percent in this case):

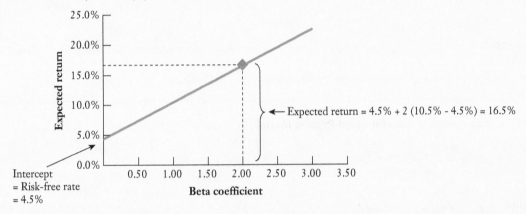

Expected return = 4.5% + 2 (10.5% - 4.5%) = 16.5%

Intercept = Risk-free rate = 4.5%

Thus, using Equation (12–6) and a beta coefficient of 2.00, the investor's expected rate of return is 16.5 percent.

STEP 2: Decide on a solution strategy

Although the expected rates of return plot along the security market line, we can solve for them directly by substituting into the CAPM formula found in Equation (12–6):

$$E(r_j) = r_f + \beta[E(r_{Market}) - r_f]$$

STEP 3: Solve

Solving for the expected return for Apple using the beta from Yahoo, the beta from MSN, a risk-free rate of 4.5 percent, and a market risk premium of 6 percent yields the following:

- Apple expected return assuming a beta of 2.90 (the Yahoo estimate of beta): 4.5% + 2.90(6.0%) = 4.5% + 17.4% = 21.9%
- Apple expected return assuming a beta of 2.58 (the MSN estimate of beta): 4.5% + 2.58(6.0%) = 4.5% + 15.48% = 19.98%

(12.3 CONTINUED >> ON NEXT PAGE)

Calculating the expected return with the CAPM equation using each of the beta estimates found in Table 12.1 for the three technology firms yields the following results:

	Beta		E(return)	
	Yahoo	MSN	Yahoo	MSN
Apple Inc. (APPL)	2.90	2.58	21.90%	19.98%
Dell Inc. (DELL)	1.81	1.37	15.36%	12.72%
Hewlett Packard (HPQ)	1.27	1.47	12.12%	13.32%

STEP 4: Analyze

The expected rate of return for the individual stocks varies somewhat depending upon the source of the beta estimate. This raises a question as to whether it makes sense to carry our estimates out to multiple decimal places.

STEP 5: Check yourself

Estimate the expected rates of return for the three utility companies found in Table 12.1, using the 4.5 percent risk-free rate and market risk premium of 6 percent.

ANSWER: American Electric Power (AEP) estimates are 8.94 percent and 8.88 percent for the Yahoo! and MSN beta estimates, respectively.

Your Turn: For more practice, do related **Study Problems** 12–8 and 12–10 at the end of this chapter.

Tools of Financial Analysis—Capital Asset Pricing Model

Name of Tool	Formula	What It Tells You
Capital Asset Pricing Model	$\dfrac{Risk\text{-}free}{Rate\ of\ Return} + \dfrac{Beta\ for}{Asset\ j} \times \left(\dfrac{Expected\ Return}{on\ the\ Market\ Portfolio} - \dfrac{Risk\text{-}free}{Rate\ of\ Return} \right)$	• Measures the expected rate of return for a risky security, where risk is measured by its systematic (or non-diversifiable) risk.

CONCEPTS IN REVIEW

12.6 Who are Harry Markowitz and William Sharpe, and what did they do that was so important in finance?

12.7 How is the portfolio beta related to the betas of the individual investments in the portfolio?

12.8 Explain the concept of the security market line.

12.9 What is the market risk premium, and how is it related to the Capital Asset Pricing Model?

Applying the Principles of Finance to Chapter 12

P Principle 2: **The Risk–Return Tradeoff** The Capital Asset Pricing Model provides a model that links the risk of an investment as measured by its beta coefficient to its expected rate of return.

P Principle 4: **Market Prices Reflect Information** Market prices reflect the risk and return expectations of investors.

MyFinanceLab

Here is what you should know after reading this chapter. MyFinanceLab will help you identify what you know and where to go when you need to practice.

What You Should Know	Key Terms	
LG1 Calculate the expected rate of return and volatility for a portfolio of investments and describe how diversification affects the returns to a portfolio of investments. A portfolio is a combination of several individual investments. The expected rate of return for a portfolio is calculated as a weighted average of the expected rates of return of the individual investments. However, the calculation of the risk of a portfolio (which is reflected in the volatility of the portfolio returns) is more complicated because diversification can influence the overall volatility of the portfolio returns. Consequently, when we compute the portfolio variance or its square root, the standard deviation, we must consider the correlation of the returns of the various individual investments in the portfolio.	Correlation coefficient, *p. 415*	A measure of the degree to which the variation in one variable is related to the variation in another. The coefficient ranges from –1 for a perfectly negative relationship to 11 for perfectly positive dependence.
	Diversification, *p. 414*	The reduction in risk that comes about by combining two or more risky assets into a portfolio where the individual assets are less than perfectly positively correlated.

Key Equations

$$E(r_{portfolio}) = [W_1 \times E(r_1)] + [W_2 \times E(r_2)] + [W_3 \times E(r_3)] + \cdots + [W_n \times E(r_n)] \qquad (12\text{--}1)$$

$$\sigma_{portfolio} = \sqrt{W_1^2\sigma_1^2 + W_2^2\sigma_2^2 + 2W_1W_2\rho_{1,2}\sigma_1\sigma_2} \qquad (12\text{--}2)$$

where	
$\sigma_{portfolio} =$	the standard deviation in portfolio returns,
$W_i =$	the proportion of the portfolio that is invested in asset i,
$\sigma_i =$	the standard deviation in the rate of return earned by asset i, and
ρ_{ij} (pronounced "rho") $=$	correlation between the rates of return earned by assets i and j.
$E(r_{portfolio}) =$	the expected rate of return on a portfolio of n assets.
$E(r_i) =$	the expected rate of return earned by asset i.

What You Should Know	Key Terms	
LG2 Understand the concept of systematic risk for an individual investment and calculate portfolio systematic risk (beta). We have made an important distinction between systematic and non-systematic risk. The distinction is important because non-systematic risk can be eliminated in large diversified portfolios. Because this risk can be diversified away in large portfolios, investors do not require a premium for holding diversifiable risk. Beta measures the average sensitivity of a security's returns to the movement of the general market, such as the S&P 500. If beta is 1, the security's returns move on average 1 percent for each 1 percent change in the market returns; if beta is 1.5, the security's returns will on average move up and down 1.5 percent for every 1 percent change in the market's returns, and so forth.	Beta coefficient, *p. 427*	A measure of the relationship between the returns of a security such as a share of common stock and the returns of the portfolio of all risky assets.
	Capital Asset Pricing Model (CAPM), *p. 425*	A model that describes the theoretical link between the expected rate of return on a risky security such as a share of stock and the security's risk as measured by its beta coefficient.
	Diversifiable risk, *p. 425*	Risk that can be eliminated through diversification.
	Market portfolio, *p. 425*	The portfolio of all risky and risk-free assets.
	Non-diversifiable risk, *p. 425*	Risk that cannot be eliminated through diversification.
	Portfolio beta, *p. 427*	The beta coefficient of a portfolio of different investments.
	Systematic risk, *p. 425*	See Non-diversifiable risk.
	Unsystematic risk, *p. 425*	See Diversifiable risk.

Key Equations

$$\text{Total risk} = \text{Systematic risk} + \text{Unsystematic risk} \tag{12–3}$$

$$\begin{aligned}\text{Portfolio Beta} =& \left(\begin{array}{c}\text{Proportion of}\\ \text{Portfolio Invested} \times \\ \text{in Asset 1 } (W_1)\end{array} \begin{array}{c}\text{Beta for}\\ \text{Asset 1}\\ (\beta_1)\end{array}\right) + \left(\begin{array}{c}\text{Proportion of}\\ \text{Portfolio Invested} \times \\ \text{in Asset 2 } (W_2)\end{array} \begin{array}{c}\text{Beta for}\\ \text{Asset 2}\\ (\beta_2)\end{array}\right) \\ &+ \cdots + \left(\begin{array}{c}\text{Proportion of}\\ \text{Portfolio Invested} \times \\ \text{in Asset } n \, (W_n)\end{array} \begin{array}{c}\text{Beta for}\\ \text{Asset } n\\ (\beta_n)\end{array}\right)\end{aligned} \tag{12–4}$$

Discussion Questions

Q12–12. (Related to Regardless of Your Major: Risk and Your Personal Investment Plan on page 413) In the *Regardless of Your Major* feature box, what are the four guidelines suggested for analyzing your personal investment decisions?

Q12–2. What did Depression-era humorist Will Rogers mean when he said "People tell me about the great return I'm going to get *on* my investment, but I'm more concerned about the return *of* my investment"?

Q12–3. Describe the relationship between the expected rate of return for an individual investment and the expected rate of return for a portfolio of several investments.

Q12–4. On a recent trip home for fall break, your grandfather tells you that he has purchased the stock of two firms in the automobile industry: Toyota and Ford. He goes on to discuss the merits of his decision and one of the points he makes is that he has avoided the risk of purchasing only one company's stock by diversifying his holdings across two stocks. What do you think of his argument? Be specific and describe to your grandfather what you have learned about portfolio diversification.

What You Should Know	Key Terms	
LG3 Estimate an investor's expected rate of return using the Capital Asset Pricing Model. The Capital Asset Pricing Model (CAPM) provides an intuitive framework for understanding the risk–return relationship. The CAPM suggests that the expected rate of return on an investment is determined by the investment's systematic risk. The model can be stated as follows:	Market risk premium, *p. 431*	The difference in the expected rate of return on the market portfolio and the risk-free rate of return.
	Security market line, *p. 430*	A graphical representation of the Capital Asset Pricing Model.

$$\text{Expected Return on Risky Asset } j = \text{Risk-free Rate of Return} + \text{Beta for Asset } j$$
$$\times \left(\text{Expected Return on the Market Portfolio} - \text{Risk-free Rate of Return} \right)$$

Note that the expected rate of return on risky asset *j* is equal to the risk-free rate of interest plus a risk premium that is specifically tailored to asset *j* by the systematic risk of the asset as measured by its beta coefficient. If the beta is equal to 1, then the expected return for the risky asset is simply the expected rate of return for the market portfolio of all risky assets.

Key Equations

$$\text{Expected Return on Risky Asset } j = \text{Risk-free Rate of Return} + \text{Beta for Asset } j \times \left(\text{Expected Return on the Market Portfolio} - \text{Risk-free Rate of Return} \right) \quad (12\text{–}6)$$

Q12–5. True or false: Portfolio diversification is affected by the volatility of the returns of the individual investments in the portfolio as well as the correlation among the returns. Explain this statement.

Q12–6. Describe what is meant by systematic and unsystematic risk. How is this distinction related to an investment's beta?

Q12–7. How is the beta of a portfolio related to the betas of the individual investments in the portfolio?

Q12–8. What is the security market line? What do the slope and intercept of this line represent?

Q12–9. Describe what the Capital Asset Pricing Model tells you to your father, who has never had a course in finance. What is the key insight we gain from this model?

Q12–10. Why would we expect the reward-to-risk ratio (slope of the security market line) to be the same across all risky investments? Assume that you are able to earn 5 percent per unit of risk for investing in the stock of Company A and 7 percent for investing in Company B. How would you expect investors to act in light of this difference in reward-to-risk ratio? (Hint: Which stock do you think investors would want to buy?)

Q12–11. Presently you own shares of stock in Company A and are considering adding some shares in either Company B or Company C. The standard deviations of all three firms are exactly the same but the correlation between the common stock returns for Company A and Company B is .5, whereas it is –.5 between the common stock of Company A and Company C. How will the risk or standard deviation of your investment returns change if you decide to invest in A and B's common stock? How will the risk or standard deviation of your portfolio returns change if you decide to invest in A and C's common stock? If the expected return on the stock of all three companies is the same, how will your portfolio's expected return be impacted by your decision to invest in either B or C along with A?

Q12–12. True or false: If the standard deviation of Company A's stock returns is greater than the standard deviation of Company B's stock returns, then the beta of Stock A *must* be greater than the beta of Stock B. Explain your answer.

Q12–13. If a company's beta jumped from 1.5 to 4.5, would its expected rate of return triple? Explain why or why not. (*Hint:* Assume the risk-free rate is 4 percent and the market risk premium is 5 percent.)

Study Problems

MyFinanceLab **Portfolio Returns and Portfolio Risk**

Go to www.myfinancelab.com to complete these exercises online and get instant feedback.

P12–1. (Related to Checkpoint 12.1 on page 416) (**Expected rate of return**) James Fromholtz is considering whether to invest in a newly formed investment fund. The fund's investment objective is to acquire home mortgage securities at what it hopes will be bargain prices. The fund sponsor has suggested to James that the fund's performance will hinge on how the national economy performs in the coming year. Specifically, he suggested the following possible outcomes:

State of the Economy	Probability	Fund Return
Rapid expansion and recovery	5%	100%
Modest growth	45%	35%
Continued recession	45%	5%
Falls into depression	5%	−100%

a. Based on these potential outcomes, what is your estimate of the expected rate of return from this investment opportunity?
b. Would you be interested in making such an investment? Note that you lose all your money in one year if the economy collapses into the worst state or you double your money if the economy enters into a rapid expansion.

P12–2. (Related to Checkpoint 12.2 on page 422) (**Computing the standard deviation for an individual investment**) Calculate the standard deviation in the anticipated returns found in Problem 12–1.

P12–3. (**Computing the standard deviation for a portfolio of two risky investments**) Mary Guilott recently graduated from college and is evaluating an investment in two companies' common stock. She has collected the following information about the common stock of Firm A and Firm B:

	Expected Return	Standard Deviation
Firm A's common stock	0.15	0.12
Firm B's common stock	0.1	0.06
Correlation coefficient	0.4	

a. If Mary invests half her money in each of the two common shares, what is the expected rate of return and standard deviation in portfolio return?
b. Answer question a, where correlation between the two common stock investments is equal to zero.

c. Answer question a, where correlation between the two common stock investments is equal to +1.

d. Answer question a, where correlation between the two common stock investments is equal to −1.

e. Using your responses to questions a–d, describe the relationship between correlation and the risk and return of the portfolio.

P12–4. (**Computing the standard deviation for a portfolio of two risky investments**) Answer the following questions using the information provided in Problem 12–3:

a. Answer question a of Problem 12–3, where Mary decides to invest 10 percent of her money in Firm A's common stock and 90 percent in Firm B's common stock.

b. Answer question a of Problem 12–3, where Mary decides to invest 90 percent of her money in Firm A's common stock and 10 percent in Firm B's common stock.

c. Recompute your responses to both questions a and b, where the correlation between the two firms' stock returns is −4.

d. Summarize what your analysis tells you about portfolio risk when combining risky assets in a portfolio.

P12–5. (**Related to Checkpoint 12.1 on page 416**) (**Portfolio expected rate of return**) Penny Francis inherited a $100,000 portfolio of investments from her grandparents when she turned 21 years of age. The portfolio is comprised of the following three investments:

	Expected Return	$ Value
Treasury bills	4.5%	40,000
Ford (F)	8.0%	30,000
Harley Davidson (HOG)	12.0%	30,000

a. Based on the current portfolio composition and the expected rates of return, what is the expected rate of return for Penny's portfolio?

b. If Penny wants to increase her expected portfolio rate of return, she could increase the allocated weight of the portfolio she has invested in stock (Ford and Harley Davidson) and decrease her holdings of Treasury bills. If Penny moves all her money out of Treasury bills and splits it evenly between the two stocks, what will be her expected rate of return?

c. If Penny does move money out of Treasury bills and into the two stocks she will reap a higher expected portfolio return, so why would anyone want to hold Treasury bills in their portfolio?

P12–6. (**Portfolio expected rate of return**) Barry Swifter is 60 years of age and considering retirement. Barry's retirement portfolio currently is valued at $750,000 and is allocated in Treasury bills, an S&P 500 index fund, and an emerging-market fund as follows:

	Expected Return	$ Value
Treasury bills	4.5%	75,000
S&P 500 Index Fund	8.0%	450,000
Emerging Market Fund	12.0%	225,000

a. Based on the current portfolio composition and the expected rates of return, what is the expected rate of return for Barry's portfolio?

b. Barry is considering a reallocation of his investments to include more Treasury bills and less exposure to emerging markets. If Barry moves all of his money from the emerging market fund and puts it in Treasury bills, what will be the expected rate of return on the resulting portfolio?

P12–7. (**Expected rate of return and risk**) Kelly B. Stites, Inc., is considering an investment in one of two portfolios. Given the information that follows, which investment is better, based on risk (as measured by the standard deviation) and the expected rate of return?

Portfolio A		Portfolio B	
Probability	Return	Probability	Return
.20	–2%	.10	5%
.50	19%	.30	7%
.30	25%	.40	12%
		.20	14%

Systematic Risk and the Market Portfolio

P12–8. (**Related to Checkpoint 12.3 on page 433**) (**Systematic risk and expected rates of return**) Table 12.1 contains beta coefficient estimates for six firms and from two different sources. Calculate the expected increase in the value of each firm's shares if the market portfolio were to increase by 10 percent (use either the Yahoo Finance or Microsoft Money Central beta estimates). Perform the same calculation where the market drops by 10 percent. Which set of firms has the most variable or volatile stock returns?

P12–9. (**Estimating betas**) Consider the following stock returns for B&A Trucking, Inc. and the market index:

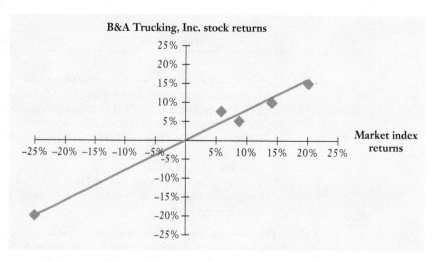

Use the visual method described in Figure 12.3 to estimate the beta for B&A. Is the firm more or less risky than the market portfolio? Explain.

The Security Market Line and the CAPM

P12–10. (**Related to Checkpoint 12.3 on page 433**) (**CAPM and expected returns**)
    a. Given the following holding-period returns, compute the average returns and the standard deviations for the Sugita Corporation and for the market.

Month	Sugita Corp.	Market
1	1.8%	1.5%
2	−0.5	1.0
3	2.0	0.0
4	−2.0	−2.0
5	5.0	4.0
6	5.0	3.0

b. If Sugita's beta is 1.18 and the risk-free rate is 4 percent, what would be an expected return for an investor owning Sugita? (Note: Because the preceding returns are based on monthly data, you will need to annualize the returns to make them comparable with the risk-free rate. For simplicity, you can convert from monthly to yearly returns by multiplying the average monthly returns by 12.)

c. How does Sugita's historical average return compare with the return you should expect based on the Capital Asset Pricing Model and the firm's systematic risk?

P12–11. (CAPM and expected returns)

a. Given the following holding-period returns, compute the average returns and the standard deviations for the Zemin Corporation and for the market.

Month	Zemin Corp.	Market
1	6%	4%
2	3	2
3	1	−1
4	−3	−2
5	5	2
6	0	2

b. If Zemin's beta is 1.54 and the risk-free rate is 4 percent, what would be an expected return for an investor owning Zemin? (Note: Because the preceding returns are based on monthly data, you will need to annualize the returns to make them comparable with the risk-free rate. For simplicity, you can convert from monthly to yearly returns by multiplying the average monthly returns by 12.)

c. How does Zemin's historical average return compare with the return you believe you should expect based on the capital asset pricing model and the firm's systematic risk?

P12–12. (Security market line) James Fromholtz from Problem 12–1 is evaluating the investment posed in that problem and wants to apply his recently acquired understanding of the security market line concept to his analysis.

a. If the risk-free rate of interest is currently 2.5 percent, and the beta for the investment is 2, what is the slope of the security market line for the real estate mortgage security investment?

b. James is also considering the investment of his money in a market index fund that has an expected rate of return of 10 percent. What is the slope of the security market line (i.e., the reward-to-risk ratio) for this investment opportunity?

c. Based on your analysis of parts a and b, which investment should James take? Why?

P12–13. (Expected rate of return using CAPM)

a. Compute the expected rate of return for Intel common stock, which has a 1.2 beta. The risk-free rate is 3.5 percent and the market portfolio (composed of New York Stock Exchange stocks) has an expected return of 16 percent.

b. Why is the rate you computed the expected rate?

P12–14. **(Expected rate of return using CAPM)**

    a. Compute the expected rate of return for Acer common stock, which has a 1.5 beta. The risk-free rate is 4.5 percent and the market portfolio (composed of New York Stock Exchange stocks) has an expected return of 10 percent.

    b. Why is the rate you computed the expected rate?

P12–15. **(Capital Asset Pricing Model)** Johnson Manufacturing, Inc., is considering several investments. The rate on Treasury bills is currently 4 percent, and the expected return for the market is 10 percent. What should be the the expected rates of return for each investment (using the CAPM)?

Security	Beta
A	1.50
B	.82
C	.60
D	1.15

P12–16. **(Capital Asset Pricing Model)** Bobbi Manufacturing, Inc., is considering several investments. The rate on Treasury bills is currently 3.75 percent, and the expected return for the market is 10 percent. What should be the expected rates of return for each investment (using the CAPM)?

Security	Beta
A	1.40
B	.75
C	.80
D	1.20

P12–17. **(Capital Asset Pricing Model)** Breckenridge, Inc., has a beta of .85. If the expected market return is 10.5 percent and the risk-free rate is 3.5 percent, what is the appropriate expected return of Breckenridge (using the CAPM)?

P12–18. **(Capital Asset Pricing Model)** CSB, Inc. has a beta of .765. If the expected market return is 10.5 percent and the risk-free rate is 3.5 percent, what is the appropriate expected rate of return of CSB (using the CAPM)?

P12–19. **(Capital Asset Pricing Model)** The expected return for the general market is 10.3 percent, and the risk premium in the market is 5.3 percent. Tasaco, LBM, and Exxos have betas of .864, .693, and .575, respectively. What are the appropriate expected rates of return for the three securities?

 P12–20. **(Portfolio beta and security market line)** You own a portfolio consisting of the following stocks:

Stock	Percentage of Portfolio	Beta	Expected Return
1	20%	1.00	16%
2	30%	0.85	14%
3	15%	1.20	20%
4	25%	0.60	12%
5	10%	1.60	24%

The risk-free rate is 3 percent. Also, the expected return on the market portfolio is 10.5 percent.

    a. Calculate the expected return of your portfolio. (Hint: The expected return of a portfolio equals the weighted average of the individual stock's expected return, where the weights are the percentage invested in each stock.)

    b. Calculate the portfolio beta.

    c. Given the preceding information, plot the security market line on paper. Plot the stocks from your portfolio on your graph.

    d. From your plot in part c, which stocks appear to be your winners and which ones appear to be losers?

    e. Why should you consider your conclusion in part d to be less than certain?

P12–21. (Security market line) Your father just learned from his financial advisor that his retirement portfolio has a beta of 1.80. He has turned to you to explain to him what this means. Specifically, describe what you would expect to happen to the value of his retirement fund if the following were to occur:

    a. The value of the market portfolio rises by 7 percent.

    b. The value of the market portfolio drops by 7 percent.

    c. Is your father's retirement portfolio more or less risky than the market portfolio? Explain.

P12–22. (Security market line) You are considering the construction of a portfolio comprised of equal investments in each of four different stocks. The betas for each stock on next page:

Security	Beta
A	2.5
B	1.0
C	0.5
D	−1.5

    a. What is the portfolio beta for your proposed investment portfolio?

    b. How would a 25 percent increase in the expected return on the market impact the expected return of your portfolio?

    c. How would a 25 percent decrease in the expected return on the market impact the expected return on each asset?

    d. If you are interested in decreasing the beta of your portfolio by changing your portfolio allocation to two stocks, which stock would you decrease and which would you increase? Why?

P12–23. (Portfolio beta and CAPM) You are putting together a portfolio made up of four different stocks. However, you are considering two possible weightings:

		Portfolio Weightings	
Asset	Beta	First Portfolio	Second Portfolio
A	2.5	10%	40%
B	1.0	10%	40%
C	0.5	40%	10%
D	−1.5	40%	10%

    a. What is the beta on each portfolio?

    b. Which portfolio is riskier?

    c. If the risk-free rate of interest were 4 percent and the market risk premium were 5 percent, what rate of return would you expect to earn from each of the portfolios?

P12–24. (Security market line) If the risk-free rate of return is 4 percent and the expected rate of return on the market portfolio is 10 percent.

    a. Graph the security market line (SML). Also, calculate and label the market risk premium on the graph.

    b. Using your graph from question a, identify the expected rates of return on a portfolio with beta of .4 and a beta of 1.8, respectively.

    c. Now assume that because of a financial crisis the economy slows down and anticipated inflation drops. As a result, the risk-free rate of return drops to 2 percent and the expected rate of return on the market portfolio drops to 8 percent. Draw the resulting security market line.

    d. Now assume that because of economic fears, investors have become more risk averse, demanding a higher return on all assets that have any risk. This results in an increase in the expected rate of return on the market portfolio to 12 percent (with the risk-free rate equal to 4 percent). Draw the resulting SML. What can you conclude about the effect of a financial crisis on expected rates of return?

P12–25. (Portfolio beta and security market line) You own a portfolio consisting of the following stocks:

Stock	Percentage of Portfolio	Beta	Return Expected
1	10%	1.00	12%
2	25	0.75	11
3	15	1.30	15
4	30	0.60	9
5	20	1.20	14

The risk-free rate is 4 percent. Also, the expected return on the market portfolio is 10 percent.

    a. Calculate the expected return of your portfolio. (Hint: The expected return of a portfolio equals the weighted average of the individual stock's expected return, where the weights are the percentage invested in each stock.)

    b. Calculate the portfolio beta.

    c. Given the preceding information, plot the security market line on paper. Plot the stocks from your portfolio on your graph.

    d. From your plot in part c, which stocks appear to be your winners and which ones appear to be losers?

    e. Why should you consider your conclusion in part d to be less than certain?

P12–26. (Capital Asset Pricing Model) Anita, Inc. is considering the following investments. The current rate on Treasury bills is 4.5 percent, and the expected return for the market is 11 percent. Using the CAPM, what rates of return should Anita require for each individual security?

Stock	Beta
H	0.75
T	1.4
P	0.95
W	1.25

P12–27. (Capital Asset Pricing Model) Grace Corporation is considering the following investments. The current rate on Treasury bills is 2.5 percent and the expected return for the market is 9 percent.

Stock	Beta
K	1.12
G	1.3
B	0.75
U	1.02

a. Using the CAPM, what rates of return should Grace require for each individual security?

b. How would your evaluation of the expected rates of return for Grace change if the risk-free rate were to rise to 4.5 percent and the market risk premium were to be only 5 percent?

c. Which market risk premium scenario (from part a or b) best fits a recessionary environment? A period of economic expansion? Explain your response.

Mini-Case

Larry Lynch has been working for a year as an analyst for an investment company that specializes in serving very wealthy clients. These clients often purchase shares in closely held investment funds with very limited numbers of stockholders. In the fall of 2008, the market for certain types of securities based on real estate loans simply collapsed as the subprime mortgage scandal unfolded. Larry's firm, however, sees this market collapse as an opportunity to put together a fund that purchases some of these mortgage-backed securities that investors have shunned by acquiring them at bargain prices and holding them until the underlying mortgages are repaid or the market for these securities recovers.

The investment company began putting together sales information concerning the possible performance of the new fund and has made the following predictions regarding the possible performance of the new fund over the coming year as a function of how well the economy does:

State of the Economy	Probability	Fund Return
Rapid expansion	10%	50%
Modest growth	50%	35%
No growth	40%	5%
Recession	5%	−100%

Larry's boss has asked him to perform a preliminary analysis of the new fund's performance potential for the coming year. Specifically, he has asked that Larry address each of the following issues:

1. What are the expected rate of return and standard deviation?

2. What is the reward-to-risk ratio for the fund based on the fund's standard deviation as a measure of risk?

3. What is the expected rate of return for the fund based on the Capital Asset Pricing Model?

In addition to the information provided above, Larry has observed that the risk-free rate of interest for the coming year is 4.5 percent, the market risk premium is 5.5 percent, and the beta for the new investment is 3.55.

Based on your analysis, do you think that the proposed fund offers a fair return given its risk? Explain.

13

Options: Puts and Calls

After studying this chapter, you should be able to:

LG1 Discuss the basic nature of options in general and puts and calls in particular and understand how these investment vehicles work.

LG2 Describe the options market and note key options provisions, including strike prices and expiration dates.

LG3 Explain how put and call options are valued and the forces that drive option prices in the marketplace.

LG4 Describe the profit potential of puts and calls and note some popular put and call investment strategies.

LG5 Explain the profit potential and loss exposure from writing covered call options and discuss how writing options can be used as a strategy for enhancing investment returns.

LG6 Describe market index options, puts and calls on foreign currencies, and LEAPS and discuss how these securities can be used by investors.

Facebook executives were not the only ones getting rich when the company went public in 2012. Several years earlier in 2005, artist David Choe was asked to paint some murals on the walls of Facebook, which at the time was a young and upcoming social media company. Sean Parker, then the president of Facebook, offered Choe the option of being paid $60,000 or with Facebook stock. Choe, who had once called the start-up social networking site "ridiculous and pointless," chose the stock option.

Choe was not an accomplished investor, but rather had become renowned for the raw and frenetic imagery he creates. Parker had long been a fan of Choe's work and had commissioned Choe to paint graphic sexual murals in Facebook's first Silicon Valley office. Although Parker was not initially pleased with Choe's earlier murals for Facebook, calling them "schizophrenically distracting," in 2007 CEO Mark Zuckerberg commissioned Choe to paint somewhat tamer murals for their next office.

It turned out that Choe was not only a graffiti artist turned legitimate muralist, but he was also a self-proclaimed risk-seeking gambler. So even though he considered himself homeless, living in casinos and hotels at the time, Choe chose to bet on the stock of Facebook. Seven years later, the option Choe picked was worth an estimated $200 million.

(Sources: "6 Things We Can Learn from The Facebook Graffiti Artist," www.forbes.com, February 3, 2012; "Facebook IPO Turns Graffiti Mural into a $200 Million Payday," www.csmonitor.com, February 3, 2012; "Facebook's Graffiti Artist David Choe Says Life Unchanged by $200 Million," www.abcnews.com, February 9, 2012.)

Put and Call Options

LG1 LG2 When investors buy shares of common or preferred stock, they are entitled to all the rights and privileges of ownership such as receiving dividends or, in the case of common stock, having the right to vote at shareholder meetings. Investors who acquire bonds or convertible issues are also entitled to certain benefits of ownership such as receiving periodic interest payments. Stocks, bonds, and convertibles are all examples of *financial assets*. They represent financial claims on the issuing organization. In contrast, investors who buy options acquire nothing more than the right to subsequently buy or sell other, related securities. An **option** gives the holder the right to buy or sell a certain amount of an underlying asset (such as common stocks) at a specified price over a specified period of time.

Options are contractual instruments, whereby two parties enter into a contract to give something of value to the other. The option buyer has the right to buy or sell an underlying asset within a given period of time, at a price that was fixed at the time of the contract. The option seller stands ready to buy or sell the underlying asset according to the terms of the contract, for which the buyer has paid the seller a certain amount of money. We'll look at 2 basic kinds of options in this chapter: *puts* and *calls*, both of which enjoy considerable popularity as investments.

In addition, there are 2 other types of options: *rights* and *warrants*. Rights originate when corporations raise money by issuing new shares of common stocks. (See Chapter 1 for a discussion of rights offerings.) Rights enable stockholders to buy shares of the new issue at a specified price for a specified, fairly short period of time. Because their life span is so short—usually no more than a few weeks—stock rights hold very little investment appeal for the average individual investor. In contrast, warrants are long-term options that grant the right to buy shares in a certain company for a given period of time (often fairly long—5 to 10 years or more). Warrants are usually created as "sweeteners" to bond issues and are used to make the issues more attractive to investors. In essence, the buyer of one of these bonds also receives one or more warrants, as an *equity kicker*.

Basic Features of Puts and Calls

Stock options began trading on the Chicago Board Options Exchange in the early 1970s. Soon the interest in options spilled over to other kinds of financial assets. Today, investors can trade puts and calls on common stock, stock indexes, exchange-traded funds, foreign currencies, debt instruments, and commodities and financial futures.

As we will see, although the underlying financial assets may vary, the basic features of different types of options are very similar. Perhaps the most important feature to understand is that options allow investors to benefit from price changes in the underlying asset without investing much capital.

A Negotiable Contract Puts and calls are negotiable instruments, issued in bearer form, that allow the holder to buy or sell a specified amount of a specified security at a specified price. For example, a put or a call on common stock covers 100 shares of stock in a specific company. A **put** enables the holder to sell the underlying security at the specified price (known as the *exercise* or *strike price*) over a set period of time. A **call**, in contrast, gives the holder the right to buy the security at the stated (strike) price within a certain time period. As with any option, there are no voting rights, no privileges of ownership, and no interest or dividend income. Instead, puts and calls possess value to the extent that they allow the holder to benefit from price movements of the underlying asset.

Because puts and calls derive their value from the price behavior of some other real or financial asset, they are known as **derivative securities**. Rights and warrants, as well as futures contracts, are also derivative securities. Although certain segments of this market are for big institutional investors only, there's still ample room for the individual investor. Many of these securities—especially those listed on exchanges—are readily available to, and are actively traded by, individuals as well as institutions.

The price that an investor pays to buy an option is called the **option premium**. As we will see, an option's premium depends on characteristics of the option such as its strike price and expiration date and on the price of the underlying asset. However, don't let the word *premium* confuse you. It's just the market price of the option.

One of the key features of puts and calls is the attractive **leverage** opportunities they offer. Such opportunities exist because of the low prices these options carry relative to the market prices of the underlying financial assets. What's more, the lower cost in no way affects the payoff or capital appreciation potential of your investment. To illustrate, consider a call on a common stock that gives you the right to buy 100 shares of a stock at a (strike) price of $45 a share. If that stock currently sells for $45, the call option would sell for just a few dollars—let's say $3 per option for the sake of illustration (or $300 since the option contract covers 100 shares). Next, suppose that a month or 2 later the stock price has increased by $10 to $55. At that point, you might exercise your right to buy 100 shares for $45 each. You pay $4,500 to acquire the shares and then immediately resell them at the market price for $5,500, pocketing a gain of $1,000. Thus, in a short period of time your $300 up-front investment grew to $1,000, a gain of 233%. The percentage increase in the stock over this period was just 22.2% ($10 ÷ $45), so the percentage gain on the option is much greater than the percentage gain on the stock. That's the benefit of the leverage the options provide.

Seller versus Buyer Puts and calls are a unique type of security because they are not issued by the organizations that issue the underlying stock. Instead, they are created by investors. It works like this: Suppose you want to sell to another investor the right to buy 100 shares of common stock. You could do this by "writing a call." The individual (or institution) writing the option is known as the **option seller** or **option writer**. As the option writer, you sell the option in the market and so are entitled to receive the price paid by the buyer for the put or call.

Puts and calls are both written (sold) and purchased through securities brokers and dealers. In fact, they're as easy to buy and sell as common stocks; a simple phone call, or a few mouse clicks, is all it takes. The writer stands behind the option because it is the writer who must buy or deliver the stocks or other financial assets according to the terms of the option. (*Note:* The writers of puts and calls have a legally binding obligation to stand behind the terms of the contracts they have written. The buyer can just walk away from the deal if it turns sour; the writer cannot.)

Puts and calls are written for a variety of reasons, most of which we will explore throughout this chapter. At this point, suffice it to say that writing options can be a viable investment strategy and can be a profitable course of action because, more often than not, options expire worthless.

How Puts and Calls Work Taking the buyer's point of view, we will briefly examine how puts and calls work and how they derive their value. To start, it is best to look at their profit-making potential. For example, consider the call described earlier that has a $45 strike price and sells for $3. As the buyer of the call option, you hope for a rise in the price of the underlying security (in this case, common stock). What is the profit potential from this transaction if the price of the stock does indeed move up to, say, $75 by the expiration date on the call?

The answer is that you will earn $30 ($75 − $45) on each of the 100 shares of stock in the call, minus the original $300 cost of the option. In other words, you'll earn a gross profit of $3,000 from your $300 investment. This is so because you have the right to buy 100 shares of the stock, from the option writer, at a price of $45 each, and then immediately turn around and sell them in the market for $75 a share.

Could you have made the same gross profit ($3,000) by investing directly in the common stock? Yes, if you had purchased 100 shares of stock. Buying 100 shares of a $45 stock requires an initial investment of $4,500 compared to the $300 investment needed to buy the options. As a consequence, the rate of return from buying the shares is much less than the rate of return from buying the options. The return potential of common stocks and calls differs considerably. This difference attracts investors and speculators to calls whenever the price outlook for the underlying financial asset is positive. Such differential returns are, of course, the direct result of *leverage*, which rests on the principle of reducing the level of capital required in a given investment without materially affecting the dollar amount of the payoff or capital appreciation from that investment. Note that although our illustration used common stock, this valuation principle applies to any of the other financial assets that may underlie call options, such as market indexes, foreign currencies, and futures contracts.

A similar situation can be worked out for puts. Assume that for the same stock (which has a current price of $45) you could pay $700 and buy a put to sell 100 shares of the stock at a strike price of $50 each. As the buyer of a put, you want the price of the stock to drop. Assume that your expectations are correct and the price of the stock does indeed drop, to $25 a share. Here again, when you exercise the put option, you realize a gross profit of $25 per share because you can buy the stock in the open market for $25 and then exercise your right to sell it for $50.

Fortunately, put and call investors do not have to exercise their options and make simultaneous buy and sell transactions in order to receive their profit. That's because the options themselves have value and can be traded in the secondary market. The value of both puts and calls is directly linked to the market price of the underlying financial asset, so the value of a call increases as the market price of the underlying security rises. Likewise, the value of a put increases as the price of the security declines. Thus, you can get your money out of options by selling them in the open market, just as with any other security.

Advantages and Disadvantages The major advantage of investing in puts and calls is the leverage they offer. This feature allows investors to profit from movements in the underlying asset without investing a large amount of money up front. Also appealing is the fact that puts and calls can be used profitably when the price of the underlying security goes up or down.

A major disadvantage of puts and calls is that the holder enjoys neither interest or dividend income nor any other ownership benefits. Moreover, because puts and calls have limited lives, there is a limited time during which the underlying asset can move in the direction that makes the option profitable. Finally, while it is possible to buy calls and puts without investing a lot of money up front, the likelihood that an investor will lose 100% of the money that he or she does invest is much higher with options than with stocks. That's because if the underlying stock moves just a little in the wrong direction, a put or call option on that stock will be totally worthless when it expires.

Options Markets

Although the concept of options can be traced back to the writings of Aristotle, options trading in the United States did not begin until the late 1700s. Even then, up to the early 1970s, this market remained fairly small, largely unorganized, and the almost-private domain of a handful of specialists and traders. All of this changed, however, on April 26, 1973, when the Chicago Board Options Exchange (CBOE) opened.

Conventional Options Prior to the creation of the CBOE, put and call options trading was conducted in the over-the-counter market through a handful of specialized dealers. Investors who wished to purchase puts and calls contacted their own brokers, who contacted the options dealers. The dealers would find investors willing to write the options. If the buyer wished to exercise an option, he or she did so with the writer and no one else—a system that largely prohibited any secondary trading. On the other hand, there were virtually no limits to what could be written, so long as the buyer was willing to pay the price. Put and call options were written on New York and American exchange stocks, as well as on regional and over-the-counter securities, for as short a time as 30 days and for as long as a year. Over-the-counter options, known today as **conventional options**, are now used almost exclusively by institutional investors. Accordingly, our attention in this chapter will focus on listed markets, like the CBOE, where individual investors do most of their options trading.

Listed Options The creation of the CBOE signaled the birth of **listed options**, a term that describes put and call options traded on organized exchanges. The CBOE launched trading in calls on just 16 firms. From these rather humble beginnings, there evolved in a relatively short time a large and active market for listed options. Today, trading in listed options in the United States is done in both puts and calls and takes place on one of 9 exchanges, including the BATS Options Exchange (BATS), BOX Options Exchange (BOX), C2 Options Exchange (C2), Chicago Board Options Exchange (CBOE), International Securities Exchange (ISE), Nasdaq OMX PHLX (PHLX), Nasdaq Options Market (NOM), NYSE Amex Options (NYSE Amex), and NYSE Arca Options (NYSE Arca). In total, put and call options are now traded on over 3,800 different stocks, with many of those options listed on multiple exchanges. In addition to stocks, the options exchanges also offer listed options on stock indexes, exchange-traded funds, debt securities, foreign currencies, and even commodities and financial futures.

Listed options provide not only a convenient market for puts and calls but also standardized expiration dates and exercise prices. The listed options exchanges created a clearinghouse that eliminated direct ties between buyers and sellers of options and reduced the cost of executing put and call transactions. They also developed an active secondary market, with wide distribution of price information. As a result, it is now as easy to trade a listed option as a listed stock.

Stock Options

The advent of the CBOE and the other listed option exchanges had a dramatic impact on the trading volume of puts and calls. Today 4.6 billion listed options contracts are traded each year, most of which are stock options. In 2011, about 92% (or 4.2 billion contracts) were stock options. That year, the total volume of stock-option contracts traded was divided among the options exchanges as follows:

Options Exchange	Number of Contracts Traded (millions)	Exchange Share of Trading Volume (%)
BATS	148.34	3.25
BOX	139.68	3.06
C2	52.82	1.16
CBOE	1,152.06	25.25
ISE	778.09	17.05
PHLX	983.49	21.55
NOM	194.20	4.26
NYSE AMEX	618.73	13.56
NYSE Arca	495.34	10.86
TOTAL	4,562.75	100

Listed options exchanges have unquestionably added a new dimension to investing. In order to avoid serious (and possibly expensive) mistakes with these securities, however, you must fully understand their basic features. In the sections that follow, we will look closely at the investment attributes of stock options and the trading strategies for using them. Later, we'll explore stock-index (and ETF) options and then briefly look at other types of puts and calls, including interest rate and currency options, and long-term options.

Stock Option Provisions Because of their low unit cost, stock options (or *equity options*, as they're also called) are very popular with individual investors. Except for the underlying financial asset, they are like any other type of put or call, subject to the same kinds of contract provisions and market forces. Two provisions are especially important for stock options: (1) the price—known as the *strike price*—at which the stock can be bought or sold, and (2) the amount of time remaining until expiration. As we'll see, both the strike price and the time remaining to expiration have a significant bearing on their valuation and pricing.

Strike Price The **strike price** represents the price contract between the buyer of the option and the writer. For a call, the strike price specifies the price at which each of the 100 shares of stock can be bought. For a put, it represents the price at which the stock can be sold to the writer. With conventional (OTC) options, there are no constraints on the strike price. With listed options, strike prices are standardized:

- Stocks selling for less than $25 per share carry strike prices that are set in $2.50 dollar increments ($7.50, $10.00, $12.50, $15, and so on).

- In general, the increments jump to $5 for stocks selling between $25 and $200 per share, although a number of securities in the $25 to $50 range are now allowed to use $2.50 dollar increments.

- For stocks that trade at more than $200 a share, the strike price is set in $10 increments.

- Unlike most equity options, options on exchange-traded funds (discussed more fully later in this chapter) all have strike prices set in $1 increments.

In all cases, the strike price is adjusted for stock splits. Strike prices are not adjusted for cash dividends, but they are adjusted when firms pay significant stock dividends (e.g., dividends paid in additional shares rather than in cash).

Expiration Date The **expiration date** is also an important provision. It specifies the life of the option, just as the maturity date indicates the life of a bond. The expiration date, in effect, specifies the length of the contract between the holder and the writer of the option. Thus, if you hold a 6-month call on Sears with a strike price of, say, $70, that option gives you the right to buy 100 shares of Sears common stock at $70 per share at any time over the next 6 months. No matter what happens to the market price of the stock, you can use your call option to buy 100 shares of Sears at $70 a share. If the price of the stock moves up, you stand to make money. If it goes down, you'll be out the cost of the option.

Expiration dates for options in the conventional market can fall on any working day of the month. In contrast, expiration dates are standardized in the listed options market. The exchanges initially created 3 expiration cycles for all listed options:

- January, April, July, and October

- February, May, August, and November

- March, June, September, and December

Each issue is assigned to one of these cycles. The exchanges still use the same 3 expiration cycles, but they've been altered so that investors are always able to trade in the 2 nearest (current and following) months, plus the next 2 closest months in the option's regular expiration cycle. For reasons that are pretty obvious, this is sometimes referred to as a *two-plus-two* schedule.

For example, if the current month (also called the *front month*) is January, then available options in the *January cycle* would be January, February, April, and July. These represent the 2 current months (January and February) and the next 2 months in the cycle (April and July). Likewise, available contracts for the *February cycle* would be January, February, May, and August; available contracts for the *March cycle* would be January, February, March, and June. The expiration dates, based on the front months, continue rolling over in this way during the course of the year. The following table demonstrates the available contracts under the two-plus-two system for the months of February and June:

Front Month	Cycle	Available Contracts
February	January	February, March, April, July
February	February	February, March, May, August
February	March	February, March, June, September
June	January	June, July, October, January
June	February	June, July, August, November
June	March	June, July, September, December

Look Up an Option Chain

Given the month of expiration, the actual day of expiration is always the same: the Saturday following the third Friday of each expiration month. Thus, for all practical purposes, *listed options always expire on the third Friday of the month of expiration.*

Put and Call Transactions Option traders are subject to commission and transaction costs whenever they buy or sell an option or whenever they write an option. The writing

FIGURE 13.1   Quotations for Facebook Stock Options

The quotes for calls and puts of a specified expiration period are listed down either side of the strike price. In addition to the last price the option traded at for the day and its end-of-day bid and ask price, the change from the previous day's last transaction price is shown. The name (Facebook) and closing price ($21.01) of the underlying stock were also shown on the webpage. (Source: quotemedia.com, accessed August 8, 2012.)

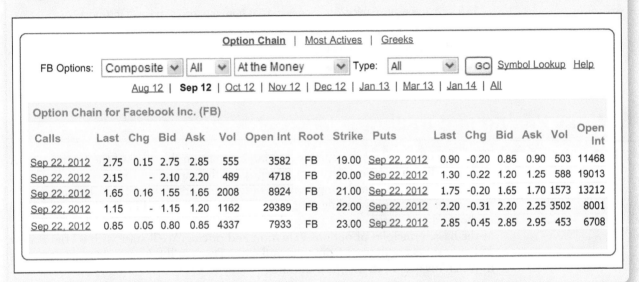

Option Chain | Most Actives | Greeks

FB Options: [Composite ▾] [All ▾] [At the Money ▾] Type: [All ▾] [GO] Symbol Lookup Help

Aug 12 | **Sep 12** | Oct 12 | Nov 12 | Dec 12 | Jan 13 | Mar 13 | Jan 14 | All

Option Chain for Facebook Inc. (FB)

Calls	Last	Chg	Bid	Ask	Vol	Open Int	Root	Strike	Puts	Last	Chg	Bid	Ask	Vol	Open Int
Sep 22, 2012	2.75	0.15	2.75	2.85	555	3582	FB	19.00	Sep 22, 2012	0.90	-0.20	0.85	0.90	503	11468
Sep 22, 2012	2.15	-	2.10	2.20	489	4718	FB	20.00	Sep 22, 2012	1.30	-0.22	1.20	1.25	588	19013
Sep 22, 2012	1.65	0.16	1.55	1.65	2008	8924	FB	21.00	Sep 22, 2012	1.75	-0.20	1.65	1.70	1573	13212
Sep 22, 2012	1.15	-	1.15	1.20	1162	29389	FB	22.00	Sep 22, 2012	2.20	-0.31	2.20	2.25	3502	8001
Sep 22, 2012	0.85	0.05	0.80	0.85	4337	7933	FB	23.00	Sep 22, 2012	2.85	-0.45	2.85	2.95	453	6708

of puts and calls is subject to normal transaction costs; these costs effectively represent compensation to the broker or dealer for selling the option.

Listed options have their own marketplace and quotation system. Finding the price (or *premium*) of a listed stock option is fairly easy since there are lots of online sources for option quotations. Figure 13.1 illustrates a quotation from Nasdaq.com for an *option chain* in which Nasdaq Facebook stock serves as the underlying asset. An **option chain** is a listing of all options, puts, and calls on an underlying asset for a given expiration period. The quotation in Figure 13.1 shows only a small subset of the entire option chain for Facebook, 5 call option contracts on the left and 5 put option contracts on the right along with their strike prices and premiums for contracts that expire on September 22, 2012. Generating a quotation for all current option contracts on Facebook produces an option chain with 323 call option quotes and 318 put option quotes.

Regardless of the source, quotations tend to be standardized: The name of the company or index and the closing price of the underlying asset are provided. The option contract expiration month and strike price are provided. The market data provided includes the option's last transaction price (or premium) of the day, the change in transaction price from the previous day's last transaction price, the bid and ask price of the day, the daily volume, and the end-of-day open interest. For example, a September (2012) Nasdaq Facebook call with a strike price of $20 was quoted at $2.15 (which translates into a dollar price of $215 because stock options trade in 100 share lots), and a September put option with the same strike price sold for $1.30.

Options Pricing and Trading

LG3 **LG4** **LG5**   The value of a put or call depends to a large extent on the price of the financial asset that underlies the option. Getting a firm grip on the current and expected future value of a put or call is extremely important to options traders and investors. Thus, to get the most from any options trading program, you must understand how options are priced in the market. Continuing to use stock options as a basis of discussion, let's look now at the basic principles of options valuation and pricing. We'll start with a brief review of how profits are derived from puts and calls. Then we'll take a look at several ways in which investors can use these options.

The Profit Potential from Puts and Calls

Although the quoted market price of a put or call is affected by such factors as time to expiration, stock volatility, and market interest rates, by far the most important variable is the price behavior of the underlying common stock. This is the variable that drives any significant moves in the price of the option and that determines the option's profit (return) potential. When the price of the underlying stock moves up, calls do well. When the price of the underlying stock drops, puts do well. Such performance also explains why it's important to get a good handle on the expected future price behavior of a stock before you buy or sell (write) an option.

Call Option Payoff Diagrams

Figure 13.2 (on page 455) illustrates how the ultimate payoffs that options provide depend upon the underlying stock price. By "payoff" we mean the gain that an investor would receive from exercising the option—the difference between the stock price and the strike price. The diagram on the left depicts a call, and the one on the right depicts a put. The call diagram assumes you pay $500 for a call option contract (i.e., 100 calls at $5 per call) that has a strike price of $50. The graph shows how the option payoff increases as the stock price rises. Observe that a call provides a zero payoff unless the price of the stock advances past the stated exercise price ($50). If the market price of the stock is below $50, no rational investor would exercise the option and pay $50 to buy the stock—it would be cheaper to simply buy it in the open market. Also, because it costs $500 to buy the call, the stock has to move up another 5 points (from $50 to $55) in order for you to recover the premium and thereby reach a breakeven point. Note, however, that even if the stock price is between $50 and $55, it's still best to exercise the option because doing so reduces the option holder's net loss. For example, if the stock price is $52, exercising the option generates a cash inflow of $200, which partially offsets the $500 option premium. For each dollar by which the stock price exceeds this breakeven point

FIGURE 13.2   The Valuation Properties of Put and Call Options

The payoff of a call or put depends on the price of the underlying common stock (or other financial asset). The cost of the option has been recovered when the option passes its breakeven point. After that, the profit potential of a call is unlimited, but the profit potential of a put is limited because the underlying stock price cannot go lower than $0.

($55), the call option's payoff goes up by $100. The potential profit from the call position is unlimited because there is no limit on how high the underlying stock price can go.

The value of a put is also derived from the price of the underlying stock, except that the put value goes up when the stock price goes down and vice versa. The put diagram in Figure 13.2 assumes you buy a put for $500 and obtain the right to sell the underlying stock at $50 a share. It shows that the payoff of the put is 0 unless the market price of the corresponding stock drops below the exercise price ($50) on the put. As the price of the stock continues to fall, the payoff of the put option increases. Again, note that because the put cost $500, you don't start making money on the investment until the price of the stock drops below the breakeven point of $45 a share. Beyond that point, the profit from the put is defined by the extent to which the price of the underlying stock continues to fall over the remaining life of the option.

Intrinsic Value

As we have seen, the payoff of a put or call depends ultimately on the exercise price stated on the option, as well as on the prevailing market price of the underlying common stock. More specifically, the intrinsic value of a call is determined according to the following simple formula:

Equation 13.1

$$\text{Intrinsic value of a call} = (\text{Stock price} - \text{Strike price}) \times 100$$
$$\text{or 0, whichever is greater}$$

In other words, the intrinsic value of a call is merely the difference between the stock's market price and the option's strike price. When the stock price is below the strike price, the intrinsic value is 0. As implied in Equation 13.1, a call has an intrinsic value whenever the market price of the underlying financial asset exceeds the strike price stipulated on the call. If a call option has a strike price of $50 and the underlying stock sells for $60, then the option's intrinsic value is $1,000.

A put, on the other hand, cannot be valued in the same way because puts and calls allow the holder to do different things. To find the intrinsic value of a put, we must change the order of the equation a bit:

Equation 13.2

$$\text{Intrinsic value of a put} = (\text{Strike price} - \text{Stock price}) \times 100$$
$$\text{or 0, whichever is greater}$$

In this case, a put has value so long as the market price of the underlying stock (or financial asset) is less than the strike price stipulated on the put.

In-the-Money/Out-of-the-Money When a call has a strike price that is less than the market price of the underlying common stock, it has a positive intrinsic value and is known as an **in-the-money** option. When the strike price of the call exceeds the market price of the stock, the call has no intrinsic value, in which case it is known as an **out-of-the-money** option. However, an out-of-the-money call option is not worthless as long as there is still time before it expires because there is a chance that the stock price will fall below the strike price. In other words, when a call is out-of-the-money, its intrinsic value is 0 but its market value is greater than 0. In such a case, we say that the option has no intrinsic value but it still has time value. In the special case when the strike price of the option and the market price of the stock are the same, we say that the call option is *at-the-money*.

As you might expect, the situation is reversed for put options: A put is in-the-money when its strike price is greater than the market price of the stock. It's considered out-of-the-money when the market price of the stock exceeds the strike price, and a put is at-the-money when the strike price equals the stock price. As with calls, an out-of-the-money put still has a positive market value as long as there is some time remaining before the expiration date.

Refer back to Figure 13.1 and you will notice that the quotation shown is for "at-the-money" options, but in fact all of the options shown are either in-the-money or out-of-the-money options. Since options are seldom ever exactly at-the-money, selecting quotations for at-the-money options generates quotes for options that are closest to at-the-money but are nonetheless either in-the-money (those highlighted in yellow) or out-of-the-money. On the day of the options quotation, Facebook's stock (the underlying asset) had a closing price of $21.01, so all call (put) options with a strike price less (greater) than $21.01 are shaded in yellow, indicating that they are in-the-money.

When firms grant stock options to their employees, they typically grant at-the-money options, meaning that the strike prices of the options are set equal to the price

ETHICS IN INVESTING

Extraordinarily Good Timing

In 1997 a finance professor conducting research on executive stock option grants discovered that firms awarding these grants seemed to display extraordinarily good timing, setting the exercise prices just before a large run-up in the stock price. Perhaps firms were withholding good news until after they awarded stock option grants, knowing that when they released the news, their stock prices would rise. A few years later, Erik Lie and Randall Heron solved the puzzle of executives' remarkable timing abilities. Some firms apparently backdated their option grants, using hindsight to set the exercise price on the one date in the prior several weeks when their stock price was at its lowest point. Backdating works like this. A firm announces on June 1 that it had granted its executives stock options on April 15, using the market price of the stock that day as the option's exercise price. In fact, the firm did not actually award the options on April 15 but rather chose that date several weeks later. That gave the firm the benefit of hindsight, meaning that the firm knew that the stock's lowest point in the preceding month or two had in fact been April 15. By the time the firm announced the option grant on June 1, the options were already in-the-money because the stock price was much higher than it had been on the retroactively set grant date. In backdating options, firms failed to disclose the true value of the option grants they awarded, which in turn affected their reported earnings and taxes.

By mid-2007, at least 257 firms had either launched their own internal investigations into options backdating or had been the subject of investigations by the Securities and Exchange Commission. Firms involved in options backdating scandals endured serious consequences. Some executives paid fines or went to prison. Other firms settled lawsuits without admitting wrongdoing, such as Broadcom, which paid $118 million to settle a shareholder lawsuit. Most of the firms investigated saw their stock prices decline by as much as 10%.

The opportunity for senior management to engage in meaningful options backdating was largely eliminated by the Sarbanes-Oxley Act, which requires companies to report option grants to senior management within 2 days. The passage of Sarbanes-Oxley in 2002 combined with the 5-year statute of limitations for securities fraud means that any additional criminal prosecution is unlikely.

(Source: Kenneth Carow, Randall Heron, Erik Lie, and Robert Neal, "Option Grant Backdating Investigations and Capital Market Discipline," *Journal of Corporate Finance*, Volume 15, Issue 5, December 2009, pages 562–572.)

of the underlying stock on the date of the option grant. However, as the accompanying Ethics in Investing box explains, many companies got into trouble for using a bit of hindsight (and failing to disclose that) when selecting their option grant dates. This practice came to be known as options backdating.

Time Value and Option Prices Put and call intrinsic values, as found according to Equations 13.1 and 13.2, denote what an option should be worth in the absence of any time value. In other words, these equations show what call and put options would be worth on their expiration dates. In fact, options rarely trade at their intrinsic values. Instead, they almost always trade at prices that exceed their intrinsic values, especially options that still have a long time to run. Thus, puts and calls nearly always have time value. In most cases, the more time there is before an option expires, the greater is its time value.

What Drives Option Prices?

Option prices can be reduced to 2 separate components. The first is the intrinsic value of the option, which is driven by the current market price of the underlying financial asset. As we saw in Equations 13.1 and 13.2, the greater the difference between the market price of the underlying asset and the strike price on the option, the greater the fundamental value of the call or put.

The second component of an option price is customarily referred to as the **time value**. It represents the amount by which an option's price exceeds its intrinsic value. Table 13.1 lists some quoted prices for an actively traded call option. These quoted prices (panel A) are then separated into intrinsic value (panel B) and time value (panel C). Note that 3 strike prices are used—$65, $70, and $75. Relative to the market price of the stock ($71.75), one strike price ($65) is well below market; this is an in-the-money call. One ($70) is fairly near the market. The third ($75) is well above the market; this is an out-of-the-money call. Note the considerable difference in the makeup of the option prices as we move from an in-the-money call to an out-of-the-money call.

Panel B in the table lists the intrinsic values of the call options, as determined by Equation 13.1. For example, note that although the March 65 call (the call with the March expiration date and $65 strike price) is trading at 7.75, its intrinsic value is only 6.75. The intrinsic value (of 6.75) represents, in effect, the extent to which the option is trading in-the-money. There is an important implication of the fact that this option trades at a price that exceeds its intrinsic value. An investor who owns this option and wants to cash out of the investment can do so by exercising the option or by selling it. Usually it is better to sell the option than to exercise it early because the option's price exceeds its intrinsic value. There are exceptions to the rule, but usually it is not wise to exercise options early. Instead, the best way to get cash out of an option investment is to sell the option.

Now look at the calls with the $75 strike price. None of these has any fundamental value; they're all out-of-the-money, and their prices are made up solely of time value. Basically, the value of these options is determined entirely by the belief that the price of the underlying stock could rise to over $75 a share before the options expire.

Panel C shows the amount of time value embedded in the call prices. This represents the difference between the quoted call price (panel A) and the call's intrinsic value (panel B). It shows that the price of just about every traded

> **INVESTOR MISTAKES**
>
> **Exercising Too Early**—Researchers have discovered that customers of discount brokers frequently make the mistake of exercising their options early rather than selling them, and they are particularly prone to this mistake when a stock hits a 52-week high. In contrast, professional options traders almost never make that mistake.

TABLE 13.1   OPTION PRICE COMPONENTS FOR AN ACTIVELY TRADED CALL OPTION

Price ($)	Strike Price ($)	Expiration Months		
		February	March	June
Panel A: Quoted Option Prices				
71.75	65	—	7.75	9.75
71.75	70	2.25	3.88	6.75
71.75	75	0.19	1.50	3.88
Panel B: Underlying Fundamental Values				
71.75	65	—	6.75	6.75
71.75	70	1.75	1.75	1.75
71.75	75	neg.	neg.	neg.
Panel C: Time Premiums				
71.75	65	—	1.00	3.00
71.75	70	0.50	2.12	5.00
71.75	75	0.19	1.50	3.88

Note: neg. indicates that options have negative fundamental values.

The Volatility Index

Because the volatility of the underlying asset plays a major role in option valuation, options traders track the volatility of individual stocks and of the market as a whole very closely. In fact, there is an index, called the VIX (which stands for volatility index), that provides an estimate of the volatility of the overall market. From about 1990 to 2007, the average volatility of the U.S. stock market as measured by VIX was close to 20% per year. But in the fall of 2008, after the failure of Lehman Brothers, the VIX index peaked at nearly 90%, more than four times its long-run average! Throughout the Great Recession the VIX index spiked several times to levels above its historical average. The VIX index fluctuated around its long-term average of 20 throughout most of 2012.

option contains at least some time value. Indeed, unless the options are about to expire, you would expect them to have at least some time value. Also, note that with all 3 strike prices, the longer the time to expiration, the greater the time value.

As you might expect, time to expiration is an important element in explaining the time value in panel C. Several other variables also have a bearing on the behavior of this premium. One is the price volatility of the underlying common stock. Other things being equal, the more volatile the stock is, the more it enhances the speculative appeal of the option—and therefore the bigger the time value. In addition, the time value is directly related to the level of interest rates. That is, the amount of time value embedded in a call option generally increases along with interest rates (and for puts, time value increases when interest rates fall).

For the most part, then, 4 major forces drive the price of an option. They are, in descending order of importance, (1) the price behavior of the underlying financial asset, (2) the amount of time remaining to expiration, (3) the amount of price volatility in the underlying financial asset, and (4) the general level of interest rates. Less important variables include the dividend yield on the underlying common stock, the trading volume of the option, and the exchanges on which the option is listed.

Option-Pricing Models Some fairly sophisticated option-pricing models have been developed, notably by Myron Scholes and the late Fisher Black, to value options. Many active options traders use these formulas to identify and trade over- and undervalued options. Not surprisingly, these models are based on the same variables we identified above. For example, the inputs used in the Black-Scholes option-pricing model are (1) the market price of the underlying stock, (2) the strike price of the option, (3) the time remaining before the option expires, (4) the risk-free rate of interest, and (5) the volatility of the underlying stock. The Black and Scholes option-pricing model prices a European call option using this equation:

Equation 13.3

Call price = (Stock price) × (Probability 1)
— (Present value of strike price) × (Probability 2)

To get probability 1 and probability 2, you need 2 more equations, plus a little help from Excel. The first equation looks like this:

Equation 13.3a

$$\text{Value 1} = \frac{\text{Natural log of}\left(\dfrac{\text{Stock price}}{\text{Strike price}}\right) + \left(\text{Risk-free rate} + \dfrac{(\text{Standard deviation})^2}{2}\right)(\text{Time to expiration})}{(\text{Standard deviation})\sqrt{\text{Time to expiration}}}$$

And the second equation is:

Equation 13.3b

$$\text{Value 2} = \text{Value 1} - (\text{Standard deviation}) \times \sqrt{\text{Time to expiration}}$$

Equations 13.3a and 13.3b calculate numerical values that must then be converted into probabilities using the standard normal distribution function. The normal distribution is simply the familiar bell curve, and the standard normal distribution is a bell curve with a mean of 0 and a standard deviation of 1. The probabilities we need in Equation 13.3 represent the likelihood of drawing a number less than or equal to Value 1 (and Value 2) from this distribution. Figure 13.3 provides a graphical illustration of the probability that we seek. Suppose we use Equation 13.3a and find that Value 1 equals 0.9. To obtain "probability 1" for Equation 13.3, we need to know the area under the curve in Figure 13.3 to the left of the value 0.9.

FIGURE 13.3

The Standard Normal Distribution

The standard normal distribution has a 0 mean and a standard deviation of 1. The shaded area to the left of Value 1 represents the probability of drawing a value at random from this distribution that is less than or equal to Value 1.

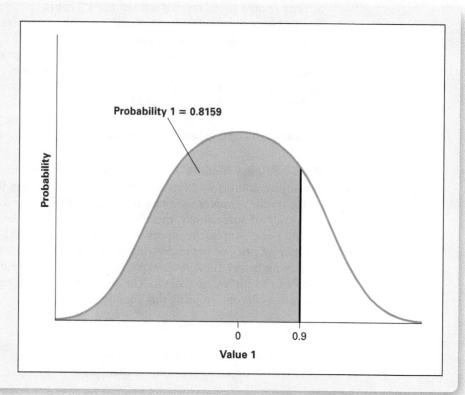

Probability 1 = 0.8159

Fortunately, Excel provides a useful function that makes it easy to calculate these standard normal probabilities. That function is denoted with = normsdist(0.9), and Excel reveals that the appropriate probability is 0.8159.

Now we are ready to price a call option using Black and Scholes.

Example

Suppose we want to price a call option that expires in 3 months (one-quarter of a year). The option has a strike price of $45, and the market price of the underlying stock is currently $44. The standard deviation of this stock's returns is about 50% per year, and the risk-free rate is 2%.

To price this option, start by solving for the quantities Value 1 and Value 2:

$$\text{Value 1} = \frac{\ln\left(\frac{44}{45}\right) + \left(0.02 + \frac{0.50^2}{2}\right)0.25}{0.50\sqrt{0.25}} = \frac{-0.0225 + (0.145)0.25}{0.25} = 0.0551$$

$$\text{Value 2} = 0.0551 - 0.50\sqrt{0.25} = -0.1949$$

Next, use Excel to find the standard normal probabilities attached to these values:

$$\text{Probability 1} = \text{normsdist}(0.0551) = 0.5220$$

$$\text{Probability 2} = \text{normsdist}(-0.1949) = 0.4227$$

Finally, plug the values for Probability 1 and Probability 2 into Equation 13.3 to obtain the call price:

$$\text{Call price} = \$44(0.5220) - [\$45 \div (1.02)^{0.25}](0.4227) = \$22.97 - \$18.93 = \$4.04$$

So, according to the Black-Scholes option-pricing model, the call should be priced at $4.04.

Trading Strategies

For the most part, investors can use stock options in 3 kinds of trading strategies: (1) buying puts and calls for speculation, (2) hedging with puts and calls, and (3) option writing and spreading.

Buying for Speculation Buying for speculation is the simplest and most straightforward use of puts and calls. Basically, it is like buying stock ("buy low, sell high") and, in fact, represents an alternative to investing in stock. For example, if you feel the market price of a particular stock is going to move up, you can capture that price appreciation by buying a call on the stock. In contrast, if you feel the stock is about to drop in price, a put could convert that price decline into a profitable situation. In essence, investors buy options rather than stock whenever the options are likely to yield a greater return. The principle here, of course, is to get the biggest return from your investment dollar. Puts and calls often meet this objective because of the added leverage they offer.

Furthermore, options offer valuable downside protection: The most you can lose is the cost of the option, which is always less than the cost of the underlying stock. Thus, by using options as a tool for speculation, you can put a cap on losses and still get almost as much profit potential as with the underlying stock.

Speculating with Calls To illustrate the essentials of speculating with options, imagine that you own a stock that you feel will move up in price over the next 6 months. What would happen if you were to buy a call on this stock rather than investing directly in the stock? To find out, let's see what the numbers show. The price of the stock is now $49, and you anticipate that within 6 months it will rise to about $65. You need to determine the expected return associated with each of your investment alternatives. Because (most) options have relatively short lives, and because we're dealing with an investment horizon of only 6 months, we can use holding period return to measure yield. Thus, if your expectations about the stock are correct, it should go up by $16 a share and will provide you with a 33% holding period return: ($65 − $49) ÷ $49 = $16 ÷ $49 = 0.33.

But there are also some listed options available on this stock. Let's see how they would do. For illustrative purposes, we will use two 6-month calls that carry a $40 and a $50 strike price, respectively. Table 13.2 compares the behavior of these 2 calls with the behavior of the underlying common stock. Clearly, from a holding period return perspective, either call option represents a superior investment to buying the stock itself. The dollar amount of profit may be a bit more with the stock, but note that the size of the required investment ($4,900) is a lot more too, so that alternative has the lowest HPR.

Observe that one of the calls is an in-the-money option (the one with the $40 strike price). The other is out-of-the-money. The difference in returns generated by these calls is rather typical. That is, investors are usually able to generate much better rates of return with lower-priced (out-of-the-money) options, but of course there is a greater risk that these options will expire worthless. A major drawback of out-of-the-money options is that their price is made up solely of investment premium—a sunk cost that will be lost if the stock does not move in price.

TABLE 13.2 **SPECULATING WITH CALL OPTIONS**		EXCEL with Spreadsheets	
		Six-Month Call Options on the Stock	
	100 Shares of Underlying Common Stock	$40 Strike Price	$50 Strike Price
Today			
Market value of stock (at $49/share)	$4,900		
Market price of calls*		$1,100	$ 400
Six Months Later			
Expected value of stock (at $65/share)	$6,500		
Expected price of calls*		$2,500	$1,500
Profit	$1,600	$1,400	$1,100
Holding Period Return**	33%	127%	275%

*The price of the calls was computed according to Equation 13.1. It includes some investment premium in the purchase price but none in the expected sales price.

**Holding period return (HPR) = (Ending price of the stock or option – Beginning price of the stock or option) ÷ Beginning price of the stock or option.

Speculating with Puts To see how you can speculate in puts, consider the following situation. You're looking at a stock that's now priced at $51, but you anticipate a drop in price to about $35 per share within the next 6 months. If that occurs, you could sell the stock short and make a profit of $16 per share.

Alternatively, you can purchase an out-of-the-money put (with a strike price of $50) for, say, $300. Again, if the price of the underlying stock drops, you will make money with the put. The profit and rate of return on the put are summarized below, along with the comparative returns from short selling the stock. Once again, in terms of holding period return, the stock option is the superior investment vehicle by a wide margin.

Comparative Performance Given Price of Stock Moves from $51 to $35/Share over a 6-Month Period:	Buy 1 Put ($50 strike price)	Short Sell 100 Shares of Stock
Purchase price (today)	$ 300	
Selling price (6 months later)	1,500*	
Short sell (today)		$5,100
Cover (6 months later)		3,500
Profit	$1,200	$1,600
Holding period return	400%	63%**

*The price of the put was computed according to Equation 13.2 and does not include any investment premium.
**Assumes the short sale was made with a required margin deposit of 50%.

Of course, not all option investments perform as well as the ones in our examples. Success with this strategy rests on picking the right underlying common stock. Thus, security analysis and proper stock selection are critical dimensions of this technique. It is a highly risky investment strategy, but it may be well suited for the more speculatively inclined investor.

Hedging: Modifying Risks
A **hedge** is simply a combination of 2 or more securities into a single investment position for the purpose of reducing risk. Let's say you hold a stock and want to reduce the amount of downside risk in this investment. You can do that by setting up a hedge. In essence, you're using the hedge as a way to modify your exposure to risk. To be more specific, you're trying to change not only the chance of loss but also the amount lost if the worst does occur. A simple hedge might involve nothing more than buying stock and simultaneously buying a put on that same stock. Or it might consist of selling some stock short and then buying a call. There are many types of hedges, some of which are very simple and others very sophisticated. Investors use them for one basic reason: to earn or protect a profit without exposing the investor to excessive loss.

An options hedge may be appropriate if you have generated a profit from an earlier common stock investment and wish to protect that profit. Or it may be appropriate if you are about to enter into a common stock investment and wish to protect your money by limiting potential capital loss. If you hold a stock that has gone up in price, the purchase of a put would provide the type of downside protection you need; the purchase of a call, in contrast, would provide protection to a short seller of common stock. Thus, option hedging always involves 2 transactions: (1) the initial common stock position (long or short) and (2) the simultaneous or subsequent purchase of the option.

Protective Puts: Limiting Capital Loss Let's examine a simple option hedge in which you use a put to limit your exposure to capital loss. Assume that you want to buy 100 shares of stock. Being a bit apprehensive about the stock's outlook, you decide to use an option hedge to protect your capital against loss. Therefore, you simultaneously (1) buy the stock and (2) buy a put on the stock (which fully covers the 100 shares owned). This type of hedge is known as a *protective put*. Preferably, the put would be a low-priced option with a strike price at or near the current market price of the stock. Suppose you purchase 100 shares of the common stock at $25 a share and pay $150 for a put with a $25 strike price. Now, no matter what happens to the price of the stock over the life of the put, you can lose no more than $150. At the same time, there's no limit on the gains. If the stock does not move, you will be out the cost of a put. If it drops in price, then whatever is lost on the stock will be made up with the put. The bottom line? The most you can lose is the cost of the put ($150, in this case). However, if the price of the stock goes up (as hoped), the put becomes worthless, and you will earn the capital gains on the stock (less the cost of the put, of course).

Table 13.3 shows the essentials of this option hedge. The $150 paid for the put is sunk cost. That's lost no matter what happens to the price of the stock. In effect, it is the price paid for the insurance this hedge offers. Moreover, this hedge is good only for the life of the put. When this put expires, you will have to replace it with another put or forget about hedging your capital.

Protective Puts: Protecting Profits The other basic use of an option hedge involves entering into the options position after a profit has been made on the underlying stock. This could be done because of investment uncertainty or for tax purposes (to carry over a profit to the next taxable year). For example, if you bought 100 shares of a stock at $35 and it moved to $75, there would be a profit of $40 per share to protect. You could protect the profit with an option hedge by buying a put. Assume you buy a 3-month put with a $75 strike price at a cost of $250. Now, regardless of what happens to the price of the stock over the life of the put, you are guaranteed a minimum profit of $3,750 (the $4,000 profit in the stock made so far, less the $250 cost of the put).

			EXCEL with Spreadsheets

TABLE 13.3	**LIMITING CAPITAL LOSS WITH A PUT HEDGE**		
		Stock	Put*
Today			
Purchase price of the stock		$25	
Purchase price of the put			$ 1.50
Sometime Later			
A. Price of common goes up to:		$50	
Value of put**			$ 0
Profit:			
100 shares of stock ($50 – $25)	$2,500		
Less: Cost of put	–150		
	Profit: $2,350		
B. Price of common goes down to:		$10	
Value of put**			$15
Profit:			
100 shares of stock (loss: $10 – $25)	–$1,500		
Value of put (profit)	1,500		
Less: Cost of put	–150		
	Loss: $ 150		

*The put is purchased simultaneously and carries a strike price of $25.
**See Equation 13.2.

This can be seen in Table 13.4. Note that if the price of the stock should fall, the worst that can happen is a guaranteed minimum profit of $3,750. Plus, there is still no limit on how much profit can be made. As long as the stock continues to go up, you will reap the benefits.

But watch out: The cost of this kind of insurance can become very expensive just when it's needed the most—that is, when market prices are falling. Under such circumstances, it's not uncommon to find put options trading at price premiums of 20% to 30%, or more, above their prevailing intrinsic values. Essentially, that means the price of the stock position you're trying to protect has to fall 20% to 30% before the protection even starts to kick in. Clearly, as long as high option price premiums prevail, the hedging strategies described above are a lot less attractive. They still may prove to be helpful, but only for very wide swings in value—and for those that occur over fairly short periods of time, as defined by the life of the put option.

One final point: Although the preceding discussion pertained to put hedges, call hedges can also be set up to limit the loss or protect a profit on a short sale. For example, when selling a stock short, you can purchase a call to protect yourself against a rise in the price of the stock—with the same basic results as outlined above.

Enhancing Returns: Options Writing and Spreading The advent of listed options has led to many intriguing options-trading strategies. Yet, despite the appeal of these techniques, there is one important point that all the experts agree on: Such specialized trading strategies should be left to experienced investors who fully understand their subtleties. Our goal at this point is not to master these specialized strategies but to

TABLE 13.4 PROTECTING PROFITS WITH A PUT HEDGE		Stock	Three-Month Put with a $75 Strike Price
Purchase price of the stock		$ 35	
Today			
Market price of the stock		$ 75	
Market price of the put			$2.50
Three Months Later			
A. Price of common goes up to:		$100	
Value of put*			$ 0
Profit:			
100 shares of stock ($100 – $35)	$6,500		
Less: Cost of put	–250		
	Profit: $6,250		
B. Price of common goes down to:		$ 50	
Value of put*			$ 25
Profit:			
100 shares of stock ($50 – $35)	$1,500		
Value of put (profit)	2,500		
Less: Cost of put	–250		
	Profit: $3,750		

*See Equation 13.2.

explain in general terms what they are and how they operate. We will look at 2 types of specialized options strategies here: (1) writing options and (2) spreading options.

Writing Options Generally, investors write options because they believe the price of the underlying stock is going to move in their favor. That is, it is not going to rise as much as the buyer of a call expects, nor will it fall as much as the buyer of a put hopes. And more often than not, the option writer is right: He or she makes money far more often than the buyer of the put or call. Such favorable odds explain, in part, the underlying economic motivation for writing put and call options. Option writing represents an investment transaction to the writers: They receive the full option premium (less normal transaction costs) in exchange for agreeing to live up to the terms of the option.

Naked Options Investors can write options in 2 ways. One is to write **naked options**, which involves writing options on stock not owned by the writer. You simply write the put or call, collect the option premium, and hope the price of the underlying stock does not move against you. If successful, naked writing can be highly profitable because it requires essentially no capital up front. Remember, though, the amount of return to the writer is always limited to the amount of option premium received. On the other hand, there is really no limit to loss exposure. That's the catch: The price of the underlying stock can rise or fall by just about any amount over the life of the option and, thus, can deal a real blow to the writer of a naked put or call.

Covered Options The amount of risk exposure is a lot less for those who write **covered options**. That's because these options are written against stocks the investor (writer) already owns or has a position in. For example, you could write a call against stock you own or write a put against stock you have short sold. You thus can use the long or short position to meet the terms of the option. Such a strategy is a fairly conservative way to generate attractive rates of return. The object is to write a slightly out-of-the-money option, pocket the option premium, and hope the price of the underlying stock will move up or down to (but not exceed) the option's strike price. In effect, you are adding an option premium to the other usual sources of return (dividends and/or capital gains). But there's more: While the option premium adds to the return, it also reduces risk. It can cushion a loss if the price of the stock moves against the investor.

There is a hitch to all this, of course: The amount of return the covered option investor can realize is limited. Once the price of the underlying common stock exceeds the strike price on the option, the option becomes valuable. When that happens, you start to lose money on the options. From this point on, for every dollar you make on the stock position, you lose an equal amount on the option position. That's a major risk of writing covered call options—if the price of the underlying stock takes off, you'll miss out on the added profits.

To illustrate the ins and outs of covered call writing, let's assume you own 100 shares of PFP, Inc., an actively traded, high-yielding common stock. The stock is currently trading at $73.50 and pays quarterly dividends of $1 a share. You decide to write a 3-month call on PFP, giving the buyer the right to take the stock off your hands at $80 a share. Such options are trading in the market at 2.50, so you receive $250 for writing the call. You fully intend to hold on to the stock, so you'd like to see the price of PFP stock rise to no more than 80 by the expiration date on the call. If that happens, the call option will expire worthless. As a result, not only will you earn the dividends and capital gains on the stock, but you also get to pocket the $250 you received when you wrote the call. Basically, you've just added $250 to the quarterly return on your stock.

TABLE 13.5   COVERED CALL WRITING

EXCEL
with Spreadsheets

	Stock	Three-Month Put with a $75 Strike Price
Current market price of the stock	$73.50	
Current market price of the call		$2.50
Three Months Later		
A. Price of the stock is unchanged:	**$73.50**	
Value of the call*		$0
Profit:		
Quarterly dividends received $ 100		
Proceeds from sale of call 250		
Total profit: $ 350		
B. Price of the stock goes up to:	**$80**	Price Where Maximum Profit Occurs
Value of the call*		$0
Profit:		
Quarterly dividends received $ 100		
Proceeds from sale of call 250		
Capital gains on stock ($80 − $73.50) 650		
Total profit: $1,000		
C. Price of the stock goes up to:	**$90**	
Value of the call*		$10
Profit:		
Quarterly dividends received $ 100		
Proceeds from sale of call 250		
Capital gains on stock ($90 − $73.50) 1,650		
Less: Loss on call (1,000)		
Net profit: $1,000		
D. Price of the stock drops to:	**$71**	Breakeven Price
Value of the call*		$0
Profit:		
Capital loss on stock ($71 − $73.50) ($ 250)		
Proceeds from sale of call 250		
Quarterly dividends 100	$ 0 profit or loss	
Net profit: $ 100		

*See Equation 13.1.

Table 13.5 summarizes the profit and loss characteristics of this covered call position. Note that the maximum profit on this transaction occurs when the market price of the stock equals the strike price on the call. If the price of the stock keeps going up, you miss out on the added profits. Even so, the $1,000 profit you earn at a stock price of $80 or above translates into a (3-month) holding period return of 13.6% ($1,000 ÷ $7,350). That represents an annualized return of nearly 55%! With this kind of return potential, it's not difficult to see why covered call writing is so popular. Moreover, as situation D in the table illustrates, covered call writing adds a little cushion to losses: The price of the stock has to drop more than $2\frac{1}{2}$ points (which is what you received when you wrote/sold the call) before you start losing money.

Besides covered calls and protective puts, there are many ways to combine options with other types of securities to achieve a given investment objective. Probably none is more unusual than the creation of so-called synthetic securities. A case in point: Say you want to buy a convertible bond on a certain company but that company doesn't have any convertibles outstanding. You can create your own customized convertible by combining a straight (nonconvertible) bond with a listed call option on your targeted company.

Spreading Options Option **spreading** is nothing more than the combination of 2 or more options into a single transaction. You could create an option spread, for example, by simultaneously buying and writing options on the same underlying stock. These would not be identical options; they would differ with respect to strike price and/or expiration date. Spreads are a very popular use of listed options, and they account for a substantial amount of the trading activity on the listed options exchanges. These spreads go by a variety of exotic names, such as *bull spreads, bear spreads, money spreads, vertical spreads,* and *butterfly spreads.* Each spread is different and each is constructed to meet a certain type of investment goal.

Consider, for example, a *vertical spread.* It would be set up by buying a call at one strike price and then writing a call (on the same stock and for the same expiration date) at a higher strike price. For instance, you could buy a February call on XYZ at a strike price of, say, $30 and simultaneously sell (write) a February call on XYZ at a strike price of $35. Strange as it may sound, such a position would generate a hefty return if the price of the underlying stock went up by just a few points. Other spreads are used to profit from a falling market. Still others try to make money when the price of the underlying stock moves either up or down.

Whatever the objective, most spreads are created to take advantage of differences in prevailing option prices. The payoff from spreading is usually substantial, but so is the risk. In fact, some spreads that seem to involve almost no risk may end up with devastating results if the market and the difference between option premiums move against the investor.

Option Straddles A variation on this theme involves an **option straddle**. This is the simultaneous purchase (or sale) of both a put and a call on the same underlying common stock. Unlike spreads, straddles normally involve the same strike price and expiration date. Here, the object is to earn a profit from either a big or a small swing in the price of the underlying common stock.

How Do Straddles Work?

For example, in a *long straddle,* you buy an equal number of puts and calls. You make money in a long straddle when the underlying stock undergoes a big change in price—either up or down. If the price of the stock shoots way up, you make money on the call side of the straddle but are out the cost of the puts. If the price of the stock plummets, you make money on the puts, but the calls are useless. In either case, so long as you make more money on one side than the cost of the options for the other side, you're ahead of the game.

In a similar fashion, in a *short straddle,* you sell/write an equal number of puts and calls. You make money in this position when the price of the underlying stock goes nowhere. In effect, you get to keep all or most of the option premiums you collected when you wrote the options.

Except for obvious structural differences, the principles that underlie the creation of straddles are much like those for spreads. The object is to combine options that will enable you to capture the benefits of certain types of stock price behavior. But keep in mind that if the prices of the underlying stock and/or the option premiums do not behave in the anticipated manner, you lose. Spreads and straddles are extremely tricky and should be used only by knowledgeable investors.

CONCEPTS IN REVIEW

Answers available at www.pearsonhighered.com/smart

13.7 Briefly explain how you would make money on (a) a call option and (b) a put option. Do you have to exercise the option to capture the profit?

13.8 How do you find the intrinsic (fundamental) value of a call? Of a put? Does an out-of-the-money option have intrinsic value?

13.9 Name at least 4 variables that affect the price behavior of listed options, and briefly explain how each affects prices. How important are fundamental (intrinsic) value and time value to in-the-money options? To out-of-the-money options?

13.10 Describe at least 3 ways in which investors can use stock options.

13.11 What's the most that can be made from writing calls? Why would an investor want to write covered calls? Explain how you can reduce the risk on an underlying common stock by writing covered calls.

Stock-Index and Other Types of Options

LG6 Imagine being able to buy or sell a major stock market index like the S&P 500—and at a reasonable cost. Think of what you could do: If you felt the market was heading up, you could invest in a security that tracks the price behavior of the S&P 500 Index and make money when the market goes up. No longer would you have to go through the process of selecting specific stocks that you hope will capture the market's performance. Rather, you could play the market as a whole. That's exactly what you can do with stock-index options—puts and calls that are written on major stock market indexes. Index options have been around since 1983 and have become immensely popular with both individual and institutional investors. Here we will take a closer look at these popular and often highly profitable investments.

Stock-Index Options: Contract Provisions

Basically, a **stock-index option** is a put or call written on a specific stock market index. The underlying security in this case is the specific market index. Thus, when the market index moves in one direction or another, the value of the index option moves accordingly. Because there are no stocks or other financial assets backing these options, settlement is defined in terms of cash. Specifically, the cash value of an index option is equal to 100 times the published market index that underlies the option. For example, if the S&P 500 is at 1,400, then the value of an S&P 500 Index option will be $100 × 1,400 = $140,000. If the underlying index moves up or down in the market, so will the cash value of the option. (*Note:* Options on exchange-traded funds are very similar to index options and will be discussed below. For now, our attention will focus solely on index options.)

Today put and call options are available on more than 100 stock indexes. These include options on just about every major U.S. stock market index or average (such as the Dow Jones Industrial Average, the S&P 500, the Russell 2000, and the Nasdaq 100), options on a handful of foreign markets (e.g., China, Mexico, Japan, Hong Kong, and the Europe sector), and options on different segments of the market (pharmaceuticals, oil services, semiconductors, bank, and utility indexes). In 2011 about 8% of traded option contracts (or 338 million contracts) were index options, and a majority of these contracts were on 5 of the leading stock indexes:

- S&P 500 Index (SPX)

- Russell 2000 Index (RUT)

- Nasdaq 100 Index (NDX)
- S&P 100 Index (OEX)
- Dow Jones Industrial Average (DJX)

The S&P 500 Index captures the market behavior of large-cap stocks. The Russell 2000 Index measures the performance of the small-cap stocks in the United States. The Nasdaq 100 Index tracks the behavior of the 100 largest nonfinancial stocks listed on Nasdaq and is composed of mostly large, high-tech companies (such as Intel and Cisco). The S&P 100 Index is another large-cap index composed of 100 stocks, drawn from the S&P 500, that have actively traded stock options. Another popular index is the DJIA Index, which measures the blue-chip segment of the market and is one of the most actively traded index options. Options on the S&P 500 are, by far, the most popular instruments. Indeed, there's more trading in SPX options contracts than in all the other index options combined. Among the options exchanges that currently deal in index options, the CBOE dominates the market, accounting for more than 94% of the trades in 2011.

Both puts and calls are available on index options. They are valued and have issue characteristics like any other put or call. That is, a put lets a holder profit from a drop in the market. (When the underlying market index goes down, the value of a put goes up.) A call enables the holder to profit from a market that's going up. Also, as Figure 13.4 shows, index options have a quotation system that is the same as for stock options, except for the fact that the strike is an index level.

Putting a Value on Stock-Index Options   As is true of equity options, the market price of index options is a function of the difference between the strike price on the option

FIGURE 13.4   Quotations on Index Options

The quotation system used with index options is just like that used with stock options: strikes and expiration dates are shown along with option prices and volumes. The biggest differences are that the option strikes and closing values for the underlying asset are shown as index levels. The closing S&P 100 Index level on the day of this quotation was 646.22. (Source: quotemedia.com, accessed August 8, 2012.)

Option Chain | Most Actives | Greeks

FB Options: [Composite ▾] [All ▾] [At the Money ▾] Type: [All ▾] [GO] Symbol Lookup Help

Aug 12 | **Sep 12** | Oct 12 | All

Option Chain for S&P 100 (OEX)

Calls	Last	Chg	Bid	Ask	Vol	Open Int	Root	Strike	Puts	Last	Chg	Bid	Ask	Vol	Open Int
Oct 20, 2012	40.40		48.50	51.00	0	150	OEX	600.00	Oct 20, 2012	5.75	-1.15	4.50	5.90	195	654
Oct 20, 2012	30.10		31.60	34.20	0	225	OEX	620.00	Oct 20, 2012	9.50	-1.70	7.90	9.60	2	421
Oct 20, 2012	19.00		17.70	19.60	0	84	OEX	640.00	Oct 20, 2012	17.10	1.10	13.90	15.90	2	317
Oct 20, 2012	8.83		7.30	8.90	0	126	OEX	680.00	Oct 20, 2012	25.00	-3.00	23.50	26.10	4	2
Oct 20, 2012	2.00	-0.15	2.15	2.70	10	937	OEX	680.00	Oct 20, 2012	84.10		38.00	40.80	0	0
Oct 20, 2012	0.70		0.45	0.75	0	489	OEX	700.00	Oct 20, 2012	90.10		56.20	58.90	0	0

(stated in terms of the underlying index) and the latest published stock market index. To illustrate, consider the highly popular S&P 100 Index traded on the CBOE.

Example

Let's say the S&P 100 Index recently closed at 587.25 and the June call has a strike price of 575. A stock-index call will have a positive value so long as the underlying index exceeds the index strike price (just the opposite for puts). The intrinsic value of this call is: 587.25 − 575.00 = 12.25.

Suppose that the call actually trades at 14.90, 2.65 points above the call's intrinsic value. This difference is the option's time value.

If the S&P 100 Index in our example (above) were to go up to, say, 600 by late June (the expiration date of the call), this option would be quoted at: 600 − 575 = 25. Because index options (like stock options) are valued in multiples of $100, this contract would be worth $2,500. Thus, if you had purchased this option when it was trading at $14.90, it would have cost you $1,490 ($14.90 × $100) and, in less than a month, would have generated a profit of: $2,500 − $1,490 = $1,010. That translates into a holding period return of a whopping 67.8% ($1,010 ÷ $1,490).

Full Value versus Fractional Value Most broad-based index options use the full market value of the underlying index for purposes of options trading and valuation. That's not the case, however, with two of the Dow Jones measures: The option on the Dow Jones Industrial Average is based on 1% (1 ÷ 100) of the actual Industrial Average, and the Dow Transportation Average option is based on 10% (1 ÷ 10) of the actual average. For example, if the DJIA is at 11,260, the index option would be valued at 1% of that amount, or 112.60. Thus, the cash value of this option is not $100 times the underlying DJIA but $100 times 1% of the DJIA, which equals the Dow Jones Industrial Average itself: $100 × 112.60 = $11,260.

Fortunately, the option strike prices are also based on the same 1% of the Dow, so there is no effect on option valuation: What matters is the difference between the strike price on the option and (1% of) the DJIA. For instance, note in Figure 13.4 that the DJIA option index closed at 96.05 (at the time, the actual Dow was at 9,605). Note also that there was a September call option available on this index with a strike price of $83—it was trading at 13.15 (or $1,315). Using Equation 13.1, you can see that this in-the-money option had an intrinsic value of 96.05 − 83 = 13.05. The difference between the option's market value (13.15) and its intrinsic value (13.05) is, of course, the time value. In this case, the time value is very low because the expiration date is not far away.

Another type of option that is traded at 10% (1 ÷ 10) of the value of the underlying index is the "mini" index option. For example, the Mini-NDX Index (MNX) is set at 10% of the value of the Nasdaq 100. "Minis" also exist for the Nasdaq composite, the S&P 500, the Russell 2000, and the FTSE 250 (an index of mid-cap stocks in the UK), among others.

Investment Uses

Although index options, like equity options, can be used in spreads, straddles, or even covered calls, they are perhaps used most often for speculating or for hedging. When used as a speculative investment, index options give investors an opportunity to play the market as a whole, with a relatively small amount of capital. Like any other put or call, index options provide attractive leverage opportunities and at the same time limit exposure to loss to the price paid for the option.

Index Options as Hedging Vehicles Index options are equally effective as hedging vehicles. In fact, hedging is a major use of index options and accounts for a good deal of the trading in these securities. To see how these options can be used for hedging, assume that you hold a diversified portfolio of, say, a dozen different stocks and you think the market is heading down. One way to protect your capital would be to sell all of your stocks. However, that could be expensive, especially if you plan to get back into the market after it drops, and it could lead to a good deal of unnecessary taxes. Fortunately, there is a way to "have your cake and eat it too," and that is to hedge your stock port-folio with a stock index put. In this way, if the market does go down, you'll make money on your puts, which you then can use to buy more stocks at the lower prices. On the other hand, if the market continues to go up, you'll be out only the cost of the puts. That amount could well be recovered from the increased value of your stock holdings. The principles of hedging with stock-index options are exactly the same as those for hedging with equity options. The only difference is that with stock-index options, you're trying to protect a whole portfolio of stocks rather than individual stocks.

Like hedging with individual equity options, the cost of protecting your portfolio with index options can become very expensive (with price premiums of 20% to 30%, or more) when markets are falling and the need for this type of portfolio insurance is the greatest. That, of course, will have an impact on the effectiveness of this strategy.

Also, the amount of profit you make or the protection you obtain depends in large part on how closely the behavior of your stock portfolio is matched by the behavior of the stock-index option you employ. There is no guarantee that the two will behave in the same way. You should therefore select an index option that closely reflects the nature of the stocks in your portfolio. If, for example, you hold a number of small-cap stocks, you might select something like the Russell 2000 index option as the hedging vehicle. If you hold mostly blue chips, you might choose the DJIA index option. You probably can't get dollar-for-dollar portfolio protection, but you should try to get as close a match as possible.

A Word of Caution Given their effectiveness for either speculating or hedging, it's little wonder that index options have become popular with investors. But a word of caution is in order: Although trading index options appears simple and seems to provide high rates of return, these investments involve high risk and are subject to considerable price vola-tility. They should not be used by amateurs. True, there's only so much you can lose with these options. The trouble is that it's very easy to lose that amount. These securities are not investments you can buy and then forget about until just before they expire. With the wide market swings that are so common today, you must monitor these securities daily.

Other Types of Options

Options on stocks and stock indexes account for most of the market activity in listed options. But you also can obtain put and call options on various other securities. Let's now take a brief look at these other kinds of options, starting with options on ETFs.

Options on Exchange-Traded Funds In addition to various market indexes, put and call options are also available on over 225 exchange-traded funds (ETFs). ETFs are like mutual funds that have been structured to track the performance of a wide range of market indexes—in other words, ETFs are a type of index fund. They trade like shares of common stock on listed exchanges, primarily the Amex, and cover everything from broad market measures, such as the DJIA, the S&P 500, and the Nasdaq 100, to market sectors like energy, financials, health care, and semiconductors.

There's a good deal of overlap in the markets and market segments covered by index options and ETF options. In addition to their similar market coverage, they perform very much the same in the market, are valued the same, and are used for many of the same reasons (particularly for speculation and hedging). After all, an ETF option is written on an underlying index fund (for example, one that tracks the S&P 500) just like an index option is written on the same underlying market index (the S&P 500). Both do pretty much the same thing—either directly or indirectly track the performance of a market measure—so of course they should behave in the same way. The only real difference is this: Options on ETFs are operationally like stock options in that each option covers 100 shares of the underlying exchange-traded fund rather than $100 of the underlying market index, as is the case with index options. In the end, though, both trade at 100 times the underlying index (or ETF). Thus, while operationally ETF options may be closer to stock options, they function more like index options. As such, the market views them as viable alternatives to index options. These contracts have definitely caught the fancy of investors, especially those who track the major market indexes.

Interest Rate Options Puts and calls on fixed-income (debt) securities are known as **interest rate options**. At the present time, interest rate options are written only on U.S. Treasury securities. Four maturities are used: 30-year T-bonds, 10-year and 5-year T-notes, and short-term (13-week) T-bills. These options are yield-based rather than price-based. This means they track the yield behavior (rather than the price behavior) of the underlying Treasury security. Other types of options (equity and index options) are set up so that they react to movements in the price (or value) of the underlying asset. Interest rate options, in contrast, are set up to react to the yield of the underlying Treasury security. Thus, when yields rise, the value of a call goes up. When yields fall, puts go up in value. In effect, because bond prices and yields move in opposite directions, the value of an interest rate call option goes up at the very time that the price (or value) of the underlying debt security is going down. (The opposite is true for puts.) This unusual characteristic may explain why the market for interest rate options remains very small. Most professional investors simply don't care for interest rate options. Instead, they prefer to use interest rate futures contracts or options on these futures contracts.

Currency Options Foreign exchange options, or **currency options** as they're more commonly called, provide a way for investors to speculate on foreign exchange rates or to hedge foreign currency or foreign security holdings. Currency options are available on the currencies of most of the countries with which the United States has strong trading ties. These options are traded on the Philadelphia Exchange and include the following currencies:

- British pound
- Swiss franc
- Australian dollar
- Canadian dollar
- Japanese yen
- Euro

Puts and calls on foreign currencies give the holders the right to sell or buy large amounts of the specified currency. However, in contrast to the standardized contracts used with stock and stock-index options, the specific unit of trading in this market

TABLE 13.6	FOREIGN CURRENCY OPTION CONTRACTS ON THE PHILADELPHIA EXCHANGE		
Underlying Currency*	Size of Contracts	Underlying Currency*	Size of Contracts
British pound	10,000 pounds	Canadian dollar	10,000 dollars
Swiss franc	10,000 francs	Japanese yen	1,000,000 yen
Euro	10,000 euros	Australian dollar	10,000 dollars

*The British pound, Swiss franc, euro, Canadian dollar, and Australian dollar are all quoted in full cents. The Japanese yen is quoted in hundredths of a cent.

varies with the particular underlying currency. Table 13.6 spells out the details. Currency options are traded in full or fractional cents per unit of the underlying currency, relative to the amount of foreign currency involved. Thus, if a put or call on the British pound were quoted at, say, 6.40 (which is read as "6.4 cents"), it would be valued at $2,000, because 10,000 British pounds underlie this option (that is, $10,000 \times 0.064 = \$640$).

The value of a currency option is linked to the exchange rate between the U.S. dollar and the underlying foreign currency. For example, if the Canadian dollar becomes stronger relative to the U.S. dollar, causing the exchange rate to go up, the price of a call option on the Canadian dollar will increase, and the price of a put will decline. (*Note:* Some cross-currency options are available in the market, but such options/trading techniques are beyond the scope of this text. Here, we will focus solely on foreign currency options (or futures) linked to U.S. dollars.)

The strike price on a currency option is stated in terms of exchange rates. Thus, a strike price of 150 implies that each unit of the foreign currency (such as one British pound) is worth 150 cents, or $1.50, in U.S. money. If you held a 150 call on this foreign currency, you would make money if the foreign currency strengthened relative to the U.S. dollar so that the exchange rate rose—say, to 155. In contrast, if you held a 150 put, you would profit from a decline in the exchange rate—say, to 145. Success in forecasting movements in foreign exchange rates is obviously essential to a profitable foreign currency options program.

LEAPS They look like regular puts and calls, and they behave pretty much like regular puts and calls, but they're not regular puts and calls. We're talking about **LEAPS**, which are puts and calls with lengthy expiration dates. Basically, LEAPS are long-term options. Whereas standard options have maturities of 8 months or less, LEAPS have expiration dates as long as 3 years. Known formally as *Long-term Equity AnticiPation Securities*, they are listed on all of the major options exchanges. LEAPS are available on hundreds of stocks, stock indexes, and ETFs.

Aside from their time frame, LEAPS work like any other equity or index option. For example, a single (equity) LEAPS contract gives the holder the right to buy or sell 100 shares of stock at a predetermined price on or before the specified expiration date. LEAPS give you more time to be right about your bets on the direction of a stock or stock index, and they give hedgers more time to protect their positions. But there's a price for this extra time: You can expect to pay a lot more for a LEAPS than you would for a regular (short-term) option. That should come as no surprise. LEAPS, being nothing more than long-term options, are loaded with time value. And as we saw earlier in this chapter, other things being equal, *the more time an option has to expiration, the higher the quoted price.*

CONCEPTS IN REVIEW		
Answers available at www.pearsonhighered.com/smart	**13.12**	Briefly describe the differences and similarities between stock-index options and stock options. Do the same for foreign currency options and stock options.
	13.13	Identify and briefly discuss 2 ways to use stock-index options. Do the same for foreign currency options.
	13.14	Why would an investor want to use index options to hedge a portfolio of common stock? Could the same objective be obtained using options on ETFs? If the investor thinks the market is in for a fall, why not just sell the stock?
	13.15	What are LEAPS? Why would an investor want to use a LEAPS option rather than a regular listed option?

MyFinanceLab

Here is what you should know after reading this chapter. MyFinanceLab will help you identify what you know and where to go when you need to practice.

What You Should Know	Key Terms	Where to Practice
LG1 Discuss the basic nature of options in general and puts and calls in particular and understand how these investments work. An option gives the holder the right to buy or sell a certain amount of some real or financial asset at a set price for a set period of time. Puts and calls are the most widely used types of options. These derivative securities offer considerable leverage potential. A put enables the holder to sell a certain amount of a specified security at a specified price over a specified time period. A call gives the holder the right to buy the security at a specified price over a specified period of time.	call, *p. 447* derivative securities, *p. 448* leverage, *p. 448* option, *p. 447* option premium, *p. 448* option writer (or seller), *p. 448* put, *p. 447*	MyFinanceLab Study Plan 13.1
LG2 Describe the options market and note key options provisions, including strike prices and expiration dates. The options market is made up of conventional (OTC) options and listed options. OTC options are used predominantly by institutional investors. Listed options are traded on organized exchanges such as the CBOE and the Amex. The creation of listed options exchanges led to standardized options features and to widespread use of options by individual investors. Among the option provisions are the strike price (the stipulated price at which the underlying asset can be bought or sold) and the expiration date (the date when the contract expires).	conventional options, *p. 450* expiration date, *p. 452* listed options, *p. 450* option chain, *p. 453* strike price, *p. 451*	MyFinanceLab Study Plan 13.2
LG3 Explain how put and call options are valued and the forces that drive option prices in the marketplace. The value of a call is the market price of the underlying security less the strike price on the call. The value of a put is its strike price less the market price of the security. The value of an option is driven by the current market price of the underlying asset. Most puts and calls sell at premium prices. The size of the premium depends on the length of the option contract (the so-called time premium), the speculative appeal and amount of price volatility in the underlying financial asset, and the general level of interest rates.	in-the-money, *p. 456* out-of-the money, *p. 456* time value, *p. 458*	MyFinanceLab Study Plan 13.3 Video Learning Aid for Problems P13.5, P13.11

What You Should Know	Key Terms	Where to Practice
LG4 **Describe the profit potential of puts and calls and note some popular put and call investment strategies.** Investors who hold puts make money when the value of the underlying asset goes down over time. Call investors make money when the underlying asset moves up in price. Aggressive investors use puts and calls either for speculation or in highly specialized writing and spreading programs. Conservative investors like the low unit costs and the limited risk that puts and calls offer in absolute dollar terms. Conservative investors often use options to hedge positions in other securities.	hedge, *p. 463*	MyFinanceLab Study Plan 13.4 Excel Table 10.3
LG5 **Explain the profit potential and loss exposure from writing covered call options and discuss how writing options can be used as a strategy for enhancing investment returns.** Covered call writers have limited loss exposure because they write options against securities they already own. The maximum profit occurs when the price of the stock equals the strike price of the call. If the stock price goes above the strike price, then any loss on the option is offset by a gain on the stock position. If the stock price goes down, part of the loss on the stock is offset by the proceeds from the call option. Option writing can be combined with other securities to create investment strategies for specific market conditions.	covered options, *p. 466* naked options, *p. 466* option spreading, *p. 468* option straddle, *p. 468*	MyFinanceLab Study Plan 13.5 Excel Table 13.5 Video Learning Aid for Problem P13.11
LG6 **Describe market index options, puts and calls on foreign currencies, and LEAPS and discuss how these securities can be used by investors.** Standardized put and call options are available on stock-market indexes, like the S&P 500 (in the form of index options or ETF options), and on a number of foreign currencies (currency options). Also available are LEAPS, which are listed options that carry lengthy expiration dates. Although these securities can be used just like stock options, the index and currency options tend to be used primarily for speculation or to develop hedge positions.	currency options, *p. 473* interest rate options, *p. 473* LEAPS, *p. 474* stock-index option, *p. 469*	MyFinanceLab Study Plan 13.6

Log into MyFinanceLab, take a chapter test, and get a personalized Study Plan that tells you which concepts you understand and which ones you need to review. From there, MyFinanceLab will give you further practice, tutorials, animations, videos, and guided solutions.
Log into **www.myfinancelab.com**

Discussion Questions

LG2   Q13.1 Using the stock option quotations in Figure 13.4 (on page 470), find the option premium, the time value, and the stock index breakeven point for the following puts and calls.
   a. The December put with a $103 strike price
   b. The December call with a $100 strike price

LG3 Q13.2 Prepare a schedule similar to the one in Table 13.1 (on page 458) for the call and put options listed in Figure 13.4 (on page 470). Briefly explain your findings.

LG5 Q13.3 Alcan stock recently closed at $52.51. Assume that you write a covered call on Alcan by writing one September call with a strike price of $55, and buying 100 shares of stock at the market price. The option premium that you obtain from writing the call is $370. Assume the stock will pay no dividends between now and the expiration date of the option.

    a. What is the total profit if the stock price remains unchanged?

    b. What is the total profit if the stock price goes up to $55?

    c. What is the total loss if the stock price goes down to $49?

LG6 Q13.4 Assume you hold a well-balanced portfolio of common stocks. Under what conditions might you want to use a stock-index (or ETF) option to hedge the portfolio?

    a. Briefly explain how such options could be used to hedge a portfolio against a drop in the market.

    b. Discuss what happens if the market does, in fact, go down.

    c. What happens if the market goes up instead?

LG3 LG4 Q13.5 Using the resources at your campus or public library (or on the Internet), complete each of the following tasks. (*Note:* Show your work for all calculations.)

    a. Find an in-the-money call that has 2 or 3 months to expiration. (Select an equity option that is at least $2 or $3 in-the-money.) What's the fundamental value of this option and how much premium is it carrying? Using the current market price of the underlying stock (the one listed with the option), determine what kind of dollar and percentage return the option would generate if the underlying stock goes up 10%. How about if the stock goes down 10%?

    b. Repeat part **a**, but this time use an in-the-money put. (Choose an equity option that's at least $2 or $3 in-the-money and has 2 or 3 months to expiration.) Answer the same questions as above.

    c. Repeat once more the exercise in part **a**, but this time use an out-of-the-money call. (Select an equity option, at least $2 or $3 out-of-the-money with 2 or 3 months to expiration.) Answer the same questions.

    d. Compare the valuation properties and performance characteristics of in-the-money calls and out-of-the-money calls (from parts **a** and **c**). Note some of the advantages and disadvantages of each.

Problems

All problems are available on **www.myfinancelab.com**

LG3 P13.1 Apple stock is selling for $600 per share. Call options with a $585 exercise price are priced at $69.00. What is the intrinsic value of the option, and what is the time value?

LG3 P13.2 Gillette is trading at $31.11. Call options with a strike price of $35 are priced at $0.30. What is the intrinsic value of the option, and what is the time value?

LG3 P13.3 Verizon is trading at $36. Put options with a strike price of $45 are priced at $10.50. What is the intrinsic value of the option, and what is the time value?

LG3 P13.4 J. Crew is trading at $36. Put options with a strike price of $27.50 are priced at $0.85. What is the intrinsic value of the option, and what is the time value?

LG3 P13.5 A 6-month call option contract on 100 shares of Home Depot common stock with a strike price of $60 can be purchased for $600. Assuming that the market price of Home Depot stock rises to $75 per share by the expiration date of the option, what is the call holder's profit? What is the holding period return?

LG4 LG6   P13.6 You believe that oil prices will be rising more than expected and that rising prices will result in lower earnings for industrial companies that use a lot of petroleum-related products in their operations. You also believe that the effects on this sector will be magnified because consumer demand will fall as oil prices rise. You locate an exchange-traded fund, XLB, that represents a basket of industrial companies. You don't want to short the ETF because you don't have enough margin in your account. XLB is currently trading at $23. You decide to buy a put option (for 100 shares) with a strike price of $24, priced at $1.20. It turns out that you are correct. At expiration, XLB is trading at $20. Calculate your profit.

XLB: Materials—$23.00

Calls			Puts		
Strike	Expiration	Price	Strike	Expiration	Price
$20	November	$0.25	$20	November	$1.55
$24	November	$0.25	$24	November	$1.20

LG4 LG6   P13.7 Refer to the table for XLB in Problem 13.6. What happens if you are wrong and the price of XLB increases to $25 on the expiration date?

LG6   P13.8 Dorothy Santosuosso does a lot of investing in the stock market and is a frequent user of stock-index options. She is convinced that the market is about to undergo a broad retreat and has decided to buy a put option on the S&P 100 Index. The put option has a strike of 690 and is quoted in the financial press at $4.50. Although the S&P Index of 100 stocks is currently at 686.45, Dorothy thinks it will drop to 665 by the expiration date on the option. How much profit will she make, and what will be her holding period return if she is right? How much will she lose if the S&P 100 goes up (rather than down) by 25 points and reaches 715 by the date of expiration?

LG3 LG4   P13.9 Myles Houck holds 600 shares of Lubbock Gas and Light. He bought the stock several years ago at $48.50, and the shares are now trading at $75. Myles is concerned that the market is beginning to soften. He doesn't want to sell the stock, but he would like to be able to protect the profit he's made. He decides to hedge his position by buying 6 puts on Lubbock G&L. The 3-month puts carry a strike price of $75 and are currently trading at $2.50.
   a. How much profit or loss will Myles make on this deal if the price of Lubbock G&L does indeed drop to $60 a share by the expiration date on the puts?
   b. How would he do if the stock kept going up in price and reached $90 a share by the expiration date?
   c. What do you see as the major advantages of using puts as hedge vehicles?
   d. Would Myles have been better off using in-the-money puts—that is, puts with an $85 strike price that are trading at $10.50? How about using out-of-the-money puts—say, those with a $70 strike price, trading at $1.00? Explain.

LG4 LG6   P13.10 P. F. Chang holds a well-diversified portfolio of high-quality, large-cap stocks. The current value of Chang's portfolio is $735,000, but he is concerned that the market is heading for a big fall (perhaps as much as 20%) over the next 3 to 6 months. He doesn't want to sell all his stocks because he feels they all have good long-term potential and should perform nicely once stock prices have bottomed out. As a result, he's thinking about using index options to hedge his portfolio. Assume that the S&P 500 currently stands at 1,470 and among the many put options available on this index are two that have caught his eye: (1) a 6-month put with a strike price of 1,450 that's trading at $26, and (2) a 6-month put with a strike price of 1,390 that's quoted at $4.50.
   a. How many S&P 500 puts would Chang have to buy to protect his $735,000 stock portfolio? How much would it cost him to buy the necessary number of 1,450 puts? How much would it cost to buy the 1,390 puts?

b. Now, considering the performance of both the put options and the Chang portfolio, determine how much *net* profit (or loss) Chang will earn from each of these put hedges if both the market (as measured by the S&P 500) and the Chang portfolio fall by 15% over the next 6 months. What if the market and the Chang portfolio fall by only 5%? What if they go up by 10%?

c. Do you think Chang should set up the put hedge and, if so, using which put option? Explain.

d. Finally, assume that the DJIA is currently at 14,550 and that a 6-month put option on the Dow is available with a strike of 144, and is currently trading at $2.50. How many of these puts would Chang have to buy to protect his portfolio, and what would they cost? Would Chang be better off with the Dow options or the S&P 1,450 puts? Briefly explain.

LG3 LG5 P13.11 Angelo Martino just purchased 500 shares of AT&E at $61.50, and he has decided to write covered calls against these stocks. Accordingly, he sells five AT&E calls at their current market price of $5.75. The calls have 3 months to expiration and carry a strike price of $65. The stock pays a quarterly dividend of $0.80 a share (the next dividend to be paid in about a month).

a. Determine the total profit and holding period return Angelo will generate if the stock rises to $65 a share by the expiration date on the calls.

b. What happens to Angelo's profit (and return) if the price of the stock rises to more than $65 a share?

c. Does this covered call position offer any protection (or cushion) against a drop in the price of the stock? Explain.

LG6 P13.12 Rick owns stock in a retailer that he believes is highly undervalued. Rick expects that the stock will increase in value nicely over the long term. He is concerned, however, that the entire retail industry may fall out of favor with investors as some larger companies report falling sales. There are no options traded on his stock, but Rick would like to hedge against his fears about retail. He locates a symbol RTH, which is a Retail HOLDRS. Can Rick hedge against the risk he is concerned with by using RTH? Using options?

LG5 LG6 P13.13 Suppose the DJIA stands at 11,200. You want to set up a long straddle by purchasing 100 calls and an equal number of puts on the index, both of which expire in 3 months and have a strike of 112. The put price is listed at $1.65 and the call sells for $2.65.

a. What will it cost you to set up the straddle, and how much profit (or loss) do you stand to make if the market falls by 750 points by the expiration dates on the options? What if it goes up by 750 points by expiration? What if it stays at 11,200?

b. Repeat part **a**, but this time assume that you set up a short straddle by selling/writing 100 July 112 puts and calls.

c. What do you think of the use of option straddles as an investment strategy? What are the risks, and what are the rewards?

LG3 P13.14 A stock trades for $45 per share. A call option on that stock has a strike price of $50 and an expiration date 1 year in the future. The volatility of the stock's returns is 30%, and the risk-free rate is 2%. What is the Black and Scholes value of this option?

Visit **www.myfinancelab.com** for web exercises, spreadsheets, and other online resources.

Case Problem 13.1   The Franciscos' Investment Options

LG3 LG4 Hector Francisco is a successful businessman in Atlanta. The box-manufacturing firm he and his wife, Judy, founded several years ago has prospered. Because he is self-employed, Hector is building his own retirement fund. So far, he has accumulated a substantial sum in his investment account, mostly by following an aggressive investment posture. He does this because, as he puts it, "In this business, you never know when the bottom's gonna fall out." Hector has been following the stock of Rembrandt Paper Products (RPP), and after conducting extensive analysis, he feels the stock is about ready to move. Specifically, he believes that within the next 6 months, RPP could go to about $80 per share, from its current level of $57.50. The stock pays annual dividends of $2.40 per share. Hector figures he would receive 2 quarterly dividend payments over his 6-month investment horizon.

In studying RPP, Hector has learned that the company has 6-month call options (with $50 and $60 strike prices) listed on the CBOE. The CBOE calls are quoted at $8 for the options with $50 strike prices and at $5 for the $60 options.

Questions

a. How many alternative investments does Hector have if he wants to invest in RPP for no more than 6 months? What if he has a 2-year investment horizon?

b. Using a 6-month holding period and assuming the stock does indeed rise to $80 over this time frame:

  1. Find the value of both calls, given that at the end of the holding period neither contains any investment premium.

  2. Determine the holding period return for each of the 3 investment alternatives open to Hector Francisco.

c. Which course of action would you recommend if Hector simply wants to maximize profit? Would your answer change if other factors (e.g., comparative risk exposure) were considered along with return? Explain.

Case Problem 13.2   Luke's Quandary: To Hedge or Not to Hedge

LG3 LG4   A little more than 10 months ago, Luke Weaver, a mortgage banker in Phoenix, bought 300 shares of stock at $40 per share. Since then, the price of the stock has risen to $75 per share. It is now near the end of the year, and the market is starting to weaken. Luke feels there is still plenty of play left in the stock but is afraid the tone of the market will be detrimental to his position. His wife, Denise, is taking an adult education course on the stock market and has just learned about put and call hedges. She suggests that he use puts to hedge his position. Luke is intrigued by the idea, which he discusses with his broker, who advises him that the needed puts are indeed available on his stock. Specifically, he can buy 3-month puts, with $75 strike prices, at a cost of $550 each (quoted at $5.50).

Questions

a. Given the circumstances surrounding Luke's current investment position, what benefits could be derived from using the puts as a hedge device? What would be the major drawback?

b. What will Luke's minimum profit be if he buys 3 puts at the indicated option price? How much would he make if he did not hedge but instead sold his stock immediately at a price of $75 per share?

c. Assuming Luke uses 3 puts to hedge his position, indicate the amount of profit he will generate if the stock moves to $100 by the expiration date of the puts. What if the stock drops to $50 per share?

d. Should Luke use the puts as a hedge? Explain. Under what conditions would you urge him not to use the puts as a hedge?

Excel with Spreadsheets

One of the positive attributes of investing in options is the profit potential from the puts or calls. The quoted market price of the option is influenced by the time to expiration, stock volatility, market interest rates, and the behavior of the price of the underlying common stock. The latter variable tends to drive the price movement in options and impacts its potential for profitable returns.

Create a spreadsheet model, similar to that presented below, in order to calculate the profits and/or losses from investing in the option described.

	A	B	C	D	E	F	G	H	I	J
1										
2						Long		100		3-Month Call Option
3						Position		Shares of		on the Stock
4						No		Underlying		Strike Price
5						Option		Common Stock		$$$
6										
7	Today									
8										
9	Market value of stock			$$		$$		$$		
10	Call strike price			$$						
11	Call option premium			$$						
12										
13										
14	Scenario One: 3 months later									
15	Expected market value of stock			$$		$$		$$		
16	Stock value @ strike price			$$						$$
17	Call premium			$$						$$
18	Breakeven point			$$						$$
19										
20	Profit (Loss)					$$		$$		

John has been following the stock market very closely over the past 18 months and has a strong belief that future stock prices will be significantly higher. He has 2 alternatives that he can follow. The first is to use a long-term strategy—purchase the stock today and sell it sometime in the future at a possibly higher price. The other alternative is to buy a 3-month call option. The relevant information needed to analyze these alternatives is presented below:

Current stock price = $49

Desires to buy one round lot = 100 shares

Three-month call option has a strike price of $51 and a call premium of $2

Questions

a. In scenario 1, if the stock price 3 months from now is $58:

1. What is the long-position profit or loss?

2. What is the breakeven point of the call option?

3. Is the option in- or out-of-the-money?

4. What is the option profit or loss?

b. In scenario 2, if the stock price 3 months from now is $42:

1. What is the long-position profit or loss?

2. What is the breakeven point of the call option?

3. Is the option in- or out-of-the-money?

4. What is the option profit or loss?

Chapter-Opening Problem

In the beginning of this chapter you read about artist David Choe, who in 2005 agreed to paint murals on the walls of Facebook headquarters in exchange for $60,000 in stock. Over the next 7 years Facebook grew into the world's largest social media company, but along the way to its $104 billion IPO there was plenty of opportunity for David Choe to cash in on his option. In April 2008 Facebook's privately held stock began trading on SecondMarket and David Choe could have at any time thereafter sold his shares.

Questions

a. Based on Facebook's 2012 IPO price of $38 per share and the reported $200 million value of Mr. Choe's shares, what was the approximate number of shares Mr. Choe received in exchange for his paintings?

b. Based on your answer to part a and the $60,000 opportunity cost Mr. Choe incurred when accepting the stock, what was Mr. Choe's implied price per share?

c. What was Mr. Choe's 7-year holding period return?

d. If instead of holding on to his shares, Mr. Choe had chosen to sell them in 2008 on SecondMarket for the initial trading price of $3.50 per share, what would have been his dollar profit and his 3-year holding period return?

Glossary

A

abnormal return The difference between an investment's actual return and its expected return.

accredited investor Investor who is permitted to invest in certain types of higher-risk investments. These investors include wealthy individuals, corporations, endowments, and retirement plans.

accrued interest Interest earned (but not yet paid) on a bond since the previous coupon payment.

agency bonds Debt securities issued by various agencies and organizations of the U.S. government.

American depositary receipts (ADRs) U.S. dollar-denominated receipts for the stocks of foreign companies that are held in the vaults of banks in the companies' home countries. Serve as backing for *American depositary shares (ADSs)*.

American depositary shares (ADSs) Securities created to permit U.S. investors to hold shares of non-U.S. companies and trade them on U.S. stock exchanges. They are backed by *American depositary receipts (ADRs)*.

amortized loan A loan that is paid off in equal periodic payments.

annual percentage rate (APR) The interest rate paid or earned in one year without compounding. It is calculated as the interest rate per period (for example, per month or week) multiplied by the number of periods during which compounding occurs during the year *(m)*.

annuity A stream of equal cash flows that occur at equal intervals over time.

annuity due An annuity in which the payments occur at the beginning of each period.

annuity future value interest factor The value,
$$\left[\frac{(1 + i)^n - 1}{i}\right],$$
used as a multiplier to calculate the future value of an annuity.

annuity present value interest factor The value,
$$\left[\frac{1 - \dfrac{1}{(1 + i)^n}}{i}\right],$$
used as a multiplier to calculate the present value of an annuity.

ask price The lowest price offered to sell a security.

asset-backed securities (ABSs) Securities similar to mortgage-backed securities that are backed by a pool of bank loans, leases, and other assets.

B

bear markets Markets normally associated with falling prices, investor pessimism, economic slowdown, and government restraint.

behavioral finance The body of research into the role that emotions and other subjective factors play in investment decisions.

belief perseverance The tendency to ignore or discount evidence contrary to one's existing beliefs.

beta A measure of *undiversifiable*, or *market*, *risk* that indicates how the price of a security responds to market forces.

beta coefficient A measure of the relationship between the returns of a security such as a share of common stock and the returns of the portfolio of all risky assets.

bid price The highest price offered to purchase a security.

blue-chip stocks Financially strong, high-quality stocks with long and stable records of earnings and dividends.

bond A long-term (10-year or more) promissory note issued by a borrower, promising to pay the owner of the security a predetermined amount of interest each year.

bond ladders An investment strategy wherein equal amounts of money are invested in a series of bonds with staggered maturities.

bond ratings Letter grades that designate investment quality and are assigned to a bond issue by rating agencies.

bond swap An investment strategy wherein an investor simultaneously liquidates one bond holding and buys a different issue to take its place.

bond-equivalent yield The annual yield on a bond, calculated as twice the semiannual yield.

book value The amount of stockholders' equity in a firm; equals the amount of the firm's assets minus the firm's liabilities and preferred stock.

broker market The market in which the two sides of a transaction, the buyer and seller, are brought together to execute trades.

bull markets Markets normally associated with rising prices, investor optimism, economic recovery, and government stimulus.

business risk The degree of uncertainty associated with an investment's earnings and the investment's ability to pay the returns owed to investors.

C

call A negotiable instrument that gives the holder the right to buy securities at a stated price within a certain time period.

call feature Feature that specifies whether and under what conditions the issuer can retire a bond prior to maturity.

call premium The amount added to a bond's par value and paid to investors when a bond is retired prematurely.

call price The price the issuer must pay to retire a bond prematurely; equal to par value plus the call premium.

capital asset pricing model (CAPM) Model that formally links the notions of risk and return; it uses beta, the risk-free rate, and the market return to help investors define the required return on an investment.

capital market Market in which *long-term* securities (with maturities greater than one year) such as stocks and bonds are bought and sold.

cash dividend   Payment of a dividend in the form of cash.

charting   The activity of charting price behavior and other market information and then using the patterns these charts form to make investment decisions.

classified common stock   Common stock issued by a company in different classes, each of which offers different privileges and benefits to its holders.

clean price   The price of a bond ignoring any accrued interest. The clean price is the present value of the bond's future cash flows, not including any interest accruing on the next coupon date.

collateral trust bonds   Senior bonds backed by securities owned by the issuer but held in trust by a third party.

collateralized mortgage obligation (CMO)   Mortgage-backed bond whose holders are divided into classes based on the length of investment desired; principal is channeled to investors in order of maturity, with short-term classes first.

common-size income statement   A type of financial report that uses a common denominator (net sales) to convert all entries on a normal income statement from dollars to percentages.

common stock   A form of equity security that represents the residual ownership of the firm.

compound interest   Interest paid not only on the initial deposit but also on any interest accumulated from one period to the next.

confidence index   A ratio of the average yield on high-grade corporate bonds to the average yield on average- or intermediate-grade corporate bonds; a technical indicator based on the theory that market trends usually appear in the bond market before they do in the stock market.

continuous compounding   Interest calculation in which interest is compounded over the smallest possible interval of time.

conventional options   Put and call options sold over the counter.

conversion equivalent (conversion parity)   The price at which the common stock would have to sell in order to make the convertible security worth its present market price.

conversion period   The time period during which a convertible issue can be converted.

conversion price   The stated price per share at which common stock will be delivered to the investor in exchange for a convertible issue.

conversion privilege   The conditions and specific nature of the conversion feature on convertible securities.

conversion ratio   The number of shares of common stock into which a convertible issue can be converted.

conversion value   An indication of what a convertible issue would trade for if it were priced to sell on the basis of its stock value.

convertible bonds   Fixed-income obligations that have a feature permitting the holder to convert the security into a specified number of shares of the issuing company's common stock.

correlation   A statistical measure of the relationship, if any, between series of numbers representing data of any kind.

correlation coefficient   A measure of the degree of correlation between two series.

coupon   Feature on a bond that defines the amount of annual interest income.

coupon rate   The amount of interest paid per year expressed as a percent of the face value of the bond.

covered options   Options written against stock owned (or short-sold) by the writer.

credit default swap   An insurance contract that pays off in the event of a credit event such as default or bankruptcy.

crossing markets   After-hours trading in stocks that involves filling buy and sell orders by matching identical sell and buy orders at the desired price.

currency exchange rate   The relationship between two currencies on a specified date.

currency exchange risk   The risk caused by the varying exchange rates between the currencies of two countries.

currency options   Put and call options written on foreign currencies.

current yield   Measure of the annual interest income a bond provides relative to its current market price.

cyclical stocks   Stocks whose earnings and overall market performance are closely linked to the general state of the economy.

D

date of record   The date on which an investor must be a registered shareholder to be entitled to receive a dividend.

dealer market   The market in which the buyer and seller are not brought together directly but instead have their orders executed by *dealers* that make markets in the given security.

debenture   An unsecured (junior) bond.

debit balance   The amount of money being borrowed in a margin loan.

debt securities   Financial instruments that represent loans to corporations. Long-term debt securities are called bonds and can be bought and sold in the bond market.

defensive stocks   Stocks that tend to hold their own, and even do well, when the economy starts to falter.

deferred equity   Securities issued in one form and later redeemed or converted into shares of common stock.

deflation   A period of generally declining prices.

defined benefit plans   A company retirement plan, such as a pension plan, in which a retired employee receives a specific amount based on his or her salary history and years of service.

defined contribution plans   A company retirement plan, such as a 401(k) plan, in which the employee elects to contribute some amount of his or her salary to the plan and the employee takes responsibility for the investment decisions.

designated market maker (DMM)   NYSE member who specializes in making transactions in one or more stocks and manages the auction process.

dirty price   A bond's dirty price equals its clean price plus accrued interest.

discount bond   A bond with a market value lower than par; occurs when market rates are greater than the coupon rate.

discount rate   The annual rate of return that could be earned currently on a similar investment; used when finding present value; also called *opportunity cost*.

discounting   The inverse of compounding. This process is used to determine the present value of a future cash flow.

diversifiable (unsystematic) risk   The portion of an investment's risk that results from uncontrollable or random events that are firm-specific; can be eliminated through diversification.

diversification   The reduction in risk that comes about by combining two or more risky assets into a portfolio where the individual assets are less than perfectly positively correlated.

dividend payout ratio   The portion of earnings per share (EPS) that a firm pays out as dividends.

dividend reinvestment plan (DRIP)   Plan in which shareholders have cash dividends automatically reinvested into additional shares of the firm's common stock.

dividend valuation model (DVM)   A model that values a share of stock on the basis of the future dividend stream it is expected to produce; its three versions are zero-growth, constant-growth, and variable-growth.

dividend yield   A measure that relates dividends to share price and puts common stock dividends on a relative (percentage) rather than absolute (dollar) basis.

dividends-and-earnings (D&E) approach   Stock valuation approach that uses projected dividends, EPS, and P/E multiples to value a share of stock; also known as the *DCF approach.*

dual listing   Listing of a firm's shares on more than one exchange.

duration   A measure of bond price volatility that captures both price and reinvestment risks and that is used to indicate how a bond will react in different interest rate environments.

E

earnings per share (EPS)   The amount of annual earnings available to common stockholders, as stated on a per-share basis.

effective annual rate (EAR)   The annual compounded rate that produces the same return as the nominal, or stated, rate.

efficient frontier   The leftmost boundary of the *feasible (attainable) set* of portfolios that includes all *efficient portfolios*—those providing the best attainable tradeoff between risk (measured by the standard deviation) and return.

efficient market   A market in which securities reflect all possible information quickly and accurately.

efficient markets hypothesis (EMH)   Basic theory of the behavior of efficient markets, in which there are a large number of knowledgeable investors who react quickly to new information, causing securities prices to adjust quickly and accurately.

efficient portfolio   A portfolio that provides the highest return for a given level of risk.

electronic communications networks (ECNs)   Electronic trading networks that automatically match buy and sell orders that customers place electronically.

equipment trust certificates   Senior bonds secured by specific pieces of equipment; popular with transportation companies such as airlines.

equity capital   Evidence of ownership position in a firm, in the form of shares of common stock.

equity kicker   Another name for the conversion feature, giving the holder of a convertible security a deferred claim on the issuer's common stock.

equity securities   Financial instruments that represent ownership claims on a business. Equity securities for corporations are called shares of stock and can be bought and sold in the stock market.

ethics   Standards of conduct or moral judgment.

Eurodollar bonds   Foreign bonds denominated in dollars but not registered with the SEC, thus restricting sales of new issues.

event risk   Risk that comes from an unexpected event that has a significant and usually immediate effect on the underlying value of an investment.

ex-dividend date   Three business days up to the date of record; determines whether one is an official shareholder and thus eligible to receive a declared dividend.

excess margin   More equity than is required in a margin account.

exchange-traded fund (ETF)   An investment vehicle traded on stock exchanges much like a share of stock. The entity holds investments in assets that meet the investment objective of the entity (e.g., shares of stock of companies from emerging markets).

expectations hypothesis   Theory that the shape of the yield curve reflects investor expectations of future interest rates.

expected inflation premium   The average rate of inflation expected in the future.

expected return   The return an investor thinks an investment will earn in the future.

expiration date   The date at which an option expires.

F

face, or par value   On the face of a bond, the stated amount that the firm is to repay on the maturity date.

familiarity bias   The tendency to invest in securities simply because they are familiar to the investor.

financial intermediaries   Institutions whose business is to bring together individuals and institutions with money to invest or lend with other firms or individuals in need of money.

financial leverage   The use of debt financing to magnify investment returns.

financial risk   The degree of uncertainty of payment resulting from a firm's mix of debt and equity; the larger the proportion of debt financing, the greater this risk.

first and refunding bonds   Bonds secured in part with both first and second mortgages.

forced conversion   The calling in of convertible bonds by the issuing firm.

fourth market   Transactions made directly between large institutional buyers and sellers of securities.

fully compounded rate of return   The rate of return that includes interest earned on interest.

future value   The amount to which a current deposit will grow over a period of time when it is placed in an account paying compound interest.

future value interest factor   The value $(1 + i)^n$ used as a multiplier to calculate an amount's future value.

G

general obligation bonds   Municipal bonds backed by the full faith, credit, and taxing power of the issuer.

growing perpetuity   A perpetuity in which the payments grow at a constant rate from period to period over time.

growth stocks   Stocks that experience high rates of growth in operations and earnings.

growth-oriented portfolio   A portfolio whose primary objective is long-term price appreciation.

H

hedge   A combination of two or more securities into a single investment position for the purpose of reducing or eliminating risk.

hedge fund   An investment fund that is open to a limited range of investors (accredited investors) and that can undertake a wider range of investment and trading activities than other types of investment funds that are open to the general public (e.g., mutual funds).

holding period   The period of time over which one wishes to measure the return on an investment vehicle.

holding period return (HPR)   The total return earned from holding an investment for a specified *holding period* (*usually one year or less*).

I

immunization   Bond portfolio strategy that uses duration to offset price and reinvestment effects; a bond portfolio is immunized when its average duration equals the investment horizon.

in-the-money   A call option with a strike price less than the market price of the underlying security; a put option whose strike price is greater than the market price of the underlying security.

income   Usually cash or near-cash that is periodically received as a result of owning an investment.

income bonds   Unsecured bonds requiring that interest be paid only after a specified amount of income is earned.

income stocks   Stocks with long and sustained records of paying higher-than-average dividends.

income-oriented portfolio   A portfolio that is designed to produce regular dividends and interest payments.

inflation   A period of generally rising prices.

initial margin   The minimum amount of equity that must be provided by a margin investor at the time of purchase.

initial public offering (IPO)   The first public sale of a company's stock.

insider trading   The use of nonpublic information about a company to make profitable securities transactions.

interest   The "rent" paid by a borrower for use of the lender's money.

interest rate options   Put and call options written on fixed-income (debt) securities.

interest rate risk   The chance that changes in interest rates will adversely affect a security's value.

investment bank   A financial institution that raises capital, trades in securities, and manages corporate mergers and acquisitions.

investment banker   Financial intermediary that specializes in assisting companies issue new securities and advising companies with regard to major financial transactions.

investment company   A firm that invests the pooled funds of retail investors for a fee.

investment value   The amount that investors believe a security should be trading for, or what they think it's worth. The price at which a convertible would trade if it were nonconvertible and priced at or near the prevailing market yields of comparable nonconvertible issues.

J

junior bonds   Debt obligations backed only by the promise of the issuer to pay interest and principal on a timely basis.

junk bonds   High-risk securities that have low ratings but high yields.

L

LEAPS   Long-term options.

level perpetuity   An annuity with a constant level of payments with an infinite life.

leverage   The ability to obtain a given equity position at a reduced capital investment, thereby magnifying returns.

leveraged buyout fund   A private equity firm that raises capital from individual investors and uses these funds along with significant amounts of debt to acquire controlling interests in operating companies.

liquidity preference theory   Theory that investors tend to prefer the greater liquidity of short-term securities and therefore require a premium to invest in long-term securities.

liquidity risk   The risk of not being able to liquidate an investment quickly and at a reasonable price.

listed options   Put and call options listed and traded on organized securities exchanges, such as the CBOE.

load fund   A mutual fund that charges investors a sales commission called a "load."

loan amortization schedule   A breakdown of the interest and principal payments on an amortized loan.

long purchase   A transaction in which investors buy securities in the hope that they will increase in value and can be sold at a later date for profit.

loss aversion   A situation in which the desire to avoid losses is so great that investors who are otherwise risk-averse will exhibit risk-seeking behavior in an attempt to avoid a loss.

LYON (liquid yield option note)   A zero-coupon bond that carries both a conversion feature and a put option.

M

maintenance margin   The absolute minimum amount of margin (equity) that an investor must maintain in the margin account at all times.

margin call   Notification of the need to bring the equity of an account whose margin is below the maintenance level up above the maintenance margin level or to have enough margined holdings sold to reach this standard.

margin loan   Vehicle through which borrowed funds are made available, at a stated interest rate, in a margin transaction.

margin requirement   The minimum amount of equity that must be a margin investor's own funds; set by the Federal Reserve Board (the "Fed").

margin trading   The use of borrowed funds to purchase securities; magnifies returns by reducing the amount of equity that the investor must put up.

market anomalies   Irregularities or deviations from the behavior one would expect in an efficient market.

market makers   *Securities dealers* that "make markets" by offering to buy or sell certain quantities of securities at stated prices.

market portfolio The portfolio of all risky and risk-free assets.

market return The average return for all (or a large sample of) stocks, such as those in the *Standard & Poor's 500-Stock Composite Index*.

market risk Risk of decline in investment returns because of market factors independent of the given investment.

market risk premium The difference in the expected rate of return on the market portfolio and the risk-free rate of return.

market segmentation theory Theory that the market for debt is segmented on the basis of maturity, that supply and demand within each segment determine the prevailing interest rate, and that the slope of the yield curve depends on the relationship between the prevailing rates in each segment.

market technicians Analysts who believe it is chiefly (or solely) supply and demand that drive stock prices.

market value The prevailing market price of a security.

maturity date The date on which a bond matures and the principal must be repaid.

mid-cap stocks Medium-sized stocks, generally with market values of less than $4 or $5 billion but more than $1 billion.

mixed stream A stream of returns that, unlike an annuity, exhibits no special pattern.

modern portfolio theory (MPT) An approach to portfolio management that uses several basic statistical measures to develop a portfolio plan.

money market Market where *short-term* debt securities (with maturities less than one year) are bought and sold.

mortgage bonds Senior bonds secured by real estate.

mortgage-backed bond A debt issue secured by a pool of home mortgages; issued primarily by federal agencies.

moving average (MA) A mathematical procedure that computes and records the average values of a series of prices, or other data, over time; results in a stream of average values that will act to smooth out a series of data.

municipal bond guarantees Guarantees from a party other than the issuer that principal and interest payments will be made in a prompt and timely manner.

municipal bonds Debt securities issued by states, counties, cities, and other political subdivisions; most of these bonds are tax-exempt (free of federal income tax on interest income).

mutual fund A professionally managed investment company that pools the investments of many individuals and invests it in stocks, bonds, and other types of securities.

N

naked options Options written on securities not owned by the writer.

narrow framing Analyzing an investment problem in isolation or in a particularly narrow context rather than looking at all aspects of the problem.

Nasdaq market A major segment of the *secondary market* that employs an all-electronic trading platform to execute trades.

negatively correlated Describes two series that move in opposite directions.

net asset value (NAV) The difference between the current market value of an entity's (such as a mutual fund) assets and the value of its liabilities.

no-load fund A mutual fund that doesn't charge a commission.

nominal or quoted (stated) interest rate The interest rate paid on debt securities without an adjustment for any loss in purchasing power.

nominal rate of return The actual return earned on an investment expressed in current dollars.

non-diversifiable risk Risk that cannot be eliminated through diversification.

note A debt security originally issued with a maturity of from 2 to 10 years.

O

option Securities that give the holder the right to buy or sell a certain amount of an underlying financial asset at a specified price for a specified period of time.

option chain A list of all options traded on a particular security. An option chain provides the current market prices and trading volumes for all options linked to a particular stock.

option premium The quoted price the investor pays to buy a listed put or call option.

option spreading Combining two or more options with different strike prices and/or expiration dates into a single transaction.

option straddle The simultaneous purchase (or sale) of a put and a call on the same underlying common stock (or financial asset).

option writer (or seller) The individual or institution that writes/creates put and call options.

ordinary annuity An annuity for which the cash flows occur at the end of each period.

organized security exchanges Security exchanges that physically occupy space (such as a building or part of a building) and trade financial instruments on their premises.

out-of-the-money A call option with no real value because the strike price exceeds the market price of the stock; a put option whose market price exceeds the strike price.

overconfidence The tendency to overestimate one's ability to perform a particular task.

over-the-counter (OTC) market A segment of the *secondary market* that involves trading in smaller, *unlisted securities*.

P

paper return A return that has been achieved but not yet realized by an investor during a given period.

par value The stated, or face, value of a stock.

payback period The length of time it takes for the buyer of a convertible to recover the conversion premium from the extra current income earned on the convertible.

payment date The actual date on which the company will mail dividend checks to shareholders (also known as the *payable date*).

perfectly negatively correlated Describes two negatively correlated series that have a correlation coefficient of –1.

perfectly positively correlated Describes two positively correlated series that have a correlation coefficient of +1.

perpetuity An annuity with an infinite life.

PIK bond A payment in kind junk bond that gives the issuer the right to make annual interest payments in new bonds rather than in cash.

portfolio beta, b_p The beta of a portfolio; calculated as the weighted average of the betas of the individual assets it includes.

positively correlated Describes two series that move in the same direction.

preferred stock An equity security that holds preference over common stock in terms of the right to the distribution of cash (dividends) and the right to the distribution of proceeds in the event of the liquidation and sale of the issuing firm.

premium bond A bond with a market value in excess of par; occurs when interest rates drop below the coupon rate.

present value The *value today* of a sum to be received at some future date; the inverse of future value.

present value interest factor The value $[1/(1 + i)n]$ used as a multiplier to calculate a future payment's present value.

price/earnings (P/E) approach Stock valuation approach that tries to find the P/E ratio that's most appropriate for the stock; this ratio, along with estimated EPS, is then used to determine a reasonable stock price.

primary market The market in which *new issues* of securities are sold by the issuers to investors.

prime rate The lowest interest rate charged to the best business borrowers.

principal On a bond, the amount of capital that must be repaid at maturity.

private equity firm A financial intermediary that invests in equities that are not traded on the public capital markets.

private placement The sale of new securities directly, without SEC registration, to private investors.

promised yield Yield-to-maturity.

proprietary trading Using the bank's capital to make speculative bets on derivatives and securities.

prospectus A portion of a security registration statement that describes the key aspects of the issue and issuer.

public offering The sale of a firm's securities to public investors.

publicly traded issues Shares of stock that are readily available to the general public and are bought and sold in the open market.

purchasing power risk The chance that unanticipated changes in price levels (inflation or deflation) will adversely affect investment returns.

put A negotiable instrument that enables the holder to sell the underlying security at a specified price over a set period of time.

pyramiding The technique of using paper profits in margin accounts to partly or fully finance the acquisition of additional securities.

R

random walk hypothesis The theory that stock price movements are unpredictable, so there's no way to know where prices are headed.

rate of growth The compound annual *rate of change* in the value of a stream of income.

real rate of return The nominal return minus the inflation rate; a measure of the increase in purchasing power that an investment provides.

realized return Current income actually received by an investor during a given period.

realized yield Expected return.

red herring A preliminary prospectus made available to prospective investors while waiting for the registration statement's SEC approval.

refunding provisions Provisions that prohibit the premature retirement of an issue from the proceeds of a lower-coupon refunding bond.

reinvestment rate The rate of return earned on interest or other income received from an investment over its investment horizon.

relative P/E multiple A measure of how a stock's P/E behaves relative to the average market multiple.

relevant risk Risk that is undiversifiable.

representativeness Cognitive biases that occur because people have difficulty thinking about randomness in outcomes.

required rate of return The rate of return that compensates investors for the risk of a particular investment. The minimum acceptable return on an investment given its risk.

required return The rate of return an investor must earn on an investment to be fully compensated for its risk.

residual owners Owners/stockholders of a firm, who are entitled to dividend income and a prorated share of the firm's earnings only after all other obligations have been met.

restricted account A margin account whose equity is less than the initial margin requirement; the investor may not make further margin purchases and must bring the margin back to the initial level when securities are sold.

revenue bonds Municipal bonds that require payment of principal and interest only if sufficient revenue is generated by the issuer.

rights offering An offer of new shares of stock to existing stockholders on a pro rata basis.

risk premium A return premium that reflects the issue and issuer characteristics associated with a given investment vehicle.

risk-averse Describes an investor who requires greater return in exchange for greater risk.

risk-free rate The rate of return that can be earned on a risk-free investment; the sum of the real rate of return and the expected inflation premium.

risk-indifferent Describes an investor who does not require a change in return as compensation for greater risk.

risk-return tradeoff The relationship between risk and return, in which investments with more risk should provide higher returns, and vice versa.

risk-seeking Describes an investor who will accept a lower return in exchange for greater risk.

rule of 72 A method for estimating the time it takes for an amount to double in value. To determine the approximate time it takes for an amount to double in value, 72 is divided by the annual interest rate.

S

satisfactory investment An investment whose present value of benefits (discounted at the appropriate rate) equals or exceeds the present value of its costs.

secondary distributions The public sales of large blocks of previously issued securities held by large investors.

secondary market The market in which securities are traded *after they have been issued*; an *aftermarket*.

security A negotiable instrument that represents a financial claim that has value. Securities are broadly classified as debt securities (bonds) and equity securities (shares of common stock).

Securities and Exchange Commission (SEC) Federal agency that regulates securities offerings and markets.

securities markets Forums that allow suppliers and demanders of *securities* to make financial transactions.

securitization The process of transforming lending vehicles such as mortgages into marketable securities.

security market line (SML) The graphical depiction of the capital asset pricing model; reflects the investor's required return for each level of undiversifiable risk, measured by beta.

self-attribution bias The tendency to overestimate the role that one's intelligence or skill plays in bringing about a favorable investment result and to underestimate the role of chance in that result.

selling group A group of dealers and brokerage firms that join the investment banker(s); each member is responsible for selling a certain portion of a new security issue.

semi-strong form (EMH) Form of the EMH holding that abnormally large profits cannot be consistently earned using publicly available information.

senior bonds Secured debt obligations, backed by a legal claim on specific property of the issuer.

serial bond A bond that has a series of different maturity dates.

short interest The number of stocks sold short in the market at any given time; a technical indicator believed to indicate future market demand.

short-selling The sale of borrowed securities, their eventual repurchase by the short-seller, and their return to the lender.

simple interest Interest paid only on the initial deposit for the amount of time it is held.

sinking fund A provision that stipulates the amount of principal that will be retired annually over the life of a bond.

small-cap stocks Stocks that generally have market values of less than $1 billion but can offer above-average returns.

speculative stocks Stocks that offer the potential for substantial price appreciation, usually because of some special situation, such as new management or the introduction of a promising new product.

split ratings Different ratings given to a bond issue by two or more rating agencies.

standard deviation, *s* A statistic used to measure the dispersion (variation) of returns around an asset's average or expected return.

stock dividend Payment of a dividend in the form of additional shares of stock.

stock spin-off Conversion of one of a firm's subsidiaries to a stand-alone company by distribution of stock in that new company to existing shareholders.

stock split A maneuver in which a company increases the number of shares outstanding by exchanging a specified number of new shares of stock for each outstanding share.

stock valuation The process by which the underlying value of a stock is established on the basis of its forecasted risk and return performance.

stock-index option A put or call option written on a specific stock market index, such as the S&P 500.

strike price The stated price at which you can buy a security with a call or sell a security with a put.

strong form (EMH) Form of the EMH that holds that there is no information, public or private, that allows investors to consistently earn abnormal profits.

subordinated debentures Unsecured bonds whose claim is secondary to other debentures.

systematic risk *See* non-diversifiable risk.

T

target price The price an analyst expects the stock to reach within a certain period of time, usually a year.

tax risk The chance that Congress will make unfavorable changes in tax laws, driving down the after-tax returns and market values of certain investments.

tax swap Replacement of a bond that has a capital loss for a similar security; used to offset a gain generated in another part of an investor's portfolio.

taxable equivalent yield The return a fully taxable bond would have to provide to match the after-tax return of a lower-yielding, tax-free municipal bond.

tech stocks Stocks that represent the technology sector of the market.

technical analysis The study of the various forces at work in the marketplace and their effect on stock prices.

term bond A bond that has a single, fairly lengthy maturity date.

term structure of interest rates The relationship between the interest rate or rate of return (yield) on a bond and its time to maturity.

theory of contrary opinion A technical indicator that uses the amount and type of odd-lot trading as an indicator of the current state of the market and pending changes.

third market Over-the-counter transactions typically handled by market makers and made in securities listed on the NYSE, the NYSE AMEX, or one of the other exchanges.

timeline A linear representation of the timing of cash flows.

time value   The amount by which the option price exceeds the option's fundamental value.

time value of money   The fact that as long as an opportunity exists to earn interest, the value of money is affected by the point in time when the money is received.

total return   The sum of the current income and the capital gain (or loss) earned on an investment over a specified period of time.

total risk   The sum of an investment's undiversifiable risk and diversifiable risk.

traditional portfolio management   An approach to portfolio management that emphasizes "balancing" the portfolio by assembling a wide variety of stocks and/or bonds of companies from a broad range of industries.

Treasury bonds   U.S. Treasury securities that are issued with 30-year maturities.

Treasury inflation-indexed obligations (TIPS)   A type of Treasury security that provides protection against inflation by adjusting investor returns for the annual rate of inflation.

Treasury notes   U.S. Treasury debt securities that are issued with maturities of 2 to 10 years.

treasury stock   Shares of stock that have been sold and subsequently repurchased by the issuing firm.

Treasury strips   Zero-coupon bonds created from U.S. Treasury securities.

true rate of interest   The actual rate of interest earned.

U

uncorrelated   Describes two series that lack any relationship or interaction and therefore have a correlation coefficient close to zero.

underwriting   The role of the *investment banker* in bearing the risk of reselling the securities purchased from an issuing corporation at an agreed-on price.

underwriting syndicate   A group of investment banks formed by the originating investment banker to share the financial risk associated with *underwriting* new securities.

undiversifiable (systematic) risk   The risk that remains even in a well-diversified portfolio. Risk that tends to affect all (or nearly all) securities.

unsystematic risk   *See* diversifiable risk.

V

venture capital firm   An investment company that raises money from accredited investors and uses the proceeds to invest in new start-up companies.

W

weak form (EMH)   Form of the EMH holding that past data on stock prices are of no use in predicting future prices.

Y

Yankee bonds   U.S. dollar-denominated debt securities issued by foreign governments or corporations and traded in U.S. securities markets.

yield (internal rate of return)   The compound annual rate of return earned by a long-term investment; the discount rate that produces a present value of the investment's benefits that just equals its cost.

yield curve   A graph that represents the relationship between a bond's term to maturity and its yield at a given point in time.

yield pickup swap   Replacement of a low-coupon bond for a comparable higher-coupon bond in order to realize an increase in current yield and yield-to-maturity.

yield spreads   Differences in interest rates that exist among various sectors of the market.

yield-to-call (YTC)   The yield on a bond if it remains outstanding only until a specified call date.

yield-to-maturity (YTM)   The fully compounded rate of return earned by an investor over the life of a bond, including interest income and price appreciation.

Z

zero-coupon bonds   Bonds with no coupons that are sold at a deep discount from par value.

Index